80-63

PR
9080
A9   Awakened conscience
1978

JUL   2000
JUN

DATE			
		JUL	0 9
		JUL X X	2015

© THE BAKER & TAYLOR CO.

AWAKENED CONSCIENCE

STUDIES IN COMMONWEALTH LITERATURE

Awakened Conscience
Studies in Commonwealth Literature

EDITED BY

C.D. NARASIMHAIAH

HUMANITIES PRESS INC.
171 First Avenue Atlantic Highlands
N. J. 07716.

Sole Distributors for USA & Canada

HUMANITIES PRESS INC.
171 First Avenue Atlantic Highlands
N.J. 07716
ISBN 0 391 00920 6

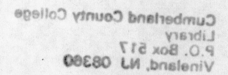

Awakened Conscience
Studies in Commonwealth Literature
© 1978, C.D. Narasimhaiah
First Published : 1978
Published by S.K. Ghai, Managing Director, Sterling Publishers Pvt. Ltd., AB/9 Safdarjang Enclave, New Delhi-110 016
Printed at Sterling Printers, L-11 Green Park Extn. New Delhi-110 016
63-8-78

To

The Writers,

Scholars and Students

who have helped to broaden

the appeal of English Studies:

from "Eng. Lit."

to "Literature in English".

Preface

THIS volume of forty papers represents approximately 50% of the contributions made at the Fourth Triennial Conference which met in Delhi in January 1977, much less does it reflect the complete proceedings of the Conference. There were poets like A. D. Hope and Chris Wallace Crabbe from Australia, Mandel from Canada and Nissim Ezekiel, Adil Jussawala, R. Parthasarathy, P. Lal, S.K. Kumar and other younger poets of promise from India, every one of whom read their own poems on the sunlit lawns of Jawaharlal Nehru University premises to undiminishing audiences of participants between the morning and afternoon sessions next to the colourful shamiana where we ate our lunch. None of these poets figure in the volume. But then, poets sing, not peddle their wares. They were the novelists' envy, and both of the critics'. However, they all met in a spirit of bonhomie and seemed to have a lot more to say to one another outside than in the meeting halls where, nevertheless, the sessions were almost always well attended. This in spite of the fact that except for Panel discussions held every afternoon participants had a choice of three discourses to attend at any point of time. The attractions of Delhi and Agra and Fatehpur Sikri had to wait for their turn till after the Conference.

The umbrella theme of the Conference announced exactly a year before was 'Commonwealth Literature as an Aid to Comparative Studies', not always strictly adhered to nor glaringly deviated from as the first few papers testify. Most papers, however, compared two or more Commonwealth works, attitudes, issues with one or the other shown to advantage. Alternatively, some papers examined how some problem of language, motif, character assumed under different skies diverse shapes, posed different questions, and generated a variety of results, all pointing to the richness of the Commonwealth experience.

It will be seen Drama and Poetry uniformly received scant attention from all Commonwealth areas. Ken Goodwin ascribes the popularity of Fiction to the nature of the medium which, unlike poetry, has access to more, and ordinarily difficult, areas of experience and reaches a much larger reading public within the country and beyond. The other possible inference is that Drama and Poetry have not achieved comparable identity, at least it is not so pronounced or pervasive. Ironically, the Commonwealth Prize is for Poetry. Which presses home the truth that prizes do not stimulate creativity, though they may help to win attention to the work. Provide what props you will, Poetry's chances are dim in competition with

Fiction.   But who will take away Poetry's prestige ?

Criticism, good criticism, that is, is a rarer commodity.   It is obvious there are not what may be called Commonwealth standards any more than universal standards. But, it seems, Commonwealth has distinct advantages over what is suggested by the term 'universal' because of a common language which eliminates the treachery of translation and reduces the gap between experience and expression. And the problems regional variations pose to a common language make it regional but happily, not too regional as the benefits of different backgrounds and larger perspectives are shot through a new imagery, idiom and rhythm which make language an inseparable part of the experience it mediates.

This is an invaluable help in the direction of evolving a Commonwealth Language and Literature with rare opportunities for sharper and more sympathetic appreciation of differences.   To date there is no more influential forum to integrate a variety of experiences and sharpen understanding of disparate responses than the Association which through its still compact triennial conferences, regional meetings and activities of national branches, with their respective journals and newsletters, keeps the channels of communication open without making too many demands on the interested scholar's time or attention.

One grievance, though, is that the regional branches do not have the resources to build up library holdings comparable, or remotely approximating, to what the Commonwealth Institute in London does. Consequently it must not seem strange, say, for an Indian scholar working on R.K. Narayan, a Nigerian on Achebe or a West Indian on Wilson Harris or Lamming, to have to journey to the United Kingdom in search of rewarding material and opportunities for fruitful discussions in their respective areas than to one of their own university centres or a regional counterpart of the Commonwealth Institute in London with holdings in the literature of its own area. ACLALS and the Commonwealth Foundation have both to apply their minds to this problem. IACLALS has made a minor beginning in the direction.

It now remains for me to thank the Commonwealth Foundation for its grants to hold the Delhi Conference and bring Commonwealth scholars together and ACLALS for subsidising publication of the present volume. The British Council, the Indian Council for Cultural Relations and Australian and Canadian embassies did more than merely show an interest—they all held colourful receptions for participants and distinguished invitees on successive evenings. The two Indian agencies, but for whom the Conference might well have flopped, were the University Grants Commission and the Jawaharlal Nehru University. The U.G.C thanks to its Secretary Mr R.K. Chhabra, with his characteristic quick grasp and sympathy, took care of the fares and maintenance of a large number of Indian academics and the JNU Vice-Chancellor Dr Nagchaudhuri with his partiality for Art and Literature did everything we wished for :

placed at our disposal conference halls, guest rooms, furniture and Campus buses as though he was animated by the spirit of Jawaharlal Nehru who, it is good to remember, conceived the idea of the Commonwealth in its present form.

K.C. Belliappa, the Secretary, brought from his vast wealth of inexperience dynamism and devotion to his work especially at a time when my own spirits were at a low ebb. And he was assisted at the Conference by our research scholars, students and the office Secretary Mr Gowdaiah. As always on such occasions, the team-work of my colleagues in the Department was at once my comfort and strength—I am particularly grateful to them for taking up the difficult task of selecting the papers for publication. Dr Ramesh Mohan, Director, Central Institute of English and Foreign Languages, has helped me in many unseen ways during the Association's existence in the country for three years; his openmindedness in bringing Commonwealth Language and Literature into a predominantly English Language Institute is one proof of it. It has been a pleasure for me to have dealings with Mr C. Cecil, the Editor, Mr O.P. Ghai the book-loving Director, and his charming son, the Managing Director of Sterling Publishers. If there are lapses in the book-production they are an inescapable aspect of the Commonwealth experience, but any good in it must promise a bright future.

C.D.N.

Contents

Introduction

C.D. NARASIMHAIAH

> Still barred thy doors ! The far east glows,
>   The morning wind blows fresh and free
> Should not the hour that wakes the rose
>   Awaken also thee ?

Of this verse by an Indian girl in her teens Edmund Gosse, the 19th century British celebrity, wrote :

'It was while Professor W. Minto was editor of the "Examiner", that one day in August 1876, in the very heart of the dread season for books, I happened to be in the office of that newspaper, and was up-braiding the whole body of publishers for issuing no books worth reviewing. At that moment the postman brought in a thin and sallow packet with a wonderful Indian postmark on it, and containing a most unattractive orange pamphlet of verse, printed at Bhowanipore, and entitled "A Sheaf gleaned in French Fields, by Toru Dutt." This shabby little book of some two hundred pages, without preface or introduction, seemed specially destined by its particular providence to find its way hastily into the waste-paper basket. I remember Mr Minto thrust it into my unwilling hands and said "There ! see whether you can't make something of that". A hopeless volume it seemed, with its queer type, published at Bhowanipore, printed at the Sapthikasambad Press ! But when at last I took it out of my pocket, what was my surprise and almost rapture to open at such verse as this :

And after quoting the lines at the top Gosse remarks with a thoughtful-ness, generosity and not altogether without a fine awareness of the critical function :

"When poetry is as good as this it does not matter whether Rouveyre prints it upon Whatman paper, or whether it steals to light in blurred type from some press in Bhowanipore".

My excuse for quoting Gosse's remarks at such length is their immediate relevance, not to India only but a considerable part of the Commonwealth. "This hopeless volume", "queer type", "published at Bhowanipore", "printed at the"—unheard of, difficult-to-pronounce—"Sapthikasambad Press", "thrust into unwilling hands", (but not always accompanied by

'surprise' and 'rapture'), "destined...into the wastepaper basket" still
describe the plight of much that comes out of the Commonwealth Pen. But
"Rouveyre prints [it] on Whatman paper" and all it entails does today seem
to make a scandalous difference in the quality of response in metropolitan
circles when one recalls that a well-known Indian journalist, till recently in charge of a most prestigious English weekly, god-like, announced to
an eager-eyed university audience his criterion for the choice of books for
review : he would take a quick look at the imprint of a book on the spine
and unless it was published by some better known British or American
firm he wouldn't touch it with a bargepole, much less consider it for
review in his columns, though, ironically much of what passed his test week
after week, more often than not, invited his arrogant assertion against itself. The colonial cringe of the kind exhibited by the editor, in sharp contrast
to the sympathy and understanding evident in Gosse's gesture, is a conti-
nual challenge to the Commonwealth writer and critic. To learn to
respond to their work adequately and convincingly is to demonstrate that
the departures from the nineteenth century insular norms were necessitated
by a recognition of the fast changing situation, itself a result of historical
forces. Not to appreciate them at this stage is to be left behind; worse, to
arrest the growth of a generation which we presume to guide. Professor
Joseph Jones, writing from his wealth of experience of world literature in
English, has diagnosed the 'precipitate exodus from English classrooms'.
He lays the blame at the doors of English teachers themselves who were
"narrowing and impoverishing our subject by the behaviour that supposedly was enriching it. Worst of all, we were gradually but quite certainly,
losing the interest of our students, processing them through short-term,
low-yield courses in which their role was chiefly that of the passive receptor...instead of seeing English as a creative, expanding discipline they
came to see it as an imposed requirement which, once satisfied, was for
the most part mercifully self-destructing." Such the justification for the
expanding circles of English studies, one of the most important of which
because of its immediate relevance, is most assuredly Commonwealth
Literature.

When the mood lasts we would do well to consider a sonnet called
'The Lotus' by Toru Dutt, that slip of a girl who could at 19 respond, as
it were, to the 'imperial' challenge (Cowper's poem is that to one like
Toru who could make a successful response) not merely from her digestive
tract and the cerebral cortex, as Eliot has elsewhere said, but from the
millennia of her race memories, hallowed by a living tradition. Behind
her is the incomparably better known—known not for any particularly
memorable poem of poems, though—William Cowper who, when he was
past 50, wrote a poem called *The Lily and the Rose*:

The nymph must lose her female friend
    If more admired than she—

But where will fierce contention end,
    If flowers can disagree ?

Within the garden's peaceful scene
    Appeared two lovely foes,
Aspiring to the rank of Queen,
    The Lily and the Rose.

The Rose soon reddened into rage,
    And, swelling with disdain,
Appealed to many a poet's page
    To prove her right to reign.

The Lily's height bespoke command,
    A fair imperial flower;
She seemed designed for Flora's hand
    The sceptre of her power.

This civil bickering and debate,
    The goddess chanced to hear
And flew to save, ere yet too late,
    The pride of the parterre.

Yours is, she said, the noblest hue
    And yours the statelier mien;
And, till a third surpasses you,
    Let each be deemed a queen.

Thus soothed and reconciled, each seeks
    The fairest British fair;
The seat of empire is her cheeks,
    They reign united there.

It was pressed on the Indian readers' attention through a miserable looking multipurpose mofussil quarterly by an obscure college teacher of English
in a small town in South India as the stimulus behind Toru Dutt's sonnet,
virtually unnoticed by any, with her much anthologised 'Our Causurina
Tree' looming large in college textbooks.   Now read 'The Lotus' :

Love came to Flora asking for a flower
    That would of flowers be undisputed queen,
    The lily and the rose, long, long had been
Rivals for that high honour. Bards of power
Had sung their claims. "The rose can never tower

Like the pale lily with her Juno mien"—
    "But is the lily lovelier ?" Thus between
Flower-factions rang the strife in Psyche's bower

"Give me a flower delicious as the rose
    And stately as the lily in her pride"—
"But of what colour ?"—"Rose-red," Love first chose,

> Then prayed,—"No, lily-white,—or, both provide;"
>   And Flora gave the lotus, "rose-red" dyed,
> And "lily-white,"—the queenliest flower that blows.

One is amazed at the young poet's enviable grasp of Cowper's poem in all
its particulars as well as of the mythological lore of two traditions which
her imagination vigorously seized in one fetch and crossed the rose with
the lily to produce the unsuspected lotus, silently proclaiming its mythical
origins and rich symbolic overtones in legend and poetry. And in the
enactment are evident Miss Dutt's audacious opening, her admirable
sense of drama, edged economy and the metaphysical with which coins the
deceptively felicitous 'flower factions' in 'Psyche's bower' resulting in
Flora's gift of lotus, 'the queenliest flower that blows,' which is at once a
triumph of her originality and a marvellously calculated triumph of her
own tradition. That her family was convert to Christianity only helps to
reinforce the conviction that neither an acquired language nor an adopted
religion can impose their own values nor distort the natural growth if the
foundations are stable—like the deep reservoirs of his own culture that
Gandhi, for instance, was aware of when he confidently affirmed his faith :
'Let all the winds of all the lands blow over my house but I shall refuse
to be blown off my feet by any.' Not surprising that Edward Thompson,
a hard-headed Oxford don and novelist of the Indian scene should have
bracketed Toru with Sappho and Emily Bronte.

Three quarters of a century after, in another part of the Commonwealth but in the same hemisphere, A.D. Hope bemoans* the plight
of Charles Harpur, his distant predecessor who, if he had the genius
of Keats, was hampered by the absence of the European tradition,
an artistocratic sensibility and the English countryside with the song
of the nightingale in it. But happily, Mr Hope himself transforms an
obvious handicap into an advantage by writing on *a* bird, any bird. What
he misses in the absence of a stable tradition and an ordered countryside
he finds in his bleak geography : in the peculiar location of his continent in
the southern hemisphere into whose tropical warmth birds migrate annually
from cool weather. Situated as he is—both geography and history generate
their own compulsions—the poet cannot look for the fall of princes
which convulse a whole kingdom and cause a tragedy, but such is his
compassion for bird and beast that it fertilises his poetic imagination which
visualises, in a minor way analogous to Valmiki's traumatic experience in
the *Ramayana*, the predicament of a bird with its loyalty divided between
its mate and its young ones and pricked by an impulse now for the one,
now for the other, it loses its way in the blue infinity of space : "the
immense complex map mocks its small wisdom" "with its vast design" and

---

* A.D. Hope 'A Note on the Ballads' in *The Literary Criterion*, Vol. VI, No. 3, pp.
47-51.

the "great earth receives the tiny burden of its death" with "neither grief nor malice". But the affective pathos is nevertheless universal, "in widest commonalty spread". And the distinction of the poet is the greater considering that he works with such slender resources for his material. In another, better known poem, "Australia" Mr Hope who, unlike the English Romantics, neither idealises his country (the dry womb of the desert obviously doesn't warrant idealisation) nor declaims but tucked away from "what they call civilization over there" and freed from "the learned doubt" and "the lush jungle of modern thought", rightly hopes that "still from the deserts prophets come"—poetry here touches prophecy, using an idiom, syntax and intonation very different from those of Yeats. It is an adverse geography, which helps to quicken his sense of history, not his but mankind's, to which he is heir and participates as one truly civilized. Another poet before him, Shaw Neilson, much less cerebral than Mr Hope, would go to "stony town" (allegorically the world) "as to a fair". "Stony town is a hard town", it's all "straight line", "and square", bereft of the joys of "the curve" but the poet is fully equipped for the contingency. The tropics that might have broken an English romantic, because there is neither the daffodil nor the skylark but only rock without water which imparts a peculiar hardiness to the scene and drives one to seek support and sustenance in mateship evoked in "merry men three I will take with me", "the girl shall go as a velvet bird with "the scent of love and cinnamon dust shaken out of her hair", and a quick-step on her tongue." If self-reliance here has not assumed the gravity and eloquence of an Emerson, Australia did not have to wait as long as that other colony across the Atlantic.

Its desert situation helped to shape the vision of the future man in its foremost novelist Patrick White who has succeeded in writing great fiction at a time when the mother country, it seems, had declined (*dried up* might be more appropriate) in literature long before it did in political prestige. In *Voss*, Patrick White's supreme triumph in his as well as Australian fiction, the reader is ushered into a Jane Austen kind of household with a wealthy businessman, his snobbish wife and marriageable daughter preoccupied with their picnics, parties and flirtations looked upon with indifference by an orphaned Cambridge-educated niece who "would work fanatically at some mathematical problem just for the excitement of it"—a bloodless substitute for life. The merchant's vision presents itself to our view in terms of "the progress we have made", "our homes and public edifices", "the solid achievement" of the men who are "settling the land". And the beefy complacency is clinched in the climaxing remark "Why, in this very room, look at the remains of the good dinner we have just eaten." Such is Mr White's legacy which he at once turns into his opportunity. The opportunity is in the enactment of the "vale of tears" and the "soul making" he effects in the lives of Laura and the German explorer, Voss, who impinge on each other's lives, in a manner unprecedented in the

Western novel, until they both grow to their supreme heights of suffering, sacrifice and wisdom. For Voss, "the country is his by right of vision"; for Laura, "she could put her head on the rude rocks and feel rested." More, she could summon the courage to adopt her servant's child disregarding wagging tongues and tell her solicitous uncle who is anxious for her future :

"My future ! It's in the hands of God."

As White puts it suggestively in the middle of the novel "common forms are continually breaking into brilliant shapes. If we will explore them." As in the choice of Voss and Laura so in that of Alf Dubbo in *Riders in the Chariot*, says Professor Jack Healy, "there is a generosity which marks the highest point in European consciousness of the aborigine in Australian literature." The inspiration may well have come from the mother country as when Alastair Niven claims that the Scottish emigré, thanks largely to the influence of Burns, who helped overseas poetry to divest itself of much pomposity, proved to be founding figures of Australian and New Zealand writing.

A.D. Hope informs in one of his critical essays that when he lectured on Australian Writing in Canada in 1958 his attack on the jingoism of Australian literature roused little enthusiasm, for that is precisely what the Canadians had no chance to witness, presumably because of an undeveloped, or a not so aggressively national, consciousness. Interestingly, there is talk of militant Canadian nationalism in certain circles today. Even Northrop Frye confesses that in reporting on modern Canadian poetry he has adopted deliberately the policy of estimating this literature not "in world but Canadian proportions" : "I have for the most part", says Professor Frye, "discussed Canadian poets as though no other contemporary poets were available for Canadian readers". "Stick a pin", says Margaret Atwood in her remarkably interesting book *Survival*, "in Canadian literature at random, and nine times out of ten you will hit a 'victim'." She continues : "*Moby Dick* told by the White Whale would be a different story". Miss Atwood speculates : "The whale would ask why is that strange man chasing me around with a white harpoon ?" Appropriately she cites the case of E.J. Pratt's *Calchalot* in which it is "the whale's not the whaler's death, we mourn".

But consider the provocation to the assumption of such defiantly nationalistic stances by critics—Frye is beyond a doubt one—whose work has rightly earned for them more than a national appeal. Reviewing a book of Professor Matthews on the Comparative Study of Australian and Canadian Poetry, *Tradition in Exile*, (1962) Professor Hope took note of the continuing expansion of English speaking people from sixteenth to nineteenth century and preferred to call literature of the overseas regions of British colonialism "the frontier literature of a single literary tradition", though he hastens to qualify his statement slightly when he observes that the comparative isolation adds to a strong local and national flavour as it grows. And soon Mr. Hope makes himself vulnerable, certainly controversial, as he lets off what sounds like a theoretical statement : It will be a provincial literature depending on the homeland and initiating little itself because of the lower level of culture in the frontier regions. Ironically, it is the same Mr Hope who has since admitted to have filled in reams of paper with the Eliot kind of verse and consigned to flames before his authentic voice was heard. Margaret Atwood affirms with her characteristic candour : "I really do not think that as Canadian writers we have a great deal to learn from recent British fiction in which I sense a widespread weariness, repetition and even triviality. We would do better to go our own way now and to make our discoveries just as African writers are making theirs".

But in using the term 'Frontier Literature', obviously Mr Hope must have had in mind countries like Canada, New Zealand and his own to which English-speaking peoples emigrated and lived in "ignorance and contempt of native peoples and cultures". Small wonder, then, that Afro-Asian peoples, awe-stricken by the sceptre and crown of that precious isle set in the silver sea, are believed to have fared far worse : they had no literature at all! Africa, thanks to its oral tradition, had none and as for India, all its history, literature, philosophy and the sciences would occupy less than "a single shelf" for that great man, Macaulay, who nevertheless, compensated for his ignorance and prejudice by his concern for its future in his memorable reference to the 'imperishable empire'. But as E.M. Forster was to observe later, this high-minded man wanted to 'improve', not 'leave', India. How could he when his country and class convinced themselves they had a mission to work out ? Not only he, but even Forster of the Liberal tradition who felt grateful to his friend Ross Masood that he "woke me out of my suburban and academic life and showed me new horizons and a new civilization", for this didn't inhibit the other, and if one may say so in a time of adulation for his *Passage*, the essential Forster. Consider the phrasing and tone of his remarks in *The Hill of Devi* :

> "Festivals are endless. Today Ganapati (the Elephant God) has a little show, the day before yesterday the bullocks were worshipped, tomorrow ladies may eat practically nothing but vegetable marrows."
> . . .   . . .
> "Yesterday after my usual early visit from 'royalty I walked to the Temple of Ram-whose-hands-reach-to-his-knees, not to be confused with the Temple of the Monkey God Hanuman (who-knocks-down-Europeans) which is close to the Guest House."
> . . .   . . .

"A great many gods are on a visit and they all get up at 4.30 a.m.—
they are not supposed to be asleep during the festival which is reasonable considering the din, but to be enjoying themselves. They have a
bath and are anointed and take a meal which is over about 9 a.m."

Compare these passages, vibrating with sarcasm bordering on sacrilege
by the reputedly suave, 'sympathetic' Forster (who almost anticipates here
the V.S. Naipaul of *An Area of Darkness*) with corresponding passages
in *Kanthapura* by an insider like Raja Rao :

"Corner-House Narsamma's son, Moorthy—our Moorthy as we always
called him—was going through our backyard one day and, seeing a
half-sunk linga, said, 'Why not unearth it and wash it and consecrate
it ?' 'Why not !' said we all, and as it was the holidays and all the
city boys were in the village, they began to put up a little mud wall and
a tile roof to protect the god. He was so big and fine and brilliant, I
tell you, and our Bhatta duly performed the consecration ceremony.
And as Rangamma said she would pay for a milk and banana libation,
and a dinner, we had a grand feast. Then came Postmaster Suryana-
rayana and said, 'Brother, why not start a *Sankara-jayanthi* ? I have
the texts. We shall read the *Sankara-Vijaya* every day and somebody
will offer a dinner for each day of the month.' 'Let the first be mine,'
said Bhatta. 'The second mine,' insisted Pandit Venkateshia. 'And
the fourth and the fifth are mine,' said Rangamma. 'And if there
is no one coming forward for the other days, let it always be mine,'
she said. Good, dear Rangamma ! She had enough money to do it,
and she was alone. And so the *Sankara-jayanthi* was started that
very day. We hastily pushed rice on the leaves of the young and
came back for the evening prayers. There used to be bhajan. Trumpet Lingayya with his silver trumpet was always there, and once the
music was over, we stayed till the camphor was lit, and throwing a
last glance at the god, we went home to sleep, with the god's face
framed within our eyes. It was beautiful, I tell you—day after day we
spent as though the whole village was having a marriage party."

Far from being a dull routine as suggested by Forster's 'Festivals are
endless' what impresses one is the all-round enthusiasm the lingam (which
to an outsider to the tradition would only have been the anthropologist's
phallic symbol in stone) evokes in the young students (despite their Ang-
licized education) and the common folk in the village to whom religion
is not a compartmentalised business but a socialising and integrating
factor, generating a sense of participation, an insistence on duty which
here, paradoxically, sounds like a privilege, because of the strong impulse
to share, celebrate and rejoice collectively which is characteristic of a
homogeneous peasant community and therefore a value to cherish.
George Lamming, the West Indian novelist, has observed, "It is the

West-Indian novel that has restored the West-Indian peasant to his true and original stature of personality" and that it is "shot through and through with the urgency of peasant life." He portrays in his *Season of Adventure* a heart-rending situation of a prostitute, Belinda, who turns out a black customer for an affluent white American. She says :

> "I don't know what all the new freedom mean," she said, "cause they all crooks the political lot, all crooks, but I see how things start to change. An' I decide to back my little boy future...."

> And she was ready for the night : this night which was her faith in the little boy's future.

If a West Indian talks of such social ills, Kenneth Ramchand (in his admirable book, *The West Indian Novel and its Background*) corrects with an insider's authority that in a society in which the position of the individual is existential this 'consciousness' is not class consciousness. And this, for him, is a point of departure from the nineteenth century English novel because 'not concerned with consolidating or flattering particular groups.'

The situation in Raja Rao's village, Kanthapura, was by no means idyllic either for the fallen woman. At the end of the commotion, only Range Gowda, the village headman, then a 'tiger to the authorities' now 'lean as an areca' tree came back; the city boys went to the city; 'the Corner-House was all but fallen', 'Rangamma's house tileless', 'Nan-jamma's house doorless', 'Bhatta has sold all his lands', 'there's neither man nor mosquito in Kanthapura', only Concubine Chinna remained 'to lift her leg to her new customers' and 'my heart it beat like a drum', says the grandmother narrator.

This is the new 'social reality' that has entered fiction in Indian-English writing. The reference to the concubine, I can vouchsafe from first-hand experience, contributed to a commotion in university circles—teachers of English in colleges, long used to paraphrasing what in their innocence (snobbery is the right word) described as the 'chaste English' of Jane Austen's provincial novel *Pride and Prejudice*, felt outraged by the 'Indian-isms'; and the reputedly high-minded public men on university bodies (where, by the way, they do not belong) demanded the withdrawal of the novel from the undergraduate syllabus because they were indignant and ashamed, by turns, that their children were taught such obscenities. But the young fellows didn't take long to see through the hypocrisies of their parents, the leaders of our newly won independence, made possible by Gandhi's mass movement thanks to which the main participants had been dispossessed of the little that was their all and turned into destitutes for whom therefore Independence made no difference, with the benefici-aries building mansions on their children's graves.

Mulk Raj Anand, as much under pressure of leftist thought as under the stimulus of Gandhi's reform movement, took the dispossessed and the destitute everywhere—in the slums of cities, in the factories, in the village, on the road and the pavement and made them enter the mainstream of life, largely through their own heightened consciousness.

Even a writer like R.K. Narayan who is said to be influenced by the English country house comedy has brought out successfully the rich potentialities inherent in mediocrity, the vagabond and the fallen woman. Consider his best known novel *The Guide* in which Narayan brings out the staying power of society itself whose hundred ills haven't destroyed the moral and spiritual base of the individual. This is done, paradoxically, not by the feverish search for identity, which in the Indian tradition is achieved essentially by assiduous attempts to lose it—its presence hindered integration with both man and God; its absence releases him from the prison of his own making. Thrown out of the railway platform, fallen from the grace of Rosie, convicted and imprisoned and, once out of prison, living in virtual isolation in a ruined temple, Raju could still rehabilitate himself and be the nucleus of regeneration for the small community by drawing stimulus from the childhood stories he had heard from his mother: she used to tell him the rains would come if there was one good man ready to sacrifice his life. Rosie, too, victim of a double betrayal, could still conquer bitterness and give vent to her generous impulse towards both. She went to Raju's rescue with her money and was overcome with anguish and remorse for her own conduct in respect of her husband : 'I would have preferred to die on his doorstep' 'After all he is my husband' became the refrain of her talk.

Raja Rao in his *The Serpent and the Rope* does something which must sound more incredible to a European ear : A young Cambridge-educated woman Savithri who smokes like a chimney, dances boogie-woogie and sings jazz, becomes like her namesake in myth, legend, and epic, not the third point of the triangle of relationships in a typical Western novel but, the agent of recognition for Ramaswami and sends him to his guru while she herself goes home to marry 'stump Pratap' because it is her *dharma*, the radar which lands the plane to safety. Such is the author's heightened sense of his past that in his last novel to date *The Cat and Shakespeare* the characters are drawn from diverse religions, castes and classes with the main character, Govinda Nair, a non-brahmin second division clerk from a ration office becomes the virtual presiding deity of the entire action. Raja Rao goes further and makes the cat, a 'pariah animal' the Mother Principle to which Man may wisely surrender, for 'Have you ever seen the kitten fall ?'

These writers have 'muddled' their way through to apprehend the 'mystery' of Indian life and virtually demonstrated the inherent limitations of Kipling and Forster who, if they had at times, some sort of sympathy, did not have the understanding to equal it. Mr Forster realised later in his life (1946) that he would not be so foolish as to say 'I understand

India' but he knew he 'loved' it, though his novel has amply shown 'love' is not enough for a *writer*.

The African writer was faced with a more formidable task : There were no Vedas and Upanishads, neither the great epics nor the bright epochs of history which he could invoke. And what chance had gesture, in speech that is, even when it was the expression of long lived experience and the accumulated wisdom of an oral tradition against a world which put its faith in the printed word ! A Joyce Cary could pass for a sympathetic commentator if, as *Time* claimed, his *"Mister Johnson* was the best novel ever written about Africa." For Cary "Its people would not know the change if time jumped back fifty thousand years. They live like mice or rats in a palace floor; all the magnificence and variety of the arts, the learning and the battles of civilization go on over their heads and they do not even imagine them." Another African expert, a renowned humanist, Albert Schweitzer, had no qualms in claiming "The African is my brother, but a junior brother," while for Kipling Africa was "half devil, half child."

Professor Wren informs that Joyce Cary's *Mister Johnson* appalled Achebe and motivated him to "tell the story he had to tell". In contrast to Cary's vision the Road in Achebe is "a simple inclusive metaphor". Achebe has seen it from the inside and shows a society that is "far more an actor in its destiny than an object that is acted upon."

As for telling the story, Achebe concedes that the English language will be able to carry his African experience. Only it will have to be a different English: "still in its full communion with its ancestral home but altered to suit its new African surroundings." Africa, like India, has different languages and innumerable dialects which shape different kinds of English all of which are necessary to articulate a rich variety of experiences, attitudes and states of mind. As Professor W.H. New has told us a literary form can "sustain not only verbal tensions but in doing so sustains social and political realities". Which brings up the question of reader-response to different kinds of works of art. To respond adequately one has to *hear* how the language works. In respect of African literature, but not only of that, you have to recognise where you have a *reading* public to-day there was a *listening* audience and learn to recognise how much of that 'orality' has passed into the printed word. Mr. New recommends a greater 'sensitivity to English in the process of being born', 'the ability to distinguish between writers who explore the suppleness of their own idiom and writers who substitute a safe vocabulary for the words which their own tongues would utter. Let me cite an example from Raja Rao's *Kanthapura*.

"Old Ramakrishnayya read chapter after chapter with such a calm, bell-metal voice, and we all listened with our sari fringes wet with tears. Then they began to lay leaves for dinner. And one boy came and said, 'I shall serve, aunt !' And another came and said 'Can I serve paysam, aunt?'... and this way and that we had quite a marriage army and they served like veritable princes."

An outsider to the experience or one without Raja Rao's kind of sensitivity to the local idiom would have falsified the experience, surely let expression corrupt experience itself by saying something like the following in the interest of what he would have thought as easy intelligibility :

"As old Ramakrishnayya read chapter after chapter in his resonant voice we were all moved to tears. Then we adjourned to dinner. We were quite a crowd. But we were waited upon by bright looking boys who were so courteous and generous with the food."

Nothing of the informative part of the earlier passage is missed here. But it is not faithful to the precise contours of experience—it is a very Indian experience, and South Indian at that. The triumph here is one of evocation as different from communication. It exemplifies a fusion of 'culture and cultural rhetoric'. In the presence of this only those speak of 'universal' standards of criticism who are insensitive to the subtle tone of voice, the rhythm, gesture, image, symbol and myth. And our backward societies are rich in speech sounds—in the cadences and intonations that constitute Commonwealth voices. And so even when written, literature in Commonwealth has an 'orality'. Consequently, to ignore this, as Professor New fears, is to be "lodged in the land of themes; we take language away from our writers at the very time they have made their language into a world of their own". Consider for instance, the traditional form of prayer in *The Serpent and the Rope* rendered into English with the relatively refined upper caste Indian habits of thought, speech, imagery, syntax or what Mulk Raj Anand elsewhere commends as the 'authentic lilts' which ally them to the consciousness of their own people.

"Rama, Rama, Sri Rama, give us wealth and give us splendour; give us the eight riches auspicious, give us an heir, give us a home and sanctuary, give us earth and gardens; those who go to lands distant, may they return, may the body be firm and innocent; give eyes to the blind, give legs to the lame, give speech to the dumb. Rama, Sri Rama, give us Thy Holy Presence".

It is contexts like this in Achebe's *Arrow of God* which makes Dr Vargo reflect indignantly on the European's cheating himself and his progeny by flattering the racial and national ego and denigrating Afro-Asian history and civilization. In his close study of priestly characters in the novels of Greene, Keneally and Achebe Dr Vargo analyses the difficulties in response as both linguistic and cultural. He finds 'no great obstacles' in the language of Greene and Keneally but despite the fact Achebe is skilful in transferring the Igbo idiom into English it would seem 'next to impossible to savour the full sophistication of his linguistic achievement without the aid of studies by knowledgeable critics'. He fears 'the chance of misreading will be in direct proportion to the distance of that novel's background from the reader's own'. In his desire to understand the frame of reference of a different culture and the entire milieu he speaks with a rare generosity and self-awareness : 'Being a Catholic and a priest, I have a particular access to the theological underpinnings of *The Honorary Consul* or the subculture of Keneally's Australian clerics. This same personal history may work against my entering into the system of theology or belief underlying the rites of Ulu.'

That is precisely the position of Mr Desani when he says 'I cannot see my book in any language other than the English language', for the 'demands of his craft' have made English, his kind of English, a necessity and therefore for him the Indian debate on whether or not to write in English is 'wasteful'. But Mr Desani himself is alive to the difficulties of communicating it to a Western audience. He brings up in his paper the examples of how 'a frightened girl in the train' and 'a defeated father of worldly wise girls' may fail to make meaning to a Western reader : they do not have a universal appeal, the appeal is local. He might well laugh at them, as he would when in R.K. Narayan's *Vendor of Sweets* Jagan, the old sweetmeat seller, renounces the world but forgets not to take the chequebook to his forest retreat, such is the ambivalence of Narayan's comedy. The renunciation is not, as is often thought, the result of a desire for indulgence in self-denial but a natural stage in a traditional Indian's life when he thinks he has fulfilled his obligations to the young. And in this case the taking of the chequebook has behind it not greed but a profound compassion for an innocent victim, the Korean girl that his son has brought with him from the States and virtually abandoned. Jagan intends to ensure her safe return home if the son should finally betray her or she should prefer to go back. It is *there* in the novel. If it is not *there*, well, the earnest reader must learn in the hard way. It is no more complex than the cross currents of Plato, Aristotle, Thomas Acquinas, the Renaissance, Reformation, Calvinism, Enlightenment, Romanticism, Transcendentalism, Symbolism, Surrealism, Existentialism, the Great Depression, Marx, Freud, Picasso and all their ramifications among the labyrinthine gifts of Europe or what A.D. Hope calls 'the lush jungle of modern thought' which an innocent teenager, child of pagan ancestors, is called upon to master in the tropics, deserts, and jungles of Asia and Africa.

Understandably, some African writers wish to concede nothing to the normal Western reader that might undermine their own position within their own heritage or compromise the integrity of their indigenous perception, for surely, they would argue, there are other ways of seeing the world than those known to Europeans.

Of Desani's practice as writer, referred to earlier, Syd Harrex has a different way of looking—one born of close acquaintance with the writing of the subcontinent. Harrex thinks that Desani has virtually turned the

novel into a performing art, just as his characters perpetually make performances of their lives, and the characters include versions of the Shakespea-
rean fool, a pretentious gull like Malvolio or Sir Andrew Ague Cheek. For
Harrex, it is a gain to the language and the literature, for 'the spirit of
comic vitality which is such an important tradition in our literature, has
been regenerated in the process'.

This is in striking contrast to what the New Zealand poet Wystan
Curnow has remarked, probably motivated by a healthy disrespect for the
contemporary poetic scene. He thinks that a considerable part of the verse
(of the sixties) is 'depressingly derivative, manneristic and spiritless.' He
has more to denounce in the poets of his generation : "if you met one of
them in the B.B.C. *Listener, Encounter* or *Poetry* Chicago you wouldn't
know whether he came from New Zealand, Nicaragua or Notting Hall
(*Essays on New Zealand Literature* ed. Curnow). This is because, according to Mr Curnow, 'Our tastes originate almost anywhere but within New
Zealand itself'. Surely, his stand is not motivated by nationalistic considerations. The concern and the commitment is born of a desire for originality and is salutary to aspiring writers everywhere in the Commonwealth
when he firmly maintains he will reject every model from another writer's
hand unless he feels 'sure of his power to surpass it, his power to create
something that employs the model for a servant' : In other words he will
'not be a literary hitch-hiker, travelling on someone else's power and no
faster than that will carry him'.

It matters little for him if 'the man-size genius fits only a pint-size
bottle'— such is said to be the reputation of a New Zealand writer. But it is
'still New Zealand literature and the world would know New Zealand much
better'. Mr Curnow, one sees, is not waving the national flag, but is pleading
for originality and self-respect in art and literature because of a deeper
concern for them in life.

One fears that this stance of Curnow will very likely embarrass Dr Syed
Amanuddin who only recognizes 'human heritage' which does 'not need a
passport, only an attitude'. Alas ! it is a hard fact of life that not attitude
but passport takes one from one's own country, keeps him there and helps
to bring him out for short or long periods. All this is true in the business
of writing as well unless one has chosen to—to so few is it given to be
content to—wander now along *A Middle Passage*, now in *An Area of Darkness*, now *In A Free State* and back again to *A Wounded Civilization* from
which, God knows where Mr Naipaul goes. A writer no less than any one
else, if any, more desperately needs his nation, region, his own village
green or, as Llyod Fernando cites, what the Tasadays of the Philippines
call 'the stump of our feelings', 'the native pith' though Mr Fernando is
quick to warn it has its hazards, but so too the 'unwary acceptance of heterogeneity', he adds. 'Roots' for one like Wilson Harris can be a very complex thing, for the 'ancestors' are not localised, they can be anywhere, 'any
race'. In the context of the African, Canadian, New Zealand as well as

Asian writers' and scholars' profound concern for preserving their identity what is one to say of the author of *Goodbye to Elsa*, Mr Saros Cowasjee's chivalrous acceptance of a young lecturer's exhortation to write something like *The Wuthering Heights* ? Raja Rao's admonition in *The Serpent and the Rope* must sound very salutary : 'Let's give to the West what we can, even if it be a tamarind seed, not this *tom-tom*', while Achebe would go as far as to 'announce not just that we are as good as the next man, but we are better'—'until we get on our feet'.

Ironically Mr Cowasjee bemoans that 'no critical tradition has emerged' from the contemporary Indian literary scene. Well, tradition can't emerge from nowhere. One would have thought Mr Cowasjee wasn't in need of telling that tradition isn't 'inherited' as an easy-going son inherits his father's real estate; and that in this case it calls for a deeper and finer awareness of the critical foundations of India than what is so easily assumed in Mr Cowasjee's remark. Nor does awareness suffice; it must enlist, besides, the determined labours of those who have the faith and the ommitment.

The Commonwealth offers possibilities for intelligent meeting of the East and the West through a yet unexplored territory which has held out promise of fruitful interaction in the ancient world by possible contact between Hellenic and Hindu ideas. The parallels are striking. Plato's concepts of 'Idea' and 'Imitation', after all, have their parallels—Bernth Lindfors remarks, the lines can be oblique, not always parallel—in the mainstream of the Indian thought from the Upanishads and Sankara to the present day. Both Aristotle's *Poetics* and Bharatha's *Natyasastra*, treatises on dramaturgy, use biological and mental images. While Aristotle made plot the soul of Tragedy, Bharatha offers *rasa*, (literally juice) a state beyond pain and pleasure. And while Aristotle apparently simplifies tragic experience by restricting it to the two dominant emotions of pity and fear, Bharatha enumerates eight primary emotions (to which a ninth has been added by subsequent authorities) and any number of derivative emotions, validated by modern European psychologists like McDougall. More, Bharatha has given the world such an invaluable critical tool as *Vibhava*, the 'objective correlative' to which T.S. Eliot has given wide currency in our own times and the resultant generation of the *rasa*, the aesthetic state of the reader, made memorable by Matthew Arnold in the celebrated phrase 'Indian virtue of detachment'. If only Western criticism comes to grips with the term *rasa* as a criterion of judgement how it can, with its tremendous prestige and influence, help to obviate tons of loose and wasteful talk of 'joy', 'pleasure', 'delight', 'instruction', 'message' which have arrested the growth of criticism apart from straying us away from the precise nature of art experience.

The work of the New Critics of America at least has its parallels in the Indian concepts of *vakrokti* (literally, crooked or oblique speech) of Kuntaka in eighth century, a term which is inclusive of Irony, Paradox, Texture and so forth; *Dhvani* of Anandavardhana, or what is for want of an appropriate equivalent called 'suggestion', also eighth century; and *Auchitya* or Propriety, probably sixth century. It will be seen the Dark Ages of Europe were peculiarly fertile for sophisticated discussions in aesthetic and critical activity in India. Add to this the traditional African and Indian approach to art, not as *accomplishment* but as *function* in which there is no distance between the makers of culture and its consumers, for as A.K. Coomaraswamy has cried hoarse, the artist is not a special kind of man but everyman is a special kind of artist (Senghor thinks everyman is a poet).

If as I.A. Richards has taught us, improvement in response is the only benefit and the degradation of response the only calamity, it follows that improvement must be sought, in a 'variety of ways'. And yet Richards who gave this sage advice himself succumbed to the tyranny of quantification in his definition of Value. Perhaps its validity and adequacy can be checked against the traditional Indian value system of the "Ends" of life with *Artha* (wealth) *Kama* (sex) and *Dharma* (righteousness) as instrumental values and *Moksha* (the completest realisation of the full potential of man) as ultimate value, because it leads to the apprehension of *that* by knowing which all else is known. Which takes one back to Plato for whom 'Idea' alone is real (for Sankara it is Brahman or That) and the world is an illusion or *Maya*. One wonders if the West by putting its faith in empiricism has not, if one may say so, stopped short of the apprehension of Reality—with social reality absorbing the energies of its best minds. One is constrained to ask if morality, even 'moral centrality', is the supreme yardstick or criterion the West in its wisdom and splendour of undoubted achievement in Arts and Science could offer ? What, then, does the West mean when it uses expressions like 'soul', 'spirit', 'spiritual', 'profoundly spiritual' ? In what relation do these stand to the 'moral' ? How does the West judge works of art like Dante's *Divine Comedy*, Melville's *Moby Dick*, Emily Dickinson's *Poetry* and Eliot's *Four Quartets*, Raja Rao's *The Serpent and the Rope*, Patrick White's *Voss* with the moral yardstick, whether in principle or perception? To say we have no yardsticks is to evade the question, for surely no one can criticise without any assumptions. One of the supreme rewards of the study of Commonwealth Literature is that it offers to our view larger perspectives and the compromises are effected not only in idiom and rhythm but in the very stuff of one's thought and feeling, when one culture absorbs elements from another, which are fundamentally alien to it and by this means 'deduce something of value about both the cultures which might not have been possible without the larger perspective'.

If the Western tradition has put its faith in social reality as the ultimate value it has been appropriately said that a tradition is there 'not to bury one but to serve as material for new departures'. History bristles with instances of literature and criticism cutting across national and racial frontiers. And so, if our endeavour is to attain a completeness of response we will not be satisfied with anything less than that; rather, we should seek it from the ends of the earth. Achebe is fully justified therefore in his demand : "I should like to see the word 'universal' banned altogether from discussions of African literature until such time as people cease to use it as a synonym for the narrow self-serving parochialism of Europe, until their horizon extends to all the world". The study of Commonwealth Literature therefore offers the best means of pooling the resources of many cultures as suggested by Achebe's vivid phrase 'humanity's heirloom' and of breaking the national barriers so as to make them available to all of us in the hope of supplementing each other's deficiencies and correcting the warps. This, then, is a significant step in the direction Professor A.N. Jeffares, the founding father of the Association, visualized for Commonwealth Literature in his introductory address to the Association's first Conference at Leeds and repeated at the second Conference in Brisbane, Australia. Let us hope the coming years can do more to reassure us of the wisdom of our choice and its vigorous pursuit by scholars everywhere within and outside the Commonwealth.

1

The Absolute
and the Image of Man in Australia :
Judith Wright and Patrick White

J.J. HEALY

UNLIKE Canada, the Caribbean and the United States, Australia is a product of the nineteenth century. It escaped the Enlightenment with its
eighteenth century brand of secular universalism. It eluded the varieties of
Christian humanism which, in one form or another, had distinguished the
seventeenth century. It had little notion of that late bloom of a rich,
medieval Christianity which informed the early presence of Quiros in the
Pacific, a presence which haunts the beginning of the European concern
with Australia : La Austrialia del Espiritu Santo : the South Land of the
Holy Ghost. The rich symbolism of Christianity, the large vistas of the
Enlightenment, yielded, in the nineteenth century, to a more historical,
literalist, and positivist conception of man and nature. There were gains in
this development; there were also losses. There were no Hookers or de
Tocquevilles in Australia, by which one means that imaginations imbued
with the universalist generosity of these men did not consider the phenomenon of man on this continent.

There are, writes Colin Horne, two versions of Australian history : a
rough and a smooth, a working class and middle class conception of Australian nationality, of Australian reality. Both developed a set of attitudes,
a concept of nation and, perforce, a view of reality which look antipathetic
from close-up, but are less so from wider perspectives. The opposition
between both groups took place across the body of an industrial society,
organised for the production of wealth, and disorganised by the inequitable
distribution of that wealth. In many ways, the debate is one of spoils and
property against a diminished conception of man beset on all sides by
determinisms : genetic, economic, historical. The great voices of opposition
to this new nineteenth century world in Europe, Kierkegaard, Nietzsche,
Schopenhauer, found little echo in Australia. Even the great voice of

definition, Marx, is absent. To the extent that there is a myth which grounds itself in Australia, it is, says Manning Clark, one of master and worker.

This may be an excessively normative way of describing the situation. But any attempt to trace the re-emergence of the absolute in Australia must emphasise the domination of positivism, especially in its aesthetic and moral implications, over the Australian imagination. Man in Australia is the man of property and of party, divorced from the kind of philosophical principle that may, in some contexts, give reflective generality to both.

There were two outstanding explanations for the inability of the Australian writer to break out of the restrictions of his inheritance. The confusions of European thought in which the connections between man and his world had become increasingly problematic and a subject of despair. Alienation; disjunction; in its more polite form dissociation of sensibility; man removed from a sense of himself, of the world; these are the prominent themes. Solutions took a number of forms : one gives up man to his material universe; one absorbs that universe into the consciousness of man himself as an embattled individual; one attempts by theories of symbolism, of dialectic, of religious mutuality, to keep the lines open across the division. The great nineteenth century question, which cuts through the advances in the physical sciences, in the social sciences, is the question of man. Does he fit in ? The energies of interrogation have been immense and a tribute to the persistence of men to have this question answered, at the same time that the answers they have come up with have fed despair.

Australia, until about 1940, remained aloof from the full force of these developments. Isolationism, White Australia, protectionist tariffs, the brave efforts to maintain a garrison community sustained by a handful of secular myths "in the optative mood", to cite Emerson's words, characterised the country. The fears were physical : the removal of the Royal Navy, invasions from Asia. The metaphysical, and with it, the moral and the metaphorical in a nuanced and supple manner, was absent. There was Brennan; there was, in London, Henry Handel Richardson, and above all, there was in Australia, through Katharine Prichard's response; through his own visit and the way his conception of man, land and myth took Australia into its orbit in *Kangaroo;* the liberating influence of D.H. Lawrence. The idiom of modernity was absent from a society that remained stubbornly attached to the nineteenth century.

The major reason why a reduced version of a reductionist and outmoded philosophy of man sustained itself in Australia so long was that it was a colonial society. This is to say that it was *one kind* of a society which permitted and encouraged certain types of sociality as distinct from others. This is important to the extent that these factors influence the kind of human relationships, the kind of Man, that becomes conceivable and graspable by the writer in a colonial situation. Hugh Maclennan put it nicely in a lecture. In the early thirties he found himself in conversation with Sir Charles G.D. Roberts about *Barometer Rising.* "This is the first Canadian novel I have read with a fully developed human being in it," said Roberts. "Animals, nature, lots of that. But no people." It is an astonishing statement. But he is right. What is it about a colonial culture that exacerbates the problem of man seeing himself in non-sticklike terms ?

I put it down to the issue of society and available sociality. George Gurvitch, a man whose great career as a sociologist was, in my opinion, supported on his brilliant intuitions during the disturbance of the Russian Revolution, has put it this way :

"Consciousness is a dialectical relationship between I, Other and We, which partially interpenetrate each other and partially converge through opposition."

The degree of consciousness which a society sustains or permits may be expressed in this way :

"Partial fusion among minds opening to each other, and among behaviours interpenetrated in a 'we', may appear in different degrees of intensity and depth. When the fusion is very weak and only integrates superficial layers of consciousness which open only at the surface and remain closed with regard to what is more or less profound and personal, sociality is *mass*. When minds fuse, open out, and interpenetrate on a deeper, more intimate plane, where an essential part of the aspiration and acts of personality is integrated in the 'we', without, however, attaining the maximum of intensity in this integration, sociality is *community*. When, finally, this most intense degree of union of 'we' is attained, that is, when the minds open out as widely as possible and the least accessible depths of the 'I' are integrated in this fusion...sociality is *communion*."

There are a number of versions of this : Buber's I-Thou; Judith Wright's reflections on Mankind and Society and her concern with naked vision. The We-phenomenon is the mediating Absolute. These are varieties of communion : a colonial society being *mass*.

At the end of the thirties glimmerings of these issues began to filter into Australia. Nettie Palmer's diary is excellent at tracing the hints. One entry dated March 4th, 1936, refers to the then Australian exile Marcel Aurousseau :

"I've never met anyone in whom literature and geography merged so significantly as in Aurousseau. One evening here he said he had more hope for Australian geography than for Australian literature—though the geography, so far, had some appalling faults and gaps. As a geographer, I think, he has an idea that a separate and fresh view of man's earthly life might be drawn from within the borders of that island of the South, the Last Sea-thing...But methods of discovery and statement must be organized, must be thorough. His mind turns to the 18th century astronomers and navigators who exercised their rapidly-expanding scientific knowledge in drawing up Australian charts and maps that are still valuable. The responsible outlook of those scientists was a new religion, humanist and rational, and he bitterly resents any cheap sneers at their limitations."

The last entry of Nettie Palmer's diary is dated August 4th, 1939, and is a tribute to the sensitive intelligence that she brought to bear, privately, on her own society.

Tonight, I've been reading over the 'Anatomy of Melancholy' with its marvellous 'Digression of Air.' Easy for Burton, dreaming by the Isis three centuries ago, to speculate remotely about us in our nonexistence: "That hungry Spaniard's discovery of Terra Australia Incognita...cannot choose but yield in time some flourishing kingdoms to succeeding ages." These are the kingdoms, no longer *incognita*; this is the succeeding age, and a difficult one; here are we, a part of mankind, and being forced to face the fact.

Here we have it : antennae reading back to the eighteenth and seventeenth centuries, seeking from these sources a new context, a new language for man in Australia : a language of the absolute, for the absolution of man from the constrictions of positivism.
Yet, these are gropings, arrows pointing in a direction rather than territory inhabited by an Australian imagination.
It is widely recognised that the late thirties saw a quickening of cultural energies in Australia. It is also a commonplace that the months between December 1941 and February 1942, which saw spectacular Japanese advances in Asia and the Pacific islands, and which culminated in the fall of Singapore and the bombing of Darwin and Broome, were traumatic for Australians. There was a fall-out of panic from these events; but in a more interesting manner there was a fall-out of consciousness, a falling into a sense of tragedy which had ramifications in different directions. The matter of Australia, as the different strands of a nationalist ideology understood it, was touched into richer possibilities by this irritation of fear. Instantaneous joinings began to take place, became possible, became necessary. The need to join European man to the Australian landscape was as old as settlement and in 1939, as remote; the need to get to the Aborigines in some undefined, mystical way was being bruited. The Jindyworobak platform of Alcheringa and Environmental Values was keen to get the separate compartments of land, Aborigine and European society teamed up for an integrated gallop into a nationalist future. Others (Eleanor Dark, Barnard Eldershaw) wished with deliberate intent to join the present Australia to its history, to make memory speak, only to be trapped by a positivist sense of history as a chamber furnished by men, objects and actions. Others (Max

Harris) sought to domesticate the cosmopolitan ghost in the colonial machine. The need to speak, the sense that what was being seen and felt was not being spoken of, was, in retrospect, overwhelming. This need expressed itself in a passionate desire to make connections. The question was : how ? The answer could not be mechanical connection; what was required was that Coleridgean imagination which seeks "to make the external internal, the internal external, to make nature thought and thought nature."

It came. With astonishing completeness, with an instaneous fusion between history, memory, land, aborigine.

Judith Wright was the poet : subsequently Patrick White would be the novelist of the absolute. Space obliges one to abbreviate the extension of the argument to include Randolph Stow, or even to make any reference to the cultural debate which centred on this theme during the fifties and sixties. For brevity I shall confine myself to one poem, "Nigger's Leap : New England" and one novel, *Riders in the Chariot*.

For Judith Wright, then, a piece of history, a poem and a comment.

In his book, *Old New England : A History of the Northern Tablelands of New South Wales 1818-1900* (1966), R.B. Walker made reference to a reprisal in October 1844 at Edward Irby's Bolivia station. The European observation was simple : "We punished them severely and proved our superiority." Later, Irby's manager commented on the pursuit of some of the aborigines to the Bluff Rock :

"The man got up to the top of the rock and threw the blacks off the rock onto the ground at the bottom. The front half of the rock was a great bit from the ground below. A lot of blacks got killed and a lot more crippled. None of that tribe was seen on the station after that."

In 1946 Judith Wright published her volume of poetry, *The Moving Image*. This included the poem "Nigger's Leap : New England."

The eastward spurs tip backward from the sun.
Night runs an obscure tide round cape and bay
and beats with boats of cloud up from the sea
against this sheer and limelit granite head.
Swallow the spine of range; be dark, O lonely air.
Make a cold quilt across the bone and skull
that screamed falling in flesh from the lipped cliff
and then were silent, waiting for the flies.

Here is the symbol, and the climbing dark
a time for synthesis. Night buoys no warning
over the rocks that wait our keels; no bells
sound for her mariners. Now must we measure
our days by nights, our tropics by their poles,
love by its end and all our speech by silence.

Did we not know their blood channelled our rivers,
and the black dust our crops ate was their dust ?
O all men are one man at last. We should have known
the night that tided up the cliffs and hid them
had the same question on its tongue for us.
And there they lie that were ourselves writ strange.

Never from earth again the coolamon
or thin black children dancing like the shadows
of saplings in the wind. Night lips the beach
scarp of the tableland and cools its granite.
Night floods us suddenly as history
that has sunk many islands in its good time.

Darkness, night, the sea, which is overrunning the range of hills, which
overran the unfortunate aborigines, is threatening to overrun Western
society in Australia in a time of world war. It is from a sense of impending
destruction, which reaches out to the roots and future of civilisation itself,
that Judith Wright discovers again, becomes vulnerable to, the silent
wounds of Australian history. Fear is the handmaid of insight :

Night floods us suddenly as history
that has sunk many islands in its good time.

In these war years, Judith Wright entered a landscape of visibilities, in
which the aborigines were an important presence. What this amounted to
was a liberation of the Australian imagination into the open field of a rich-
textured history. Only in this kind of open field could the aborigine be a
lived and living presence. "Nigger's Leap" becomes literally and imaginatively, a symbol, a moving image, providing an opportunity for synthesis in
a dark time.

The connection between the liberation of the Australian imagination
and the Aborigine has been brilliantly examined by Patrick White in *Voss*
and *Riders in the Chariot*, to the extent that in the latter novel an Australian Aborigine becomes the Australian imagination. To understand Alf
Dubbo one has to grasp the peculiar situation of Jackie caught between the
aboriginal tribe and Voss.

When Jackie, at the instigation of the tribe, severs Voss's head into the
dust, he does so in an attempt to "break the terrible magic that bound
him remorselessly, endlessly, to the white men." The death of the explorer
leaves hanging the great question: do dreams breed? If Jackie is an answer,
dreams do breed and white maggots do not dry up. Jackie carries with him,
whether he likes it or not, the burden of a new consciousness. He has con-
tracted this from his association with the visionary white man, who had
sowed a certain magic and an obtrusive possession into the autochthonous
world of the aborigine. The tribe buys an immunity with the sacrifice of

Jackie. There is no return for him—to the tribe, to Jildra, or to the countrymen of Voss :

> "Jackie promised himself great happiness in talking to old Dugald.
> As he approached Jildra, he began to sing. To his disappointment,
> however, he discovered that Dugald had become so old he was again
> young, and he, Jackie, was weighed down with the wisdom of age. So
> he did not tell Dugald much beyond some uninteresting facts concern-
> ing the mutiny of the white men. All else he kept to himself.

> "For it is not possible to communicate lucidly with men after the
> communion of souls, and the fur of the white souls had brushed the
> moist skin of the aboriginal boy as he shuddered in the brigalow shrub.
> He was slowly becoming possessed of the secrets of the country, even
> of the spirits of distant tribal grounds. The children of Jildra ran
> screaming from him and hid in the gunyahs, and when he went from
> there, whole tribes of strange natives would beat the trees as he appro-
> ached, or sit in ashy silence round their fires as he recounted to their
> unwilling ears tales of the spirit life.

> "But of his own, the great spirit by which he was possessed, that
> would sometimes look in from the outside, through his eyes, but which
> more often would writhe inside him, like warning life, or gush and
> throb, like blood—of that spirit he would never tell, because nobody
> was to know of it but himself.

> "So Jackie came and went. He became a legend amongst the tribes.
> Of the great country through which he travelled constantly, he was the
> shifting and troubled mind. His voice would issue out of his lungs, and
> wrestle with the rocks, until it was thrown back at him. He was always
> speaking with the souls of those who had died in the land, and was
> ready to translate their wishes into dialect. If no other blackfellow
> learned what those wishes were, it was because his fear prevented him
> from inquiring of the prophet."

Jackie has become one of those favoured creatures of Patrick White's
fictions, a Seer—unsought, sensed, unseen. He has penetrated the core of
mystery that momentarily embraced Palfreyman and his compatriots. The
prophet as Pariah; the outcast as seer; Jackie as Alf Dubbo.

Himmelfarb is in the washroom. He looks at the open book, forgotten,
and reads :

> "And I looked and behold, a whirlwind came out of the north, a great
> cloud, and a fire infolding itself, and a brightness was about it, and out
> of the mist thereof as the colour of amber out of the mist of the fire."

Alf Dubbo, his workmate, comes to collect his book to find Himmelfarb
aglow.

> "Is it your book ?" asked the Jew.
> Then the blackfellow did something extraordinary.
> *He spoke.*

Alf, moving beyond Jackie, *speaks*. White has spiralled his preoccupations
of *Voss* into *Riders in the Chariot*. Voss himself has become a quaternity.
These shards of his visionary search, Laura, Jackie, Judd and Le Mesurier,
have broken into the brilliant shapes of Himmelfarb, Dubbo, Miss Hare
and Mrs Godbold. The saint, the eccentric, the artist, and the outcast, become the *illuminati* of a stubborn and blind world. The desert and Voss,
Voss in the desert, have been transposed through Alf, to the city.

> "Alf Dubbo now went bush, figuratively at least, and as far as other
> human beings were concerned. Never communicative, he retired into
> the scrub of half-thoughts, amongst the cruel rocks of obsession. Later
> he learned to prefer the city, that most savage and impenetrable terrain,
> for the opportunities it gave him of confusing anyone who might at-
> tempt to track him down in his personal hinterland."

Alf has taken over the shifting and troubled mind of Jackie, and he does
so as the aborigine who has been touched into uncertainty and deprivation
by contact with white civilisation, of whom Jackie was the prototype. White
is structuring *Riders in the Chariot* with the confidence of a world already
opened up. Jackies flows inevitably into Alf, just as Alf draws into his own
fate that of the aboriginal group he leaves behind at the river bank of his
youth. He is born into a time when the autochthony of his tribal ancestors
in *Voss* is at best a sentimental memory. It is appropriate, therefore, that
he should be burdened with the demands of a silent, wordless art. The seer
articulate, or, as the nature of the book requires, the seer articulating.
Dubbo is the artist as painter, who circumnavigates the treacheries of language into the traditional aboriginal medium of paint, who finds a language
of silence for a world of silence.

Riders in the Chariot continued the attack on the great Australian
Emptiness that White began to address seriously in *The Tree of Man*, that
he earthed in the founding elements of Australian history in *Voss*. The
Second World War seems, in White's view, to have exacerbated the
Emptiness : "Now it was the eyes that disturbed most, of the white people
who had always known the answers, until they discovered those were wrong.
So they would burst out laughing, or break into little snatches of tinny
song." Australia as a country of the blind is drained of its gods, those of
Alf's forbears and of Himmelfarb's faith. Himmelfarb activates, by his very
presence in the emptiness, its capacities for good and evil. He draws into
visibility the significant impoverishment of Harry Rosetree, Mrs Flack, Blue

and of society in general. Alf is the watcher, the displaced indigene, watching the reactions of Himmelfarb, watching the reactions *to* him. Contemporary Australia is portrayed in *Riders in the Chariot* as an *agon* of shy recognition between an Aborigine and a Jew, the brackets of reality between which that society founders in unreflective materialism. It is an echo of what has often been noted of the literature of the United States since 1945—written at its most profound by Jewish and Negro writers, it is a literature which can find words in the waste land of technology because these writers have had forced on them an image, a condition of man suffering. Dubbo strikes one as a figure of crucial importance in the personal and cultural vastation which informs so much of the book. Ralph Ellison expressed an intention in his essay, "Twentieth Century Fiction and the Black Mask of Humanity," which may be applied to Dubbo : "on the moral level I propose that we view the whole of American life as a drama acted out upon the body of a Negro giant, who lying trussed up like Gulliver, forms the stage, and the scene upon which and within which the action unfolds. If we change the figure of the giant to that of a sensibility, and that of the stage to a canvas, we catch the active and the passive dimensions of Alf Dubbo's role in *Riders in the Chariot*.

Alf, who watches and interprets the world, absorbs it into his own existence. He, who inherits the roles of Voss and Jackie, inherits the wisdom and insights of Himmelfarb. That inheritance, the right to have it and the struggle to attain it, emerge in his encounters with the Reverend Timothy Calderon, Mrs Park, Mrs Spice, Hannah, Humphrey Mortimer, and his attempts to capture the significance of these encounters on canvas. The career of Alf, therefore, addresses itself simultaneously to the deprivations of a society and an impairment of self. Everything in the novel flows into Alf, and whatever consolidation emerges from it, flows quite literally from him.

Alf Dubbo, in White's scheme, is the great re-threader of the sundered fabric of man in Australia. At the beginning he is himself a torn creature, caught between the imposed abstractions of Mr Calderon's Christ and the rich but discrete memories of youth in an aboriginal community. He was drawn to the Gospels :

"And he would fail, as he had always failed before, to reconcile those truths with what he had experienced. Where he could accept God because of the spirit that would work in him at times, the duplicity of the white men prevented him considering Christ, except as an ambitious abstraction, or realistically, as a man."

Between impotence and duplicity, between abstraction and realism, there is neither release nor transcendence. That is Alf's condition, and White seems to imply that it is an aspect of Australian life. Alf's relation to it as artist may be likened to Voss's relation to it as an explorer. Voss was trying to overcome a land and to move beyond human limitations. In the process he

discovers the weakness of his arrogance. Voss set out from Sydney as Man
tidied into Will. He would force a cross-grained universe into concession.

He fails and is broken into a recognition of this failure, which in his
last moments, takes the form of the world flowing in on him with great
beauty, and he flowing out to it with a rich contemplative love. The abstractions of Voss, which had criticised so thoroughly the realism of Mr
Bonner, are themselves reduced by suffering to an insight of love which
negates them. The assault on the physical, the social and the metaphysical
in *Voss*, becomes in *Riders in the Chariot* a confused courting. The change
from German explorer to Aboriginal artist brings about a difference of
emphasis, to the extent that the metaphysical carries, in *Riders in the
Chariot*, overtones of the spiritual, of craft, peculiar to the task White has
imposed on Alf Dubbo. Alf is the artist as "lieur", used in the sense that
Sartre has in mind in an essay on Merleau-Ponty : "In many archaic religions, there are holy persons who exercise the function of *lieur* (binder).
Everything must be attached and tied by them." Outside of the mediation
of Alf's paintings there is little interpretative clarity in *Riders in the Chariot*.
Inside them a radical process of redefinition takes place.

Alf's observant eye reconstitutes the world of an Australia locked into
a paralysis of imitation and abstraction. Three quotations illustrate the
direction and thrust of the argument White tried to develop through him.
The first comes at the point when Alf is sitting in the public library and
comes across, once more, the Frenchman's portrait of the Apollonian
chariot.

"He realised how differently he saw this painting since his first acquaintance with it, and how he would now transcribe the Frenchman's
limited composition into his own terms of motion, and forms partly
transcendental, partly evolved from his struggle with daily becoming,
and experience of suffering,"

The second occurs at the end of his career when he is wrestling once more,
and finally, with "the Chariot-thing", which he comes to see with clarity :

"So the firmament was again created. First the foundations were laid
in solid blue, very deep, on which he began to build the gold. The road
ran obliquely, and cruel enough to deter any but sure-footed horses.
The latter could have been rough brumbies, of a speckled grey, rather
too coarse, *earthbound* might have been a legitimate comment, if their
manes and tails had not streamed beyond possibility, and the skein of
cloud shed by their flanks appeared at any point to catch on the rocks
of heavenly gold."

Alf can overcome his grotesque experiences with Mr Calderon and Mrs
Spice and Hannah because he has hit the spiritual condition for seeing.

"Because he had grown physically incapable of hating, his capacity for wonder led him to embrace objects he had refused to contemplate until now. So he would examine the face of Humphrey Mortimer, for instance, with the same interest that he might have brought to bear on a flock of pastured maggots, or block of virgin land. Everything, finally, was a source of wonder, not to say love."

Alf finds his way to a kind of immanent transcendence, in which there is unimpeded traffic between the physical and the spiritual, in which both translate into each other. This kind of conciliation takes hold of the Great Australian Emptiness of Mrs Flack and Mrs Jolly, depriving it of its venom, even though leaving its inanity intact. Alf orchestrates sterility and chaos into meaning.

The fact that Alf is an aborigine is not superfluous for White. Given the Australian context of the novel, and the kind of seeing and healing that he felt was important to it, Alf was destined to be aboriginal. He was a logical successor to Jackie, with whom he joined in providing a removed but indigenous view of the society raised by Europeans over the bones and rights of the aborigines. The product of injustice and the subject, initially, of a distracting philanthropy, Alf was indispensable as the litmus of suffering and seeing in contemporary Australia. In a restricted sense, White might have managed with the portrait of an artist of the type he created in Hurtle Duffield in *The Vivisector*. But although there are continuities of conception between Alf and Hurtle, the latter is freed of Alf's crucial responsibilities as "lieur" in a special social, historical and moral world. The "rough brumbies, of a speckled grey, rather too coarse, *earthbound*," the face of Christ that Alf darkens, the ringtail possums and the furry animals that express, almost totemically, Miss Hare in his last paintings, glance back to the earth that Dugald and Jackie touch with such assumed kinship at Jildra, and to those aborigines "beginning to appear, their shadows first, followed by a suggestion of skin wedded to the trunk of a tree," that haunt the expedition in *Voss*. Alf brings a whole aboriginal view of the world—perhaps it would be better to say a sensitivity to it—to bear on the drama of a White Australia he has been witnessing, and some of the values to which it was theoretically committed. He redeems the love of Mr Calderon's Christ *into* the land that is obviously such a threat to the minister's fragile pieties. The fact that Alf dies and his paintings are dispersed before being seen for what they were is an irony, but it is not an important one.

Patrick White's strength as an author is that he has an acute eye for the symbolic shapes of human experience. This, I think, is a moral quality, primarily, but it is one which, in Patrick White, moves with ease at a social and an historical level. It would be possible to recognise that *The Aunt's Story* and *The Solid Mandala* are more central to his talent than *Voss* or *Riders in the Chariot*. In the first pair of novels there is a preoccupation with the problem of reality from an epistemological and individual point of view; in the second pair, it is with the problem of reality *in Australia*, from a social, an historical, as well as an individual viewpoint that White is concerned. That was an ambitious homecoming for his talent, and it was inside this particular homecoming that the aborigine featured. At the point in his work when he found himself engaged with Australia he found the aborigine looming large with special privilege inside the *structure* of Australian history. Structurally and morally, which is to say in symbolic terms, the aborigine was central to an understanding of white Australia. It is understandable that a backward glance to the nineteenth century should swirl around the aborigine, and that a contemporary glance, informed by Dugald and Jackie, should discover the figure best placed to uncover the futilities of modernity in Alf Dubbo.

What is of interest from our point of view is that a process of consciousness that began with the German Blitz on London and a reading of Eyre's *Journals*, should eventuate in Alf Dubbo as the vehicle for an integrated conception of man in Australia, embracing black and white, innocent guilty, past and present. An aboriginal artist has been the medium and agent of the assertion of that tradition of contemplation, the lack of which Grant deplored in North America and which, indirectly, White deplored in Australia. Alf Dubbo remains, even more than the triumph of Himmelfarb, Patrick White's peace with Australia, with himself in Australia. There is insight as well as privilege in his choice of Alf as seer and cement of *Riders in the Chariot*. Boldrewood had stumbled into the pervasive presence of Warrigal as the linking agent of *Robbery Under Arms*. There is an enormous difference, however, between the accidental recognitions of fear, and the intentional recognitions of a man opening up the implications of a culture with a vision of clarity. Because White has seen the activity of Australian history and the formation of a particular society *whole*, from the viewpoint of a reflective consciousness of considerable depth, he is able to see the *part* that the aborigines have performed in that whole. And since that history and that society are still open, and constitute a field of value as well as fact, the role that the aborigine *can* play is much greater than his factual existence in nineteenth century Coranderrk or twentieth century Redfern would suggest. In an essay on the problem of the relation of the writer to his time, William Walsh quoted Samuel Hoare's essay on Paul Valery :

"the poet....is compelled to form with the complexity of the modern world a host of relations, not merely physical or social but also intellectual, which are not easily resolvable into a unity. He is torn in a number of directions: he has to exist upon a great many planes of being. So has the ordinary person, but the difficulty for the modern poet is to take up an attitude in which these activities are synthesised. He has to reach a point from which they can be viewed in some relation and seen to fit together...."

The direction of Patrick White's fiction has been to discover and sustain this attitude of engaged detachment, from which the elements of Australian experience could speak with coherence. In placing the burden of synthesis and order on Alf Dubbo in *Riders in the Chariot*, he was imputing to him the intimacy and difficulties of his own creative effort as a writer in Australia. There is generosity in this choice which marks the highest point in the European consciousness of the aborigine in Australian literature. History does not stop at these moments, but it does pause sufficiently for a clearing of comprehension to open up. The blindness that diminished Bennelong and Bungaree was most seriously retracted by White's penetrating revisions of aboriginal man in the figures of Dugald, Jackie and Alf Dubbo. Above all, Alf Dubbo.

2

The Politics of Cross-Cultural Dependence in Language and Poetry

DANIEL MASSA

Waqghet hi imrammti, l' ili zmien nibni,
Ma htatlix mghallmin, 'mma qataghli tafal merhi;
Fejn tmajt insib il-gebel sibt tafal merhi,
Waqghet hi, imrammti.

Waqghet hi imrammti, nizzlet hi s-sisien;
Ma htatlix l-imghallmin, 'mma qatghetli il-gebel;
Fejn tmajt insib il-gebel sibt tafal merhi.
Waqghet hi imrammti, l'ili zmien nibni.
U hekk waqghet hi, imrammti ! w'erga' ibniha.[1]

I assure you I did not wander in here by accident thinking this was a class taking Arabic. I have been reading two stanzas from the middle section of the earliest poem in Maltese—Caxaro's "Cantilena" dated middle of the fifteenth century, but discovered only recently by Dr Godfrey Wettinger and M. Fsadni (1966).[2]

It is the allegorical lament of the master-builder whose magnificent edifice, a long time abuilding, has collapsed. In some ways the "Cantilena" could be read as the allegory of Malta, for long the epicentre of periodic shifts of power in the Mediterranean, with its language, literature and politics now shifting this way, and now that.

The Maltese language itself finds its immediate source in the Arabic dialect of the North African Maghreb [Morocco, Algeria, Tunisia]. Written in Latin script, with a morphology and syntax that is essentially Semitic, with various Romance accretions and borrowings, it is basically the product of two eras of cultural dependence brought about by the conquest of the Maltese archipelago by the Arabs in 869-70 A.D., and by

Count Roger the Norman in 1090 A.D.

As far as we can tell, our earliest literary tradition was Arabic for even after the Norman Conquest Arab civilisation and culture flourished, and it was only after 1249 when Frederick II cleared many Mohamedans out of the island that the overall majority became once more Catholic. It was at this time that Malta's administration was linked to that of neighbouring Sicily, and that the languages of civil and religious administration became Latin and subsequently Italian in its Sicilian variant.[3]

However, the language spoken by the community remained exclusively Arabic based—but an Arabic that was visibly shifting further and further away from its Maghrebenic source in North Africa. Thus the only non-Semitic word in Caxaro's "Cantilena" is *ventura*—fortune—in : "The man who changes his neighbourhood/surroundings can also change his fortune"; but the form (though defined as Mozarabic[4]) approximates that used in Sicily and Spain at the time, and shows Caxaro's response to Malta's dependence on the Aragon/Castille fief to which Malta and Sicily then both belonged.

The next surviving poem of any importance is that written by G.F. Bonamico (1639-1680), when Malta was held by the Knights of St John. Dedicated to Nicolas Cotoner,[5] this panegyric stressed Malta's dependence on the foreigner who is responsible for the island's colonial heritage. Addressing the grandmaster, Bonamico states :

There would be little pleasure in this island,
Had there not been someone to keep her company...
Had there not been someone to guard her
She would cry hunger like a slave. (1672 *circa*)

Since that time, we have had dependence in both manner and matter, accepting the lessons of colonialism both as metaphor and as experience. Thus the panegyric, the hymn, the didactic poetry fostered by paternalistic rulers who governed Mediterranean Malta till 1964, when it became independent within the British Commonwealth and started afresh a post-colonial search for individual and possibly national identity.

Anthropologist Jeremy Boissevain has correctly stated that these rulers inhibited questioning and punished dissent :

"whether Romans, Arabs, Knights or British [these rulers] often provided the basic necessities of life. That is, they arranged for the importation of scarce foodstuffs and provided a certain amount of employment. Nonetheless, they all wielded big sticks that made discussion with them very one-sided. This inequality of power has encouraged in Malta a tradition of *dependency on outsiders, and their culture.*"

This has been especially so since the Treaty of Amiens (1802) when, following the Blockade and the expulsion of the French, the Maltese

National Congress freely acknowledged as their legitimate sovereign the King of Great Britain.[7]

But there have since always been a dissenting minority, especially among the landed and the upper class bourgeoisie and therefore the better educated, who insisted that Malta's emotional, political and cultural tradition lay with Italy and the Italians; that indeed since

"Roman times, Malta was one with Sicily, with which it had been once joined geographically."[8]

Since the middle of the fifteenth century, Maltese scholars had to go to Italy so that, in its Tuscan form, Italian dominated culture learning in Malta.[9] with the result that practically throughout the whole of the *nineteenth* century we had a host of uninspired and uninspiring Maltese poets writing in Italian, often responding to the colonial situation with the "literature of panegyric and dependence."

We have the strange amorphous growth of the Maltese poets influenced mainly by the Arcadian Italian poets Metastasio, Zappi and Lemene[10] penning hymns and odes to their English rulers. One such poet is Giuseppe Testaferrata Viani (1767-1837) whose *La Musica* celebrated in Tuscan mellifluous verse the outgoing virtues of George III of England; Cesare Vassallo (1800-1882) wrote an Ode of a similar nature on the Coronation of Queen Victoria; while yet another (Giuseppe Depiro, 1794-1830) stressed *that other great dependence*, the Roman Catholic Church, by his "Ode al sommo Pontefice Pio IX".

The link between Maltese and Italian poetry was strengthened when numbers of exiled Italians arrived towards the middle of the nineteenth century,[11] among them the poets Luigi Fabrizi Carlo *Porta* and Giovanni *Berchet* who used poetry as a political weapon.

It is just this stand which the 'irredentisti' Maltese poets, those who thought Malta's destiny lay with Italy, were later to take against a British Imperialism, that in trying to impose its own language, to the exclusion of the 'parent' Italian culture, forced the language problem which in its turn helped strengthen and consolidate the Maltese vernacular.

Arturo Mercieca, poet and later Chief Justice, deliberately trying to insulate his inherited Italian religious and cultural identity, addressed *La Giovine Malta* this way in 1901 :

"The Maltese shall never consent to seeing the banishment from their shores of the most beautiful and musical language [Italian] that ever was spoken...we shall never renounce that language which (when still in the cradle) resounded among us, when the troubadors sang the amorous songs of Ciullo d'Alcamo and Pier della Vigna among our rocks in the charmed nights of the Middle Ages, nor shall we ever renounce that idiom which we proudly acknowledge to be ours, the divine art of Dante and Manzoni......The Maltese will refuse to amalgamate with a people [the English] that differs from them considerably in habits, thought, climate and especially religion. They are determined to conserve integral and insurmountable the linguistic barrier which serves as the firm fulcrum for their character."[12]

Mercieca's nationalism was of course Italian rather than Maltese—but he found a host of other writers (bilingual but monocultural) ready to join the fight, using poetry as a political tool. These, with very few exceptions, borrowed their patterns from Italian neo-classical metrics and were technically limited and mediocre.

This was true even of the Italian poetry of Dun Karm, our national poet whose stature assumed the first rank only after he started writing in Maltese in 1912. The importance of Dun Karm cannot be sufficiently stressed. Although strongly influenced by Italian literature, especially Manzoni, Monti "e un po dell settecento veneziano",[13] although an Italian monocultural to a significant extent, Dun Karm worked unceasingly to convince his contemporaries that this "hated Arab dialect" was a language fit for literature. His attempt to retrieve the essentials of the native past, far from being retrogressive, was vitally necessary; in seeking to discover the strength of a previously neglected linguistic heritage he was putting first things first.

In this he was helped, perhaps unwittingly, by British language policy. In 1934, the Malta Constitution (Amendment) Letters Patent banned Italian (until then the language of the Courts) as one of the two official media and substituted it by Maltese. Henry Frendo recently put it this way :

"In de-Italianizing Malta, the British forced the birth of a more homegrown product. In resisting assimilation and colonialism, pro-Italians and others engendered a national political conciousness upon which a body politic could feed. Paradoxically, the Maltese language emerged as a synthesis of the pro-English and pro-Italian rivalry. The Maltese vernacular served as a social and emotive bond, and became a natural unifier."[14]

With a few notable exceptions such as Gan Anton Vassallo's *Il-Gifen Tork* (1842) and Dwardu Cachia's *Katrin ta' l-Imdina* (1890), Maltese poetry was very mediocre. It is only when the language was consolidated that it began seriously and quantitatively to be written.

There was still one major obstacle to be cleared—its rigidly anachronistic pattern, for although all the "great poets" and "small-scale" ones sought to cultivate a "pure" Arabic-derived vocabulary (apparently blissfully unaware of the "fascist" implications of upholding a concentrated linguistic purity), they still adopted verse forms from *conventional*, and seldom contemporary, Italian metrical models, "just as painters and sculptors still followed Baroque forms",[15] the generative seed that contained pre-existing patterns which determined the growth and development of the Maltese species. This is partly due to the fact that the revered Dun Karm, steeped in Classical and neo-Classical forms, fashioned his best poetry within that rigid tradition; partly due to the fact that his manipulation of the vernacular was so effective that all other poets leonised him and sought to imitate even his metrics, and sometimes style and theme as well. Dun Karm's achievement may have inhibited the growth and new directions of those who followed. It is the kind of difficulty plants have here in India when growing under the shade of the big banyan tree.

Another possible reason is that the *rigid conventionalism of verse forms* adopted *mirrored the rigidity of social and religious institutions* that characterised the period preceding the April '58 riots, *that conventionalism of themes* admirably reflected the inner meaning of the nation's experience then obtaining : and therefore the charge of anachronism is muted. Samuel Johnson might have put it this way: if they were anachronistic it is because Malta itself, in relation to the rest of the world, was anachronistic. Their *closed forms* and *non-contemporary* preoccupations reflected their outdated monoculture.

The War had killed many things, among others *irredentism*, but not, it seems, religious and political orthodoxy, nor yet the cult of dependence on neo-classical Italian patterns.

In 1943, the "first" professor of Maltese[16] tried to shift the core of dependence from Italian to English by using the outcome of the War specifically to suggest the "Planning [of] an Anglo-Maltese Culture." Speaking at the British Council, Guzè Aquilina stated that the War had demonstrated that Malta was not a geographical "appendix" to Sicily, but a "very mortal appendicitis" to the whole of Italy.[17]

Malta, he argued, had since the Treaty of Paris in 1814 formed part of the British Empire and there were various educational and cultural adjustments "that had to subserve this historical necessity in order to avoid perpetuating a state of educational incompatibility."[18] He noted particularly the advantages of English language in Malta : indispensable for this, that and the other but especially indispensable as the treasure-house of one of the world's greatest literatures.[19] Guzè Aquilina added :

> "Historical experience has taught us two lessons : first, to accept domination as the inevitable destiny of our islands...second, to thank Providence for aligning us to the greatest power of the time ..."

Aquilina went on to say :

> "I had often wondered at the irritating apathy of the Imperial Government that did nothing worthwhile for a better knowledge of English speech and ways in Malta."[20]

He thought that much of the harm done could be remedied by the British

Council, and a British policy in education that consciously planned the development of an Anglo-Maltese culture. It was then that English gradually assumed overall importance in the Primary Schools, and English literature (especially Romantic poetry) in private and government Secondary Schools, often to the almost total neglect of Maltese, such that the same professor in a controversy that raged in the last 30 days stated that Convent Schools particularly had done the nation a disservice by "serving the interests of God and the British Empire."[21]

I have quoted Professor Aquilina at some length because I believe he was *formative* of the modernist attitudes that were to appear later in Maltese poetry. His stature commanded respect, and his directions and signposting were at least read—they were on the syllabus.

In introducing the first edition of the anthology of Maltese verse— *Il-Muza Maltija*—in 1948, Aquilina noted correctly that the inherited traditional metrics, metaphor and imagery were showing signs of tiredness and looked forward to "new rhythms" latent in the Maltese language; mentioning particularly the modernist patterns of G. Manley Hopkins, Ezra Pound, T.S. Eliot, Stephen Spender and Wordsworth. This was another, perhaps more important move towards the planning of an Anglo-Maltese culture, for whereas his previous speech was published in an academic journal, *Scientia*, and therefore had a restricted audience, *Il-Muza Maltija* was compulsory reading in government Secondary Schools and University.

But the "split" inherent in the goal of a bi-culture had to wait a few more years, literature and culture running parallel to socio-religious and political developments, and it was the Malta Labour Party's series of splits that indirectly helped usher modernity into literature.

Upto the mid-50's as Jeremy Boissevain has noted[22] "the unifying influence of the Church in a small isolated community" had been reflected in the homogeneity of Maltese life. This in turn had been reflected in the literature, religious and often gushily patriotic, that sought to justify the ways of God and the Establishment to man; but when the *political break-away* core of the Mintoff "split" came to power as the more radical Malta Labour Party, the edifice of traditional homogeneity and orthodoxy collapsed, just like that of the master-builder's whose foundations had shifted. Church state relations came to a head, the head broke to a sore, ecclesiastical interdicts were clamped on Party papers and Party officials, and politically the "split" went down the middle. To add to this, after an *initial ambivalent* failed attempt at "wholeness in marriage", integration with Britain with representation at Westminster, the Malta Labour Party refused further to acknowledge British domination as a historical necessity and adopted the '*break with Britain*' resolution.

These splits, important in themselves as corrosive of socio-political-religious allegiances and structures, could not by themselves have led to the modernist revolution in literature. They were linked, however, to widespread industrialisation in the three years of Labour power on a scale unknown before [infrastructure, road-building, tourism]. This, I think, is important for literature because most forms of artistic creation undergo *radical* changes in *quickly-developing industrial habitats,* due not simply to the emergence of new techniques in mass-media communication [Television came to Malta around this time] but as the direct result of the fact that *accelerated industrial production* provokes fundamental changes, and change and experiment become a central preoccupation.[23]

As a matter of fact, Francis Ebejer's first novel, *A Wreath for the Innocents,* (written in 1957 and published in London '58), draws a picture of a Maltese girl, Lucija, whose tender sensibilities are torn to shreds as she gets caught up inside the socio-politico-religious maelstrom of that time. In Ebejer's, *The Evil of King Cockroach* (written '58, published '60), Rosie, who is an extension of Lucija in the first book, makes her first tentative steps into the new emergent Malta.

Ebejer, faintly existentialist, was obsessed by the rape of the land, for so long virgin and untouched by either indiscriminate industrialisation or Tourism described in his finest English novel, *The Eye of the Sun* (written 1959, published '69). In 1961, Ebejer wrote a play *Vakanzi tas-Sajf* (*Summer Holidays*) which raised a storm of controversy about its preoccupations and its technique and therefore caused new interest in the arts in general. This was later further fanned by *Boulevard* (written 1963, produced '64), the finest and certainly the most avant-garde play in the Maltese language. Polemic and discussion, praise and vituperation went on and on.

It was also after *Vakanzi tas-Sajf* that modern painting started to flourish—Emvin Cremona (who incidentally did the scenery and decor for *Summer Holidays*), Antoine Camilleri, Alfred Chircop, Portelli; soon to be followed by sculptor Anton Agius and ceramist Gabriel Caruana. It is possibly not too large a claim for Ebejer to state that the interest generated by *Summer Holidays* and *Boulevard* marked the first light of what is usually referred to as "the new dawn".

Further impulse for change on the ultra-religious front was the second Vatican Council, and on the political independent status for Malta in September 1964 under a *conservative* Nationalist Administration—the younger poets charged impatience and dissatisfaction at a continuing paternalistic philosophy that still peddled religious, political dependence as though it were still a historical necessity.

This is Kenneth Wain questioning in the year of independence :

On Television they claimed
the new democracy
a flag rose
in the arena
a tired bird
—the end of a history of crutches ? (*On Independence*)

Before independence, we had had sporadic attempts at more 'open' forms in poetry (Achille Mizzi and Peter Serracino Inglott). In 1964 'open form' poetry arrived, and the first volume in the *Kwartett* series (edited by Victor Fenech) was printed in 1965. It seemed as if the long-planned for Anglo-Maltese literature (Professor Aquilina incidentally wrote the introduction to the book) was with us, but only partially, for though the four poets in *Kwartett* (J.J. Camilleri, Victor Fenech, Charles Vella, and myself) had all studied in England, and influences of Pound, Eliot and Dylan Thomas were traceable in this poetry, they were really much more concerned with discovering the hidden rhythms inherent in Maltese word-building and sentence-structures that had remained unused or fitted ill with the "closed forms" of neo-classical Italian metrics.

Maltese word-formation is basically more concentrated than either Italian or English, and when dealing with pronouns, which are often linked, the contrast is even more pronounced. These are some examples :

i.   *I understood her* (3 words, 5 syllables) would in Maltese just read as *Fhimtha* (1 word, 2 syllables).

ii. *I understood the king* (4 words, 6 syllables) as *Fhimtu r-re* (3 words, 3 syllables).

iii. *I gave them [to] her* (5 words, 5 syllables) as *Tajthomlha* (1 word, 3 syllables).

iv. *I thought [that] she was pregnant* (6 words, 7 syllables) as *Hsibtha tqila* (2 words, 4 syllables).

In more formal speech, language can be much less concentrated, so that *Hsibtha tqila* (4 syllables) can become *Jiena hsibt li hija ḱienet tqila* (10 syllables). But in speech, the tendency is for even further concentration. Final syllables are hardly sounded at all, so that our 6-word 10-syllable formal Maltese in *I thought she was pregnant* can not only be reduced to 2-words 4-syllables, but also to just 2-syllables-plus in normal flow.

Let's put it this way. If I were ordering/writing this formal paper along these lines, the process of gestation and composition would have taken me very much longer than it did take me, but as for reading/communication time—why, I would have finished 20 minutes ago. The exercise would have been to say as much as possible, in as many ways and on as many levels, in as little time and space as possible.

The difference in syllabification can be even more pronounced in Italian.[24] Now when you remember that traditionally our poetry was usually patterned on Italian octosyllabic and hende-casyllabic verse (our *vers tat-tmienja* and *tal-hdax*), when you add to that the fact that most young poets were insistently dropping all link words except those absolutely essential (and sometimes even those absolutely essential), you will realise the kind of condensation that imagery, metaphor and concept had to suffer. It was a case of torturing the roots to make them bear fruit, pressing words and images into each other so that they clash dialectically and gain an explosive force.

It is this more than anything else which in 1965 made *Kwartett* walk resolutely out of traditional forms without as much as a "by your leave". The result on the Maltese poetry scene, not least because of the resulting *ambiguities*, was a shattering revelation. We had pitched battles, ancients versus moderns, bourgeoisie versus booboisie. The new poets were described as "rebellious, unscrupulous, law-shattering boobies."[25]

Controversies raged, but the critics who counted came down in favour of the new-wave poets, emphasising the questioning, dissenting, cerebral, symbolistic, avant-garde, mass-media technique of dissolving images into each other in the fashion of film, pressing words into each other in the manner of fireworks;[26] a corpus that brought Maltese poetry for the first time in line with contemporary movements abroad. The critics' headlines were indicative : "Literature of our Time,…Exercise for the Mind…Poetry of Great Promise…Poets for Today…New Trends…New Branches…Poetry of Experiment."

The other young poets eagerly took up the call, forming the Movement for the Promotion of Literature (1967), publishing *Il-Polz*, taking poetry to the people in frequent sessions of jazz and poetry in halls, church squares, historical sites, seaside resorts. After this the shedding off of formalism and the closed forms of tradition came naturally.[27] The move towards more open forms followed in a succession of publications, the most notable, after *Kwartett*, being *Dhahen fl-Imhuh* (1967, which also proclaimed the writers' manifesto : Gorg Borg, Oliver Friggieri, Albert Marshall);

> *L-Ghar ta' L-Enimmi* (1967, Achille Mizzi)
>
> *Antenni* (1968, Mario Azzopardi, J.J. Camilleri, Victor Fenech, Ray Mahoney)
>
> *Prizmi* (1968, Lawrenz Cachia, Philip Sciberras)
>
> *Kalejdoskopju* (1969, Pawlu Cachia, Charles Flores, Charles Xuereb)
>
> *Nistaqsi* (1969, Bernard Mallia)
>
> *Analizi '70* (1970, Mario Azzopardi, Victor Fenech, Oliver Friggieri, Daniel Massa)
>
> *Mas-Sejha tat-Tnabar* (1971, Mario Azzopardi, Oliver Friggieri, Achille Mizzi)
>
> *Rumminiet Jittewbu* (1971, Albert Marshall)
>
> *Dwal Fil-Persjani* (1972, Mario Azzopardi, Joe Friggieri, Oliver Friggieri, Ray Mahoney, Philip Sciberras)
>
> *Mal-Hajit tas-Sejjieh* (1975, Marjanu Vella)
>
> *Demghat tas-Silg* (1976, Mario Azzopardi)

It is indicative of the close-knittedness of the Kwartett-Antenni group that 8 of these 12 books are shared collections mostly in threes and fours.

It is also indicative that although all the poets in these collections are bilingual and bi-cultural, they insist on *wholeness*, a whole *personality* that "shall not be a whore to a foreign cult",[28] their main concern the redis-covery of the strength inherent in linguistic heritage and Maltese identity.

It is ironical, therefore, to note that having shaken off traditional dependence, taken new directions, there was *simultaneous to the deepening of experience in post-independence* a crisis of self, a crisis of identity, a disease in the psyche "marda bla fejqan tal-Egojizmu",[29] an interesting retreat into the self that followed from the continued rejection of even the more liberated mores and realities in post-independent Malta.

Their vision, identity, consciousness, is fragmentary, certainly ambi-guous and multivalent, often incomplete and particularly schizomorphic, similar to that of the *Novissimi* movement in the Italian poetry of the '60's.[30] They were, despite their efforts at taking the poetry to the people, mainly poets of private individual search, not public statement; or as Professor Lloyd Fernando, discussing similar predicaments, put it during this conference they were

> "writers who dealt with contradictions, dilemmas, minor tragedies in a confusing bicultural context where ultimate goals are undiscernible, and the meaning of the past is inexplicable. They document the detailed realities of private lives, their works represent the diverse partial visions of artists who may be talented enough but lack a driving thoroughness of perspective to raise their achievement to the first rank."

Their schizomorphic visions arising from a fragmented identity and con-sciousness[31] are often unrelated except through recurrent characteristics that assume the role of catalyst or constant. First in (a) *desecration, deforma-tion*, rendering in grotesque images dehumanising abstractions[32] or

> once I died in protest
> resurrected by the cry of black gorillas
> howling in a breathless orgy with virgins clean.

> > (Malta, *The New Poetry*, pp. 18-19)

Second in (b) enigmatic symbolism that often confuses one's identity with that of another, but which in this case is often linked to retreat, what the pundits would term the return-to-the-womb. There are many wombs available, and it's interesting that poets of this particularly Christian island, so small that unless you're careful you are possibly liable to step into the sea accidentally, should often choose the fish as one particular variant of the Freudian womb.

Achille Mizzi speaks of the "man-fish" that is swallowed in the wide,

or not so wide, expanse of the sea.[33] Mario Azzopardi does it repeatedly,
"Did they tell you *I'm a fish* a million years old ?"[34] or in another poem,
after the tragedy the fisherman cannot know or tell whether the bubbles on
the face of the sea were caused by the "breathing of a fish, or the breath
of a drowning man."[35]

I have been amphibian in *Matrix*. Consequent upon this idiosyncrasy I
have in *Design for a New Arras* been, like Pinocchio, recently swallowed
by a whale :

> Come up Jonas spit no more but take a ticket
> wind it round your finger and swallow
> at first draw you'll win a silver-plated blacktail
> still with jump in it Robespierre
> or a wine of your choice (say Barolo '64)
> to go with your Lobster Thermidor[36]
> and souze yourself get pist
> for the bout of the beasts is
> about to begin

and belatedly and thirdly the "constant" of this fragmented identity is
found in (c) a "gratuitous" semantics of deviation that mirrors the process
of disintegrating structures outside and within the poet's personality.[37]

The linguistic experiment itself was often proclaimed to be an important
constituent of poetic experience, in so far as the experiment ensured
perennial attempts and *provisional solutions*. Looking back, I think we were
at times insufficiently aware that heterogeneity, sometimes in the shape of
too quick an acceptance of contemporary trends, threatened a formlessness
that could hardly be satisfactorily replaced by a running emotional line (one
critic called it an emotional "sore".) In the heat of controversy we sometimes failed to strike a balance between valid linguistic experiment and less
valid gimmick, failed to distinguish between natural growth and indiscriminate grafting, between fireworks and a damp squib.

With chaotic structures and heterogenous blends of material, ideologies,
motives drawn from the recent productions of the Novissimi in Italy, Yuri
Pankratov and Yevgeni Yevtushenko in Russia, the poets of the 'beat'
generation, Gregory Corso, Jack Kerouac, Ginsberg, Ferlinghetti, the
Liverpool music and the Liverpool poets, Maltese poets especially Albert
Marshall, Mario Azzopardi, and Achilie Mizzi aimed at giving the literary
equivalent to the contemporary social and moral disorder, often felt/ex-
pressed as a pathological condition in the typical schizomorphic forms/
symptoms of hysteria and paranoia, that urge retreat : they often felt more
comfortable *inside the whale*.

This incidentally happened in the best plays and novels published after
Independence, and I have elsewhere[38] traced the career of the hero whose

immaturity leads him progressively into

(a) retreat from the *performing community*
(b) *impotence-cum-sterility syndrome*
(c) a *descent into psychopathology* that ultimately leads
(d) to absolute polarisation expressed in terms
(e) of (i) escape abroad or (ii) suicide.

These several preoccupations are evident in much of the best post-independence poetry, the chaotic structures of form and content leading to a negative condition that does not provide an alternative social order, but only a sense of malaise,[39] a negative yearning to "grow backwards" that rejects the confusion of the present.

This has persisted right to the present day, as seen in the most recent collection of poetry, Mario Azzopardi's *Demghat tas-Silg* (1976), where the angry young poet of the '60's, stridently protesting against tradition now emerges as a more skilful poet, less committed, more withdrawn, a craftsman who has, through sacrifice, gained more control in a form that remains open. In most of his new poems—*Zirkon, Dghajsa tal-Latini, repubblika, resurrezzjoni*—understatement takes over from brash protest to register facets of deep emotion.

His is often beautiful poetry of rejection, deviationist but brilliant, with rhythm and imagery that haunt. But Azzopardi is now more than ever the psychic alienate concerned with freeing himself of a past of dependence—a past that he subjectively regards as very much the present.

In the "Gzira tal-Mohba" section, Azzopardi registers again a rejection of traditionally accepted social and religious mores that leads him this time not only to muted satire of the Establishment (*Demghat tas-Silg*, pp. 44, 47, 88, 100 *et passim*) but also of those least able to defend themselves, the inadequate, the unaware, the unfulfilled (pp. 40, 43, 45, 50, 54-55, 81 *et passim*). He finds there can be little valuable communication with "the Semitic crowd cursing", and its representatives of unhealthy normality. Whatever sympathy Azzopardi might once have had for his people and his land changes now to scorn (pp. 45, 47-48, 107)—a negative attitude, resulting from a subjective vision that shuts him off from communication and initiates a process of inwardness that often retreats into paranoia (*Novena lil Van Gogh*, pp. 104, 98, 61-72).

This in itself, as well as possible misinterpretations by sociologist critics, ought perhaps to sound a warning that it is possibly time to retreat from the philosophy of retreat; I can sense two directions : first the *partial collapse of subjectivism* in the poets (Mizzi, Azzopardi and myself) as well as in the novelists (Ebejer, Sammut) *will lead to* some *kind of objectivisation* that finds its shining examples in Nathalie Sarrante and Robbe-Grillet, but this will be a road too intellectually demanding to be taken up so early or sustained for long; and a second easier one towards some kind of acceptance of the community, a wholeness of vision to replace schizomorphia; in which case socio-political events might again come to the rescue.

A few weeks ago, Mr Mintoff and the Malta Labour Party were returned to power with a narrow majority (just over 51% of the votes cast) and declared the birth of a new "socialist generation".[40] This will, I am sure, make for significant changes not only on the socio-political situation but also, and again indirectly, on the cultural front.

With the spread of socialist propaganda and literature, the growing popularity of Russian and Chinese "positive" literature (Mayakovsky, Lu Shun), we will have attempts at a literature patterned on socialist realism, where as in Mayakovsky, writers

> Measure each Action
> by the Final
> Purpose.[41]

But my feeling is that if we want to establish any degree of independence that is not merely subjective we shall have to go for the "virile maturity" of Critical Realism resisting the temptations of socio-political simplifications. Aware of the limitations of our society, freeing ourselves now from too morbid a preoccupation with self, we move towards a community of conviction realised perhaps first in terms of art, where dependence is not merely restriction, where contact with community provides sustenance for, as well as erosion of the ego, where schizomorphic visions combine in relevant mosaic, and a design for future building is attempted :

> In double-handed grip
> I seized a pebble with sea-made blades
> in my clutch it kindled like oil-spill
> unfroze like a rose
> opened up in my mind like spray of red brass
> and I drew a sketch of a new arras.[42]

We are now watching the terrible clash of the Symplegades; through which the poet's soul must pass—identified with neither side.[43]

REFERENCES

1. G. Wettinger and M. Fsadni, *Peter Caxaro's Cantilena*, Malta, 1968, p. 37.

2. *ibid.*, pp.7-8.

3. G. Mangion, *Un Contributo di Letteratura Regionale : La Letteratura Barocca a Malta*, Bari, 1970, pp. 311-313.

4. O. Friggieri, *Kittieba ta' Zmienna*, 1976, p. 200.

5. See G. Mangion, *Giovan Francesco Buonamico*, Florence, 1971, pp. 299-300.

6. *Ferment* (January 1969) p. 19.

7. 15 June 1802.

8. Bernabo Brea, *Sicily before the Greeks*, London, 1957, p. 25.

9. G. Wettinger and M. Fsadni, op. cit., p. 33.

10. O. Friggieri, op. cit., p. 10.

11. *ibid.*, p. 206. See A . Corbelli, "Esuli Italiani a Malta", *Risorgimento Italiano*, 1929.

    G. Mangion, *Governo Inglese, Risorgimento Italiano ed Opinione Pubblica a Malta (1848-1851)*, Malta, 1970, p. 62ff.

12. O.F. Tencajoli, *Poeti Maltesi d'Oggi*, Rome, 1932, p. 147.

13. *ibid.*, p. 81.

14. H. Frendo, "Language and Nationality in an Island Colony", *Canadian Review of Studies in Nationalism*, Autumn, 1975, p. 31.

15. P. Serracino Inglott, *Pangs of Birth, Fangs of Doubt*, Mimeo, University of Malta, 1974, p. 12.

    Cf. idem., *Contemporary Art in Malta*, Malta, 1973, Introd.

16. M.A. Vassalli was appointed first professor of Maltese on 21 February 1825.

17. *Scientia*, IX No. 4, 1943, p. 85.

18. *ibid.*, X No. 1, 1944, p. 39.

19. *ibid.*

20. *ibid.*, pp. 41-2.

21. *Sunday Times of Malta*, December 1976-January 1977.

22. *Hal-Farrug*, New York, 1969, 99-100.

23. J. Duvignaud, *The Sociology of Art*, London, 1972, p. 124.

24. G. Curmi, Journal, Faculty of Arts, University of Malta, 1964, p. 223.

25. *The Malta News*, 16 January 1969.

26. *Antenni*, Malta, 1968, p. 104.

27. P. Xuereb, *Biblijografija—IL-Poezija bil-Malti 1964-1974*, University of Malta, 1976, iii.

28. D. Massa, "Underground" published in A. Niven, *The Writer in Exile*, Brussels, 1975.

29. A. Marshall, "Psiko", *Dhahen Fl-Imhuh*, Malta, 1967, p. 63.

30. A. Frattini, *Dai Crepuscolari ai Novissimi*, Milan, 1969 pp. 333-378.

31. See M. Azzopardi's "identifications" with eagle, fish, moth "I have died a lot of times" in *Demghat tas-Silg*, pp. 92, 97, 100, 102. *Malta : The New Poetry*, 1971, p. 19.

32. See Hugh Friedrich, *Die Struktur Der Modernen Lyrik*, Hamburg, 1956.

33. See *L-Ghar ta' L-Enimmi*, "Foetus" and "Huta", pp. 34, 37.

34. *Demghat tas-Silg*, p. 77. Cf. "natura morta 1.30 p.m." p. 98.

35. *ibid.*, p. 103. "Gharqa". Cf. Also pp. 36, 45, 48, 57-8, 66, 71, 80, 83, 85, 90.

36. Written on the eve of Malta being proclaimed a Republic.

37.   See A. Marshall, *Dhahen fl-Imhuh* pp. 63, 65-66.

38.   "Contemporary Maltese Literature—An Interim Report" Mediterranean Symposium II. 24-26 June 1976 : Malta.

39.   O. Friggieri, *Dhahen fl-Imhuh* pp. 58, 59; A Mizzi, *Ghar ta' L-Enimmi*, pp. 9, 20, 29, 31, 34, 58.

40.   *Malta Labour Party Electoral Manifesto*, Malta, 1976.

41.   "Action" can be supplemented by "Detail".

42.   Daniel Massa, "Design for a New Arras".

43.   J. Campbell, *The Hero with a Thousand Faces*, New York 1956, pp. 387-391.

3

The Scottish
Element in
Commonwealth Literature

ALASTAIR NIVEN

MAY I take it as an historical commonplace that the Scottish contribution
to the establishment, maintenance and disintegration of the British
Empire was quite out of proportion to the population of Scotland at any
given time in the imperial adventure ? The population of Scotland in 1700
was just over a million to England's five-and-a-half millions; it increased in
the nineteenth century from about one-and-a-half millions to nearly four-
and-a-half millions; and in this century it has topped the five-million mark
to England's current approximate figure of nearly fifty millions. Yet during
this period economic deprivations at home, especially after the Jacobite
failure of 1745 and the conversion of the Scottish lairds to a policy of
largescale sheep-farming instead of tenanted crofting, combined with the
lure of material success in the southern part of the United Kingdom to
lead to what David Craig, in his indispensable book *Scottish Literature and
The Scottish People*, calls 'a landslide of people away from Scottish soil'.[1]
Many of these folk eventually found their way to Canada, especially to
Nova Scotia and to the prairies. At the last ACLALS Conference, in
Stirling twenty-one months ago, Robert Robertson spoke of his own Scot-
tish ancestry and detected in some of the immigrant literature of the
prairies a crucial Scottish element.[2] This character I hope to enlarge upon
in a moment. Other Scots *emigrés* went, of course, to Australia and to
New Zealand. Church of Scotland missionaries play an important part in
Christian developments in Ghana and Malawi. India had its share of
Scottish administrators, one of whom, Mountstuart Elphinstone, wrote distinguished histories which can be grouped with the work of that other Scot
who served in India, Lord Macaulay, as seminal histories in the nineteenth
century.

My intention in this paper is less to concentrate upon the literary

achievement of Scotsmen abroad than to mark a Scottish inheritance which
I feel to be an intriguing element in much of the literature with which
members of ACLALS concern themselves. Let us not forget, however,
how Scottish literature was greatly enlarged by its contacts overseas.
India, by its colonial circumstances, attracted the interest of Scottish
writers from the eighteenth century onwards starting with Alexander Dow's
tragedies, *Zingis* (1769) and *Sethona* (1774), both of which were performed
at Covent Garden. Sir Walter Scott, whose influence over English language
literatures perhaps exceeded any other writer's in the nineteenth century,
set one of his last novels, *The Surgeon's Daughter* (1827), almost entirely
in India, though he never visited Asia.

Several interesting Scottish authors did work in India and drew from
their experience there in the memories, novels, treatises and verse they
contributed to Scottish literature. As much as one man can, Dr John
Leyden (1775-1811) exemplifies the type. Leyden came from farming stock
in the Borders area. Like many of his background he found his way to
Edinburgh University by dint of hard scholarship, and there he quickly
established himself as an outstanding linguist and classicist. He began to
contribute elegies, odes and many translations from classical and Oriental
languages to the *Edinburgh Magazine*, that influential journal which found
its way to every corner of the Empire. (The role of the *Edinburgh Magazine*, *Edinburgh Review*, *Blackwood's Magazine* and the *Scots Magazine* in
encouraging knowledge of the Empire, often through stories and poems,
needs to be stressed, and in return the dissemination of copies of these
journals to many different places must have affected the style and subject
of local writing.) Leyden was coadjutor to Walter Scott in Scott's first
major published work, *Minstrelsy of the Scottish Border*, and by the time
he left for India in 1803 he had edited the *Scots Magazine* for some
months. His decision to come to India was entirely the result of professional disposition : the range of languages to be studied there fascinated
him. Leyden lived in India for the remaining eight years of his life, dying
eventually of a fever at the age of thirty-five. By then, as Scott put it, 'his
extensive researches into Oriental languages and Antiquities exceeded that
of any man......who ever made them his study'.[3] His mastery of nearly
twenty Asian languages may, by today's standards, seem superficial but it
allowed him to translate from, and hence to introduce to the western
world, the works of Hindi, Bengali, Persian, Malay, Arabic, Tamil and
many other eastern authors. On each occasion the translation is crafted
into the standard mellifluousness of classical couplets or Scott-like quat-
rains. Here is part of the 'Lament for Rama', taken by John Leyden from
the Bengali :

I warn you, fair maidens, to wail and to sigh,
For Rama, our Rama, to green-wood must fly;
Then hasten, come hasten to see his array,

For Ayud'hya is dark when our chief goes away.

All the people are flocking to see him pass by;
They are silent and sad, with the tear in their eye:
From the fish in the streamlets a broken sigh heaves,
And the birds of the forest lament from the leaves.

His five locks are matted, no raiment has he
For the wood, save a girdle of bark from the tree;
And of all his gay splendour you nought may behold,
Save his bow and his quiver, and ear-rings of gold.

Exotic, plangent, a little sentimental, but clear and incisive in its rhythms and attentive in its detail : that is Leyden's contribution to translation. As the *Memoir* of Leyden frankly puts it in the 1875 Centenary edition of his poetical works, 'We thus place him in the first rank of linguists, but when we come to his *poetry*, we must fall back somewhat. No mind has yet been first in everything'.[4]

Through the last 160 years there have been many figures like John Leyden in Scottish literary affairs. The best-known include John Galt (1779-1839), whose novels of country life in Scotland have been brilliantly rediscovered by the Scottish-New Zealand critic Professor Ian Gordon : Galt settled eventually in Canada; R.L. Stevenson (1850-94), whose travels in the South Pacific reveal a man restlessly discontented with Edinburgh parochialism; John Buchan (1875-1940), the most successful adventure writer of his day and for the last five years of his life the Governor-General of Canada; and we ought in our own time to remember Edwin Muir, Muriel Spark and the popular romantic novelist, Mary Stewart, who have spent many years abroad. More important for us are those Scots who settled abroad because they could not find a livelihood at home : not the dilettantes and the administrators, but people like Alexander MacLachlan and Susanna Moodie in Canada, James Brunton Stephens and Mrs Aeneas Gunn in Australia, or William Langton in New Zealand, and the countless anonymous adaptors of Scottish ballads and folk songs who gave to their countries a minstrel tradition which survives more vigorously there than it does now in Scotland. These people became part of the cultural fabric of the nations they helped to settle.

Ballads and songs have always been a particularly rich part of the Scottish folk tradition. Valuable folkloric research has been done on the influences inherent in the Negro songs and ballads of the southern states of America, transmitted to the slaves by the many Scottish people who settled in the South. In Nova Scotia and Ontario, as one might expect, the links with the Scottish oral tradition are especially strong. Some of the ballads which Scott recorded in his *Minstrelsy*—'Katharine Jaffray', for example —are still actively used in these provinces. The tradition is dying fast, however, and only very old people now seem to recall the Anglo-Scots ballads and Jacobite songs which were passed down, particularly among

Catholic families, from the mid-eighteenth century onwards. A typical repertoire today will include familiar songs like 'Barbara Allen' and 'Loch Lomond' as well as many less obvious pieces which have been passed to the singers in a direct family descent from a Gaelic source. Specific identification can sometimes be made between Ontario songs and Hebridean songs. A well-documented folk-singer like Mrs Grace Arlington Fraser, of Glengarry County, Ontario, sings the following refrain :

> The day is fine, the wind is fair,
> And it's swiftly flows the tide.
> The boat is sailing o'er the main
> To bring me far from Canada.

This is merely an inherited adaptation from the o·iginal Gaelic which, if translated directly into English, goes :

> The wind is fair, the day is fine,
> And swiftly, swiftly runs the time;
> The boat is floating on the tide
> That wafts me off from Fiunary.

We find the folk-song element impressing itself upon many twentieth-century Canadian poets. Here, for example, are a few amateur verses by an Orkney exile in Alberta, Thomas Johnston, lines not addressed, I feel sure, to the Australian author of *The Female Eunuch* :

> Germaine, the sweet, the pure, the true,
>   My blessing ever goes with you.
> Where e'er you roam. by land or sea,
>   Still ever happy may you be.
>
> Though storms may rage and winds may blow
>   And war is raging here below
> Deep down into your bosom's core
>   May peace still reign for evermore.
>
> May he who loves you ever be,
>   Faithful and kind and cherish thee,
> And may you be a faithful wife,
>   To cherish and comfort him through life.[5]

The verse is weak and the sentiments stereotyped, but in connecting the stability of love with the wandering and vicissitudes of exile the poet expresses the commonest association in expatriate folk-song. Inevitably verse of this kind is nostalgic, often in language as much as subject.

Alexander MacLachlan (1818-1896) was not himself a pioneer though his father was; he had died whilst returning to Scotland to bring his family out to Canada.   MacLachlan's most famous poem, 'The Emigrant' (1861), deals with the fortunes of a Scotsman who has left his native country fifty years earlier.   The poem starts with a lofty paean to Canada :

Land of mighty lake and forest !
Where the winter's locks are hoarest;
Where the summer's leaf is greenest,
And the winter's bite the keenest;
Where the autumn's leaf is searest,
And her parting smile the dearest;
Where the tempest rushes forth
From his caverns of the north,
With the lightnings of his wrath,
Sweeping forests from his path;
Where the cataract stupendous,
Lifteth up her voice tremendous :
Where uncultivated nature
Rears her pines of giant stature...

These crisp Longfellow-like rhythms and the impeccably resonant diction give way to the simpler melody of a Scots lament :

Oh, sad was the morning
    When I cam awa'
And big were the tears frae
    My e'en that did fa';
My mother was weepin',
    My father was wae,
And farewell, my laddie,
    Was a' they could say;
While the tears o'er their haffets
    Were fa' in like rain,
For they thocht that they never
    Would see me again.

The influence of Robert Burns is strong here and helps to divest the poetry of much pomposity.   Yet the long narrative resumes its formal poise soon after, though it is surprisingly versatile in its range of metre.   Indeed, the Burnsian streak of Scottish melancholy runs throughout, evident even in the most polished couplets :

Why left I my country, why did I forsake
The land of my hill for the land of the lake ?

Ben Ledi !   Ben Lomond !   Ben Awe !   Ben Venue !
Old monarchs, forever enthroned in the blue,

Ben Nevis !   Ben Avon !   the Brotherhood hoar,
That shout through the midnight to mighty Ben More,
Though lovely this land of the lake and the tree,
Yet the land of the scarred cliff and mountain for me.

It would be cynical to deny the genuineness of feeling here, but why does
the narrator of 'The Emigrant' need to stay in Canada if he pines so much
for the beauties of the Scottish bens ?   There is no word in the poem of
poverty or Glasgow or the clearances.   This emigrant left 'at Fortune's
call......I was then a happy boy,/Earth a scene of hope and joy.'   In one
bound we are in the heather-scented atmosphere of countless Caledonian
Societies throughout the Commonwealth—a half-picture of Scotland which
Scotland's own 'kailyard' writers at the turn of the century were happy to
sustain and which the worldwide popularity of her best known entertainers
like Harry Lauder has done little to discourage.

The same tone exists in much of the versifying by Scottish *emigrés* who
have been claimed as founding figures of Australian and New Zealand
writing.   There are exceptions, though you cannot read the early New
Zealand poet, John Barr (1809-1889), without detecting the sense that a
new community needed a roughspoken bard to celebrate its luck in establishing comparative prosperity and welfare beside the wretchedness of what
has been left behind.

There's nae place like Otago yet,
    There's nae wee beggar weans,
Or auld men shivering at our doors,
    To beg for scraps or banes.
We never see puir working folk
    Wi' bauchles on their feet,
Like perfect icicles wi' cauld,
    Gawn starving through the street.

                              ('There's Nae Place Like Otago Yet')

This is the work of a man who has no illusions about the Scotland he has
left behind.

When to New Zealand first I cam,
    Poor and duddy, poor and duddy,
When to New Zealand first I cam,
    It was a happy day, sirs.
For I was fed on parritch thin,
My taes they stickit thro' my shoon,
I ruggit at the pouken pin,
    But couldna mak it pay, sirs.

But now it's altered days, I trow,
    A weel I wat, a weel I wat,

The beef is tumbling in the pat,
   And I'm bath fat and fu', sirs.
At my doors cheeks there's bread and cheese,
I work, or no', just as I please,
I'm fairly settled at my ease,
   And that's the way o't noo, sirs.

('New Zealand Comforts')

His successor Jessie MacKay (1864-1938) has some of the plainspoken recognition that Scotland cannot be viewed in a haze of beneficence.

They tore us oot o' Scotland, they flang us in the west
Like a brain's thread o' beads, an' we downa look for rest.

('For Love of Appin')

Barr's and MacKay's confidence in the pioneering spirit recurs in several of their poems, expressed in simple Scots vocabulary from which dialectical difficulties have been ironed out. By contrasting their work with the virtually contemporary achievements of MacLachlan or Thomas Johnston we can begin to see in the Scots literature of the Commonwealth the same separation of two distinct strands of sentiment, the one raw, energetic, yet often lyric, the other tending to blandness, nostalgia and even whimsy, which has frequently been detected in the modern writing of Scotland itself. Just as the tougher language of modern Scottish poetry, initiated by Hugh MacDiarmid, Scottish fiction, from George Douglas Brown's *The House With The Green Shutters* onwards, and Scottish theatre today, in the plays of Hector MacMillan and Tom Gallacher, seems finally to have ousted the type of sentimentality exemplified by the verse lyrics of Marion Angus or Compton MacKenzie's *Whisky Galore* or J.M. Barrie's *Mary Rose,* so in Commonwealth writing the smell of the heather and the sound of the pibroch has been finally eradicated from all but the most amateur writing.

We see something of the conflict between these different demands upon literature of Scottish descent in the verse of Australia's James Brunton Stephens (1835-1902) whose regret for Scotland was coupled, in poems of real craftsmanship though some heavy-handedness, with a sense of Australian nationhood. The conflict exists more positively in the work of a considerably better poet than Stephens, John Shaw Neilson (1872-1942). Neilson's father came to Australia from Scotland as a boy, working all his life either as a self-employed farmer or as a contract labourer, and his mother was Scottish by ancestry. The poet himself, who imbibed the works of Robert Burns and Thomas Hood when still a lad, was for most of his working life an itinerant labourer, though in late middle-age he found clerical employment in Melbourne. John Shaw Neilson is best known for lyrical verses which often seem about to break into song :

Sing me the song that never dies,
  Of little love blinded and bold,
Blossoms unblemished and blue skies
  And the green going into gold.

                                                ('The Dream is Deep')

At the end of the nineteenth century there were still Gaelic-speaking
Australians, though they did not survive as communities in the way that
some Cape Breton villages in Canada have done to this day.   Neilson's
forebears spoke Gaelic, though he did not himself, so that it seems reasonable to detect in both the mood and the structure of his poems a Gaelic
element.   There are many examples of Gaelic intonation in Neilson's
poetry,[6] but I want to demonstrate, too, a struggle, of which I think he is
aware in his verse, to avoid soggy nostalgia and yet to be true to his Celtic
inheritance.   His poems are not explicitly about Scotland—you would not
expect them to be as he did not go there—but laments for a lost homeland
run through his work, reflecting not only his own life as a wanderer but
something of the uprooted exile too.

Mourners move onward from the gloom—
  Not for himself the lover sings :
Give us, they cry, the birds, the bloom,
  The long light on our journeyings.
Star follows star in the dull grey,
Deep is the dark, it drinks the day :
  For very love of God he sings.

                                                ('The Lover Sings')

Some of Neilson's best work are poems in portraiture.   There is 'Old
Granny Sullivan'—'The boys and girls that Granny knew, far o'er the seas
are they;/But there's no love like the old love, and the old world far away';
'Old Nell Dickerson'—'They young folk heard the old folk say/'twas long
ago she came;/Some said it was her own. and some/ it was another's
shame'; and the narrator of 'The Poor, Poor Country'—'My riches all
went into dreams that never yet came home.' This sense of being far from
the places of youth, warmth and innocence partly expresses a romantic
poet's natural sense of human decline, but partly, too, the sadness of
losing a former country.   The particular kind of nostalgia we find in Shaw
Neilson's lyrics and ballads owes a lot to the Scottish literary tradition,
both to Burns in Scots and to the Gaelic songs.   His poetry is much
concerned with death, which he perceives, as it is seen in Gaelic poetry,
more as a fading into shadows or dream than as an absolute finality.

The man God made he dreameth deep
  Down in his heart.   High in the air
His heaven lies.   How shall he sleep ?

He had a dream—the dream was fair ?

('The Dream is Deep')

Yet this Celtic lyricism, recognisable in early Yeats too, can descend into posturing, into the sort of sentimentality we find on Caledonian calendars :

The highlands, the hilltops,
    They make the heart bare,
Burned out with wishing for
    That country out there.

('The Winter Sundown')

John Shaw Neilson's joy in nature and in its often secret activity derived substantially from his Scots inheritance. Though he often lacks the robustness of the best songs and ballads of Robert Burns, his poetry shares with them an elegiac tone which has been assimilated in much sub-sequent Australian verse by poets with a similarly relevant Scots ancestry; in A.D. Hope, Chris Wallace-Crabbe and Les Murray.

There are many connections between Scotland and the development of Commonwealth poetry which I do not have space to explore here, but I must at least indicate the predominant influence of Walter Scott. Through-out the nineteenth century his ballads, songs and verse romances were possibly more widely read overseas than the work of any other British poet. He became the model for aspiring versifiers in all parts of the English-speaking world, but with especial importance in India. Look at Henry Derozio (1809-1831) or Michael Madhusudan Dutt (1824-1873), for example, in whom elements of Scott's diction are obvious. It is only fair for me to point out that I am currently supervising an able postgraduate student, Prabhu Guptara, whose thesis will be that the nineteenth century Indian poets in English went beyond mere imitation of Scott (or Byron or Wordsworth) to achieve an original synthesis of eastern and western poetry. Their awareness of Scott cannot be refuted, however, demonstrable in their fondness for his octosyllabic metre and in their echoing of his nostalgia for the past : in Derozio's poems on India or in Madhusudan's 'The Captive Ladie', which is set in an artificialised eleventh century. Derozio, it may be worth nothing, was taught for many years at Dhurmtollah Academy by the Scottish scholar-poet, David Drummond, and he later became a life-long friend of John Grant, the Scottish editor of the *Indian Gazette*. Madhusudan had early contacts with Scotland by sending some of his first poems to *Blackwood's Magazine* in Edinburgh.

It would require a much longer work than this brief paper to list the many Scottish pioneers who either, like Mrs Aeneas Gunn (1870-1961) in her story of endurance in the Australian outback entitled *We of the Never-Never* (1908), wrote accounts of their adventures which have passed into the national literatures of the territories they came to, or who, like the famous Mrs Fraser who has cropped up in many Australian attempts to come to terms with the foundation of the country, including Patrick White's latest novel, *A Fringe of Leaves* (1976), were to become transmuted into myth figures for subsequent generations of writers. Mrs Susanna Moodie (1803-1885) manages to be both, an estimable author and the inspiration for one of Margaret Atwood's best poems. Susanna Moodie's *Roughing It in the Bush, or Forest Life in Canada* was published in 1852, though it recounts incidents of fifteen years earlier. English by birth, Susanna Moodie was married to an Orcadian and imbibed many of his qualities of insularity, fortitude and thrift. Her ear for Scots speech and her shrewd eye for comic detail make hers among the most lively pioneer descriptions to be found in any of the former dominions. Her agony at leaving Britain, her dubious view of most Canadians and all Yankees, her misery with the cold winters and her delight at the wild summer landscapes come across in a varied prose which, at its best, deserts Victorian self-respect for a briskly intimate manner. Not least of her skills is a vivid bringing-to-life of the many Scottish folk she encountered, both the passengers on the ship out, 'who were chiefly honest labourers and mechanics from the vicinity of Edinburgh', and individuals like Bell, her servant, or Dr Harrison, the advocate of dandelion coffee. Some readers of Mrs Moodie's recollections find them prissy or dour, but they undoubtedly form a major source for our knowledge of mid-nineteenth century domestic life in Canada and of the essential Scottish element within it. Margaret Atwood's *The Journals of Susanna Moodie* (1970) recreates Susanna Moodie for a modern audience.

Mrs Moodie, who considered herself Scots by marriage though Canadian by initiation, is only one of many emigrants who made a distinctive contribution to the founding of a local literary tradition. She and her husband, after they abandoned the 'bush', helped for a brief period to run a literary journal, *The Victoria Magazine*. One can think in the South African context of Thomas Pringle (1789-1834), a former editor of *Blackwood's*, who wrote the interesting *Narrative of a Residence in South Africa* (1834) as well as a number of poems which Sir Herbert Warren describes in *The Cambridge History of English Literature* as 'little known in Scotland or England' though 'a great and good influence in South Africa';[7] of Pringle's predecessor Gordon Greig, who, as early as 1824, founded the *South African Commercial Advertiser*, the first independent newspaper in that part of the world; in New Zealand, of Dugald Ferguson (1833-1920) whose documentary novel *Vicissitudes of Bush Life in Australia and New Zealand* (1893), has the authentically masculine *timbre* of the pioneering world; or in India of Maria Graham (1785-1842), author of *Journal of a Residence in India* (1812).

The list of Commonwealth novelists who derive from a Scottish tradition, as opposed to simply bearing Scottish family names, is a matter for interpretation. I think there can be no denying the centrality of the

Scottish voice in the emergence of Canadian fiction especially. The Canadian novel has tended to be strongly regionalised, with a distinctively Quebecois, Jewish, Ukrainian or English tone predominating in many of the best examples. Three Canadian novelists have essentially Scottish personalities, Frederick Niven (1878-1944), Hugh MacLennan (b. 1907) and Margaret Laurence (b. 1926). Niven's first novels, *Dead Men's Bells* (1912), *Ellen Adair* (1913), and *Two Generations* (1916) are essentially contributions of Scottish literature and in this connection it is fair to mention that there is a prestigious prize awarded annually to a Scottish novelist in his memory. But after Niven left Scotland for Canada he continued to use Scottish characters in his work and to wrestle with what had always been a great anguish for him : that though one might intellectually reject its creed a terrible irony asserted itself whereby Calvinism moulded one's fears and obsessions for the whole of life. His autobiography, *Coloured Spectacles* (1938), emphasises Niven's Scottishness, especially in his conflict with what, in *Ellen Adair*, he had called 'the curse of Calvin and a misconceived Christ.'

Hugh MacLennan has always made much of his Scottish family background—'three quarters Scotch, and Highland at that'—but what he ascribes to this ancestry is less specific than in Niven's work. He claims to derive the general power of his imagination from a Celtic source whilst maintaining that Calvinism has thwarted the expression of much true fiction in Scotland itself. MacLennan's characters often have strongly Scottish names—Neil MacRae in *Barometer Rising* (1941), Huntly MacQueen in *Two Solitudes* (1945), Matt McCunn in *The Precipice* (1948), Archie MacNeil in *Each Man's Son* (1951), George Stewart, the narrator of *The Watch that Ends the Night* (1959) and Laura Sutherland in *Return of the Sphinx* (1967).

Though a compulsive folk-memory constantly draws him back to the Scottish highlands, we also find in MacLennan's writing an anxious fear of Calvinism. Here is Dan Ainslie, in *Each Man's Son*, driven by his inherited Calvinism to deride his own ancestors with impotent fury :

"A shaking rage began to mount within him. There is no God, he kept repeating to himself. God is nothing but an invention of mad theologians who have told generations of men that He is the all-seeing Ancient of Days who at the same time damns men and loves them. The theologians, not Jesus, have tried to convince us that God, out of His infinite loving-kindness and tender-mercy, out of His all-wise justice, has decided that nearly all human beings must be scourged in the hope that a few of them, through a lifetime of punishment, might become worth saving.

"Now he had something specific to be angry about, and Ainslie let his rage build upon itself. Underneath all his troubles, he told himself, lay this ancient curse...The fear of the curse had led directly to a fear of love itself. They were criminals, the men who had invented the curse and inflicted it upon him, but they were all dead. There was no one to strike down in payment for generations of cramped and ruined lives. The criminals slept well, and their names were sanctified."[8]

This citation of 'Calvinism' for its power to shape yet damage whole generations recurs many times in Canadian novels, not only in those by Niven and MacLennan but in Sinclair Ross's famous tale of ministerial claustrophobia, *As For Me and My House* (1941), and in Margaret Laurence's *The Stone Angel* (1964), and in a score of lesser works. Ross's novel is by now a modern classic, widely accepted as a brilliantly poignant analysis of provincial snobbery and spiritual pride. Its skilful narrative form imposes under the reader an inevitable responsibility to judge the characters, who are presented with ingenious ambiguity. The novel has much in common with *The House With The Green Shutters*, a grim extension into a prairies setting of an essentially Scottish moral tone. As for *The Stone Angel*, perhaps no Commonwealth novel has more acutely rendered one of the principal dilemmas which Calvinism sets, how to make something out of our lives when the Lord may have directed a different destiny for us. Hagar Shipley's discontent with herself and her strange incapacity to make herself charming—'*Bless me or not, Lord*', she prays at the end, '*just as You please, for I'll not beg*'[9]—may not, to many readers of *The Stone Angel*, seem to have much to do with Scotland, but I doubt if anyone who understands both the prairies and the shaping spirit of the modern Scottish intellect will miss the connection.

The authority of the manse is just as prevalent in early New Zealand fiction though it has tended to fade in more recent writing. William Langton's *Mark Anderson : A Tale of Station Life in New Zealand* (1889) exemplifies the type, one of several Otago novels at this time which are imbued with presbyterianism : though the formal sentiments can contrast strangely with the vivid roughness of some of the Scots dialogue. Alexander Bathgate (1845-1930), a Dunedin solicitor, expertly caught the manner of the Scottish sheep-shearers in New Zealand in his novel, *Sodger Sandy's Bairn* (1913).

I am anxious that this paper should not dwindle into a list of names : but I trust that enough has been indicated, in what I have been saying, of the many connections that exist between Scotland and the literature of the Commonwealth. The principal inheritance seems to me to be threefold. Disadvantageously to the earlier development of some writing in the Commonwealth was a tendency to fall for the same kind of sentimentality which for so long glutinised Scottish literature itself. But the impact of traditional Scottish folk songs and ballads upon the emergence of an oral tradition in Australia and Canada cannot be underestimated; it even has its place in the evolution of oral culture in black communities. Finally, the rigorous and chastening effect of Calvinism has been influential, especially in the prairie novel of Canada. Add to this the unique strength of the Scottish intellectual contribution to scholarship in the Commonwealth and we perceive a loose-knit but substantial importance to the subject I have been considering. I have not here assessed the extent of Scottish criticism within the study of Commonwealth writing. Nor have I begun to look at Scotland and Scots people as a subject for authors uncommitted to any particular Scottish literary influence, though from Samuel Foote's play *The Nabob* (1772), concerning a Scotsman working in India, to Wilson Harris's *Black Marsden* (1972), with its personal but authentic evocation of Edinburgh, we can see that for two hundred years few other countries have had a more constant attraction to the writer's imagination. I hope that this paper has isolated some key motifs in a large composition, any one of which would be a valid subject for research and evaluation.

REFERENCES

1. David Craig, *Scottish Literature and the Scottish People*, 1680-1830, London, Chatto and Windus, 1961, p. 273.

2. R.T. Robertson, 'My Own Country : Prairie Immigrant Literature', Chapter in *The Commonwealth Writer Overseas* (ed. Alastair Niven), Brussels, Librairie Marcel Didier, 1976, pp. 75-85.

3. Sir Walter Scott, in a testimonial sent by him in favour of the Rev. Alexander Murray's application for the Hebrew Chair at Edinburgh University.

4. Thomas Brown, 'Life of John Leyden', A Memoir accompanying *The Poetical Works of Dr John Leyden*, Edinburgh, William P. Nimmo, 1875.

5. Thomas Johnston, from 'Written to Mrs Perreal', Poem in *Canadian Scottish Songs and Poems* by Thomas Johnston, Calgary, Alberta, 1920.

6. A.R. Chisholm, the editor of Neilson's poetry, has instanced specific phrases of Gaelic influence :

    > In the far days, when every day was long,
    > Fear was upon me and the fear was strong,
    > Ere I had learned the recompense of song.
    >
    > ('The Gentle Water Bird').

    The phrase 'Fear was upon me', which occurs twice in this poem, matches word for word the Gaelic expression 'Bha' (was) 'Eagal' (fear) 'orm' (upon me) and typifies the passive inclination of Celtic writing both in Scotland and Ireland. Chisholm discusses this and other linguistic points in the introduction to his edition of *The Poems of Shaw Neilson*, Sydney, Angus and Robertson, 1965.

7. Sir Herbert Warren, 'South African Poetry'. *The Cambridge History of English Literature* (ed. Sir A.W. Ward and A.R. Waller), Vol. XIV, Part III, 1964, p. 374.

8. Hugh MacLennan, *Each Man's Son*, Toronto, MacMillan Laurentian Library. 1971 (1st pub. 1951), pp. 222-223.

9. Margaret Laurence, *The Stone Angel*, London, MacMillan, 1964, p. 263.

4

"East is East and West is West" : Points of Divergence in African Literary History

BERNTH LINDFORS

IF literature is an art of cultural self-definition, then it can be assumed that different cultures will produce different literatures in the process of defining their own identity. Also, the same culture may produce different literatures at different moments in its history. But how will these literatures differ ? Will artists select themes that are singularly suited to their times and approach them through a variety of forms ? Will they select a favourite form and try to shape their statements to fit the contours that this genre imposes upon creativity ? Or will a single gifted individual put such an indelible stamp on the imagination of his society that it is impossible to recall his era without associating it with his own remarkable achievements?

Literatures which have existed for centuries are usually subdivided into "periods", each dominated by a particular theme, form, figure, or by some combination of such features. English literature, for example, is said to have an Elizabethan period in which drama flourished and lyric poetry soared, a Romantic period in which poetry eclipsed prose and drama, a Victorian period in which the novel asserted its supremacy over all other forms. These periods are often given the name of their chief exponent : the age of Shakespeare, the age of Wordsworth, the age of Dickens. Similarly, in French literature we find an era of classicism followed by such eras or "movements" as romanticism, realism, naturalism, symbolism, surrealism, existentialism, etc., each with its own discrete characteristics, its own masterworks, and its own place in European intellectual history.

Can such periods be postulated for some of the new literatures that have sprung up in the twentieth century, many of them within our own lifetime ? If so, is it possible to distinguish between particular emerging literatures by using formal, thematic or biographical criteria, even when the nations and individuals creating such literatures have undergone very similar historical experiences ? In short, what idiosyncrasies define a new national or regional literature and how did these idiosyncrasies come into being ? The large, polymorphous field of "Commonwealth literature" affords an interesting arena for such speculations, but I intend to confine most of my remarks to only one corner of this field—the continent of Africa—and I shall begin by briefly straying outside the boundaries of the Commonwealth to comment on a literature of cultural self-definition first produced by African and West Indian writers in French in the 1930s and 1940s—the literature of Negritude.

Negritude has been aptly described by Jean-Paul Sartre as a movement expressing "anti-racist racism".[1] The Black Man, long regarded by Europeans as an inferior being, eventually rose up and insisted that he too belonged to the human race, that his culture, though different from that of Europeans, had equal validity, integrity, morality and beauty. Instead of feeling ashamed of his blackness, he began to affirm it, discovering positive value in those ingrained racial characteristics which had always been denigrated by whites. Emotion, rhythm, earthiness, "soul"—these were qualities as laudable as any the impersonal, abstract, rational European world could offer. To be black, unapologetically black, proudly black, was not only beautiful but essential for all colonised Africans and West Indians who wanted to free themselves from the racial tyrannies of the past. Only by creating a revolutionary new self-image could they achieve psychological as well as political independence.

The negritude movement found initial literary expression in the form of poetry. Much of the imagery and music of this poetry was new, but its structure tended to be conventional. Aimé Césaire's *Return to My Native Land* was heavily influenced by French Surrealism,[2] and Lèopold Sédar Senghor's early verse bore the clear imprint of Paul Claudel, Saint-John Perse and Walt Whitman.[3] It was as though these young black lyricists, in seeking to sing a new song, felt compelled to pitch it in a recognisable key so that French ears would be able to accept it as melodious and well-composed. They were committed artists fighting a battle against European racism, but to fully engage their enemy, they had to choose weapons already familiar to Europe. Their selection of an approved idiom of the French intellectual elite may have been as much an effort to gain the confidence and respect of the colonial master as it was an attempt to protest against alien cultural domination by eloquently expressing African ideas in an authentic African style, albeit in a non-African tongue. The Negritude poets were domesticated radicals who set out to be revolutionary by exploiting orthodox forms. They had to prove themselves indisputably French in order to effectively assert their *africanité*.

The writers who came later had considerably more freedom to manoeuvre, but a good many of those who emerged in the French African colonies in the years prior to independence opted for a particular narrative form : the satirical novel.   Mongo Beti, Ferdinand Oyono, even Camara Laye in his Kafkaesque *Radiance of the King*, found that lugubrious laughter was a satisfying way to deal with the many ironies that confront individuals who have imperfectly assimilated a new culture.   Through the antics of a fumbling hero, these authors could attack the social absurdities to which colonial Africans were constantly exposed.   Since they were writing in a postwar era, when European imperialism had already been partially discredited, they could approach the subject of colonialism with irreverence. There was no longer any need for the colonised to impress the coloniser with a display of respect for French culture.   It was far more acceptable now simply to laugh at some of the horrible mistakes that had been made during this awkward historical encounter.

The writers who emerged in the English African colonies prior to independence were a more sober-sided lot.   The novel was their favourite form too, but they used it to tell tragic stories of the past.   The two most influential writers of this period—Chinua Achebe of Nigeria and (James) Ngugi wa Thiong'o of Kenya—believed that the role of the African writer was to help his people understand what really happened to them during the colonial era.   The fictional historical chronicles they created were thus another type of politically committed literature.   As Achebe once said :

> Even those early novels that look like very gentle recreations of the past—what they were saying, in effect, was that we had a past. That was protest, because there were people who thought we didn't have a past.   What we were doing was to say politely that we *did*— here it is...One big message of the many that I try to put across, is that Africa was not a vacuum before the coming of Europe, that culture was not unknown in Africa, that culture was not brought to Africa by the white world. You would have thought it was obvious that everybody had a past, but there were people who came to Africa and said, "You have no history, you have no civilisation, you have no culture, you have no religion. You are lucky we are here. Now you are hearing about these things from us for the first time." Well, you know, we didn't just drop from the sky. We too had our own history, traditions, cultures, civilisations. It is not possible for one culture to come to another and say, "I am the way, the truth, and the life; there is nothing else but me." If you say this, you are guilty of irreverence or arrogance. You are also stupid. And this is really my concern.[4]

So the historical novel with a tragic ending became a means of reinterpreting the African past, thereby counteracting the European myth of African barbarism. This was another form of "anti-racist racism."

All the types of writing discussed so far were produced in reaction to the European presence in Africa. All were expressions of the spirit of nationalism which swept across Africa in the last decades of the colonial era. This partly explains why they were all so much alike in cultural thrust and political orientation despite the differences of form that mark the Anglophone and Francophone contributions. Indeed, the similarities so outweigh the differences that it is probably legitimate to speak of a single African literature in European language emerging during the colonial period. Anglophone and Francophone artists may have displayed a preference for different forms but the message they articulated was essentially the same. This was an anti-colonial literature written in colonial times and in colonial tongues.

After independence these literatures grew and changed but the speed and direction of their transformation was so conditioned by local circumstances that it is now becoming possible to distinguish between some of the national and regional literatures that have been written in the same language. At least one can attempt to do this with the Anglophone literatures that have grown up in West and East Africa. Some of the Francophone literatures of West and Central Africa can no doubt be analysed in much the same way, but it would complicate an already complex argument to attempt it here, so I shall concentrate only on West and East African writings in English.

First, it must be emphasised that these literatures had a lot in common after independence, too. A mood of disillusionment and pessimism permeated both areas, finding reflection in such works as Chinua Achebe's *A Man of the People*, Wole Soyinka's *Kongi's Harvest*, Ayi Kwei Armah's *The Beautyful Ones are Not Yet Born*, Ngugi wa Thiong'o's *A Grain of Wheat*, David Rubadiri's *No Bride Price*, and Robert Serumaga's *Return to the Shadows*. Political satire was the dominant mode of literary expression throughout Anglophone Africa in the 'sixties, but this time the criticism was directed against Africans themselves, particularly politicians who were now viewed as villains and rogues rather than idealistic nationalist leaders. The major form was still the novel but poetry and drama were being used to some extent to sound the same theme. Chinua Achebe, in an essay published in 1966 entitled "The Black Writer's Burden", tried to explain why it was necessary for African writers to shift their attention from the past to the present :

Most of Africa is today politically free; there are thirty-six independent African States managing their own affairs—sometimes quite badly. A new situation has thus arisen. One of the writer's main functions has always been to expose and attack injustice. Should we keep at the old theme of racial injustice (sore as it still is) when new injustices have sprouted all around us ? I think not...The black writer in independent Africa is thus facing his first real challenge...We must seek the freedom to express our thought and feeling, even against ourselves, without the anxiety that what we say might be taken in evidence against our race.[5]

This was the black writer's burden in both East and West Africa in the 'sixties—to expose and attack the new political injustice openly.

What changed the literary situation in West Africa was a total breakdown of law and order in the mid-sixties that resulted in a rush of military coups and, in Nigeria, erupted into an ugly civil war. Most of the literature published by Nigerian writers in the 'seventies has been inspired or influenced by this traumatic experience. There have been stories of heroism and villainy, of man's inhumanity to man, and of the outside world's complicity in divisive Third World conflicts. Writers appear to be striving to comprehend the significance of what their nation experienced as well as to document some of the horrors of war. This has been a profoundly serious literature and one which has taken a number of artistic forms. During and immediately after the war there was a gush of poetry and short-story writing. The country's leading novelist, Chinua Achebe, who lived in Biafra throughout the war, switched to these shorter forms because he found it impossible to concentrate on long fiction.[6] Also, the Igbo students who returned to the University of Nigeria at Nsukka, a town formerly in Biafran territory, rapidly filled several anthologies and literary magazines with verse and stories about the human consequences of armed conflict. But at the same time, Wole Soyinka, the country's leading dramatist, who was in prison during much of the war, found it possible to explore war-related themes in four different forms—drama (in *Madmen and Specialists*), poetry (in *Shuttle in the Crypt*), novel (in *Season of Anomy*), and autobiography (in *The Man Died*). In recent years more Nigerian authors have returned to writing novels but mainly to tell stories of battlefield heroics and behind-the-scenes corruption. Satire has made a comeback but lighthearted humour is still hard to find. Nigerian literature remains a rather sombre chronicle of contemporary confusion.

In East Africa, on the other hand, the dominant literary idiom has become laughter. It ranges from the harsh, grating snort of the satirist to the gentle chuckle of the humorist to the madcap giggles of the clown. Even some of the most serious social themes—political murder, organised crime, government corruption—are being treated comically in East Africa today. But such literature is not necessarily frivolous or lightweight. Several East African authors have mastered the art of saying something very heavy with a smile.

The first was Okot p'Bitek whose *Song of Lawino* and later songs established a precedent which many other East African authors have elected to follow. Combining a traditional oral form of poetry—the lament or autobiographical song of grief—with wide-ranging socio-political commentary relevant to modern East Africa, p'Bitek has been able to attack such contemporary vices as "apemanship" of European ways, ethnic conservatism, social irresponsibility, moral bankruptcy, intolerance of human diversity, and mindless totalitarianism. In doing so, he has pioneered an entirely new form of cultural criticism, one which puts into the mouth of a singing persona the private thoughts behind the public attitudes of his day. No West African poet has yet sung in this register.

Another form which distinguishes East African writing from its West African counterpart is the amoral urban picaresque narrative. West Africa has rural picaresque narratives such as Nkem Nwankwo's *Danda*, town picaresque narratives such as John Munonye's *A Dancer of Fortune*, and even a few urban picaresque narratives such as Cameron Duodu's *The Gab Boys*, but it has nothing to compare with the pop novels of Charles Mangua, *Son of Woman* and *A Tail in the Mouth*, in which a totally immoral, self-seeking trickster-hero tries to keep himself afloat in a disordered world. Mangua's heroes are city-slickers who must learn early how to survive by using their wits. Through them we are given a kaleidoscopic view of modern East African society and urged to laugh at what we see. Mangua's main purpose is not to criticise but to entertain. He is willing to tolerate immorality if it is good for a few laughs.

Allied to the urban picaresque narratives are the civil service melodramas that David Maillu has popularised in East Africa. In works such as *Unfit for Human Consumption*, *After 4 : 30*, and *No !*, Maillu focuses attention on the lives of minor bureaucrats and office workers in Nairobi who are struggling to make their way into the middle class. Usually they slip and fall, ruining their prospects for the future. There is a heavy didactic note in these melodramas but readers seem to be attracted to them more for their frank and funny descriptions of erotic encounters than for their morality. In telling these stories Maillu has exploited both of the most popular East African literary forms—the satirical solo song introduced by p'Bitek and the urban picaresque narrative developed by Mangua. Maillu, who publishes his own books, seems to be trying to cater to the reading interests of the masses.

Several other forms of popular writing have also appeared in East Africa in recent years, each with an avid following. Transafrica Publishers and Heinemann East Africa have issued brief paperback romances about the love affairs of airline stewardesses, nurses, nightclub singers, and the like. Mwangi Ruheni and Hilary Ng'weno have turned out fast-paced mystery and detective fiction. Several publishers have begun flirting with, and in a few cases fully embracing, the tawdry thrills of cheap pornography. Indeed, a whole sub-literature on prostitution has evolved, some of it written as grassroots social commentary by "serious" authors such as p'Bitek and Okello Oculi. The trend in East Africa seems to be toward producing a literature that will be read by the common man.

Of course, this is nothing new. West Africa has had such a literature for more than a quarter of a century. Popular romances were available in Ghana before the Second World War, Onitsha market literature first appeared after the war and flourished in the late 'fifties and early 'sixties, and Cyprian Ekwensi published *Jagua Nana*, one of the liveliest prostitutions of West African fiction, in 1960. What is most significant about the recent explosion of pulp literature in East Africa is that it is being used not so much as an escape from the realities of the present day but— at least in the hands of the most thoughtful writers—as a means of con- fronting those realities. It is a popular literature with a social purpose, a literature taken rather seriously by many who read it. Yet it scores its points primarily through humour and through the exploitation of poetic and deliberately episodic narrative forms. It laughs at the human predica- ment instead of grumbling gloomily about man's inhumanity to man, as does the elite literature of contemporary West Africa.

Different social and political conditions in East and West Africa appear to be largely responsible for these differences in literary orientation. Except in Uganda, East Africa has not undergone the kind of convulsive political transformation that Nigeria, Ghana and Sierra Leone (to name only the nations most productive of literature in English) have experienced. One is tempted to speculate that East African literature could easily be soured by civil war too. Yet there are indications that this impulse has been resisted by writers who have been exposed to a form of tyranny more vicious and ruthless than almost any other on the continent. I am referring, of course, to the Ugandans who have witnessed the gory rise of Field Marshal Idi Amin Dada. There is an incipient anti-Amin literature grow- ing up in East Africa but it is taking characteristic East African forms. Okot p'Bitek is now composing a satiric *Song of Soldier*, and another Ugandan writing under a pseudonym has produced a hilarious animal fable called "The Amazing Saga of Field Marshal Salim Fisi and Friends"[7] which features a despotic hyena in the role of military dictator. The impulse, even in literature devoted to the maniacal and macabre, is to laugh. There may be tears behind the laughter but there is not as much blatant bitterness as in West African writing. The humour in East African literature may reflect a need or determination to maintain a buoyant mental attitude, even in the face of severe adversity. Compared with their West African counterparts, East African authors appear to be optimists at heart.

Such basic distinctions, if proven to be correct, may ultimately help to define the differences between specific regional or national literatures in Africa. But these distinctions must also be viewed in much broader spatial and temporal terms. So far, writers in tropical Africa working in English and French have produced two kinds of literature: one in response to European cultural imperialism, the other in response to African social transformations after independence. In other words, this body of diverse writings, viewed as a single entity, can be said to have a colonial period and a post-colonial period. In other areas of the continent which have undergone a different historical experience—North Africa, South Africa, and the former Portuguese colonies, for example—one finds literatures which share some common ground with East and West African writings but which also depart radically from the patterns already described. Furthermore, one can find other areas of the world—the Caribbean, India, Oceania, for instance—which have produced literatures remarkably similar yet markedly different. The literary scholar who attempts to isolate the distinctive characteristics of a regional or national literature in any language must not lose sight of the larger picture into which his own unique configuration of discrete elements fits. For while the study of a particular literature may be helpful in defining a specific culture, its ultimate aim should be to teach us something significant about the expressive arts common to all mankind.

REFERENCES

1. See Jean-Paul Sartre, *Black Orpheus*, Paris, Presence Africaine, n.d. This essay was originally written as an introduction for Leopold Sedar Senghor's *Anthologie de la nouvelle poesie negre et nalgache de langue francaise*, Paris, Presses Universitaires de France, 1948.

2. For discussions of the nature of this influence, see Eric Sellin, "Aime Cesaire and the Legacy of Surrealism," *Kentucky Foreign Language Quarterly*, 13, 1967, supp. p. 73, and Emile Snyder, "Aime Cesaire: The Reclaiming of the Land", *Dahousie Review*, 53 (1973-74), 730-32.

3. For a recent discussion of these influences, see Sylvia Washington Ba, *The Concept of Negritude in the Poetry of Leopold Sedar Senghor*, Princeton University Press, 1973, Chapter 5.

4. "Interview with Chinua Achebe", *Palaver: Interviews with Five African Writers in Texas*, ed. Bernth Lindfors et al., Austin: African and Afro-American Research Institute, University of Texas, 1972; p. 7. Cf. Ngugi wa Thiong'o, "The Writer and His Past", *Homecoming: Essays on African and Caribbean Literature, Culture and Politics*, London, Heinemann, 1972, pp, 39-46.

5. Chinua Achebe, "The Black Writer's Burden", *Presence Africaine*, 59, 1966, 131-39.

6. Achebe, *Palaver*, p. 12.

7. Excerpts have been published in the August and September 1976 issues of *Joe* magazine.

5

'Mister Johnson' and the Complexity of 'Arrow of God'

ROBERT M. WREN

Chinua Achebe's *Arrow of God* is the most complex, richly-textured novel to come out of Africa. It is considerably finer in this respect than its predecessor from Nigeria, the Englishman Joyce Cary's *Mister Johnson*.[1] Discussion of Cary's novel in this context is inevitable because it is one of the novels that Achebe says appalled him and motivated him to tell "the story that we had to tell."[2] I do not deny the faults of *Mister Johnson*. But nevertheless I propose a rather detailed analysis of its virtues. This prior discussion will illuminate the rather greater virtues of Achebe's novel and illustrate as well the cultural presumptions of the two authors and the contrast between them.

However delightful, even splendid, the character of Johnson may seem to the British reader, to the African, Johnson is a European monster, a culturally vacuous stage Irishman dressed in black skin and voiced with a bad approximation of West African pidgin English. But in a vitally important sense, the novel is not about him at all; it is about Rudbeck, colonial officer, symbol and activist of Progress : he will build a road, not because the road is needed, not because it is wanted, not because it is ordered, but because—in some inarticulated way—he thinks that to Build a Road is Good. Johnson is the operative agent of the Road, for he gives Rudbeck the means to build it. Because Johnson is so purely instrumental, the novel almost breaks in two : the Rudbeck story with the making of the Road, and the Johnson story, with its awful ending—the execution of the appreciative black by a white who would have done as much (with the same feeling) for a sick dog.

The Johnson story can be largely disregarded here. That Johnson helped Cary to go on to better things—notably Gulley Jimson in *The*

Horse's Mouth—cannot be denied, and the literary critic would be ungrateful indeed to deny that Johnson's character has literary validity. But it wholly lacks African validity, and for that reason Johnson's antics are as offensive as the affectionate pet name Rudbeck's wife gives him—Wog. He is a gollywog, a little black Sambo, if you like, that Cary's skill has made seem alive and even, at times, splendid. His splendour, of course, lies in his odd, anarchistic ability to create for Rudbeck what Rudbeck cannot create for himself : the Road. It is this, the Road, that is the centre of the present discussion.

Cary makes it very clear that Rudbeck's passion for roads has no ideational base. Early in the novel the reader learns from the first resident he served under "that to build a road, any road anywhere, is the noblest work a man can do."[3] It is also something, when it is done, that you can see. Later Rudbeck is unmoved by the doubts of another resident, Blore, to whom "motor roads (are) the ruin of Africa." They are like railways earlier, which "spoilt the old Nigeria wherever they went."[1] What is this "old Nigeria"? It is never defined. In the novel it seems to be no more than the old town of Fada, which (in a passage made famous by critics who despise it) "is a pioneer settlement five or six hundred years old, built on its own rubbish heaps, without charm even of antiquity. Its squalor and its stinks are all new."[5] Cary is fully conscious of the irony. Such a place may be transformed romantically, as it is not only by men like Blore, but even by Rudbeck's wife Celia. To her it seems "the house of unspoilt primitive, the simple dwelling-place of unsophisticated virtue."[6]

Yet Cary makes it clear that she and Blore are justified in a measure that they themselves do not understand. There is—Cary emphasises this —something like virtue, certainly unsophisticated, in Fada. The Government Office staff does not seal the mail bags. Cary explains why : "There has never been a mail robbery in Fada, and there never will be until civilisation and private enterprise are much further advanced."[7] Cary's point is in its own way romantic, for by European standards Fada is thoroughly corrupt. In the Waziri, for example, Cary paints a portrait of an intelligent and vicious manipulator of money and power. The family of Johnson's wife Bamu are potentially utterly corrupt. Cary illustrates this through the way Bamu's brother Aliu sees the world: "All things are stubborn and dangerous; all men, except one's own family, find their chief pleasure in tormenting the helpless stranger. After all, what else could anyone do with a stranger, except to fleece him ?"[8] So the lack of stealing in Fada is not a matter of virtue; it is more a matter of technique, of style, of technology : thieves do not steal until they learn how.

It is now possible to see in part what it was that—while it repelled Achebe, as is only just—engaged him as well. Unlike the mass of colonial novelists, Cary struggled to fit the colonial into a practical African context that the colonial did not and could not comprehend. It is an African context devoid of mysterious drums in the night and unspeakable rites,

without fabled treasure, white goddesses, Prester Johns, and the white
man's burden. It is—and for this it deserves praise—unique in that the
African world is recognisably the world of ordinary affairs, and yet still
beyond the colonial officer's understanding. It is irrelevant that Cary's
understanding is so limited. He saw that the British officers, whether
benign or malign, did not know what they were doing, and however much
Cary misunderstands the Africans, he understands the colonial official
extraordinarily well. And, most importantly, he saw the significance of
their mindless actions. His symbol, richly worked out, for this significance
is the Road.

It is unnecessary here to detail the road or its construction. Cary lets
the location remain vague—it will link "Fada direct with Kano and
Sokoto,"[9] perhaps, which means an end to isolation at least. Construction
of the road requires financial ingenuity—misappropriation to be exact—on
Rudbeck's part, and the genius of leadership that Johnson can provide.
But why the road should be built at all, and what the result will be—these
questions are unarticulated because Rudbeck cannot directly imagine them.

Early in the novel, Rudbeck's passion for road-building seems harm-
less. The first clear indication that something is amiss is seen when even
the Emir, a man of vast limitations, recognises a danger in the road and
in the zungo, the primitive inn that is built for travellers. He and the
Waziri hate both. The road they say "will bring thieves and rascals, (and)
the zungo will encourage them to stay." Johnson is seen to disagree, but
in the light of Cary's ironic comment above on stealing and civilisation,
the defence is an implicit attack :

"You are not civilised, Waziri, You don't understand that people must
have roads for motors."'
"Why, lord Johnson ?"
"Because it is civilised. Soon everyone will be civilised."[10]

The implications of this "civilisation" are clear. At a high point in the
novel, Rudbeck is surprised : a lorry from the north appears and the
driver, not knowing he is the first, goes through without pause. Rudbeck
"has not realised perhaps that the road would open itself." The road has
become an operative entity. The next day, Rudbeck has cause to reflect :

He is surprised to find how much his court work has increased in the
last three months, not only with cases due to the new road, such as disputed bargains, complaints of extortion, adulteration, fraud, highway
robbery; but purely local ones, such as theft, assault, quarrels between
villages, disputes between chiefs and their people, disputed claims to
all kinds of rights; and even wife-beating, kidnapping, and divorce.
There is a crime wave in Fada...[11]

Civilisation—embodied in the road, in commerce (in "free enterprise")—
has come, and it has activated the potential for crime that was inherent; it
is like the infection of a virus that attacks but one organ and thereby sic-
kens the whole man.

As Cary saw, and as Achebe understood, the intention was good. It
was to *civilise through commerce*, a proposition Rudbeck would never have
articulated, but one which underlay, philosophically, "the white man's
burden" as Englishmen saw it. "The missionaries," according to the
historian J.F.A. Ajayi,

> placed emphasis on...trade because they believed it would inevitably
> lead to the formation of...a class who would...carry out the social
> reforms the missionaries...would rather not meddle with.   Commerce,
> (said one missionary), will aid the "change in Society which the Gospel
> seeks...will erect new standards of responsibility and thus remove one
> of the strongest props of polygamy."[12]

The absurdity of the last proposition should not blind us to the fact that,
earlier in this century, to doubt the essential idea would be to doubt the
moral base of English society itself. Trade is good. What promotes trade
is good. The road is good.

Yet, when it is finished, when it has "opened itself," it seems to speak
to its creator :

> "I'm smashing up the old Fada—I shall change everything and every-
> body in it. I am abolishing the old ways, the old ideas, the old law; I
> am bringing wealth and opportunity for good as well as vice, new
> powers to men and therefore new conflicts. I am the revolution. I am
> giving you plenty of trouble already, you governors, and I am going
> to give you plenty more. I destroy and I make new. What are you
> going to do about it ? *I am your idea. You made me, so I suppose you
> know.*"[13]

Rudbeck does not know. He is caught in a web of interconnectedness, the
existence of which he never imagined. To build the road, to increase
trade, even to break "tribal" isolation—these he might have understood as
goods, but to see (as he seems finally to see), that unexpected and unwanted by-reactions actually enforces his objectives while reversing or negating
their value, leaves Rudbeck looking at the ruins of a society he set out to
help.   Under his innocent hand, things fall apart.

When he has done the job, then he sees what he has done. In anguish,
he raises the question to a superior :

> "We're obviously breaking up the old native tribal organisation or it's
> breaking by itself. The people are bored with it."

"Yes, yes, and I'm not surprised," Bulteel says.

Rudbeck is greatly surprised. "Don't you believe in the native civilisation?"

"Well, how would you like it yourself ?"

Bulteel smiles...

"Then you think it will go to pieces ?"

"Yes, I think so, if it hasn't gone already."

"But what's going to happen then ?   Are we going to give them any new civilisation, or let them simply slide downhill ?"

"No idea," Bulteel says cheerfully.[14]

It is this idea that Achebe seized upon.   George Allen, the district officer of the last chapters of Achebe's first novel, *Things Fall Apart*, is more pretentious than Rudbeck and more ruthless, and he is less cheerful than Bulteel, but it hardly matters : he is the master, and he does not know, guess or suspect the outcome of his actions.

It is obvious that Rudbeck's "new civilisation" and Bulteel's insouciance are functional if not moral equals in failing to solve the problems that the road has created.   There is no answer to the Road : "You made me, so I suppose you know."   Nobody knew.   Cary the novelist was aware, as Cary the colonial officer perhaps was not, that one act is the cause of many effects, most of them unlooked for.   This is a fundamental principle of the contemporary science of Ecology, and the operative word is *pleiotropy*, a genetic term which identifies the astonishing capacity of the biological gene to produce—usually by interaction—an immense variety of physical manifestations in the living organism.

Pleiotropism. applied to the things that men do, is suggestive of that circumstance in human life when a single aberrant—or mutated—gene produces a living monster. Nature has made an error; commonly the error dies.   When man acts—as Rudbeck does in building the road—it is as if a wild gene were loose, transforming the social body.   Rudbeck's is the rational prognosis : the social body will die; an ancient and viable civilisation (whether Englishmen would care to live in it or not) is doomed.

Chinua Achebe found *Mister Johnson* "appalling" as a novel about Africa[15]—for reasons, I think, that are irrelevant to the pr:ceding discussion.   He adopted what I take to be Cary's central proposition : The colonial powers undermined a healthy civilisation, constructed over centuries, and, witnessing its destruction, were unwilling or unable to put anything in its place.   This is not to say that Achebe lifted the proposition boldly from Cary.   As will be seen below, he took a single aspect (the disintegrative effect of colonial intervention) as the base for his first novels, and then evolved, entirely in his own terms, a new and more comprehensive pleiotropic concept, which came to be embodied in his finest novel—easily one of the finest novels of the century—*Arrow of God*.   This was not in any likelihood a conscious process.   As I will show elsewhere, the generation of *Arrow of God* was an immensely complex process, its scope drawn from a cumulative awareness which Achebe gained through wide-ranging investigation and experience.   For the present, it is enough to say that Cary's appalling novel was the base upon which Achebe work-ed his transformation.

The first step in the transformation was the writing of Achebe's first novel, *Things Fall Apart*.[16]   The title is an immediate reflection of Cary's disintegrative theme.   The essential element is the same : a community into which colonial power intrudes, rending the social fabric.   On the other hand, Achebe's Umuofia is not merely geographically distant from Cary's Fada, it is also a different realm of experience.

The geographic difference is significant but should not be overempha-sised.   Fada—a fiction, of course—lies somewhere south of the cities of Sokoto and Kano, and well to the north of Ilorin.   It is, one may suppose, in Borgu (where Cary served); a town with an Emir of Fulani descent and Islamic religion, with a rural animist population of farmers and pastora-lists.   Such is the western part of today's Kwara State in Nigeria, as seen with an alien eye, superficially.   In Fada, colonial rule was "indirect"; the British officer ruled the Emir, and the Emir ruled the people.   Resistance, such as it was, to the colonial authority was embodied by Cary in the intelligent, wily, and pederastic Waziri, a man as sophisticated in his poli-tics as in his sexual taste.   The time would seem to be near 1920—a little before rather than later.

Umuofia seems a different world—and in at least two ways, it is.   It too is fictional, but the reader is to imagine it thirty or forty miles east of the great Niger River market city Onitsha; one would not improbably find it somewhere in the vicinity of Awka today.   Umuofia is a dispersed town composed of nine villages; commonality of ancestry links the nine into a clan.   Rule is vested in the commonality of citizens, particularly men of substance, while grave decisions were reserved for the ancestors, embodied in terrible masked figures, sacredly impersonated by great men of the clan.   All men are farmers, wealth is counted in yams and wives, and the colonial power—when the novel begins, around 1900—has not yet been felt.   Such is the superficial difference of Umuofia from Fada.

The other difference is more profound.   For all the richness of Cary's imagination, his African characters are outside of his understanding.   His Fada is two-dimensional, carefully observed, precisely pictured, without depth.   From his superior vantage, Achebe creates an Umuofia in which each practice, each ritual, each formality is detailed functionally.   Fada is rich in African oddities; Umuofia is rational, ordered.   Cary acknowledges the old African "civilisation" of Fada, but allows the reader to doubt that it really exists except as a kind of satisfactory stagnation.   Achebe shows on the other hand that behind the colonial's confused awareness of savage practices and unspeakable rites, jungle drums and cries in the night, is a dynamic, rich, and generous culture.   It has one great flaw : fragility.

This fragility is little indicated in the plot of the novel, which is of little concern here.   A fiercely ambitious man, violent because he fears weakness, Okonkwo alienates his eldest son by the ritual murder of the boy's foster-brother, and the white man's church is established in time to capture the disaffected child.   Okonkwo makes a final effort to free the community from the newly-established colonial government, fails, and hangs himself.

Around this plot, however, is woven a firmly textured community life which slowly unravels in the second half of the novel as the invaders' presence and power becomes increasingly pronounced, increasingly evident, challenging and even forbidding practices which are indispensable to the design of the culture.   The title, from Yeats' "The Second Coming", reflects both what the novel shows and what Cary predicted :

Things fall apart; the centre cannot hold;
Mere anarchy is loosed upon the world...

The agent of this anarchy is, of course, impersonal. It is not Cary's Rudbeck, nor is it the George Allen of *Things Fall Apart*, a man both ruthless and insensitive—insensitive as Rudbeck, but without doubts. Achebe portrays good white men as well—the Reverend Mr Brown is nicely if briefly sketched—but it does not matter; Brown is no less disruptive than Allen. Cary suggested the essential impersonality very well when he said of Rudbeck :

He understands that people in themselves, full of goodwill and good sense, can form, in an organisation, simply an obstructive mass blocking all creative energy; not from any conspiracy or jealousy, but simply from the nature of rules and routine, of official life. He accepts this cheerfully and says to Bulteel, "Ours is not to reason why."[17]

Implicitly, Achebe accepted this point of view in *Things Fall Apart*; in *Arrow of God*, it is explicitly operative.

Before proceeding to *Arrow of God*, however, it would be well to note, briefly, the sequel Achebe wrote to his first novel.   In *No Longer at Ease*,[18] Okonkwo's grandson extends his father's disaffected separation from the traditions of Umuofia. Obi Okonkwo—British educated—embodies anarchy : he can live by neither the traditions of the colonials nor those of his own ancestors. He idealises both and is trapped by their contradictions.

In many ways, *Arrow of God* is a truer sequel to *Things Fall Apart* than *No Longer at Ease*. It is as if between the two novels, Achebe saw what he had failed to do in the first. His point of view changed. The society of *Things Fall Apart*, for all its richness and variety, had this in common with Fada's : it was static—or at least seemed to be through part one, more than half the novel—just as Cary's town had in some fashion been what it was at the start of *Mister Johnson* throughout the indefinite past. The "old native tribal civilisation" was in both novels somehow fixed, permanent until Europeans came to tamper with it and thereby destroyed it.

The context of *Arrow of God* in contrast is greatly expanded in both time and space. Umuaro, the town that is the centre of the action of the novel, itself has a history that retreats into "the very distant past, when lizards were still few and far between";[19] this history is an essential dynamic to the progress of the novel. The missionary who helps bring about the denouement is motivated to his aggressive evangelicalism by the martyrdom of his relative during the previous century. The district officer is willing to risk and perhaps sacrifice his chances for honours in the service by his opposition to foolish misapplications of colonial political theory; he is not wise, he is not understanding—but he is not stupid. He too has a history.

Spacially, the novel is energised by violence and peacemaking both at great distances and at hand; this spaciousness is functional to the history and part of it. The present essay can deal with only a small part of the history, only enough to illustrate the proposition announced above, that in this novel Achebe has embodied a pleiotropism that pervades the entire novel, that is not, as in *Mister Johnson*, only an aspect. The power of the Road in *Mister Johnson* is brilliantly conceived, the Road is a powerful symbol and makes a profound point, but Johnson's splendour and his crimes, like his death, seem scarcely relevant to the power of the Road : Johnson's happy anarchism doomed him on page one. In *Arrow of God* there is no one event, no point in time, no thing that sets the pleiotropic organism into decisive action. A multitude of events—a hundred arrows in the hand of the god—bring about the rite of passage that is the substance of the novel.

Briefly, the action concerns the priest of Ulu who must deal simultaneously with the adherents of the rival god Idemili, adherents who hold great political power, and with the district officer, Captain Winterbottom, who has chosen Ezeulu to be his warrant chief in Umuaro. The priest declines the chieftaincy even though it would give him the power to dominate his enemies. Instead, imprisoned for his obstinacy, at government headquarters far from home, he conceives a higher retribution for his enemies and the enemies of his god : during his captivity two new moons pass, two sacred yams remain uneaten, and the yam harvest to be called by the priest in the name of Ulu cannot proceed. Umuaro is faced with immediate famine. Climactically, the Christian mission offers absolution from the wrath of Ulu to those who bring thank offerings to Christ, and Ezeulu, seemingly abandoned by his god, rises into "the haughty splendour of a demented high priest."[20]

Even in briefest outline, the story suggests complexities : the rival gods and the warrant chieftaincy are the two most obvious, and the present essay will deal with those alone; the larger context will be dealt with in subsequent essays.

The rivalry of Ulu and Idemili is, with one exception, seen in the novel as an immediate thing—not new, of course, not restricted to the present priests, but without a specific beginning. Ezeulu and Ezidemili (*eze* meaning, in this context, priest) do in fact have different histories and different powers, in accord with the histories of their gods. The origin of Idemili is never discussed in the novel, but in Achebe's 1974 revised edition the insertion by the author of a single word defines the history in a way that can be confirmed by evidence outside the novel, in the town of Achebe's birth, Ogidi. At the point of the revision, Ulu is speaking directly to his priest, at a time when Ezeulu has been contemplating appeasing the townspeople by permitting the harvest. "Go home and sleep," the god says, as if speaking to an unruly child, "and leave me to settle my quarrel with Idemili, whose envy seeks to destroy me so that his python may again come to power."[21] The operative revision is the word "again"; in earlier editions, Idemili had no claim to power, but the change implies that Idemili was supreme before the coming of Ulu.

Unlike Idemili, Ulu was created—the origin of Idemili will be suggested shortly. Indeed, the creation of Ulu was at the same time the creation of Umuaro. Unlike Umuofia, whose nine villages shared a common ancestor and therefore constituted a clan with powerful common loyalties, Umuaro was the union of six relatively antagonistic villages. Years of victimisation by the fierce warriors called the Abam had forced an unwilling unity, and medicine of the utmost power was used to create the new ruling, guardian deity named Ulu. This unity, forged by fear, made Ulu great because the united villages succeeded in resisting the Abam, and Ulu was beyond challenge as long as the Abam were to be feared.

At the time of the action of the novel—around 1921, with an episode five years earlier—Ulu is still supreme, but that supremacy has been undermined. Ezeulu's formidable antagonist, supporter of Ezidemili, Nwaka, speaking during that early episode, calls attention to Ulu's loss of primary function :

"We have no quarrel with Ulu. He is still our protector, even though we no longer fear Abam warriors at night..."[22]

No explanation is given in the novel for this peculiar circumstance, but if the people of Umuaro knew only by distant hearsay why the Abam no longer raided, Achebe as author certainly knew exactly why. The action that stopped the Abam was the beginning of European penetration of that hinterland which is the place of the story, until not long ago called Iboland—now the Nigerian Anambra and Imo States.

The Abam were highland allies of the great Iboland traders, called collectively the Aro. It was in late 1901 that the British launched a huge military exercise against the Aro in the belief that the Aro ruled Iboland; control of the Aro would then mean control of the entire territory.[23] The assumption was wrong, and more than fifteen additional years were required before the British could say that every Ibo village was secure under government rule—but the crucial change had already occurred : the subjection of the Abam and their allies, and—far away in Umuaro—for fifteen years the villagers had learned that they need fear the Abam no longer. Without fear of the Abam, there would be no great fear of Ulu, so Nwaka could carry his contempt for Idemili's rival to an astonishing extreme :

> "...we have all heard how the people of Aninta dealt with their deity when he failed them. Did they not carry him to the boundary between them and their neighbours and set fire on him ?"[24]

This virtual threat, though not made publicly, nevertheless caused some to tremble for Nwaka, but Ulu, for whatever reason, took no action to meet the threat then. The novel does not say, but perhaps Ulu could not.

What Achebe has shown, by indirection, is that colonial interference with the Aro and the Abam in 1900 decisively weakened the one spiritual power that united the people of Umuaro a hundred uncharted miles away, and prepared, all unwittingly, the death of the god twenty years later. The occasion of Nwaka's threat was the opposition of Ezeulu to a proposed war, strongly advocated by Nwaka, against the neighbouring town of Okperi. In spite of Ezeulu, the war began. But it was ended by a second, more immediate interference from government : Winterbottom and his soldiers (strangers, black men from the north, though the novel does not say this) intervened, collected all the guns in Umuaro, and broke them. Then, after listening to the evidence of Ezeulu, Winterbottom awarded the land in dispute to Okperi. Five years later, the priest's testimony against his town stood as another threat to his god, Ulu—who, it must be recalled, was not only protector in war but also guardian of the agricultural year in peace.

Idemili is commonly identified in the novel as the god to whom the python is sacred, but that does not account for his origin. The story of how a village ceased to exist after certain villagers unwisely cooked a python for food concludes only with the observation that the village was doomed because "the royal python was sacred to Idemili; it was this deity that had punished Umuana."[25] The answer to the origin lies outside the novel, but is significant. Oral testimony among elders in Achebe's home village of Ikenga, in Ogidi town, attests that since time immemorial all the clans of the region drained by a tributary of the Niger which has as its source the spring called *ide* have revered Idemili (literally, *pillar of water*). The spring feeds the python as well as all the people of the region.[26] Thus, unlike Ulu, Idemili is clearly autochthonic in Achebe's home; if Achebe has moved Idemili some miles to the east, he has done so with the free license of fiction.

In brief then, the quarrel between Ulu and Idemili was the quarrel of the no-longer-needed protector against the autochthonic deity. The British action in breaking the power of a warlike community at one extreme of Iboland, in good time destroyed the power of a god essential to the ecological cycle of a community unheard of and unthought of by the colonials and their government. Things fall apart once again, it is true, but now the fragility of the cultural defenses has distant as well as immediate causes, the society and its gods were dynamic before the British came. Indeed British intervention can be seen as one factor in the great change; certainly not, as in the earlier novel, the sole cause.

The Abam raids and the British subjugation of the Aro respectively caused the creation and caused the fatal weakening of Ulu. In its turn, the institution of the Warrant Chieftaincy—or rather the attempt—exacerbated the internal quarrels of Umuaro and thus led indirectly to the triumph of Ezeulu's enemies and, ironically, the Christian church.

The scope of this essay does not permit full development of the warrant chieftaincy concept as it was applied in south-eastern Nigeria. Briefly, the governor of Nigeria, Sir Frederick Lugard, had come to believe that all Africans had in some natural fashion come to be organised in hierarchical states, despotically ruled by kings. Where something like that state of affairs did exist—Lugard thought he had found it in Uganda and in the Fulani-ruled portions of northern Nigeria (including, one must suppose, Cary's town of Fada)—the British appointment of a "Resident" to "advise" the ruler insured British control while maintaining the appearance of traditional political organisations. But the policy, called "indirect rule", was not applicable (whatever Lugard thought) everywhere. As Achebe's Winterbottom, in disgust, put it :

> "We do not only promise to secure old savage tyrants on their thrones
> —or more likely filthy animal skins—we not only do that, but we now
> go out of our way to invent chiefs where there were none before..."[27]

What disturbs Winterbottom is that he must appoint a chief in Umuaro, a town which, however little Winterbottom understands, he knows has no chieftaincy institution. His choice is Ezeulu, because of the testimony he gave in the land-war dispute five years earlier. Winterbottom described what happened :

> "I should mention that every witness who testified before me—from
> both sides without exception—perjured themselves...Only one man—a
> kind of priest-king in Umuaro—witnessed against his own people. I
> have not found out what it was, but I think he must have had some
> pretty fierce tabu working on him."[28]

To Ezeulu, the "tabu" was his god Ulu; to Ezeulu's enemies, the tabu was his mother, a daughter of the opposing town in the land dispute.

Winterbottom, naturally, found for Umuaro's enemies on Ezeulu's testimony, and when he could no longer resist demands from the government at Lagos that he appoint a chief, he chose the priest. Ezeulu's enemies expected no less; they saw him as the friend of the white man, not of Umuaro. This was unbearable to the priest and, as has been indicated before, he found the means of his revenge upon his people while imprisoned. But his failure to call the yam harvest, instead of vindicating himself and Ulu, created the first great opportunity for the Christians—and in but a single season, the mantle of priesthood fell from the descendant of priests to a stranger, John Jaja Goodcountry, and his god of the Christians, for Goodcountry sanctified the harvest that Ezeulu had denied.

Only two of the threads that make up the intricate web of Achebe's ecological complexity have been explored. Others have been touched upon or hinted at. The Aro expedition of 1900, the Church Missionary Society (Goodcountry's employer), the Church in the coastal towns of Bonny and Opobo (obliquely identified in the missionary's names), the abuses of the warrant chiefs (Winterbottom is all too familiar with one appointed chief who has become rich through extortion), all contributed. Yet there is much that a short essay cannot notice : the strains with Ezeulu's household, the intellectual propositions which both maintain and endanger Ulu's power, the appeal of the white man's education, and, of course, much more.

But what should be clear is that Achebe has adopted and transformed Cary's pleiotropism. Instead of the Road as a single inclusive metaphor that shows but one thing—how the British wrecked a "civilisation" that they neither respected nor saw any reason to respect—Achebe has looked at something of the same kind of event from the inside, and shown that it is not a road (though a road is built in the novel) that transforms a society, but the interaction of forces, ancient and new; that the British did not contribute a dynamic to a static culture, but rather contributed to a process of change long in progress. They gave to it a direction it would not otherwise have taken, of course, but—in contrast to Cary's vision—Achebe shows a society that is far more an actor in its destiny than an object that is acted upon.

REFERENCES

1. Chinua Achebe, *Arrow of God*, 1964, 1974, revised edition, Heinemann ; Joyce Cary, *Mister Johnson*, 1939, 1962, Penguin.

2. Achebe, "Named for Victoria, Queen of England," *New Letters*, XL, 1973) reprinted in *Morning Yet On Creation Day*, London, Heinemann, 1975, p. 70.

3.   Cary, p. 52.

4.   Cary, p. 51.

5.   Cary, p. 110.

6.   Cary, p. 111.

7.   Cary, p. 57.

8.   Cary, p. 20.

9.   Cary, p. 162.

10. Cary, pp. 94, 95.

11. Cary, p. 181.

12. J. F. Ade Ajayi, *Christian Missions in Nigeria 1841-1891: The Making of a New Elite*, 1965, Longmans, p. 18.

13. Cary, p. 186 (italics added).

14. Cary, p. 185.

15. Achebe, "Named for Victoria," p. 70.

16. Achebe, *Things Fall Apart*, 1958.

17. Cary, p. 10.

18. Achebe, *No Longer at Ease*, 1960.

19. Achebe, *Arrow of God*, p. 14

20. *ibid.*, p. 229.

21. *ibid.*, p. 192, Cf· earlier editions, chapter sixteen.

22. Achebe, *Arrow of God*, p· 28·

23. J. C. Anene, *Southern Nigeria in Transition 1885—1906* (Cambridge, 1966), pp. 229-30.

24. Achebe, *Arrow of God*, p. 28.

25. *ibid.*, p· 48·

26. Oral testimony of an elder of Iᴋenga, Ogidi town, and Emmanuel Chukwuka Agulefo, my host and translator, to whose generosity and helpfulness I am greatly indebted.

27. Achebe, *Arrow of God*, p. 26.

28. *ibid.*, p. 38.

6

The Indian Sensibility
in English

WILLIAM WALSH

LET me begin with one or two generalities. First, by sensibility I mean
what Remy de Gourmont defined as

> le pouvior général de sentir tel qu'il est inégalement développé en
> chaque étre humain. La sensibilité comprend la raison elle-méme, qu
> n'est que de la sensibilité cristallisée.

I take this, then, to be that special combination of thought, feeling, value
and assumption, that particular flavour of taste and sentiment, that
characteristic mode of action, which reveal the nuance and crystallise
the tone and temper of a literature. In literature, that is to say, we find
embodied, concretely and insistently present, not 'a philosophy', not some
abstract doctrine or partial metaphysic, but a rich complex of 'beliefs',
'the picked experience of the finest minds,' the great writer's intricate
apprehension of reality—'the idea', as Henry James said, 'which deeply
lurks in any vision prompted by life'.

I am aware that to speak about Indian literature in English in the
space of some twenty minutes would require a Confucian concision and
a Thomistic inclusiveness, not to speak of courage—or rather nerve—
beyond the ordinary. I shall not attempt even a long footnote on an unwritten literary history. For what, after all, is literary history? It is
hardly history in the historian's sense, for that is always subject to the
sprawling intervention of life. Literary history seems to exist in an enclosed, solipsistic world bounded by library shelves and filled with dusty
air. It consists of the accumulation of influences, the confluence of sources, the marriage of books and the generation of papers. It forces upon
the writer a special manner, that of the alert and confident lecturer. The
literary historian on this scale cannot but affect to be blandly omniscient

and imperturbably clever, a blend of Lord Buddha and Lord Keynes. Like the lecturer he has to set about briskly putting to rights the untidiness of a hundred years in fifty minutes : in the interests of history—literary history, that is—he can hardly even admit the existence of that large category of authors who are merely boring. Tedium is taboo.

I can only be savagely abstract and egotistically arbitrary, and suggest a few tips and themes which seem to me appropriate for the student to consider. The first, and most profound, is the English language itself. Literature in the end is only—only !—the most powerful, the most human, the subtlest and the most inclusive use of the language. It was only when the language itself had been organically nourished by the life of the people and brought to a point of readiness, early in Chaucer and mature in Shakespeare, that these two geniuses could appear. How true is the comment that Shakespeare did not invent Hamlet, but discovered him in the English language.

Literature can be read as the self-illuming chronicle of the state of the language. New movements in literature are new uses of language, and this is as true of Chaucer, of Shakespeare, of Donne in the seventeenth century, of Pope in the eighteenth century, as it is of Wordsworth in the nineteenth and Lawrence in the twentieth. The new mind requires the new voice, and the new voice is discovered by the writer's genius for intimately registering the idiom of his own world.

It is this new voice in the choir of literature in English which I recognise in the work achieved in India in the nineteenth and twentieth centuries. Let me offer some examples of the distinct sensibility, of the new voice, within the context of which we speak. Everybody knows Indians were writing in English before Macaulay's *Minute* and before Lord William Bentinck endorsed it in 1835 as government policy : '... the great object of the British Government ought to be the promotion of European literature and science among the natives of India, and all funds appropriated for the purpose of education would be best employed on Indian education alone.' Rammohun Roy (1774-1833) was as much responsible for this policy on the Indian side as Macaulay was on the British. Rammohun Roy was the first of that notable line of Indian sages who have expressed themselves in English. His vigorous English, Victorian yet with a measure of eighteenth century energy, the staple of which was an extensive vocabulary, a slightly abstract diction, and long, balanced, supple sentences, carried with it some of the certainties, as well as the structure, of the contemporary sermon and admirably fitted his double intention : which was, first, to reform Hindu religious thought and practice by introducing into it a stricter, Protestant ethos, and second, to associate with a profound loyalty to the Hindu spirit a more open attitude to Western categories of thought, particularly scientific thought. He argued, therefore, with energy and determination, for women's rights, religious toleration, the freedom of the Press, for the radical improvement of the conditions of peasants, for science, education, and democracy in the manner of the best of the disinterested and liberal Victorians. Rammohun Roy was a large-minded, independent, and gifted journalist of an admirable type who introduced a sharper bite into the languid Indian intellectual scene and offered to his successors a prose which was a model of clarity, energy, and point. He inaugurated that tradition in which Indians have found a sense of peculiar intimacy with the English language, making it a second natural voice for the Indian mind and sensibility.

Another and grander sage was Vivekananda (1862-1902), a man of profound spiritual force, powerful intellect, great learning, and Franciscan candour, who wrote, given the period and a national bias towards the nebulous, in a remarkably strict and athletic way. He detested abstractions and his analysis and evocation of the ancient Indian spiritual tradition, which he wished both to recover and to revivify, is made with the utmost precision and concreteness. He resisted an undignified and philistine submission to Western, pragmatic thought, just as he had no sympathy with a simple nostalgia for the past. He was a moralist not just a moral philosopher, a thinker not just a theorist, a speculative critic not just a man of erudition deeply familiar with European philosophy. His intelligence, that is to say, had an active inclusive character; it had, as well, an attractively sardonic sharpness. "The Hindu man drinks religiously, sleeps religiously, walks religiously, marries religiously and robs religiously.' 'No single individual before Gandhi and Nehru... did more to de-hypnotise a complacent, slumbering people,' wrote the critic C.D. Narasimhaiah.[1]

A modern version of the Indian sage, a very different and even fanatically individual version, is Nirad C. Chaudhuri (b. 1897). The development so exhaustively detailed in his *The Autobiography of an Unknown Indian* (1951), which belongs incontestably to the line of Roy, Vivekananda and Aurobindo, is not just an evolutionary one in which a Western Protestant astringency displaces the warm appeal of an Indian past—although it certainly *is* that. It is also a more personal and strenuous achievement which involves, on the one hand, hacking out an area of freedom and manoeuvre from a choked jungle of inheritance; and on the other, constructing a fresh identity which would join a questioning Western mind to a temperament laced with Bengali fury. The instruments of demolition and of building, and the elements out of which the new self was to be made, were concepts and principles, usages and styles, which Chaudhuri found, not in the imaginatively cramped local British population, or the restricted Anglo-Indian tradition, but in the immensely more inclusive source of the English language and its literature. It was an undertaking which required on the part of Chaudhuri not only intellectual energy and analytical skill but also courage, will, stamina, and a quite unabashed interest in himself. The psychological composition or structure which results is a triumph of self-education and a model of the formative power of language, of its capacity to disturb and rearrange at the depths of the personality. It is also—like *The Autobiography of an Unknown Indian* itself and the whole literary production of which it is a part—a monument to the creative clash of two civilisations.

It was in the 1930s that the Indians began what has now turned out to be their very substantial contribution to the novel in English, and one peculiarly suited to their talents. Let me make a comment about no more than a handful of these writers.

R.K. Narayan's fiction makes explicit two of his deepest convictions about human life. In the first place is his sense of the way in which, at every stage of his life, the isolated individual faces the enormous, fundamentally indifferent crowd. Streams of people flow round the single stone. This contrast is present in many places in Narayan's work. He speaks in *Waiting for the Mahatma* of how 'one heard night and day the babble of the big crowd moving on the market road'; and the bitter conclusion of the comedy of *The English Teacher* is that 'a profound and unmitigated loneliness is the only truth of life.' 'Unmitigated loneliness' amid 'the babble of the crowd'—it is this in the end that we feel in *The Guide* as Raju stands up to his knees in the water at the extreme of strength, of his consciousness, and even of his life.

The sense of individual alienation is distinct from—may seem at odds with—the other perception which operates constantly in Narayan's work, though nowhere, perhaps, so strongly as here. Narayan is intensely aware of the way in which human character is constituted—not simply influenced—by the expectation of others. There may be a distinction in logic between these two insights but there is not one, as our own lives confirm, in actuality. Character *can* develop, can improve or degenerate, because a person feels himself to be not just a point in a continuous line of humanity but in some fundamental way at a distance from and set off against the rest. And character does develop by means of responses to the cues offered by others. Nor is the model of this response simply that of a reaction to a stimulus. The novel is closer to the form of answer to question. It is less a psychological bond and more a dramatic construction. We can become what others expect of us only because we are ultimately isolated and separate.

For Narayan, then, the very conditions of human growth are individual discrepancy and communal collaboration. It is this double insight which the career of Raju embodies and justifies. At its conclusion the confidence man has become the man deserving of confidence. He stands at the end up to his knees in water utterly isolated from the enormous crowd, and yet it is his collaboration—uneasy, desperate, and finally total—with the expectations of the people that turns their immense illusion into something like the truth. And the hint in the last words of *The Guide* that rain is on its way is Narayan's method of suggesting that there is some measure of objectivity, of endorsement by reality, in Raju's transformation. It has the approval of the gods, of life.

Mulk Raj Anand belongs to the tradition of the nineteenth century writer—not necessarily just the British tradition, for one is aware of a distinctly European set of influences operating on him, particularly French and Russian influences—in his approach to the novel, in his techniques, his weaving together of theme and event, in his sensibility and in his hope for what the novel may publicly achieve. He is particularly of this tradition in point of his fluency. Creation appears to be no agonising struggle for him, communication something he engages in with an unstrained and vivid enthusiasm; and the facility of a Russian writer. He is nineteenth century, too, in his conception of the novel, seeing it as an organisation strongly based on a double foundation of character and circumstance : character, I repeat, which has to be clearly defined and then developed, largely through the causality of the other constitutive force, social circumstances and influences, usually of a harshly oppressive sort. He has, too, a natural disposition towards the picaresque. The trilogy, *The Village* (1939), *Across the Black Waters* (1940), and *The Sword and the Sickle* (1942), takes the peasant boy, Lal Singh, from his North Indian village and a life stifled by suffocating layers of custom and religion, into the ferocity of the 1914-18 war and the crass commercialism of Europe, and then back again to India to a new political stance towards life.

The defect which constricts his real creative capacity is the habit of allowing his moral and social purposes to become separate from the particular actuality of the fiction, so that they frequently lead a collateral rather than a unified existence. This is accompanied by a certain passivity on the part of the characters, apt no doubt when they are the victims of circumstances, which they so frequently are, but out of place in those parts of his work where the individual should be more energetically active in the working out of his own nature.

As a writer Mulk Raj Anand lacks the concrete sagacity, the *finesse*, the 'appetite for the illustrational'—to use Henry James's phrase—which marks everything that R.K. Narayan writes; nor does he have that sense of the metaphysical nature of man we find in the other distinguished novelist, Raja Rao. But he has a deep feeling for the the deprived, a grasp of the social structure of his society, and an extraordinary fluency of communication. This fluency of communication has something Russian in it.

How different in every particular from Mulk Raj Anand is Raja Rao, a member of an old Brahmin family, born in Mysore in 1909 and roughly a contemporary of the two senior novelists, Mulk Raj Anand and R.K. Narayan. He has, however, a completely different literary character. He is not, like Anand, a politically committed writter, and he is very different from Narayan in being poetic, metaphysical, Lawrentian *Kanthapura* focuses on the intensity of Indian life, its physical immediacy, its traditional swaddling, and its religious murmurations. *The Serpent and the Rope*, his most elaborate work, gives no impression at all of any constricted or meagre talent. On the contrary, it strikes the reader with its flowing, outgoing abundance. It is a meditation, but a dramatic one, on the nature of existence, profoundly 'philosophical', but not at all abstract or theoretical. Its tone is strikingly individual, a blend of Indian tenderness and French clarity. The action, or the meditation, since external events do not have high status in the novel, swerves from India to France to England and takes in an astonishing number of authentic, sharply realised characters. It is a novel in which the examination of human nature is done through the intense diagnosis of its hero, Rama—Southern Brahmin, tubercular, intellectually brilliant, spiritually sensitive, and profoundly sad.

A delicate and exact vehicle for Rao's talent is *The Cat and Shakespeare*, a *novella* of patterned complexity and sardonic poetry. There is no vague wash of feeling round the edge of this book, no conceptual cloud floating in the air. The racial and poetic wisdom which is everywhere implicit is thoroughly absorbed into the details of the fable, and the cat, the rats, the wall, the ration shop, as well as the characters, Ramakrishna Pai, Govindan Nair, Abraham, John, Saroja, Shantha, can each be, in Henry James's terms, 'a strikingly figured symbol' because each is also 'a thoroughly pictured character'. Moreover, the innumerable literary and philosophical hints, analogies, the muted quotations and obscure connections which echo and re-echo everywhere are used with a musical propriety quite different from any explicit or academic pointing.

If Anand is the novelist as reformer, and Narayan the novelist as moral analyst, Raja Rao is the novelist as a metaphysical poet.

So far I have seen the Indian sensibility in English under the figures of the sage and the novelist. I now turn to the third figure in this trinity, the poet. And indeed it seems to me that if the achievement of Indian literature is in the novel, its promise is in the poetry. Let me take no more than three names, Nissim Ezekiel, R. Parthasarathy, and A.K. Ramanujan.

About Nissim Ezekiel himself we have to remember that he is an Indian Jew of Bene-Israel origin, belonging to a community long established in India, and that in his own family English was indeed the language of the home, and his use of it from the earliest days was instinctive and natural. But of course it was a language disconnected from a society constantly using and changing it, a language which to a greater degree than with native speakers had to rely for enrichment on books rather than a living use. Perhaps this accounts in Nissim Ezekiel both for the quality of inhibition one sometimes detects in his verse, and the occasional oppressive sense of deliberation and control his poetry communicates.

If Ezekiel has on one side the inhibiting discontinuity of a gap between himself and the living, used language, he has on another side a second but very different, creative discontinuity. This is constituted by his being of Jewish descent in a Hindu culture. It is both a theme of his poetry and a source of considerable energy in it. Nissim Ezekiel in the Indian scene is a permanent expatriate, but one who has freely elected to stay. Displaced by his own spiritual past, he is in place by an act of the will. His eye is familiar with, but at a distance from, the object, and his specifically Indian poetry is both inward and detached, a combination making for a peculiar strength and validity.

> The Indian landscape sears my eyes.
> I have become a part of it
> To be observed by foreigners.
> They say that I am singular,
> Their letters overstate the case.
> I have made my commitments now,
> This is one : to stay where I am,
> As others choose to give themselves
> In some remote and backward place.
> My backward place is where I am.

('Background, Casually')

One is aware of a double impulse in the poet, which on the one hand keeps him at a distance from his environment as he clutches his private history and aspiration, and which on the other, by means of a free and painful act of will, reconciles him to his environment.

Coolness, detachment, objectivity : these are the marks of Ezekiel's harsher notations of Indian life, as in the poem on the misused, anonymous maidservant, or the one on the grandfather standing in the monsoon water supporting the grandchild who has learned to sleep on his shoulder. They are also, together with a fastidious distaste for anything loud or ornate, and a balancing sense of proportion and perspective, the marks of his more affectionate recording, particularly in the context of the family, where his work shows that specially Indian candour and joy in family relationships that we observe in the writing of Narayan and Raja Rao.

Nissim Ezekiel's work calls to mind a remark of George Santayana : 'Art supplies constantly to contemplation what nature seldom affords in concrete experience—the union of life and peace.'[2] This poetry, itself a discipline of contemplation, certainly affords to the contemplative reader what concrete experience offers to this exquisitely equipped observer— occasions for the union of life and peace. The impression the poems give is one of intense, active tranquillity.

Parthasarathy, like Nissim Ezekiel, is totally without that swelling euphoria of the late romantic tradition as it manifested itself among nineteenth century poetic Indians. A kind of melancholy is common to them both, calmer in Ezekiel, more nervy in Parthasarathy. Disappointment is his principal theme, whether with the edgy complications of love, with the insoluble problems of composition or, as with England, in face of the actuality of what he expected. He accepts disappointment with an

irritable but unprotesting glumness, a slightly morose recognition of the
way things are.   A proportion between his themes and his temperament
makes his work a singularly faithful projection of his nature, and accounts
for the absence of fabrication and externality in it.

His naturalness and honesty of feeling are helped by his delicate skill
in managing an idiomatic and unpretentiously modern line and voice.
The span of the instrument may not be great but the cleanness and direct-
ness of the speech actively engage the reader's sympathy and persuade him
to cooperate in accepting whatever modification of line or voice is necessary for the poet's purpose.   A tiny illustration of what I mean is the last
line of the poem 'Stairs' : 'Only/the heart isn't hospitable anywhere.' The
line is cool and grey, but saved from flatness by the natural break after
'Only', by the faint doubleness of meaning also contained in 'Only', and
by the active and passive meanings conflated in 'hospitable'.   In fact, it
turns out not to be simple or flat, and to have just that degree of complexity appropriate to one brooding, not with passion but with a sort of
moderate melancholy on his checked, imperfect experiences of love.   A
second example in which the theme joins Parthasarathy's interest in his
own past to his agitation about problems of composition shows again this
natural, scrupulous and restrained line, and his gift for making a contemporary idiom suggest with precision the character of his personal
experience :

> Much experience, they say
> dulls the mind :
>   the hands touch,
>   the lips meet
> at the evocation of a word.
> Only we haven't the words
> to bring it off.
>
> But stumbling on experience
> I chanced on an implement,
> a supererogatory silence.
>
>   ('A Supererogatory Silence')

And the essential bias of that experience, it seems to me, is the fascination with the element of foreignness in his experience.   He is both
attracted to and frightened by what is alien and distant in his life, whether
this is in India, or the England his love affair with the English language
took him to, or with the India he discovers when he is away, or the strange
Tamil he decides to cultivate on his return, whether it is his experiences
of love or his awareness of himself.

> The street in the evening
> tilts homeward

as traffic piles up.
It is then I stir about :
rise from the table
and shake the dust from my eyes.

Pick up my glasses
and look
For myself uneasily.

('Complaint')

The quality of difference breaks upon him with such shock because of the cold and accurate objectivity with which he sees, a capacity responsible for the glass-like quality of his language. His imagery even when it is in the form of metaphor is essentially composed of similes, aids to clearer sight. The consciousness of what is alien or different or remote is produced by his historical situation, his education, and the special circumstances of his life. But it is also accounted for by a poetic personality which glides silently through experience, observing its properties with meticulous exactitude and an uneasy sense of not being at home.

Finally, let me mention A.K. Ramanujan. His poetry is intimate, concrete, and dismissive of anything puffy or obese, and it brings into the Indian literary scene a welcome note of confident, individual, and independent voice. His images are sharp in content and outline. His arrangements of images and scenes, each distinct in itself, have a strong quality of inner continuity, and give the appearance of life seen by an accurate, poetic eye. He writes an alert and grainy poetry, whose touch is abrasive, whose sight is microscopic, whose movement is distributed, cogent, and strong. The title of one of his finest poems, 'Small-scale Reflections on a Great House', conveys the peering quality of his minutely accurate findings. His poems on relatives and insects, on grannies and ants, show his devotion to the intense, the diminutive, the angular. His intricate, ironic reflective skill makes him, like Nissim Ezekiel, not only one of the most impressive of Indian poets in English, but the embodying and focusing of a true Indian sensibility.

In these poets, as in the novelists who preceded them, and indeed in the sages who came before them, we see realised in the English language the power of the Indian inheritance, the complexity of the Indian experience, and the uniqueness of the Indian voice. We see an Eastern sensibility wholly at home in a Western art.

REFERENCES

1. *The Swan and the Eagle*, Simla, 1969, p. 58.
2. George Santayana, *The Life of Reason, or the Phases of Human Progress*, New York, Charles Scribner's Sons, 1905, London, Constable, p. 174.

WITHIN "Commonwealth Literature" there are examples of writers who,
having disdained conventional ideas about form and idiom, acquired
reputations for originality or eccentricity, yet subsequently earned "a
local habitation and a name". This has happened—in the case of the
poetic quasi-novel—to such writers as Amos Tutuola, Raja Rao, and
Wilson Harris. But it has not happened to G.V. Desani, whose remarkable but neglected novel, *All About H. Hatterr*,[1] is the subject of the ensu-
ing discussion. When this novel was being written just prior to 1948
there were very few "Commonwealth" writers, outside the British stream,
with whom Desani could have creatively compared himself. In the novel,
he and Hatterr are men with fantastic appetites for Forster's theory of
"only connect", but are writing and living in acute cultural isolation and
disjunction. Yet Desani did connect as he applied his bizarre imagination
to the question of the cultural relevance of the English literary tradition
to modern India. In so doing, he analysed the pertinent issue of the role
of the modern artist who, in his relations to his society, felt estranged
while belonging or belonging while estranged. This artist's daemon had
special significance for Asian, African and Caribbean writers who were
possessed by the comic or tragic significance (for their respective societies)
of the contradiction of cultures theme.

Raja Rao, Desani, Tutuola and Harris, among stylistically experimental novelists from the newer literatures in English, demonstrated that
foreign backgrounds could contribute to creative English originality of
expression, particularly in realms of verbal gesture such as rhetoric, local
idiom, and folk metaphor. These novelists did not so much write as
perform on behalf of their imaginations : Tutuola and the early Raja
Rao in simulated oral recital; the later Rao and Wilson Harris in dialect
soliloquy and metaphysical symbolism; and Desani in a theatrical, farcical

pastiche of these styles, and more.   In *All About H. Hatterr*, Desani ex-
perimented with language idioms, techniques of comedy, and cultural
themes based on the mixed-race, divided-self viewpoint.   These areas,
twenty years later, became the province of an emerging comparative
criticism.

Against this background, then, I should now like to turn my attention
to *Hatterr*, inviting you to entertain the following "PRESUMPTION":
namely, that beneath the novel's surface cavalcade of wit and fantasy, of
language-fission and mad Hatterr's adventures, complex issues are seriously alluded to.   That said, let us proceed to the "LIFE-ENCOUNTER"
with the text.   This is an experience which I have shared with a colleague[2]
and undergraduates.

The present generation of Western students, with its interest in India
and faith in the healing powers of Eastern religions, comprises an ideal
audience for Desani who (as early as 1948 when the first version of
Hatterr was published) seems to have been conscious of the comic possi,
bilities in addressing his novel to mystic-eyed Indophiles. In my experience-
Hatterr has a shock-wave effect on contemporary students. They are
vastly amused by certain sequences, but the humour of the book leaves
them feeling bewildered. They betray, you might say, the same symptoms
they did on first reading *Catch 22*.   Some of Hatterr's more painful
experiences, however comic, can strike the feeling reader as traumatically
close to the bone.   In this sense, Desani's vigorous humour, like Joseph
Heller's, is cathartic.   Desani, too, is capable, as Emily Bronte put it, of
turning the universe into a "mighty stranger", of reproducing the sensation of surreal nausea which can accompany existential loneliness:

> "I am scared, old feller.   I still hear the drums I used to hear when I
> was in the school.   Sometimes, just drums.   Sometimes, I see things.
> My mum. I see her. Sometimes, like I remember her. Sometimes, just
> her skeleton.   Soft porous bones, like honeycomb, and awful-smelling
> blood oozing out of them.   The other night I saw her, like I remember
> her, but with lumps of raw meat hanging from her chest and her
> elbows. She had no eyes. Just blood-stained holes and filled with bits
> of pointed glass. Wounds, lacerations, and bites all over her. As if she
> had been savaged. Her head was split, just like an orange, same colour.
> She called me Baby. She was crying, poor darling!   Then I heard the
> dreams. They seem to be saying 'Come to mamma !Come to mamma !'
> ...I felt as if my mouth was full of pus. It was horrible. I wished I
> were dead. I wished I knew where my poor old mum was !" (pp. 222-
> 223)

Well may you ask, was it for this that Auden and Isherwood ascended
F6?   Nevertheless, the passage does illuminate Desani's understanding of
his Western-educated audience. He employs acceptably absurdist allegory

to diagnose the disease of modern life. We recognise, in this instance of post-Freudian *angst*, one of the characteristic moments of self-recognition in twentieth century literature : isolate man's psychically-horrific separation from the lost Mother who is an inexplicably violated figure in a violent, irrational world. Hatterr is seeking an alternative to such nihilism. Many of us may be disposed to hope that a cure is to be found in the mystical philosophies of India, but are not sure whether Desani is endorsing or mocking our faith in a Light from the East.

Let us return, therefore, to the quoted passage in context to see what light Desani throws on the problem. The passage is followed by further conversation between Hatterr and Banerrji :

> "Please, Mr H. Hatterr," said my brother, "please, I think, this is one of the most pathetic sad things I have heard..."
> "Don't, old feller, don't ! No tears, old friend...I haven't had my mother to love me...I am afraid, can't you see ?"
> "Please have faith in God. God loves helpless people."
> "I can't help it, old feller. I can't help loving God. Even if He isn't there, even if He doesn't care, I can't help loving Him...I think He looks after my mum, like my dad used to."
> "Yes."
> "But it won't always be like that, old feller. I don't ask God any favours...I will pick up the strings...I shall find her, old feller. My mum." (p. 223)

Here, then, the hero and his preceptor decide that the solution to the modern neurosis is to be found in God and spirituality. However, what is one to make of Desani's presentation of this, once having identified the amusing parallel with Victorian melodrama, the cliches which deflate the life-affirming spirit of resolution, and the hit-tune mode of Hatterr's speech :

> "I can't help loving God.
> Even if He isn't there,
> Even if He doesn't care,
> I can't help loving Him."

Is the spiritual alternative to nihilism merely an occasion for comedy, is the question posed seriously only to be deposed satirically, or does Desani's comic plan affirm the value of the spiritual quest ?

So far, then, we have seen in the passages quoted how Desani has presented the reader with a recognisably contemporary vision of reality followed immediately by a "melodramatic gesture" (see p. 6), which in turn culminates in the following philosophical gesture :

Satan acts through *apparent* goodness, through *rahasyam*, doctrine and righteousness, and religion : the *apparent* spirituality : the *false* Karma

Yoga...The Fiend, in the urgent purpose of applying pain-plaster to
man...approaches a victim, *soft ! soft !* like a pussyfoot, and often
through human agents, who, though themselves minus the demonic
strain, and Al chaps—yet, subserving and ministering to Evil—*are* the
Fiend incarnate ! (pp. 223-224)

The would-be student of Hinduism recognises that here is a "vicious mole
of Nature" passage which should be regarded with caution, if not scepti-
cism. Is the passage. he may ask, a parody of Vedantic and Christian
terminology ? Or is Desani, through Hatterr, making a valid point about
the deviousness of Evil operating through the medium of goodness, as in
the character of Hamlet ? Certainly, in view of Hatterr's experiences of
victimisation through the machinations of charlatan holy men and psychotic saints, it is a legitimate conclusion for him to arrive at. But what are
we to make of the fusion of Hindu and Christian concepts, philosophical
absurdity or enlightening synthesis ? Any interpretation of *Hatterr*, I
believe, must come to terms with these questions. Let us now proceed,
therefore, to a detailed consideration of the novel bearing in mind that
Desani treats his central themes of cultural symbiosis and the ironic discrepancy between appearance and reality (as exemplified in the last
passage) in the spirit both of Shakespearian comedy and absurdist
humour.

Having read as far as the above statement concerning Evil (the end of
Chapter V), we have formed a picture of Hatterr as a man who is utterly
human in his frailty, illusions, desires and philosophical confusion. Hatterr
has been deceived and punished as a result of either his belief in the goodness and honesty of mankind, or his own vices of egoism, and each major
experience has been reviewed in the light of a universal problem. Consequently, the empathetic reader feels some obligation to identify with
Hatterr as a fallible Everyman.

Born to suffer because he is a classic case of psychological and cultural
identity crisis, Hatterr is, like the disciple Baw Saw, "a love-brat, a mixed
Oriental-Occidental sinfant" (p. 101) who oscillates between a dream of
eternal sahib-hood in "the seat of Mars, that damme Paradise" (pp. 35-36)
and decisions to go "completely Indian" (pp. 33, 47). He is a baptised
Christian who asserts "Been a member of the Club. Have drunk to royalty
in the company of sahibs. Damme, I am a sportsman, and bound to
noblesse oblige!" (p. 67), yet Indianises his soul to seek after Truth. But
he lives in a world of outer as well as inner contradiction, a world where
irrationality and mystery prevail :

"To hell with Reason ! To hell with judging !
After the evidence of human cussedness...and the blind ambition
of man...I just accept all this phenomena, this diamond-cut-diamond

game, this human horse-play, all this topsy-turvyism, as *Life*, as *contrast*.

As to *Truth*, the great generalisation is, *"dam' mysterious ! Mum's the word !"* (p. 154)

The world is *maya* : "things are not what I thought they were, what they seemed they were, and what might-have-been I wish they were !" (p. 36). Life is an absurdist fantasy, or circus act : "Never in my life did I do a turn with a lion. Yet, there was I, being a living plate to one ! That's *Life*, if anything is !" (p. 79). But, living as Hatterr does, prone to neurosis in the age of anxiety, he must need have faith in the psycho-medical or Freudian approach to man.

These facets of Hatterr's characterisation thus indicate that he is a twentieth century fictional type — the psychologically vulnerable picaro, or at least a parody of it. The sympathy Desani elicits for his hero is qualified by the detachment of comedy. As a spirited eccentric and bizarre fall-guy, Hatterr is like Falstaff to be laughed at as well as with. But because Desani's comic technique is absurdist as well as traditional, Hatterr appeals to a modern audience. Indeed, when Desani's novel first appeared, it most probably appealed to *avant-garde* readers who reacted favourably to the novel's absurdist humour. Today absurdism is an established tradition in the novel (Joseph Heller, Kurt Vonnegut, Spike Milligan, etc.) and the mass media (*The Goon Show, The 1948 Show, Monty Python*). But in 1948 Desani was ahead of his time. Heller waited. But, given that both were writing during World War II ("Though I was attending a world war, the first row, I worked," Desani says, p. 14), it seems likely that the English-language tradition of absurdist humour originated as a psychologically self-protective response to the barbarism and irrationality of war.

To understand the dynamics of Desani's style of comic absurdism, we must consider Desani's conception of the novel as *gesture*, and the special relationship between joking and gesturing which this entails. Underlying Desani's definition of comedy in terms of gesture, is a distinction between "overt" and "subtle" gesture, not unlike that which Hatterr refers to on an embarrassing occasion when Always-Happy insults Hatterr's manhood (p. 132). In Desani's case, overt gesture is a dramatic concept, while subtle gesture relates to his functions as author.

Consider the word "gesture" as it applies to physical actions and expressions of personality, consider the very theatrical qualities of Desani's writing, and it follows that *Hatterr* is aptly described as a dramatic gesture. Desani has virtually turned the novel into a performing art, just as his characters perpetually make performances of their lives. At the centre of the novel are Shakespeare's "All the world's a stage" image and the Hindu idea of *maya* as a kind of play, illusion, or game in which the players are "such stuff as dreams are made of." Hatterr being his "autobiographical" with a parody of *Hamlet*, and sums up his history in theatrical terms : "It is one of those Life's little panto-comedies, against which there lies no appeal...damme, clowning and vaudeville-turning !" (p. 31). He is tricked into taking part in a circus lion-taming act, and is constantly taken in by people who act roles which contrast with their true natures. His experiences illustrate the thesis that life is fundamentally absurd; theatrical, "human horse-play". Life seems a dramatic or illusory law unto itself, and would be incomprehensibly so, in Hatterr's view, were it not for the law of Contrast. And he concludes his memoirs exclaiming, but not without an all-important sense of wonder and thrill of exultation, "What a Show !" (pp. 276-277).

The case for regarding Desani's novel as dramatic overt gesture is further strengthened by the evidence of his technique of character portrayal. Desani's characters are incorrigible gestures. They include versions of the Shakespearian fool—particularly the pretentious gull like Malvolio or Sir Andrew Ague Cheek—whose comic behaviour recalls the meaning of the verb *to gesture* in the sense of to be affected, strut, act, perform. Desani is alert to the comic dynamism or pathetic frailty of the human personality, to the gesture accentuations in speech and behaviour. This talent is mainly expressed in his portraits of Hatterr and himself. Author and protagonist are accomplished gesturers. The same is true of such minor characters as "the Indian extreme-wing" newspaper editor, Chari-Charier, who, having been "struck off from All Souls' College", "has a very high regard for struck-off gentlemen" :

The sort of feller who didn't glance, but hypno-stared; didn't knock, but smashed in; didn't fish in a river, but drained it off....
Journalistic appetite, animal magnetism, and sardonique were written all over him. (p. 48)

The gesturer may be, like Desani himself, a persuasive illusionist with ulterior motives who manipulates his audience with a false appearance. Always-Happy, for example, who will milk money from the faithful by displaying Hatterr as a Celibate-Castrate :

His entire revelation, apropos the mein kampf against my sex-mania, sounded like a super-horsepower De Quincey autobiographical!...
The cad was so convincing on the side of detail!...
"...Many a *sadhana* did the Bitter-one perform to overcome his unspeakable urge. He was not free. He wallowed in lust when awake, and in dreams, seductive female forms, forms devoid of clothing, haunted him!..."
...he gave no respite to the audience....mentioning the most intimate organs of my body to elaborate and enlarge.... (pp. 143-144)

Hatterr is thus the comic butt of a gesturer who fabricates an absurdly false appearance which must dispossess Hatterr of his indentity (not to mention his sexual organ). The process is duplicated, moreover, when Banerrji, on hearing Hatterr's account of the episode, regards him incongruously as an embodiment both of Freud's theories and the Indian ideal of saintliness (a brilliant, hilarious scene, but regrettably too long to quote here; see pp. 146-149).

Combining a faith in the moral power of compassionate gesture with a theatrical style of expression, Banerrji is Hatterr's perfect comic foil. He is typically Indian, Desani suggests, in uniting a passion for theory with a respect for morality. This takes the form of a sublimated obsession with sex. Hence he endorses Freud's theories while condemning sexual freedom outside marriage. His philosophy of life is also impregnated with his garbled devotion to Shakespeare. In fact, he is modelled on a Shakespearian type : the satirised man of learning, like Holofernes or Don Armado. And just as Shakespeare's buffoons comically corrupt the classical tradition, or the language of sophisticates, Banerrji is notorious for his adaptations of Shakespeare. For example, when Hatterr says he is looking for "clean fun", Bannerji replies : "To sleep, perchance to dream ! Aye, there's the rub ! The Bard knew it." Clean fun may lead to misconduct. Moments later he comments, apropos circus horses : "The Bard has rightly said, A horse ! A horse! My kingdom for a horse ! I am myself entirely devoted to the turf !" (p. 67).

Desani's comic analysis of overt and subtle gesture, as evident in his portrayal of Hatterr, Banerrji and Always-Happy, extends to his presentation of social systems and cultural mores. By having Eurasian Hatterr looking at the West through Eastern eyes and vice versa, he portrays misunderstanding at multi-national as well as multi-personal levels, and thus subjects the theme of the deceptive nature of appearances to a bizarre form of comic scrutiny. In comedy-of-manners vein, Desani gives us passages like the following on the mystical significance of the English old school-tie :

Baw Saw : Why do the occidental males wear neck-wear ?
The Sheik : It is a mystic symbol and is called the Neck-tie. Their system of mysticism is called Etiquette. Accordingly, their women suffer equality with men : and assume leg-wear, the Garter ! mystically baptised the Honi. (p. 104)

The novel abounds with such satiric cameos. They come naturally to Desani, as does the Indian-English mode of expression. Moreover, the hybrid constitution of his hero justifies the polyglot style, thus enabling Desani to display his virtuosity in the realm of linguistic gesture and articulate a variety of babu, sahib, cockney, pidgin, learned, oratorical, rhetorical idioms. Such a style, freed from the conventions of orthodox English, has refreshing vitality, while the mixture of cultures that has produced it is a rich source of fanciful description and incongruous comparison. Hatterr depicts himself in idiosyncratic language. He describes himself as acting on a "Hereford and Angus bull-power impulse" (p. 34), or shuddering "like a badly-packed bale of agitated eels" (p. 146). Banerrji exhibits similar audacity in manipulating the language of absurdity, hyperbole, *non-sequiture*, and conceit. When Hatterr showers him with "poetic words", Banerrji replies opportunistically : "They show that you are deeply moved. But after his Worship's show comes the Council's dirt-cart" (p. 44). The speech and prose styles of Hatterr, Banerrji and Rembeli are a violent yoking together of Victorian portentousness and bizarre egoism, as they connect anything and everything, using whatever principle of association—pun, sound pattern, rhetorical echo—comes readily to hand. Vivid phrases like "his sumptuous Boswelling (i.e., beau-swelling) of Woman" (p. 172) are characteristic of Desani's imagistic predilections. His delight in theatrical verbal wit in a picaresque mode is reminiscent of Smollett in *Humphrey Clinker*.

The examples of Desani's style, characterisation, theatrical comedy and absurdist humour, which I have provided so far, may suggest that *All About H. Hatterr* is little more than a disorganised pantomime, a chaotic stream of verbal exhibitionism and public gestures, such as the surface of Indian life often seems to the foreign visitor; and that to apply to the novel the label "picaresque" is a sleight-of-hand defence of Desani's *apparently* anarchic presentation of experience.

On the contrary, I would argue that, underlying Desani's exuberant performance there is shrewd design and a sophisticated view of reality and imagination. Just as Smollett incorporates the *Clinker* plot in an epistolary form, so Desani frames Hatterr's adventures in a Hindu treatise format. Thus, Hatterr's seven adventures with the seven sages follow the "digest", "instruction", "presumption", "life-encounter" pattern, which is in fact a kind of dialectic progression from illusion, through defeat to enlightenment. Each adventure illustrates Desani's central thesis concerning the "contrast", "human horseplay" and "diamond-cut-diamond" "design" of life It is a thesis with many a philosophical and literary echo, and recalls the dialectic argument of Hopkins' poem "That Nature is a Heracletian Fire" which culminates in the celebrated "immortal diamond" image. Hatterr remains an authentic picaro throughout : knowledge comes through suffering; he must experience wretchedness and injustice to learn the facts of life. From these facts he derives a lesson at ironic odds with the prevailing moral code, particularly with respect to the way people should behave towards each other. But he remains faithful to the quest motive, and his search for Beauty and Truth culminates in a unique interpretation of the universe.

To realise this is to come to terms with the problems Desani poses for his readers : particularly the problems of authorial credibility, of distinguishing the author from his characters, of deciding whether any of the profundity of Shakespeare's great theme survives after Desani has put it

on the comic chopping-block, of deciding whether his parody of traditional knowledge amounts to anything more than a performance in which
hoaxing the reader as victim is the real point. These problems, I believe,
result in part from Desani's skill in manipulating philosophical concepts
from an absurdist point of view. Because Desani purports to be a liar, we
must always consider the obverse of any claim he makes, as when he says:
"I don't think there's such a something as the Leg of the Literary Public.
S o-*o* : the question of pulling it cannot arise" (p. 18). Once the reader
appreciates all these difficulties, however, he comes to see that *Hatterr* is
a work rather like the "problem play" in which questions of justice, truth
and existentialism are being analysed in a curiously original fashion.

   In *Hatterr*, as in much modernist art, theories of imitation of life or
truth seem to be supplanted by a notion that the artist's function is to
doubt his capacity to arrive at truth, but to arrive at that doubt through a
process of poetic paradox. Desani's preface, in which he confesses his
addiction to lying, would seem to introduce his novel about the quest for
truth with an unusual irony. When you compare this with Defoe's preface
to *Moll Flanders*, Desani's irony must be viewed as either more complex
or less reliable than Defoe's. Defoe's preface, with its posture of moralistic decorum, is lucid irony : his editorial point of view is plainly the opposite of what it appears to be. But is the same true of Desani's preface ?

   Sometimes the distinction between what Desani says and what he
means is obvious, as in the fictive claim that Hatterr is a *real* person who
has written an autobiography, while he, Desani, merely functions as a non-
interfering editor. On the other hand, Desani enjoys perplexing the reader
with paradox : if he is, as he maintains, an incurable liar, how can we believe him when he implies that he is *not* telling the truth ? Of course, this
can be interpreted as a promising Beckett-like foundation for a novel in
which the author intends to demonstrate that truth is despairingly inaccessible to the methodology of reason and logic.

   A major point about Defoe's comic irony was that his lie was so out-
rageous that the intelligent reader could identify with him in enjoying the
spectacle of Moll's promiscuity masquerading as moralistic propaganda,
and realising that Defoe was undermining the puritanical morality which
Moll's moral lesson was supposed to reinforce. Paradoxically, then, through
comic irony, the exaggerated lie is a way of pointing out the truth quite
specifically. In contrast, the modern manner of irony is often complicated
by ambiguity, and so testifies to the confusion man feels in the face of his
psychological complexity, the absurdity of life and the incomprehensible
character of the universe. In the light of these definitions, then, Desani
must be regarded as a modern rather than classical ironist. But he is not a
romanticist; he doesn't romanticise the irrationality of life; indeed, he
analyses it with comic satire, conscious of the contradictions inherent in
transcendental doctrines.

   At the same time, however, Desani apparently adopts a contradictory

position for himself. That of not knowing whether he is author or character; that of a self-aware liar who regards himself as having an acute consciousness of "the whole truth" (p. 13). In a key passage, Desani poses
with characteristic affrontery the problem of how seriously he is to be
taken by the reader :

> "The trump card of us Balaamite fellers is the mumbo-jumbo talk : the
> priestcraft obscurantisms and subtlety : (...*Wherefore, pious brethren,
> by confessing I lie, yoiks* ! *I tell the truth*, sort of topholy trumpeting-
> it, by the pharisee G.V. Desani : see the feller's tract All About....,
> publisher, the same publishing company) : a language deliberately
> designed to mystify the majority....while....we....the masters of perplex-
> ing parable-speech, remain the all-knowing, never-puzzled minority !"
> (p. 120)

This statement would seem to suggest that Hatterr's judgement of Desani
is Desani's judgement of himself, while at the same time attributing to
Hatterr an independent enlightenment that merits serious consideration.

Thus, although Hatterr is himself a victim of Desani's satire, he also
shares something of the latter's omniscience. He perceives, for example,
that excessive enthusiasm to the point of absurdity characterises the
attempts by some Asians to worship beauty, truth and art. Thus Hatterr
caricatures mystical fanaticism, Indian Wordsworthianism and Lit. Crit.,
oriental Lawrencianism, the Kama Sutra libido, Hindu philosophical formalism, and pundit poetry readings. Hatterr views sceptically such
mountebanks as Giri-Giri, who "can, and does, fall in love with any visible
or invisible object" (p. 168); Sri Harrow-voo, who "invented an Indian
form of Tyrolese and Swiss yodelling" (p. 165); and the bards The Roarer
and The Killer, who are exponents of "poetica erotica" (p. 243).

Although transcendental and poetic feelings are hilariously caricatured,
Hatterr's own lyrical aperceptions of Nirvana are presented in a charitable
spirit of comedy. We observe the spiritual side of his personality evolve
towards self-realisation and philosophical enlightenment which, I believe,
cannot be dismissed solely as hilarious nonsense. Whereas Hatterr's initial
experience of yoga in the lion's den is comically far-fetched, I don't think
the author of *Hali* is being derisive in the scene in which Hatterr experiences the Hindu version of Keats' Beauty-Truth equation :

> The Indian sunset !....
> That night, I knew the holy river....
> She the high-wrought, she the fascination, the comely, flower-decked,
> dew-laden Fair....
> ...I heard a piercing scream....a cry of anguish, of a cobra, cornered
> by an adversary !...and I listened to a thing sobbing....
> This, all this, this contradiction, this merging of beauty with brutality,

this non-separation between Evil and Good, this unity, this oneness, this evidence, made me feel, perhaps, there *is* no Good : and there *is* no Evil !

Perhaps, both are just phases : two ends of a line, two facets of the same die. (p. 125-31)

In passages like this Desani seems to imply that, despite Hatterr's comic incongruity, Hatterr's suffering, his aesthetic and spiritual tumult, do matter, Hatterr achieves enlightenment through internalising experience, not through having it thrust upon him.

Thus, from Chapter V to the end of his autobiographical, Hatterr evolves a subtle argument about Evil. He argues that Evil is an element in the diamond-cut-diamond part of design, and that a rummy angle to *contrast* is that Evil has to take the form of disguise in order to triumph. But disguise, gesture, appearance, are part of Maya, and ultimately illusory. He arrives at a Hindu rationale for a Christian concept. Satan's problem is his inferiority complex. Man's problem is that Satan operates through the appetites which God gave man in the first place : particularly, appetites for drink, women and luxury goods. This leads Hatterr to question whether such ideas as "the just society" or "personal salvation" are futile dreams. Does Hinduism provide man with a philosophical licence to sin, given that sin, being evil, is unreal ? In the end, the Hatterr life-urge survives the vultures of pessimism. He doesn't despair. In this sense, Hatterr is, as Anthony Burgess says, "heartening". In facing the problem of Evil, Hatterr is fallible fallen man, but more sinned against than sinning. Yet, paradoxically, his redemption is accomplished because he is a fallen sinner. Using an audacious mode of logic, combined with a scrupulous Indian respect for law, Hatterr synthesises two positive elements of Hinduism and Christianity—namely, the doctrine of the illusoriness of Evil and the paradox of the fortunate fall.

What a show ! Let a god or a human deliberately court hell, commit Evil,...contrast'll come to him and *deliverance* from *whatever* state he happens to be in !...

Hell, can you imagine the depth of red on Lucifer's face when he finds Himself in Heaven ? Yet, that's where the Feller is heading for ! Free board and lodge ! That's Law. That's *Contrast*. That's *Compulsion.* No escape !

He'll be *Law-bound* to commit good !...It'll be Hell for Him....in *contrast* to us fellers....

Maybe, I will cheat Satan yet; by understanding Law. A legal fight ! I will be His accessory, and abound in what feels good and fine. I will win His favour, and acclaim, by committing the seven deadly sins : the eighty heresies : and *never* repent ! And when my turn comes

to go to Hell (as assuredly it must come), I'll be *feeling* it Heaven, and
know no pain !

Maybe, thereby, *Avidya* ! *Avidya* ! Illusion ! Error ! I will be
serving His Adversary ! And maybe, the same law-understanding cosmic Clerk of the Court, Charitas, Aminus curiae, will judge me. Thus:
"H. Hatterr, accused. Broke the law of Christian Behaviour by allying
himself with Satan. But observed the Law of Consequence by going to
Hell. Not guilty of breaking Law. *Recommendation and reprieve* :
Both he, and his Master Satan, reprieved, lauded and esteemed, for
serving the Purpose of the Lord, by being *Awful Examples*." Perhaps,
in a not too distant enlightened age, we'll be cannonised ! (Miracle 1).
A new gnosis ! (pp. 276-277).

Hatterr's ironic self-apotheosis receives support from Desani's systematic destruction of cherished illusions about Eastern and Western cultures.
Many contemporary heroes in Hatterr's situation are stereotyped romantics
who, in the face of the massive failure of reason in our time, submit themselves self-destructively to the Irrational. Hatterr, however, is tough
beneath his vulnerable surface, and exists not with a sentimental existential
whisper, but with an affirmative : "Carry on, boys, and continue like hell !"
(p. 278).

Possibly, Desani sees Hatterr's creative logic as a reasonable substitute
for that conventional rationality which fails to explain man to himself in
an absurdist universe. And Desani probably regards comedy as a healthy
protection against romantic capitulation to the forces of chaos.

Desani's absurdist humour is both an original and a classical response
to modern existence : original in that he is a pioneer of absurdist humour,
both linguistically and psychologically; classical in the sense that he has
spoken to our age in a voice authentically of our age about problems of
existence which many regard as central to our age. His comic hero is
ennobled by the rage for order (seeing surprising design in the contrast of
things), by his inexhaustible capacity for wonder at the "damme" unex-
pectedness of things, by his Aurobindo-like search for synthesis, by his
incurable humanity :

                                                        ...and

This Jack, joke, poor potsherd, 'patch, matchwood.
    immortal diamond
        Is immortal diamond.[3]

Regarding the novel, *All About H. Hatterr*, we can perhaps best conclude by asserting that it is a work with a dual ending : Hatterr's, which
we have just discussed, and Desani's. Both endings, moreover, are likely
to be interpreted differently by different readers : a farce (overt gesture) or
a lying game (subtle gesture), in which the search for truth is never taken

seriously; as a comedy with a philosophical conclusion to the effect that the ultimate truth is that life is absurd; or as a comedy which masks a belief that there is more to life than farce and absurdity, but that reality cannot be encapsulated in orthodox logical or rational formulation.

Whichever conclusion you favour, you cannot avoid deciding what role Desani assigned to himself in Hatterr's drama.

This being the case, we may well conclude that, at the end of the novel, Desani has become the butt of his own joke. This follows from a consideration of the following points. Desani is a self-confessed liar who blantantly denies that his authorial role is of great consequence. As a picaresque author, he provides an appropriate first ending (Hatterr's philosophical triumph), but implies (by the addition in 1972 of a new final chapter) that Hatterr's triumph is open to question. We had thought that Hatterr was the accredited hero (we have a moral preference for him over the other characters). But when we realise that Desani has manipulated us into this position, we prefer to identify with him as a congenial sophisticated consciousness who takes an omniscient view of life's irrationality. Thus Desani emerges as the true, ultra-modern hero. Or is he, in fact, the anti-hero ? Are the psychological butts of his comedy, in fact, elements of himself, of his ridiculous incompatibility with his environment, as his preface would seem to confirm ? If such is indeed the case, the final laugh is at the expense of the absurdist author-hero, who, while creating fantasy situations and manipulating fantastic gestures in a fictive universe, has no power to control life's events, and consequently resorts to satirising others and mercilessly ridiculing himself.

So, finally, we are left with a choice between Hatterr's eccentric attempt to wrest meaning from external reality and Desani's masochistic joke concerning life's sound and fury.

But, either way, the spirit of comic vitality, which is such an important tradition in our literature, has been regenerated in the process. And, even if Desani's comic gesture fails in the end to disguise a belief that his own absurdist condition is the ultimate reality, that life is an illusion and art the illusion of an illusion, nevertheless Desani has reminded us that the metaphysical problem that so intrigued Shakespeare in his last play, a comedy, is no less fascinating to day.

REFERENCES

1. Penguin Books, 1972 (Introduction by Anthony Burgess). All page references are to this edition.

2. Ron Shepherd, some of whose thoughts on the novel have inevitably found their way into this paper.

3. Gerard Manley Hopkins, "That Nature is a Heracletian Fire . . .", *Poems and Prose* (ed. by W. H. Gardner), Penguin Books, 1975, p. 66.

8

Inside the
Outsider

MEENAKSHI MUKHERJEE

MUCH of Henry James' work embodied an experience that was unique in the literature of his own time. But, as our century becomes old, we note that writers who express the awareness of more than one culture have become an increasingly common phenomenon. Today it is not at all rare to find a writer for whom the multicultural situation is not only a subject-matter but a mode of perception as well. Without it, he would cease to be creative.

Even without going so far as George Steiner who holds that "the modernist movement can be seen as a strategy of permanent exile" (*Extraterritorial*, Penguin Books, p. 26), and who places Nabokov, Burgess and Beckett at the centre of this movement, we can easily find instances of some novelists in the Commonwealth countries who are not easy to place in any given literary tradition. Most of our assumptions about literature being the expression of a national sensibility, explicable in terms of history and geography, have to be reshuffled when we tackle G. V. Desani's *All About H. Hatterr*, or confront the works of V. S. Naipaul and Ruth Prawar Jhabvala, or read *The Nowhere Man* (Kamala Markandaya) and *Bye Bye Blackbird* (Anita Desai) and *Wife* (Bharati Mukherjee). These novelists cannot be discussed in terms of one nationality alone. Whether they are 'peregrine' writers or stationary, their apprehension of reality has been affected by the experience of more than one country and conditioned by exposure to more than one culture.

At the same time they are different from a writer like Raja Rao, because even though he explores an intercultural situation in *The Serpent and the Rope*, his protagonist, whether he is in Europe or in India, invariably responds to experience from an Indian anchorage. The writers mentioned earlier do not reveal any such mooring. Hence, for better or for worse, we are left only with the individual writer, unlabelled, "unhoused", to be judged for what he is by himself, without much aid from his communal or national affiliations.

Ruth Jhabvala has stated her purpose very clearly in a *New York Times* (April 20, 1975) piece : "When one writes about India as a European, and in English (as I do), invariably one writes not for Indian but for Western readers." Yet one wonders if she can be regarded as an European or western writer. No totally western writer would have persistently explored an India-based cross-cultural theme for twenty years as Jhabvala has, etiotating and refining it continuously until in *A New Dominion* (1972) the presentation of the theme is no longer an alive human situation but like a lonely game of chess in which the same player makes the moves from both sides. Trusting the tale and not the teller, we must ignore what Jhabvala may say about her intentions. Her presumed audience has surely not determined her writing to the extent her own situation as a writer has. Forster, too, obviously wrote about India "as an European and in English", but it never seems relevant to ask whether *A Passage to India* was written for an Indian or for western readers.

For whom does V. S. Naipaul write ? His early Trinidadian novels were not well-received in the West Indies, which is perhaps understandable, but even the British critics were uncomfortable because "during the fifties it was considered rather bad form in literary circles to approach an undeveloped country in a spirit of sophisticated humour" (Francis Wyndham in *The Listener* quoted by William Walsh : *V. S. Naipaul*, p. 13). But he continued to write and a readership developed which could accept him on his own individual terms. In spite of his fear of 'Trinidad' and his early awareness that he was born in a wrong place, Naipaul will never be a British writer, because his consciousness is shaped by his West Indian childhood. His observation has been refined and sensibility sharpened by the double exposure and this would probably explain his concern with other cultures too—India, for example, to which ten years after *An Area of Darkness* he returns compulsively to dissect this intransigent land and people with a mind that delights in discrimination. *In a Free State* (1971) he deals with several intercultural situations in such depth (Englishmen in Africa, Indians in USA, West Indians in England) that the geography and the theme coalesce to give us a truth that is almost poetic in its haunting intensity.

Bharati Mukherjee, a newcomer to this area of greyness, has sounded a new note in self-orientation by claiming that she is a North American novelist (see interview published in *Sunday*, September 1976). Yet her two novels so far have obsessively excavated the consciousness of her transplanted protagonists—the Indian who returns after a long stay abroad in one, and the Indian who has gone to live in North America in the other. It will be interesting to keep track of how she chooses to match her talent and her resources hereafter.

The reasons why these writers transcend nationality are many and complex. Increased mobility and easy availability of books, films and other forms of art from outside the country—these are of course the obvious factors. In India there must be very few creative writers in any language today who are not exposed to English, and are not influenced, directly or indirectly, by non-Indian sources. Other than the shrinkage of the globe there must be subtler forces at work too which drive the writer back upon his own individual consciousness. The delayed, or 'relayed' effect of existentialist thought, the realisation that the nineteenth century variety of social realism is getting obsolete, the awareness of 'self' as something different from the community—these and many other un-isolable factors must have contributed towards the emergence of the 'post-national' phenomenon in fiction.

One identifiable result of this process in certain writers is concentration on words, on using language in such a way that words become in themselves a reality. G. V. Desani is an example in whose novel language and theme cannot be separated, because the cross-cultural, multilingual situation is both the matter and the form of *All About H. Hatterr*. The hero of the novel is an Anglo-Malayan orphan living in India, and the bizarre pattern of parody, pastiche, punning and playfulness of the narrative style becomes synonymous with Hatterr's peculiar predicament. A comparable absorption with language can be seen in the works of Krishna Baldev Vaid, whose situation is indeed unique, because many years after settling in America, teaching English literature in a University there, he still writes in Hindi, but he also translates his Hindi novels into English, recreating in a remarkable degree all the linguistic idiosyncrasies. In an interview he was asked if the fact of staying away from one's language heightens his sense of style. Vaid replied "...not always invariably, because I am sure there have been hordes of writers in exile who lost not only their style but whatever talent they had started out with. There is always that danger. But those who survive that—Henry James, James Joyce, Beckett, Nabokov, Pound—are all stylists par excellence. And they all have one thing in common—they make love to their language without any inhibition and a lot more fervour and foolishness than those who have never been separated from theirs." (See *Vagartha*, October 1973). And in Vaid's writing, specially in the two volumes of *Bimal in Bog*, language and theme get so close sometimes that concern with style and the concern with substance cannot be separated. Naipaul in *The Mimic Men* says in a different context : "So writing for all its initial distortion, clarifies and and even becomes a process of life."

The second way in which the 'unhoused' sensibility sometimes operates in fiction is through abandonment of the traditional techniques of realism. In *The Nowhere Man*, *Bye Bye Blackbird* and *Wife* the characters are self-obsessed in various degrees, each shut up in his involuted existence. The objects of the external world are not blurred; they appear bright and clear, and are used as marking periods, as it were, in their mental processes. External reality and fantasy blend in a surrealistic design transcending causality.

In spite of what the blurbs say, neither *The Nowhere Man* nor *Bye Bye Blackbird* is really about Indian immigrants abroad. One is a study of individual suffering where the immigrant situation is a metaphor for loneliness, just as the multilation of the protagonist's fingers by leprosy is a metaphor of both inward corrosion and outward isolation. Srinivas in *The Nowhere Man* is an old man leading an innocuous existence in a shabby neighbourhood of London, who suddenly becomes the victim of racial hatred. There is mounting tension towards the end of the novel culminating in a fire which kills Srinivas as well as his tormentor. It is not this dramatic incident which is important in the novel, but the narrative style : the subtle texture of the language, the ability to linger over the contour of experience, to catch the fleeting but revealing moment. This circling around in verbal arcs before coming to the core of experience might exasperate the reader at times, but without this extravagant web woven out of words, the particular introspective world of this work could not have been created. Unlike some of Kamala Markandaya's own earlier books, *The Nowhere Man* has to be taken seriously as a novel, and the reason lies in her emphasis on the inward consciousness, the superimposition of memory upon the present, and the refusal to be bound to documentary realism.

Bye Bye Blackbird belies its publisher's claim of being "a powerful love-hate story of the unfortunate Indian immigrants." It is concerned more with individuals than with a community, and the most acutely realised character is an Englishwoman who has cut herself off from the mainstream of English life by marrying an immigrant Indian. A complex hypersensitive woman like the heroines of Anita Desai's earlier novels, Sarah Sen undergoes the suffering of daily duality for having to inhabit two incompatible worlds. In the process of switching roles morning and evening she feels the unreality of her existence : "her face was only a mask, her body only a costume." The novel has many weaknesses, not a few of them due to serious editorial lapses, but even in the present unfinished state its departure from the expected tradition of realism through absurd situations and fantasies is disturbing and powerful. Each detail underlies in some way or another the separateness of individuals who can never really know each other. If *The Nowhere Man* is about suffering, *Bye Bye Blackbird* is about loneliness, both done from a point of view where the question of national sensibility is irrelevant. Although adjustment or lack of adjustment to a culture is their repeated theme, these writers are not insiders in any culture.

Bharati Mukherjee's novel *Wife* which became available in India very recently also demonstrates this departure from traditional realism. The Bengali middle-class girl who gets married to an IIT-trained engineer and then migrates to America is a familiar stereotype in India today. But it is not the novelist's aim to document a sociological case-study of culture shock. The central character is acutely self-conscious and the world she conjures up does not reach out beyond the field of her vision. The background of the novel is strictly confined to the small island formed by the central character's consciousness. From the deliberate destruction of a foetus to the murder of a husband, from TV commercials to day dreams about suicide, from advertisements in glossy magazines to Indian gatherings of the tribe in New York, the novel moves back and forth nimbly between fantasy and reality. Living in another person's house, trying out other persons' clothes, eating beef, inability to keep the potted plants alive, all these realistic details assume grimly comic symbolic overtones by the end of the novel.

But exactly the reverse of this can happen too. Instead of concentrating on the inward life and disregarding social realism, the novelist who by temperament or circumstance is an outsider can move to the other extreme of completely excluding the private consciousness to look at experience only from the outside, describing it in a style that is deliberately devoid of all suggestions. This is Prawar Jhabvala's method. She writes in a cultivated dead-pan language, emphasising details of incidents and objects while underplaying the complex workings of the human mind. For twenty years and through eight novels and four collections of short stories she has maintained this detached clinical stance.

Born of Polish parents in Germany, educated in England, she has lived most of her adult life in India. To this extent her background offers an interesting parallel to V. S. Naipaul's who was born of Indian parents in the West Indies and was educated in England. But unlike the changing locale and theme of Naipaul's works, Jhabvala has consistently written about the interaction between Indian and Western characters in India. Unlike the writers who probe into the interior landscapes of the mind, Jhabvala's landscape is very much externalised, the dust and the heat a necessary and tangible part of her theme. She brings what she calls an European sensibility to work upon material which is non-European, and all her work is born out of this tension. She is a prisoner of India and this incarceration is her creative impulse.

A typical Jhabvala situation (repeated many times in her novels and short stories) is an English or American woman seeking spiritual solace in India. This suits her purpose and manner perfectly : her confident double-edged irony exposes with fine impartiality the neuroses of those who are seeking solace and the hypocrisy of those who are offering it.

One of her repeated concerns is 'What India does to a foreigner,' and she has presented numerous case studies of Europeans under the Indian sun. It reappears even in *Heat and Dust* which in other ways is a deliberate effort to wrench herself out of her groove. Early in the novel there is a casual description of a foreign tourist who says that all Indians are dirty and dishonest : "She had a very pretty open English face, but when she said that it became mean and clenched, and I realised that the longer she stayed in India, the more her face would become like that."

But this is change on a very obvious level. *Heat and Dust* explores other more insidious changes and for the first time Jhabvala goes back to colonial India to add an extra dimension of time for the confirmation of a pattern she had so far traced only in terms of contemporary India. While Jhabvala is incomparable in her keen observation of contemporary behaviour, for documenting the life of the past she relies nearly on literary sources and Forster's influence is unmistakable in the setting (Satipur/Chandrapur), characters (Rivers/Heaslop), in the incidents (the picnic) and in the representation of Indian speech through odd rearrangement of syntax. But the differences are just as important. Unlike Forster's novel where "outside every arch there is another arch, beyond every echo a silence," Jhabvala writes totally without tonal reverberations. Beyond the local and the temporal, *A Passage to India* is basically about a significant human experience. *Heat and Dust* lacks any such dimension. Because her observation is so acute and her irony so scathing, one wishes she would go beyond documentary realism to a more abiding version of reality, where the characters will matter not just because they are Indians or British but because they are authentic human beings, where the author's device of detachment will not become a barrier to understanding.

Prawar Jhabvala's novels read singly impress the reader with their superb technical skill and cold brilliance of understatement, but their cumulative effect is one of barrenness. Perhaps her failure to develop during the twenty years of her career points to one hazard that the root-less writer is prone to. While in some writers absence of a single homo-genous culture base sharpens their sensibility, in some others it might result in arrested creative vitality.

Prawar Jhabvala is an extreme case of the outsider in the Common-wealth context. Her situation is far too unique to offer a model, but it certainly warns the writers who are outside a literary tradition that in order to exploit their situation they must peregrinate and remain 'un-housed' and not get caught in their own self-created grooves. Their true triumphs happen, as they have in the case of Naipaul, by reaching and remaining in a free state.

9

James K. Baxter and the Terror of History :
the de-colonisation of a New Zealander

PETER ALCOCK

In 1966 the New Zealand poet James K. Baxter published from Oxford an unpoetically titled volume *Pig Island Letters* (Pig Island is an unflattering local term for our country). Earlier volumes have such 'poetic' titles as *Beyond the Palisade* (1944, his first), *Blow, Wind of Fruitfulness* (1948), *The Fallen House* (1953), *In Fires of No Return* (1958). In this last year, 1958, Jim—as he is still universally known in New Zealand—held a six-month UNESCO Fellowship in India out of which, in 1961, came *Howrah Bridge and Other Poems*. That book is in two sections; in Baxter's own words on the dust-jacket : 'the first part was written some time ago by a man who thought he was a New Zealander; the second part lately, in the past two or three years, by a man who had become, almost unawares, a member of a bigger, rougher family. The poems written in India mark this change.' The dust-jacket also of *Pig Island Letters* repeats in full this quotation (in the context of an account of Baxter) although there is no overt Indian material at all in this book, which, on the other hand, demonstrates—significantly—for me a completely achieved maturity of technique.

I had better now quote two poems. First, to satisfy your just curiosity, the title poem of *Howrah Bridge* :

Howrah Bridge, *to my wife*

Taller than the stair of Qtub Minar
These iron beams oppress the eagle's town.
Bare heels will dint them slowly.
And swollen Gunga's muscles move
Beneath, with freight of garbage,
Oar and sail, the loot of many lives.

In the unsleeping night my thoughts
Are millet falling from an iron pan,
While you, my dear, in Delhi lying down
Enter the same room by another door.
The rupee god has trampled here;
The poor implore a Marxist cage.
Dragon seed, the huddled bundles lying
In doorways have perhaps one chilli,
A handful of ground maize.
King Famine rules.   Tout and owl-eyed whore
Whose talons pluck and stain the sleeve,
Angels of judgement, husk the soul
Till pity, pity only stays.

Out of my wounds they have made stars :
Each is an eye that looks on you.

Second, a poem from *Pig Island Letters* (first in *The London Magazine*),
evaded by anthologists but, for me, a small masterpiece of cadence and
timing, 'Tomcat' :

Tomcat

This tomcat cuts across the
zones of the respectable
through fences, walls, following
other routes, his own,   I see
the sad whiskered skull-mouth fall
wide, complainingly, asking

to be picked up and fed, when
I thump up the steps through bush
at 4 p.m.   He has no
dignity, thank God !   has grown
older, scruffier, the ash-
black coat sporting one or two

flowers like round stars, badges
of bouts and fights.   The snake head
is seamed on top with rough scars :
old Samurai !   He lodges
in cellars, and the tight furred
scrotum drives him into wars

as if mad, yet tumbling on
the rug looks female, Turkish-
trousered. His bagpipe shriek at
sluggish dawn dragged me out in
pyjamas to comb the bush
(he being under the vet

for septic bites) : the old fool
stood, body hard as a board,
heart thudding, hair on end, at
the house corner, terrible,
yelling at something. They said,
'Get him doctored.' I think not.

Trivial and self-regarding this self-image may be, but endearingly self-
deprecatory and comic also and, I think, superbly, totally, assured and
relaxed.   But is this *all* Baxter has to say ? He can use 'the snaffle and
the curb all right', he has a splendid 'bloody horse'—but *where* is he
going ?

Some retrospect may give perspective. Baxter's first book, so accurately
titled *Beyond the Palisade*, that is, beyond the walls of colonial conformity,
established him as a powerful rhetorician :

> 'O lands seen in the light of an inhuman dawn...'

or :

> 'In this scarred country, this cold threshold land,
> The mountains crouch like tigers...'

or :

> 'Fell the wild swan :   from havenless crags of sky
> Fell to no cool lagoon...'

Of such poetry our, then and now, premier poet of an older generation,
also major anthologist (*A Book of New Zealand Verse*, 1945, 1951; *The
Penguin Book of New Zealand Verse*, 1960), Allen Curnow wrote: 'It seems
to me that since Mason in 1925 no New Zealand poet has proved so early
his power to say and his right to speak !'   And-but ?-also : 'Like a few
younger English poets...he seeks the eloquent rather than the inquisitively
precise word !'[1]

Modelling, it seemed at times, his life upon the Rimbaud of Cwmdonkin
Drive, Dylan Thomas, in his own words in 'fountains of Bohemia and the
night'[2], Jim moved from success to success through succeeding years but
always, amid the increasing plangencies of his sombre and rhythmical
chant, one may detect on the one hand 'the rhetorical British voices of the
1940's[3]—MacNeice, Thomas, Barker, Auden, also Yeats and Hardy—on
the other a floridity implicit in Curnow's careful phrase 'the eloquent...

word.' Our most guarded and reticent poet, Charles Brasch, wrote as late
as 1966 : 'I am disturbed by what I take to be due in part to Mr Baxter's
copiousness : that he writes poetry rather than poems…I have the
impression that a number of them have been chopped off arbitrarily from
a continuous poetic conveyor-belt.'[4] The matter is complicated by a certain
quasi-prophetic portentousness, partly a distortion of Baxter's earnest
pacifist heritage (his father was an unhonoured national hero of passive
resistance in World War One—of which more later); Jim himself converted
to the Church of England in 1948, year of his marriage to a Maori wife,
and to Roman Catholicism at the start of 1958, his Indian year. This and
a frequent gloom make his earlier verse, for me, all too often, in his own
quotation from Ezra Pound, 'sonorous, like the farting of a goose.' *Blow,
Wind of Fruitfulness* was sometimes unkindly called *Blow, Wind of Fright-
fulness*. And here are the last two of nine much-praised and anthologised
melodious and highly 'poetic' stanzas of 'Poem in the Matukituki Valley' :

Sky's purity, the altar cloth of snow
On deathly summits laid; or avalanche
That shakes the rough moraine with giant laughter;
Snowplume and whirlwind—what are these
But His flawed mirror who gave the mountain strength
And dwells in holy calm, undying freshness ?

Therefore we turn, hiding our souls' dullness
From that too blinding glass : turn to the gentle
Dark of our human daydream, child and wife,
Patience of stone and soil, the lawful city
Where man may live and no wild trespass
Of what's eternal shake his grave of time.

I could attempt a stronger case by offering more of this admired poem. It
seems so clear to me that Baxter has 'Adopted what [he] would disown,/
The preacher's loose immodest tone.'[5]

It would be unfair to bore you with obviously producible evidence for
an obviously tendentious thesis. Suffice it to allege that Jim was capable
of producing some very picturesque gardens of the imagination—with
never a real toad anywhere. Or say that he needed, perhaps, to reverse
the proverb and turn a rather sleazy synthetic silk purse of 'poetry' into
the bristling pig's ear of 'language charged with meaning to the utmost
possible degree.' It is *Pig Island Letters* that, from the springboard of
Howrah Bridge, begins, both in style and content, to achieve this.

After such generalisations then, about almost the first two-thirds of
Baxter's poetry in point of style, let me attempt some similar retrospect
for content; I am singling out some particular concerns.

In 1951, at an important New Zealand Writers' Conference, Baxter gave an address, 'Recent trends in New Zealand Poetry' (subsequently published), that became prophetic towards its close :

"In this country we are in a peculiar situation. New Zealand is now an island in more than geographical terms. Our standard of living is high, while that of the peoples of Asia and Europe is appallingly low. We are removed from the immediate scene of war and starvation. It is possible without obvious absurdity for our politicians to call our country a Happy Island, in some degree a just one. But poets are different from politicians; their value depends solely on their insight. If they do not speak the truth, they may live unmolested—but their work will perish. I believe that our island is in fact an unjust, unhappy one, where human activity is becoming progressively more meaningless...

"The typical dilemma of the modern poet is one of divided aims. A man who is working as a schoolteacher, a tradesman, or a government official in a society which he knows to be unjust, cannot dare to think clearly on moral issues; for the society is part of his physical and even psychological security. If he breaks with the society and departs into the Wilderness in customary Romantic style, then he loses brotherhood with all but similar outcasts. What Justice demands is something more difficult—that he should remain as a cell of good living in a corrupt society, and in this situation by writing and example attempt to change it."[6]

Derivative though he is, from W.H. Auden (*The Enchafed Flood* came out that year) I still see here the enlarging *personal* concern for 'social reality' that will, in my view, prove a rock on which his final achievement may rest. For such a concern is not comfortably compatible with excess of rhetoric, lives uneasily with classical allusion, enforces prolonged consideration of realities outside oneself.

Two small critical paperbacks on Baxter are available in New Zealand: one by Father John Weir, academic and posthumous editor of Baxter, essentially a university thesis, *The Poetry of James K. Baxter*; the other by Vincent O'Sullivan, poet, academic, editor of Oxford's *Anthology of Twentieth Century New Zealand Verse*, simply called 'James K. Baxter' in a new series 'New Zealand Writers and Their Work.' The starting point in each is similar : 'An alcoholic grave-robbing friend said to me the other day, as we sat and watched the milkbar cowboys come and go—"I took the wrong turn round the cabbage-tree, Jim, a long time ago; and since then I've not been able to change it." He was mythologising his life; and that's what a writer does. The trouble is, I can't demythologise it. What happens is either meaningless to me, or else it is mythology...' Both critics also quote as a revelation of Jim's temperament : '...the sense of having been pounded all over with a club by invisible adversaries is generally

with me, and has been with me as long as I can remember...'[7]   Both
refer also to similar experiences in two poems, 'The Cave' and 'The Hollow
Place' as, in Weir's words 'the foundation of much of Baxter's best verse,'[8]
in O'Sullivan's terms 'the most important paradigm in Baxter's work.'[9]
Father Weir on another page says simply and, to me, significantly, 'No
other New Zealand writer has expressed as keenly as he the conviction
that man inhabits a fallen state.'[10] O'Sullivan roundly and at length
asserts : 'The greater part of Baxter's work relates at one point or another
to this archetype, to the seasonal cycle and the *rites de passage* which are
at the core of most mythologies. The journey towards or through the
secret door, the gates, the tomb, the maze and the return not to a new
world so much as the old seen as if for the first time—these proliferate in
Baxter's work,...Baxter's verse, like that of Robert Graves in his "To
Juan at the Winter Solstice", carries "one story and one story only".' It
is the story of his own personality exchanging unshaped experience for the
form of myth. He refers to Northrop Frye and to Joseph Campbell's
assertion, in his *The Hero with a Thousand Faces*, of a universal
'monomyth' in human culture, citing Campbell's description : 'The
standard path of the mythological adventures of the hero...a magnification
of the formula represented in the rites of passage : *separation—initiation—
return* : which might be called the nuclear unit of the monomyth.'[11]

Though I am unsympathetic—as will appear—to this approach I had
better supply you with the evidence. From 'The Cave' (in *Blow, Wind of
Fruitfulness*) I will quote only the last of four stanzas, perhaps unfairly to
emphasise the *regression* in lines 2, 3, 4; the narrative essentially is of
finding a small cave 'sunless kingdom/Where souls endure the ache of
Proserpine' and entering where 'The smell of earth was like a secret
language/That dead men speak and we have long forgotten' :

The whole weight of the hill hung over me;
Gladly I would have stayed there and been hidden
From every beast that moves beneath the sun,
From age's enmity and love's contagion :
But turned and climbed back to the barrier
Pressed through and came to dazzling daylight out.

I think neither a notable poem but, from *Pig Island Letters*, 'The Hollow
Place' can serve also to demonstrate Baxter's great *technical* improvement
—laconic, relevant, dramatic :

The Hollow Place

On the waste low headland
Below the road, above the plunging sea,
I would climb often round the crumbling face
Where flax bushes precariously

Gave something to grip :   then I'd stand
Alive in the hollow place
That meant...well, I must describe it ; a bent cleft
In limestone rock above a pool
Of fluttering scum; bushes to the left,
And an overhang.   The passage was dark and cool,
Three yards long perhaps, hidden from any eye
Not acquainted;   and the air
Tainted by some odour as if the earth sweated
In primeval sleep.   I did nothing there;
There was nothing to do but listen to some greater I
Whose language was silence.   Again and again I came
And was healed of the daftness, the demon in the head
And the black knot in the thighs, by a silence that
Accepted all.   Not knowing I would come again,
My coat of words worn very thin,
Knocking, as if lame,
With a dry stick on the dumb
Door of the ground, and crying out :
'Open, mother.   Open.   Let me in.'

O'Sullivan remarks also, I think importantly, on the recurrent presentation in Baxter of 'the individual aware constantly of his loneliness...   In
poem after poem one is in the presence of that recurring shape of the
isolated man on his journey towards death, and perhaps rebirth'.[12] We have
already noticed Jim, prophet alone in the wilderness, in 'Matukituki Valley'.
Many and varied are such poems of isolation, from 'The Bay', where he is
'waiting for the taniwha'—a traditional Maori water-monster—to such
perhaps transitional and later poems as 'Crossing Cook Strait' and 'At
Akitio'.   In a fascinating late (1971) interview with John Weir (to which
reference will recur) Baxter uses these words :   'I find that my own mind
more and more gravitates towards this position of silence, death, eternity.
whatever you like—the point of peace actually...*rangimarie*, the state of
peace.   To be there, in that gap ! And the poems will come from there at
times like water out the rock.'[13]   Or let me quote a most witty and agreeable poem (again from *Pig Island Letters*) exemplifying finely that liberation
from rhetoric and 'poetry' of the later Baxter (though also the influence of
Gary Snyder), 'The Cold Hub'.

The Cold Hub

Lying awake on a bench in the town belt,
Alone, eighteen, more or less alive,
Lying awake to the sound of clocks,
The railway clock, the Town Hall clock,
And the Varsity clock, genteel, exact

As a Presbyterian conscience,
I heard the hedgehogs chugging round my bench,
Colder than an ice-axe, colder than a bone,
Sweating the booze out, a spiritual Houdini
Inside the padlocked box of winter, time and craving.
Sometimes I rolled my coat and put it under my head,
And when my back got frozen, I put it on again.
I thought of my father and mother snoring at home
While the fire burnt out in feathery embers.
I thought of my friends each in their own house
Lying under blankets, tidy as dogs or mice.
I thought of my Med. Student girlfriend
Dreaming of horses, cantering brown-eyed horses,
In her unreachable bed, wrapped in a yellow quilt.
And something bust inside me, like a winter clod
Cracked open by the frost.   A sense of being at
The absolute unmoving hub
From which, to which, the intricate roads went.
Like Hemingway, I called it *nada* :
Nada, the Spanish word for nothing,
Nada; the belly of the whale; *nada*;
Nada; the little hub of the great wheel;
Nada; the house on Cold Mountain
Where the east and the west wall bang together;
Nada; the drink inside the empty bottle.
You can't get there unless you are there.
The hole in my pants where the money falls out,
That's the beginning of knowledge; *nada*.
It didn't last for long; it never left me.
I knew that I was *nada*.   Almost happy,
Stiff as a giraffe, I called in later
At an early grill, had coffee, chatted with the boss.
That night, drunk again, I slept much better
At the bus station, in a broom cupboard.

This line of argument also, by the way, illustrates admirably Lionel Trilling's dictum 'On the teaching of modern literature' (reprinted in *Beyond Culture*, 1965) : 'I venture to say that the idea of losing oneself to the point of self-destruction, of surrendering oneself to experience without regard to self-interest or conventional morality, of escaping wholly from the societal bonds, is an "element" somewhere in the mind of every modern person who dares to think of what Arnold in his unaffected Victorian way called "the fulness of spiritual perfection."[14]

All this foregoing material does indeed seem to suggest Baxter's domination by compulsive pattern, by this 'monomyth', by a *'rite de passage'* scheme of separation-experience-return, though there seems not ever to be any 'return' and the 'experience' also lacks realisation.

I don't find such a view satisfactory; it is very much less than the whole story. I recall Father Weir's comment : 'No other New Zealand writer has expressed as keenly as he the conviction that man inhabits a fallen state.' But this Judaeo-Christian tradition of 'the Fall' is purposive, becomes dialectic of identity, has traditionally its therapy, redemption, in-built : 'Whatever is hateful to you, do not do to your neighbour. That is the entire Law. The rest is commentary; go and learn.'[15] Or, for that is a Jewish source, for Jew and Christian alike : '...you shall love your neighbour as yourself; I am the Lord....'[16] Or I return, in our own age and discipline, to Lionel Trilling's related comment (in *Sincerity and Authenticity*) on a recurrent problem in our alienated West of sanity and 'reality' :

> "But who that has spoken, or tried to speak, with a psychotic friend will consent to betray the masked pain of his bewilderment and solitude by making it the paradigm of liberation from the imprisoning falsehoods of an alienated social reality ? Who that finds intelligible the sentences which describe madness (to use the word that cant prefers) in terms of transcendence and charisma will fail to penetrate to the great refusal of human connection that they express, the appalling belief that human existence is made authentic by the possession of a power, or the persuasion of its possession, which is not to be qualified or restricted by the co-ordinate existence of any fellow man ?"[17]

Now too the rather melodramatic title of this paper may be considered. Such a 'monomythic' Baxter might superbly exhibit what has been notably called by Mircea Eliade in his *Cosmos and History* (1959)—originally *The Myth of the Eternal Return* (1949)—'the terror of history', an attitude that 'neither the objects of the eternal world nor human acts, properly speaking, have any autonomous intrinsic value,' abnegation of 'that individuality whose creative spontaneity, in the last analysis, constitutes the authenticity and irreversibility of history.'[18] Baxter's true progress seems utterly opposite to this. I think that perhaps the approach I am quarrelling with consists in seeing a man's life as determined by its beginnings; I would rather look from the end—Baxter died in 1972—and see how this end transfigures the beginnings.

For Baxter's end was very strange indeed. Never an addict of suburban colonial conformity, in 1962 he became a postman ('Tomcat' records him returning from his rounds), in 1966-67 he held for two years the Robert Burns Fellowship at the University of Otago for a full-time practising writer. 'When that expired he took part in catechetical work in Dunedin for a year before helping to establish a Narcotics Anonymous group in Auckland in 1969. In 1970 he was living alone at Jerusalem, a tiny settlement up the Wanganui River.'[19]   It was in that remote place that, in October 1972, forty-six years old, Baxter was buried amid an attendance estimated at eight hundred people, before the national television cameras, with a full Maori funeral or *tangi* rarely given a white man, with an emotional commemoration by what may be termed New Zealand 'hippies' and with a Roman Catholic Requiem Mass celebrated by nine priests.

It had been in 1969 that Baxter, in his own words : 'realised I was slowly dying in the comfort of my home, smoking cigars and watching television.' So he walked out of the door with a duffel bag holding a change of clothes and the Bible in Maori.[20] Through the next three years the image of a bearded, threadbare Baxter, sandalled or barefoot, living with 'junkies' in Auckland, then in Wellington, then retreating with a small and shifting community to derelict wooden farmhouses in this Maori village, site also of a ninety-year-old Catholic convent of some fame, steadily gained through our media a mixture of fame and notoriety as the best we could locally produce as a kind of *guru*. It is the three principal books of this period, with a little additional material contemporary but not in those, that finally consolidate his writing : *Jerusalem Sonnets* (1970), *Jerusalem Daybook* (1971) and the posthumous *Autumn Testament* (1972). I'll now consider these; first the medium then—a slightly violent separation—the message.

His message is simple. His 'enlarging concern for social reality' was mentioned earlier after quoting, from the 1951 Writers' Conference, his rather sour report on New Zealand society and prescription of becoming 'a cell of good living in a corrupt society.' Alongside his poetry of isolation, rumination, 'wilderness' situations, slowly develops an alternative concern for society, thus for its colonial alienations and structures, thus for the processes of history in our time. Even as early as *Blow, Wind of Fruitfulness* he is capable of opening a poem 'The Returned Soldier' (we New Zealanders have been in all the available wars; one of our own historians has labelled us 'Prussians of the South Pacific) 'The boy who volunteered at seventeen/ At twenty-three is heavy on the booze.' Several other poems take up this particular theme of the 'returned soldier', perhaps notably and 'transitionally'. 'The homecoming', where the (for me) outworn poeticisms of Homeric allusion are yet applied to such a reality. In a kind of doggerel Jim also turned to vernacular ballads, 'Lament for Barney Flanagan, Licensee of the Hesperus Hotel' or 'Ballad of Calvary Street' :

On Calvary Street are trellises
Where bright as blood the roses bloom,
And gnomes like pagan fetishes
Hang their hats on an empty tomb
Where two old souls go slowly mad,
National Mum and Labour Dad.

(The final line refers to, relatively, conservative and radical political parties). It is this 'social concern', infinitely more finely but quite unrhetorically orchestrated, that floods Baxter's final writing. From letter 2 of *Pig Island Letters* :

> From an old house shaded with macrocarpas,
> Rises my malady
> Love is not valued much in Pig Island
> Though we admire its walking parody...

His medium is over a hundred 'sonnets', interspersed with prose and some other poetry, using 'carped, carved, little two-lined stanzas',[21] unrhymed, inherited from a poet Baxter had much time for—Lawrence Durrell (e.g. in *The Tree of Idleness*, 1955, and in the sequence 'A soliloquy of Hamlet')—and influenced, unavoidably, by Robert Lowell. In his own words in 1965 : 'I find Lawrence Durrell and Robert Lowell particularly helpful...Durrell loosens up the chains of association, helping me to avoid heavy aphorisms about Time or God, and keep the eye on the invaluable sensory image; Lowell has helped me to use words as a straitjacket to contain the violent experiences of the manic-depressive cycle.'[22] The 'little two-lined stanzas' come first in the Indian volume, *Howrah Bridge*, in 'Elephanta' (eleven of them), then, back to a New Zealand setting, in 'Election 1960' and 'A Dentist's Window' (only eight each, approaching the 'sonnets'), all, in their different ways, responses to undoubted 'social reality' !

Pig Island Letters consolidates Baxter's transformation. Three sections comprise the title sequence (one in couplets), fourteen poems (four in couplets, one a 'sonnet') including 'The Hollow Place' and 'The Cold Hub' already quoted, a vernacular 'ballad', and three dramatic sketches of social episodes—'A Takapuna Business-man Considers his Son's Death in Korea', 'Thoughts of a Remuera Housewife', and 'Henley Pub'; the final section has some rather technically elegant verse, partly on ancestral and autobiographical themes, several reprinted from *The London Magazine*, including 'Tomcat'. It is from here he goes to Jerusalem.

For such a journey there are precedents. First, the '60s were a heyday throughout the West for 'alternative societies'; the tradition of post-Romantic bourgeois protest to which Jim had long been close would ease such a move. Second, whether one thinks, as Catholic, of St Francis, or, as poet, of Villon, the life of poverty had, before our bourgeois world, an honourable tradition. Third, this part of Jim's life is rich in Maori values (of which more later) of tribal and communal loyalty, notably *aroha*, 'communal love', so evidently absent in suburban relations, and *korero*, traditional speech, so patently lacking in our communication. There is a fourth strand also I think not recognised—India. Baxter himself has already been quoted that there began his sense of 'a bigger, rougher

family' than the Pig Islanders. One of our best critics, C.K. Stead, specifically locates in the *Howrah Bridge* volume 'a new voice...that of the
mature Baxter', quoting one particular poem, 'This Indian morning'. On
this topic I myself wrote to Baxter's widow; she replies : 'I myself am
quite convinced that India was a sort of crossroads, and Jim, being the
kind of person he was, had no choice but to turn in the direction of a new
and then unknown destination—Jerusalem. I'm not now just referring to
a particular spot on the map. The immediate and obvious effect on him
as a writer produced Howrah Bridge, but this of course was only the tip of
the iceberg. And this is what India did to Jim the man. I mean ordinary
man. It didn't shake him *to* his foundations...but *from* his foundations.
And it took nearly 10 years to find himself again in a new relationship to
God and man.'[23] I would further quote, without comment, an admittedly
minor posthumous poem not demonstrably located in India, 'The Communist Speaks' :

The Communist Speaks

Do not imagine I could not have lived
For wine, love or poetry,
Like the rich in their high houses
Walking on terraces above the sea.

But my heart was caught in a net
Woven out of strands of iron
By the bleak one, the thin one, the basket-ribbed
Coolie and rickshaw boy

Who has not learnt the songs that ladies like,
Whose drink is rusty water,
Whose cheek must rest on a dirty stone,
In whose hands lie the cities of the future.

A few pages back in this same posthumous volume (largely of '*pre-*
Jerusalem' work, *Runes*, 1973) comes, in couplets, 'Mother and Son'. Here
Baxter, before Jerusalem, soliloquises in his childhood home :

    ...As I did in my 'teens
I listen again to the Roman-lettered clock

Chiming beside the statue of Gandhi
Striding towards God without any shadow

Along the mantelpiece.[24]

And here also may be found the origins of 'Jerusalem'. For Baxter came
of remarkable parentage. 'My mother had a Newnham M.A. degree in
Old French; and my father was a self-educated Otago farmer who recited

Burns and Shelley and Byron and Blake and Tom Hood and Henry
Lawson when the mood took him.'   His mother's father was, furthermore, a remarkable early New Zealand professor and author also of
Utopian fiction; his own father, Archibald, published his searing experiences as a conscientious objector in World War I, 'in memory of days that
we can't yet afford to forget', with the title, *We Will Not Cease*, and a two-
stanza title-page epigraph from the *Jerusalem* of William Blake.   Jim tells
of the 'Scriptures' of his pacifist socialist home '—Tolstoy and Gandhi and
the New Testament suitably interpreted—'.[25]

An extremely interesting interview with Baxter in 1971, already quoted
earlier, has Father Weir recording him on *Pig Island Letters* : 'I wanted
that : just someone speaking authentically...—I thought "That book will
break the critics' teeth." I felt happy about it.' His attitude to poetic
formalism is close to that of D. H. Lawrence (his Introduction to *New
Poems*) : '...these very formal poems are rather circular : they're all
closed on themselves in a way, the perfect round, ...I prefer one that is
like a house with all its doors open...' And of development after *Pig
Island* he says : 'But the "Jerusalem" poems are different. They are more
uneven. I'm not concerned with their quality, only with saying something.'
He talks of 'social poetry, poetry of community' and adds 'I would not be
so desperately concerned with how well the poem is made as I once would
have been.' Later, 'And then the poem has strength because it is true.'
And again, quoting Yeats' "Now I must wither into the truth", he
remarks, '...and that is a statement of liberation, I think ... to become
oneself, an old man standing on the ground, in my case with bare feet—
that may be ostentatious. But then if one speaks, perhaps it's one's own
voice and not the echoes of other people any longer. ...the lush plant
hardening into a strong stick,...Truth is what I would consider important,
not the way one appears in the eyes of other people.' Earlier answering
Weir's comment, 'a fundamental anarchy...at the centre of your way of
life,' Baxter affirms 'the fundamental anarchy at the heart not a way of
life chosen but of life itself not chosen.'[26] 'Life' is totally Baxter's choice
at his death.

Further roads to the heart of 'Jerusalem' can be traced in the useful
criticism of Charles Doyle, former New Zealand poet and Catholic friend
of Jim, now a Canadian academic whose Twayne World Authors book on
Jim has just appeared. Having paid due attention to Baxter's 1951
address, of the Jerusalem venture he finds the 'type' in the Sacrament of
the Mass, in the community and identity this enacts.[27] Another former
New Zealander, David Moody, observes : 'Implicit there is the conviction
that Self and Society have the one root, one life, one fate.'[28] In prose at
the beginning of *Jerusalem Daybook* Baxter writes of a 'theology of
communality'; towards the end, of 'a theology of kenosis', that is, 'self-
emptying'.

The great enemy for him is now a state 'when communities are everywhere ceasing to exist, and only a desacralised, depersonalised, centralised Goliath remains to demand our collective obedience'. To this his response is partly Maori :

I do not relish the role of David, in confronting that Goliath, who numbs the soul wherever he touches it. But I find myself curiously, perhaps absurdly, cast in the role. And the five water-worn stones I choose from the river, to put in my sling, are five spiritual aspects of Maori communal life—

arohanui :   the Love of the Many;

manuhiritanga :   hospitality to the guest and the stranger;

korero :   speech that begets peace and understanding;

matewa :   the night life of the soul;

mahi :   work undertaken from communal love.

I do not know what the outcome of the battle will be.
My aim may be poor. But I think my weapons are well chosen.'[29]

The response is also traditionally Catholic : 'I have been engaged for some time, with the help of God, in an experiment that involves the love of the Many. In that haphazard community that has grown up where I live, there are one or two principles that seem necessary and permanent...

'If we are to rebuild the sacramental universe our civilisation has shattered to pieces—I see no way of doing it except by sharing the things we possess. Then we are using them as God wishes them to be used...'

Another principle is that people should love one another, and display love in a physical manner. There are good reasons behind this.[30] If one thinks, further, of *korero*, and of his statements to John Weir in favour of poetry 'like a house with all its doors open', Baxter can be placed in that major modern tradition of 'open' poetry I would myself conveniently originate with Wordsworth—'What is a Poet ? ...He is a man speaking to men'—but which has been significantly placed by Baxter's admired Robert Lowell (in a recent US anthology) first in 'the translations of the Bible... supreme poems, written when their translators merely intended prose and were forced by the structure of their originals to write poetry; then Whitman, whose "Song of Myself" is the only important long nineteenth century American poem, then Lawrence's bird and animal poems, Pound's Cantos, and most of William Carlos Williams. These works would have lost all their greatness and possibility in meter.'[31]

New Zealander C. K. Stead says of *Jerusalem Sonnets*, 'The beauty of these poems is subtle : even, for all the rough contour of the voice, delicate.' And again, 'They are not poems of doctrine but poems of experience.'[32] O'Sullivan calls them '...a triumph of *tone*. This is the talk of everyday, the natural talk for the mundane yet extraordinary part

of God's interpenetrating the most simple of our acts'.[33] I am myself
reminded of Allen Curnow's observations about the tasks of poetry, back in
1945 in his Introduction to that same pioneer *Book of New Zealand Verse*
where Baxter (then 19) was hailed as our new poetic 'wonder-child' : '…it
is the *uses* of poetry we need to realise : and that what is admired but
does not change the imagination, has been wrongly admired.'[34]

Baxter's personal task now can be seen also as not only, in my view, a
de-mythologisation of his living—an increasing assertion of moral autonomy and liberation from dominance by inner compulsions—but also, of
possibly special interest to this Conference, of 'de-colonisation' of a
colonist—in his assertion of an authentic emotional life and steady denial
of that 'tyranny of externality' which, extreme in colonies, has been the
bane of the Western world for the last three centuries. His renunciation
of 'the work ethic', of narrow Calvinism, of racist pride, of sterile conformity, is complete. Further, in his writing as in his living—the two become
one—mundane accident becomes unique, unrepeatable, theophany; time
becomes linear, teleological, theodicy, that is, traditionally, what the West
has had presented to it as 'history'. A 'monomythic' Baxter may indeed
demonstrate 'the terror of history'; the anti-heroic protagonist of
'Jerusalem' *becomes* 'history'.

These three books (there is some other material)—*Jerusalem Sonnets,
Jerusalem Daybook, Autumn Testament*—add up to over a hundred and
fifty pages to which there is now no time to do justice; they may at least
be sampled. The range is wide—comic, domestic, bawdy, tragic, mundane,
profound—all these; the common substance is humility, their salt is
humanity. Baxter sets his own epigraph before the first book : 'If that
Jerusalem which is unbreakable friendship with God has not been established first in the heart, how can the objective Jerusalem of c mmunal
charity be built so as not to fall ?' Some Maori terms need explanation
(two of the books have extensive glossaries, incorporating also two Indian
terms—there is no time to follow other Indian references—*Ram, avidya*).
Jim himself was *Hemi te tutua*—Jim the nobody, worthless person; his
'tribe', so-called, or community were *nga mokai*—the fatherless—or more
hopefully *Ngati-Hiruharama*—the people of Jerusalem; a *wharepuni* is a
tribal meeting-house; *Wahi Ngaro* is the Void, Space, a term in Maori
creation chants; *Te Atua* is God. I think only the first of the following
half-dozen 'sonnets' has made any of the anthologies so far—others may
be more dramatic, intense, spiritual—but even this handful torn from
context should offer the sensitive ear some of this purity, simplicity,
integrity that has raised the poetry of New Zealand to an as yet not fully
comprehended stature.

Poem for Colin—I

The small grey cloudy louse that nests in my beard
Is not, as some have called it, 'a pearl of God'—

No, it is a fiery tormentor
Waking me at two a.m.

Or thereabouts, when the lights are still on
In the houses in the pa, to go across thick grass

Wet with rain, feet cold, to kneel
For an hour or two in front of the red flickering

Tabernacle light—what He sees inside
My meandering mind I can only guess—

A madman, a nobody, a raconteur
Whom He can joke with—'Lord', I ask Him,

'Do You or don't You expect me to put up with lice ?'
His silent laugh still shakes the hills at dawn.

(Jerusalem Sonnets)

Poem for Colin—37

Colin, you can tell my words are crippled now;
The bright coat of art He has taken away from me

And like the snail I crushed at the church door
My song is my stupidity;

The words of a homely man I cannot speak,
Home and bed He has taken away from me;

Like an old horse turned to grass I lift my head
Biting at the blossoms of the thorn tree;

Prayer of priest or nun I cannot use,
The songs of His house He has taken away from me;

As blind men meet and touch each other's faces
So He is kind to my infirmity;

As the cross is lifted and the day goes dark
Rule over myself He has taken away from me.

(Jerusalem Sonnets)

The Problem of Keeping Dogs, No. 2

It's no good my raving on about it;
The dogs amble into the wharepuni,

Rastus, Trash, Rooter, and the ones who have no names,
Lollop on the beds, drop shit on the verandah,

Shove their noses into the flourbag—well, I don't like fleas,
And I shout at them, boot their arses,

And meet the astonished eyes of twenty-five dog-lovers
Saying, 'What's wrong with you, Hemi ?'

I'm not St Francis; I don't want to run a dog farm;
I plot against the lives of our animal companions—

Last night I heaved a rock at a cat
That climbed through the broken boards in the cottage.

And shame sits on my back—even to raise my head
To the winter stars, is to hear them saying, 'What's wrong
    with you, Hemi ?'

                                   (Jerusalem Daybook)

Autumn Testament No. 5

Wahi Ngaro, now the ego like a sentry
At the gate of the soul closes its eyelids

For a moment, as today when
A crowd of ducks rose flapping at the place

Above the rapids where I go to bathe
Naked, splashing the water on my thighs,

And later I walked barefoot over the smooth boulders,
Thinking, 'There need be no other Heaven

'Than this world'—but rain spat soon
Out of a purple cloud, and I hid under

The willow leaves and bramble, as Adam did
Once from the Father.   I brought back for Francie

A sprig of wet wild mint
That should go well tomorrow with the potatoes.

                                   (Jerusalem Daybook)

Autumn Testament No. 23

The heat moves into my bones again
Here on the edge of the verandah

Father Te Awhitu mended hour by hour
With new boards where the rain had rotted them

Pouring down from a roof that has no spouting,
And when I asked him why, replied, 'Mahi mo Te Atua'—

'Work done for God'—the day the house was ready
I lit the stove in the front room,

That cost me twenty dollars secondhand in Wanganui
And had a broken lid—wood, stove, matches,

The first flame rising—so the house became
Inhabited with the flame of non-possession

That burns now and always in the heart of the tribe,
Too simple a thing for the world to understand.

Autumn Testament No. 38

Last night a grey nimbus round the moon,
Today the rain comes from the west;

The leaves on all the trees look greener,
Rangimotu is burning piles of dry grass in his garden,

The flames go up to the low heaven,
And Wehe shouts to him from the door of her kitchen,

'You, come in out of the rain !' He only smiles
And goes on raking.   I carry up the hill

A milk bottle full of sauce, bread and a parcel of sausages;
I plug the jug in and wait for it to boil

While the girls lie in bed.   'I like the rain.'
'I like it too.   Aren't you afraid, Hemi,

Of catching the "flu" ?'   'Not exactly.
It's only that—' The rain comes down in a dense white curtain.[35]

REFERENCES

1. Allen Curnow, ed., *A Book of New Zealand Verse*, 1945, 2nd ed; Christchurch, Caxton Press, 1951, p. 47.

2. James K. Baxter, *Pig Island Letters*, London, Oxford, 1966, p. 8.

3. Vincent O'Sullivan, James K. Baxter, Wellington, Oxford, 1970, p. 13.

4. Charles Brasch, "Phrases and Poems", *N. Z. Monthly Review* 74, (December 1966, p. 22.

5. W.H. Auden, *New Year Letter*, London, Faber, 1941, p. 24.

6. Baxter, *Recent Trends in New Zealand Poetry*, Christchurch, Caxton Press, 1951, pp. 16, 17, 18.

7. *Idem*, "Notes on the Education of a New Zealand Poet" in *The Man on the Horse*, Dunedin, University of Otago, 1967, p. 121.

8. John Weir, *The Poetry of James K. Baxter*, Wellington, Oxford, 1970, p. 25

9. O'Sullivan, p. 47.

10. Weir, p. 12.

11. O'Sullivan, pp. 9, 48.

12. *Idem*, p. 15, 22.

13. Weir "An Interview with James K. Baxter", *Landfall* 111, September 1974, p. 250.

14. Lionel Trilling, *Beyond Culture*, 1965, rpt; Harmondsworth, Penguin, 1967, pp. 40-41.

15. Often cited response of Rabbi Hillel, 1st century A. D.

16. Leviticus 19, v. 18.

17. Trilling, *Sincerity and Authenticity*, 1972, rpt, London, Oxford, 1974, p. 171.

18. Mircea Eliade, *Cosmos and History*, 1949, rpt; New York, Harper, 1959, pp. 3, 46.

19. Weir, p. 14.

20. *New Zealand Herald*, 24 October, 1972.

21. Louis Johnson, ed., *New Zealand Poetry Yearbook*, Volume Eleven, Christchurch, Pegasus Press, 1964, p. 12.

22. Baxter, in Charles Doyle, ed., *Recent Poetry in New Zealand*, Auckland, Collins, 1965, p. 29.

23. Personal letter, 23rd October 1976.

24. Baxter, *Runes*, Wellington, Oxford, 1973, p. 30.

25. *Idem* (1967), pp. 122, 123.

26. Weir (1974), pp. 244, 245, 249, 250.

27. Doyle, "James K. Baxter: the Jerusalem Writings", *The Literary Half-Yearly*, 18, 1977, pp.110-116.

28. David Moody, "For James K. Baxter", *Meanjin Quarterly* 32, June 1973, p. 221.

29. Baxter, *Jerusalem Daybook*, Wellington, Price Milburn, 1971, pp. 53-4.

30. *Idem, The Six Faces of Love*, Wellington, The Futuna Press, 1972, unpaged (pp. 41-2).

31. Robert Lowell, "On Freedom in Poetry", in Stephen Berg and Robert Mezey, eds., *Naked Poetry: Recent American Poetry in Open Forms*, New York; Bobbs-Merrill, 1969, p. 124.

32. C. K. Stead, "Towards Jerusalem", *Islands*, 3, (Autumn 1973), p. 15, 16.

33. O'Sullivan, p. 43.

34. Curnow, p. 49.

35. The sonnets are, respectively, from *Jerusalem Daybook*, 1970, rpt; Wellington, Price Milburn, 1975, pp 9, 45; *Jerusalem Daybook*, p. 33, *Autumn Testament*, Wellington, Price Milburn, 1972, pp. 17, 25, 32.

10

Peter Nazareth's
'In a Brown Mantle' :
Novel as Revolutionary Art

G.S. AMUR

AN Indian reader's immediate reaction to novels like Achebe's *A Man of the People*, Ngugi's *A Grain of Wheat* or Peter Nazareth's *In a Brown Mantle* is to wonder why there are so few novels like them in Indian writing in English. The pattern of political and social change in India, as we know, has had close similarities with that of the rest of the Third World and the problems too have been very much the same, but while the representative African writer is generally a committed writer, the representative Indian writer—R.K. Narayan for example—is essentially an uncommitted writer. Peter Nazareth perhaps speaks for all his fellow African writers when he says :

> ...When writing about people in the changing African society of today, unless the African writer is perfectly satisfied with the *status quo*, he will be committed, whether explicitly or implicitly.[1]

What are the reasons for this basic difference ? Is it because, as V.S. Naipaul has suggested in that much misunderstood book, *An Area of Darkness*, the Indian writer's attitude is one of 'total acceptance,'[2] or is it because of a fundamental difference in ethos and sensibility which makes the Indian writer turn to the fable rather than the novel proper ? Or, is it merely a question of literary influence ? For example, Conrad, who has been such a formative influence on the African writers, has never had much of an appeal to the Indian writer.

Peter Nazareth, the East African novelist and critic, is a committed writer and *In a Brown Mantle*,[3] his first novel, is an attempt toward what Trotsky has called 'revolutionary art', an art whose concern is the dynamics of a new epoch and which reflects all the contradictions of a revolutionary social system. Nazareth has learnt his art not only from Conrad but even more specifically from Naipaul. Of Naipaul's *The Mimic Men* he says :

> The novel is of particular relevance to anybody in an ex-colony going through a period of rapid political change.[4]

He finds Naipaul's experiment with technique of particular interest to the Third World writer :

> In writing this novel, Naipaul faced the same problem that other Commonwealth writers of today face. What literary technique is one to adopt so as to present the confusing and explosive realities of today in an organised manner ? How is the writer to select a vantage point in order to present a pattern out of apparent chaos, a chaos he is so involved in that he may not be granted a sense of perspective in his daily life?[5]

Nazareth solved his own technical problem successfully when he chose Joseph D'Souza as the narrator for his novel. In *The Mimic Men*, Ralph Singh, the narrator, is too much of a participant and the tone of the novel is totally affected by his own disillusionment. This no doubt gives the novel an extraordinary intensity but it somewhat vitiates its value as an objective document. In Achebe's *A Man of the People*, which Nazareth had certainly read before he wrote his own novel, the narrator, a young man called Odili Samulu, is not only immature but, as Arthur Ravenscroft has noted,[6] lacks a moral identity distinct from that of Chief Nanga, the central character. This results in a simplification of the author's vision. Nazareth, who had studied both his models carefully, chooses a narrator, who is distinguished from both the central characters, Robert Kyeyune and Pius Cota and, as a Goan African, has a separate racial identity as well.

The novel is in the form of Joseph D'Souza's memories which he records as an act of confession and expiation during his period of political exile in London, away from his mother country, Damibia. It turns out to be a political novel because of D'Souza's involvement with the life of his country during a revolutionary period of its history, the Independence movement and its aftermath. Nazareth takes pains to create the little Goan world within Damibia in all its complexity, because D'Souza's Goanness has a special value in the novel. It differentiates him not only from the Africans but also from the other Asians in the novel and provides him with an acute insight into the racial and political situation. The shrewd African leader, Robert Kyeyune, chooses D'Souza as his adviser and organiser, not only because he is a brown man, but specially because he is a Mugoa and not a Muindi.

The Indian element in the novel, apart from the Goans, is limited to the family of Mohan Shah, the industrialist. But the Goan community, with its Institutes, parties and scandals, is a real presence. Nazareth goes into the 'bitter history' of the race, records its customs and beliefs and analyses its psychology. The Goans in general, like the Narrator's own father, accepted authority and white rule, avoided politics and stuck to the Civil Service. D'Souza, the Narrator, is not by any means a typical Goan. Kyeyune recognises this instinctively when he presents him to his people. 'He is a brown man outside, but he is all black inside'. Though the manner in which he is sucked into active African politics from the security of the British Civil Service is absurdly dramatic, it is not altogether incredible in the context of his background. Very early in his life, at the age of fourteen, he had been exposed to the influence of Pius Cota, the Goan radical from the neighbouring Azingwe, who was always urging the Goans to throw in their lot with the cause of African independence, and he had received his message: 'I hope you will one day become a politician and throw in your energies for justice.' Later, at St Jude's, a Mission School, he had had his first taste of politics when he successfully organised student strikes. In retrospect, D'Souza recognises the value of this experience and says :

> I had learned to appreciate the power of a mass of people when they could be persuaded not to cooperate with authority. I also had a foretaste of that queer mixture of idealism and calculating craftiness I was to meet when I started working with Kyeyune. (40-41)

D'Souza's encounter with John Waddimba, a member of "Mene Mene," a terrorist movement in the neighbouring Azingwe, and his participation in the general strike which forced the University authorities to permit Pius Cota to address the students, had further deepened his political awareness. Like most other Goans in Damibia he had joined the Civil Service but he had been soon fed up with it and had been thoroughly disillusioned with its method of dealing with real problems.

Unlike the idealistic Pius Cota and Robert Kyeyune who, despite their racial difference, were fully committed to their cause, D'Souza preserves his detachment, which he recognises to be a racial as well as a personal trait :

> I was detached, far away, watching myself talking and acting and making myself speak as though through ventriloquism. It was precisely this detachment that gave me a sense of perspective, which apparently was such an asset to Kyeyune. (p. 56)

D'Souza likes to think of himself as the Brown Abstraction complementing the sensual impulse in Kyeyune. There are, of course,

moments in his association with Kyeyune when his mantle of detachment
drops as, for example, when his naive aspiration for political power is
frustrated, and, much to his chagrin, his enemy, the Cow, is appointed
Minister for Interior and Defence Matters, but generally he keeps his
cool and, when the situation gets hot, leaves the country. His nationalism is genuine and the sentimental note in his final goodbye to the
country, 'Goodbye Mother Africa, your bastard son loved you,' is not
altogether false, but unlike Pius Cota, his fellow Goan, he is incapable of
total commitment.

D'Souza believes that his gift for abstraction is an Asian gift, but he
is essentially a product of Western education, and his values are of the
West. Unlike Cota or Kyeyune, he is not prepared to shed his individualism and merge with the masses. So, he takes to flight. After Independence, he is sucked into the sewers of corruption and has to pay the
price by leaving his home and country and condemning himself to the
life of an exile in London, a city he strongly dislikes.

Nazareth's choice of an ironic participant-narrator with a sophisticated intelligence and a gift for comic detachment, enables him to see the
social and political contradictions in East Africa in a clear perspective.
This is as true of his presentation of the historical phenomenon as of the
chief protagonists involved in them. It is shown, for example, that
Damibia is not a classic case of exploitation and that its independence
movement, unlike that in the neighbouring Azingwe, is somewhat
spurious. 'Our Independence movement,' the Narrator recalls, 'was
mainly a revolution one shouted and drank one's way into.' If in other
countries the formation of a political party which sought to be the expression of the masses had preceded the Independence movement, in Damibia
the leaders acquire an instant party by putting together all the power
blocs. The PCP projects a leftist image but collects funds from the
Western powers to fight the elections. The PCP victory is manouevred
through the distribution of gifts and free booze and all kinds of polling
irregularities. When at last the country becomes independent, it has
little meaning for the poor masses. A mission doctor working upcountry
reports to the Narrator that when he asked one of them what he thought
of Independence, he was told that Independence was the name of
Kyeyune's wife! The aftermath of Independence reveals similar contradictions. The immediate task before the leaders is to create a Civil Service,
but they find that the Africans who replaced the British, thought very much
like the British. After all, they had been selected by the British. A
People's Army comes into being, but since there are no foreign aggres-
sions to fight off, the Army gets busy looking after itself. There is, what
the Narrator calls, 'conspicuous consumption' everywhere and there is a
deluge of foreign aid and, in its wake, an army of foreign technicians. Everyone, including the Narrator, is caught in the quagmire of corruption.
The Minister for Interior and Defence Matters goes abroad and buys

a golden bed for his wife and causes a major scandal. The inevitable crisis follows and Kyeyune, the only good man in the Party, is shot at while leaving to attend a session of Parliament. The Narrator sums up the situation and says, 'We lost the advantages of capitalism without gaining the benefits of socialism.' In short, the Revolution had failed.

The Narrator is of course a well-informed man and is aware of Fanon's work, but perhaps he is too close to the events to realise that this phase in the history of Damibia is an inevitable phase. Fanon has written that the process of decolonisation is a programme of complete disorder,[7] and, therefore, what happens in Damibia is not unusual. The Narrator, a typical example of the Westernised intellectual Fanon described in his book, does not show an adequate awareness of the problems a decolonised country faces when it wants to make a complete break from the past, particularly when all the institutions it inherits are the ones created by the colonist. His vision is clear but narrow and too deeply coloured by his own disillusionment to be entirely true.

Against this background, it is very much to the credit of the novelist (and the Narrator) to have balanced his vision of cynical disillusionment by affirmations in terms of human personality. Robert Kyeyune, the Leader, conforms in many ways to the prototype presented to us by Fanon. He has become Leader by his hard work, spirit of sacrifice and an exemplary patriotism. The Narrator speaks of him as 'a radical in the typical African manner.' He has a record of successful strikes and boycotts behind him, and he knows his enemy well. He is always 'one jump ahead of the colonial Government'. Above all, he has the gift of involving the people in the movement he leads. As the Narrator puts it :

Kyeyune could reach out to the very soul of these organisms. It was as though he kept emitting radio waves and all of them receiving sets attuned to the same wave length... One was continually renewed and refreshed by their direct faith and lack of sophistication. (pp. 46-47)

Kyeyune's conformity to the type continues even after the achievement of Independence. Fanon has said :

The leader who has behind him a lifetime of political action and devoted patriotism, constitutes a screen between the people and the rapacious bourgeoisie since he stands surety for the ventures of that caste and closes his eyes to their insolence, their mediocrity and their fundamental immorality.[8]

So, his own ministers, army officers and even the trusted special adviser, the Narrator, steal under his very nose, and he can do nothing about it.

Kyeyune is a product of history and the pattern of his rise and fall is determined by the play of historical forces in the context of a country in the process of decolonisation, and the Narrator reproduces all the subtleties and contradictions of the phenomenon. But Kyeyune is far from being an abstract symbol. He is one of the most fully realised characters in the novel.

The other affirmative symbol in the novel is Pius Cota, a pure and uncompromising revolutionary. Fanon has described this type as well :

> The native who decides to put the programme into practice and to become its moving force, is ready for violence at all times. From birth it is clear to him that his narrow world, strewn with prohibitions, can only be called in question by absolute violence.[9]

Cota is inflexible in his commitment to the cause of political and social justice to the Africans and he is prepared to pay the price for this commitment. He is a dedicated nationalist, Pan-Africanist and socialist. He is one of the main forces behind the terrorist movement in Azingwe, but after the country's Independence, his very idealism proves to be a thorn in the side of his former comrades, and he is destroyed.

The Narrator's approach to Pius Cota varies from irony to sentiment. He is put off by the extreme revolutionary zeal of his fellow Goan and prefers the more human Kyeyune who knew how to relax. It is only after Cota's death that he comes to recognise his full value.

Writing about Paule Marshall's *The Chosen Place, The Timeless People*,[10] Nazareth praises Miss Marshall's skill in interweaving individual characters with historical forces.[11] He has done this superbly in his own novel and, in the process, has given us a fine example of revolutionary art.

Let me in conclusion come back to the question I raised at the beginning of this essay. Why do we have so few novels in Indian writing like *The Mimic Men* or for that matter *In a Brown Mantle* ? Our attempts at the political novel, Bhabani Bhattacharya's *Shadow from Ladakh*, Manohar Malgonkar's A *Bend in the Ganges* or Khushwant Singh's *A Train to Pakistan*, for example, are too contrived to be real and lack the pulsating life of the African novel. Our best political novel is Raja Rao's *Kanthapura*. But even in this novel, while it is true that Raja Rao has succeeded in creating a political myth out of the national struggle for independence, there is hardly an attempt at an analysis of political motivation or a clarification of an original political vision. Our political novels all tend to be historical novels. They are, unlike their African counterparts, unduly solemn and heavy. They seem to have been motivated not by concern for the living moment in all its baffling complexity but by the intention to produce the Great Indian Novel out of the material of history.

REFERENCES

1. Peter Nazareth, *An African View of Literature*, Illinois, Northwestern University Press, 1974, p. 2.

2. V.S. Naipaul, *An Area of Darkness*, Harmondsworth, Penguin Books, 1968, p. 216.

3. Peter Nazareth, *In a Brown Mantle*, East African Literature Bureau, 1972.

4. *An African View of Literature*, pp. 76-77.

5. *ibid.*, p. 78.

6. William Walsh (ed.), *Readings in Commonwealth Literature*, Oxford, 1973, p. 187.

7. Frantz Fanon, *The Wretched of the Earth*, Harmondsworth, Penguin Books, 1974, p. 27.

8. *ibid.*, p. 135.

9. *ibid.*, p. 29.

10. Paule Marshall, *The Chosen Place, The Timeless People*, London, Longman, 1970.

11. Peter Nazareth, "Paule Marshall's Timeless People", *New Letters*, 40 : I, October 1973, pp. 113-131.

11

The Commonwealth Writer
and his Material

CLARK BLAISE

WHAT follows is intended as a personal statement from a non-existent creature—a "Commonwealth Writer"—about a faintly-visible subject called "Commonwealth Literature." Since I am not a scholar or literary critic, I have no way of knowing how earnestly debated the point may be; I only know that there are Canadian, Jamaican, Nigerian, Australian writers, and there are a few whose allegiance is more to the language than a national tradition (Vladimir Nabokov and Samuel Beckett spring to mind), and there are a few who do not balk at terms such as "West Indian","West African",or "Indian English". There is none, however, who claims the "Commonwealth" as his inspiration, his nightmare, his identity or his market. A category of literature without conscious (or admitted) practitioners, claiming participants from every race, religion and national background, from six continents and Oceania, either points to a sponta-eous fertility that is humbling, or a loose Platonism that is embarrassing. In either case, we are spouting polite gibberish unless we can counter the obvious and fundamental objection that we are manipulating fragile con-structions with the bluntest of instruments, from a very great distance.

The blunt instrument is our presumed common medium of the English language. I'm not referring to the area of "English Usage" or regional varieties of English—specialised vocabularies and dialects are in fact wel-come concretenesses—I am talking about our understanding of funda-mental English words within a sophisticated literary context. The "New Criticism" sets a rigorous standard, but it implies a unity of culture; Com-monwealth Literature, if nothing else, shows that language can be pared from culture. Language is at best an approximation, dependent on other cultural signs for perfect communication ; when these signs are missing, or misinterpreted, our common language is a source of confusion and obscurity. And how do we, as literary critics and not as sociologists, as writers and not apologists, see that it doesn't happen ? I confess that I do not know.

Examples are everywhere, and before concentrating on the works of V.S. Naipaul, whom we have all read, I will make a small point with a recent (1974) Canadian work that probably only Canadian specialists have read, *The Disinherited* by Matt Cohen.   (This is a comment only on the problem of book-distribution; the only Canadian author available in India is Mordecai Richler, in Penguins.   Only Patrick White and V.S. Naipaul are fully available here).   *The Disinherited* is, like many Canadian novels, a multi-generational farm saga, radiating outwardly from the hospital bed of the dying pater-familias, Richard Thomas. (Readers of Patrick White's *The Eye of the Storm* will recognise the form, though other parallels are missing).   In three following quotes, three different characters are recalling different houses in their lives :

The house was long gone now, there was a supermarket there instead.

'We could meet in Winnipeg and you could show me the house where you grew up.'
'It's gone.'
'I feel like I don't know you anymore,' he said.

The house he had lived in, a three storey redbrick house with an always freshly-painted verandah, had been torn down to make way for a zoology building.

What I feel is suggested by these flat, repetitive ruminations on vanished houses is nothing less than the emotional core of the book.   In fact, it relates to the only kind of "tragic consciousness" we are likely to find in Canadian writing of this moment; land-tragedy, the spectacle of a people waking up in a burning house. Acutely alert now, they can only save their skins and count their losses. They've lost everything else; it's a supermarket now. But I can imagine the editor's blue pencil falling heavily on such lines, calling them "indulgent" or "melodramatic", if the editor happens to be in London or New York. Americans already know it's a parking lot, a laundromat, a Macdonald's Drive-in—sad, but so what ? Leave the balladeering to the folk-singers (many of whom, strangely, are Canadians making it big in the US market, peddling a pop-poignance rooted in that same Canadian sense of tragedy. It's easier to set such feelings to music, *a la* Joni Mitchell, Gordon Lightfoot, Leonard Cohen and Buffy Ste-Marie than to commit them to prose). I confess this, even as I do it myself—there *is* something wistful, ineffectual and adolescent in such sentiments, true as they may be. It sells records, not books.

The special recognition that Canadian readers have felt in the works of Alice Munro (*The Lives of Girls and Women*) and Margaret Laurence (*The Diviners*, and others) is, I suspect, related to their ability to create and pass on intact that vanished small-town world, where ambitious girls fought against ignorant authority for a chance to escape. And the bitter knowledge that the escape was a new imprisonment, and that they had achieved nothing in their escape but a degrading survival—that too is passed on, and in an archly conservative society like Canada's, quickly takes on the sober density of revelation. Canadians *do* yearn to go home again.

To an inattentive US reader, these concerns with the personal past are likely to be dismissed as mere nostalgia, something that Americans are even better at than Canadians. But you don't usually find in modern US writing—except in other authors for whom the land was "manured with blood", like Faulkner—the sense of loss and tragedy in the mere replacement of the woods with a highway. [Faulkner in any case, offers a fruitful parallel with many Commonwealth authors. He too was staking a first literary claim, having to render virgin territory for "foreign" readers, while at the same time counteracting the inherited misconceptions of generations. Vision and revision; Canadians, West Indians, Africans, Indians, and Australians, like Jews, like women, have as much to *undo*, as they have to introduce. This leads to the temptation of didacticism, which Faulkner, Lawrence (D.H.), Canadians (Hugh MacLennan, the early works of Hugh Hood), women, Indians, and everyone else, every other visionary, is prey to. More on that later.]

To clarify the distinction between US and Canadian attitudes towards childhood memories, one need only dip into Saul Bellow's latest novel, *Humboldt's Gift*. Beautiful evocations of Division Street Chicago of the 20's and 30's are followed by equally haunting images of the jungle it has become. But always the tone is exuberant, inquisitive—a supermarket you say? What *kind* of supermarket? Bellow evokes contemporary Chicago in all its glass canyons and smog with the same inspiration that Wordsworth found in trees. (Modern Torontonians, on the other hand, have succeeded in banning new high-rise construction in their downtown, and speak longingly of a time, only half a generation ago, when all of downtown Toronto was the level of a three-storey suburban mainstreet.) When, in *Humboldt's Gift*, Charlie Citrine's eight-year-old daughter asks him, "What was it like, way back then?" Charlie is eager to respond. Too eager—his answer springs from the spirit of Doctorow's *Ragtime*, an answer so complete that it famishes the very possibility of an echoing nostalgia. It parodies the past :

"We had coal stoves," I tell her. "The kitchen range was black with a nickel trim—huge. The parlor stove had a dome like a little church, and you could watch the fire through the isinglass. I had to carry up the scuttle and take down the ashes."

"What did you wear ?"

"A leatherette war-ace cap with rabbit-fur flaps, hightop boots with a sheath for a rusty jack-knife, long black stockings, and plus fours. Underneath, woolly combinations which left lint in my navel and elsewhere."

(But when she goes on, asking what *else* it was like, Charlie instead describes her and how she reminds him of his wife, a lady who is one of his many tormentors. "I shall have to lay aside these emotional data," says Charlie Citrine. The renunciation of such data, I think, would be impossible for a Canadian of this moment. There is too much pressing in on us, too many things that are uniquely ours and have never been expressed for us to leave them out. Charlie [Bellow] doesn't have to worry; he can make a bow in the direction of the past, then get on with the troubles of being Charlie Citrine in Chicago in the 1970's.) The differences between our two literatures may seem small at first, but there is nothing small in the differences of our intent. Our common use of English, even among countries as similar as Canada and the US disguises our differences, poses a deeper barrier to clear appreciation, than would an overtly foreign language.

Here is a scene from V.S. Naipaul's first novel, *The Mystic Masseur*. The hero, Ganesh, is beating his wife :

It was their first beating, a formal affair done without anger on Ganesh's part or resentment on Leela's; and although it formed no part of the marriage ceremony itself, it meant much to both of them. It meant that they had grown up and become independent. Ganesh had become a man; Leela a wife as privileged as any other big woman. Now she too would have tales of her husband's beatings; and when she went home she would be able to look sad and sullen as every woman should.

This is an extraordinary scene, and not in the way the author might have thought. Naipaul, then only 24, perhaps did not trust it himself, and felt the explanation was necessary. But the intervention is disfiguring; it attempts to spare the feelings of the benevolently-disposed British reader, while forgiving the characters their quaint behaviour. The compromise is curiously brutal—the beating is "explained" as a masochistic pleasure for Leela, allowing her full participation in her new role of wife. "Wife" is synonymous with "she-who-is-beaten." That Trinidad is a wife-beating and child-beating culture is obvious, but what wife-beating *means* (i.e. how we, as readers, are supposed to take it) is here overlooked. Can we take the author at his word—"a formal affair without anger or resentment"? What does that do to their humanity ? What does it do to our trust in our own sense of human nature ? What does it do to the tone and fabric of the book ? We know how to deal with casual wife-

beaters in *our* literature—we know it's a short-hand for brutality bordering on the degenerate. But how to deal with it here ?   Naipaul tried to
tell us, but the language was too fluent, too soothing, and the effect was
the opposite of its intention.   And worse, the explanation condescends
towards what would become Naipaul's truest material—inarticulate grief,
impotence, rage, and the sham of "manhood" in corners of the world
that deny scope, comfort, power, or dignity.

And the question goes begging. What exactly *does* a beating mean, in
Trinidad ?   Trinidadian literature is bloody with wife-and-child-beatings,
murders, floggings, and horse-whippings; even without V.S. Naipaul we'd
be asking the question to Shiva Naipaul (*The Chip-Chip Gatherers*), or
the ghost of the late ˙ Harold Laddoo (himself murdered on a return to
Trinidad, after his first novel, *No Pain Like This Body*). Beating is obviously a form of communication, but how do we, reading it in the original
language, begin to translate ?   It is a problem faced by all writers in the
Commonwealth who lack a sufficient "home audience"; how to be true to
your material and still make it accessible.   How to make it accessible
without turning unnecessarily mystical, didactic, or condescending.

Early in *A House for Mr Biswas*, we come upon a simple statement :
"He had no ambition."   The full context is a paragraph describing Mr
Biswas' adolescent reading :

> The heroes had rigid ambitions and lived in countries where ambitions
> could be pursued and had a meaning. He had no ambition, and in
> this hot land, apart from opening a shop or buying a motor bus,
> what could he do ?

He had no ambition ! The phrase may just as well be in Hindi for
most of us; the situation has no meaning. We are accustomed to long
fictions on the "theme" of *accidea* and sloth : the Russians, Italians,
French and North Americans have done it to death. It is one of the great
levers of irony—a lazy man is a special case, an oddity, one through whom
our obsession with work and personal advancement can be effectively
satirised.   But Mr Biswas is typical, not eccentric.   To lack ambition and
not to be troubled by it, or psychoanalysed for it—in fact, to inhabit a
culture in which ambition is treated as an affliction—would be a hell for
most North Americans. (And Trinidad *is* a hell, in the way "The South"
was a hell for Quentin Compson, but not just because it is backward,
aimless, or historically mutilated.   Naipaul has his own theories and has
written fourteen books in seventeen years to put them across.   This paper
is not about Naipaul's quarrel with history, but about the difficulties we
may have in extracting even the simplest ones from his books).   We learn
later in the book of two other traits of Mr Biswas—*flaws*, we would certainly say—the first being that he is never satisfied with what he has.
(This may seem like "ambition" but it doesn't go that far; it is a dispa-

ragement of effort, not an incentive). The second is that he always blames others for the sourness of his fate. Three rather primitive, shallow traits, we might think. Yet we are talking of a complicated man. There is a catalyst working in Biswas and in Trinidad that remains out of sight, one that deepens and mystifies even the simplest components. Individually, we might think we understand each of those traits; we have met them in a dozen books (*Dubliners*, for a start, by another islander struggling in exile to master his material). Mr Biswas is unique. What Naipaul created was a disturbing new kind of person for whom we had no category. Call it "West Indian Hindu", but we have learned in the past fifteen years that he lives on every continent and in our cities, and now, even in ourselves, and we still don't know him. Biswas is an allegorical man, whose single brief life encapsulates a new collective experience. The feeling lies on the threshold of articulation in *Biswas* (the best place for it), caught in Mr Biswas' many contradictions. Mr Biswas is a wife-beater who is also a sensitive journalist. An opportunist, a cheat and a conniver who is nonetheless as helpless as any shlemiel before the financial machinations of others. A superstitious ritual-observing religious cynic. A passive man with a ferocious temper. A faithful married man for whom "sex" as a drive, a pleasure, a need, or a burden, is never discussed, never even presented. The list of contradictions could be extended infinitely in every direction—he is the newest creation in English-language fiction, a character for whom all of our catch-words : "bitter", "alienated", "sensitive", "moody" are equally applicable and unconfining. Undefining, "Touching and pathetic", "tragic-comic", critics have called him, acknowledging indirectly their inability to do justice to anything but their own bafflement. Unconsciously, they soften and universalise the portrait, in order to facilitate the wide acceptance they feel he should have. But there will be no easy acceptance for such a book; Naipaul will have to educate us—as Joyce, Faulkner and Lawrence did—by the example of his own work. In *Biswas*, Naipaul drew as close to a character and a culture as the English language permitted; it is vivid because of that. And it remains just slightly elusive, I feel, because the English language is....finally, English. It can cope exquisitely with the intricacies of Anthony Powell's 12-volume *Dance to the Music of Time*, but it can't quite fix the potential of Mohun Biswas, Trinidad journalist. For his next novel, *The Mimic Men*, Naipaul would plot a new strategy.

The Mimic Men is Naipaul's *Portrait of the Artist*, the work of exile and cunning, a first-person statement from a fully self-conscious, non-wife-beating (in fact, deserted husband), articulate "Caribbean" intellectual. Ralph Singh is the Humbert Humbert of third world politics, bringing to shoddy goods a fine, even noble sense of the tragic and the absurd. ("Industrialization in territories like ours," he writes, "seems to be a process of filling imported tubes with various imported substances."). This time there is no mistaking the meaning of simple words or actions (nor will there be in succeeding novels; Naipaul has left "folk material" well behind him); the language of *The Mimic Men* comes from the pages of *Encounter* and the *New York Review of Books* :

> Occasionally I read a letter in *The Times*, a communication on a great topic from a mean address; I recognise a name and see with enormous sympathy the stirring of some chained and desperate creature.

(The "creature" could well have been Mohun Biswas or Ganesh Ramsumair; the early novels had been told, as it were, from Caliban's consciousness. Ralph Singh is Prospero.)

> To be born on an island like Isabella, an obscure New World transplantation, second-hand and barbarous, was to be born to disorder. From an early age.... I had sensed this. Now I was to discover that disorder has its own logic and permanence.... Even as I was formulating my resolve to escape, there began that series of events which, while sharpening my desire to get away, yet rooted me more firmly to the locality where accident had placed me.

> The pace of events, as I see it, is no more than the pace of chaos on which strict limits have been imposed.

Naipaul had turned another corner (each of his novels, after the second, has been a personal "breakthrough"; perhaps he'll never 'consolidate his gains' like a Joyce, or perhaps he uses his travel and history books as meditations, much in the way that Camus tested his theories in drama and fiction. In any event, Naipaul's travel writing and his personal journalism tend to match the voice of Ralph Singh; Naipaul travels, it often seems, to confirm as much as to discover). Despite the "aged eagle" eloquence of *The Mimic Men*, I find it the least successful of Naipaul's "island" novels. (Least successful, I should add, on its own terms; it is a magnificent novel). It contains the most quotable lines and the most vividly-etched scenes, but there is a deadness around its edges. Ralph Singh does not fully convince, either as an ex-politician or an exile, or land-developer; his banishment to London to write his memoirs at forty is something of a pose, a convenient way of gathering up his several selves into a single narrative. Next to the brilliant childhood section, the London material is forced, plausible only because Naipaul is an eloquent professional. But the evocation of growing up exceptional on an island that could not accommodate it—"a ship-wrecked leader of his people", the mad-school-master's son who secretly reads *The Migrations of the Aryan Peoples* and fantasises himself a Rajput warrior, who believes that a special fate has singled him out and will not let him live and die anonymously on that barbarous shore—*that* is what rings with absolute clarity. *The Mimic Men* would seem to be the archetypical "Commonwealth

Novel" (thinking of its parallels with Margaret Laurence's *The Diviners*, *Portrait of the Artist*, *The Vivisector*, and doubtless, many others). Ralph Singh and Morag Gunn both manage their escapes, both succeed in the world beyond their wildest aspirations, both are disillusioned, and both settle down, in their forties, claiming peace, to write their books. The only difference is that Trinidadians cannot return to cabins in the woods, either in Trinidad or in India, and Canadians can. It is a happy situation for Canadian authors, though perhaps baleful to their growth. For Naipaul there is still no "home-audience", not even a "home"; only a still-fresh, inexhaustible subject-matter. To be able to return home comfortably and to have an audience who understands instinctively, is, potentially, to see one's country as no longer odd, no longer a nightmare to be wakened from.

In the past ten years, Naipaul has written only two novels : *In a Free State* and *Guerrillas*, both in their way brilliant, and though "difficult", they are neither elusive nor didactic. Naipaul seems to be moving to colder detachment and to an obliteration of all his earlier, autobiographical material. His islands or developing nations, are now merely backdrops (but living ones) to universal, "white" conflicts. The last Indian to appear in his fiction is Santosh, the narrator of the story ' One Out of Many" in *In a Free State*, and Santosh, as Indian, performs an act of complete self effacement. He begins as a Bombay pavement-dweller who accompanies his master to Washington as a domestic. He runs away, becomes a well-paid restaurant cook, and marries (bigamously) a Negro chamber-maid who saves him from deportation. In forty pages he goes from baggage-porter in the hills of India to slum-dwelling American, "soul-brother" to the people he still calls *hubshis* that he lives among. The story is funny, but Santosh's lesson is coldly sober : he has learned "I have a face and a body and I must feed the face and clothe the body for a certain number of years. Then it will be over." And in *Guerrillas*, "Trinidad" and its several disguises disappears just as silently. As Roche, the ineffectual South-African liberal tells his soon-to-be-butchered girl-friend, Jane : "When you're out in the country, in the old estates, and you see the country people walking to church or rocking in their hammocks or drinking in their little bars, you don't think it's that kind of country. But every country is that kind of country...." That is a powerful phrase; behind its simple dismissal lie a dozen books dedicated to the uniqueness of Naipaul's various Trinidads. From Saroyanesque delight in "his people's " dialect and idiosyncracies, to elegant, mordant epithets, he'd found ways of remaining "West Indian", even in exile. Then suddenly, he is free.

Commonwealth writers are all from islands, and we each make cases for the special absurdity of our isolation. French-Canadians yield nothing to Bhojpuri Hindus of Trinidad; nor do Australians, nor Parsis, nor Polish-born wives of Parsis—the Commonwealth will eventually prove more cosmopolitan than Manhattan ever was. Our fates have been something to fascinate, frustrate, and preoccupy us for a literary lifetime. Our material has been tractlessness, our grasping for compasses, our envy of those who were born knowing what they were, or never having to ask. Writers like Joyce and Naipaul were there to show us it was an honourable obsession. And now they show us it is not the end.

12

Mates, Mum, and Maui :
The theme of maturity in
three antipodean novels

CHRIS TIFFIN

THE necessity for the young to leave the nest and strike out on their own
is a natural pattern which has long provided a metaphor for the human
family. With Samuel Butler's *The Way of All Flesh* the idea that maturity
consisted in this was canonised in the novel and given the added piquancy
of a departing kick aimed at the parents' pants. D.H. Lawrence follows
the model in *Sons and Lovers* as does Joyce in *A Portrait of the Artist*.
For the colonial writer in an emerging country the pattern is particularly
attractive because it offers a way of depicting both personal and national
aspirations in a multi-layered fiction. However, as not every culture will
subscribe to the same ideas of maturity at a personal level as they do at a
national level, the result is a tension which creates thematic richness on
the one hand, but considerable technical difficulties on the other. I wish
in this paper to demonstrate something of the range of treatments of the
theme of maturity by choosing novels by Randolph Stow, Witi Ihimaera
and Albert Wendt. Of the three, Stow's is the most traditional and the
most direct in its treatment. Both Ihimaera and Wendt, who explore
social and racial conflicts as well as personal ones, find their fictional forms
through importing distinctive elements from other cultures and incorporating them into the novel.

Stow's *The Merry-go-Round in the Sea* is about the inevitable loss of
childhood vision and the growth into more complex ideas of time and the
self. With leisurely, straight-forward narrative it follows the development
of Rob Coram from age six to age fourteen, concentrating more upon
the dispersal of his childhood fantasies than upon the replacement
of them by anything more positive or substantial. Rob at the
start is a precocious child, the solidity of whose world is guaranteed by an
extensive though distanced family, by the model of his older cousin, Rick,

and by his complete sensuous identification with the environment. Rob's immediate family is strangely remote. His father appears infrequently, and when he does Rob notices him as one might an interesting stranger. On a couple of occasions when his father manifests ingenuity, such as in the rescue of Rob from the river, there is as much surprise as admiration in his reaction. His mother is more pervasive in the book, but her role is scarcely more important than that of any of the other relatives. She and Rob are intimate—they know each other's moods and conversational ways to the extent that Rob is prematurely bored by the relationship, being able to predict when he can get his way, and when she is 'dangerous'. His substitute parents are drawn from the wider circle of the family, and consist of his aunt Kay who likes men and is eternally knitting or repairing socks for them, and most of all his cousin, Rick, who is fifteen years older than him. As his mother remarks, "He seems to be trying to turn himself into a carbon copy of Rick." (p. 260) This substitution is brought out clearly in an early scene as Rick leads the horse on which the six-year-old Rob is riding.

He looked down on Rick walking ahead in the road, being nudged now and then by Goldie's nose, but not turning... The day, the summer would never end. He would walk behind Rick, he would study Rick forever. (p. 36)

Rob, then, is insulated from the parental problems faced by Ernest Pontifex or Stephen Daedalus, but only because he has transferred his vulnerability to his expectations of Rick. Rick becomes his primary guarantee of protection and his hope of timelessness and stability, but he also draws reassurance from his sense of the natural world. This is a very visceral novel replete with the multitudinous sights, sounds, but especially smells that surround the growing Rob. As they do with an animal, they serve to identify and demarcate his territory. His world is that of the area round Geraldton extending out to the family properties which he sometimes visits. Beyond that to the east lies Australia, a sad romantic land carpeted with the bleaching bones of its true heroes, the noble suicides. The war news has no impact on him until Broome, a town that has affinities with his world, is mentioned. But the primal element of Rob's physical world is the sea, "the first sound, the beginning and ending of all his circling days." (p. 47) It, too, is a guarantee of the stability of his life and of his immunity from upheaval and change. But circular patterns, as in Stow's previous novels, are deceptive if not outright destructive, and the aimlessness of Rob's life, whatever the sea might promise, will not be allowed to continue forever. For the moment, though, Rob is allowed his illusions, and Stow typifies them by the merry-go-round of the title which becomes the central symbol of the book. Rob is devoted to a merry-go-round, or rather, roundabout, in a park by the sea.

He identifies with this the mast and stays of a sunken barge in the harbour
and imagines it to be a timeless, self-propelling roundabout, perfect and
primal, on which he could live forever with his chosen parent substitutes.

> He would swim miles and miles, until at last the merry-go-round would
> tower above him, black, glistening, perfect, rooted in the sea. The
> ' merry-go-round would turn by itself, just a little above the green water.
> The world would revolve around him, and nothing would ever change.
> He would bring Rick to the merry-go-round, and Aunt Kay, and they
> would stay there always, spinning and diving and dangling their feet
> in the water, and it would be today forever. (p. 25)

This emphasis on changelessness, the suspension of the happy present,
is the start of a rearguard action against the proposition of linear time
that Rob has already accepted intellectually. While he still entertains the
desire to perpetuate the moment riding behind Rick, or imagines the most
perfect of all suspensions as the effortless, circular movement of the magic
roundabout in the sea, he has discovered the inexorable irreplaceability of
each moment.

> He was thinking of time and change, of how, one morning when he
> must have been quite small, he had discovered time, lying in the grass
> with his eyes closed against the sun. He was counting to himself. He
> counted up to sixty, and thought : That is a minute. Then he thought :
> It will never be that minute again. It will never be today again.
> Never. (p. 14)

And Stow comments : "He would not, in all his life, make another discovery so shattering."

The bulk of the novel, then, is occupied not with Rob's discovery of
this metaphysical truism, but with the implications of it for Rob's own
life. His self-containedness is almost impenetrable, but there are breaches
of it, the most noticeable being caused by the second world war, which
overshadows the novel. Rob is first aware of the war as the generic
source of irritations and omissions. He notices it first when the tiny
Japanese flowers which expand in water are no longer available. The war
is the explanation given for the family's maid not being replaced when
she leaves to marry. More crucially it is why he cannot travel out to
inspect his merry-go-round in the sea, as that part of the beach has
become a barb-wire enclosed army reserve. The war causes other upsets
in his way of life and in his surroundings. The tennis court is dug up for
an air raid trench, and the whole family prepares for an evacuation inland
which never takes place. But the most important change is the four-year
absence of Rick who leaves for the war the morning after the boy's ride
on Goldie, and who is captured by the Japanese with the result that for

most of the four years his family do not know if he is alive or dead. Rob
has difficulty in comprehending this absence. He is unused to anyone not
being a free agent, and is appalled at the thought that anyone would dare
to harm an Australian, much less a Maplestead. Rob's world expands as
places like Thailand take on a distant meaning, but for the most part he is
still confined by his physical world. He has vowed that he will not forget
Rick, but Rick's face becomes harder and harder to recall until only a few
jokes and smells and places will bring back the memory.

   In the meantime other developments take place. There is still a circularity about his days, but his experiences expand. Time manifests itself as
more mysterious than he had realised. The amnesia that results from a
fall from a tree blots out not only the day or two afterwards, but also the
twenty minutes or so before. Time therefore not only moves forward
inexorably but can reverse as well to efface incidents that have already
happened. Equally startling is the sudden recollection of a visit to Perth
which had passed out of his consciousness. Both the land and the sea
start to yield up mysteries. The poison fish he catches which spikes him
so painfully teaches him that "there's some funny things in the sea."
Similarly the land reveals its darkness when he is lost in the paddocks, a
metaphysical darkness which precipitates him towards maturity. He
learns that it is possible to die of that darkness, and that one does not cry
after learning that.   There are less painful surprises, too, such as the sight
of the deer in the early morning mist. But for all this, and for all the
unease he feels at his growing awareness of sex, and his self-consciousness
about being teased by his friends, his world continues largely intact. He
remains a simple sensibility responding to scents and sounds of the country,
his continued simplicity guaranteeing him against any major upset.

   The boy then was little more than a body, a set of sense organs. To
   himself he had little identity, and to his friends none at all, as they had
   none to him.   They knew each other by sight and hearing, by certain
   mannerisms. In absence, they ceased to exist for one another. (p.125)

   The return of Rick seems to offer a continuation of the stable life. At
first sight Rick appears no different despite his aunt's warning to Rob that
he might be, and Rob is ready to accept him back in the same hero-mould.
Rick too with his quote from Donne in Rob's autograph book

   Thy firmness makes my circle just
   And makes me end, where I begun

seems ready to accept a return to the *status quo*. But this does not last
long Rick *is* different, despite the boy's protests that he must not be, and
the differences are all anti-heroic ones. He can't sleep at night, he cries,
he has moods of brooding reminiscence, he faints at the sight of the pigs

being castrated, and there are moments when he seems to hate Rob. Rick is so central to Rob's sense of fitness and security that these unheroic weaknesses "disturbed him and left him without bearings." (p. 166) But Rick is even more profoundly changed, for not only has he developed feet of clay as far as both Rob and the family are concerned, but also he starts repudiating the other props of Rob's life : family and country. While Hughie has little trouble settling back into a comfortable existence, Rick cannot. He finds Australia "a good country to be a child in" because "it is a childish country." (p. 250) But he has lost his innocence in the war, and to an adult, Australia is "an Anglo-Celtic vacuum in the South Seas," (p. 250) characterised by "arrogant mediocrity, shoddiness and wowserism. (p. 281) Nor can the claims of the past or of the family hold him any longer. When Rob complains, "If you liked us, you wouldn't mind those things you're talking about," (p. 281) Rick repudiates all ties. "Look, kid, I've outgrown you. I don't want a family, I don't want a country. Families and countries are biological accidents. I've grown up, and I'm on my own." (p. 281)

The defection of Rick is the most serious upset that Rob in his fourteen years has been exposed to. There have been moments of disturbance earlier, and moments when he wished he could turn back the clock. He wishes the harnessing of atomic power could be unlearned, he wishes he had not seen Rick cry. But Rick's leaving brings home the implications of Rob's discovery of linear time eight years earlier. If each minute comes once and never again, then there is no circularity, suspension, nor final return and the stable institutions of hero, land and family which implied that circularity, which made that circle just, are specious and illusory. Ultimately, in the growing up process there is nothing and no one on whom to depend except the self. Rick's departure implies Rob's own eventual departure, perhaps in quite a different way, if he too is to "get a soul." (p. 175)

Appropriately, Stow returns to his merry-go-round symbol to make his final comment.

> The boy stared at the blue blur that was Rick. Over Rick's head a rusty windmill whirled and whirled. He thought of a windmill that had become a merry-go-round in a back yard, a merry-go-round that had been a substitute for another, now ruined merry-go-round, which had been itself a crude promise of another merry-go-round most perilously rooted in the sea. (p. 283)

Originally, Rob's dream had been a merry-go-round "glistening, perfect, rooted in the sea." The final version shows Rob aware of the ambiguous nature of such a vision. Not only is he left with a reminder of a makeshift substitute for a time-ruined promise of his dream—fully four removes from reality to ideal—but he recognises it now as "perilously rooted", with the twin senses of precariously and dangerously, for if the dream is clutched too long it retards and destroys. The family think Rick "immature", but Stow intends his escape from a perfunctory marriage and then from the country to be anything but this. The lesson is intended for Rob, too. Although he has lived in the shelter of family and in identification with the sounds and smells of the land, although he has created his own mythology of Australia with its carpet of bleaching bones and self-destructive hero-poets, although he has forged his hero in Rick, none of these can obviate for long the demand by linear time that he repudiate such solace and security.

There is no triumph in such a conclusion. Neither Rick nor Rob shows any indication that they are on the verge of forging anything particular in the smithies of their respective souls. Rick's departure seems to be an escape rather than an apotheosis, and Rob's final vision is tinged with the sweet sadness of the passing of intimations of immortality. This is, I think, a romantic novel farewelling the ecstasies of youth, and for Stow farewelling a country which, like Rick, he feels he has outgrown. The novel identifies and defines maturity, confronts the demands of inexorable reality, but lingers over the childhood experience. The "blue blur" of Rick at the conclusion is no longer the blue of immense possibility but only the blue of Australian distance, and like Rob the novel concludes with no more and no less than the "agreeable sadness" (p. 269) of knowing that one is young but that one will not be young for long.

Witi Ihimaera's first novel, *Tangi* (which means a funeral or wake), is told through the consciousness of a young Maori who has maturity thrust upon him at the death of his father, and there is little doubt that maturity here means fulfilling a responsible, even patriarchal role in the family group. Many times the novel repeats the father's injunction, "The eldest always looks after the younger ones of the family," (p. 21) and the son, Tama, responds with a vow to become like a giant Kauri sheltering the family. But although Tama's consciousness is the chosen vehicle for the narrative it is not the centre of interest. The novel shows the form of grief rather than analysing the grief itself. For all its tearing of hair and rending of garments, it is a novel less about personal sorrow than about the way a group restores itself after the loss of one of its members. One of the characters in Ihimaera's second novel says of an old man, "Everyone's been so lucky to have him so long."[1] The individual is shared and valued by the group, so when an individual does die the loss is felt by all and is to be demonstrated by all. In the Maori culture the ritual of the *tangi* provides the method of demonstration. By choosing the viewpoint of the eldest son, the orthodox successor, Ihimaera has been able to internalise with remarkable success the public, traditional lore of the Maori funeral. The novel is an individual treatment of a ritual which seeks to exorcise the loss of the individual and to reconfirm the coherence and mutual support of the group.

Since the sort of material Ihimaera has to organise affects the way he goes about it, it is worthwhile to sketch the process of grief exorcism. Also it should be remarked in passing that Ihimaera is explicit that the *tangi* is a ritual to be gone through. Early in the novel Tama speaks of his path to the Underworld, and as the novel approaches the *tangi* itself, the refrain emphasises the self-conscious confronting and purging of individual sorrow.

> And one step further now.
> No don't stop. If you stop, even for a moment, the grief will possess you completely, and you must complete this journey. You are your father's son, the eldest. (p. 145)

This is important because it puts in much better perspective the explicitness of the emotion about which reviewers have been defensive. The point is that articulating the sense of loss is a way of concretising and ultimately overcoming it. The sociologists can probably do it with bigger words, but simply extrapolating from this novel we can see a number of different stages or elements in the formal process of grief. (It is interesting to note how many of them crop up in a form like the pastoral elegy.)

First there is the refusal to believe in the fact of death. The shearers cannot accept what they hear. Tama is stunned :

> —Dad, dead ?
> No. Not my father. Not Dad. (p. 4)

The women-folk demonstrate their refusal to believe by hysterics or by continuing to talk to the corpse as though he were still alive. The children simply cannot understand. The next element is the expression of guilt for injustices done to the deceased and for opportunities lost of honouring, helping or showing affection to him. Tama's regret for not returning to help on the farm is much reiterated at the start of the novel. The most pervasive element in the process is the demonstration of personal loss in the wildest and most extravagant terms. Anger or fierceness may be involved, and the demonstration is made through extreme and even cosmic comparisons.

> I try to smile back. My lips curl only with sorrow.
> There is no joy in the world now that Dad is dead. (p. 62)
> World, surround me with a rush of silence. Let no sounds of joy or happiness come to me. There should be no world now that Dad is dead, nor any joy...(p. 70)

> Your father is gone now and the world is filled with darkness. He was
> a good man, the axis of your universe, the sun giving light to your
> day. Now clouds obscure the sun. All the world laments with you.
> And this place has become desolate with ashes and sorrow. (p. 144)

Next there is a recapitulation of what has been owed to the deceased.
Kopua's first reaction is to list what Rongo had done for him, while much
of the novel is devoted to substantiating Tama's claim that his father was
"so completely the sculptor of my life." (p. 47)

Two features of the grief process are recognisable from the pastoral
elegy, but with significant modifications : the declaration of alienation from
one's fellows following the death, and the reproach against time. Tama's
alienation from others is mentioned often enough, but unlike Shelley's
Adonais there is companionship in mourning. Tama is not alone in his
emotional exclusion from the world as he approaches his sister, Mere.

> We see only each other. All these other people embracing and meeting
> one another are only shadows existing on the edge of our universe. I
> stumble through them. I walk along the barrier towards my sister.
> Her face is wet with tears. (p. 106)

More significant is the treatment given to Tama's *pakeha* girl-friend,
Sandra, who belongs to the world of Wellington, the world of Tama's
temporary defection from the family. She is summarily abandoned both
by Tama and by Ihimaera, being given only one or two oblique mentions
until she telephones late in the book. In the crisis of death none but the
family matters. All else is alien, and will continue to be for Tama since
he will return to head the family. Whoever Sandra is, and whatever
relationship they have had, she becomes suddenly alien and irrelevant.

If group mourning mitigates the isolation of the individual mourner,
so too it modifies the resentment at time. The underlying ethic of the
novel demands an acquiescence in the process of time, and so its swift
rapacity is attributed to Tama's own thoughtlessness. "Those forever
years when father was always with [him]" (p. 101) have blinded Tama to
his father's aging. "He seemed always the same as if life had just streamed round him and left him unchanged." (p. 96) There is anger in the
grief process, but it is less impotent reproach than a fierce pride in what
has been achieved in the time allowed. The final words of the novel
encapsulate this beautifully.

> Farewell, Rongo ! Farewell ! Farewell ! Farewell !
> It is a cry of aroha, swelling louder and gathering in strength.
> It is an acclamation for our father.
> It is the final farewell, echoed by earth and sky.
> It is a roar of pride, before the slow descending of the sun. (p. 207)

Earth and Sky, the primal parents and progenitors of natural law, are invoked to place this death in its proper context. This is the climax of the *tangi*. Rongo has been buried, along with all his possessions, and the mourners, having demonstrated their solidarity, are about to disperse to take up their lives again. The pride comes from the sense of value and worth in the deceased, in the family, in the self; an assertion of positiveness in the face of the unavoidable fact of individual decline and death.

The last three stages of the ritual are especially important in Ihimaera's version. Physical activity, or the promise of it, is a way both of declaring respect for the dead and of controlling personal grief. Thus Kopua's voice is "fierce" when he announces he is coming back immediately for the *tangi*. Similarly, the usually stuffy Auntie Arihia is galvanised into energetic action, as Mere relates.

> She yelled out : Where's a knife, somebody give me a knife, I'll show you fullas how to peel spuds !......She kept everbody going, and she really ripped into some of the boys when she saw them being lazy. (pp. 128-9)

More important, perhaps, is the way Tama is made to participate in the actual burial. The custom of pall-bearing by the adult male bereaved is widespread in western culture, but this does not answer to the therapy of helping to dig the grave which Uncle Pita, the master of ceremonies, enforces on Tama. This provides the ultimate exposure to the fact of death which must be undergone before the regenerative emotions can reassert themselves.

> I begin to dig. Slowly at first. The clay has not been reached yet. My tears begin to fall, warm and scalding. For this is where father will lie. Here, in this cold earth. Here. And he will be gone forever. (p. 174)

This reaches the ultimate level of purgation. The remaining steps are the regenerative ones of receiving reminders of solidarity and support from the group, and the diffident assumption of the new role into which one must step as a result of the death—in Tama's case to become a Kauri to his family.

Beneath the working out of this grief exorcism lies Ihimaera's fundamental theme of the coadjunction of ends and beginnings. From the opening sentence, "This is where it ends and begins," to the final one, "It is a roar of pride, before the slow descending of the sun," he reminds us that each beginning is simply a termination seen from a different viewpoint. Moreover, with his constant stress on the communal rather than the individual, beginnings and endings lose even their partial identity and merge as simply points in the flux of existence. Human life and its termi-

nation in death bring us our most acute awareness of time, and in learning
to cope with death we learn to cope with time, in fact with existence.
Hence the pertinence of the creation myth to the story. The primal father
and mother, Sky and Earth, are conjoined in an ageless embrace while
their children crawl about them in darkness. Eventually they are forcefully separated by one of their sons, and light is let into the world marking
"the time of separation and the dawning of the first day." (p. 26) Separation, then, from the inception of time has been associated with hope and
with beginning. It is one of the fundamental rhythms to which we must
attune ourselves if we are to achieve happiness. And, says Ihimaera, the
Maori respects that rhythm in his code of family tutelage, "The oldest
always looks after the younger ones in the family."

The ritual of mourning, then, whether in the Maori or any other cooperative society, has a function which implies pattern or shape beneath
the endless repetition of traditional words and gestures. To some extent
these patterns translate into fiction, but much more is required of the
novelist if he is to avoid confusing or boring the reader. The real-life
tangi is a participatory ritual; a novelistic version must be a virtuoso performance.

The principal device which Ihimaera uses to shape the material is the
convenient one of the two journeys : the plane flight home on hearing the
news of his father's death, and the train journey back to Wellington after
the *tangi* to finalise his affairs there before returning to the farm,
and to the family, for good. The one journey shows his immediate
reaction, the other the later overview. These two journeys are detailed
in sections that alternate almost strictly (there are only three exceptions)
until right at the end of the novel when they fuse. The initial homeward
journey is grief-choked, terse, and suffused with a sense of disembodiment
and unreality. (An air journey seems a particularly appropriate vehicle
for this.) Tama is preoccupied with his grief, profoundly isolated from
his fellow-travellers, and subject to fragmentary invasions of memory.
Ironically he is seated next to a widow who is travelling to see her newly-
born first grandchild. There are few sustained flashbacks in these sections,
the thrust being to depict the immediate assimilation of grief through the
processes I suggested earlier.

Significantly the second journey is outward. Initially grief makes one
turn inwards, but the morning comes again. Consequently, even though
Tama's destiny is back with the family, Ihimaera shows the journey to
Wellington rather than the final one (presumably only a few days later)
back to Waithui. The weather on the plane flight has been sombre and
rainy except for the suspension above the clouds. Now the blue sky is
continually opening out as the train emerges from a valley or rounds a
mountain. The pace, appropriately, is more leisurely; the memories more
expansive and more ordered. Instead of the nightmare flashes, the whole
of the family's life—as itinerant workers, in town, on their own farm, in

town again for the children's education—is dealt with in order and at considerable length.   The irony of the plane travellers going to a birth and a death gives way to a generation parallel on the train when Tama sees in the young girl being farewelled by her Nanny, himself setting out for Wellington four years earlier, and knows that they have a common solace in the Maori family.

> Perhaps this girl will never see her Nanny again.   She will go to the city and enjoy life, forgetting about her Nanny.   Then maybe the telephone will ring or a telegram will come... Then she will know where her heart lies as I know where my heart will always be.   At Waituhi, my whanau. (p. 94)

This speculative parallel of himself with the young girl is only one of a number of parallels of character and incident with which the novel is structured.   Most of these are concerned with the idea of necessary separation.   The earlier death of his grandmother, Nanny Puti, foreshadows the death of his father, but so too do the incidents of his being lost—once in the city, a second time less painfully in the country.   As separation is inherent in life, not all of the examples are devastating, or even particularly painful.   The parting from the neighbour who wades across the river with the morning's baking, the daily separation when the father goes to work or the children to school, even the removal of the sleepy children to their own bed when the father returns late from work, all create a continuum of divisions which mitigates the sense that death. the ultimate parting, is a perverse obscenity in life.   Even the family's itinerant life, with its many partings and arrivals, while contrasting with Tama's aimless four years in the city reverberates with the overriding images of the two journeys to create a sense of solid purposiveness beneath the flux : "of pride before the slow descending of the sun."

I have suggested that Ihimaera exploits traditional material.   This is especially true of his images, and there seem to be only two in the whole novel which strike the reader as fresh and individualistic.   Both are recurrent and functional, and the more striking because of their solitary splendour.   The first of these is the image of the train window which Ihimaera uses like Alice's looking-glass.   It is at once a reflective glass in which Tama sees himself, the frame through which he sees life passing by him, the passageway into memories of the past, and finally it coalesces with the photograph of his father as a young man in which he sees himself and acknowledges his succession to the headship of the family.   The second is the compelling image of fingers grasping. In a book so concerned with partings and the way to accommodate them, the fingers mark the final point at which contact is relinquished.   They are tenuous but tenacious.   The motif is first used at Waithui station as the train leaves for Wellington, breaking the farewell grasp of Tama and his mother.   It takes on a natural, geographical note as the train leaves a gorge. "The valley widens, and with splayed fingers, takes one final grasp of the earth. The train roars past the fingertips into Nuhaka." (p.68) It stands for the intimidating power of the town over young Tama, which diminishes as he grows older and more confident.

> When I was a small boy it seemed very large. Its long main street intersected other streets which splayed out towards the sea and hills like long thin fingers. As I grew older however, Gisborne seemed to get smaller as if the fingers were curling slowly into the palm of the city. (p. 81)

Life, too, opens its fingers to Tama, but this is the false invitation of the aimless city. Finally the motif finds its appropriate place at the *tangi*, first with Wiki leaving scratches on the wood of the coffin, and then with the stubborn grief of Tama's mother at the moment of burial.

> He speaks to Mum. She shakes her head and clutches more tightly at father. Uncle Pita speaks to her again and holds her shoulders. My sisters too, they come to prise her away.
> Her fingers claw at the casket as she breaks her clasp.
> Her head arches back, her hands reach up to tear at the sun. (p. 186)

Ihimaera's prose style requires a study in itself which neither my competence nor your indulgence would permit here, but it is worth making two brief points. In the first place only a superb stylist could hope to suspend disbelief and maintain interest in such necessarily excessive and repetitive material, and Ihimaera is just that. Sometimes the prose imitates a child's enthusiasm and wonder : "And afterward, Dad even took us all to the pictures, even Mum. And at night time too !" (p. 83) Sometimes it is flat and fragmented to capture the disorientation of grief :

> I look ahead. The road curves round the bay. The car turns onto the highway leading to the airport. Far in the distance I see the runway. A plane is about to take off. It gathers speed, then lifts into the grey sky. There is a thunderous rumble as it passes overhead. (p. 63)

Sometimes it is formally and richly poetic :

> Your mother looks old in the light. Her eyes are red-rimmed with weeping. Her body is thin and wasted away with grief. But she is still beautiful. She is the Earth. Her hair is silver with the mists of the hills. Her eyes are like shimmering waterfalls. The contours of her face are the sculpted landscapes of earth. Her moods are the seasons. This is her winter unending, the most bitter season of all. (p. 152)

The second point I would make is the skill with which Ihimaera makes his transitions from one journey to the other and from the past to the present. Two children waving at a railway crossing take Tama back to his own childhood with his sister. The nervous plane passenger tells him casually that one soon gets over a bereavement and reprecipitates his struggle to control his grief. The schoolboy on the train taking off his cap reminds him of his own schooldays. His final return home will find his sister, Mere, waiting for him just as she was at Rongopai airport, and just as she was when he returned home from school each day. The transitions are carefully prepared and consumately executed.

Tangi is a pre-emptive novel. The material could be treated in this way only once, so it is especially gratifying that it has been done so well. While the translation into poetic English prose is Ihimaera's own, one never loses sight of the fact that this is a public ritual and that the novel imitates the patterns and functions of a real-life *tangi*. In its almost exclusive use of stock images, its constant, even daring repetitions, its incorporation of traditional song and its exploitation of mythology, it contradicts many of our expectations of the modern novel and forces us to rethink our definitions. Its sense of maturity is based upon a cooperative culture, but is conveyed through an individual consciousness. The result is extravagant but compelling.

Both Stow and Ihimaera have written what one might call non-processive novels. Ihimaera, certainly, is a recorder of a particular clearly-perceived culture which, like Wordsworth or Hardy or Achebe in their times and places, he wishes to preserve from oblivion, and whose values he wishes to assert. Stow seems to be writing a more personal recapitulation of childhood experience, and perhaps a self-justification of his voluntary exile. In neither case does one feel the sense of concerted enquiry that one does in Wendt's novel. Stow and Ihimaera profess certain values, Wendt (and his reader) discover them. This makes Wendt's novel a more difficult and demanding one, but implies as well an additional level of excitement.

Sons for the Return Home deals with the love affair between a young Samoan and a white New Zealand girl, his return to Samoa and ultimate rejection of his country. At first the girl makes all the advances and the protagonist is antipathetic. However her persistence eventually overcomes his reluctance, they commence an affair, carefully guide each other along the edges of their respective social circles, visit each other's homes, and pass an idyllic month touring the North Island of New Zealand during which she becomes pregnant. On their return they inexplicably separate for a couple of weeks until one night she summons him to a middle-class party where she tries to goad him into fighting a former boyfriend. He declines and leaves, she follows him out and after passionately pummelling him for a few seconds reiterates that she rejects her former circle for him, and reveals that she is pregnant. She declines his offer of marriage for fear that that would trap him into what might become a loveless marriage like her parents', and so although they both want to marry, she decides to go to Australia, think things over, have an abortion so there will be no hint of compulsion or possibility of later recrimination by him, and then come back and marry him. She does this but is overcome by guilt and does not return, saying that while she does love him intensely, to return would be to destroy him with her guilt. He is distraught, beats up the former boyfriend, and a little later finishes his studies and returns with his family to Samoa where he is unhappy both in the village and in Apia. On discovering that his mother had mischievously promoted the girl's abortion realising that this would alienate them rather than prepare for an unambiguous marriage as the girl expected, he feels the last tie with his family broken, and in an enigmatic final scene he returns to New Zealand, a more experienced and now totally detatched young man.

Just as Ihimaera used an individual consciousness to portray a collective ritual, so Wendt focuses on a single personality to present a theme which in part repudiates the importance of personality. The first indication the reader has of this tension is the anonymity of the characters who remain throughout "he", "the girl", "his mother" etc. Since the practice is awkward and risks confusion, one must ask what gains there are. Perhaps it is easier to deal with delicate autobiographical incidents in this way, but there is no reason to believe that Wendt is coy. On the other hand this is the saga of a family's outward voyage, conquering and triumphal return. The pattern is epic, and the anonymity accentuates this. For a similar purpose Patrick White suppresses the name of his character in the opening pages of *The Tree of Man*. But there is an important thematic reason too, for the persistent anonymity of these characters who in other respects are carefully detailed through action, dialogue and motive or obsession suggests a two-tiered view of human life which Wendt is exploring. Even as it reveals man's vulnerabilities, a psychological study necessarily implies the importance of individuals. The Polynesian view is less flattering to the single soul, for whereas there may be value in the collective, the individual is subsidiary. However, instead of praising the family as Ihimaera does, Wendt exploits the ironical tension which results from considering the individual simultaneously as a developing self-exploring consciousness and as an insignificant pawn of fate or chance. The coalescence of these two ideas produces the intellectual verdict that life is absurd, but for the Polynesian this does not destroy its positiveness, nor does it obviate the need to find a practical, individual attitude or stance. The coherence of one's stance to life can be termed maturity.

Like Stow's, Wendt's concept of maturity involves repudiation of land and family, and seizing upon lines like "this was now the only right way for him to break away from her and the safety of home and country, and

to be what he was," (p. 214) one could be forgiven for thinking their
ideas coincide. But in each case the repudiation is in response to more
profound problems. With Wendt's hero it is not the metaphysic of time,
but rather the range of forces—social, racial, familial and personal—
which retard one from achieving insightful honesty. Maturity for Wendt
involves courage, clear-sightedness, the ability to bear responsibility, and
the willingness to lend oneself freely to the chaotic rhythms of life. The
first three are active and invite a psychological portrayal. The last is a
wise passiveness much more difficult to portray in traditional ways, and
for this Wendt invokes Polynesian mythology.

Ken Arvidson has pointed out that the Polynesian god, Maui, seems
to provide the key to the novel.[2] He is mentioned in the final line and
has appeared throughout the story, being associated in particular with the
young man's assertion that Polynesian mythology is based upon the absurdity of life. (p. 99) Maui is the Polynesian version of Prometheus, the
dynamic underworld force and breaker of taboos, the irreverent yet
effective provider of fire, land and protracted daylight. His role in the
novel is to suggest a mischievous unorthodoxy associated with Wendt's
idea of maturity. This is apparent at a number of levels and can be
clearly seem if one opposes the lines of succession here and in *Tangi*. In
Tangi "the eldest son looks after the younger ones" and Tama is the
eldest son of Rongo who was also the eldest son. Wendt's hero by
contrast is the youngest son of a youngest son of a youngest son,
and the law of succession in this novel is accordingly different. "In
every generation it is always the youngest sons in our family who must
carry on... They have always proved the most gifted." (p.32-3) The hero is
a Maui figure, for Maui himself was a youngest son in whose informality
and unpredictability Wendt finds an image for the fluid and illogical
pattern of life. I'd like to quote from a folklorist to bring out this
underworld element in Maui. She is contrasting him with the much more
establishment god, Tahaki.

Maui is such a direct contrast to Tahaki that it seems as if the feeling
were, "Well, if I can't be as good as Tahaki, I'll be as bad as Maui."
Maui is essentially a hero of the Polynesian proletariat and the non-
conformists. He was the youngest of a large family of male children,
an ignominious position in Polynesian society. He defied an endless
number of taboos in a society in which the word taboo originated.
Maui who in defiance of gods and every obstacle stole fire for mankind
and raised the sky did more lasting good for mankind than Tahaki
who, with everyone's goodwill and assistance, simply conformed to
social standards.[3]

But Maui is as important for Wendt in his defeat as in his triumphs.
In achieving so much, but still ultimately defeated by death, Maui becomes

an emblem for foredoomed human aspiration which at first sight may not seem to differ greatly from that of Tamburlaine or Manfred. But there is an important difference of tone, a note of acceptance yet resilience and irreverence which is foreign to western culture. Maui combines the stature of Prometheus with the folksy mischief of Robin Hood, and this is what Wendt seeks to capture in his rendering of the story, and especially in that final line, "He imagined Maui to have been happy in his death." (p. 217)

Maui's career embodies both assertive and acquiescent aspects and thus serves as appropriate figure for the maturity to which the young man grows. This may not be immediately obvious since first and last we see him as an isolated figure, but there is a significant difference between the two states. At first he is defensively alone, refusing any contact except that of his family. Despite the cynical self-confidence he manifests on the football field, despite the defensive, clinical sexual experience he has had, despite his independence in choice of a course of study, he is still emotionally unformed and his stance of non-involvement is a negative defence. This stance is eroded by the marathon advances of the girl, and through her he comes to understand himself and New Zealand racial tensions more clearly. The increased insight does not, however, prevent him from acceding to the abortion which alienates him from the girl. When he returns to Samoa his *pakeha* experience prevents him from accepting the easy pre-eminence in which his mother glories. Nor does the town offer any sort of compromise because he is too aware of the hypocrisy and cultural debasement there. He has no alternative but to leave again, and the revelation of his mother's complicity in the abortion provides a convenient opportunity for him to ritually renounce home and family.

This renunciation is a more positive one than that in Stow's novel because it involves both the assertive and acquiescent elements. The gesture of renunciation was a "slap of his forgiving hand" (p.215). The myth of Maui too, although it enshrines the mystery of individual death, is given a positive rendering as if to spell out that even though life is contradictory and ambiguous it is still good and still demands acquiescence. Thus one version of the Maui story concludes :

And thus did the laughter of his companions at the last and most scandalous of his exploits deprive mankind of immortality. For Hine-nui always knew what Maui had it in mind to do to her. But she knew that it was best that man should die, and return to the darkness from which he comes, down that path which she made to Rarohenga.[4]

The young man, for all his apparent isolation and inactivity, is transformed by the end of the novel through losing not illusions (like Rob Coram) but intolerance and prejudices. At the most obvious level, the racial, he has become less aggressively antagonistic to the Maori and less passively or defensively antagonistic to the *pakeha*. To do this he had to free himself of the personal and racial mythology which often crops up in Wendt's fiction. These sectarian self-images are destructive to the individual not only because they are misleading in detail but because they seek to impose a pattern on life where none exists nor can exist. Personal or racial myths may have practical uses and applications in the short term but ultimately they imply a non-acquiescence with life. Other intolerances are less obvious : that against people in general, seen in his stance of non-involvement; that against the physical self seen in his sexual prudishness and jealousy; and ultimately intolerance of life itself in acceding to the abortion.

More interesting is the accession to courage by the young man. In his short stories Wendt seems to regard courage as the universal Samoan virtue, but there is a spectrum of courage. At one end is the physical courage demanded of Pili by his grandfather in the short story, ' Pint-Sized Devil on a Thoroughbred.'' After making Pili return day after day to a fight with an older boy until he wins, the grandfather explains :

> Victory is a matter of guts plus technique, but mainly guts. Fear is nothing. It's matter of working at it. Chipping it away until you're scared no more and your guts are the guts of a man.[5]

Somewhere in the middle of the spectrum is a combination of physical and psychical courage as in "A Cross of Soot." In this story Wendt shows a boy playing round a jail persuading one of the prisoners to tattoo a star on his hand. Only a cross has been completed when the prisoner is led away to be executed, something which is not referred to directly by the other prisoners, but which the boy intuits. The brave bearing of pain thus becomes associated with initiation into knowledgeable maturity, and when the boy returns home his mother is about to scold him but desists seeing a new awareness in his eyes. This coalescence of insight and courage reaches its fullest exploration in the ascetic view of the long story, "Flying-Fox in a Freedom Tree." The dying Flying-Fox describes a landscape he once saw which symbolises the rigorous perspicacity that metaphysical courage can attain, and which, I think, corresponds to the dispossessed suspension of the young man in *Sons*.

> You travel for miles through forest and so many villages where the people have ruined the beauty, and then... And then It is there. You feel you are right in it at last. Get me ? Like you are there where the peace lies, where all the dirty little places and lies and monuments we make to ourselves mean nothing because lava can be nothing else but lava...I felt like I had been searching for that all my miserable life. Boy, it made me see things so clear for once. That being a dwarf or a saint does not mean anything......That we are all equal in

silence, in the nothing, in lava.[6]

This universal *néant* which suppresses personality and the forces which form personality is of a different order from the wall of self-protective silence with which the hero surrounds himself for a good part of the book. The one is a denial of the processes of life, the other is an acceptance of them. The self-conquering demands insight and courage, and in the dispossession of what has formed and constrained us we witness to life. As the father puts it,

> We forget too easily what we are, and—most of all—the beauty we are capable of when we heal ourselves. There are no evil spirits or wrathful gods; we are, in the first instance, not victims of circumstance either. We are all equal in our affliction and our guilt. We secrete the poison of that affliction. (p. 208)

The individual, then has no one to blame, he is totally responsible. So many of the more overt concerns of the novel, sexual reticence and jealousy, parental imposition, racism, are distractions from a vital and positive self-acceptance. Self-acceptance involves a denial of the formed personality, just as Wendt's protagonist is denied a name. To win through to the emancipation the young man achieves, one needs to shed family, race, country, not just as security blankets as in Stow's novel, but at the more profound level of elements of the personality. Only then is one capable of that acquiescence in fate that could imagine "Maui to have been happy in his death." (p. 217)

Courage, then, is a major part of Wendt's concept of maturity. It is the elusive, vital courage that rejoices in personal responsibility, extirpates from the personality outside influences of all sorts, and above all adopts a wry fatalism which does not struggle querulously with what life offers. The conclusion to the novel is difficult because Wendt's concept is difficult rather than confused or vague. It is a demanding novel, at least for a western reader, simply because Wendt's theme has suggested a retreat from traditional characterisation and a much greater use of a mythological pattern. But it is in precisely this way that the English novel is enriched through contact with other cultures, so it is a demand that we are committed to meet.

Each of these novels is concerned with the passage from a naive to a mature attitude to life. The starting points of the protagonists are quite different, of course, as are the authors' ideas of in what exactly maturity consists. But even more interesting and important is the diversity of method and technique found in the three novels. This is Stow's most relaxed novel in which he all but abandons the symbolic stridence of the previous two, yet he has never written so physically, to present the world, or rather Rob's section of Australia, as a plethora of sounds and shapes and smells and scenes for animal action. Ihimaera fuses two radically different types of event, an individual literary creation and a collective ritual into a form which is as startling and individual as was *Tristram Shandy* or *Such is Life*. Wendt writes an intricate exploration of cross-cultural values drawing upon both Polynesia and the West for elements in his fictional method. It is, when you think about it, an extraordinary diversity. The English novel is alive and well, and living in the Antipodes.

REFERENCES

Page references of the novels discussed are to the following editions :

The Merry-go-Round in the Sea, Macdonald, 1964.

Tangi, Heinemann, 1973.

Sons for the Return Home, Longman Paul, 1973.

1. *Whanau*, Heinemann, 1974, p. 45.

2. *Landfall*, XXVIII, no. 3 (Sept. 1974), p. 259.

3. Katharine Luomala, "Notes on the Development of Polynesian Hero-Cycles", *Journal of the Polynesian Society*, vol. 49 (1940), p. 373.

4. Antony Alpers, *Maori Myths and Tribal Legends*, John Murray, 1964, p. 70.

5. *Flying-Fox in a Freedom Tree*, Longman Paul, 1974, p. 132.

6. *ibid.*

13

Towards Place and Placelessness: Two Journey Patterns in Commonwealth Literature

HELEN TIFFIN

As historical fact, empire creation and colonial settlement involved on the part of conquerors or settlers a journey with a beginning in the old world and an arrival in a new. The arrival in new worlds involved for settlers and conquerors a dislocation of geography, climate and race, and was usually primarily destructive of that new environment and its native inhabitants. The dream of empire, as opposed to the processes of its institution, was primarily strategic and economic, though not a few idealists saw it as the ultimate dream of union of far-flung places and peoples. This dream of empire contains the creative potential the historical fact denies—the perception of difference in race or geography more frequently led to the destructive imposition of an alien order on a subject people, than to the realisation of the dream of creative union. The operation of the concept of white destiny in Empire and Commonwealth was usually a destructive and divisive factor in the economic, social, and even metaphysical spheres. The potential for creative union inherent in race, religion and sex was discarded in favour of divisive imposition of the conquering white value system.

In this century in the literary as well as the political sphere, there has been a movement towards "decolonisation". And the process of decolonisation, as Frantz Fanon noted, is not exclusively social and political; it is, above all, spiritual. "Decolonisation is the veritable creation of new men.... the thing which has been colonised becomes man during the same process by which it frees itself."[1] Fanon is here stressing not just the spiritual implications, but the importance of the very process of achieving this end, rather than *arrival* at the state of "decolonisation". The journey itself is emancipation.

Commonwealth literature is a literature of former colonies. Like the original settlers and conquerors it did in its early stages look almost exclusively backward towards the homeland[2] in a desperate clinging to what was safe, known, and culturally sanctified. But with the rise of national feeling, the beginnings of "decolonisation" in Fanon's sense, colonial man, former agent of white European destiny, found that the colonial situation had foisted on him a twofold necessity—to reject what of his old tradition was inapplicable in the new environment, and, secondly, to arrive at some spiritual understanding of his new world by imaginative surrender to it. He must reject the historical past in favour of the geographical present. In so doing he often found himself in a "timeless" land, timeless because not of *his* historical traditional time, and terrifying in its vastness not just by an accident of British and new world geography, but also because of the vast spiritual and imaginative distances to be covered before his new land could be spiritually his "place."

In one sense, ex-colonial literatures have been involved in the potentially independent and divergent processes as specific self-definition and national (re)creation, but it is noteworthy that the very destructive and divisive forces of the *creation* of Empire have, in its historical demise, been those which give the emerging national literatures firm bases for creativity and thus comparable interests within a Commonwealth context. Not just the language, but the history has been imposed, and the destructive processes of that imposition, with the concomitant of linguistic union has issued in what are recognisably comparable "decolonisation" patterns in the literatures of Canada, the West Indies, Africa, India, Australia, the Pacific Islands.

One of the most frequent patterns is, not surprisingly, that of the journey of the former representative of white destiny through the vast new landscape with a native of that place. In the course of the journey the historical colonial pattern of destruction and division outlined above is usually reversed. The white parent or overlord is led like a child through the harshness and danger of the new environment, to gain no economic advantage whatsoever, to sometimes lose his own language and adopt that of his native companion, and to dispense with his own narrower Christian concepts in favour of those of the native companion (whose relationship to his gods is appropriately connected to this specific land) or an amalgam of all religions. The process of coming to spiritual terms with place is thus one of the systematic destruction of what is axiomatic to the concept of white destiny—the superiority of the white race, his right to land and people for economic gain, his imposition of his language, and an alien religion not nurtured in that soil and in that sky. The journey most frequently 'ends' ambiguously, with a tentative discovery of a new self, not as an assertive individual, but in a communal or collective way, involving a union with the land and its original inhabitants, and a rejection of former divine rights over it. Most frequently too, the cost is life. The price of this process of spiritual union or rebirth is appropriately death, but the death is creative, not destructive, in its issue. A rejection of the western notion of explanatory teleology of history in favour of the unthinking experiential present is usually implicit, and the journey is above all one from a destructive self-consciousness to a creative unselfconsciousness. To imaginatively accept and be accepted by the new environment, conquering or colonising man must arrive at the same unconscious spiritual union with it, that the evolution of centuries 'unconsciously' effected for the native inhabitant. Ideally, too, the creative potential of race, religion and sex is restored in one form or another in the course of such journeys, so that the original historical dream of unified 'empire' is resuscitated in the imaginative literature of an independent Commonwealth. Man is united with different men, with new land, with appropriately local gods.

John Buchan's last novel, *Sick Heart River*, is superficially an Empire or Commonwealth novel in the old sense. As latter day Empire builder and adventurer, and later Governor of Canada, Buchan was the tolerant British Empire idealist. *Sick Heart River* comes from a man unconsciously committed (albeit tolerantly) to racial, political and religious white destiny. While the novel seemingly upholds these values, the pattern of the narrative has elements of that later journey of decolonisation. Buchan's work provides an interesting starting point as it straddles the border between the novel of Empire adventure, and the journey of 'decolonisation' in Commonwealth literature.[3]

Sir Edward Leithen, on hearing that he is suffering from terminal tuberculosis, decides to "die standing as Vespasian said an emperor should" (23).[4] Ex-statesman, sportsman and Empire adventurer (always in the cause of right) he resolves to the last to "play up, play up and play the game," to die actively engaged in rescuing the underdog in a far-flung outpost of empire. This is his last 'show', and he remembers the other 'shows' of his life, those undertaken with Richard Hannay, Sir Archibald Roylance, and Lord Sandy Clanroyden. These familiar Buchan names, are, like many of the cliches Buchan uses, the hackneyed nomenclature of Empire, and the attitudes and language of Leithen in his recollections are similar.

> Leithen remembered Sandy's doings in South America; Blenkiron had been in that show, and he had heard about his being a sort of industrial dictator in Olifa, or whatever the place was called. (p. 24)

Sandy Clanroyden "had just been to Cambridge to talk to the Explorers' Club, and had come back with strong views about modern youth."(p.13). "Industrial dictator", "Whatever the place was called", "explorers club" —this is, one suspects, not just Leithen and Sandy, but Buchan, and it is certainly the Buchan of earlier works.

But this "show", Leithen's in *Sick Heart River*, is an altogether differ-

ent adventure from his former exploits or from those of Hannay in Africa
or the Scottish vales.   The trouble here is internal, imaginative, between
man and land and man and God, not the adventurous encounter between
man and man.   It is not "dirty work".   The trouble is in Galliard's own
mind (p.27). Thus Leithen moves from the external patterns of flight, pursuit and encounter in the service of divisive European values, to a journey
of the soul through the Canadian wilds in pursuit of a man whose own
problem is one of dislocation and dislodgment from land and from
God.   And as the journey continues into the Canadian heartland, the
external action, even as the physical rigours of the journey increase, becomes less important than the internal journey of the souls of the men
engaged in that journey.   But this soul-action is inevitably tied to the
specifics of the Canadian north, and the union or reunion of man's spirit
with that of the land.

From the Ravelston dinner in all its titled and commercial splendour,
Leithen travels to "the borderline between the prosaic world, and the
world as God first made it out of chaos" (p. 66).   Out of the world of
ordered Empire he is plunged into a "horrid lushness—an infinity of mire
and coarse vegetation and a superfluity of obscene insect life" (p. 85).
The world he finds is "timeless", "colourless", and "formless", a kind of
placeless eternity in which man seems utterly lost. This dislocation of the
old order is Leithen's first step towards a real spiritual place in this place-
lessness, the 'recipe' for which is stated by Father Duplesis early in the
novel.   For Leithen and Galliard, however, there is a long way still to
go and a series of quite deceptive points of arrival.

Like the Mounties, Leithen finds his man, but seeing the valley of the
Sick Heart River he fells th t "This....feat obscured the fact that he had...
found Galliard, for setting out on one task he had incidentally accomplished a greater" (p. 162).   His name as an explorer of Empire will be
memorialised.   But it is a false goal and a false boast.   The valley is life-
less; closed, muffled, immured.   There is no breath of wind, and with
the exception of the demented Lew, no living creature to be found.

Nearly all was subfusc, monochrome, and yet so exquisite was the
modelling that there was nothing bleak in it; the impression rather was
of a chaste, docile luxuriance. The valley bottom, so far as he could see
it, seemed to be as an orderly garden. The Sick Heart was like a Highland salmon river, looping itself among pools and streams with wide
beaches of pebbles, beaches not black like the enclosing cliffs, but shining white.   Along its course, and between the woods, were meadows of
wild hay, now a pale russet against the ripple of the stream. (p.160)
and,

Here, in this fantastic sanctuary was nothing of North America. Apart
from the sheer containing walls, the scene might have been a North-

umbrian pasture in an English December.   (p. 169)

The Sick Heart is not the river of life, but the stagnant and sterile river of death, for it represents an alien English idyll, as well as the green and pleasant Christian promise.   It is not of the Canadian north, the spiritual and physical reality of ice and snow, hardship and conifers.[5] It represents the old world from which new world man must turn if he is ever to come to terms with his new environment and with himself. Return to the green and pleasant is a creative dead end.   Rebirth and union and reunion in the Canadian situation can only be worked out in direct confrontation between man and the rigours of the north, an exercise not just of endurance and geography, but of colonial spiritual necessity. There is, as Lew says, "no chance of salvation if you die in this cursed hole" (p. 187).

Leithen, leaving the valley, has still the ultimate discovery to make. Earlier in the novel Father Duplesis was asked, "Don't you feel crushed by this vastness ?" "No", he replies, "because I live in a little world. I'm always busy among little things." (p. 103) The north, which dwarfs humanity, also magnifies it. (p. 204)   At first it is the dwarfing, the pettiness of it all that worries Leithen :

> In coming into the wilderness he had found not the majesty of Nature, but the trivial, the infinitely small—an illiterate half-breed, a rabble of degenerate Indians, a priest with the mind of a child.   The pettiness culminated in the chapel, which was as garish as a Noah's Ark from a cheap toyshop. (p. 113)

But even in these early stages he dimly perceives the principle of ultimate union which the north demands :

> He had been right in doing as he had done, coming out to meet death in a world where death and life were colleagues and not foes. He felt that in this strange place he was passing, while still in time, inside the bounds of eternity. He was learning to know himself. (p. 117)

Though he later feels this union represents a falsity against which he must pit his remaining strength, he nevertheless finds his "salvation" in a familial union with the Hares, the "rabble of degenerate Indians", and the priest with "the mind of a child". He has found the balance between the infinite inanity of the Northern Canadian vastness and the apparent trivial inanity of the insignificant human life which peoples it.

The great white explorer-father, (and he remains to the end something of this), has however been with his native guides, the Frizelles, through the ritual of decolonisation and subsequent rebirth. He has given up fame and destiny to help save the lives of the native inhabitants of the north, and come to adopt them as his family.   This is of course the ideal metaphor for the old ideal of Empire, and it is on this level that much of the novel operates. The independent intrepid self-sufficient Englishman adopts his weaker brethren as his children, the world-family.

But, just as Fanon stressed *process* rather than arrival in the politics of "decolonisation", so here too in the structure of the novel it is process or journey that is of prime importance. And during this journey Leithen is led "like a child" through a novel landscape of barren terror by the two half-breed guides, Lew and Johnny Frizelle. During the journey, that archetypal colonial quest through the new landscape of the mind for place and thus spiritual peace, Leithen rejects the past (the English countryside, and finally his old notion of the prime importance of the European war) and squarely faces the new, balancing perfectly geography and native inhabitants, working out in his own journey and in his last task of understanding, that most important native balance of the Canadian north—the spiritual magnitude of the physically small. Though Lew and Johnnie lead Leithen on his journey, they too must participate to some extent in the ritual initiation the north demands. They are after all only *half*-breeds, not natives. While Leithen and Galliard struggle towards Sick Heart River, Lew and Johnnie find that section of the journey easy. But Lew has trouble climbing out of the Sick Heart Canyon, and only then can the brothers Frizelle help in the rehabilitation of the Hares, their poll tax as half-breeds to full spiritual placement in their familiar wilds. Leithen, from whom the Voss-like payment of life itself for this understanding and reconciliation has been demanded, dies in early spring, but his own rebirth into understanding of and union with the Canadian environment has been assured, more in the ritual processes of the journey than in the Christian platitudes of his eulogisers.

Galliard's quest is, apparently, a very different one from Leithen's. His is that of the urban sophisticate, who having rejected his true origins, finds in middle age that he must return for penitence and reconciliation with his "native" land. But on both quests the protagonists of alien ancestry, if not alien birth, are led into the wilderness separately by the two half-breed brothers. The blood tie between Lew and Johnnie emphasises the spiritual link between Galliard's quest and Leithen's. Both men become "children", Galliard even more so than Leithen, as their journeys progress, and both find their salvation in the north with the Hares, via the false goal of the Sick Heart. Reunited with his wife at the end of the novel, Galliard is asked of the north, which he came to find, and which almost killed him,

"You don't fear it any more ?"

"No. It has become part of me, as close to me as my skin. I love it. It is myself." (p. 316)

Reunion is Galliard's fate—union with the community of the Canadian north and its inhabitants is Leithen's reward.

> Each....now held at last in his arms what he had been forever seeking
> and what he had eternally possessed.[7]

But only by the rejection of material possession, and of the attributes of white destiny can coloniser or conqueror spiritually possess the new land.

Leithen's journey began as a self-centred idea of "making his soul" by dying standing.   It ends in a spiritual union with a native tribe of northern Canada.   Heriot's journey in Randolph Stow's *To the Islands* seemingly begins as a journey of individual expiation in atonement for a three-fold human guilt, but it ends with Heriot's fitful understanding of the inapplicability of such concepts as guilt and atonement in the Australian desert setting.   In *To the Islands*, the figure of old-style Empire-white destiny is Heriot, who undertakes, with a native interpreter-guide, Justin, a journey towards a qualified salvation of soul, arrived at through a coming to terms with place, with the native people of that place, and in particular with their aboriginal metaphysic of existence.   Though this journey might be seen as one of expiation, it is instead a rejection of expiation as irrelevant once the nature of man-man, man-land, and man-god relationships have been understood.

Heriot has all his life been obsessed by two things : the notion of guilt, generally human and racially specific, and the fear of being deceived. But it is in his previous attempts at expiation for this guilt that he has been repeatedly deceived. By the time he begins his desert flight and pilgrimage in *To the Islands* he is running from a three-pronged guilt : the guilt of having been born at all; the racial-historical-colonial guilt for the massacre at Onmalmeri, and his personal guilt over his attempted "murder" of Rex. To atone for the guilt of birth itself, Heriot had become a missionary and was deceived into believing that his service in this field would also atone for the colonial-race guilt of the Onmalmeri massacre.   Instead, his career led him into the perpetration of a more horrifying, because more personal, re-enactment of the first murder, ("brother" against "brother") and of the colonial historical crime, when he throws the stone at Rex.   Once again he has been deceived, as his missionary life of atonement has only led him to a personal recommission of the crime.

Heriot flees with the rather fuzzy hope that in his wild pilgrimage through the desert he may actually atone at last for all these crimes and reach the aboriginal islands of the dead.   But his journey with his native "good deeds" Justin, is an atonement of a different kind.   The peace he makes with the land and with his aboriginal brothers is one of the communal geographical attunement, not atonement. What Justin teaches Heriot, as he leads him, (and again the white father is led like a child by the native guide), is that his guilt-ridden soul is still inapplicably European.

The aborigines (and particularly Justin) teach the former mission director that guilt is a man-centred European concept which finds no place in aboriginal life and lore. Heriot must consciously re-learn, ancestrally speaking, the unselfconscious attunement to the land and its ways by which Justin and the other aboriginals live.

"I want to give myself to the country," (p. 107)[8] Heriot declares, and "I'm exploring." But initially he is too steeped in the attitudes and traditions of the past to do anything as spiritually exploratory as surrendering to the country. There are the old lessons to be discarded, and the new to be slowly learnt. Thus, aboriginal chants and words gradually replace the *Lyke Wake Dirge*, and the linguistic bric-a-brac of the European past. The symbol of white authority, the gun, struggled over by Heriot and Justin, is finally relinquished to the native. The past is left behind, the present reigns. Like Leithen, Heriot is a dying man, "willing to be managed by Justin for the rest of his life." (p. 89) And like Leithen too, he is subject to extreme changes of mood in attitude to the journey itself, to the native people and to the land. It is all a necessary part of the discarding of the past in a new and alien environment. Even Gunn who searches for Heriot feels "freed of the past and future" as he travels into "the strange country of austerity and luxuriance" (p. 145). Dixon searching for Heriot at Onmalmeri (a wrong choice because this is not a journey of atonement), sees himself for the first time as

> a stranger, cast without preparation into a landscape of prehistory, foreign to the earth. Only the brown man belonged in this wild and towering world. (p. 100)

Only Heriot embarks fully on this pilgrimage of place which will lead him beyond the extremes of mood and perception, (austerity and luxuriance, death and life, crime and guilt) to a unified vision of the process of the world. It is interesting to note here that Leithen in *Sick Heart River* describes the very different Canadian landscape in comparable terms. While nothing would seem more removed from the snowy slopes of northern Canada than the West Australian desert, it is the common condition of the perception of the land by the Europeans in terms of divisive extremes which unites the two. And the movement in both novels is towards the reconciliation of the divisive extremes of European perception through the journey with the native interpreter guide.

As well as discarding the past and its values, Heriot must learn from Justin, the land, and the bush people a metaphysic of existence to replace the one he is haltingly discarding. The two major lessons Heriot learns from his companion are the acceptance of killing (and thus of death) that is necessarily involved in the 'journey' of life; and a sense of true community with the aboriginal people he has for too long "ruled" without really loving.

Seeing in the natural world a malice which he believes to be the way of the universe, Heriot sympathises with dingoes because he felt "they lamented their dingohood as he is humanity." (p. 173) It follows from this attitude that he senses deliberate malice in the hovering hawks :

> 'What are they doing ?' he asked, suddenly frightened and old.
> 'They just looking at us. They not cheeky.'
> 'Why are they following me ?'
> 'They follow anyone, old man.'
> 'No', Heriot said shakily, 'they're following me, they're waiting for me to die.' He screamed at the hawks : 'Get away, you filthy vultures, go on ! I'm not going to die !' But they wheeled still.
>
> 'Don't look at them,' Justin advised, 'they go away soon, they got their own countries.'
>
> 'Shoot them,' Heriot commanded. 'Where's the rifle ? Give it to me   Why are they watching me ?'
> 'They all right, old man.'
>
> 'Filthy birds ! Look at them,' Heriot raged, 'watching me. They're going to follow us, all the way. Why don't you shoot them, damn you ?'
> 'They always around,' Justin said. (p. 117)

The attitudes are extreme because they attribute the self-conscious motivation of man to the natural world. It is in Justin's attitude to this world and to the necessity of killing that Heriot begins to sense some wisdom. After Justin kills the goose, Heriot

> saw with ineffable sadness the claws of the brilliant yellow legs bent like dying hands, the perfect and ingenious groovings on the edges of the beak. 'That was pretty,' he said, 'and happy.'
>
> Justin fondled it, tender and proud. 'Good little geese,' he said with affection. 'You was pretty fella, eh ? Poor old geese.'
>
> 'You love the things you kill,' Heriot said, 'but you never regret killing them. I've noticed that always about you people, how you love your prey. There's some wisdom there.'
> 'They pretty,' Justin said. (pp. 171-72)

Just as Heriot must learn that the natural world does not operate in human terms, he must also retrieve his own humanity from the destructive ruins of Empire-colonisation and white destiny. Still wanting gratitude, because he is accustomed to the role of ruler, arbiter and gift giver, he at first offers friendship, and then despises the bush woman when he does not receive the expected gratitude for his profer of friendship :

'I am one of you,' he said. *'Ngaia bendjin.'*

But she understood neither language, and did not look at him.

'I am your friend,' he said.

She reached out to touch her dog, which was growling, but did not move her head.

'Ah, you thing,' he said resentfully, 'you thing of dirt and wrinkles and pubic hair.' (p. 128)

Heriot is obviously not "one of them", but in sudden recognition of her blindness, his human compassion completely overcomes the divisive and destructive leftovers of white destiny, and in feeding her, he does become for the first time "one" with the bush people, "naked brown woman by naked white man." (p. 128)

The two lessons Heriot has learned from Justin, the inevitability of killing, with love rather than guilt or in anger, and his sense of real community with the land and its people meet in this spiritual reconciliation with Rex. Heriot has in one sense loved the Rex whom he attempted to kill, but the nature of white Christian guilt has made it impossible for Heriot to connect the two—love and killing—before his "lesson" from Justin. And Heriot's dream after feeding the old woman presages his eventual vision in the cave of aboriginal bones. The dream is one of pursuit, surrender, and hence resolution of extremes and polarities :

...his strength was gone and there could be no more climbing, he could only cling and pray as the breakers rose towards his feet.

The sun blinded with the spray of them, time died, there was nothing but the light and the agony of waiting.

Now I become nothing, whispered Heriot, now and forever, for ever and ever, I am no more. He closed his eyes, waiting, clinging to the rock. No more, no more.

Then the intolerable sweetness washed over him. His hands slackened as he cried out, in astonishment and joy.

I am all light, cried Heriot, I am torn, I am torn apart, all light, all glorious light.

All elements and colours in him were resolved, each to return to its source below the enormous swell. (p. 132)

While his claim earlier in the novel "No more white man. I am a blackfellow, son of the sun" (p. 116) is premature, he nevertheless approaches at the end, if not absolutely achieves, in the aboriginal/death cave by the sea, the partial apotheosis prefigured in the dream. The "victory" as in *Sick Heart River* is in a minor key and ambiguous as well; but it is nevertheless a triumph of child over man, of the unselfconscious over the self-conscious, of native over the stranger, of the spiritual over the material, and the community (with land and man) over the individual; the present over past and future.

It is significant that Heriot is a missionary, for the role played by the Christian religion in the disjunction between man and man, and man and land was no mean one in colonial areas. As well as unlearning the inapplicable European traditions in this now inappropriate landscape, Heriot unlearns his Christian concepts (so man- and guilt-centred) in favour of the cave of skulls and the possibility of the Islands. Leithen and Galliard gave up their heroic and commercial role, to achieve comparable results as, like Heriot, they were led away from the divisive aspects of the colonial past to confrontation with the communal present of the new land. The symbols of authority are discarded and the child-European is re-educated by the interpreter guide into a sense of communal timelessness where the divisive forces of Empire building are annihilated.

In his 1973 introduction to *The Whole Armour* and *The Secret Ladder*, Wilson Harris writes that vision is

> a capacity to re-sense or rediscover a scale of community.
>
> That scale, I would think, needs to relate itself afresh to "monsters" which have been constellated in the cradle of a civilisation—projected outwards from the nursery or cradle thus promoting a polarisation, the threat of ceaseless conflict and the necessity for a self-defensive apparatus against the world *out there*.
>
> In some degree, therefore, we need to retrieve or bring those "monsters" back into ourselves as native to psyche, native to a quest for unity through contrasting elements, through the ceaseless tasks of the creative imagination to digest and liberate contrasting spaces rather than succumb to implacable polarisations.
>
> Such retrieval is vision.[9]   (p. 8)

Harris is thus consciously concerned with what I've called the "decolonisation" process leading to retrieval of community suggested as central to *To the Islands* and *Sick Heart River*.

In *Palace of the Peacock*, Donne and his crew literally re-enact the exploitative colonial voyage of an earlier crew drowned in the rapids, and now revived "to a man" to retrace the stages of that journey. The seven days of their "historical" journey are also symbolically the seven days of creation, or more accurately, *re*creation. Donne, slaver and 'Empire builder', concerned solely with economic advantage and self-interest, is forced into forcing the Arawak woman to accompany his crew as guide to the Mariella-El Dorado they are seeking. The Arawak woman is herself the Mariella for which they are searching, both El Dorado. and the

Guyanese spirit of place.

Progressively, the destructive and divisive barriers of colonial-conquest legacy between native and European are broken down :

> Her race was a vanishing one overpowered by the fantasy of a Catholic as well as a Protestant invasion. This cross she had forgiven and forgotten in an earlier dream of distant centuries and a returning to the Siberian unconscious pilgrimage in the straits where life had possessed and abandoned at the same time the apprehension of a facile beginning and ending. An unearthly pointlessness was her true manner, an all-inclusive manner that still contrived to be—as a duck sheds water from its wings—the negation of every threat of conquest and of fear—every shade of persecution wherein was drawn and mingled the pursued and the pursuer alike, separate and yet one and the same person. It was a vanishing and yet a starting race in which long eternal malice and wrinkled self-defence and the cruel pursuit of the folk were turning into universal protection and intuition and that harmonious rounded miracle of spirit which the world of appearances had never truly known.[10] (p. 72)

With this increasing blurring of all boundaries of even time and space, the crew find themselves becoming a part of the unconscious unifying and communal tendency of the universe.

On the final day of creation the metamorphosis is complete—an alchemy of soul has made European intruder one with God, man and the land through the journey with the interpreter guide. It is important too to note that the central point of view in the novel, originally divided into the narrator and the character of Donne, has now become one. The narrator represents Donne's spiritual potential, long shackled by the greed for gain uppermost in his character at the outset of the journey. But after the seven days of recreation with the reversal of the conquering processes of white destiny, the two are reunited with the spiritual side triumphant.

Harris uses images of metamorphosis and alchemy to underline the inevitable nature of the journey. The base metals of Donne's original purpose are transformed into the gold of communal soul through the alchemy of the journey upriver with the Arawak woman. It is significant that this journey is by river, in contrast to Heriot's and Leithen's which were overland, and that the interpreter guide in this case is a woman. As well as lending itself more appropriately to ideas of alchemy and metamorphosis, the river with its own directional flow, its rapids and currents expresses the inevitable nature and outcome of the quest. While Donne, the acme of white destiny, pursues the folk for his own economic ends, he is not only forced to be led by them and be pursued by them, but is inevitably carried away from his original economic goal towards his spiritual arrival at the palace of the peacock. And the Arawak woman who guides him and his crew is agent, end, and process, of their destiny.

Palace of the Peacock introduces, and Harris' later works continue to explore in more detail, the connection between sex and the destructive force of Empire. Mariella (who is both place and person) has been ill-treated by Donne, and bears the marks of his abuse. Nonetheless, it is Mariella who leads Donne to the carpenter's room where he sees a woman with a child at her knee—the nativity image of the recreation, this time in positive terms, of the creative sexual potential inherent in the old historical situation :

> The room was as simple as the carpenter's room. Indeed as he looked he could not help reflecting it was simpler still. Bare, unfurnished, save for a crib in a stall that might have been an animal's trough. Yet it all looked so remarkable—every thread and straw on the ground, the merest touch in the woman's smile and dress—that the light of the room turned into the wealth of dreams.
>
> The woman was dressed in a long sweeping garment belonging to a far and distant age. She wore it so absent-mindedly and naturally however that one could not help being a little puzzled by it. The truth was it was threadbare. One felt that a false move from her would bring it tumbling to the ground. When she walked however it still remained on her back as if it was made of the lightest shrug of her shoulders—all threads of light and fabric from the thinnest strongest source of all beginning and undying end.
>
> The whole room reflected this threadbare glistening garment. The insubstantial straw in the cradle, the skeleton line of boards made into an animal's trough, the gleaming outline of the floor and the wall, and the shift the child wore standing against the woman's knee—all were drawn with such slenderness and everlasting impulse one knew it was richer than all the images of seduction combined to the treasuries of the east. Nothing could match this spirit of warmth and existence. Staring into the room—willing to be blinded—he suddenly saw what he had missed before. (pp. 138-139)

Just as Donne's whole destructive quest is also a potentially creative one, so even the sexual abuse of Mariella contains the creative potential for a fulfilling love. Sex (like the Christian religion) contains the potential for true communion, and the exciting promise of sexual love and nativity is conveyed in this passage through images associated with the historically divisive but potentially creative and unifying Christian religion.

Again, then, we have the representative of white destiny, the interloper, led on a quest into the heartland of a new world by an interpreter guide. Again it is a quest which begins as one thing and inevitably ends as something else. Donne's initial quest for a material El Dorado is metamorphosed into one for a spiritual El Dorado before he is aware of the change. Significantly, all three quests end with a rejection of historical time in favour of an eternal present, and all end with a conscious or unconscious unity established between interloper and native. "Implacable polarisations" have, in Harris' words, been transformed into "rediscovery of community" in a timeless world. To achieve this, Harris stated, it was necessary to "retrieve or bring these monsters back into ourselves as native to psyche." Buchan did not really face these "monsters" squarely—he still saw what Harris would regard as the divisive monsters of history as triumphs of Empire, but he did, nevertheless, have his hero embark on a "rediscovery of community" with concomitant abnegation of implacable polarisations. Stow looked generally at the monsters, and at the difference between true creative rediscovery of community and guilt-ridden atonement for crime. Harris deals directly and symbolically with the economic and sexual historical monsters, and, like Buchan and Stow, has the implacable polarisations transformed into a world *without* history, a timeless eternity of community.

Albert Wendt in *Sons for the Return Home* depicts a different kind of "Commonwealth journey" with the native. I began by talking of the ideal of community inherent in the idea of Empire, and conversely,"the monster polarisations" of historical Empire. I then examined how, in Commonwealth Literature, the historically divisive steps were imaginatively re-examined and redrawn, as the white interloper journeyed through the new landscape with a native of place. In such a way the self-styled arbiter of world destiny was reduced to the status of a child, and re-educated by a native companion to a stance more appropriate to the spirits of the new place. This achieved state in the Australian, Canadian, and West Indian instances was, broadly, one of community and timelessness.

But there are several other kinds of journeys implicit in the Commonwealth-Empire experience and apparent in the Commonwealth Literary traditions. After the racial and geographical dislocations incurred in the slave and indentured labour experience, many Africans and West Indians journey not to find a home through coming to terms with the spirit of a new place, but attempt to recapture that lost and fractured past by returning to India or Africa, and such journeys have found their imaginative expression in the literature.

But in this century there has been another interesting journey, frequently undertaken, and quite pervasive in the various literary traditions. This is also a journey, apparently also backwards, to the imaginative homeland, most frequently, of course, to England. West Indian, African, Indian, Canadian, New Zealand and Australian writers have written of the hopes, disillusionments and qualified successes involved in this journey. The interpreter guide has appeared less frequently in such journeys, because it would seem, the colonial 'returning' to his imaginative homeland does not as frequently lack the spiritual sense of place that empire-builders going out to foreign countries did. The colonial who makes this pilgrimage to Britain brings to that 'home' a concept, deeply rooted, and tragically false, of the spirit of that place. Spiritual initiation here is most frequently replaced by the rigours of adjustment to a painful economic and social reality. But even where disillusionment is the result of such a journey, perpetual exile is often implicit. The colonial, finding too many (however unsatisfactory) homes, finds himself at home in none.

When the unnamed hero of *Sons for the Return Home* journeys with a white 'native' New Zealander, (and she is 'native' only in the sense that the spiritual metamorphoses involved in the journeys undertaken by Leithen, Heriot and Donne may now be taken for granted) through the New Zealand landscape, he undergoes an initiation that relates him, through the girl, to the New Zealand white and Maori community, and to the land itself. But this time it is an initiation which results not in his unity with a communal timelessness, but in his confirmation as a homeless exile.

Sons for the Return Home is, in many ways, a novel about rituals and their meaning, both Samoan and European, but the one most significant for the hero is that ritual of initiation into the New Zealand environment undertaken in the form of a journey. It is this more than anything else that cuts him off from unselfconscious response to the Samoan community, and which leads to his eventual loneliness and exile.

The protagonist's[11] initial dislike of white and Maori New Zealanders is gradually eroded in his growing relationship with the girl. But as yet he feels nothing for the country itself, and is divorced socially from its native Maori inhabitants. As a child he was brought from Samoa to New Zealand by his parents, a journey in search of a sort of portable El Dorado. With the gold New Zealand will provide, they will return to the fa'a Samoa, the Samoan way of life, with a much improved social standing. From the outset then, the protagonist's life has been dislocated, and he has been left without a home. His parents try to remedy this deficiency by constantly reminding him of the paradisal ways of home : yet it is only the ritual of the pig-killing that he really remembers. As far as memory is concerned then, the beginning of his life, or, at least his memory of it, is involved with the experience of death.

Both birth and death are the significant features of the journey the hero makes with the girl. It is presumably on this journey that she becomes pregnant, and it is during the journey too that she angers him by shooting the hawk :

> This was the first live hawk he had seen, and he was beginning to comprehend the beauty of fear, the awesome depth of freedom. Poised in the sky, the hawk seemed to be holding up the earth. The silence trembled as it dropped lower, stopped, lowered again... Perhaps to the Maoris the hawk had been a god, he thought. Then he remembered that the hawk had come with the pakeha.

The rifle shot severed the silence which held the hawk and the hills together, and echoed across the sky. He scrambled to his feet. For a hopeful instant he thought the hawk would continue to balance the earth on its delicate axis, but it folded and plummeted, like a fist, down from the sky into the gully.[12] (p. 94)

Potentially creative acts and images in the novel all have their destructive counterparts. The new life created for him by the girl and with the girl is destroyed by her. The abortion is a cutting off of the freedom into which he and the girl have been liberated by their sexuality. The assertive sexuality in the novel is presented as a deliberate break with the missionary and W.A.S.P. past, but the real creative union it promises is aborted by the Samoan-Christian past through the influence of the mother, who is determined that her sons return home.

But this return, too, is aborted for the protagonist in his inability now to relate to the fa'a Samoa. Self-consciously he sees it as a falsely seductive facade too long fostered in his imagination by his parents. The plane has

disgorged him on the shores of a country real only in myth or fairy tale or dream. Beyond the airstrip, reminiscent of backdrops in a Technicolor movie of the South Seas, palm trees rolled up to the foothills. (p. 171)

Not only is the landscape a Hollywood construct, but the promised communal reunion is aborted. He cannot uncritically and unselfconsciously bask in the glory of his relatives' eternal present. In the end he returns to New Zealand, a lonely exile.

Sons for the Return Home, with its celebration of the creative joy of sexual union, its undercutting of the economic value orientation of the older generation, its attack on the Christian church (it is in the ugly church in the heart of Wellington that the girl tells him she is going to have the abortion); its creative ritual of initiation (closely associated with ideas of freedom and death) follows something of the imaginative pattern of Buchan's, Stow's and Harris' works. But images of cruxifixion and abortion pervade the novel, and while in one sense the creative potential of the present is seen as having been aborted by the past—Harris too stresses the need for liberation from history before man can be creative in the eternal present—there is contained in *Sons for the Return Home* the continuing Commonwealth and world problem of the international experience. The journey is one of birth for the protagonist into the New Zealand landscape, but it is this central part of his New Zealand experience that divorces him from his original homeland—it is death to the fa'a Samoa and only abortive birth into the New Zealand world.

What Wendt seems to be saying is that the process of initiation in the journey with the native inhabitant, so potentially creative, is also potentially destructive. For the coloniser, the experience of initiation gave him spiritual and imaginative footing in his adopted land, but for the colonised or the transplanted, the dream of that homeland of promise across the sea exercised a destructive social, imaginative, and economic pull away from his original homeland or the land of his enforced adoption. While "decolonisation" then reversed the movement of the historical monsters of empire, it could not fully erode the imaginative pull of the land of white colonisers. The moment of perfect free balance between any two worlds is a tragically short one. Man plummets to earth to find that neither the sky nor the earth is really his. In adopting the new, he loses the old, and his fate is, like that of Naipaul's protagonists in *In a Free State*, the condition of perpetual exile. In the "global village" of the twentieth century, this is increasingly becoming not just a problem for colonial man, but for the world generally.

Obviously I have not had time to begin to do justice to these four works. I have tried rather to examine briefly two patterns of the journey with the native that I feel provide a very valid basis for comparative study. The first pattern has been noticeably pervasive in Commonwealth literature in the past; the second will probably become increasingly so in the future. Both however involve the same elements of the journey of the "interloping" protagonist with a native inhabitant to reach the spirit of place, usually through a reactivated sense of community in a timeless landscape. Where the creative side of this process is aborted as in the second type of journey, the protagonist is left in a state of terrifyingly timeless and placeless exile. Both are two sides of the same "decolonisation" coin of Empire.

REFERENCES

1. Fanon, Frantz, *The Wretched of the Earth*, London, Macgibbon & Kee, 1965, pp. 29-30.

2. This is particularly true of some early Australian and early Canadian literature, and for that matter, that other colonial literature, American literature. Where it is not true, a deliberate act of rebellion is involved, as in the Australian convict ballad.

3. This pattern is also a typically Canadian one. There is always the temptation of the green and pleasant which must be rejected in favour of the rigorous confrontation with the extremes of the Canadian climate.

4. Buchan, John, *Sick Heart River*, London, Hodder & Stoughton, 1945. Following page references are to this edition.

5. In Raddall's *The Nymph and the Lamp*, the extreme environment, Sable Island, is a very different one. But the pattern of the narrative which involves a reconciliation with these extremes, and the rejection of the green Annapolis Valley for them is very similar.

6. It is interesting that Leithen's 'condition' has been exacerbated, if not actually caused by his experience in the European war.

7. Harris, Wilson, *Palace of the Peacock*, London, Faber & Faber, 1960, pp. 152·

8. Stow, Randolph, *To the Islands*, Harmondsworth, Penguin, 1962. Following page references are to this edition.

9. Harris, Wilson, *The Whole Armour* and *The Secret Ladder*, London, Faber & Faber 1973, p. 8·

10. Harris, Wilson, *Palace of the Peacock*. Following page references are to the 1960 edition·

11. Wendt makes life difficult for the critic by referring to his hero throughout as "he", and to the girl as, simply, "the girl". While he is dealing then with community minorities (even the girl is a minority in the 'establishment' society represented by her father) he thus gives his central characters and their fate a general application.

12. Wendt, Albert, *Sons for the Return Home*, Auckland, Longman Paul, 1975. Following page references are to this edition.

14

Mosaic and Monolith :
A comparison of Canadian and Australian
poetic responses to the Great Depression

LEE B. THOMPSON

IN researching the topic of 1930s Canadian poetry, I once came upon a *Canadian Forum* editorial which berated Canadians for self-pity and exhorted them to consider themselves lucky in comparison with the sufferings of their Commonwealth sisters—particularly Australia. There was no time then for more than a mental note, but I later returned to the material, curious about how Canadian and Australian poets compared and differed in their response to this phenomenon known as the Great Depression.

Certainly there were numerous factors to support the expectation that the Canadian and Australian poetic response, of whatever sort, would be similar. First, there was the Commonwealth link, involving not only parallel experience in colonialism (including the famous Colonial Cringe) but also a shared mother country and traditions. Both countries knew the pains and voiced the laments of emigration and exile, the rigours of a fresh start in a seemingly "empty", gigantic, and frequently forbidding land. As well, Canada and Australia have literary histories coincident in many respects. Dr John Matthews's comparative study of the nineteenth century has brought forth illuminating comparisons,[1] concluding with the comparable literary nationalism of the late decades (the Confederation poets in Canada; O'Dowd, Lawson, the Sydney *Bulletin* in Australia). Both countries went through a fairly sluggish literary period in the early twentieth century, followed by a resurgence of activity in the 1920s (the Montreal Group in Canada; the *Vision* group in Australia) with endless controversy over the proper priority of nationalism and cosmopolitanism in art. Both countries were then economically hard hit by the Depression and suffered publishing cutbacks which reduced the poetic output of the decade.[2] In each case the relatively low-profile 1930s were

followed by a "renaissance" in the war years, characterised by an outburst of new periodicals, by a moderate degree of technical modernism in
poetry, and by common poetic interests in the psychological, the mytho-
poeic, and the socially realistic.   Further, Canada and Australia are both
steeped in a narrative tradition which favours the linear sequence of a
beginning, middle, and conclusion, whether the bush ballads of Banjo
Paterson and the sea adventures of Kenneth Slessor in Australian poetry
or the historical accounts of E.J. Pratt and Klondike yarns of Robert W.
Service in Canadian verse.   Spanning all these developments and decades
in both countries was a rural orientation, a preoccupation with themes of
landscape, and a perhaps related wariness of precipitant change of any
kind—the quality of being, as F.R. Scott has written, "emphatically
middling."[3]   All of these ingredients argued for similarity in the two
nations' poetic responses to the Depression.

Upon reflection, however, it seemed fully as reasonable to anticipate
some noticeable difference, specifically a much more vocal social poetry
in Australia than in Canada.   Reasons for this assumption were several,
beginning with the abovementioned greater severity of conditions in Depression Australia than elsewhere, a factor which would presumably incite
proportionately greater passion in poets.   In addition, there were the
world-renown Australian traditions of mateship and of conscious egali-
tarianism, which would naturally lead the Australian to ponder and care
about his brother's plight.   Out of the convict past had grown a fundamentally working-class society said to recognise no masters, said to reject
old world class distinctions.

Our writers [writes T. Inglis Moore] have not merely protested against
social wrongs, but also made a very positive demand for social justice,
largely because they felt with [Joseph] Furphy that the "petrified injustice" of the old world should have no place in the new.   The vision
of an Australian Utopia gave an added edge to the writers' social
criticism.   From the eighties onward injustice has been condemned as
being unaustralian as well as being undemocratic.[4]

Historically there was the nineteenth century "Poetry Militant" of Bernard
O'Dowd, the mateship principles of Lawson and Daley, the social concerns
of Mary Gilmore, as promising foundations for a social orientation in
1930s Australian poetry.   The critics speak eloquently of Australian
humanism, of the Australian Dream which "emphasises man's duty to his
brother, and man's basic equality, the mutual trust which is the force that
makes society cohere."[5]   Canada, having no "mystical cult of mateship",
would presumably have less likelihood than Australia of producing
socially-conscious poets, even in times of obvious social stress.   Remember
as well Australia's much stronger Popular Tradition in literature, which
would presumably lead literature to reflect social conditions and the

problems of current living, of the common man, more rapidly than Canada's elitist, Academic Tradition.

On the instinctual level, the area of the Grand Generalisation, one might also be led by Australia's image as an outspoken, vigorous, and active nation to expect vocal social protest from her poets. This would compare with the poetic reticence expected from Canada, a nation regarded even by herself (probably foremost by herself) as orthodox, self-effacing, compromising, born of dully respectable origins next to the drama of convict beginnings and outback sagas.

On, at last, to the actuality of the 1930s, we find that all these hypotheses and expectations serve primarily to account for aberrations from the mainstream of poetic practice during the Depression. The two countries' poets do exhibit different reactions to the Depression, but, in a reversal of expectations, it is the Canadians who reflect the hard times more directly and forcefully.

In Canada, as my selection of the titular word "mosaic" suggests, one sees in the Depression a dramatic range of responses to current events. A substantial number of writers, ultraconservative and anxious to preserve their art and their world in the face of rapid change, hold firmly to traditional themes and even avoid the unsettling rhythms of free verse or other modernist techniques. The more philosophical of these poets are prepared to discuss their studied "escapism" in lucid prefaces and articles, lest they be interpreted as fools oblivious to reality. For example, the author of *Anne of Green Gables* observes wryly, "The critics condemn my books because of what they call lack of realism. My reply to them is that sunsets are just as real as pigsties and I prefer writing about them."[6] Numerous other intelligent rationales arise at this time for a choice of unremittingly non-social themes in verse, viewpoints shared and amplified by Australian poets. But for the moment, let us stay with the image of a Canadian Mosaic.

At the other end of the spectrum are the explicit, energetic social poets who take very seriously Leo Tolstoy's pronouncement that "Art is not a disembodied element feeding on itself, but a function of social man indissolubly tied to his life and environment." Such major Canadian poets as Dorothy Livesay, A.M. Klein, and F.R. Scott sometimes strain their verse far beyond the graces of their usual forms and themes in their determination to express indignation or to comment ironically upon social injustice. And they begin their outcry early in the decade, in clear and immediate response to Depression conditions.

In Australia, by comparison, one finds only the tiniest proportion of explicitly social poetry, and almost invariably by poets of extremely minor reputation. Admittedly the major figure, Mary Gilmore, can be found writing poignantly of poverty or babies dead from rats and starvation, but a reading of her early, pre-World War I poetry shows this to be part of a continuous concern for deprivation rather than a new consciousness springing specifically from the Dirty Thirties. The inception of three short-term socialist "little magazines", *Yesterday and Most of Today*, *Pandemonium*, and *Point*, parallels the equally short-lived Canadian *Masses* and *New Frontier*, but the Australian magazines are not supported by her poets (Slessor, FitzGerald, McCrae) as are their Canadian counterparts (Kennedy, Livesay, Smith). Thus in Australia one can find smatterings of social poetry but it is an extremely isolated fragment of the total poetic picture and is not much contributed to by any of the major Australian poets. In Canada, while not the dominant choice as a rule, the social theme is vigorously and extensively employed by important poets.

It is in the middle ground that the Canadian poets most demonstrate the Mosaic response : while insistent upon the continuance of traditional themes of home, love, death, the cosmos, more poets than not at least try their hand at social topics. Some, like E.J. Pratt, Art Smith, and Robert Finch, are obviously slightly ill at ease in this area, but feel they should, at least nominally, fulfil a poet's function as spokesman of his times. Evidence of social awareness in Canadian poetry is extremely widespread by the end of the thirties; more than half of the poets from this period (minor as well as major) still available for examination demonstrate specific concern with the troubles of the decade. The Canadians reveal themselves in these years of stress as a moderate people inclined neither to complete escapism nor to radicalism but to a conservative synthesis of the best of both.

Australia, much more "the Monolith", interestingly does not exhibit the dramatic diversity of the Canadian poetic response. Australian poets in the 1930s tend to avoid quite uniformly direct social commentary. The major poets—Kenneth Slessor, R.D. FitzGerald, Hugh McCrae, Douglas Stewart, Peter Hopegood, Rex Ingamells, Shaw Neilson—turn to history, myth, adventure, and cosmic abstractions for their materials. In their work, fleeting references to the present tend to serve other than social purpose. T. Inglis Moore's statement regarding the "proletarian preference" in Australian literature turns out to refer almost exclusively to the novel, the short story, and drama,[7] and H.M. Green subtitles his study of the "Fourth Period : World Consciousness and Disillusion (1923-1950)" with such categories as "Poet Balladists" or "Poets of Love" but without a "Social Poetry" distinction at all.[8] Vincent Buckley has observed that

In the best Australian poetry of the thirties, man is viewed as an animal who seeks not primarily a social status and stability, but the conquest of time and space.... [Australian poetry in the Depression] is concerned not so much with man's place in society as with his place in the context of nature. It is concerned to establish the possibility of human action rather than the reality of certain human states.[9]

Given our prior expectations, particularly the proletarian tradition of the country, why *did* Australian poets choose so decidedly to eschew social verse, while their Canadian fellow poets insisted equally firmly upon an eclectic approach ? I offer to you a baker's dozen of theories; none of these explanations individually answers the question, which is not only a literary but also a cultural and historical one, but in combination they create a framework, the materials for an answer.

An artist may reflect his social awareness as movingly by a studied avoidance of social themes as by their constant use. So one must begin with the type of attitude in which both Canadians and Australians and indeed the whole world shared: the universal human impulse loosely tagged "escapism". Certainly some thirties writers on both sides of the Pacific operate in apparently blithe unawareness of the grim era, and innumerable sunny spirits quietly refuse to or can not bear to dwell on painful reality. Many, however, are making a considered choice in stressing life's beauty and downplaying the imperfect. Canadian Amy Roddick writes:

> This world may be most evil; still I think
> There's promise in a day that lauds the sun :
> So decked Spring woods, why search the skeleton
> Beneath embroidering green and pearly pink... ?[10]

Similarly, Australian Flexmore Hudson writes:

> I know, Australia, most of you go poor
> and I am angry: yet I still exult
> you have the courage of our desert trees
> that heave green leaves from famisht sands
> undauntedly surviving drought
> and fire and flood. I love you, I am by
> in all your sorrows, feel your setbacks, share
> your pioneering pride. I promise I shall ever
> sing your land's beauty and the greatness of your soul.[11]

The decision to emphasise the positive is in itself frequently a political or philosophical position, involving a Keatsian sense of poetry's divine mission to "be a friend/ To soothe the cares, and lift the thoughts of man" Or, as Horace would have it, "to delight and to instruct": numerous writers the world over feel that depressing people with social truths is simply no way to combat the Great Depression and that instruction is impossible without pleasure. In a twinkling, the fate of the world as they know it rests upon a resistance to debased, disturbing, degrading social visions—all very well in prose but unsuitable to the heights of Poesy.

Allied is a fear that the social poet's concentration on the lowest aspects of human experience, his descent to the commonplace, will be irreversible. Thus, this sort of thinking, far from a mindless or cowardly retreat from Truth, represents rather a concerned attempt to preserve and to exalt man's potential, to build morale, to keep a place for delicate sensibilities in a gray, unromantic modern world.

Canada and Australia somewhat more exclusively share in a tradition which is rural rather than urban, agricultural rather than industrial. This has meant in both countries a greater emphasis upon man's relationship with the soil than with his society. In the 1930s when the drought-ridden Canadian terrain no longer produces, the entrenched vision of the bountiful earth, of benign nature, continues to appear in verse (although not in fiction). Even the stark landscapes inspired by the bleak beauty of the Group of Seven paintings concentrate on a world far removed from industry, breadlines, and the mounting tensions of the prewar years. Meanwhile, in Australia, urban problems seem to drive the imagination almost literally into the wilderness. Frank Hardy, discussing "Environment and Ideology in Australian Literature", remarks on the profound impact of the Depression on his generation, but notes :

It is interesting that even in the 1930's most of Australian literature was still largely set in the bush. Books were still very few and far between on the big cities where the majority of Australians lived.[12]

The severity of the Australian countryside, no harsher than usual in the Great Depression, is viewed by gymnastics of morality as a pure, unsullied, purgative place in comparison with the squalor and indignity of cities. Judith Wright points perceptively to this anti-city and anti-social strain as an undercurrent of the bushman legend, and we see it survive beyond the Depression years, as in A.D. Hope's famous poem, "Australia". I quote in part :

And her five cities, like five teeming sores,
Each drains her : a vast parasite robber-state
Where second-hand Europeans pullulate
Timidly on the edge of alien shores.
....
Yet there are some like me turn gladly home
From the lush jungle of modern thought to find
The Arabian desert of the human mind,
Hoping if still from the deserts the prophets come,

Such savage and scarlet as no green hills dare
Springs in that waste, some spirit which escapes
The learned doubt, the chatter of cultured apes
Which is called civilization over there.[13]

Rejection of the corruption, filth, and sin of cities and elevation of the virtues of the countryside can also be traced in Canadian, American, and British literature. What seems to be a uniquely Australian development is the rejection that occurs of civilisation *per se*. The Americans often regard Europe as the postlapsarian garden whose snake they plan not to import, although some, like Henry James, waver considerably between the two. Yet they have a concern with material progress which distinguishes the American from the Australian distaste for "civilisation". However many affinities US and Australian literature share, one does not find in American literature much calling for prophets from "The Arabian desert of the human mind". And the Canadian poet in fact seeks to perpetuate (and all too frequently carefully mimic) what the Australian is capable of dismissing as "the chatter of cultured apes". Naturally this pattern—anti-city, anti-social, anti-civilisation—reduces the likelihood of an Australian poet's interest in socialism.

A partially related point, and one on which the Canadians and Australians have more commonality, involves their parallel self-concepts as nations different from the US and Europe. Murray-Smith speaks of the Australian distaste for a "sickened Europe and a vulgar America"[14] and there is evidence in both literatures of a self-image that gives priority to the moral and spiritual over the materialistic. Notice that I am talking of self-image, not historical truth. What it means, however, in terms of social poetry, is the sentiment that one should rise above the temporal, emphasise the eternal, and not write that nasty, ephemeral stuff the Yanks and the Brits are producing. Therefore one finds in both Canada and Australia but perhaps even more strongly in Australia a sense of being "out of time", out of the immediate, living in *The Timeless Land*, "The Lonely Land", a preoccupation shared by Pratt, Smith, Finch, Slessor, FitzGerald, Wright, and countless others. *Sub specie aeternitatis* and with a value system claiming to give little weight to the temporal and crassly material, what would be the point of gloomy poems decrying specific abuses, transitory problems, full of dated insights and passé references?[15]

A factor which may well have inhibited a social sense in the poets of both countries is geography. Lacking contact with one another, frequently working in an isolation which prevents the interchange of ideas and exposure to the techniques and interests of others, writers not surprisingly only very rarely venture out of the inherited ways. In Canada there are some links through the university system (an advantage of the Academic Tradition) but this does not operate as vitally in Australia, where the major writers are less often academics, more usually labourers, members of the working class. Shaw Nielson, for example, farms, wields a pick in a quarry, works as a nearly-blind attendant for the Melbourne County Roads Board. Or if well-educated, they are often, like the Palmers or H.H.R., part-time exiles in other lands. Australia is legendary for the globe-trotting penchant of her citizens.

As well, Canada has organisations like the Canadian Authors' Association to provide a literary network. By comparison, only Australian writers, like Nettie Palmer, with incredible amounts of energy and a determination to foster a native literature, seem able to keep up any contact with fellow Australian writers. John Tregenza notes the lack of communication or literary coteries even during the Australian boosterism of the 1920s,[16] a period when Canadian writers, Scott's satiric "The Canadian Authors Meet" suggests, are in all too cosy and self-congratulatory contact.[17] "Australian writing," Judith Wright elaborates,

has on the whole been the product of non-professionals and usually of solitary workers. Our poetry grew up sporadically; we have had no patrons, few critics of importance, small and rather uninterested audiences. There has been no important literary centre, except for a few eddies of influence in the capital cities. Universities, libraries, even 'little magazines' to publish poetry, have not been until recently important factors in the growth of our literature. This lack of a focus, of any central point of reference, has meant that writers here have been more isolated and more self-centred than in countries where a tradition was established and literature was honoured.[18]

Combined with Australia's less developed literary communications system are the internal dissension of the interwar years, the Melbourne-Sydney polarities, and the supreme lack of interest in one another's work which Mrs Palmer occasionally laments. Furnley Maurice's *Melbourne Odes* introduces in 1934, for instance, a new urban emphasis which has no appreciable effect on his contemporaries.[19] Thus physical and psychological distances contribute to make poetic social protest in Australia a highly individual and unreinforced phenomenon. The reverse operates in Canada insofar as poets like Smith and Pratt are influenced by their socialist colleagues to produce some social verse. Even the grand old Confederation poets, Sir Charles G. D. Roberts and Duncan Campbell Scott, open themselves to the new trends in this period. And the lower ranks of versifiers respond gradually in the course of the decade to the example set by the best of Canadian poets. The humbler levels of Australian Depression poets, following the leaders, are lured into voyage poems, the songs of Pan, and contemplations of the Universe.

This leads us to the pronounced fascination in Australian poetry with classical myth and allusion, with the fantastic, and with the historical (this last especially in the 1930s, when it focusses particularly on the aboriginal and on long narratives of the early explorers like Cook). Given the intrinsic charm of such themes, it is little wonder that Australians prefer them to topics of the mundane, "depressing" present. Like Canadians, they have a heritage of English poetry which makes references to nymphs and satyrs a familiar device and both countries' poets in the 1940s become heavily involved in modern forms of mythopoesis. The Australian evolution of opinion about myth has been somewhat different from Canada's, however. Beginning with the Confederation poet's attempts at a diction and imagery more appropriate to the realities of the Northern landscape, Canadians have become more and more self-conscious about the use of imported and unnatural references in literature. At the same period and later, Bernard O'Dowd and others are staunchly defending the Australian right to take advantage of any myth or allusion thought pleasing. In his long poem, "The Bush", O'Dowd argues :

> Ye, who would challenge when we claim to see
>   The bush alive with Northern wealth of wings,
> Forget that at a common mother's knee
>   We learned, with you, the lore of Silent Things.
> There is no New that is not older far
> Than swirling cradle of the first-born star :
> Our youngest hearts prolong the far pulsation
>   And churn the brine of the primordial sea :
> The foetus writes the précis of Creation :
>   Australia is the whole world's legatee.
>
> . . . .
>
> Who fenced the nymphs in European vales ?
>   Or Pan tabooed from all but Oxford dreams ?
> Warned Shakespeare off from foreign Plutarch's tales ?
>   Or tethered Virgil to Italian themes ?
> And when the body sailed from your control
> Think ye we left behind in bond the soul ?
> Whate'er was yours is ours in equal measure,
>   The Temple was not built for you alone,
> Altho' 'tis ours to grace the common treasure
>   With Lares and Penates of our own![20]

So, where the cautious and self-effacing Canadian begins to feel presumptuous about borrowings, the assertive Australian feels free to seize whatever appeals to him. Why *not* nymphs in the Outback ? Interestingly enough, the viewpoints of the two countries will later coincide once again on nationalistic grounds, that one should select the materials which most define the nation's distinctiveness. Canada has first flirted with this insistence on Canadianness in the nineteenth century movement known as Canada First. Australia develops the bush ballad and the bushman ideal in the nineteenth century but waits until the 1930s to see the attempt at Australia First and the Jindyworobak movement led by Rex Ingamells.

As for the historical impulse, poets in Canada and Australia have always tended toward the narrative. In the Australian context aboriginal history is a unique item and is recognised in the 1930s to be an indispensable part of her nationalism. (This differs from the Canadian experience, where even today the history of our native peoples, Indian and Eskimo, plays only a peripheral part in poetic expression.) The history of Australia generally also becomes the vogue in the 1930s, inaugurated by Kenneth Slessor's *Five Visions of Captain Cook* and followed by a host of voyager poems, the "conquest of time and space" to which Buckley has referred. (For this there is a prominent Canadian equivalent, E.J. Pratt, but Pratt's "Titanic", "The Roosevelt and the Antinoe", "Brébeuf and His Brethren" and so forth have not had the same legion of imitators.) In overview, Australia, to a greater degree than her Commonwealth sister, turns to history as material for her poetry.

Myth, fantasy, the historical—whether in the name of aesthetics, the poet's freedom of choice of theme, national consciousness-raising, or explorations of that which outlasts the transitory troubles of a decade—all of these popular poetic topics serve to draw the Australian away from the comparative gloom of contemporaneous events and to place a blessing upon his choice of "then" or "once upon a time" over the unattractive "now". John Tregenza even theorises that nationalism and the preoccupation with the outback and aborigines and history are directly due to the disagreeable modern times. He posits that these subjects function as "both a religion and an escape", representing

an urgent desire for escape from cramping Australian city life—a desire even for purification from the evils of modern civilisation. For the notable difference between the nationalist movement of the old *Bulletin* days and the modern Jindyworobak movement, seems to be that, in the former, writers wrote about the outback and its people as their normal environment, while the latter seems to have consisted of a rediscovery of the character of the outback by writers brought up, for the most part, in the city or the settled areas.[21]

In the same way as the continuing preoccupation with classical and historical subjects may be said to exist in both countries but to be clearly much stronger a factor in the poetry of Australia, so the tradition of stoicism may be acknowledged as applicable to both but particularly dominant in the Australian mentality. It is Australia which has coined the phrase finally immortalised in the title of Joseph Furphy's novel, *Such is Life*. "Such is Life," said with a shrug and perhaps a wry smile. It seems to have derived from a compound of history, geography, and climate : history, in that Australians felt themselves cast involuntarily as convicts into a hostile environment; geography, in that only 10% of the land was considered arable and there were large unconquerable geographic features to which the human mind had no choice but to submit; and climate, with its droughts, floods, and bushfires (what Judith Wright terms

"The Terrible Three which haunt all Australian thought and writing"),
the factors which multiply the injustices of life and destroy the principle of
"just deserts".   This is an extremely large area in which to theorise glibly,
particularly as the Canadian experience (with the substitution perhaps of
snow for floods or Indian raids for bushfires) appears no different. I suggest, somewhat tentatively, that the difference here lies in attitude to the
land. Judith Wright speaks of the Australian exploitative response to
nature :

> Our attitude to this continent has always been that of the master,
> intent on profit and the quick dollar; our emotional homeland was for
> very many years not here at all, but thousands of miles overseas, and
> hence we have usually regarded this country as a property to be ex-
> ploited, rather than an inheritance to be cherished.[22]

Her observations are supported by some of the 1930s Australian poetry I
have encountered which is moved to protest not the Depression but the
Australian's rape of his land.[23] It would appear that the Australian will
or desire for self-actualisation is in this regard a very strong one, comparable to the American, and that frustration by the elements and the
past could be expected to cause a greater element of anger and disgust
than in Canada, where the attitude to nature has been, at least on the
intellectual level, considerably humbler. Such an hypothesis gains strength
when one considers how much more at home satire is in Australia than in
Canada,[24] and to what a degree irony is Canada's more comfortable
posture. The ironic vision lingers a bit in hope; the truly entrenched
stoic, abandoning eventually even the hope of satire, becomes silent, turns
to other things. This stoicism in itself becomes an enormous relief valve
for social indignation, in that there is vast satisfaction in coping with
adversity in an impassive, controlled manner—an Australian variation on
the British stiff upper lip, perhaps ? The bush ballad, another way to vent
feelings, both derives from and perpetuates the stoic sense of such-is-
life.   Again the likelihood of social poetry dwindles.
Judith Wright, later in her discussion of man and land in Australia,
touches on an emptiness which may also be pertinent to our topic.   Of
the lack of love or commitment for the landscape, she argues :

> This fact is probably one of the most important in considering
> the whole attitude of our society. An exploitative relationship with
> one's environment is bound to have its effect on every aspect of human
> feeling towards that environment, and even to extend towards one's
> relationship with one's fellowmen. Visitors often comment on the
> emptiness of Australian life, its emphasis on externals, and its lack of
> inner direction. I suggest that the root of this may easily lie largely
> in our relationship with the country itself....[25]

Nettie Palmer mentions this as well in her journal entry of July 24, 1933 :

> How to explain the thinness of our skin and our distrust of any theme
> that might penetrate to the bone? How to explain our literary bar-
> loungers and their demand for the light and sunshiny? There was the
> hostility shown to Stewart Macky's play, 'John Blake,' one professor
> saying that drama should never touch the convict-period; there was
> the hullabaloo raised when Katherine's [Pritchard] 'Coonardoo' began
> to be published serially, so many letters of protest arriving that the
> editor was thrown into a panic. We are still at a stage when any casual
> person takes for granted he can tell a writer what subjects are tabu
> and what acceptable.[26]

Supposing these views are accurate, the poetry of protest—always an
arduous experience for the sensitive reader—would not be a much favoured mode. (Lest this point, albeit from the mouths of Australians, cause
offence, I hasten to add that Canadians have similarly been accused of
shallowness, of a resistance to meaty philosophical and artistic questions,
of a chilling reserve which impedes fellow feeling or social warmth. The
world's image of Canadians does not stress our powerful intellect or our
cuddliness.)

The point about stoicism helps to explain why the late nineteenth
century socialist reformers like O'Dowd and Lawson have made so little
permanent impact and do not form a solid enough foundation for social
poetry to build upon in the 1930s. Of Lawson, Wright says, "He is that
paradox, a revolutionary writer who is never quite convinced that revolution will bring the Utopia he wants."[27] He is, she claims, "deeply pessi-
mistic about human nature and its fate."[28] This paradoxical pessimism
puts Lawson in the flow of a stream of Australian pessimists. One notices
as a stunning reversal of an equally strong Australian optimism the recurring sense of "Them" and of a malevolent universe, to which the reaction
is sometimes a "Byronic brooding", as in the case of A.L. Gordon or
Barcroft Boake.[29] Australia for these individuals comes to be a sort of
penance or perpetual, irreversible purgatory ("The Land Where the Dead
Men Lie"), to which one responds stoically, bleakly. One is brought
back to the already mentioned Australian notion of the "failure of civilisation" and the concomitant rejection of the world. Bad times, needless
to say, for the social imperative.

It seems reasonable that if pessimism was an impediment to social
verse in Australia, then optimism would be its ally. Yet such is not the
case. T.I. Moore identifies "affirmation of life" and "earth-vigour" as
major moods opposing pessimism and stoicism in Australian literature,[30]
and one is reminded of another phrase that Australians have contributed
to the English-speaking world, the irrepressible optimism contained in
the words "She'll be right." But the effect on poetry is one of vision, of

rose-coloured spectacles, another stage in the progress of the Great Australian Dream, what one critic calls the "never-questioned picture of
Australia as the Land of the Dawn, the egalitarian paradise."[31]   Moore
argues at one point that this Great Australian Dream, in his words the
"picture of a cosy classless community living in cheery mateship," was
disintegrating from the 1890s onward and dead by 1930, but later says
that even into the 1940s "the perfectionist Dream lived on."[32]   James
McAuley's well-known "Terra Australis" demonstrates this idea of Australia as the arena for greatness, the unsullied place where all is still
possible and men may yet achieve their divine potential.

> Voyage within you, on the fabled ocean,
> And you will find that Southern Continent,
> Quiros' vision—his hidalgo heart
> And mythical Australia, where reside
> All things in their imagined counterpart.
>
> It is your land of similes : the wattle
> Scatters its pollen on the doubting heart;
> The flowers are wide-awake; the air gives ease.
> There you are home; the magpies call you Jack
> And whistle like larrikins at you from the trees.

Temporary economic setbacks and social inequities come to seem, in this
perspective, merely trials set to enhance the final attainment of the Australian Millenium.   Again the poetry of social protest would be regarded
as inappropriate.

With the exception of dutiful occasion poems, generally from second-
rate versifiers, one finds little of this authentic rapture, this national
vision, in Canada's twentieth century.   As the Canadians tend away in
verse from the extremities of a negative, even sardonic, view of the universe and their own landscape, so they avoid as intuitively any visions
about the nation's destiny.   Canadians have never stopped feeling slightly
embarrassed at Laurier's turn-of-the-century pronouncement, "The twentieth century belongs to Canada."

It should be mentioned that while Australia and Canada share a burst
of literary boosterism in the 1920s, Australia uniquely experiences a movement which lends special and enduring reinforcement to optimism in the
1930s.   This is the phenomenon, centred around Norman Lindsay, variously known as Vitalism, Gaiety, Enthusiasm for Life, or Delight of the
Present Moment.   Clustered about a periodical called *Vision*, its focus is
on celebration of life rather than critical examination of conditions, a
Nietzschean cult of beauty, uninterested in social responsibility and answering only to the self.   This group has widespread impact,[33] lasting long
after such core members as FitzGerald and Slessor, Jack Lindsay and

Leon Gellert have diverged in thought and practice. The lingering of Gaiety is a factor peculiar to Australia in accounting for a lack of direct poetic response to the Great Depression. Canadians have the minor cult of Havelock Robb's "Abbey Dawn" but its scale and influence are infinitesimal next to Norman Lindsay's Vitalism. Prominent poets like Hugh McCrae, William Baylebridge, James Devaney, Dorothy Mackellar, Dulcie Deamer, Peter Hopegood, and "Ricketty Kate" write their verse of affirmation, of Greek and Roman myth, of dream and pastorale, serenely and virtually without interruption from the late nineteenth century through the 1930s. In Canada even the high priestess of romanticism, Audrey Alexandra Brown, feels under pressure to discuss and explain her "pedestal" above the common round and the current anguish.[34] One wonders whether a previous surge of Gaiety in Canada would have relieved Ms Brown from the need for self-justification, a need most Australian poets, an independent breed, evidently never feel. But Gaiety in Canada? The mind boggles.

Now, it is possible that the independence from current events that persons like Dulcie Deamer exercise derives not only from lack of peer pressure in this specific area but also from the entrenched Australian tradition of rugged individualism, the "cult of the independent, sun-tanned bushman, of mateship and self-reliance...."[35] According to Judith Wright and others, in Australia "...the picture of the hard-riding independent bushman be [comes] almost as formalised as that of the American cowboy..."[36] and the fact that the appeal of this image survives through the 1930s is demonstrated by the enormous popularity in print and film of the adventures of Arthur Upfield's half-caste private eye, Napoleon Bonaparte, a manly and resourceful lone wolf. Canada has tended to operate more with a corporate instinct than the individualistic one found in the US and Australia. The Mounted Police, the missionaries, the surveyors, the Red River settlers, the United Empire Loyalists, the railway workers upon the Great Canadian Dream, the component members of the ethnic mosaic—all are groups rather than individuals, and Canadians are inclined to want to know a person's affiliations, in order to fit one into his 'proper' category. Hence the hyphenated Canadian : French-Canadian, Italian-Canadian, Ukrainian-Canadian, and so forth. I have not encountered this insistence on grouping in the Australian consciousness, and that seems consistent with the idealisation of the sturdy, self-reliant, solitary bushman. Canada, by comparison, has never really had a Lone Ranger, a Mike Hammer, or a "Boney".

Mateship and self-reliance : they appear to the foreigner almost antithetical. One of the thorniest problems an outsider faces in puzzling out the lack of Australian social poetry in the Depression is the need to account for mateship. This distinctive Australian institution preaches the equality of man and the importance of fellow feeling. One is told that"...

the chief difference between, say the Australian and American dreams"
is this :

> Where the American dream made use of the competitive individualistic
> element in life, the freedom of any man to become richer and better
> than his fellows by hard work and emulation, the Australian dream
> emphasises man's duty to his brother, and man's basic equality, the
> mutual trust which is the force that makes society cohere.[37]

Well, if that's the case, shouldn't the thirties poet, swept up in the sentiments of mateship, be writing virtually nothing but protest and commitment verse? The reason "why not" lies in the actual nature of mateship,
its roots in mutual trust. "Mutual trust," one Australian has written,
"implies for us equality between man and man, equality of a kind that
transcends the necessary difference of circumstance and work and intelligence and income." [Notice "the *necessary* difference of circumstance and
work and intelligence and income."] The cult of mateship rests upon the
practical notion of two individuals, each doing his own work and having
faith that the other will do *his* part, facing things doggedly, side-by-side. It's
the work—or the suffering and deprivation—that links and is jointly borne.
Mateship does not lift burdens off others or wax vocal against the existence of burdens; it simply provides moral support, does its bit and trusts
the next fellow to lend his hand to the task. It is self-reliance of the
"buddy" system. And an indispensable part of this system are the equality
and the independence—structure, compulsion, the authoritarianism which
arises in most strong union organisations, all are anathema to this outspoken (tho' not unsung!) comradeship.

Essential as well is the silence of this mateship. One sees in *The
Sentimental Bloke* and other sources the profound opposition to sentimental verbalising, the entrenched ideas that silence is masculine, that speech
is feminine and weak,[38] that complaint represents a loss of masculinity.
Paul Grano, in a poem called "Sacrament" captures the combined values
of silence, of stoic endurance, and of the mystical capacity of the harsh
land to purge and cleanse :

> To stress and rue
> Of men in strife with men;
> To hidden pain in tenement,
> To callous factory and street—
> To these
> I turn again,
> Strong with this sacrament,
> Sweet with the unction of the hills,
> Cool with the vestment of the plains,
> Clean with their silences.[39]

Silent stoicism : with this sort of tradition, small wonder it is that the Australian poets feel ill at ease with themes of social protest.[40]

I have used the word "solitary" in describing the bushman ideal and certainly solitude is unavoidable in bush life. Critics speak of an Australian "flaunted preference for the enforced virtues of solitude and simplicity in hard but pure surroundings" and the way it "led for a time to a kind of hermit-cult, an anti-social glorifying of the lonely life in contact with the realities of the elements, and a rejection not only of the 'artificialities' of the city, but even of society itself."[41] This relates importantly to our previous discussion of the anti-social impulse in Australia but also serves as a link with Australia's larger geographic situation. As the individual in his microcosmic bush existence is isolated, so in the macrocosm Australia, antipodean, is isolated. And Australia has rather enjoyed her sense of splendid isolation, the notion of distance and safety from the contamination of the rest of the world. Geoffrey Blainey, in his book on this subject entitled *The Tyranny of Distance*, notes that isolationism even from Asia is the norm until as late as World War II, when the presence and the threat become too palpable to ignore. Moore claims that by the 1930s the Great Australian Dream was shattered, the fallacy of isolationism utterly exposed.[42] Judith Wright counters, however, that this didn't sink into writers' heads until later, and blames that in part on the dominant influence of "the barren reiteration of *Vision's* Nietzschean and anti-intellectual notions."[43] For whatever reasons, the Australian resists for a remarkably long time acknowledgement of his place and his country's role in the troubled modern world. Nettie Palmer, in the final entry of her published diary, writes :

August 4th, 1941.... For me, the war is something that has been going on remorselessly since July, 1936, when that sudden attack came at Barcelona. Looking back over my journal, I can't help noticing how little it has been concerned with purely literary questions since then. But is there, I wonder, any such thing as 'pure' literature? Isn't it just a conception of people who look on writing as an escape from the living world? Perhaps a painter or a musician can cut himself off, in his work, from what's going on around him, but a writer can't. I remember thinking, when we came home from Europe, that our writers were trying to do just that, but lately all I know have had this sense of the ground quaking beneath them as acutely as I have.... here are we, a part of mankind, and being forced to face the fact.[44]

In Canada, poets are gradual in their adoption of social themes, but their advance is a process of an entire decade, not a sudden surge of interest at the end when the looming war obliges an awareness. Physically and economically linked to the United States in the frequently uncomfortable relationship which has been likened to a mouse sleeping with an elephant, Canada has also historically felt immediately involved in the fate of Mother England. She may not have often felt she could alter world events, but Canada has always felt implicated in and vulnerable to global conditions. Thus isolationism has been a perspective never really viable for Canadians, even as a luxurious illusion.

Connected with the matter of isolationism is a difference between Australian and Canadian attitudes to foreign literary influences. The history of Australian literature shows a marked strain of resistance to foreign influences for several reasons. The first is rooted in a hurt reaction to convict status (more legendary than true, it appears, but no less potent for all that) : the outcast turning a defiant face to his former family and telling them to shove off. This is combined with the natural process of maturation, as the child colony, to assert its growing identity, rejects the parent. It becomes a part of a nationalist pattern to write "distinctively Australian" poetry, to define the self by its difference from the dominant (m)other. If the rage in Britain is the social verse of Spender, Auden, and Day Lewis, one should be writing anything but. P.R. Stephensen in a 1935 essay entitled "The Foundations of Culture in Australia" shows his intentions in his subtitle, "An Essay towards National Self-Respect" and his one issue of *Australian Mercury* (1935) has the same goal. Then Rex Ingamells in 1937 initiates the Jindyworobak movement with its nationalist little magazine *Venture* (Adelaide, 1937, 1939-40), and in a milestone essay called "Conditional Culture" denounces "subservien[ce] to the spirit and idiom of English poetry."[45]

In his conclusion to *Tradition in Exile*, John Matthews observes :

Australian poets writing in the present century have been less influenced by foreign trends than were their Canadian contemporaries. Australian poetry did not pass through a phase in imitation of T.S. Eliot, for there were native traditions established that were more influential.[46]

While it should not be deduced from this that Canadian poets spent any time in the Wasteland (their imitations being stylistic rather than thematic), Canada has undeniably—in comparison with Australia and particularly with the rebel United States—played the consistent role of dutiful daughter through to the present day. A dearth of dramatic convict origins is part cause of this propriety, and so is the psychological proximity of Canada to England, compared with Australia's palpable remoteness. Largely, however, it is a matter of self-definition : whereas the Australian identity is tied up at times in rejection of the Motherland, the Canadian identity, often achieved by differentiation from the US, has lain mostly in underscoring links with the UK. In poetry, this has meant that patriotism and nationalism have historically been connected not with repudiation of British models, but with careful imitation of British, non-Yankee, practices. This colonialism unquestionably has slowed the development of an indigenous tradition in Canadian literature. The offshoot, in terms of the topic at hand, has been the acceptability of British-style, thence Canadian-style, social poetry.

That some poets in Australia are simply oblivious to the verse (protest and otherwise) written in other countries is testified to by the inception of three 1930s journals directed expressly to remedying that unawareness : *Manuscripts* (of Geelong and Melbourne, 1931-5), *Stream* (of Melbourne, 1931), and *So This is Adelaide* (1931-2). None, it appears from John Tregenza's account, have much impact and despite high quality, are fairly shortlived.[47] The same sort of insularity naturally occurs in Canada, but to the present day one can hear complaints that it is easier to get a book from Blackwell's of London than McClelland and Stewart of Canada, so possibly availability is greater in Canada than in far-flung Australia.

Another possibility remains, to explain the lack of social poetry in thirties Australia. In a seminar on the interwar period, Australian academics in the 1960s pondered an absence of World War I themes in Australian literature. Their conclusions were reported as follows :

Given the necessary time lag to permit artistic assimilation of the experience of war (*All Quiet on the Western Front* appeared as late as 1929), it was suggested in discussion that Australian writing about the war was inhibited by three factors—

1. The very real horror of the war to those involved on the Western Front, a horror best to be forgotten.

2. The growth of the Anzac Legend, a legend sufficiently unreal to turn many writers away from it.

3. The onset of the Depression, a social trauma sufficiently immediate and profound as to obscure the war.

Their next sentence is a suggestive one : "The onset of World War II, in turn, probably served to obscure the Depression in like fashion."[48] In both Canada and Australia, one must look to the 1940s, 50s, 60s to find accounts of the Depression—usually in prose.

Finally, Vincent Buckley offers to us an interpretation of the Australian mentality which admits its general political apathy and the prevalence of a sentiment of every man for himself but argues in Australia an ongoing humanism. "Left-Wingery with us," he writes, "has not been what it was in England : the concern of a decade; it has been on the contrary a recurrent strain, a constant aspiration in our poetry."[49] From that viewpoint the Australian poet would have no need to trot out protest poems as though he had just discovered injustice. From the earliest days on Botany Bay, one might say, he has embodied his social sense and his protest in every bush ballad he has devised; there is nothing new for him to say.   Canadians, perhaps dwelling longer in a state of innocence, cry out more loudly when global reality begins to pinch, when the soil no longer produces, when the work ethic is betrayed on a scale which cannot be ignored.

In the Great Depression, when the social imperative demands utterance, writers of both nations incline to prose—essay, novel, short story.   Katherine Pritchard in Australia and Earle Birney in Canada represent a considerable body of writers who feel the one medium more suitable than the other for direct social statement.   But poetry is, by the sacred light in which many sincerely regard it, a powerful gauge of what people think and what they value.   We find, in conclusion, that the factors influencing the poet's choice of them are multiple and complex—extending deep into the geographical, the historical and the social nature of the country.   The blend, the interweave, the overlap of these factors is an extremely subtle one, begetting endless analysis.   No single component dominates but a definite poetic profile does emerge in terms of social themes : in Australia, a comparative Monolith of Silence; in her sister, Canada, a Mosaic of Response.

REFERENCES

1. John P. Matthews, *Tradition in Exile*, Toronto, U. Toronto Press, 1962.

2. J.K. Ewers, *Creative Writing in Australia*, Melbourne, Georgian House, 1945, p. 85 says that the 30s had a great surge of publishing, but this is contradicted by John Tregenza, *Australian Little Magasines 1923-1954 : Their Role in Forming and, Reflecting Literary Trends*, Adelaide : Libraries Board of South Australia, 1964, p. 27.   It appears to have been only nationalistic or escapist materials which prospered.

3. From the poem, "Audacity" (1964), used to describe Canada, but echoed in the words of Vincent Buckley about Australian poetic conservatism, "There has been nothing of this [British] changeability, [nothing of its concomitant extravagance in the work of Australian poets." *Essays in Poetry*, New York, Books for Libraries Press, 1969, p. 44.

4. T.I. Moore, *Social Patterns in Australian Literature*, Berkeley, U. California Press, 1971, p. 261.

5. Judith Wright, *Preoccupations in Australian Poetry*, Melbourne, Oxford U. Press, 1965, introduction, p. xxi.

6. L.M. Montgomery, address to the Toronto Women's Press Club, 1936.   Cited in

Lee Thompson, " 'Emphatically Middling' : A Critical Examination of Canadian Poetry in the Great Depression", unpublished Ph.D. thesis, Queen's University, Ontario, Canada, 1975, p. 137.

7. Moore, *ibid.*, p. 258.

8. H.M. Green, *A History of Australian Literature Pure and Applied*, Vol. II : 1923-1950, Sydney, Angus and Robertson, rpt. 1962.

9. Buckley, *ibid.*, pp. 36, 37.

10. Amy Roddick, "Above Brick Walls," *I Travel to the Poets' Mart*, Montreal, Dougall, 1936, p. 26.

11. F. Hudson, "Song of an Australian, Part III" in *The Oxford Book of Australian Verse*, ed. William Murdoch, Melbourne, Oxford, rev. 1945, p. 272.

12. Frank Hardy, "Environment and Ideology in Australian Literature," in *Literary Australia*, ed. Clement Semmler and Derek Whitelock, Melbourne, Cheshire, 1966, p. 75.

13. A.D. Hope, "Australia," in *A Book of Australian Verse*, ed. Judith Wright, Melbourne, Oxford, 1956, p. 132f.

14. S. Murray-Smith, "The Novel and Society," *The Literature of Australia*, ed. G. Dutton, Adelaide, Penguin Books, 1964, p. 101.

15. Nor is that Australian and Canadian attitude, for all its implicit smug self-congratulation, as snobbish as it may seem to some. One thinks of W.H. Auden at age 64 looking back on his political verse and confessing to a *New York Times* reporter : What embarrasses me is the question, 'Who benefited ?' And the answer is me. The poems didn't change one thing.... As a poet—not as a citizen—there is only one political duty, and that is to defend one's language from corruption.
                                                                "People", *Time Magazine*, 1 Nov., 1971

16. Tregenza, *ibid.*, Chapter 2.

17. F.R. Scott, "The Canadian Authors Meet" in *Canadian Anthology*, ed. C.F. Klinck and R.E. Watters, Toronto, Gage, 1966.

18. Judith Wright, "Inheritance and Discovery in Australian Poetry," in Semmler and Whitelock, ed., *Literary Australia*, p. 6f.

19. Douglas Stewart, *Poetry in Australia*, Vol. II : Modern Australian Verse, Sydney, Angus & Robertson, 1964, introduction.

20. Bernard O'Dowd, *The Bush*, Stanzas 54 and 57.

21. Tregenza, p. 50.

22. Wright, "Inheritance and Discovery...," p. 3.

23. E.g., Brian Vrepont, *The Miracle*, 1939.

24. Buckley, *ibid.*, p. 38 : "We are antipodean and therefore bluff; irony has little place in our poetic personality."

25. Wright, "Inheritance and Discovery....", p. 3.

26. Nettie Palmer, *Fourteen Years : Extracts from a Private Journal 1925-1939*, Melbourne, Meanjin Press, 1948, p. 121.

27. Wright, *Preoccupations....*, p. 70.

28. *ibid.*, p. 71.

29. *ibid.*, pp. 60, 61.

30. Moore, *Social Patterns....*, p. 289.

31. Wright, *Preoccupations*, p. 78.

32. Moore, *Social Patterns*, pp. 286, 289.

33. Murray-Smith, *ibid.*, p. 440.

34. Audrey Alexandra Brown, *Poetry and Life, an Address Given at the CIA in Vancouver*, Macmillan, Private Printing, 1941.

35. Wright, *Preoccupations*, p. 77.

36. *ibid.*

37. *ibid.*, introduction, xxi.

38. The modern slang term for complaint, "bitching", seems to be in this stern macho tradition.

39. Paul Grano, "Sacrament", *Jindyworobak Anthology, 1939*, Melbourne, Jindyworobak, 1940.

40. Buckley, *ibid.*, p. 45.

41. Wright, *Preoccupations*, p. 54.

42. Moore, *Social Patterns*, p. 286.

43. Wright, *ibid.*, p. 135.

44. Palmer, *ibid.*, p. 250.

45. Rex Ingamells, "Conditional Culture," in *The Writer in Australia : A Collection of Literary Documents 1856 to 1964*, Melbourne, Oxford U. Press, 1969, p. 252.

46. Matthews, *ibid.*, p. 190.

47. Tregenza, *ibid.*, pp. 44, 45.

48. Semmler & Whitelock, eds., *Literary Australia*, Appendix, p. 182.

49. Buckley, *ibid.*, p. 53.

15

The Novel and a
Vision of the Land

NICK WILKINSON

PEOPLE everywhere feel the need to define themselves in relation to the landscape they inhabit. In the past, the land was encompassed by means of mythology, with heroes and supernatural beings giving meaning to particular aspects of the land, and sometimes to the whole dimension of the occupied terrain. India is famous for its great mythology of the Himalayas as the abode of the gods, and the Five Rivers the locks of Siva's hair. Hinduism also encompasses very local mythologies, such as that of Kenchamma in Raja Rao's *Kanthapura*. The Icelandic sagas were composed in the face of a hostile and extraordinary environment. In Africa and Oceania the origin myths describing the first beings nearly always associate them with special geographical features. Even Tolkien, in his *Lord of the Rings* carefully (but simplistically) links the nature of his different beings to the kind of terrain they inhabit. For the peoples who have been dispossessed, the mythologised memory of their homeland exerts a powerful influence on their whole way of life.

In many ways, the British Empire was constructed by the dispossessed, and the appeal of "Home" was so strong for many colonialists that they managed to persuade some of their subjects that their real Home was Britain, and not their own land. Selina, in Abrahams' *A Wreath for Udomo*, is a fictional character seduced by this lure, and Nirad Chaudhuri a living person (not to speak of the many self-exiled authors from the Caribbean). From this sentiment, even more than economic arguments, the Commonwealth was forged. It is still a considerable influence on writers in Commonwealth countries in which English is an official language. However, dispossession is a much more vital factor in those countries populated by outsiders : the white Commonwealth and the West Indies; and it has nowhere been as successfully encompassed as in America. America has forged both historical and literary mythologies for itself, and one of its most vital literary traditions lies in the creation of literary worlds which encompass areas of the land and the cities. In contrast to this, Commonwealth writers have not busied themselves with creating new literary mythologies for their lands, but rather have allowed the image of "Home" to serve as their mythic source. Thus we have characters like Hagar in the Canadian Margaret Laurence's *The Stone Angel*, who accepts her father's dreams of the Scottish Highlands and so never comes to terms with the land (represented by the Shipley farm), but clings instead to her house and memories. Halloran, in Keneally's *Bring Larks and Heroes*, is one of the few early transportees in Australia who "did not resent the grotesque land, did not call it evil because it was weird."[1] Yet he constantly dreams of Home. And in Rhys's *The Wide Sargasso Sea*, Antoinette is driven mad by the husband from Home who lacks the powers of strength and healing she had hoped for from the Homeland : and she ends up a prisoner in the country house in England.

The myth of Home enables many Commonwealth writers to evade the challenge of coming to terms with the lands they inhabit, but they are also hampered by the presence of the remnants of the indigenous peoples who had once held a mythology which had tamed the lands into their own. These aborigines hover accusingly in the works of many Commonwealth writers, especially in recent fiction. The Canadian Indian image of the past so haunts the characters in Leonard Cohen's *The Beautiful Losers* that it splits their consciousness and drives them into a distracted search for meaning and consciousness.[2] The Amerindians appear and fade through the Guianan novels of Wilson Harris, embodying the elusive power of the Folk; and in Australia the aborigines obsess the background of novels by Patrick White, Keneally and Randolph Stow. The myths and the mysteries of these peoples remain beyond the possibility of use and absorption by the new owners of the land (significantly, White's Alf Dubbo and Keneally's Jimmy Blacksmith are both adopted by priests early in life and so are alienated from their own background); yet their very presence challenges any attempt to create a new mythology of the land. Moreover, the temper of modern Western culture and its own literary form, the novel, militate against a traditional mythologising based upon heroes and supernatural concern. Recent attempts to encompass the ancient mythologies of their own lands have been made by Andrew Sinclair in *Gog* and *Magog* and Anita Desai in *Voices in the City*, and it is just at this level that the novels fail.

Nevertheless, a few Commonwealth authors have faced the task of endowing the land and the characters they create with an archetypal resonance, but have done so in an attempt to come to terms with their alienation and dispossession. They have made use of a tradition in the English novel, stretching through Emily Bronte to Conrad and Lawrence (and many lesser lights) in which character and landscape are interfused in a direct relationship. In *Wuthering Heights* and

Nostromo particularly, the aspects of the land and sea-scape both define and extend the consciousness of the characters—and sometimes overwhelm them. Lawrence extended this relationship even further into a mystical vision whereby character and landscape ideally become fused into aspects of one overriding reality (in *The Plumed Serpent* and "The Woman Who Rode Away"). What, in *Women in Love*, for example, is treated as symbolic, with aspects of the landscape clarifying and extending the significance of the immediate situation of the characters (as in the "Moony" chapter or Gerald's death on the ice), in the later works becomes a marriage between the "natural" forces in man, his immediate landscape, and, ultimately, the whole universe. And this universe is seen as a complementary, yet restless balance of forces which achieve harmony in moments of conjunction. Patrick White and Wilson Harris in particular, have developed upon this literary tradition, and Randolph Stow has hammered out his own apocalyptic vision upon it. The mystical worlds which these authors create are very different, but they seem to have been fed by many of the same sources (which also interested Lawrence) : esoteric Christianity and Judaism, alchemy, Jung, perhaps even theosophy. Other writers, such as Hugh Maclennan of Canada, have followed a more familiar mainstream of Christian thought : as he concludes in *The Watch That Ends The Night*, "It came to me...that to be able to love the mystery surrounding us is the final and only sanction of human existence."[3] This serves, however, as a conclusion, rather than a driving literary principle which would form the whole significance of his work.

Wilson Harris, however, does approach his writing and his philosophy wholesale. In the Guyana Quartet he aims to map out a literary and mystical world for Guyana, encompassing its history, the diversity of its peoples, and its geographical reality of the coastal plain, the mountain interior, and the great rivers. This is a world whose edges are subject to brutal and rather erratic seasons and whose heartland is almost seasonless, where there is a simultaneity of birth and death, growth and decay; a world where water and life are frequently opposed instead of merely dependent.[4] In this world, the individual consciousness and its apparent significance is almost totally submerged into the total flux of nature, and its struggle for some solid reality and cohesion is merely an aspect of the wider struggle of life. As Michael Gilkes writes of Harris :

> the purpose of his work is to convey the conjunction of disparate elements which contribute to his complex vision of reality as a 'oneness' in which both Man and Nature (animate and inanimate) participate.[5]

By using this as his basis, Wilson Harris is able to give a new literary expression to the ancient mystical precept that the bulk of mankind lives enmeshed in a world of appearances, subject to the surface forces of nature. Only the man who achieves a profound or true consciousness can break through this surface and align himself with the deeper, constructive patterns of the universe.   The crew in *Palace of the Peacock* have their spiritual eyes opened by their trial in the rapids (the "straits of memory," p. 73) and begin to be aware of "that harmonious rounded miracle of spirit which the world of appearances had never truly known" (p. 72). The basic narrative framework of *Palace of the Peacock* is a seven-day journey into the Interior in an open boat by Donne and his crew following the fleeing Arawaks.   This journey precisely echoes an earlier, historical journey, in which the boat was wrecked and all perished.   This is clearly a journey of the spirit, a journey to discover the real meaning of an act in the past; and a search for the lost Folk and their mythic resources. Donne and his crew represent the hodgepodge of different peoples, products of the colonial period when so many races were intermingled, whose place is normally the coastland.   However, the complex mixed strains of their ancestry endow them with a special potential : like an alchemical mixture, they need only the crucible (the boat) and a catalyst (the old Arawak woman from Mariella) to fuse and purify into the spiritual essence of humanity.   Different members of the crew are "purified" by death (though their spirit, their essence, remains in the boat) until all are dissolved into a final vision of death and pure being in a well of pure water— the Palace of the Peacock (or the Rainbow of Lawrence) where all the hues are one.   Some of the characters are twinned, like Donne and the Dreamer-narrator who are brothers and Schomburgh and Carrol who are father and unacknowledged son, as dark and light sides of the Hermes figure of alchemy; but they are separate identities which are in need of fusion and resolution, each incomplete because of the inheritance of their confused racial ancestry, yet peculiarly fit for spiritual regeneration by becoming whole.

In many ways, *Palace of the Peacock* can be seen as a reverse image of *Heart of Darkness* where Marlowe's river journey is from apparent wholeness to dissolution and acknowledgement of the primitive at the heart of his being.   It is Donne's primitive colonial behaviour of aggression and oppressive authority (especially sexual) which had led to the Amerindians of his lands fleeing into the interior : the river journey is made to contact them and bring them back.   From the damaging divisions of the coastal colonialism they achieve a unifying vision of the one in the many. This implies the total acceptance of the multi-layered personality, and is achieved in the country's heartland.   The contrast can be seen even in some of the details, such as the work involved in guiding the respective craft: Marlowe treats it as his work, as a means of evading serious thought and the challenges to his being, while the boat crew, in fighting the rapids, achieve a vision of wholeness.   In *Heartland*, a sort of epilogue to the Guyana Quartet, Harris returns to answer the profound colonial insult of *Heart of*

Darkness by exploring more fully the human significance of the inland water in the depth of the tropical vegetation. Stevenson, initially disoriented by the still waters above the cataract and the indifferent jungle, is shocked out of his selfishness by his encounter with the dead da Silva and the Amerindian woman giving difficult birth (to the son of Donne, perhaps). He fails to catch fish, symbol of the gift of the spirit, to give to the woman; and then finds that she has simply departed. After his initial disturbance at her indifference to him and his offerings, he faces the forest with an awakened sense of its possibilities and vanishes into the interior.

Through the multivalency of his approach, Harris attempts to marry the various traditions of religious esotericism which have come to him through his mixed cultural heritage with the actual geographical features of the country. Guyana is conceived of as a confluence, the node of a gyre to which all has come and from which all can emerge, and whose individual features can offer models for spiritual ascent. Sharon, in *The Whole Armour*, achieves a spiritual and sexual consummation with Christo, the shamanistic jaguar-man (significantly, the only character who is taken in and taught by the Caribs), and her vision is described geographically :

> The feeling in her stroking fingers made her see far away across the moonlit river—as if she rode in the beam of light-sliding hollows and rising features, growing into stones and foothills. It was along this very mysterious backbone and watershed—between ancient terror and new-born love—that the frightful jaguar of death had roamed, leaping across emotional tumbling rivers from crag to crag, across Devil's Hole Rapids and the Nameless Falls, greenheart ravines steaming with mist, blue mountains frowning in cloud, coming as far as the heart of Brazil into Venezuela's Orinoco and Guiana's Potaro, Mazaruni, Cuyuni and Pomeroon. Her fingers travelled across the map of Cristo's skin, stroking the veins in every ancestor's body.[6]

Even more specifically, Harris outlines his spiritual method through the musings of the semi-autobiographical Fenwick in *The Secret Ladder* :

> Fenwick had named his dinghy *Palace of the Peacock* after the city of God, the light of gold set somewhere in the heart of Brazil and Guiana. He liked to think of all the rivers of Guiana as the curious rungs in a ladder on which one sets one's musing foot again and again, to climb into both the past and the future of the continent of mystery.[7]

Each rung of a mystical ladder is complete with its own ladder of spiritual dimensions, to be mounted by meditation ("musings") and moments of vision, and each of the Quartet novels attempts to embody this. However, he started on his highest rung and vision in *Palace of the Peacock*, and subsequently seems to have abandoned a full seven-fold mystical cosmology.

In order to attain the necessary density and multi-layered significance of the events upon which he works, Harris has necessarily dissolved the accepted forms of fiction. Instead of developing a sequential chronological development of action, he takes points in a narrative and extends multiple dimensions around them. All his layers of significance and meaning are considered as coexistent, potentially capable of being focused upon at any point of a novel. But the literary form is extensive by its very nature, and only limited points can be presented, in sequence. Harris attempts to overcome this by moving freely (and sometimes jerkily) across different planes within individual sentences to emphasise the simultaneity of significance. This makes his writing extremely difficult to comprehend in detail and in development—but then, the esoteric works which have influenced him have always been deliberately inaccessible to any but the determined seeker.

Patrick White, on the other hand, uses a far more conventional chronological novel form, and chooses to express his mystical vision through the developing reverberations of his characters' progress. He indicates these reverberations through his peculiar choice of subjects for description and attention: many of his descriptions choose as their object aspects which seem the least likely out of the range of normal possibilities—such as the way people live in their clothes and adjust them for comfort, rather than describing the clothes themselves. Much like Lawrence, White focuses attention through the consciousness of special characters whose mode of vision is set apart from that of "normal" members of society. In fact, he usually places them initially against a "normal" view, such as Miss Hare's appearance at the Post Office[8] at Sarsaparilla, when she is commented upon by the postmistress to an elegant visitor, in *Riders in the Chariot*. Whereas Lawrence's protagonists are usually super-sensitive, White's characters are usually socially disabled as well. He is fascinated by the way they manage to turn their way of seeing into a vision, and how they perceive and absorb their own experiences. This is especially clear in his fascination with the artistic processes in the painter. His method is necessarily oblique, an accumulation of hints and details which often seems to take place at the periphery of his characters' lives or strike at a tangent to the actual events. This serves to make many of White's characters extremely shadowy (to themselves as much as to the reader), and they undergo experiences which have no clear outline and whose significance remains open-ended. It is this vagueness, allied to an authorial eye which is very sharp for odd detail (especially details of social behaviour), which Patrick White manipulates to suggest the workings of a mystical dimension. This dimension is much more distant from the immediate world than that of Wilson Harris, and in many ways is a much more specifically human achievement. While he reveals a knowledge of mystical and esoteric texts (especially through Himmelfarb in *Riders in the Chariot*), White does not make use of the formulae which these have evolved for the ordering of spiritual experience: instead, he concentrates upon his characters' rare moments of spiritual vision which are treated as transient moments of achievement. They can occur in a brothel, in the desert, at the death of an old Jew, in the heart attack of an old farmer. Unlike Harris's moments of vision, however, they are not essentially apocalyptic, or even purposive in normal terms: they do not lead the characters into a "better" life, or even offer a controlling dynamic for living a life. Miss Hare simply vanishes and her house is dismantled to make way for the soulless bungalows of suburbia; and while Voss becomes a legend at his death, Laura Trevelyan, who knew his soul most intimately, falls "to wondering aloud whether she had brought her lozenges". Their visions "disturb the air", to intimate to others their sometime existence; but they offer no answers or even the possibility of answers, merely a chance of a fleeting vision of a purposive universe.

The austerity of this mystical vision, hammered out, it would seem, in the writing of *Voss*, is at the opposite pole from Harris's baroque eclecticism, and echoes the totally different geography of Australia. Australia's heartland is a burned out desert, inimical to modern man. It offers no riches, no answers, not even the sudden negative of a Malabar cave, because, illogically, it can support life for the human beings who adapt to its ways, the Aborigines. Like the land, the life of the Aborigines seems to be an attenuated mockery of the colonialists' values: the desert at the core of their experience emphasises the insignificance of individual lives, and denies the values attributed to them in the busy world of the Australian whites. If there are true constants behind the lives of individuals, or even individual cultures, these must necessarily be implacable and barely concerned with humanity at all. It is only the "chance" communion of visionaries, brought together in a vital tangent of their lives, (usually when circumstances have weakened their natural defensive barriers), which sparks the moments of mystical vision. This does not in itself establish a community, or form a context in which the vision can be caught or stimulated by repetition or ritual, for each life remains strictly individual and isolated and goes its own way. Only Voss and Laura, in the telepathic sympathy established through their extremes of suffering, manage to exchange something of their natures before Voss dies.

Because Patrick White is so preoccupied with the ways his characters mould and are moulded by their lives, he becomes deeply involved in the landscape of Australia as an inescapable part of the Australian psyche. It is through his characters that the desert, the townscapes, the suburbs, the farmlands and the odd anomalous pockets of individual lifestyles are observed. Through the integrity of this observation, these locations achieve an independent literary validity, and some of the characters achieve a fully mythic character. In the earlier novels, White seems to be deliberately striving after this kind of resonance, which makes *The Tree of Man* rather overblown, and threatens *Voss* with moments of monumental immobility. With *Voss*, as his most ambitious, self-consciously "Australian" work out of his system, White has been able to concern himself with his deeper preoccupations : the mystical possibilities of the most dispossessed, especially the "holy innocents" in *Riders in the Chariot* and *The Solid Mandala*, and of the "private" artists in *Riders in the Chariot* and *The Vivisector*—themes which had appeared already but left undeveloped in *The Tree of Man*. Around the main characters are arranged their surroundings, vital contexts against which their behaviour is formed or clashed: the suburbs and towns with their small-minded hostilities and internecine cruelties.

The novel which made this possible, however, was *Voss*: it faced the heart of dryness, and came out in terms which are fully mystical as the means of encompassing it. The enterprise is deliberately mythic. As Laura pens her last direct address to Voss before falling into her spiritual and physical agony, she writes :

> It would seem that the human virtues, except in isolated, absolved, absurd, or oblivious individuals *are* mythical. Are you, too, my dearest, a myth, as it has been suggested ?[9]

Voss achieves his mythic power precisely because he embodies all these exceptions which Laura wrote down, and seems to lack ordinary human virtues especially when he practises them so ruthlessly. Voss, socially inept, obsessively self-righteous and believing only in the God in himself, speaks his truth; and he is confronted by Laura Trevelyan, doubting, perceptive, willing to give way to the whims of her inferiors, but who can also be implacable in her truthfulness.

> It had become quite clear from the man's face that he accepted his own divinity. If it was less clear, he was equally convinced that all others must accept. After he had submitted himself to further trial, and, if necessary, immolation.
>
> I shall worship you, suddenly said the voice of the cold girl.
>
> It was she who had wrestled with him in the garden.[10]

As Voss pits himself against the desert, the only worldly feature grand enough to challenge his immense certainty, his body dries out while his will clarifies. His acts grow deliberately, challengingly Christlike, and the imagery grows stiff with Christian symbolism. Eventually, his body is almost dead, laid in a humpy, and he admits his weakness:

> He himself, he realized, had always been most abominably frightened, even at the height of his divine power, a frail god upon a rickety throne...

Now, at least, reduced to the bones of manhood, he could admit to all this and listen to his teeth rattling in the darkness.[11]

Then he looks up at the "nails" of the Southern Cross "eating" into the sky. Even

at one stage the spear seemed to enter his own hide, and he screamed through his thin throat with his little, leathery strip of remaining tongue. For all suffering he screamed.

Oh, Lord, let him bear it.[12]

He achieves a "luminous state" of visionary harmony with his "wife" Laura:

Of greater importance were his own words of love that he was able at last to put into her mouth. So great was her faith, she received these white wafers without surprise.[13]

The communion of his faith, received by Laura Trevelyan in her sickness, is modified from its original harshness by her gentleness and sensitivity: it is finally translated into the useful "knowledge and strength" of a headmistress. Her inner certainty of Voss is confronted by Colonel Hebden who is appointed to "scientifically" pin down Voss's actual achievements, but who is consistently thwarted both by the reality of the events themselves and the tendency of all who knew Voss to mythologise him into the Devil or Christ.

Mythologising the land has always been done in terms of suprahuman powers and superhuman men. The land must take its place within a wider framework, so that its peoples can see it as part of the order of all things. Some writers had already attempted to stretch the range of the bourgeois literary form, the novel, to embrace the suprahuman through its human preoccupations. Individual authors in the Commonwealth have extended these efforts which they have inherited, and recharged the ancient traditions of mysticism to assist them. Wilson Harris has leaped into the esoteric systems and wrapped himself in the multifaceted robes of the shaman, while Patrick White has chosen the lonelier road of contemplation. For both, the achievement has been a difficult emotional mapping of their heartlands. But as Laura Trevelyan points out towards the end of *Voss*:

Knowledge was never a matter of geography. Quite the reverse, it overflows all maps that exist. Perhaps true knowledge only comes of death by torture in the country of the mind.[14]

REFERENCES

1. Keneally, Thomas, *Bring Larks and Heroes*, London, Quartet, 1973, p. 27.

2. F.M. Macri extends this interpretation further in his article *"Beautiful Losers* and the Canadian Experience", *Journal of Commonwealth Literature*, VIII, 1. He observes : "The whole pattern of the fight for life, of the dangers of annihilation, of the split being striving for unity, is observable in *Beautiful Losers*. The process usually begins in the past, and the knowledge attained in the struggle is its most important element, for it teaches that liberation from alienation precludes the possibility of any pure existence." Wilson Harris and Patrick White both go *through* alienation to achieve a level of pure existence.

3. Maclennan, Hugh, *The Watch That Ends The Night*, Toronto, Macmillan, 1959, p. 372.

4. Gerald Moore, in *The Chosen Tongue* shows clearly the significance of the geography and life-cycles of Guyana in Harris's work, especially in the chapters "Coastland" and "Heartland".

5. Gilkes, Michael, *Wilson Harris and the Caribbean Novel*, Longman Caribbean, 1975, p. 3.

6. Harris, Wilson, *The Whole Armour and The Secret Ladder*, London, Faber, 1973, p. 88.

7. *ibid.*, pp. 151-2.

8. Post Offices and the postal system seem to occur frequently in Patrick White's novels. Perhaps they relate to his own attempts to communicate. They are certainly tied to his preoccupation with the vulnerability of actual pieces of paper on which words are committed—as is shown very clearly in Voss's declaration to Laura which is torn up by the uncomprehending aboriginal messenger.

9. White, Patrick, *Voss*, London, Penguin, 1960, p. 329.

10. *ibid.*, p. 144.

11. *ibid.*, p. 390.

12. *ibid.*, p. 392.

13. *ibid.*, p. 393.

14. *ibid.*, p. 446.

16

Time in the Third World :
A Fictional Exploration

PETER NAZARETH

MY first novel, *In a Brown Mantle,* begins with the attempted assassination of Robert Kyeyune, the President of an African country, Damibia. After reading the headlines about the attempted assassination and coup, we realise that the story is being told by a narrator, Deo D'Souza. Deo D'Souza is a Goan who was born and grew up in Damibia; he had been a politician in Damibia but is now in exile in London. Like all Goans in East Africa, he is a Roman Catholic and feels the need to confess. He feels guilty— why? He wants to know why, and so do we. In telling his story, his mind goes backwards and forwards in time, making comments, recalling persons, talking about history, not in any chronological order but in an apparently haphazard way. In fact, he is holding a dialogue with himself. At the end of the novel, he comes back to the present: his exile. As in a poem by T.S. Eliot—the title of the novel is taken from *The Waste Land*—the end is the beginning. Time in the novel is a spiral, and the way we come back to the beginning is not through linear movement but through psychic time. Deo D'Souza's "internal time" is not the kind measured with a clock: it covers 450 years of Portuguese rule in Goa, several decades of British rule in Damibia, a few years of political independence with continued economic dependence, and exile to the mother country, all of which impinge on his consciousness. The economic and political dependence on outside forces, continuing with the assistance of some adventurers and social climbers, leads to this spiral time for the narrator. The more things change, the more they seem not to change.

My novel is easy to read because a narrator takes you along in conversational language. I believe like Sandipan Chattopadhyay in having a transparent prose style to which a reader gets stuck "like an inspired fly on a panel of glass." The problem of readability is more complex when

we turn to *The Combat* by Kole Omotoso of Nigeria.   In this short novel,
Omotoso deals with the Civil War in Nigeria which followed the two
coups of 1966.   The novel starts off with a detailed, realistic account of
a common man, the taxi-driver Chuku.   This is followed by a sensuous,
detailed description of a cheap meal eaten by a boy, Isaac.   We get the
impression that the novel is going to be a naturalistic account of the
disruption the coups and Civil War caused to the lives of the common
people.   This does not happen. Shortly after the beginning, it is announced that a coup has taken place; the details are from the first coup of
1966, dovetailing into the second coup, as though the two coups are one.
Chuku's response to his friend's information about the second coup is to
say, with a laugh, "That na my business?" Reversing his car to drive off,
Chuku unknowingly kills Issac, who was sitting on the bumper of the car
to eat his little lunch. Ojo follows Chuku on a motor-cycle and challenges
him to a duel to exact revenge for the killing of Isaac.

Thereafter, the novel keeps changing form, from realism to moral fable
to allegory. The forthcoming combat becomes a symbol for the fratricidal
Nigerian War, but this is not a static symbol we can identify comfortably
because more symbols and incidents keep bubbling up to reinforce the
idea that both friends and all parties concerned will lose out.   One such
incident is as follows: we discover that the two friends had both slept
with a woman, Moni, and both claimed to be the father of her son.   The
courts were trying to decide who was the father and who Moni belonged
to.   When preparations for the fight hot up, the courts decide to award
the child to Ojo and the mother to Chuku.   But Chuku now needs the
child because he had agreed to send the boy to Russia for education in
exchange for Soviet military aid in his forthcoming combat, while Moni,
now grown large, refuses to go with Chuku because she is too big for one
man. Meanwhile, Ojo had gone to the South Africans for help, as
Biafra had apparently done in real life.   Very soon, everyone from the
outside world is involved in the build-up to the fight—the outside powers,
the outside reporters, outside gamblers, adventurers, etc. The combat
gets so completely out of hand that the combatants make heroic, ideological statements that have nothing to do with the cause of the combat.
Chuku says,

> "Moreover Ojo Dada is the agent of colonialists, imperialists, neocoloni-
> alists.   Through him some outside monster is going to take over the
> running of our lives here.   I must prevent this. This is my duty and I
> am ready to sacrifice my life for it."

Towards the end, when it is time for the combat, Moni, now called
Dee Madam, collects the body of Isaac, whom everybody had forgotten
and who turns out to be the boy in dispute, her son.

We have the evidence of *The Edifice* and *Sacrifice* to show us that

Omotoso is not a careless writer but a careful craftsman. Time in *The Combat* is not linear, and the novel ends at the beginning. Time itself seems not to have moved because the situation and events are such that the more things appear to change, the more they remain just where they are. The two coups have changed nothing for the ordinary people, represented by Isaac. (The name is significant: Abraham was asked by God to sacrifice his son Isaac.) The novel is spiral shaped: everything is drawn into the vortex of the forthcoming combat, which will change nothing.

Only two coups and one Civil War had taken place in Nigeria when Omotoso had written *The Combat*, in the first decade of Independence. What would happen if the pattern continued and a hundred coups took place in as many years? What happens when a new set of generals comes in and says the same idealistic things about the reasons for the coup as the ones they overthrew, who themselves had said the same things as the ones they had overthrown?... *ad infinitum*. This would be like the situation in Columbia, Latin America, and we would get a novel like Gabriel Garcia Marquez's *One Hundred Years of Solitude*. Garcia Marquez uses a more exaggerated technique than Omotoso, a technique called "marvellous reality" or "magical realism". As the Peruvian writer Jose Bravo said in a talk on marvellous reality in Latin American writing at the International Writing Program, Iowa City,

> The author then proposes a game, a delirious game that dissolves reality and makes objective all the marvellous or inadmissible there could be in a text. Imagination flies making it possible for marvellous reality to live with objective reality in the same plane with the same value. Dreams stimulate this symbiosis, nightmares intensify the possibilities of the absurd, delirium takes reality to unimaginable, unimagined limits.

The Latin American reality is one of nearly four hundred years of exploitation, the last hundred of which has been economic. There is no dignity in this kind of underdevelopment, and reality becomes absurd as people trying to save the situation only keep it the same. Elections become a farce, and they are rigged anyway. In the tradition of the picaresque hero, Colonel Aureliano Buendia in *One Hundred Years of Solitude* rides off to fight and save the village and the country. This is what happens to him :

> Colonel Aureliano Buendia organised thirty-two armed uprisings and he lost them all. He had seventeen male children by seventeen different women and they were exterminated one after the other on a single night before the oldest one had reached the age of thirty-five. He survived fourteen attempts on his life, seventy-three ambushes, and a firing squad. He lived through a dose of strychnine in his coffee

that was enough to kill a horse.   He refused the Order of Merit, which
the President of the Republic awarded him.   He rose to be Commander in Chief of the revolutionary forces, with jurisdiction and command from one border to the other, and the man most feared by the
government, but he never let himself be photographed.   He declined
the lifetime pension offered him after the war and until old age he
made his living from the little gold fishes that he manufactured in his
workshop in Macondo.   Although he always fought at the head of
his men, the only wound that he received was the one he gave himself
after signing the Treaty of Neerlandia, which put an end to almost
twenty years of civil war.   He shot himself in the chest with a pistol
and the bullet came out through his back without damaging any vital
organ.   The only thing left of all that was a street that bore his name
in Macondo.

Although the words and sentences of this passage are moving us forward, we do not seem to be getting anywhere.   We see the total meaning-
lessness of Colonel Aureliano Buendia's fight.   After fighting on and on,
he comes to the conclusion that the only difference between the Liberals
and the Conservatives is that the Liberals go to mass at five o'clock and
the Conservatives at eight!   So much for democracy in an underdeveloped
country, says the novelist; it is merely a choice, which is rigged anyway,
between Tweedledum and Tweedledee—the military being no solution.
    The sinister reality behind this bizarre situation is largely economic.
One day, a "Gringo" named Brown comes to visit Macondo and is given
bananas to eat.   He comes back to start a flourishing banana business
belonging to an outside company.   The workers, led by José Arcadio
Segundo, decide to go on strike to protest the lack of sanitary facilities
in their living quarters, the non-existence of medical services, the terrible
working conditions and the fact that they are paid not in money but in
scrip which is good only for buying Virginia ham in the commissaries of
the banana company.   When the case begins, all sorts of legal tricks are
used to fool the workers.   Mr Brown has been forced by the workers to
sign an agreement.   When he appears in court, he is in disguise, his hair
is dyed and he speaks Spanish; the judge rules that he is not Jack Brown
and that, therefore, the agreement was not signed by Jack Brown.   Later,
after new demands by the workers, the lawyers produce a death certificate
to prove that Mr Brown died after being run over by a fire engine in
Chicago.   Eventually, it is established by a decision of the court and set
down in solemn decrees that the workers did not exist.   When a great
strike breaks out in response to the situation, the military shoots unarmed
people. Thousands of people are killed :

Trying to flee from the nightmare, José Arcadio Segundo dragged
himself from one car to another in the direction in which the train

was heading, and in the flashes of light that broke through the wooden slats as they went through sleeping towns he saw the man corpses, woman corpses, child corpses who would be thrown into the sea like rejected bananas.

History is rewritten so that nobody remembers or knows of the massacre. The people killed seem to have vanished through a hole in time as though they never were.

No wonder, then, that Ursula, the wife of José Arcadio Buendia, who lives to be over a hundred, often comments on time. "It's as if time had turned around and we were back at the beginning," she says. The author emphasises this spiral time by constantly coming back to the scene of Aureliano Buendia facing the firing squad. The novel ends with the last member of the family reading some encyclicals and discovering that he would never leave the room for the moment he finished reading them, "the city of mirrors (or mirages) would be wiped out by the wind and exiled from the memory of men at the precise moment when Aureliano Babilonia would finish deciphering the parchments, and that everything on them was unrepeatable since time immemorial and forever more, because races condemned to one hundred years of solitude did not have a second opportunity on earth." Time seems to swallow itself up, like a snake swallowing its own tail until the snake itself disappears.

Garcia Marquez takes the story further in his latest novel, *The Autumn of the Patriarch*. The patriarch is the ruler of a Latin American nation who rules for—who can figure it out ? Perhaps a hundred years, perhaps two hundred. He runs a home for overthrown generals and cheats them in dominoes; only one person is permitted to beat him in dominoes, a man who had lost an arm saving the leader from an assassination attempt : that is until he is roasted and served at a state dinner to the guests. "His time is Macondo time," says Gregory Rabassa, Garcia Marquez's translator. Rabassa adds that the patriarch is a meld of many dictators and we can all find our dictators in him. The whole novel was written in six convoluted sentences.

The spiral concept of time can also be found in the fiction of white writers from the Third World. A good example is the first novel by Michael Henderson of New Zealand, *The Log of a Superfluous Son*. The Superfluous Son is Osgar Senney, a New Zealander who has signed up as a supernumerary on a ship, the 'Hindbad', to look after cattle being shipped from New Zealand to Korea. On one level, the whole story takes place over sixteen days, from December 21, 1965 to January 6, 1966. On another level, however, the story goes through several time layers so that "time" is often simultaneous :

The sea lisped against the Hindbad's plates. Latitude 0°. Drake, Magellan, Raleigh, da Gama, Dana, Conrad, Columbus—an eternal

thalassocracy buoyed him up. Latitude 0°. Es-Sindibád, Captain Marr-
yat, R.M. Ballantyne, R.L.S., Jack London, O'Neill, Gulliver bright as
a spume on the bow-wave !

The voyage therefore is a voyage of exploration through time. Michael
Henderson is concerned not just with linear time but also with underlying
historical, psychic and mythic time. Thus Osgar Senney says in his poem,
used as a motif to the novel, "Why must I fill my log of time/with such
unfitting information ?" We are told that Auckland "played hide-and-
seek behind its history", reminding us of the levels behind the facade.
Thus "time" in the novel is multi-layered and the author uses all the novelistic techniques to explore these layers : reference to a diary kept earlier
by the protagonist, dreams, drunken thoughts, repetition of phrases and
images, anagrams, ancient spellings, literary echoes, parody, symbolic
names, phrases from other languages, etc. These techniques are organised
into a whole as taut and suggestive as a poem. Much of the externalised
action must be imagined, thus achieving the effect of timelessness by not
tying down the action to specific details. Henderson has taken New
Zealand to be the furthest outpost of the white man's empire in space and
time. The voyage of Osgar Senney therefore becomes the questioning not
merely of the personal self but also of the whole of the white man's empire,
throughout time. Thus the protagonist's name is significant. His first
name is not "Oscar", a mistake made by some of the sailors, but an old
English name meaning "Divine Spear", given by his mother who had died
as a result of ill-treatment by her husband. His second name suggests
"senna", the dried leaves of a certain plant used as a cathartic. Osgar
Senney seems to be suffering from spiritual exhaustion of the whole of the
white man's world. Hence most of the action is internalised for Osgar
Senney represents a whole world.

Osgar has worked in the Ministry of External Affairs, where he had
had to lie about New Zealand's involvement in Vietnam. Finally, he cannot stand it any more and tries to find expiation by joining a ship taking
cattle to Korea. His job is to look after the cattle and clear out the dung.
Symbolically, Osgar is trying to clear the Augean stables.

Osgar's diary is an old medical diary given to him by his grandfather,
Dr. Ernest Happenstance. Each entry, made during the early, "glorious"
rule of Elizabeth II, is punctuated by complaints and commercial remedies, which symbolise the sickness of the society. Each date in the novel
also has symbolic significance. It is no coincidence that the novel starts
on December 21, the feast of St Thomas, the Doubting Apostle, or that
the favourite cow named Goldie gives birth to a calf during the Christmas
period, or that the novel ends on Epiphany. There is a Christian structure
underlying the novel. Thus, in keeping with the multi-layered nature of
time in the novel, Osgar is running away not only from his past but also
from his present in the form of a girlfriend who has an angelic name,

Angie. The heaven Angie represents is one of settling down into bourgeois, unquestioning comfort : so the doubter runs to probe the wounds. One of the three wise men in the novel is called the Cologne King. His Christmas gift to Osgar : in a whorehouse in Guam, he tells Osgar that the ship is too dangerous and may fall apart at any time. He says the ship was made out of the front and the back of the two abandoned ships which had been built hurriedly for the Second World War. "Our can was dere war effort, son, dere masterpiece for Uncle Sam," he says. "It wasn't made for no shipyard, it was made for de graveyard." So Osgar sees that there is no escape. His attempt at enjoying himself with the black whore, whom he chose in preference to the white one, does not work : no longer can he exploit the non-white with a clear conscience.

Osgar's voyage shows him that there is no escape from his past for the past is not a personal one he can put on and take off. At the same time, it is personal in that one cannot excuse one's own moral crimes by blaming history. As Martin Fierro says satirically regarding Vietnam, history will absolve President Johnson, who will blame Kennedy, who will blame Eisenhower, who will blame Truman, through the corridors of time until it will be decided that the Vietnam war started before the birth of Christ. Osgar is guilty and he knows that the time for petty, chauvinistic, top-dog, exploitative nationalism is past. We are all in a ship that was built dangerously and could sink at any time. This is also the conclusion of Henderson's fellow-writer from New Zealand, the Samoan Albert Wendt. Wendt achieves the effect of timelessness in his novel *Sons for the Return Home* by having characters who are nameless.

A writer whose work Michael Henderson's closely resembles is Wilson Harris of Guyana. In all his novels, Harris deals with reality through recurrent, spiral time. His novels usually contain a story about a journey into the awesome interior of Guyana, where man faces primordial forces of nature. Simultaneously, the journey becomes one into the interior of the soul and the psychic possibilities of each individual as part of a larger community. The characters begin to resemble one another, to appear as reincarnations of people from the past, and to recognise their kinship with one another. *The Secret Ladder* ends as follows :

In our end...our end...our end is our beginning...beginning...beginning. Fenwick awoke. It was the dawn of the seventh day.

This quotation echoes the last line of T.S. Eliot's "East Coker" from *Four Quartets*, which itself is an echo of the motto of Mary Queen of Scots. The seventh day brings to mind the Judaeo-Christian myth of creation. But Harris's presentation of time comes from multi-layered myths, including those of the Arawak and Carib Indians who were practically exterminated. Harris prefaces his retelling of the myth of *Quiyumucon*, "By Quiyumucon the Caribs meant First Cause or ancestral time."

Analysing *Ascent to Omai*, the Guyanese critic, Michael Gilkes, says,

> At this point the reader has the curious impression of looking *forward* into the past from the present and *backward* from the present...into the future...Past, present and future now co-exist.

The reason for this, Gilkes tells us, is that "[Harris'] own attitude to history...rejects the 'dead' time of the historians : the catalogues of deeds 'that measure man as a derivative industry-making animal, tool-making animal, weapon-making animal' : and looks instead towards a re-appraisal of history in the light of *intuitive* logic which deals with the latent, unpredictable impulses affecting present and future. Historical time becomes relative, factual events become symbolic, linear thematic development becomes cyclical."

A modern Indian is the protagonist of William Lawson's first novel, *Zepplin Coming Down*. (I am referring, of course, to those people who were discovered by Columbus when he lost his way trying to get to India.) This is Codac, who, as his name suggests, uses art to keep reality at a distance. Action takes place on two planes : the present, in California, where Codac is separated from his lover, and the past, in France, when he was with her. As reality closes in on Codac, as the Zepplin of his fantasies comes down, the two times merge. Codac is arrested during a demonstration and thrown into jail. Immediately, he is on the barge he and his lover had travelled on in France. Can he escape the disaster of the Zepplin ? Will he be saved like Werner Franz, saved by the cold water tanks exploding over him ?

Another Third World novelist in the First World is Ishmael Reed. Many elements have gone into the style of Ishmael Reed : films, comics, the tall tale, but most of all, the traditions of Africa. Thus Reed calls his writing Neo-Hoodoo, and among the deadly enemies of his protagonists are all forms of Western cultural, religious and political oppressions, including excessive rationality and socialist realism. Hoodoo (or Voodoo) comes from Vodun, the African god. Reed claims that some of his work, such as "D Hexorcism of Noxon D Awful", is solidly in the tradition of African witchcraft : he used hoodoo to put the hex on the Noxon figure, in 1969. He says of his second novel, *Yellow Back Radio Broke-Down*, that the time sense is akin to the time one finds in the psychic world "where past, present and future exist simultaneously". In this novel, the Loop Garoo Kid is simultaneously an African mythical figure and a parody on the popular film and comics wild-west cowboy, Lash LaRue, who could do amazing things with a whip.

In Reed's fourth novel, *The Last Days of Louisiana Red*, time certainly is simultaneous. The action involves characters from African religion, Greek mythology, black Americans from today, political leftists, and academics. One of the characters is Chorus, who is looking for revenge against Antigone for destroying his role.   He finally meets up with her on a plane and shoots her.   "Antigone" is Minnie the Moocher, who resembles Angela Davis.   Another character is Papa Legba, the Yoruba God Legba or Eshu; he is a detective trying to find out who murdered Ed Yellings, who was just "taking care of business".   Papa Legba takes advice from an Indian god, who is in the form of an animal in the zoo. What is the significance of the title of the novel ?   Louisiana Red is a hot sauce that is poured by the exploiters on the Third World peoples to keep them fighting among themselves "while above their heads, fifty thousand feet, billionaires flew in custom-made jet planes equipped with saunas tennis courts swimming pools discotheques and meeting rooms decorated like a Merv Griffin Show set."   Such a description of the work misses the wild humour of Ishmael Reed, who must be one of the funniest writers today.   However, underlying all this humour is a time that is not linear : it is simultaneous, past and present, psychic and real.   Reed says that like an African necromancer, he is using the past to prophesy about the future.

Ayi Kwei Armah of Ghana and Africa has chosen in his fourth novel, *Two Thousand Seasons*, to tell the collective story of the Africans in the collective voice and with a non-Western sense of time.   For example, the collective voice says,

> A hundred seasons we spent in this slow flowing.   In our minds the terrors of the immediate past grew not so pressingly terrible.   Fewer among us woke up in the middle of their sleep screaming against the murders we had suffered.   A new generation had grown to produce children, and on the surface these children did not come bearing scars. Our wounds were covered over by new growth.

Having had enough of suffering at the hands of predators, the people decide to move away from all exploiters, including those within themselves. Their time is not to be measured by any clock but by their own ontological system and their suffering.   Like all the other authors mentioned in this paper, Ayi Kwei Armah is dealing with the Third World reality.   In the words of that classic analyst of the Third World, Frantz Fanon, "There's nothing save a minimum of readaptation, a few reforms at the top, a flag waving : and down there at the bottom an individual mass, still living in the middle ages, endlessly marking time."

    Does this mean that when exploitation and self-exploitation end in the Third World, and by implication in the First and Second Worlds, the novelists of the Third World will move away from a spiral presentation of time ?   Does it mean that they will move towards some form of artistic simplification such as socialist realism ?   This is a hypothetical question. Certainly, Ishmael Reed and Wilson Harris would resist, and it is to be doubted the others would accept dictated simplification.   For the present time, however, time in the Third World must find its own artistic expression.   In the inner world of Codac,

But the memory, arriving obliquely at unlooked for bits of information, slips past the censors and delivers up raw truth, leaning with a controlling angle back through time so that the tidied-up past, stored like letters to impress the family at home, is shaken into its true structure.

REFERENCES

This paper draws from the following critical works by Peter Nazareth :   *The Third World Writer*, East African Literature Bureau, Kampala/Nairobi/Dar-es-Salaam, 1978.

'The Tortoise is an animal, but he is also a wise creature' published in *Umoja*, A Journal of Black Experience, ed., Ernest N. Emenyonu, University of Colarado, Boulder, Colorado, USA, Vol. II, No. 2, July 1975.

"Time in the Third World", paper presented at a symposium on Time and Man, Michigan State University, East Lansing, Michigan, April 24, 1976, published in *Mana Review*, a South Pacific Journal of Language and Literature, ed. Subramani, Suva, Fiji, Vol. 1, No. 2. Dec. 1976.

"White Man's Burden", published in *Commentary*, Journal of the University of Singapore Society, ed. Kirpal Singh & Pauline Baratham, Singapore, Vol. 1, No. 4, May, 1976.

Other references in the paper are as follows, page numbers for the larger quotations provided in brackets :

Ayi Kwei Armah, *Two Thousand Seasons*, East African Publishing House, Nairobi, Kenya, 1973 (p. 78).

Jose Antonio Bravo, "Latin American Reality and its Problems with Respect to Narrative (Special Orientation to Magical Realism)", trans. Connie Sue McDuffee, paper presented at the International Writing Program, University of Iowa, Iowa City, April, 1974.

Frantz Fanon, *The Wretched of the Earth*, trans. Constance Farrington, Ballantine Books, New York, 1973.

Gabriel Garcia Marquez, *One Hundred Years of Solitude*, trans. Gregory Rabassa, Bard Books, Avon, New York, 1971 (p. 104, p. 284).

Gabriel Garcia Marquez, *The Autumn of the Patriarch*, trans. Gregory Rabassa, Harper & Row, New York, 1976.

Michael Gilkes, *Wilson Harris and the Caribbean Novel*, Longman Caribbean, Trinidad/Jamaica/London, 1975 (pp. 135/36, p. 132).

Wilson Harris, *Ascent to Omai*, Faber & Faber, London, 1970.

Wilson Harris, *The Secret Ladder*, Faber & Faber, 1963.

Wilson Harris, *The Sleepers of Roraima*, Faber & Faber, 1970.

Michael Henderson, *The Log of a Superfluous Son*, John McIndoe, Dunedin, New Zealand, 1975 (p. 84, p. 85).

William Lawson, *Zepplin Coming Down*, Yardbird Wing Editions, Berkeley, California, 1976 (p. 212).

Adil Jussawalla, ed. *New Writing From India*, Penguin, Baltimore, Maryland, 1974.

Peter Nazareth, *In a Brown Mantle*, East African Literature Bureau, 1972.

Kole Omotoso, *The Combat*, Heinemann, London, 1972 (p. 58).

Kole Omotoso, *The Edifice*, Heinemann, 1971.

Kole Omotoso, *Sacrifice*, Onibonoje & Book Industries (Nig.) Ltd., Ibadan, Nigeria, 1974.

Ishmael Reed, "D Hexorcism of Noxon D Awful", from *Amistad 1*, ed. John A. Williams & Charles F. Harris, Vintage Books, Random House, New York, 1970.

Ishmael Reed, *Shrovetide in Old New Orleans*, a collection of essays, Doubleday & Co., New York, 1978.

Ishmael Reed, *The Last Days of Louisiana Red*, Random House, New York, 1974.

Ishmael Reed, *Yellow Back Radio Broke-Down*, Bantam Books, New York, 1972.

Albert Wendt, *Sons for the Return Home*, Longman Paul, Auckland, New Zealand/ Victoria, Australia, 1973.

17

From the Village to the City :
the song of the road
The treatment of the Village in two modern novels
of Bengal and Sri Lanka

A.J. GUNAWARDANA

THE village is a recurrent theme in literature. How writers perceive the
village, the values they attach to it, the way it shapes their work, of course
change from culture to culture and from period to period. But certain common attitudes prevail. What I shall attempt in this paper is to locate and
assess the significance of one such common attitude in two very popular
and highly regarded non-English language novels from two neighbouring
societies—Sri Lanka and Bengal, two cultures which are related closely
enough to provide a realistic basis for comparing the two works.

The first novel I have chosen is *Pather Panchali* by Bibhutibhushan
Banerji, now a work internationally known because it is the story of
Satyajit Ray's celebrated film of the same name, and the translation
made available by UNESCO. The other is *Gamperaliya*, a Sinhala novel
by Martin Wickremasinghe. *Gamperaliya* does not have the same international reputation, though it has been translated into Russian and made
into an outstanding Sinhala motion picture which won the first prize at
the second international film festival held in New Delhi thirteen years ago.
Gamperaliya itself, however, is only now in the process of being translated
into English. (I am currently engaged in that task.) Before proceeding
any further, I should mention that my knowledge of *Pather Panchali* is
limited to the English version.

Let me begin with *Gamperaliya*, the work that is the closer to me of
the two. First published in 1947, *Gamperaliya* marks the maturing of the
Sinhala novel as an art form as well as a sophisticated mode of social
commentary. Sinhala fiction dates back only to the last decades of the
nineteenth century, though literary prose has been known in the language
for several centuries. The novel grew quite rapidly, but it entered man's

estate, as it were, and began to command the respect and attention of the literati only with the publication of *Gamperaliya*, making it a landmark in the history of Sinhala fiction. That it should deal with village life is perhaps no accident. "The Changing Village", the title used in the film, is an inadequately suggestive equivalent for "Gamperaliya". "Gampera-liya" means "upheaval in the village" (*gam*=village; *peraliya*=distur-bance or upheaval.) The upheaval amounts to the emergence of one social class in the village and the decline of another.

The narrative revolves round the fortunes of a village family of high social standing, by tradition and general acceptance (there is no question of caste) the most important and highest ranking members of the village community, who are very conscious of their position, taking every care to guard it. They are a sort of aristocracy in the village. In the beginning, they are fairly prosperous, but their wealth based on land gradually dec-lines. Towards the end, they are reduced to near-penury; however, their family pride remains, though somewhat battered. There is a second family, regarded by the first to be lower in social status, which rises up in the world. The changing relationships among the members of the two families form the core of the novel.

The head of the aristocratic family has an honorific title—*Muhandiram* —and is looked upon by the villagers as their leader. He has two unmar-ried daughters and a young son. The Muhandiram's wife is a kindly mat-ron greatly respected by all. Their house, an impressive edifice with a long history, is called "Mahagedara" (=the big house) by the villagers. The second family consists of Piyal, a young man of some education, and his widowed mother. Piyal is a frequent visitor at Mahagedara. He teaches English to the girls and is in love with Nanda, the younger of the two. Through an intermediary, he proposes marriage, and is cavalierly rejected by Nanda's parents because his family is socially inferior to theirs. Piyal's grandfather had been a vegetable vendor who sold his merchandise house to house.

Greatly wounded by the treatment he received from Nanda's family, Piyal leaves the village and finds employment in Colombo (the capital city). Nanda falls ill (it is not suggested in any way that she has emotional ties with Piyal; there is no romantic love in the novel). The prolonged, costly treatment Nanda needs eats into the dwindling assets of her family. The parents are eager to give her in marriage, but there is no dowry to accom-pany her. Eventually, she is married off to Jinadasa, a groom of unble-mished family background. Jinadasa, however, has no regulur occupation; like the family he marries into, Jinadasa lives off his patrimony, a precari-ously meagre one. The Muhandiram passes away soon afterwards, leaving only the crumbling ancestral house to his family. Nanda has a baby which dies within a few days of birth, the victim of a midwifely misadventure. Now at the end of his tether, Jinadasa sets out to start a trade in a distant rural community. He fails and never returns.

Tissa, the Muhandiram's son, has been attending English school in a nearby town. He is forced to stop after his father's death because the family can no longer spend any money for his board and lodging. He idles away his time at home, going about with village acquaintances and friends, much to the annoyance of his mother. Subsequently, he too leaves the village, goes to Colombo and finds a job. It is understood that he will not only help support his impoverished family, but also continue his education.

Meanwhile, Piyal has established a business of his own in Colombo and is prospering. And his desire for Nanda has grown rather than diminished over the years. He renews his plea for Nanda's hand. In the end, he is accepted—believing Jinadasa to be dead, Nanda marries Piyal. This, however, is not the end of the story. One day, Nanda receives a telegram saying that her husband is seriously ill in a hospital many miles away. She rushes to the hospital, only to be shown Jinadasa's body in the mortuary. The novel ends with Piyal's taunting remark that it was *his* money which was used for Jinadasa's obsequies.

Pather Panchali has less of a story to summarise. Bibhutibhushan Banerji's novel is primarily about the coming of age of a young boy, Opu. *Pather Panchali*, with no plot to speak of, consists of a series of events which shape the awareness of the boy and help determine his future. Opu is born to a very poor Brahmin family in a small, remote Bengali village. His father, Horihor, a man of religious learning, is rather inept at making a living. The family exists just above the starvation line—there are times when the mother is compelled to make do with boiled leaves. Opu's mother, Shorbojoya, treats the "old auntie", a destitute old relative, in a very callous fashion partly because of their constantly straitened circumstances—there just isn't enough food to go round. The world of the child, in some ways a highly joyous and endearing one, is linked to the adult world by this crushing poverty. Very little happens in the book which does not in some way stem from the condition of dire indigence—from Horihor's regular absences from the house to Opu's sister Durga's habit of stealing. In the end, after Durga's death, Horihor takes his family away from the village, to seek a new life in the faraway city of Benares.

How is the village seen and experienced in each novel ? What attitudes towards the village are manifest in them ? Needless to say, there are many contrasts between the two; but they also converge at several points. And it would seem to me that the affinities are more significant than the differences.

We should begin with the observation that both novels are greatly admired as works of realism. Realism, in fact, is generally considered the most distinguishing quality of the two novels. Insofar as the Bengali work is concerned, this has been well stated by the late T.W. Clark, co-translator :

> The merits of Banerji's work rest on the ease with which it is written, with its naturally executed changes of style, and on the vivid and sympathetic realism of its portrayal of the day to day life of the two children, their parents and other members of the village community.[1]

Life in a remote, rural corner of Bengal comes alive in Banerji's novel—mainly through events that are congruent with the experiences of two children. A good deal of what is in the book is seen from the perspective of Opu and Durga. It has also been remarked that the realism of *Pather Panchali* is not contaminated by mawkish sentiment. This again is true. Emotion is always well disciplined. Consider for example the scene where the news of Durga's death is conveyed to Horihor :

> He looked round the house, went from room to room, and then slowly a feeling of disappointment began to creep into his eager and delighted voice. "Where are the children ? Are they both out of the house ? They can't be surely !" He sounded impatient. Shorbojoya could bear it no longer. She burst out crying. "Durga," she sobbed. "My poor, poor Durga ! We've lost the poor darling. She's gone and left us. Where have you been all this time ?"[2]

This ends the scene. I cannot of course comment on the quality of the translation, but it is quite clear that the author is in firm control of his material. Or take Shorbojoya's treatment of the old auntie. Our sympathies are with the old woman, but we are not made to shed tears over her fate. Durga's errant ways and the punishments that are meted out to her could have become an exercise in the pathetic. But they do not. Such examples can be multiplied. They all add up to the impression that the writer has a firm, unflinching grip on reality which does not relax even in situations of great emotional compulsion. This strength becomes especially admirable when it is remembered that *Pather Panchali* is a work which was first serialised in a popular journal, and that its two main characters are children.

Equally high praise can be bestowed on *Gamperaliya* as a work of realism. The novel has a seemingly sensational plot. Nanda marries a second time while her first husband is still alive, though of course unconsciously. There are many occasions for tears (several funerals) and for passion as well. The dead body of Nanda's first husband turns up in a hospital mortuary. There is unrequited love and a dramatic decline in the fortunes of the principal family. This is the very stuff of melodrama; but Wickremasinghe can never be charged with the melodramatic exploitation of his material.

Not long after the Muhandiram's sudden death, his wife cleans up his writing bureau and discovers a number of letters written to him by a village woman, one of them inviting him to an assignation. The existence of such a liaison is subtly hinted at earlier but never revealed until this chance discovery. For the Muhandiram's wife, this affair is a cause for both shame and anger; her sense of family pride has been rudely violated. At the end of the novel, when he is told by Nanda that she paid for Jinadasa's funeral, Piyal bursts out : "So it was all done with *my* money !" a remark for which he later begs Nanda's forgiveness.

Incidents of this kind enrich the texture of characterisation; such instances abound in *Pather Panchali* too. Shorbojoya, in many ways a good mother, behaves most unkindly to the old auntie who has no one else to help her. And Horihor does not remonstrate; indeed, he does not seem to notice Shorbojoya's cruelties.

There are no heroes or heroines in either novel, and from this angle both works show a modern consciousness. Wickremasinghe used to remark that there aren't good people or bad in his fiction; he treated them all alike. The same observation holds for Banerji's book. He too "treats all his people alike." Stated differently, neither author idealises or romanticises the village and its people. They are shown as an uncommitted observer perceives them.

The authors' handling of character and incident enhances the realism, as do their descriptions of social intercourse and the natural environment. This last aspect is more evident in *Pather Panchali* than in *Gamperaliya*. Many of Opu's encounters are with nature. The following passage is typical.

It was nearly fifteen minutes walk to the Moat Lake, and to get there they [Opu and Durga] had to go along a narrow path through almost continuous jungle. It is true that there were many mango and jackfruit trees there, but they were very old, and underneath them was an almost impenetrable wall of thorn bushes and other undergrowth. Scarcely anybody went there to look for mangoes because it was such a lonely and remote place. Old creepers as thick as ropes hung from tree to tree, and it was far from easy to ferret out the mangoes that had fallen into the tangle of undergrowth beneath the giant old fruit trees. To make things more difficult they could not see very well, what with the thick black storm clouds overhead and the dark shadows where the trees sagged down over the bushes below.[3]

Even this description of raw nature is entirely straightforward and unromantic. A similar tone is to be found in *Gamperaliya*.

In these different ways then, *Pather Panchali* and *Gamperaliya* can be taken as good examples of realism. It is on this basis that the two novels are customarily appraised. *Gamperaliya* is praised for its faithful portrayal of the rise of a new social class in Sri Lanka and *Pather Pan-chali* is valued for its sensitive depiction of the joys and travails of child-hood. This valuation is undoubtedly true, yet there is an underlying thread which goes beyond realism and binds the two works closer to-gether. This link is a specific attitude towards the village.

The vast body of modern literature tells us that realism can range between two poles, moving from the relentlessly detailed depiction of the totality of observed reality to the highly selective presentation of chosen segments of life. *Pather Panchali* and *Gamperaliya* may seem to be closer to the first extreme than to the second. As we have already indicated, most critical evaluations laud the novels for being 'true to reality.' Neither novelist, it would appear from these assessments, has a thematic axe to grind—although Wickremasinghe's austere prose does sometimes stray into patches of ethical discourse. At one point, for example, he explicitly blames Nanda's parents for adhering to outmoded values which, he argues, hasten the family's decline. Such occasions apart, the novels are thought to be "value free" in that the authors do not articulate any particular viewpoint about the village. The two novels, it is said, merely mirror village life without distorting it or colouring it.

In fact, however, both novelists express clear, and almost identical, views of the village which are by no means devoid of value judgments. One convenient way of discovering these is to consider the writers' relationship to their material. We might begin by noticing that both novels have strong autobiographical resonances. The autobiographical element in the Bengali work can be summed up in the words of Clark :

> It should not be supposed that *Pather Panchali* is pure autobiography, but it is near enough to it to breathe a realism which pure fiction, even the greatest, can seldom achieve.[4]

There is, of course, no simple equation between Opu and Bibhutibhushan; but what is known of the writer's boyhood in a Bengali village, with a Durga-like cousin and parents cast in the same mould as Horihor and Shorbojoya, warrants Clark's assertion.

As for the Sinhala novel, the correspondence between the autobiogra-phical and the fictional cannot be so clearly established with respect to the characters. Wickremasinghe was born to a family not unlike that of the Muhandiram in social standing and economic circumstances. And there is an unmistakable resemblance between Wickremasinghe and Tissa, the young son of the Mahagedara family.

It hardly needs to be underlined that Banerji and Wickremasinghe write about the worlds of their childhood. Wickremasinghe was born in 1891; *Gamperaliya* begins with the Sinhala New Year festivities of 1904 (the date is given) and covers the next decade. Banerji was born four years later and his novel deals with approximately the same period, though specific dates are not mentioned.

Yet by the time they wrote their novels, Banerji and Wickremasinghe had long been city-dwellers. Both left the village in their late teens—Banerji to continue his schooling, Wickremasinghe to earn a living. They began writing early in life, and they were not only prolific but highly successful as well. It was from the vantage point of the city that they looked back upon and dramatised the experiences of their childhood. Their treatment of the village—the long view of rural Sri Lanka and India—stems from their status as ex-villagers, as artists and intellectuals who made it in the city. This obvious truth is crucial to an understanding of what the novels "say".

Consider what happens to Opu and Tissa, the surrogates of Banerji and Wickremasinghe respectively. Opu migrates with his parents to distant Benares. It may be argued that he has no choice in the matter—being small, he has to follow his parents for whom the city spells "a new world, a new way of life, and a new prosperity."[5] But we are not left in any doubt that given the choice, Opu would have had no hesitations about moving out of the village. For him too, the city does symbolise the fulfillment of certain vague aspirations. Young as he is, Opu feels a yearning to leave the village. In groping, unconscious ways, he shares his mother's picture of Benares "where everything is made of gold, where no one is poor."[6] But more :

> Suddenly he was voyaging to England like that man in the *Bangbashi*. His ship had sailed from Calcutta. Sagar Island in the mouth of the estuary was behind them, and they were threading their way through a host of little islands in the middle of the sea. The dark green line of coconut palms on the shores of Ceylon was already in sight, and on the far horizon he could make out blue mountains in a strange land, which reddened as he watched them in the light of the setting sun. All was change! New sights! And still he journeyed on, further and further into the unknown.[7]

Horizon is a key word. In an earlier chapter we read :

> One day at this time Opu stood staring over the grassy plain to where in the far distance the blue sky came down to earth over a line of trees; and as he looked that peculiar sense of far-awayness came over him again. He had not been able to describe it before, neither could he now. All he could do was to shout to his sister when she came up out of the water. "Look, Didi! Look right over there!" and point with his finger to where field and horizon met. "There it is ! On the other side of that tree there ! It's a long way off, isn't it?"[8]

Such perceptions and flights of fancy are no doubt meant to suggest the early awakening of the boy's imagination. They suggest something else too : an inarticulate desire for space, for room to grow. In physical terms, this entails leaving the village, a consummation beautifully symbolised by the railway line, which ultimately is the means of transporting Opu and his family to the city. As he runs with Durga to see the railway line for the first time, Opu feels "really free...free of the restrictions of the small circle which had hitherto imprisoned him, and his young blood thrills to the joy of release."[9]

The young imagination, fed upon stories of Jelekha, Sarayu, Grace Darling and Zutphen Sidney, envisions all those lands where somebody is waiting to welcome him, knows instinctively that "one day the call would come, and that he would go."[10]

To break out of the village, then, is the most natural thing to do; it is the boy's manifest destiny. And it is not questioned or contemplated in any serious manner. Opu's only regret is saying good-bye to Durga, not leaving the community or the woods and rivers he was so fond of. The "song of the road" beginning in the village must inevitably lead him out to the wide, beckoning world beyond.

In *Gamperaliya*, Tissa's departure from his native village seems equally natural, as much a manifest destiny as it is for Opu, though perhaps rather more matter-of-fact. Unlike Opu, Tissa has been educated for some years in an urban school. What he garners from his reading—he too is a voracious reader like Opu—turns him against the traditional beliefs of the village. Despite close familial bonds, Tissa returns to the village only twice during his first four years in Colombo. Although Wickremasinghe attributes this to Tissa's lack of leisure, it does suggest a kind of alienation from the village. Moreover, as he begins to write, it is seen that Tissa's interests are in the realm of ideas. He sets out to expose what he regards as the irrational aspects of traditional beliefs. Intellectually, Tissa divests himself of the village which seems a deadweight, while his spiritual ties with the culture of his boyhood seem tenuous at best.

City and village orbit closer together in *Gamperaliya* than in *Pather Panchali*. The railway line borders the village; the highway to Colombo divides it. Urban styles and fashions are not unknown to the village gentry. Interestingly, for the Mahagedara family Colombo remains a distant place—romantic, different, faintly exciting. Yet they do not appear to be overly concerned about Tissa. That Tissa should go to seek employment in Colombo, that he should be critical of traditional beliefs and values, is all taken for granted by them.

Tissa is a peripheral figure in the plot structure of the novel, but that he should thus draw away from the village physically and intellectually can hardly be called idiosyncratic. For him too, "a song of the road" had been sung, and this carries him to the metropolis, which from then on becomes his natural habitat, as his gifts as a writer begin to flower.

The economic imperatives behind the general phenomenon of migration to the city are well known, having been studied in depth and detail in many societies. In the two novels, these are quite obvious and specific. Tissa goes to Colombo for employment (he works as a salesman and clerk in a store) and does reasonably well, though he has no interest in business and in accumulating wealth, unlike the entrepreneur Piyal. In *Pather Panchali*, Shorbojoya's assumptions about the city ("The picture she had of Benares was of a place in which everything was made of gold, and where no one was poor..."[11]) may be naive, but Horihor, who has been there before, is sure that "life would be much more comfortable for them"[12] in Benares. As a learned and respected Brahmin priest, he expects to receive more patronage and a regular income in the city.

What is rather more striking is the cultural dimension of the changes depicted in the two novels. For both Opu and Tissa—the artist as juvenile and young man respectively—the exit from the village is shown as a positive act, a necessary step in the growth of their minds and personalities Tissa begins to extend his reading, to cast an analytical eye on the life around him and write occasional essays and short stories after his arrival in the city. In Opu's case, the developments that occur in the city area taken up in a later work, and are hence outside the scope of the present essay.[13] But there can be no doubt about the fact that Opu must get out of the village in order that his mind may grow. An unschooled village woman tells Opu's mother :

What is there in Nishchindipur [Opu's village] to stay for ? I certainly would not advise you to stay. Besides, it's not a good thing to let yourself get bogged down in one place. It makes you so narrow, doesn't it ? and prevents your mind from developing.[14]

It is important to note that neither writer seems to feel any need to justify in extensive fashion his protagonist's move to the city. For Banerji and Wickremasinghe, it is axiomatic that any youth with intellectual or artistic gifts must automatically follow this route, as they themselves did in real life. In a word, they present a critical but not unsympathetic evaluation of the village from the perspective of men who have made a successful transition to the city—to the wide, intellectually stimulating, artistically challenging world outside the confines of tradition.

To describe *Pather Panchali* as a loving but unsentimental evocation of a childhood in a village, and *Gamperaliya* as a faithful portrayal of the emergence of a new social class is to reduce the scope of the two novels. Both works record a most dynamic phase in the artistic and intellectual history of their societies, and speak of profound and fundamental social drives which, among other things, helped to generate a new consciousness and a new literature. Banerji and Wickremasinghe consider the journey out of the village as a liberation, not only from economic deprivation, but in things of the mind as well. The city becomes the logical destination for the new generation of intellectuals and artists.

REFERENCES

1. Clark, T.W. and Tarapada Mukherji, translators, *Pather Panchali* by Bibhutibhu-shan Banerji, Indiana University Press, Bloomington and London, 1968, p. 16.

2. *ibid.*, pp. 255-56.

3. *ibid.*, p. 105.

4. *ibid.*, p. 17.

5. *ibid.*, p. 298.

6. *ibid.*, p. 281.

7. *ibid.*, p. 279.

8. *ibid.*, p. 132.

9. *ibid.*, p. 134.

10. *ibid.*, p. 280.

11. *ibid.*, p. 281.

12. loc. cit.

13. It should be noted that both *Gamperaliya* and *Pather Panchali* belong to larger fictional entities. *Gamperaliya* is the first part of a trilogy which traces the fortunes of the Mahagedara family into the second and entirely urban generation. Opu's later career is taken up in *Aparajita*.

14. *ibid.*, p. 292.

18

Naipaul and Narayan :
The Sense of Life

D.V.K. RAGHAVACHARYULU

BOTH Naipaul and Narayan have established themselves as masters of the comic mode in fiction, portraying the life of their particular societies by means of a realism strongly rooted in the locative impulse and vividly rendered through an almost optic precision of closely observed nuances of human behaviour and attitudes. Both Malgudi and Trinidad or Port of Spain emerge as symbols of a mystic space which controls the physical and psychological centres of action in the novels, conferring on their narratives the quality and force of ritual. In tracing the locutions of human response to the crises of change and the contingent involutions in experience, both novelists have employed comic distance as a strategy of detachment and as a route to objectivity and truth. Here, however, they seem to part ways and the cognate nature of their art ends. The life of the novel is, in the sense of life revealed and dramatised, directed towards vastly different ends in the two writers. The radical vision of experience projected by the pressure of events and existential choices they generate as well as the alterations in the stance of human personality in the flux of life is fundamentally different in each.

One aspect of this difference lies in whether or not in either case the clock of the novel is wound up to a higher potential of human awareness acting beyond the sensuous cognition of people and their affairs in the machinery of life. Naipaul uses the novel form as a ritual of extinction and exorcism, whereas Narayan employs it as a ritual of initiation and renewal. Comedy at once distorts and clarifies, and even distorts in order to clarify, the human situation; and as a process in itself it leads us ultimately to a perception of the reality behind the appearance, the dignity behind the absurdity, and the value behind the pain of being human. Penetrating beneath the mask of incongruity and disorder, the comic artist denominates a sense of identity and order which do not smother but re-

revitalise the multitudinousness of life. In other words, we expect comedy in the final analysis to extend, not contract, to enhance, not diminish, our sense of life and its possibilities. Thus viewed Narayan's comedy employs limitation as art, whereas Naipaul's uses art as limitation. Narayan's humour is gentle, tender and gregarious; but Naipaul's comic wit is harsh, anguished and isolative. We may admire Naipaul; but we love Narayan.

At the first reading, the sheer brilliance of *A House for Mr Biswas* dazzles us. The well-wrought work seems to be an ultimate and an absolute in itself. Its minutely particularised background and the vividly realised characterisation seem to be intimately interwoven into the texture of the novel. But soon we realise how nightmarish the background is, and how monstrous the hero has been, and what a nugatory, antagonistic relation they enact towards life. Break the narcissistic enclosures of personality, you enter into the solipsistic circle in which life is suspended and arrested. Cut through the areas of darkness, you are enmeshed in a benighted void. The author, speaking through the narrator's editorial voice, fixes our attitude and judgment in respect of everything. The Prologue builds up a retroactive effect by means of a tone that mocks its own creation, proclaiming the obsequies in the form of a plenary last judgment over the life and fortunes of Mr Biswas.

> Ten weeks before he died, Mr Mohun Biswas, a journalist of Sikkim Street, St James, Port of Spain, was sacked. He had been ill for some time. In less than a year he had spent more than nine weeks at the Colonial Hospital and convalesced at home for even longer. When the doctor advised him to take a complete rest, the *Trinidad Sentinel* had no choice. It gave Mr Biswas three months' notice and continued, up to the time of his death, to supply him every morning with a free copy of the paper.
>
> (*A House for Mr Biswas*)

The passage demonstrates a disconcerting seepage of stylistic libido which acts as a destructive agent, mutilating, disfiguring and trampling down upon the created world of art. The comic pose is exposed by the harsh entification of experience and the singularly inappropriate, almost graceless feedbacks of the life-situation. The frightening insistence on the naturalistic contour of time (ten weeks; some time; less than a year; even longer; three months' notice; up to the time of his death; every morning) enacts a terrifying feeling of *tedium vitae*. Even more, it indicates an ordering of moral priorities which draws our attention away from human aspiration and our identification with it, producing a kind of alienation effect. The doctor's advice that Mr Biswas take 'a complete rest' may have solved the *Sentinel's* managerial problem; but the usage smacks of necrophilia and administers a severe *coup-de-grace* to the objectivity of the point of view technique. The egregious innuendo forces the crisis and mystery of personality out of the historical focus, desensitising the whole felt life of the novel, and extinguishing all promise of aesthetic charity. The Prologue, one feels, wrenches the whole human saga out of its heroic potentiality and moral significance. Artistic authenticity and human concern as well are deliberately destroyed by the pejorative tone adopted by the biographer. And what is left of comedy, when the perception of the tragic is taken away ? Instead of subtle 'hasya', we have gross 'apahasya' and we are set on a voyage to fools' paradise.

Naipaul's objectivity seems to stem not from historical altitude, but from a wry histrionic *hubris*. We are made conscious everywhere that the novelist takes up a position far away from the polluting touch of his own characters. This attitude is at work in the description of Mr Biswas's house, which its owner claims to represent 'a portion of the earth' he has possessed, to be passed on as an inheritance to his children. The image that emerges out of the Prologue is that of a place which is disconnected from the protagonist's own feeling. It stands out not even as a haunted house; it has, on the contrary, the acrid air of 'the absence of ghosts.' This may be a part of the hero's situation itself; but the author administers the last unctions with sadistic indirection so as to isolate us from it. Behind the curtain of death, what is man's worth ? Mr Biswas leaves behind him a host of grotesque remnants which celebrate not a life lived, but the wreckage of a life-time littered across a gruesome void. The kitchen-safe, the typewriter, the hatrack, the book-case, the morris suite, all a grimy *memento mori*, constitute not so much a personal chronicle as a palimpsest of successive, miscellaneous futilities. Life is reduced to mere thingdom, the detritus of a derelict, doomed existence, an unredeemed past, malevolently viewed and truculently expunged out of living memory abetted by a cynically accented irony. Naipaul's distortion darkens rather than clarifies Mr Biswas's aspiration for order and identity, for the novelist's design falsifies by disinfecting the living pattern and its detail. Our sympathy is attenuated, not extended, and we cannot freely participate in the author's stupendous cosmic chuckle. Naipaul's calvinistic blends of satire and burlesque, if the tone of the Prologue is any indication of his artistic intentions, make it difficult for the reader to establish any feeling of reciprocity with his hero, who is perspectivised as a non-man, not even an anti-hero. Mr Biswas turns out to be a victim not so much of his own life circumstances as of his biographer's ritual comminations.

Naipaul's areas of darkness are hopelessly mythridated vortices of being, from which no purgatorial awareness emerges and no resonance of human motion is generated. The solemn mimicry of his characterisation touches no chord of life. He reduces all the vital centres of human action, society, family and self to a funereal ubiquity of material surfaces. His adverse intimation and contrary awareness of everything, his antagonistic attitude to his own creative genius, pre-empt all potentiality of human relationships evolving a sensitive apprehension of human affiliation, succession and continuity. Heartiness, gratitude, affection, concern and charity seem to have no place in his world. He presents Mr Biswas's world as a gross spoiler's world obsessed with the abstractions of designing, self-regarding appetite and power, a world foreclosed to the opportunities of growth, differentiation and contact. There is panic, but no pain here; complicity, but no mutuality; anger, but no commitment. It is not surprising that Anand, who represents the author's *persona*, just before fading out of the story, reflects:

> So later, and very slowly, in securer times of different stresses, when the memories had lost the power to hurt, with pain or joy, they would fall into place and give back the past.
>
> (*A House for Mr Biswas*)

This ahistorical view of a usable past excludes any organic sense of a living tradition clarifying the present or fructifying the future.

Naipaul's presentation of Mr Biswas's married life has no trace of tenderness, let alone love; there is only a twisted, wounded kind of feeling which abhors the contact of flesh and desire. Biswas and Shama are thrown together into a marriage of mutual inconvenience, petulance, privation and punishment. They are ashamed of their connection, and dwindle and disappear separately into a world of contrition and connivance. Children are a menace : they are found strewn all over the landings and darkling corners of the house, like slimy shapes lurking in lascivious ambush to strike at their elderly foes. Life tends to be an abomination of 'alien growths, alien affections'. All joy has fled from the table, as Mr Biswas himself says at one point in the narrative; the shy, discomfiting coming together of all the Biswases under their own roof enacts no sense of belonging. Such is Naipaul's apocalypse of the householder's self-actualisation. We are not with the characters, but perpetually against them. We are in the interior of a crystal, an amazingly wrought artifice whose very perfection shuts out all sense of life and light. The story of Mr Biswas, because of its imperviousness to human touch, seems to be an ultimate in dark comedy, where *jugupsa*, not *karuna*, is the regnant *rasa*, which generates moral horror and revulsion.

That the muse of comedy can offer a different route to detachment other than a cult of aesthetic untouchability, that its moral resolution can turn on *santa*, and not *jugupsa*, contemplating human deficiency and enormity with sympathy and charity is illustrated in the art of Narayan. Narayan's world has a recognisable logic of our own world with which we can have a relationship of reciprocity. Spoilers, cozeners, mavericks, fools, knaves and clowns thickly populate this world, too; and it has its soured householders, foiled adventurists, footloose truants, cunning buccaneers and ambiguous mystics. The whole spectacle of freckled human nature with its connective tissue of motive and behaviour is offered to view with unflattering clarity. But it leaves in the end the implications of a life which does not exclude a healthy metabolism of response and potentiality. We have the feeling of being gently led in and out of a Vanity Fair. No slaughter-house this, where the whiplash of satire crackles on exposed human flesh. We do not diminish into a twittering world of unenzymed shadows; the comic deflation does not flatten out the lively ambiguity of the human situation; nor are the characters denigrated by mockery into flimsy, wafer-like effigies. There are steady ignitions of recognition which bring the characters and ourselves into a kind of aesthetic brotherhood. Life is not stymied and impoverished into a pallid inventory of impassive and affectless things, there is no Kafkaesque liquefaction of the boundaries of reality. It is rather enhanced to its higher, its certainly more agreeable potentiality.

As in Jagan, the sweet vendor's Goddess of Radiance, there is in Narayan's world a movement into life even out of stone, an influx of comic grace out of the comic traumas administered by the human situation. And as in the case of Raju, the Guide, who hears the thunder in the distant Mempi Hills the moment he enters the river, and feels the worthiness of the awful daring of an instant's surrender to the will of others, so we catch the glimpse of a life clarified in creation and enhanced by epiphany. Sarayu in Malgudi is never sunken; we are knee-deep in life where the sense of the past flows like an *antarvahini*. Not that the ugly underside of life is wished away by some heuristic fantasy of permanence. There are distraction, delusion, panic, hysteria, resigned disappointment, cursed spite, unctuous piety, moral hypocrisy and the thousand gorgon heads of power, appetite and evil in the Malgudi saga. But they are all somehow balanced out in the life of the novel. Narayan never mutilates or disfigures his creations; and his comedy, whether wildly funny, or ironically muted, never withers away into an acrimonious satire or a cynical farce. There is no titanic author-figure dwarfing, let alone trampling, the created world. We are [not sucked away into a sieve of unelemented, cloacal, life-denying blackness.

Contrast, for instance, with Naipaul's, Narayan's portrayals of married life and familial affections, his fine etching of the feeling of inheritance, the action of human sensibility and sentiment under the stress and strain of events. His objectivity in all these does not force us into retreat or recoil; rather it creatively re-engages us in life. Here, for example, is Krishna, the English Teacher, waiting to meet his wife Susila, with tremulous expectation and lyrical concern :

I was pacing the little Malgudi railway station in great agitation. I had never known such suspense before. She was certain to arrive with a lot of luggage, and the little child. How was all this to be transferred from the train to the platform ? and the child must not be hurt.

I made a mental note, 'Must shout as soon as the train stops : ''Be careful with the baby!'' ' This seemed to my fevered imagination the all important thing to say on arrival...

A whirling blur of faces went past me as the train shot in and stopped... I hurried through the crowd, peering into the compartments. I saw my father-in-law struggling to get to the doorway. I ran up to the carriage. Through numerous people getting in and out, I saw her sitting serenely in her seat with the baby lying on her lap. 'Only three minutes more!' I cried. 'Come out !' My father-in-law got down...and in a moment I was beside my wife in the compartment.

'No time to be sitting down : give me the baby,' I said. She merely smiled and said : 'I will carry the baby down. You will get these boxes. That wicker box, bring it down yourself, it contains baby's bottle and milk vessels.' She picked up the child and unconcernedly moved on... I cried : 'Susila, mind the door and baby'. All the things I wanted to say on this occasion were muddled and gone out of mind...

(The English Teacher)

Shot through the texture of the whole experience is the incremental movement of human feeling, spurred by a sense of human concern : 'Be careful with the baby'; 'Susila, mind the door and the baby!'; and even the concern about the wife's not being concerned (She picked up the child and unconcernedly moved on).   The platform, the compartment, the whorl of faces, the boxes, the bottles and the doorways, the whole enjambment of inventoried things, is subsumed into the ritual of reunion and substantiated by the covenant of married love.   The husband's clumsiness and awkwardness are comic; but as we flow into his consciousness on the axis of his concernedness, the touch of human nature glorifies the comic embarrassment.   Life proclaims itself, gathering around the vacant cores of time.   There is nothing of this tenderness, attractive charity, in Naipaul's handling of Mr Biswas's whole married life.   Mr Biswas's overtures to his wife are clinically paradigmatic, matters of a strictly observed ritual distance.   Even the erotic confidences he exchanges with his wife change gratuitously into conspiratorial name-calling sessions. Take the following, for instance :

'I got a name for another one of your brother-in-laws,' he told Shama that evening, lying on his blanket, his right foot on his left knee, peeling off a broken nail from his big toe. 'The constipated holy man.'

'Hari ?' she said, and pulled herself up, realising that she had begun to take part in the game.

He slapped his yellow, flabby calf and pushed his finger into the flesh.

The calf yielded like sponge.

She pulled his hand away. 'Don't do that. I can't bear to see you do that. You should be ashamed, a young man like you being so soft.'

'That is all the bad food I eating in this place.' He was still holding her hand. 'Well, as a matter of fact, I have quite a few names for him. The holy ghost. You like that ?'

'Man !'

'And what about the two gods ? It ever strike you that they look like two monkeys. So, you have one concrete monkey-god outside the house and two living ones inside. They could just call this place the monkey house and finish, Eh, monkey, bull, cow, hen. The place is like a blasted zoo, man.'

'And what about you ? The barking puppy dog ?'

'Man's best friend.' He flung up his legs and his thin slack calves shook. With a push of his finger he kept the calves swinging.

'Stop doing that !'

By now Shama's head was on his soft arm and they were lying side by side.

(*A House for Mr Biswas*)

Well, here is a picture of married love, indeed ! It doesn't have even the energy and grace of animality, notwithstanding the zoomorphic imagery in the passage. The intrusion of grotesque, deformed human flesh reduces sex to the rape of demons, the concupiscence of Rakshasas. *Sringara*, which is believed to be the zenith of *rasas*, is violently distorted and scurrilously dehumanised. Mr Biswas's nuptial logomachy and his sniping are not certainly part of a lover's quarrel; they are part of an ignominious contest, a venal game of skills he has to exercise in order to show the energy of his own inertia to advantage against putative enemies. There is a rage of the beast in him, and at the very springs of life, he is, as it were, caught in the death-wish.

Naipaul's habit of fixing up and placing his characters and situations in terms of objects and things is well-known. But his inventories are mere hyphenated accretions and their effect is to repudiate the sense of life. Narayan, who too uses the technique to produce the impression of solidity and specificity, works towards life rather than away from it. Thus for example, even while play-acting, Nataraj's description of his family estate renders it into a comic genealogy implying the continuity rather than the abruption of tradition and inheritance, beyond the physical perquisites.

A rattan easy chair on which my grandfather used to lie in the court-
yard, watching the sky, was claimed by my second uncle whose wife
had started all the furore over the property. She also claimed a pair
of rosewood benches which shone with a natural polish and a timber
wooden chair that used to be known as the bugproof chair. My
father's third brother, as a compensation for letting us go, claimed a
wooden almirah as his own and a 'leg' harmonium operated by a
pedal... Our grandfather had lent a hundred rupees to a local dramatic troupe and attached their harmonium as their only movable
property after a court decree, lugged it home and kept it in a corner
of our hall. He died before he could sell and realise its value, and his
successors took the presence of the harmonium in the corner of the
hall for granted until this moment of partition.

(*Man-Eater of Malgudi*)

The bizarre history of the furniture is lively comedy. Yet underlying it
all is the historical sense. The heirlooms do not turn into mummified
totems without any evocative life of their own. They dramatise the lively
maze of dynastic continuity. On the contrary, as seen earlier, Naipaul's
household effects spell out dissolution, displacement and the withering
away of personality. Hence the Biswas children have no identification
with them; they recall no usable, living past which can be meaningfully
integrated into their present. Their inheritance hurts them with a sense
of lethal dispossession and disinheritance.

Or, compare the existential thrusts which Narayan's Raju and Naipaul's
Biswas make in their stories, and what they do with the crisis of choice
forced upon them by life. Raju, the quondam Railway guide, turned into
the spiritual guide, fulfills his title by an act of reshaping his will to live
even if that should involve self-mortification, and eventually death.

For the first time in his life he was making an effort; for the first time
he was learning the thrill of full application outside money and love;
for the first time he was doing a thing in which he was not personally
interested. He felt a new strength to go through his ordeal.

(*The Guide*)

Raju, unlike Mr Biswas, has an open, accessible personality; confronted
with the last choice of his life, he views it as another first act of self-
education and recondite gesture of disinterested action. His strength
comes from his metamorphic self-perception, his capacity to attune himself
to the unexplored possibilities of life, as also from Narayan's final narrative balancing of the novel's tension between what Alan Friedman calls
the stream of consciousness and the stream of conscience. But Mr Biswas
acts differently, or rather he is made to act differently, so as to leave no
room for a fertilising human ambiguity capable of perceiving the human

core of existence. He is entirely one-dimensional, a syncopated individual, in whose secret intimations of life, if any, no one can ever participate. He never achieves a breakthrough from the novel into life, from abstraction into personality. The last things in his life-cycle are as inauspicious, contorted and etiolated as the first.

> But bigger than them all was the house, his house. How terrible it would have been, at this time, to be without it : to have died among the Tulsis, amid the squalor of that large, disintegrating and indifferent family; to have lived without even attempting to lay claim to one's portion of the earth; to have lived and died as one had been born, unnecessary and unaccommodated.
>
> (*A House for Mr Biswas*)

It's a weird, suffocating tale of an unfinished man, whose history is one of might-have-beens. And indeed he ends as he begins : unnecessary and unaccommodated. Biswas is unable to see through the hiatus in his own personality between fantasy and actuality, because throughout he opts out of life—a life which, however, muddled and complicated, might at the same time be enhanced and accredited by the presence of other human beings. He snaps all connections with life. His house is a metaphor of his loss of self and of society. All this Naipaul makes *vachya* through his Prologue and allows no room for the existential ambiguity to resolve itself in terms of irony. On the contrary, Narayan leaves ambiguity to resolve the meaning of Raju's action, which gains for him a society, though he has risked his self. Biswas, in the confusion of his orgiastic self-conception, cannot even fulfill his name : the faithful, well-beloved. Where Raju is a creation, Biswas seems to be an ejaculation.

The attitudinal and artistic differences between the two writers may undoubtedly be attributed to the widely differing situations inherited and contexts inhabited by them. Narayan proceeds from the assurance of a stable society, with his imaginative universe resting on the assumption of a cosmic permanence. The manifold of change, modification and variation could always be referred back to it for clarifying, without needless distortion, the conflicts and ambiguities in the predicament of his characters. Naipaul, on the contrary, is dealing with an unstable, mutable and unformed society, which is more a process in the making than a settled system of values and traditions. In this derelict and featureless society, he is several degrees removed from his inherited as well as acquired past. Compelled to choose among competing societies, he has chosen to repudiate both as areas of darkness affording him no meaningful shock of recognition. Necessarily, he contemplates the human scene as a disinherited and displaced outsider straining to discover and denominate a world elsewhere, an imaginative heterocosm where survival takes precedence over permanence, and anger and anguish all too readily overtake charity and serenity to enable comedy to attain the ends of tragedy.   He has to distort in order to clarify; and in the process the distortion prevents clarification; and for the idea we fail to see the object. This obviously builds up an intolerable tension within the artist's consciousness, because of which his cognitive objectivity fails to convert itself into its preceptual counterpart.   Consequently, the sense of life fails to triumph over the forbidding constructs of art.

Naipaul himself seems to be aware of the abrasive tension within himself, which the dramatises in *An Area of Darkness* as well as *Middle Passage*. There is an episode in *In a Free State,* which also reveals his creative deadlock.   In the Epilogue to the novel, the journalist-narrator comes to the rest-house.   Tempted by the offer of a sandwich or an apple by the tourist lodgers, an Arab entertains the guests by scaring away the desert children gathered around with a camel-whip. This is repeated in a macabre pantomime, until the shouts of the man with the whip turn into resonant grunts.   The narrator is enraged by the tourists' sadistic unconcern, and before his reason could foil the natural impulse, he snatches away the whip and stops the gruesome circus. But he realises that his gesture would not stop the inhumanity.

I felt exposed, futile, and wanted only to be back at my table... It happened quickly; there had been no disturbance. (*In a Free State*)

Naipaul as an artist seems to be embarrassed by his own natural human concern.   And this may prove a fatal flaw in an artist who is endowed with great gifts.

19

The Poem as Autobiographical Novel :
Derek Walcott's 'Another Life' in relation
to Wordsworth's 'Prelude' and Joyce's 'Portrait'

EDWARD BAUGH

THIS paper is not so much a true comparative study as it is an attempt to define the nature of one literary work, Derek Walcott's long poem *Another Life* (1973), partly by reference to two other works, Wordsworth's *Prelude* and Joyce's *Portrait of the Artist as a Young Man*. My concentration on *Another Life* will be increased by the fact that I shall take largely for granted the audience's familiarity with *The Prelude* and the *Portrait*.

All three works are portraits of the artist as a young man. All are about how the artist/the poet is shaped by his early environment and experiences. All are outstanding examples and investigations of the importance of memory to art and of the relations between the two. All are crucially concerned with the question of the connection and separation between the artist-self and all that is not-self (society, the world, Nature, as the case may be), the tension between isolation from and involvement with the outer reality. In all three the dedication to art takes on explicitly religious overtones and raises the question of the relationship between poetry and religion, the question of poetry as quasi-religious or even substitute religion, although the idea of a conflict as such between art and religion belongs more properly to *Portrait* and *Another Life* than to *The Prelude*, as does the notion of the poet as *maudit*, accursed and outcast, a sacrificial saviour/victim.

The high praise with which most critics have greeted *Another Life* is exemplified in the following observation by Kenneth Ramchand :

> The literary event of the West Indian year [i.e. 1973] was the publication of Derek Walcott's long poem, *Another Life*. It contains more metrical variety and experimentation, and in its feeling out of language and experience it is more compressed and less self-indulgent than the

only other poem in English that approaches it for stature, but the most convenient way of suggesting its richness and importance is to describe it as Walcott's and the West Indian's *The Prelude*.[1]

Perhaps the use of the word "stature" makes the praise excessive, and for present purposes let us substitute "kind" for "stature" and say that *The Prelude* is the only other poem in English that approaches *Another Life* in kind. As a poem which is also an autobiography (as distinct from "an autobiographical poem"), Walcott's work is a rarity for which one is hard put to find any precedent in English other than *The Prelude*. (In Roy Pascal's study of the art of autobiography, *Design and Truth in Autobiography* [1960], the only example of an autobiography in verse is Wordsworth's). But Walcott's work is even rarer, and its experimental nature more pronounced, when we perceive the extent to which it moves towards the novel while remaining without question a poem. It is a poem which is an autobiography which is a novel. The significance of this formulation depends on our recognising autobiography as a literary form in its own right. *Another Life* is not only Walcott's *Prelude*; it is also, perhaps even more so, his *Portrait of the Artist*, a *Portrait* modified by Joyce's other works, especially *Ulysses*. But to the extent that it is genuinely an autobiography, as distinct from being just autobiographical, *Another Life* is closer to *The Prelude* than to the *Portrait*, the remarkable fact in this connection being that autobiography proper otherwise invariably takes prose as its medium of expression. On the other hand, the nature of *Another Life* as poem is distinguished partly by its attempt to resemble a novel.

However much *The Prelude* approaches the novel or creates its own mode, it still sets itself, though shiftingly, within traditional poetic modes, such as epic, pastoral and descriptive-reflective. But *Another Life* takes its bearings as much from narrative-autobiographical prose (and here we may mention also specifically Pasternak's *Safe Conduct*) as from *The Prelude* or any other long poem which has influenced it (e.g. Dante's *Divine Comedy* and Pound's *Cantos*). *Another Life* is Walcott's *kunstler-roman*. Besides, the *Portrait* is a much more explicit and pervasive influence on the subject-matter of *Another Life* than is *The Prelude*; and Walcott very consciously *uses* Joyce at certain points to help him shape his poem.

Of course, the fact that Walcott can be as experimental as he is is partly the result of the fact that he is writing more than a century and a half later than Wordsworth, which means that he has been able to benefit from a process of experimentation which Wordsworth may be said to have set in motion. Ultimately, *The Prelude* is perhaps more innovative or daring in relation to its time than is *Another Life*; *The Prelude*'s self-consciousness and hesitancy about its own validity and about what sort of a creature it is would suggest this. And Walcott's interest in the ever-fresh question of the relationship between poetry and prose, an interest of which *Another*

Life is the supreme product, also establishes him as an heir of Wordsworth.

But to understand the *modus vivendi* of *Another Life* it is useful to know
something about how it came into being. In its issue for September 1965,
the *London Magazine* published an autobiographical essay by Walcott
entitled "Leaving School".   The editor, Alan Ross, had asked Walcott to
be one of a number of internationally known poets contributing to a series
of articles on this topic. As it happened, Walcott's period of leaving
school coincided with what he calls in that essay his *annus mirabilis* and,
in *Another Life,* his "golden year".   It was a time marked by the bloom-
ing of his first "great" love affair (with the Anna celebrated in the poem),
by the tragic and traumatic fire of Castries (another major event in the
poem), as well as by the first flush of the maturing of his poetic gift, concretely realised in the publication of his first book of poems.   The impression which these developments made on him was heightened by the fact that
this golden year was brought to an abrupt, if in retrospect inevitable end
by his departure from St Lucia.   The turn in his life which the departure
involved gave to the period just before the departure a climactic quality
which would enhance the shape and symmetry and underscore the other-
ness of the "other" life recounted in the poem.

The commissioned act of putting down his memories of this special
period released in Walcott a flood of recollection, more than could be
contained in the brief essay which the *London Magazine* wanted.   It also
gave him the idea of disburdening himself of those memories by writing a
fullscale autobiography, the story of his St Lucian life.   So, in addition to
writing the essay, he began, in April 1965, to write what was to be the
first version of *Another Life*.   By early November he had filled a quarto-
size exercise book of 76 pages in closely written longhand and had started
on a second such exercise book.   Up to that time the work was proceeding
as a prose memoir, and was to that extent conventional; but in January
1966 the Ms (which I shall call Ms One, to distinguish it from subsequent
Ms drafts of the work) begins to break into verse, after an entry in which
Walcott reflects on the difference between verse and prose.   Thereafter,
verse alternates with prose until the former takes over completely, as the
work makes up its mind that what it wants to be is an autobiography
which is also a poem and, as such, rather more unusual in its mode than
it had originally set out to be.   Through various subsequent drafts, Walcott reworked the whole thing as a poem.   A comparison between the
published poem and Ms One, especially the prose part of it, is obviously
most illuminating for an appreciation of the work in each of its three
existences—as poem, as novel and as autobiography.   The extent to which
he reshapes the original, to release the poetry that he came to see as latent
in it, is instructive to an understanding of the poetic process. On the other
hand, the extent to which he keeps close to the original prose style helps
us to appreciate the particular quality of the finished poetry and the way

in which the work as a whole tries to appropriate some of the qualities and principles of prose narrative.

The fact that this autobiography became a poem was not as radical a transformation as might at first appear. From the beginning it was highly selective, governed by a strong sense of shape, of its own inner shaping as an autonomous and pleasing object in itself. As such, it was from the beginning far removed from the run-of-the-mill, pedestrian (in nature if not in detail) sort of autobiography, autobiography as the annals or day to day account of a life, trying to "set it all down", laundry lists and all, on the assumption that if a person is famous or important any information about him will be interesting. In eventually becoming a poem, *Another Life* was only heightening or taking to an extreme conclusion a process that had been manifest in itself from the beginning, a process of transforming mere autobiography into art. The greatest autobiographies tend to share this characteristic, of being works of art in their own right, not just historical records. As Roy Pascal says,

> ...One demands from the best [autobiographies] more than an account of personalities, events, and circumstance. These must become the framework, in some sense embodiment, of the personality of the writer as a man pledged to life, and one must be set free from them as historical facts, and from the concern with their accuracy as historical documents, in order to savour the quality of the central personality.[2]

Another Life is certainly "the embodiment of the personality of the writer as a man pledged to life," as is *The Prelude*, and we recall how Stephen Dedalus ends his narrative :

> Welcome, O life ! I go to encounter for the millionth time the reality of experience and to forge in the smithy of my soul the uncreated conscience of my race.

And *Another Life* is also particularly interesting for the way in which it liberates itself from historical facts *qua* historical facts, even while being dependent on them and staying so true to them, conveying a strong sense of precise and vivid recall of persons, places, events and objects. In this respect comparison with *The Prelude* is one index of *Another Life*'s relative closeness to a novelistic approach, as well as of a relatively greater challenge that Walcott set himself. His poem presents proportionately far more of concrete and circumstantial detail, far more of the sort of "surface" reality which one normally associates with the novel rather than with poetry. People and places are named, *located*, far more than in *The Prelude*; consequently, while Walcott's poem is no less of *inner* autobiography than Wordsworth's, it is at the same time more of *outer* autobiography. Wordsworth was more cautious about documentary detail; and despite any suggestions to the contrary which the *Preface to the Lyrical Ballads* may have contained, verse was still quite definitely verse and something quite distinct from prose; so tic-tac-toe became "strife too humble to be named in verse."[3]

At least one reviewer, Peter Porter, thinks that *Another Life* is weighted down by historical facts, that, in short, the autobiography gets in the way of the poetry—"this sort of enterprise is doomed to failure. The facts separate from the lyricism even while you are reading."[4] But a cursory reading of the poem is unlikely to reveal how much selectivity has gone into the making of it, a selectivity confirmed by comparing the poem with Ms One as well as with the essay "Leaving School". For example, although the latter is much shorter than the poem, it mentions, usually by name, many people who had some influence on his life, but who are not referred to in the poem. There is proportionately more factual information of this kind in the essay than in the poem. The same is true of Ms One. To take a small example—one of the minor characters, Emmanuel Auguste, "the inveterate reciter who had seen Barrymore's Hamlet,"[5] gets more than a page in Ms One, of description and analytical comment; in the poem he is "caught" in thirteen short lines. Incidentally, one of the bits which Walcott wisely excluded from Ms One is a passage in which the Joycean debt is explicitly dealt with. Although the debt is acknowledged self-mockingly, the passage does not rise above mere pastiche :

Wonder what Harry thinks ? Liz a good bit. When he enters that's trust in his eyes or doubt. What've you been working on ? My poems, master. What drinks have you had too, I bet ? Or did you go down the steps to the kitchen to the servant's room and make a tack ? Would he believe watching the blue out there most of the morning was some kind of work and hearing, like it was for the first time Mozart. Tall windows, dusty that the light glares through thickly, making the place a vault, my own cathedral kind of, and all the sounds outside although they say this morgue is damp. Knowing with the music, the battered old typewriter, Royal ribbon, that there're sounds outside, the names of sounds and things, like oleanders and the rusty old barrack roofs, and like gold leaf, Andreuille, as if the whole morning were an old manuscript, gilt and curlicued that I opened alone A phony little monk with prickings under his brown habit. Reading Joyce, you have, of course. Even Stephen, Son of a pastiche. Some article I read by whatshisnamenow, in a Life and Letters yes, predicting that someday a new Ulysses will come forth out of these emerald, ethnic isles, and sure then he had put his finger on me. Imitation, imitation, when will I be me ?

(p. 93)

Anyway, all the selectivity that went into the making of *Another Life* works in the interest of shape, proportion, concentratedness, poetry. It must also be noted, against criticisms like Porter's, that such "facts" as the poem records are never there merely as circumstantial detail, merely because they are vivid memories. Whatever facts are documented are there because they mean something, because they contribute to the self-image which the poet is projecting. At the least, they are there to enhance the poem's sense of *locatedness* and actuality, the feeling of a particular time and place. *The Prelude* has been rightly defined as "spiritual autobiography"; curiously enough, in the very first sentence of Ms One, Walcott described the work on which he was embarking as "the spiritual history of [a] region" :

> So, from a green book held in the hands of an astigmatic master, in those mornings of my life when I imagined myself a painter, the spiritual history of this region begins.

Another Life is not only, like *The Prelude*, a self-portrait, it is also the portrait of a society, and the Joycean presence in the work helps to give resonance and shape to the narrative of a love-hate relationship between the artist and his society.

The sociological analysis works with the use of physical detail and the skill at character-drawing to increase the novelistic quality of the poem. It reminds us of a novel to the extent that it captures in such depth and with such clarity the character of a society. And the gallery of characters, precisely observed, from the swift, cameo portraits to the large, rounded study of Gregorias, adds to the sense of a sociological, *peopled* density such as we normally associate with the novel. And even though the people and the landscape exist as metaphors for aspects of the poet-protagonist's mind, they are also solidly *there*, an external reality distinct from the protagonist's consciousness, forming a resonant background against which and in reaction to which that consciousness defines itself.

The deliberate novelistic tendency in the poem has been glimpsed by some reviewers. Laurence Lieberman says, "Walcott is at his best when he exercises novelistic skill in presenting his gallery of West Indian characters, an inexhaustible storehouse of types and classes."[6] And Claire Tomalin observes, "Sections of the poem can indeed be read as a novel of what was then colonial but now, more subtly, provincial life..."[7] This novelistic quality is also visible, not only in the relatively superficial fact that the work is divided into "chapters", but, more importantly, in the way in which it tries at times to bring verse close to prose, or to incorporate into verse some of the qualities usually thought of as being more natural to prose. Seen in this light, the poem is a kind of fulfilment of a long-standing fascination which the novelist's craft has held for Walcott the poet. We might almost say that his verse has to some extent been motivated by an envy of prose, or at least a hankering after that hard-to-define area where both media merge. From the early fifties, when he began to write the sonnet sequence "Tales of the Islands", a remarkable experiment in the area under discussion, he was consciously addressing himself to the problem. The "Tales" first appeared in *Bim*, No. 26 (Jan.-June 1958). In their preface to that number, the editors quoted from a letter in which Walcott explained his intention in the sequence in terms of the notion of poetry competing against prose, of "do[ing] away with the prerogative of modern prose in narration." He spoke of trying to get into the "Tales" the "factual, biographical plainness" and "dispassionate observation" which he associated with prose, while at the same time preserving certain features associated particularly with poetry, in this case "selectivity". Later, he will single out other typical aspects of poetry as reasons for his relishing of certain novelists such as Hemingway, Nabokov and Joyce. Of Nabokov he writes :

> That book [*Lolita*] introduced me to a writer who in an adopted tongue, had a command of prose as etymology equal to Joyce's, a sense of parody, a systematic derangement of words into ambiguities that is close to madness; those uncontrollable voices in the head that the poet must learn to listen to or to shut off at the right time...His mind, like any true poet's, is anagrammatic, obsessed by puzzles, puns, by ambiguities, and like any poet who turns to fiction, indifferent to plot, since the puzzle of life is too straightforward, simple and repetitive.[8]

As it happens, one of the "Tales of the Islands", the story of the *loupgarou*, reappears, in an expanded version, in *Another Life*. The later version realises the full measure of the intention or inclination inherent in the earlier version, and is a good illustration of how far Walcott has advanced in terms of the idea of taking poetry towards prose fiction. Whereas in "Tales" the story shows the sonnet being used as a poetic equivalent of the short story, or rather the embodiment of the germ of a short story, in *Another Life* it becomes literally a short story, entitled "The Pact", within the novel, so to speak. The traditional verse-music which still suffuses the original sonnet-story is absent from "The Pact", the style of which is drier, harder. Besides, the brevity of the sonnet seems to force the poet to rely rather much on generalities in order to encompass the story. The greater scope of "The Pact" allows him to work more through specific, descriptive detail, thereby giving greater depth to the background and action. The larger space for manoeuvre and development which "The Pact" affords, even though as short story it is still very brief, also allows for the dimension of *duration* or *sequence*, which a short story, no matter how short, usually has as an essential characteristic.

Reading "The Pact", one is reminded of a comment which Walcott made in a review of a collection of short stories :

If only because of its concentration of language and mood, the short story is the nearest thing to poetry. Its last great practitioner was Hemingway, who approached it with the exactness of lyric.[9]

And in a review on Hemingway Walcott praised Hemingway's style for its "concentration of language and mood," which he found to be "as intense as the method of poetic composition," as well as for its "physical immediacy."[10] A similar immediacy is felt in *Another Life*, rather more than in *The Prelude*, felt even in the movement and tone of the language, and helps to increase the sense of concentration and intensity even when the verse seems near to prose :

If there was one thing Manoir's watchman hated
more than the merchant, it was the merchant's dog,
more wolf than dog.   It would break loose
some nights, rooting at the warehouse,
paws scuffing dirt like hands for some lost bone.
Before he struck it, something dimmed its eyes.
Its head dilating like an obscene rose,
humming and gemmed with flies, the dog
tottered through the tiled hallway of the house
towards its bed.[11]

Informing a passage like this, we feel the rhythm and intonation of the speaking voice, although it is not colloquial. We do not doubt its validity as poetry, but if it had been presented as prose it might have seemed no less valid.

Often, too, in *Another Life*, the basic prosy style works by an impressionistic method which itself creates an effect of concentratedness. For example, in chapter 6, the account of the boat-trip down the coast runs with the stream-of-consciouness of a passenger on the boat (Joyce again), a blending of the consciousness of the poet-narrator with that of the priest whom he is observing. In its movement, the passage evokes the mood of the experience, the sense of monotony-in-variety as the silently observing eye takes in the continuous succession of images, the shoreline, the passengers and the monotonous sea. The introduction of direct speech, including dialogue, at certain points, not only adds depth and vividness to characterisation, but also adds to the novelistic quality.

But there are times when the style becomes quite formal, more overtly and traditionally poetic. There is, for example, the epic sweep and thunder of the passage, stylistically unique in the poem, which recreates the heroic/suicidal leap of the Carib Indians at Sauteurs. And there is the grave, plangent music of two passages (the ones beginning "Who could tell, in the crossing of that pair" and "And which of them in time would be betrayed") which are in effect love lyrics and could, if taken out of context, stand on their own as complete poems. These passages rely noticeably on the iambic, as does the deliberately paced blank verse of the section describing the young poet-lover being rowed across the harbour for a rendezvous with his beloved :

> Perched on the low stern of the rented shallop,
> he watched the barracks on the hill dilate
> with every stroke behind the oarsman's ear.
> The rower, silent, kept his gaze oblique-
> ly fixed on the wharf's receding beacon,
> a mannequin with a skirt of lacy iron, and
> in the opaque, slowly-colouring harbour
> the one sound was the plump plash of the oars,
> each stroke concluding with the folded gurgle
> of an intaken breath. Weakly protesting,
> the oarlock's squeak, the gunwale's heaving lurch,
> the pause upheld after each finished stroke,
> unstudied, easy, pentametrical...[12]

But if the basic pattern here is iambic pentameter, its gravity also has about it a flexibility and "naturalness" which make it seem "unstudied" and "easy".

All such passages express moments of high emotion and tension in the poem, or moments when narrative "peaks" into lyric. They help to account for that variety and richness which Ramchand finds in the work, and they seem to fit effortlessly into a novel which is also a poem. Curiously enough, Walcott has said[13] that for him *Another Life* fails somewhat, precisely because it needed to resort to these more obviously poetic and lyrical passages, and to the extent that it resembles a suite, an orchestration of various styles, as do Eliot's *Ash Wednesday* and *Four Quartets* and Brathwaite's *Arrivants*. He had hoped, he says, to sustain one relatively dry, plain, prosy narrative style throughout, more as Pound had done in the *Cantos*. But the *Cantos* are themselves a monumental failure; and Wordsworth, "plugging away" at his blank verse to maintain the poetry of *The Prelude*, ended up with many unsatisfactorily and unintentionally prosaic bits. Besides, *Another Life* as we have it is perhaps more truly Walcott than it would have been if he had succeeded in his hope. For as that work itself so fully acknowledges, he thrives on the condition of dividedness, and one kind of division in him is that between what I have called an envy of prose and a deep-rooted love of and facility in rich verbal music and the mighty line.

We cannot leave the subject of richness in *Another Life* without mentioning its metaphorical richness. The complex artifice and interplay of images not only promote the qualities of physical immediacy and concentratedness, and enrich the texture of the poem at any given point;

they also help to secure the unity and close-knit quality of the poem as a whole, and act as a dynamic, shaping principle.   Ultimately, it is perhaps this metaphorical richness and principle which most ensure the integrity of the work as poetry, no matter how close the style may sometimes get to prose.   At the same time, Walcott's near-obsessive pursuit of metaphor and ambiguity and irony, a pursuit which we heard him remarking in certain novelists, is one of the features which make his poem radically different in texture from Wordsworth's.   As W. Graham says,

> [Wordsworth's] poetry has few of the qualities that lend themselves to the fashionable analytical techniques which seize so readily on the interplay of metaphor, irony and other forms of figurative language.[14]

In this respect *Another Life* is almost the opposite of *The Prelude*; but I hope that I have sufficiently suggested that it is hardly just a "fashionable" poem; indeed, it is in some ways most unfashionable.

At the beginning of Ms One, Walcott has a marginal note indicating what he was aiming at : "A prose, if possible, like wrought iron, hard, but figured ..." Those words, intended to describe what he wanted his prose memoir to be, remain a useful epigraph for the poem which he eventually wrote.

REFERENCES

1. *Journal of Commonwealth Literature*, IX (Dec. 1974), p. 131.
2. *Design and Truth in Autobiography*, London, 1960, p. 20.
3. *The Prelude*, 1850 version, Bk I, p. 513.
4. *Observer*, 5 August 1973, p. 28.
5. *London Magazine*, V (September 1965), p. 7.
6. *Yale Review*, LXIII (October 1973), p. 120.
7. *New Statesman*, LXXXVIII (20 December 1974), p. 908.
8. *Sunday Guardian* (Trinidad), 19 April 1964, p. 15.
9. *Trinidad Guardian*, 26 February, 1964, p. 5.
10. *Sunday Guardian*, 10 March 1965, p. 15.
11. *Another Life*, London & New York, 1973, p. 27.
12. *ibid.*, p. 85.
13. In conversation with the author.
14. W. Graham, *The Prelude, Books I & II*, Oxford, 1968, p. 78.

20

Folk Humour :
A comparison of the comic ballads
of Australia and Kerala (India)

K. AYYAPPA PANIKER

THE ballad is perhaps the most localised of all forms of poetic expression and humour is the most parochial and culture-dependent feature of literature. It would thus seem apparently futile to try to enquire into similarities between Australian ballads and the ballads of Kerala from the point of view of humour. But the ballad is also the most widely distributed of all literary forms, basically extra-literary, a manifestation of what is most cosmopolitan in culture. The modes may vary just as the languages may vary, but the basic tendencies—although not their actual realisations—must show certain essential similarities. The present paper is a preliminary enquiry into the nature of humour in Australian and Kerala ballads and folksongs. No attempt is made here to define ballads or to distinguish ballads from folksongs. The main effort will be to discover points of similarity and dissimilarity between the basic springs of humour in the folk poetry of these two parts of the Commonwealth.

The term "Australian ballads" is here meant to refer to those written in English, whether of individual or of communal authorship, whether orally circulated or available in print. Thus these ballads are the common possession of the inhabitants of Australia, emerging mainly from the Anglo-Saxon stock, speaking the English language and settled permanently in some part of the Australian continent. 'Australian' therefore refers to nationality, geographical entity, language, culture and race. Racial or linguistic (dialectal) differences within Australia will not have any important bearing on the present study.

No two parts of the Commonwealth are more widely different than Kerala and Australia. It would be impossible to list all aspects of this difference. Kerala ballads such as those now available to us in print belong to a historical period before the arrival of the English in Southern India.

They clearly belong to the pre-British days of Indian history. Several of them belong to tribes which are even today totally immune to Western thought, except perhaps in certain tribal areas where missionaries have taken the message of Christ. The differences in language, culture, race, climatic conditions, historical background, etc. would certainly point to major comprehensive differences between the ballads of Kerala and those of Australia. The only sense, therefore, in which such an enquiry as the present one can be meaningfully conducted, is in trying to see certain fundamentals of human experience affecting the folk imagination that contribute to humour, in spite of all these differences. It would also help to identify what makes people anywhere and everywhere laugh, the basic features of situation or language that have this special appeal to man, the only laughing animal in the world.

As everywhere else, there are more tragic ballads than comic ballads in Australia too. While it is true that the early settlers brought with them the songs they had learned in England before being sent out on colonial service or as convicts, there were attempts to give a characteristically Australian effect to the singing of those ballads. Whether it is thus only the Australian adaptation of British ballads or literary ballads written by Australian poets, gifted or otherwise, the comic ballad was more realistic and closer to the colonial soil than the serious one. In "A Note on the Ballads", A.D. Hope observes :

> The humours and tragedies, more often the humours of life in the bush and the country town were their usual subjects, shearing, gold-prospecting, drinking sprees at the shanties and pubs, well-sinking and mustering, horse-breaking and droving. But if they were unpretentious, most of them make agreeable reading because they could tell a lively story in verse, and if they represented a low level in poetry, they were often poetry at that level and not mere doggerel or pedestrian verse.[1]

This general assessment would apply to the ballads of Kerala too. They have a vitality which has preserved them and their flavour intact through centuries, despite political, religious and cultural upheavals. *Vadakkan Pattukal*—the ballads of the north—(north here means the northern part of Kerala) are an exceptionally brilliant collection of folk poems of anonymous authorship which have acquired an epic stature through the creation of a great number of heroic figures whose war-life and love-life form their main subject. Their chief quality is vitality and vigour. William Walsh's rather reserved praise for the Australian bush songs also highlights their qualities of vigour and poetic authenticity :

> The earliest bush songs, the manner of which was taken up and sophisticated by Peterson and Lawson, were the anonymous chants of convicts and workers adapted from contemporary cockney doggerel

and sentimental Irish ballads. Even so these songs of convicts, miners, and stockmen had a simple vigour and bite, and it was this note which Paterson and Lawson developed and refined... The idiom and scene of Paterson's ballads, their unselfconscious use of local life and theme, their muscular buoyancy, these together with the bleaker quality of Lawson's ballads became part of the national memory and part of the poetic inheritance of far more significant Australian artists.[2]

The Kerala poet Vallathol Narayana Menon, writing over fifty years ago, gave the same kind of praise to the rich folk heritage of Malayalam. In a poem called "The Songs of Old Times", he wrote :

When our mother Kairali long ago
was just a sweet little child,
when she used to frisk about
making her anklets jingle
whatever way she liked
with no serious thought to it :
the old songs that she used to sing then
with her sweet throat still moist
with the white milk of her mother,
were like a delicacy to every ear.

Their lack of sophistication is purely relative. In fact they—both Australian ballads and Malayalam ballads—are sometimes exquisitely sensitive to the beauties of the mind as well as those of nature. The comic ballad particularly is an expression of the vital relationship the lower class people, before the industrial revolution spoilt it, had cultivated between the human mind and external nature.

In Malayalam poetry we sometimes speak of two traditions : one, the classical *manipravala* tradition of Sanskrit-influenced Malayalam, using the themes and forms of the predominantly Aryan Hindu puranic lore; and the other, the popular "semi-literate" song tradition of basically Dravidian elements, choosing themes and forms at least partially independent of the upper class Brahmin-oriented culture. The elite tradition preferred standard Malayalam or the Namboodiri dialect or a mixture of this with Sanskrit; whereas the folk tradition favoured the use of the regional dialect with what might be called substandard or corrupt forms of the colloquial variety of Malayalam closer to the Tamil forms. It seems in Australia too there was a trend that favoured European-based tradition while the ballads formed the basis for Australianisation, Judith Wright hints at this national schizophrenia in *Preoccupations in Australian Poetry* :

After Kendall's death, the split in the Australian consciousness took its most obvious shape, on the one side in the 'bush balladists' who for the first time began to express what was happening to European charac- ter in the new conditions of Australia, on the other side, in Christopher Brennan's withdrawal from all such manifestations of 'nationalism' and his attempt to rejoin the mainstream of European thought.[3]

The conflict between the cosmopolitan and the national or (regional) is evident in both cultures, but what is interesting in both is the affinity and affiliation of the balladists to the latter. The confrontation surfaced cen- turies earlier in Kerala, the older settlement, than in Australia where the colonisation process was still in full swing in the 19th century. But the features were not dissimilar. The non-elite tradition was basically oral and in intimate contact with manual labour and everyday reality. This is of very great importance in determining the nature of ballad humour. The folk poems were rendered with the accompaniment of drums in the villages by illiterate or semi-literate people performing dance in the open air as part of some traditional ritual. A well-known Australian bush song illustrates this point :

I humped my drum from Kingdom come
To the back of the Milky Way;
I boiled my quart on the Cape of York
And I starved last Christmas Day.

I cast a line on the Condamine
And one on the Nebine Creek;
I've driven through bog, so help me bob,
Up Mungindi's main street;

I crossed the Murray and drank in Cloncurry
Where they charged a bob a nip.
I worked in the Gulf where the cattle they duff,
And the squatters let them rip.

I worked from morn in the fields of corn
Till the sun was out of sight,
I've cause to know the Great Byno
And the Great Australian Bight.

I danced with Kit when the lamps were lit,
And Doll as the dance broke up;
I flung my hat on the myall track
When Bowman won the Cup...

I pushed my bike from the shearer's strike,
Not wanting a funeral shroud;
I made the weights for the Flying Stakes

And I dodged the lynching crowd...

One may compare this with the following Malayalam folksong :

The time is gone, the time is gone
the waterfowl
is hopping away
behind the screwpine.
When I went there
there was neither this nor that;
when I went there
they made me do the fence which was not there;
when I went there
they made me dig the pond which was not there;
when I went there
they made me thatch the unthatched roof.
For half a pint of toddy
they drove me to death;
For half a tender coconut
they drove me to death;
the time is gone, the time is gone;
the waterfowl
is hopping away
behind the screwpine.[4]

The tendency to render even pain in terms of rhythmic chant is common to both Australian and Kerala ballads. The careful accumulation of telling details taken from every day reality also enlivens both kinds. While there may not be any matter for laughter here, both poems are free from languishing sentimental whining. The rhythm is well sustained.

The way these people faced the deprivations of life reflects their fundamentally optimistic outlook of life. In the Australian ballad "The stringy-bark cockatoo", we have a lighthearted treatment of an extremely unpleasant situation :

For breakfast we had pollard, boys, it tasted like cobbler's paste,
To help it down we had to eat brown bread with vinegar taste,
The tea was made of the native hops, which out on the ranges grew;
I was sweetened with honey bees and wax for the stringybark cockatoo.

For dinner we had goanna hash, we thought it mighty hard;
They wouldn't give us butter, so we forced down bread and lard.
Quondong duff, paddy-melon pie, and wallaby Irish stew
We used to eat while reaping for the stringybark cockatoo.

When we started to cut the rust and smut was just beginning to shed,
And all we had to sleep on was a dog and sheep-skin bed.
The bugs and fleas tormented me, they made me scratch and screw;
I lost my rest while reaping for the stringybark cockatoo.

At night when work was over I'd nurse the youngest child,
And when I'd say a joking word the mother would laugh and smile.
The old cocky, he grew jealous, and he thumped me black and blue,
And he drove me off without a rap—the stringybark cockatoo.

The same smiling attitude to the harsh realities of life is seen in this snatch
of a Malayalam song :

Mother gives us coffee in the morning
     pure black coffee
But if you want sugar in it
     you have to go to the market, my friends.
Mother gives us porridge in the morning
     the left over porridge of the previous night
But if want any solid crumb
     you have to go to the market, my friends.

In the treatment of love, sex and marriage, women are given an upper
hand in the comic ballads of both Australia and Kerala. The ballad of
"The German Girls" shows how the young man learns a bitter lesson :

I once fell deep in love, sir,
     In a true Colonial way,
With a German girl who played and sung
     In the "Union" Bar all day;
I'd just arrived, was green as grass,
     Not badly off for tin,
So this German girl first drew me out !
     And afterwards took me in,
As she sat in the Union Bar,
And played on an old crack'd guitar,
     I soon 'pon my soul
     Made a very large hole
In my cash at the Union Bar.

And with her in that Bar, sir,
     With an old guitar apiece,
Were two younger girls (her sisters)
     The "fast young men" to fleece;
And when a song was finished

They'd not a minute wait,
But make those spoons "fork out" their tin,
    By sending round their plate,
And my fair one who played the guitar
(The best of the whole three by far)
        smiled quite fondly on me
        As I'd shout for the three
In that confounded flash Yankee Bar.

I shepherded that girl, sir,
    And soon got in such a flame,
That I fancied every fellow there
    Was going to jump my claim;
The prospect too I liked too well
    It made my heart quite flutter,
And think I was on, not in a line,
    And dead upon the gutter;
As I sat in the Union Bar,
And watched my love play her guitar;
        I considered it great
        To go round with the plate,
For the lady who played the guitar.

One day I sought that Bar, sir,
    To have my usual chat,
But no German girls were there, sir,
    They'd gone to Ballarat—
I shouted to the barman,
    Got tipsy, pain to quell,
Asked him if he knew where they'd stop,
    He said he couldn't tell,
But thought if it wasn't too far
To go up myself by Cobb's Car,
        I should be bound to see
        The whole of the three
Of them playing in some Yankee bar.

Though cash was getting low, sir,
    I went straight and paid my fare,
Off started the next morning
    And arrived in safety there.
Commenced my search, spent all my tin,
    Got very drunk as well,
But late at night I bowl'd them out,
    In the Bar of Bath's Hotel,

And when once more I heard that guitar,
By joy I was carried so far
    That my cash being run out,
    I stuck up a shout
For the whole crowd in front of the bar.

Young men list to the sequel,
    And a warning take in time,
Don't get sweet on German girls
    Like those who're in my rhyme.
For when I'd no more cash to spend,
    And drop into the plate,
She said I was a shicer,
    And got another mate;
And now when we meet in a bar
(She still sings and plays the guitar)
    She'll wink at her mate,
    Who'll come round with the plate
For the lady who plays the guitar.

There is a Malayalam folk song in which a girl is slyly approached by a young man as she is walking across a paddy field. It is in the form of a dialogue. The young man asks her to move closer to him and take cover under his umbrella, but she cleverly manages to counter his requests with witty evasions :

Who's going there along the causeway
With bangles on the arms ?
    Oh, it's the slave girl
    of my lord of the farm.
Throw away those bangles, girl,
and come under this umbrella.
    The umbrella is just for a day,
    but my bangles are for ever.
Who's going there along the causeway
with palmleaf rolls in the ears ?
    Oh, it's the slave girl
    of my lord of the farm.
Throw away the palmleaf rolls, girl,
and come under this umbrella.
    The umbrella is just for a day,
    but the palmleaf rolls are for ever.
Who's going there along the causeway
with silver anklets on the feet ?
    Oh, it's the slave girl

of my lord of the farm.
Throw away the silver anklets, girl,
and come under this umbrella.
    The umbrella is just for a day,
    but the anklets are for ever.

The motif of the clever girl outwitting her lovers is a recurring one in
Australian ballads also.   In this respect "Colonial Courtship" is in the
main tradition of the comic ballad :

The best of this colony is,
    The brides have no fine affectation,
In saying "I will" they're "all there",
    And they don't faint upon the occasion;
A bottle lots of 'em will use,
    And it seems to come in very handy,
You might think it's Preston salts,
    No fear ! the smell tells you it's brandy.

The bride's mother too will be there,
    She's not overcome by emotion,
Her spirits you find she keeps up
    By old tom or some other lotion;
And sometimes her voice will grow thick,
    In her speech there's a wond'rous obstruction,
But her friends are to blame for it all,
    For they ought to allowance her suction.

Some brides upon their wedding night,
    In colonial parlance get "tight", sirs,
And then in that state they evince
    A strong inclination to fight, sirs,
They've been known to take tumblers up
    And shy them in every direction,
But bless their dear hearts, we all know
    It's proof of colonial affection.

What a rum lot the gals are out here,
    They jolly soon get colonised, sirs,
I twig their rum capers sometimes,
    And feel not a little surprised, sirs,
As regards love and marriage out here,
    I'm fairly licked clean off my perch, sirs,
One day they pick up a chap,

The next day he's walked off to church, sirs.
If at home you should flirt with a girl,
    In a twinkling the old bloke, her father,
Asks what your intentions may be,
    And isn't he down on you, rather;
The mother leads you on a string,
    And sticks to you like bricks and mortar,
For she's always talking to you
    About her accomplished young daughter.

The courtship lasts some little time,
    And then of course you pop the question,
She immediately bursts into tears,
    And calls it a cruel suggestion;
She falters out "Ask my papa",
    When you beg her to be your dear wife, sirs,
And in two or three weeks from that time,
    You find that you're tied up for life, sirs.

But things are far different here,
    The girls don't consult their relations,
What's father or mother to them,
    They follow their own inclinations;
If you name the day here to a gal,
    Don't think off her perch it will lick her,
For nine out of ten will reply
    "Lor, Sammy, can't it be done quicker ?"

Another Malayalam folk song that reveals the same presence of mind and witty evasiveness on the part of a girl is in the form of a coaxing invitation extended by the landlord to a low-class untouchable girl and her polite but sharp repartees. At the end of the poem she tells her upper-class lover that all his sly secret gifts to her have no real worth and that if he will give up his secretive approach and openly offer to marry her in the proper manner she will have no objection to go and live with him. The forward lover quails at this, and his ignoble attempt is thus foiled by the girl's cleverness.

The anti-elitism of the comic ballad, directed against snobbery and gentility, of which there was plenty both in the Australian and the Kerala social set-up, seems to be a universal ballad feature. The discomfiture of the dishonest, the pompous and the vain is seen in the ballads of many nations. There is thus a corrective social purpose in ballad satire. The give and take between a cunning barmaid and a clever customer is the subject of a famous Malayalam folksong. The girl's name here is Kali.

Kali did trick me
She put water in the toddy
And I in turn tricked her
I gave her fake money.

This takes us to the drinking song, one of the fertile sources of ballad
humour.   Hugh Anderson has pointed out the enormous popularity of the
drinking song. "One characteristic," he says, "of bush workers which
reappears in song after song is the enjoyment of drink. In actual fact,
men employed far away in the bush for months or even years at a stretch
had teetotalism forced upon them. This prohibition is said to have had a
reforming effect, but in many the absence of drink seems to have merely
worked up a craving that burst at intervals into an alcoholic spree."[5]   In
Malayalam there is a boat song refrain shouted by boatmen as the tempo
rises and they row their fastest under the stimulus of the drink they have
had, only to complain that they haven't had enough :

Hooray ho ! it's all gone
All my toddy is gone.

The Australian ballad "Poll the Grogseller" is a good example of humour
associated with alcoholic drinks.

Big Poll the Grogseller gets up every day,
        And her small rowdy tent sweeps out;
She's turning in plenty of tin people say,
        For she knows what she's about.

Polly's good looking, and Polly is young,
And Polly's possessed of a smooth oily tongue;
She's an innocent face and a good head of hair,
And a lot of young fellows will often go there;
And they keep dropping in handsome Polly to court,
And she smiles and supplies them with brandy and port,
And the neighbours all say that the whole blessed day
        She is grog-selling late and early.

The non-tragic ballad often tends to look at life through idealistic
spectacles. The glorification of work is a frequent motif. "The Stockmen
of Australia" thus presents an idealised picture of the Australian cattle-
raisers.

The stockmen of Australia, what rowdy boys are they,
They will curse and swear an hurricane if you come in their way.

They dash along the forest on black, bay, brown, or grey,
And the stockmen of Australia, hard-riding boys are they.

    Chorus : And the stockmen, etc.

By constant feats of horsemanship, they procure for us our grub,
And supply us with the fattest beef by hard work in the scrub.
To muster up the cattle they cease not night nor day.
And the stockmen of Australia, hard-riding boys are they.

The bushman similarly praises himself to the skies.   The romantic idealisation of the bushman is the subject of the Australian ballad, "The Bushman".

When the merchant lies down, he can scarce go to sleep
For thinking of his merchandise upon the fatal deep;
His ships may be cast away or taken in the war,
So him alone we'll envy not, who true bushmen are.

    Chorus :   Who true bushmen are,
                Who true bushmen are,

So him alone we'll envy not, who true bushmen are.

"The Squatter of the Olden Time" is concerned with the glorification of the Australian settler :

I'll sing you a fine new song, made by my blessed mate,
Of a fine Australian squatter, who had a fine estate;
Who swore by right pre-emptive, at a sanguinary rate,
That by his rams, his ewes, his lambs, Victoria was made great—
Like a fine Australian settler, one of the olden time.

Apart from the exploitation of particular social themes and psychological types, the comic ballad seems to exaggerate certain features so as to make the situation or character provide humour even when there is no social satire intended.   The good humour in which the world is viewed in the poems is free from all bitterness.   There is sheer celebration of life as, for instance, in the Malayalam ballad of the "Kanika hunter" :

The little hunter of Kanika
Do you see the costume of the little hunter ?
He's all gartered up from his knee to his back
with hunting tools and arrows.
He sees a short-tailed monkey

He shoots at it and puts it in his swag.
With raw meat broiled and with toddy
He puts aside a portion
Dancing and dancing this hunter of Kanika
This hunter who's drunken is going away
This hunter of Kanika is dancing his way
Do you see the costume of the little hunter ?
Dancing and dancing is the hunter of Kanika,
The hunter of Kanika is dancing his way.

This has some features in common with the situation of the Australian trap of the ballad "Song of the Trap" :

Hey for glorious bygone days,
    For ever past, but famed in story;
At hunting covers for licences,
    There I was in all my glory.
The new chums I'd put in a fright,
    To nail 'em I'd jump down a shicer,
But a trifle soon made it all right,
    And no one ever was the wiser.

Sometimes I don an old blue shirt,
    Disguise myself up like a digger,
And with hands encrusted o'er with dirt,
    I cut a precious curious figure.
To those who sell grog on the sly
    My visit proves a wholesale warning,
Some brandy I contrive to buy,
    And I send a summons in the morning.

Chorus : Hey down, ho down, derry derry down,
    The life of a trap passes gaily O.

It is true that in the Kerala setting we have never had the major social types that figure in Australian ballads such as the swagman, the bushranger, he trap, the squatter, the stringybark, the golddigger, the shearer, the stockman, etc. but their psychological counterparts are not hard to find.

There is great similarity between Australian and Kerala ballads in the means employed to generate humour. In quite a number of these ballads, humour is conveyed by choral passages and refrains made up of nonsense verses meant to highlight the rhythm and to sound humorous. The chorus of "The Whaler's Rhyme", for instance, goes like this :

With ra-dum, a ra-dum, a rub, a dub, a dub,
Drive him back to the tar-boy's tub.

The chorus of "The Song of Old Joe Swallow" by Henry Lawson is a more sustained piece meant to underscore the rhythm in the manner of the bush song :

> Chorus :
> Then it's yoke up the bullicks an' tramp beside 'em slow,
> An' saddle up yer horses an' a-ridin' we will go.
>> To the bullick-drivin', cattle-drovin'
>> Nigger, digger, roarin', rovin'
>> Days of long ago.

Among the songs used in the folk-play series in Malayalam known as *Kakarissi* we have near-nonsense rhymes suggesting fast rhythms which reveal a light-heartedness in tone :

> The bastard, the bastard of our household
> He'll pound the rice, he'll eat the bran
> With country sugar he'll eat even more
> He'll poke his head into the mortar and lick it up
> Kar Ka them in tha thom.

Another fast-moving chorus in the same play goes on as follows :

> Idukkali of Korandipallil
> didn't have a bath even after menstruation
> didn't menstruate even after a bath
> let her bathe when she bathes
> I'll get a piece of cloth
> Kar ka thom in tha thom.

Pure verbal humour which plays with the sound of words is also seen in both groups of ballads. Each language may realise this in its own way. Bernth Lindfors and Oyekan O Womoyela have referred to several examples of "tongue twisters, tonetwisters and Wellerisms". For instance,

> Opolopo opolo Ko mo pe opolopo opolo
> lopolo lopolopo

When uttered with variation in tone on individual words, this would mean in free translation : "Many frogs do not know that most frogs have brains."[6] Here is a tongue twister in Malayalam :

> Cheru kara valavinorilayuthalathel
> Pathirupathanchilayuthalanga.

[Meaning :   There are some twentyfive unripe utha¹a fruit on the young
uthala tree standing at a turning in Cherukara (place name)]
Something like the same zest for word play may be found in the Australian
ballad, "Stringybark and Greenhide".

> I sing of a commodity, it's one that will not fail yer,
> I mean the common oddity, the mainstay of Australia;
> Gold it is a precious thing, for commerce it increases,
> But stringybark and greenhide can beat it all to pieces.

Our enquiry has shown not that there are some stray and curious
similarities between certain Australian ballads and Malayalam ballads, but
that whatever similarities they have are perhaps common to the ballads of
all races and languages. This investigation has brought to light that,
despite obvious differences arising from parochial features of culture and
language, ballads have certain inalienable common springs—and one of
these is their humour.   The ingredients may vary from place to place and
language to language, but the common core is unmistakable.

REFERENCES

1. A.D. Hope, "A Note on the Ballads", *The Literary Criterion*, vi; No. 3 (1974);
    William Walsh, ed. *Readings in Commonwealth Literature*, London OUP, 1973,
    p. 329.

2. William Walsh, *Commonwealth Literature*, London OUP, 1973, pp. 117-8.

3. Judith Wright, *Preoccupations in Australian Poetry*, Melbourne OUP, 1965; paper-
    backs pt. 1966, p. 47.

4. The translations of Malayalam ballads given here have been specially made by the
    present writer for the purpose of this paper.   They have not been published before.

5. Hugh Anderson, *Colonial Ballads*, Melbourne Cheshire, 1955, p. 121.

6. Bernth Lindfors and Oyekan Owomoyela, "Yoruba Word Play : A Tongue-
    Twister, A Tone-Twister and a Wellerism", *Southern Folklore Quarterly*, 39 (1975),
    p. 169.

21

Invective and Obliqueness in
Political Poetry :
Kasaipwalova, Brathwaite, and Soyinka

K.L. GOODWIN

IN modern Commonwealth literature studies a clear hierarchy of interest
governs the main genres (as understood in European terms). The greatest
interest by far has been directed to fiction (chiefly the novel); then comes
drama; and poetry trails the field. This hierarchy by no means parallels
the actual volume of work produced, nor does it, in many countries, represent the hierarchy of local interest, but there can be little doubt that the
one typically Western genre, the novel—and that a late developer even in
the West—has dominated international sales and international critical
interest.

The reason is no doubt partly a reflection of word-wide reading
habits and the conventional wisdom of publishers. But with literature
from the Third World (especially as read by their former colonisers and
by those sharing the same language) a further reason is the desire to
combine instruction with delight. Growing up in a country controlled by
unsympathetic foreigners, the experience of competing cultures, victimisation through racial prejudice, the sense of alienation, the struggle for independence, the establishment of an independent nation, disillusion with the
new political rulers, and the movement to political and social revolution—
these are the common subjects of Commonwealth novels during the last
two decades. One reason they have been so popular is the desire to convey to fellow nationals and to readers from the colonial powers the feelings of the colonised. A good deal of care is often expended in the early
chapters explaining the local tribal or village scene to those unfamiliar
with it.

Even Chinua Achebe, who is in general a very subtle and skilful
novelist, has sentences such as 'Among the Ibo the art of conversation is
regarded very highly, and proverbs are the palm-oil with which

words are eaten' or 'Fortunately among these people a man was judged according to his worth and not according to the worth of his father.' (*Things Fall Apart*, chapter 1).

The poet's opportunities for conveying information of this kind are more limited, and as a result the understanding, or at any rate appreciation, of poetry tends to be less readily available to an international readership. This distinction between the novel and poetry is, however, irrelevant to a consideration of the local political impact of poetry.

That poetry can have an important political impact is evident, for instance, from the history of British literature. Spenser, Milton, Dryden, Blake, Shelley, William Morris, Auden, and Spender represent a variety of forcefully conveyed political beliefs, some conservative, some radical, some in the service of the state, some seeking to overthrow it.

Political commentary and invective are more common in francophone and Latin American poetry than they are in Commonwealth literature in English, though there is a small number of much anthologised classic pieces. The best-known are probably Wole Soyinka's 'Telephone Conversation' and David Rubadiri's 'Stanley Meets Mutesa'. Another that deserves to be as well known is the *nanga* song composed by the blind Acoli poet, 'Adok Too' (Omal Lakana), in 1938, which earned him two years' gaol.[1]

I should like to draw attention to some of the variety and some of the problems of contemporary political poets by considering the work of three poets from widely different political environments. John Kasaipwalova is a Trobriand Islander who, after writing a number of plays, short stories, poems and polemical articles, returned to the Trobriands to become executive officer of the Kabisawali Movement (for self-help in a communal manner).[2] His two main poetry publications are *Reluctant Flame* (1971) and *Hanuabada* (1972).

Kasaipwalova is a writer of invective and satire, mostly in Whitmanesque lines and verse paragraphs. He is an observer of local circumstances, an absorber of black power rhetoric, and a dreamer in Blake-like symbols. The observation of life in Port Moresby is both sharply focused and deeply felt, whether it is metaphorical and symbolic in expression, as in *Reluctant Flame,* or conveyed mostly by simile, as in *Hanuabada.* The two styles can be compared in these brief descriptions of the material and cultural deprivation of town blacks.

Black faces staring mutely by the dusty bus stops
Our envy hateful hearts crying tears to see them speed past in arrogance
Black shoulder bleeding from the copra bags
Our silent spear strikes inside to see the fortnight scraps
Black angelic voices singing the strange alleluia
Our soul damning itself to feel the memory of sensual dance and song

Black bodies madly showing off long white stockings shirt and
                                                                    trousers
Our laugh spirits cries to wear fully the colours we know...

(*Reluctant Flame*)

In *Reluctant Flame* the poet as *persona* is submerged in the group
personality on whose behalf he speaks. The writing is frequently cast in
the balanced antiphonal pattern evident in this quotation. *Hanuabada*,
on the other hand, is a much more personal set of poems, and the rhetoric is less incantatory :

When my awkward feet first walked the streets of Moresby
My eyes did not see you in your tight corner
My eyes, my mind and my body counted and followed every car instead
Like a sea gull capsizing up and down in the whirlwind.
How can they be so countless like a flowing stream ?
Why the palefaced drivers so stone faced and blind
To the pleading eyes and bare toes of my brother natives covered in dust
As we sullenly walk past Chinese shops toward Koki [an open-air
market] in the burning sun ?

(*Hanuabada*)

Kasaipwalova's specific observation of the local scene is occasionally
displaced by the conventional borrowed rhetoric of United States and
Third World Black Power. 'I hate you as a panther hates a motherfucker...
Here your boot is on our necks', 'Big beautiful black shouting bursting
open,' 'Firm beautiful black hands stoning police things' (*Reluctant Flame*),
and 'these white devils that trample you and use you like a prostitute'
(*Hanuabada*) represent intensely felt attitudes expressed in someone else's
language. Even in these instances, however, Kasaipwalova submerges the
borrowed language in his own observation or wry humour.

The most striking quality of *Reluctant Flame* is its creation of two
symbols, mask and flame, that vehemently and inevitably oppose each
other in mythical combat. The mask is bloodless, cold, and cold-engen-
dering; it stares, commands, and stifles Papua New Guinea culture and
values, suppressing the flame that the poet tries to cultivate. Under the
influence of the chilling mask the poet 'drop[s] the bush knife for the pen',
has his soul captured by Christianity, lusts after white women, and has his
whole mode of vision altered. 'I accept pain for pleasure,' he says, 'and
call my vomit my "good character".'

In rhetorical invective of this kind it is perhaps easier to characterise
the oppressive alien culture than to characterise the indigenous one. The
first two lines of the poem

> Cold bloodless masks stare me, not for my colour
> But for my empty wealth house and passion logic

offer a highly elliptical account of the contrast between the two cultures. Later, Kasaipwalova refers to 'the spirits of my grounds and waters' as offering help to tend the flame, for 'inside each mountain lies a tiny flame cradled and weighted by above'.

The flame is not, however, a nationalistic belief in the value of being rooted in the soil of one's native land. Kasaipwalova's flame is one with the flame of revolt by blacks everywhere against white domination :

> Look how the flame came from the ghettoes
> The flame kept down by chain and hunger
> Once reluctant now creeps obviously into the pale coldness
> Chubby Checker gave Elvis the twisting flame to throw
> Ray Charles gave the Beatles the explosive pulse to shake the total
> stiffness
> That children tempered by this flame will scorch and burn their elders
> Listen carefully, this is but one arm of the reluctant flame
> Burning and melting the icy bloodless body

> My flame take your fuel from these brother flames
> Let not the oceans drown your linking pipe
> You will grow, you will grow, you will grow like a boil on pale skins
> Maybe your vibrant lava will flow to burn anew the world
> When Johannesburg and New York is in flames
> and the black vomit will fertilize this barren soil

'The spirits of my grounds and waters', then, do not constitute the flame; they will merely help the poet to cultivate the flame in himself. The flame is one of revolt against an alien culture, not one of pride in the soil. The land is, in fact, at present a barren land, needing to be fertilised by revolution.

In another ambiguity, this time unresolved, the author asserts that the revolutionary flame comes out

> from heaven nor from the green mountain
> It IS the unseen vibrant rhythm from my pulse deep down down inside
> Crying violently for me to open my eyes and the time.

The source, then, is not only not the spirits and not the land; it is also not a black-world revolution or a national uprising. It is a personal rhythm of revolt, to which the poet must surrender himself in frenzied love.

The last two and a half pages of the poem bring together three emotions : resentment and shame at those—typified by the police—who have sold out to white values; a sense of tender affection for black love, black music, black gaiety, and black community; and an impassioned vision of destroying the oppressors' culture when the reluctant flame is able to 'burn into my heart a dancing flame'.

Both Edward Brathwaite and Wole Soyinka are more informed, allusive, and oblique writers, sensitively aware of the history, both chronicled and fabled, of their own countries, familiar with European civilisation and its literature. Both are able to create poems set simultaneously in the past and present (and sometimes the future) and Brathwaite, in his poem sequences, creates a multiple *persona*, mythic and actual, racial and personal, detached (third person) and involved (first person), plural (we) and singular (I).

Brathwaite has denied being influenced by other Caribbean poets, but acknowledges his indebtedness to novelists. 'The major influence was perhaps the West Indian novelists who from the very beginning have been putting the speech of our people into our ears; in contrast to our poets who have, on the whole, been very concerned with "English" poetic complexities rather than with the concerns of the West Indian people as a group/community.'[3]

Although Brathwaite's disclaiming of 'English' poetic complexities (except for the influence of T.S. Eliot) in his own work is disingenuous, there can be no doubt that 'the concerns of the West Indian people as a group/community' and 'the speech of our people' are major elements in his work. Brathwaite is not, of course, the only Caribbean poet to use such material, but he does so with perhaps more finesse, more sociological awareness, and more control of the point of view than others. In his work dialect is never used merely as clever imitation. If his disillusioned compatriot says

Yeah man !
and the old man gone
old Uncle Tom gone
rain making souse

of his balls in the soil.
But he's real cool,
man, while we sweat
in this tin trunk'd house

that we rent from the rat
to share with the mouse :

Castries' Conway and Brixton in London,
Port of Spain's jungle

and Kingston's Dry Dungle

Chicago Smethwick and Tiger Bay.
                           (*Rights of Passage*, p. 39)

he is not merely being linguistically demotic or modish.   He is jibing at
his own naivety and being jibed at by the poet.   Brathwaite's major point
is that after securing agreement about colonial oppression and the deracination that it produced, there is no further agreement possible about identity or the way forward.   One can only try on and poke fun at a number
of actual or conceivable *personae*.   Even the Uncle Tom *persona*, usually
thoroughly scorned, can be presented sympathetically later in *Rights of
Passage*.   In 'The Cabin', the returned expatriate visits an old shack once
inhabited by a former slave.   It is now scheduled for demolition to make
way for a characterless Housing Estate.

> No one
> knows Tom now, no one cares.
> Slave's days are past, for-
> gotten.   The faith, the dream denied,
> the things he dared
> not do, all lost, if un-
> forgiven.   This house is all
> that's left of hopes, of hurt,
> of history....
>
>   (p. 72)

The poet is the only one who realises how important the fabric of history is
in informing modern consciousness.   In the last section of the poem he re-
works the three crucial concepts of 'hopes', 'hurt', and 'history' into an
explanation of why Tom's achievement ought to be remembered and a
lament that it will not be.

> It was not shame that built this hurt,
> collected local stone
> to build the fence
>
> conceived the plaster,
> reared the tamarind tree :
> Its brittle leaves, green speechless
>
> fritters, only mock
> this shack's dilapidation and the hopes of one
> whose life here, look
>
> how snapped, how
> broken, will not be

recorded on our cenotaphs or
books.

(p. 73)

In the first line of this passage there is a good example of Brathwaite's
use of the unexpected word.   The listener is meant to hear 'hut' as well as
'hurt', of course, for Tom's experience of hurt is epitomised by the hut he
built.   Brathwaite here wants to say two things with the one word, and
his careful preparation has made it possible and effective.   Careful preparation is apparent, too, in the last couple of lines.   The dilapidated shack
is the last vestige of evidence for Tom's existence.   Brathwaite has told us
earlier that 'no one knows/where Tom's cracked limestone oblong lies', and
this oblivion is obviously not going to be corrected by the erection of a
cenotaph or the writing of books.

Tom's cabin is on the edge of the village.   In the next poem, 'Mammon', the poet comes, apparently, to the centre, in a pilgrimage to his
father's house.

So in this tilted alleyway
that rolls in debris to the sea
I kick my way among the wealth
of fish smells, fish bones,
to my father's home.

(p. 74)

It is an opening in which rhythm and phrasing are constantly belied by
Brathwaite's diction. 'Tilted', apart from its description of an angle, still
has a touch of the glamour of the joust or tournament about it, a glamour
standing in stark contrast to the mundaneness of 'alleyway'.   The second
line contains a similar ironic contrast, a similar disturbance of expectations.
The phrase 'rolls in...to the sea' sets up an expectation of some grandiose,
abstract noun to fill the gap—something like 'glory' or 'grandeur'.   One
thinks of the elevation of tone in Coleridge's lines about the stately plea-
sure-dome decreed

where Alph, the sacred river, ran
Through caverns measureless to man
Down to a sunless sea;

or in Arnold's evocation of the haunts of Apollo as being

where Helicon breaks down
In cliff to the sea,

But Brathwaite sets up associations of this kind only to destroy them. The word he chooses is 'debris' : the alleyway 'rolls in debris to the sea'.

A similar point can be made about various other phrases in this verse-paragraph. Brathwaite speaks of 'the wealth/of fish smells', of the sun 'prowling/among the rocks and fowls', of 'the thick/necked sweating God', of 'the three R's/taught : Reading, a little Riting,/and some Rural lust', summing up the items of schoolboy life in a finely ambiguous phrase : 'the immemorial legacies of dust'. 'Legacies of' can mean 'legacies from', 'legacies consisting of', or even perhaps 'legacies bequeathed to'. All three meanings are intended, and again there is the ironic juxtaposition of something desirable (legacies) with something apparently worthless (dust). Man's achievements—and here Brathwaite seems to allow his generalisation to spread beyond the specific settlement he is speaking of to embrace all mankind—end in literal and metaphorical dust.

The comparative point that emerges from this analysis is an obvious one. Brathwaite's passion is as fierce as Kasaipwalova's but he has a far more complex understanding of the historical and social circumstances he describes, a far more critical attitude to stereotypes, a far wider multicultural experience to draw on, and a more resonant, witty, and ironic language.

If Brathwaite has a set of key words used with incremental additions of meaning throughout a sequence ('history', 'whip', 'wind', 'worn', 'wave', 'heart', 'memory', 'chains', 'break', 'freedom', 'fear', 'hope', 'protest', and 'ground' for example), Wole Soyinka has a set of favourite images that he reverts to again and again, generally with a meaning that either is fairly constant or develops. Grey, the colour of the great rocks surrounding his home town, Abeokuta, is the prevailing hue of his work. Dawn is seen often as light flickering between spears or staves of grass or palmtrees. All kinds of airy filaments—spiders' webs, fronds, and feathers, for example—are familiar objects in his poetry. Small and delicate creatures—ants most commonly of all—are frequently encountered. Archetypal images of rain and water; the sun; day and night; the earth and its metals, fruit, and nuts; the road; blood; and wine are all very common. And surgery and madness seem always at hand.

Soyinka is, of course, a much more private poet—and perhaps a less popular one—than either Kasaipwalova or Brathwaite. That does not necessarily mean, of course, that he is less effective as a political poet. By comparison with the other two he represents himself as far more tortured, more visionary, more tense and nervous, more acquainted with breakdown. His satire is more sorrowful than scornful; his attitude to life not only ambiguous (like Brathwaite's) but suffused with a sense of the mystery and fragility of life. If Brathwaite achieves at times epic magnitude, Soyinka's mode is personal and tragic, self-critical but not self-pitying.

Like Brathwaite, Soyinka often needs the frameworks of time and distance to separate him sufficiently from events for assimilation to occur and understanding to begin. 'Massacre, October '66' uses the setting of the lake at Tegel, on the north-west outskirts of Berlin, a few weeks after the renewed massacres of Ibos in northern Nigeria. His interpretation of what has happened is confessedly fragmentary and ambivalent. The fragmentary quality is conveyed by the image of 'Shards of sunlight' with which the poem begins and ends, and by the broken play of light and fallen leaves on the surface of the lake. The ambivalence arises chiefly from the syntax, which at times is capable of quite contradictory interpretations. As he walks by the side of the lake the poet feels that there is

> Time to watch autumn the removal man
> Dust down rare canvases
>
> To let a loud resolve of passion
> Fly to a squirrel, burnished light and copper fur
> A distant stance without the lake's churchwindows
> And for a stranger, love.
> ....
> I borrow seasons of an alien land
> In brotherhood of ill, pride of race around me
> Strewn in sunlight shards. I borrow alien lands
> To stay the season of a mind.

The first ambiguity here is whether the availability of time to watch the leaves fall and the squirrel interact with the light is to be approved of or deprecated. The lineation of

> a loud resolve of passion
> Fly to a squirrel

suggests deliberate bathos, accompanied by self-loathing at the trivialising of emotion, but the lovely description of the light being burnished by the squirrel and the fur made coppery by the light suggests pure esjoyment of the scene for its own sake.

'A distant stance' may refer to that of the poet, the squirrel, or Nigeria—perhaps all three are intended. But the most stunning ambiguity of all concerns 'love'. Is it to be taken as coordinate with 'stance' (A distant stance, ... And ... love') or with 'churchwindows' ('without the lake's churchwindows/And...[without] love') ? The meanings here are entirely contradictory, but both may be intended. The poet, moving away from the broken coloured patterns on the lake, but seeing instead the brilliant colour of the squirrel, may experience a feeling of love—for nature, for the squirrel, or for humanity. And at the same time—such is the intricacy one has to expect in Soyinka—he may, deprived of the play of colours in the lake feel that, in this alien country, oppressed by the thought of the massacres in his homeland, he is unloved and incapable of loving.

The last stanza of the poem is similarly ambivalent. 'Brotherhood of ill' and 'pride of race...in sunlit shards' seem to apply to the Germans, the Nigerians, and himself. The setting at Tegel, the very land itself, in-indeed any and every alien land available, is useful 'To stay a season of a mind.' The lands may, presumably, be either actual or imaginary, but the chief ambiguity lies in 'stay'. It seems to mean to stop (in order to scrutinise), to steady (in order to bring into focus), and to postpone or ward off (as in a stay of execution). It seems to me not unreasonable to assume that all these meanings can operate simultaneously. Soyinka's atti-tude to himself apropos the massacres is a vacillating one, hinted at (as in so many of his poems) by the images of broken light, stated in syntax that is deliberately ambiguous.

Where Kasaipwalova is direct and unambiguous in what he says (grant-ed the use of satire and of occasional stereotypes), Brathwaite brings a multitude of points of view to bear on his material, sometimes simulta-neously. In Brathwaite we are often aware of the author's attitude to a character's attitude to a mythical interpretation of what may have hap-pened. In Soyinka the same multi-layering of the point of view can also occur, but what is more remarkable in his work is the simultaneous hold-ing by the poet of contradictory ideas and the expression of those contra-dictory ideas through a single set of words. It is not a matter of the wittily ambiguous use of a single word, as in Brathwaite, but the contradictory ambiguities of whole statements. His verse is, then, at the farthest possible remove from the discursiveness possible in the novel, and it is likely to reach far fewer readers than many Nigerian novels. Kasaipwalova and Brathwaite, using more techniques from the novel (and from song and dance, for that matter), are likely, because of a potentially larger reader-ship, to have a broader based effect as political poets.

REFERENCES

1. See Okot p 'Bitek, *The Horn of My Love*, London, 1974, pp. 12-13.

2. See John Kasaipwalova, 'Philosophy and Historical Reality of Kabisawali' (pp. 16-17) and Ulli Beier, 'Kabisawali : The Impact of a Self-help Movement on Cultural Life in the Trobriand Islands' (pp. 18-24) in *Gigibori*, 2, No. 1 (April 1975).

3. *Contemporary Poets*, London and New York, 1970, p. 129.

22

Diminishing Satire :
A Study of V.S. Naipaul
and Mordecai Richler

VICTOR J. RAMRAJ

THE easily discernible similarities between the experiences and works of
Mordecai Richler of Canada and V. S. Naipaul of the West Indies call
attention to themselves and suggest the possibilities of more specific,
organic comparative studies of these two novelists. Both are of the same
generation, both belonged to racial minorities in their respective countries,
and both protested against and rejected certain values and attitudes of
their race, suffering consequently feelings of loneliness and estrangement.
They initially saw their countries as cultural backwaters unconducive to
the artist, and sought refuge in the literary and cultural richness of
London. Here, though lost and lonely, they found an environment more
encouraging to the realisation of their talents. Both at one time or
another were reluctant to be pinned down as writers of a particular region
or a particular race, choosing to be known as writers pure and simple.
Both are critical of aspects of their societies, and are in turn chastised by
some of their countrymen for their apparently unnationalistic stand.
These and other parallels of varying significance (both have semi-autobiographical works on a particular street, both were published—until
recently—by Andre Deutsch, both are distrustful of political causes) help
to establish the viability of undertaking comparisons of Naipaul and
Richler, and the unforced nature of such comparisons. These patent
parallels in themselves, however, are not the main focus of this paper.
My primary concern is with examining the character and quality of their
satiric vision and tone in their novels—a sphere of their work which
reveals telling affinities and divergences.

   Naipaul and Richler have reputations as satirists of the shortcomings
of their respective countries and peoples—reputations, I feel, acquired

less through their novels than through their many journalistic reports and essays and other non-fiction works, where severe unambiguous strictures on their societies are certainly evident. Richler's primary target is the barren cultural climate of Canada during his adolescence. He quotes with perverse frequency (and with apparent disregard for chronology) Dr Johnson's dismissal of the dominion as a "region of desolate sterility... a cold, uncomfortable, uninviting region, from which nothing but furs and fish were to be had." And he likes to groan with Samuel Butler in *A Psalm to Montreal* "O God ! O Montreal !"[1] Naipaul describes his society, in *The Middle Passage*, as a place that is unimportant, uncreative, cynical, where intrigue is substituted for talent. He epigraphically quotes, with implied endorsement (and with Richler's apparent disregard for chronology) James Anthony Froude's dismissive comments on the nineteenth century West Indies : "There are no people there in the true sense of the word, with a character and purpose of their own."[2]

These unambiguous strictures from Naipaul's and Richler's essays and journals cannot be ignored, yet we should not allow ourselves to be per-suaded to see them as necessarily accurate reflections of their presentation of, and attitude to, their respective societies in their novels. Novelists' non-fiction pieces do often complement and illuminate their fictional efforts; in Naipaul's and Richler's case, however, we should be wary of too readily admitting this—for several reasons. In the first instance, they certainly do not shy away from revealing the shortcomings of their parti-cular society in their novels, but this is not prompted by any perverse hatred; as serious novelists, they attempt to reflect the total experience— both good (it is important to emphasise this) and bad—of the societies fictionally examined. Nevertheless, the very fact that they are writing from within about insecure, new societies gives their critical assessment the inherent stigma of mocking betrayal and repudiation—a stigma under-scored by the publication of their novels outside their countries. As Nai-paul has stated in *The Middle Passage* : the West Indian society wants and is given writers who have "so far only reflected and flattered"[3] its prejudices rather than objectively examine what it is and where it stands. And Richler, with the Jewish minority primarily but not exclusively in mind, says : "A Gentile in my position, can ridicule the pretensions of the middle class and their clergy with a degree of impunity. He has, it's true, to face the tests of accuracy and artistic worth but never will be called an anti-Gentile. My people unfortunately, are still so insecure here that they want their artists to serve as publicists, not critics."[4] Shunning the publicists' function, Richler adds : "Most Jewish writers annoy me because they write about the Jews in a honeyed way; it's like writing about the poor for the rich as Saroyan did to a large extent."[5]

Naipaul and Richler do make firm and important distinctions between their fiction and non-fiction. In an essay published in 1968, Richler issued this racy *caveat emptor* to the readers of his journalistic censure of Canada :

> Still, being a Canadian writer abroad offers a writer a number of built-in perks. I have, through the years, been turning over a useful penny in the why-have-you-left-Canada interview, that is to say, once a year
>
> I make a fool of myself on TV for a fee.
>
> Most recently a breathless girl from Toronto sat in my garden, crossed legs distractingly as the TV cameras turned, smiled cutely, and said, 'I've never read anything you've written but would you say you were part of the brain drain ?'
>
> Sure, baby. I also assure her that I'm an Angry Young Man. A black humorist. A white Negro. Anything.
>
> 'But why did you leave Canada in the first place ?'
>
> I daren't tell her that I had no girl friends. That having been born dirty-minded I had thought in London maybe, in Paris certainly, the girls...Instead, I say, 'Well, it was a cultural desert, wasn't it ? In London, I could see the Sadlers Wells Ballet, plays by Terence Rattigan. If overcome with a need to see the Popular Stars of Prague, I could hop on a plane and jolly well see them.[6]

His essays, articles, and reports, together with his excursions into script writing for the cinema and television represent, as Richler himself puts it, "time out". They enable him to buy time for his novels of which he says : "I am a writer vain enough to think my real office is to write fiction."[7] In the foreword to *The Middle Passage*, Naipaul points to a fundamental distinction in the creative process of fiction and non-fiction : he hesitated to accept Dr Eric Williams' offer to write a non-fiction work because the "novelist works towards conclusions of which he is unaware; and it is better that he should...I felt it as a danger that having factually analysed the society as far as I was able, I would be unable to think of it in terms of fiction and that in anything I might write I would be concerned only to prove a point."[8] We are reminded here that non-fiction appraisals generally lack the wider complex, ironic perceptions of the novel, and that they tend to reflect, in T.S. Eliot's words "the man who suffers" rather than "the mind which creates."

Both Richler and Naipaul have disclaimed the satirical intention. In an interview with Derek Walcott in 1965, Naipaul said : "I am not a satirist. Satire comes out of a tremendous optimism. One simply does not indulge in satire while one is awaiting death. Satire is a type of anger. Irony and comedy, I think, come out of a sense of acceptance."[9] Reform in society, he says elsewhere, "begins with the direct vision and the compassion of a Chekov or a Dickens." In a later interview with Robert Lowell, he mentions "true satire" as distinct from "satire" which is malicious and cruel. By 'true satire' I feel Naipaul means the wider, understanding ironic vision for he says that "true satire grows out of the largest vision.... that 'all embracing Christlike' vision...."[10] Richler, too, though he does not deny satirical pieces in his novels, protests against an interviewer categorising him as satirist pure and simple. This, Richler observes, ignores his larger concern with the novel of character and with being the loser's advocate rather than his castigator, which he sees to be the novelist's primary moral responsibility.[11] This preference is reiterated in Richler's essays and interviews. Significantly, he stated of the early writings of himself and his coterie (which included Terry Southern and David Burnett), that satire (which does not require knowledge of the psyche and inner complexity of the individual or society but only of the moment of folly and vice) was shrewdly settled upon because it did not "betray knowledge gaps of day to day experience."[12] Satire, then, can be used by Richler as a stylistic device rather than a straight expression of attitude.

The satirical vision springs from firm convictions of what is right and wrong, unimbued with any hesitancy, vacillation, or ambivalence. The satirist in the published form of his work does not weigh, balance, and sift evidence, resolve queries, wrestle with doubts like a member of the judicial bench; he more closely approximates the prosecutor, who having convinced himself of the accused's guilt sets about to convict him relentlessly. As Basil Willey says : the satirist "must, whether deliberately or not, miss precisely these aspects of the ignoble thing which in fact make it endurable to the non-satiric eye : that is to say, he must ignore the explanation of the thing satirised."[13] It is interesting to note in relation to their political stance that Richler and Naipaul are unhesitantly convinced of the rightness of only two or three causes : Naipaul said to Derek Walcott : "You cannot commit yourself unless your cause is absolutely pure. I think there have really been only two good causes within recent times : against Hitler and possibly in South Africa."[14] And Richler says : "We've lived through two great horrors, in our time, the murder of the Jews and Hiroshima, and the rest disappears....one must...figure out where he stands in relation to [them]...."[15]

What informs Richler's tone from his very first novel is less a satiric and more an ambivalent vision. Though satire appears sporadically but sharply, and though he has written (in *Cocksure*) the most serious Canadian satirical novel and therein has employed one of the most grotesque satirical images (of Star Maker) in contemporary literature at large, nevertheless his ambivalent, vacillating, conflicting vision does restrictively affect any sustained, cogent satire in his novels. All Richler's protagonists from Andre Bennett of *The Acrobats* to Jake Hersh of *St Urbain's Horseman* are questing, troubled souls searching for values in a world where absolutes have disappeared. And it becomes difficult to chastise satirically when yardsticks of judgment have not been decided upon.

In *The Acrobats* and *A Choice of Enemies* Richler's protagonists, Andre Bennett and Norman Price, conduct their search in post-war Europe where causes and ideologies are seen by the young Richler to inform and govern human relationships. Satire plays a very minor role in these novels for the protagonists are not sure of what is evil and what is good, what should be censured and what should be sanctioned. The title of *A Choice of Enemies* reflects their predicament. Richler is concerned with the pain, the frustration, the disillusionment, the bewilderment, and the ennui of his seekers, one of whom does not live long enough to realise that truth is not to be found in ideologies and political causes. In *The Acrobats*, Andre does make one emotional outburst against Canadian culture, but Richler focuses on the impassioned anger and resentment of his troubled protagonist, intending no controlled satiric distancing. Perhaps the only piece of cogent satire is a brief dig at four dignitaries at a Spanish fiesta who sit aloofly from the ubiquitous misery around them, and whose mechanical, orchestrated behaviour is satirically set against the passion and spontaneity of the street dancers. But this is a digressive piece, not wholly digested within the novel. *A Choice of Enemies* has a measured, unruffled, contemplative tone. Sometimes it rises to mild sardonicism through the character of the protagonist (the main consciousness of narration), but it is his very character which prevents this mild sardonic attitude from becoming satirical. An aloof, contemplative man, Norman Price reprimands himself for not being more generous and tolerant; and to avoid being considered cold and detached, he makes every effort to be pleasant. The one cogent satiric passage is again digressive and undigested here : Richler briefly satirises cultural programmes on Canadian television through Charlie Lawson, a character viewed with sympathetic concern by the author and protagonist in the rest of the novel.

Son of a Smaller Hero and *The Apprenticeship of Duddy Kravitz* are Richler's two novels wherein the Jewish society of Montreal features prominently. Some aspects of this society annoy and dismay Richler, but others appeal to him. He does not sweepingly or indiscretely poke fun at the inhabitants. He observes the members of this richly complex society in all their guises and forms, sympathising with their predicament at times and censuring them when they deserve it. The censured in his novels are the materialistic, the pompous, the dullards, and the bigoted. In *Son of a Smaller Hero*, Richler, however, is less concerned with satirising these shortcomings than with the struggles of Noah Adler, another unanchored, questing soul who embodies the contradictions and ambivalences of someone seeking himself. Noah does reject several aspects of his Montreal Jewish society, but his criticism is never sharp or vicious, for in fact he does not know what to believe in. It is not until the end of the novel that he has found something to adhere to (and even then what he has found is vague). Throughout the rest of the novel he experiences an emotional bind in his relationship with the Jewish community, rejecting it and accepting it, seeking to escape from it yet returning to it for assurance. In this quandary, Noah is unable to administer firm chastisement; and, instead of becoming a persecutor of his people, he reveals himself to be a troubled, tormented young idealist in this *bildungs-roman*.

Certain readers of Richler's other Montreal Jewish novel, *The Apprenticeship of Duddy Kravitz*, believe that Richler mocks and censures the young Jewish protagonist, presenting him as a money-grabbing *pusherke* from the Montreal ghetto. But Richler has said otherwise : "A character like Duddy Kravitz possibly has enormous strength in that he's not, in that book, sufficiently perceptive or sensitive to believe in his own death, and that does give acquisitive money-making people a lot of strength and energy and vitality, which I both *admire and despise*."[16] And elsewhere he candidly states of Duddy : "I don't think of him as fundamentally unsympathetic."[17] An examination of the novel bears out Richler's response to his protagonist. He is portrayed almost simultaneously as a waif of circumstances and environment (no morality is imparted him; he has no mother, of whom he asks for with pathetic recurrence; he is ignored by members of his family who favour his brother, Lennie, the designated doctor of the family; he is considered a cipher socially and academically), and as a man of free will who chooses the wrong way of life (Uncle Benjy's letter, read posthumously by Duddy, underscores this). Richler shows that Duddy, in order to escape the harsh and oppressive realities of his environment—a business jungle, where survival of the fittest is the law—must play according to the questionable values of that environment, and then ironically become himself a victim of those values. Unnecessary and unaccommodated, overlooked and ignored, Duddy seeks to lose his status as a nonentity in the eyes of his unheeding family and environment. The only way he knows how is by taking his grandfather's platitudinous advice literally : a man without land is a nobody. Towards the end of the novel, Uncle Benjy on his deathbed is Richler's voice, and he realises that Duddy's obsession with land is not that of a money-grabbing *pusherke* for Duddy has just refused his financial offer; Duddy's tooth-and-nail struggle for land is only an expression of his need to be wanted and heeded. Though Richler doesn't sanction Duddy's unscrupulous efforts to acquire Lac St Pierre, he does suggest what would have happened to him had he not fought the business jungle by its rules : the manqué comedian Cuckoo Kaplan, the gullible Lennie, and the disillusioned Mac-Pherson (with whom the novel significantly opens) all succumb to the jungle. Duddy himself in fact almost did; at one point he suffers what appears to be a nervous breakdown, and is overwhelmed by *ennui*.

In his study of Duddy Kravitz it is a remarkable achievement on

Richler's part that he succeeds in never making Duddy satirically repellent when he shows his vices and in never making him a romanticised, sentimental figure when he presents him as a poor creature who cannot help but be moulded by his social environment. Richler is aware both of the worst and of the possibility for good in his protagonist, and he is neither his castigator nor his advocate. He does not intend that the reader should make a simple sympathetic identification with, or an easy rejection of, the young protagonist. Such responses would be a gross simplification of Richler's achievement and energising ironic vision. Were Duddy a real-life acquaintance of the reader it is true that he would be on his guard against Duddy; however, with Duddy contained between the covers of the novel, Richler invites us to shed our biases and to look objectively at him, though like the author we may not be able to make up our minds about whether we should admire or despise him. There are the inevitable Richlerian certain set pieces of satire on social pretensions and hypocrisies; and two characters with some thematic and structural functions—Cohen and the Boy Wonder—are satirised. The predominant tone of the novel, however, is characterised by an energising ambivalence.

In *The Incomparable Atuk*, Richler leaves the Montreal Jewish world for Toronto's cultural scene. He shows here that the Canadian society is walled in by a narrow nationalism which encourages the fabrication of national heroes and heroines of pedestrian proportions, creates an insularity that seeks to exclude all outside influence (particularly that of America), and fosters the parochial cultural man. This is a work, however, which though it is not equated with his journalistic articles, is dismissed by Richler as a light novel, a holiday piece, "more of a spoof."[18] It is not satire primarily but farce, wherin laughter is used for laughter's sake rather than to mock or ridicule. Richler is certainly caricaturing attitudes and manners, drawing creatively from the pseudo-cultural type, but often his characters cease to represent something and they just are. They are not so much satirical caricatures as originals, however unreal they may be. Often, too, Richler becomes so absorbed with his zany plots and zestful situations that he is distracted from whatever censuring intentions he may have had. One obvious illustration is the situation in which Sergeant Jock Wilson of the Royal Canadian Mounted Police finds himself towards the end of the novel. Initially, Richler appears to be using him as a means of satirising the ineptitude of this police force and the fastidiousness and officiousness with which it undertakes to entrap communist students. But any potential satire gives way to farce in the scenes of mistaken identity where Jock and Jean-Paul McEwen, both masquerading as their opposite sex, fall in love. In the final hilarious farcical scene of this sub-plot, whatever satirical butt there was disappears completely as Richler, following this episode to its most unlikely extreme, tells of Sergeant Jock, disguised as a woman,

winning the Miss Canada crown, and preparing, on orders from his supe-
riors, for the Miss Universe contest.

St Urbain's Horseman, Richler's latest novel (if we omit his recent
children's novel, Jacob Two-Two and the Hooded Fang), has as its protagonist Jake Hersh, a character who is a culmination of all Richler's
troubled seekers. The novel is a therapeutic work, dramatically embodying a revaluation of attitudes and opinions held by Jake Hersh (who is
more than partially identifiable with Richler) up to his thirty-seventh year,
which would appear to be a climacteric period of his life. The complex
feelings and attitudes of this cogitative, temperamental, vacillating, self-
contemptuous protagonist are Richler's main concern; whatever censure
is given by the protagonist is more a reflection of himself rather than
an objective, controlled satiric comment on his society. Jake's responses
to his wife's pleasure in, and his own ignorance of, gardening is one clear
indication of this. Having uprooted peony tubers and rose bushes, which
were not as Jake thought and Nancy pointed out to him, barren, cancer-
ous growth, he resentfully thinks of her as an "Ontario hick." He sulkily
describes Nancy strolling with their Scottish gardener as "two bores of
a Thomas Hardy novel delighting in rustic trivia, exchanging their gentile secrets, the text derived from the Protocols of the Elders of the Com-
post Heap."[19] Later, he is appalled that he could think in such terms of
Nancy whom he devotedly loves. (Their relationship provides some of
the warmest, most tender passages in the novel). He accuses himself of
being too touchy and too resentful. That Jake could so abusively think of
the woman he loves and admires and in no way wants to mock and censure, does prepare us to see that his abuse of others is not the mockery and
ridicule of satire but groping attempts on his part to comprehend his inner
discordance and inconsistency. Jake re-examines with growing ambivalence—which accommodates tolerance and lessens rebuke—the vices and
follies of his multitudinous family, of the Jewish community at large, and
of his country. Perhaps his comments on Canadian culture is the clearest
indication of this. As a youth, Jake Hersh, whose experiences are very
close to Richler's, flees Canada, mocking its picayune standards. Before
embarking for London, Jake and his friend, Luke, serve their artistic
apprenticeship in Toronto. They scoff at the cultural society and at the
second-rate artists, particularly at Jenny's husband, Doug Fraser.
However, the more mature Jake, through whose consciousness this scene
is presented and who indulges in an ongoing revaluation of his life
throughout the novel, stands objectively apart from the young Jake,
implicitly suggesting that such scoffing is the attitudinising of bright, cocky,
young men at whose feet lies the world. Later, Jake states explicitly :

Fulminating in Montreal; he could agree with Auden that the
dominons were tiefste Provinz. Scornful of all things home-baked,
he was at one with Dr. Johnson, finding his country a cold and

uninviting region. As his father had blamed the *goyim* for his own inadequacies...so Jake had foolishly held Canada culpable for all his discontents.[20]

Despite four set pieces of satire—the parody of *The Good Britons*, the Hampstead Heath baseball match, the English lawyer Ormsby-Fletcher, and the Canadian Immigration Officer urging the English to migrate to Canada—the predominant tone of the novel is dictated by this mature, tolerant, accommodating vision.

In Richler's first three novels, *The Acrobats*, *Son of a Smaller Hero*, and *A Choice of Enemies*, humour is found almost exclusively in short, satiric set pieces, making it easy to assess its function. It is not until *The Apprenticeship of Duddy Kravitz* that humour appears pervasively and organically, concomitantly creating an elusiveness of tone and attitude. This pervasive, organic humour is manifest from Naipaul's very first novel (whether we consider this to be *The Mystic Masseur* or *Miguel Street*) and the critical problem—which began with the publication of the novels, as the early antithetical reviews show—is to determine whether his laughter is sympathetic or mocking, or perhaps just farcically purposeless. Naipaul has described his first three novels, *The Mystic Masseur*, *The Suffrage of Elvira*, and *Miguel Street*, as apprenticeship works, and certainly where his attitude and tone are concerned this is an apt assessment, for he does not have a consistent tone shifting from satirical laughter to the warm laughter of comedy and to the sheer fun of farce—though there is a strong leaning towards tolerance and understanding. The young novelist, who like Ralph at Isabella Imperial, was taught to look at his world through British eyes yet is intimately aware of the constricting circumstances of the colonial society, who opted out of Hindu metaphysics but whose protagonists (Ralph, Biswas, Ganesh) reflect Hindu fatalism, is trying to find the proper vision with which to come to grips with the complex experience of his society.

A significant technique of satire is caricature, exaggeration, and distortion of character and behaviour to accentuate the particular shortcoming requiring reprimand and censure. In these early novels, many of the characters appear to be satirical caricatures and exaggerations but, as Naipaul points out, familiarity with the West Indies immediately contradicts this : "The social comedies I write can be fully appreciated only by someone who knows the regions I write about. Without this knowledge it is easy for my books to be dismissed as farces and my characters as eccentrics."[21] Naipaul goes on to explain that personages who appear to be distortions in his work are really based on 'characters' and eccentrics whose existence is fostered by the circumstances of the society :

... Trinidadians are more recognizably 'characters' than people in

England. Only a man's eccentricities can get him attention. It might also be that in a society without tradition, without patterns, every man finds it easier "to be himself." Whatever the reason, this determination of people to be themselves, to cherish their eccentricities, to reveal themselves at once, makes them easy material for the writer.[22]

This cautionary remark to the reader is certainly applicable too to the gallery of richly delineated eccentrics in Richler's novels, as indeed it is with Dickens' characters.

The principal ironical technique in *The Mystic Masseur* is Naipaul's employment of dual points of view in telling of Ganesh's successful climb from an obscure mystic to the Honours List. We are given Ganesh's interpretation through brief recurring excerpts from his autobiography, *The Years of Guilt*, wherein he sees himself marked by fate and destined for greatness. The narrator's account, on the other hand, tends deflatingly to examine the more mundane, environmental reasons and Ganesh's own wiles and skulduggery as contributing factors to his success. The irony here could be considered satirical. However, this juxtaposition of points of view is not balanced, the narrator's being very prominently the main focus of narration, and recurringly the ironical juxtaposition fades out as Naipaul presents Ganesh as a lovable rogue in the mould of Chaucer's Pardoner. It is likely too that employing two points of view constitutes a fairly serious consideration (though not to the extent of his examination of Ralph's father's rise to prominence as a cult leader, in *The Mimic Men*) of the extent to which the individual's course of life depends on his innate qualities, environmental factors, and fate or chance. There are certain scenes with satirical overtones (though, like the Government House reception scene, these could be considered to be harmlessly farcical as well), but in his study of Ganesh, Naipaul is not wholly lacking in tolerance, positing as he does environmental condition and chance as extenuating factors in Ganesh's tainted progressive march to fame :

If he had been born ten years earlier it is unlikely, if you take into account the Trinidad Indian's attitude to education at that time, that his father would have sent him to Queen's Royal College. He might have become a pundit. If he had been born ten years later his father would have sent him to America or Canada or England to get a profession—the Indian attitude to education had changed so completely— and Ganesh might have become an unsuccessful lawyer or a dangerous doctor.[23]

In *The Suffrage of Elvira*, Naipaul weaves a complicated but deliberately contrived story which humorously examines the advent of democracy and adult suffrage in one of the remoter fictional constituencies in

Trinidad.   There is little cogent satire here, for though Naipaul acknowledges Elvira's electioneering rogueries, he does not chastise or reprimand
the Elvirans.   In fact, he appears to be suggesting in this ironical passage
that perhaps the fault lies with those who too hastily introduced adult
suffrage in a community not quite ready for it :

> A long grey van pulled up.   It belonged to The Trinidad Film Board,
> who were shooting scenes for a Colonial Office documentary film about
> political progress in the colonies, the script of which was to be written,
> poetically, in London, by a minor British poet.[24]

This is the only comment of its kind in the novel for Naipaul refuses to
take himself seriously. He once mentioned in an interview : "I would
dearly like to become frivolous again. I would love to write another
Suffrage of Elvira."[25] It is worth noting, also, that the electioneering
games, though they constitute the central fable, are in fact not the sole
concern of the novel. There are as many scenes dealing frivolously with
family misunderstandings, neighbourly quarrels, breaches of etiquette,
lovers' meetings, peeping-toms, and other incidents not integrally related
to the political theme. When the political activities are considered, we
get a rollicking picture of rogues battling rogues. The novel is all one
huge joke, narrated in a fast-paced, pervasively dramatic style. It does
reflect Naipaul's awareness of the absurdity of the Elvirans, and his
preference to see the fun that is in it rather than the satirical possibilities.
     There are many similar light-hearted sketches in *Miguel Street*, but
the laughter in most of the sketches is the tolerant, sympathetic laughter
of one aware of the joys and sorrows of the inhabitants of the Miguel
Street slum during and immediately after the Second World War. The
seemingly effortless sense of irony with which Naipaul describes the traits
and behaviour of these characters and the situation in which they find
themselves is the main source of humour in ths novel. The irony is
rendered innocuous by Naipaul's use of the young narrator, who, though
mischievous, is a kind-hearted lad.   It is not the rhetorical irony of satire,
but philosophical irony which underlines the predominantly sad incongruities of life. In sketches dealing with many of these personages (such
as Black Wordsworth, Laura, Elias, Bolo) there is an essential pathetic
note beneath the humour. Of the three apprenticeship novels, *Miguel
Street* is the warmest, and its commingling of humour and pathos most
closely prefigures the tone of *A House for Mr Biswas*.
     In this later novel, the satiric tone is just one aspect of an intricately
constructed, ambitiously conceived novel that abounds in a reticulation
of moods, atmospheres, tones, and paces. One is conscious of Naipaul's
personal involvement in the plight of his protagonist; *a propos* of which,
the irony serves the stylistic end of aesthetic distancing, enabling Naipaul
to see his characters with a clear, objective, yet indulgent eye; it is seldom

the cold detachment of satire. Naipaul understandingly portrays Mr Biswas's struggle to free himself of the Tulsis who frustrate his efforts to achieve some measure of individuality and independence. Yet, though Mr Biswas—whose consciousness provides the main focus of narration—mocks the Tulsis, Naipaul lets such mockery characterise the frustrated little man as well as reflect at times unsavoury aspects of Tulsidom. In fact, Naipaul makes us aware of what a despicable, unreasonable man Mr Biswas can be now and again. He is not a characterless ingénu used as a satirical device against the Tulsis, but rather is himself the focal concern of the novel. Naipaul explores at arm's length, like Richler in *St Urbain's Horseman*, the nature and motivation of his protagonist's sardonicism : a little man with few skills, no physical stature, little education, and with no supportive family, he tries to preserve through his satirical wit his eroding individuality in a society where he is considered unnecessary and unaccommodated from birth. Anand is very much his father's son in this respect : "Though no-one recognised his strength, Anand was among the strong. His satirical sense kept him aloof... it made him unassailable."[26] Like Noah's anger with his Jewish family, Mr Biswas's resentment of the Tulsis is more the animadversion of a frustrated man, and is seldom given unqualified authorial sanction or a controlled, objective satiric presentation.

Naipaul's penultimate novel so far, *The Mimic Men*, and Richler's *St Urbain's Horseman* reveal several parallels, some of which are pertinent to our comparative examination of the nature and development of their satire. Both are contemplative, therapeutic novels written by protagonists at climacteric periods of their lives. Both constitute a revaluation of attitudes and values, and a patent rejection of the easy satirical tone. Naipaul does see the ridiculous aspects of political life in *The Mimic Men*, but as Ralph Singh (who, like Jake Hersh, is more than partially identifiable with his creator) says : "I wish to avoid satire... It is that the situation satirises itself, turns satire inside out, takes satire to the point where it touches pathos if not tragedy.[27] A darkening vision envelopes this novel. The light air of the early novels, which later commingled with the pathos of *A House for Mr Biswas* (and *Mr Stone and the Knights Companion*), disappears almost completely in this confessional work. Here of course is one point of divergence from Richler's *St Urbain's Horseman*, for laughter, though predominantly sympathetic (except in set, digressive passages) is still present in Richler's novel. These novels indicate another, more significant point of divergence between the two novelists. While both do still have a sharp eye for human follies and vices, they choose not to employ a primary satirical stance towards the experiences of which they write. Both develop a tolerance. But while Richler's growth away from satire comes from an ambivalence which appears in his very first work and intensifies in the later novels consequent upon his and his protagonists' realisation of their own frailty which makes them more

accommodating of the faults of others, Naipaul's springs from a realisation that blame cannot be readily apportioned to man, for in certain
conditions man seems to have little control over circumstances and
naturalistic forces. *The Mimic Men* is an intensification of Naipaul's
efforts to posit extenuating circumstances of chance and environment for
Ganesh's conduct in *The Suffrage of Elvira*. He would agree with Philip
Toynbee's observation that satire "will surely remain as a means of human
expression as long as there is human folly and wickedness to satirise. But
there are periods when satire falls into abeyance, not through lack of
follies and wickedness, but because things have gone too far for satiric
treatment : disaster seems to be out of proportion to any degree of human
responsibility."[28]

REFERENCES

1. See, for instance, Richler's *Canadian Writing Today*, Harmondsworth, Penguin, 1970, pp. 15-16.

2. Epigraph, *Middle Passage*, London, Deutsch, 1962.

3. *Middle Passage*, p. 87.

4. "We Jews...," *Maclean's*, 12 October 1960, p. 79.

5. Interview with Nathan Cohen, *Tamarack Review*, Winter 1957, p. 23.

6. *Hunting Tigers Under Glass*, Toronto, M & S, 1969, pp. 27-28.

7. *ibid.*, p. 14.

8. *Middle Passage*, p. 5.

9. *Trinidad Sunday Guardian Magazine*, 6 August 1967, p. 8.

10. "Documentary Heresy," *20th Century*, Winter 1964, p. 18.

11. Taped interview with Earle Toppings, *OISE*, Toronto, 1970.

12. *Shovelling Trouble*, Toronto, M & S, 1972, p. 36.

13. *Eighteenth-Century Background*, N.Y., 1941, p. 107.

14. Interview with Derek Walcott, p. 5.

15. Interview with Donald Cameron, in *Conversations with Canadian Novelists II*, Toronto, Macmillan, 1973, p. 117.

16. Graeme Gibson, Interview with Mordecai Richler, *Eleven Canadian Novelists*, Toronto, M & S, 1973, p. 290. (italics mine).

17. *ibid.*, p. 270.

18. Interview with John Metcalf, *Journal of Canadian Fiction*, Winter 1974, p. 74.

19. *St Urbain's Horseman*, Toronto, M & S, 1971, p. 284.

20. *ibid.*, pp. 301-302.

21. "The Regional Barrier", *TLS*, 15 August 1958, p. xxxvii.

22.   *ibid.*, p. xxxvii.

23.   *The Mystic Masseur*, London, Deutsch 1957, p. 200.

24.   *The Suffrage of Elvira*, London, Deutsch, 1958, p. 207.

25.   Interview with David Bates, *The* (*London*) *Sunday Times Supplement*, 26 May 1963, p. 13.

26.   *A House for Mr Biswas*, London, Deutsch, 1961, p. 372.

27.   *The Mimic Men*, London, Deutsch, 1967, p. 250.

28.   Philip Toynbee, quoted in *Contemporary Satire*, ed. D.J. Dooley, Toronto, M & S, 1971, p. 14.

23

'In God's Name' :
Ironic Forms of Religious Drama
in Canada and Australia

PATRICIA MORLEY

IN 1975 I was privileged to see performed two dramas which left an indelible impression. Both plays were extremely moving. Both broke new technical ground. Each restated an ancient truth: that man prefers to mould his God in his own image in order to advance his own ends; and that behind man's cruel and petty posturings stands a mystery of genuine love and power to which we turn only too rarely.

The plays in question are Ron Blair's "The Christian Brothers" and Jean Herbiet's "De la manipulation de Dieu". Blair is Australian and Herbiet, French-Canadian. Both dramatists are concerned with man's inhumanity to man in the name of God, and with the hypocrisy of much of the behaviour that claims to be religious. Both are also concerned with the search for mercy, love, truth, and transcendence.

Australian drama begins to mature in the seventies. Dramatists such as Ron Blair, David Williamson, Jack Hibberd and Peter Kenna are helping to provide the country with a cultural mirror, a sense of identity, and a healthy streak of irreverence. A society should be able to laugh at itself.

At thirty-four, Blair's record is uneven but impressive. By 1975 he had written five plays, three of them apprentice works, one solidly good piece (*President Wilson in Paris*), and the outstanding short drama mentioned above. I rank "The Christian Brothers" among the best short plays I have seen or read in thirty years of theatre-going. Blair's progress is not chronological, since "Owning Things", one of the relatively amateur plays, was written *after* "The Christian Brothers". "Flash Jim Vaux" is a ballad opera, set in late eighteenth-century England and early nineteenth-century Australia. "Kabul" is a historical melodrama set in that volatile corner of India between 1839 and 1842.[1] Both of the latter plays have a confusion of scenes and incidents. The characters are stock ones : a pander, a whore, a foolish judge, a blade, a dullard, and so on. "Flash Jim" attempts the theme of the convict as Everyman seeking freedom. The symbol is less successful than the music and light-hearted social satire. Britishers, as one song goes, put business before pleasure, even on their wedding night. The debt to James Joyce is apparent when corpses come to life and cemeteries turn into pubs.

"The Christian Brothers" is an incredibly strong, beautiful, *painful* portrait of life. One human life, with its fears and yearnings and emotional responses, becomes archetypal. The mood is simultaneously comic and tragic. Above all, the play is honest. It cuts deep and clean. At one level we see a comic exposé of modern Australian society, a confrontation between a narrowly defined religious orthodoxy and a sports-loving materialistic majority. At another level we see ourselves : lonely, hungry for love and understanding and recognition; fearful that we have not lived up to our own self-image; terrified of ageing, death, and oblivion.

The play is a technical *tour de force* : two acts, one scene, one actor. The setting is a Christian Brothers' school in Sydney; the action, a schoolroom in session. Peter Carroll as the Christian Brother successfully evokes an entire class-room of boys. The one prop (other than blackboard and desk, crucifix and portrait of the Virgin Mary) is a plain chair, 'occupied' by a difficult pupil who finds himself heir to the bulk of the teacher's rage. So real is the invisible student that we find ourselves wincing when he is strapped or cuffed, horrified when his 'ear' (alias the corner of the chair) is knocked against the blackboard, and anxious when the upturned chair lies unmoving on the floor.

Laughter mingles with terror and compassion for the human condition. References, incidents, anecdotes, are perfectly in keeping with the class-room situation while doubling as symbols. The play's opening lines, memory work from Keats' "Ode to a Nightingale", refer to heartache and oblivion; the history lesson on the French Revolution serves as a reminder that hardship can make men despair of the goodness of God: and the play closes with the Catholic litany, a chanted prayer for mercy. 'The human condition' has become a cliché, but the artist can reveal the essence of that ever-changing ever-constant condition so that, as Conrad puts it, we are forced to *see*.

The Brother labours under the delusion that he is self-disciplined while his students are not. In actual fact, his anger is continually erupting into uncontrolled rage. His monologue reveals the life of the Roman Catholic school, the society in which it functions, and the emotional needs of the teacher who has taken vows of poverty, chastity, and obedience. The students, largely unconscious representatives of their secular society, provoke his scorn. The Brother sees them as lazy, lustful, materialistic and self-indulgent. Ironically, the Brother's physical violence suggests a kind of sublimated lust, and it is apparent that he envies his materially successful former students.

Most pathetic is his fear of sex and his compensating reverence for the

Virgin Mary. The Brother produces a magazine picture of a young woman in a bathing suit, suggesting that those who leer at it are headed straight for hell. He burns it on stage. Later, he describes a personal vision of the Virgin which moved him to enter the novitiate. Still later, the exact details of this vision are repeated while the vision is ascribed to another Brother, one who "now wonders whether or not it was some self-induced miasma, an adolescent mirage." In the first telling, the details are intriguing and comic : the steady emanation of light ("giving off a sort of hum like high tension cables"); the gift of tongues for the benefit of opportunely present Armenians and Chinese; the woman's beauty. In the repeat performance, the comedy is blacker. We wonder how much of the Brother's vocation stems from a genuine faith and how much, at this point in his life, from the lack of an alternative. Has he the courage to leave the order ? He quotes his doubting colleague, or alter ego, he of the vision, as saying ''There's nothing more comic than an old man who is both broke and looking for a wife." Suggestions of ageing, of losing faith, of loneliness and aimlessness run as a muffled refrain throughout the play.

The timing is superb, and the play's success belongs in part to this factor. Slow, reflective passages alternate with sudden rages. There is a constant tension between laughter and horror, sympathy and fear. An anecdote from the Venerable Bede concerning the Saxon belief that life is like being at a feast in a well-lit hall surrounded by darkness is followed by the Brother's boosting of easy orthodoxy as the surest way to the banquet. One "Hail Mary" is spoken while the Brother is blowing his nose, followed by a brisk "Right !" One of the beatings is played against the Brother's concern for the souls of his charges. A lesson in French verbs provokes his wrath at the apparently prurient jokes. The bells which mark off the different periods get steadily closer together until near the end; the last period is long. The patterns in both mood and pace are expertly orchestrated.

One symbolic action is the Brother's removal of his soutane following his worst rage and the beating of the boy. The Brother is concerned to show that clothes do not make the man; that he is "still a man and still a brother" without his habit; still "disciplined" and "responsible"—ironic emphases both. The removal of some of his clothing suggests a psychic stripping, but Blair leaves it ambiguous as to whether or not the Brother's self-knowledge has increased.

The ending is surreal. The Brother gently lifts the chair and proceeds, to the accompaniment of the litany, *to paint it blue*. In the discussion with the director and playwright which followed the August 28, 1975, Sydney production, members of the audience spoke freely of "the metaphor of the chair", yet seemed to assume that the metaphoric identification of chair and boy had ended prior to the painting episode. Not so. At the end of the play, the chair is the individual boy who has been beaten now being soothed; it is all the boys ever taught by the Brother; it is himself, tragically isolated from them by his vocation; and, finally, it is all sufferers. Balm of Mary's colour is spread like ointment over pain, accompanied by the timeless chant. Blair's satiric portrait indicates that he does not subscribe to the Christian Brother's version of Christianity, yet Blair's own vision is deeply religious (I would go further and say *Christian*) in a mystical way.

"Owning Things" is an amusing four-acter which becomes increasingly blacker as the action progresses. The play takes place on a weekend in a rundown residential hotel near the Sydney harbour. Its characters are the tenants, the manageress Doreen, and the owner. The title plus the two epigraphs on the cover of the typescript set up expectations which are not fulfilled : the lines from Walt Whitman note the advantages of being an animal, free from "the mania for owning things"; the John Lennon quotation speaks idealistically of universal sharing and brotherhood. The play, however, is a bleak portrait of people who own nothing but who are also lacking in love for their neighbours. The anti-materialism of the epigraphs contradicts the practical and emotional plea for cheap housing. In short, there are unresolved tensions and the play seems at cross-purposes with itself.

The action involves the owner's attempt to sell the old house at a large profit. If he succeeds, he can afford to take his sick child to London doctors, but the tenants will be homeless. Doreen's canary, incapable of surviving outside its cage, is a facile symbol for the tenants, losers all, who seem incapable of surviving outside the crumbling hotel. There are some socialist speeches but these are mostly undercut. It is not really a didactic drama. The attack on big business and capitalism seems half-hearted. Some of the scenes are good theatre, but much of the humour is local, such as the thrusts at inter-city rivalry. The emotional weight of the play is carried by Doreen and a tenant called China. Despite Doreen's strength, some of her speeches seem fatuous, such as "In this house, the brotherhood of man only lasts as long as the beer and when the last bottle's gone, God help us all." The final line goes to a tenant—"I'm not as young as I used to be"—and the play concludes with the melancholy sound of the harbour foghorn. The pathos of this melodrama is well spiked with black comedy. But the overall prospect is grim. No real vision of hope, either religious or secular, lightens its gloom.

President Wilson in Paris is a surreal farce with a disturbing message : "We are all predators and live a little more by killing others. Most people can afford to exercise power only in their dreams..." In "Flash Jim Vaux", the pick-pockets and fences have their own stock exchange, a comic parody which implies that regular financiers are thieves. "Owning Things" plays other variations on the theme of predators. China tells the hotel owner that "By owning this place, you own us too." He concludes : "I'd like to see his kid get better —who wouldn't—it's us or them." *President Wilson* (1973) is a black little drama which suggests that all is not

for the best in the best of all possible worlds. "We are all predators."
Blair dramatizes love by showing its appalling absence.

President Wilson is nothing if not ingenious. There are only three
characters, and each of them plays two *personas*. Wilson and his wife
Edith appear initially as their historical namesakes in Paris for the 1919
Peace Conference—believable, if a bit mad. When a prowler who turns
out to have been lured there by Edith's newspaper ad is forcibly co-opted
into playing Wilson's aide, our view of events is sharply dislocated.
Wilson and his wife become a deranged couple in contemporary Sydney
while they continue to act their 1919 role. Tired of the game, they
eventually kill the burglar with a deadly injection. Drunk with their own
fantasies and exhilarated by power, the pair become Hitler and his mistress
as the play ends.

Technically, the play is clever. Its patterned irrationalism links it to
the European Theatre of the Absurd, as does the blackness of its comedy.
In an Introduction, Blair writes : "It is primarily an entertainment. If
people detect a comment on the presidency and power politics in the
Kennedy-Nixon era, so much the better; but *President Wilson in Paris* is
neither a study of Woodrow Wilson nor a clinical case study of a
lunatic."[2] An entertainment, certainly, and a parable. Of our shadow
selves.

Like Blair, Jean Herbiet is concerned with man's predatory nature.
"De la manipulation de Dieu" reveals how Western man, since becoming
Christian at least in name, has not ceased to manipulate his God for his
own ends and to prey upon his fellow men in God's name. *Western
Christendom*: the play reflects a Canadian sensibility indirectly, as the semi-
universalist stance is one to which Canadians, with an educational system
which was until recently particularly lacking in nationalist bias, are prone.

The play is a spectacle for voice, masks, and marionettes. It is an
extraordinarily vivid and affecting piece of theatre, drawing on the
resources of music, dance, mime, formal poetry, large puppets worked by
silent animators, and human actors. Four gorgeously robed Readers are
enthroned two and two at the stagefront sides. I saw the play performed
in French and my oral French is negligible. I thus experienced it almost
as one would an opera. And experienced in this way, *it worked*. I was
reminded that theatre is not dependent upon logic but upon eye and ear;
upon action, passion, emotion and image. Speaking of an earlier play,
"Job's Kit" (1967) Herbiet said that he thinks of spectacle first of all, and
wished to portray "certain sonorous images."[3] The appeal to eye and
ear is typical of his work.[4]

Herbiet is currently the Artistic Director for French language theatre
at the National Arts Centre, and a professor of theatre at the University
of Ottawa. As a director, he has produced some two score plays. As a
playwright, his published works include *Job's Kit* and *Terre des Hommes*.
"Elkerlouille", "La Rose Rotie", and "De la manipulation de Dieu"

have not yet been published. As actor, director, designer, playwright and teacher, Herbiet has been actively involved in theatre for some twenty-five years.

"De la manipulation" is the fourth co-production with Felix Mirbt of Montreal. Mirbt is a German-born builder and manipulator of puppets, a craft-artist of impressive originality and skill. The play owes much of its success to his genius. The wise and dignified face of Mirbt's beautifully formed Galileo, for example, conveys the whole grandeur and tragedy of life. As in the Japanese *bunraku*, the puppet is far more 'real' than the three humans who support it.

A sentence from the Programme Notes of the French Canadian play is equally applicable to "The Christian Brothers". It reads, "God is not attacked nor are the Christian religions." Religions ? The plural might puzzle an idealist, but Herbiet and Blair are realists in this respect. Both are from Catholic backgrounds and illustrate the tensions in their areas between Protestant and Catholic. Blair's Christian Brother darkly suspects that the Australian Examiners for the School Leaving Certificate are Protestants and Masons, ever ready to fail a Catholic student unwary enough to reveal his religious affiliation through his answers. One of Herbiet's scenes takes the form of a TV quiz where the contestants are a Protestant and a Roman Catholic nun. The TV hosts take for granted a long-standing animosity between the two groups, and do their best to aggravate it further. As for the claim that God and Christianity are not attacked, those who understand the plays have no need of the remark, and those who do not will disregard it. Herbiet described his play as an attempt to prompt members of the audience to reflect on God and man.[5]

The fourteen scenes of Herbiet's play depict historic events in Western Christendom in roughly chronological order. They include the Nativity, the Crusaders, Joan of Arc, the Spaniards in Mexico, the Wars of Religion, the trial of Galileo, and the nineteenth-century potato famine in Ireland. As in "The Christian Brothers", the range of mood is enormous, but the prevailing tone ironic. Man's hypocrisy, and the gap between ideal and action, is constantly evoked. Ironic juxtaposition is characteristic of each dramatist.

The initial scene of Herbiet's drama is both the birth and the crucifixion of Christ. Man is born to die. Five blue-jeaned workers in yellow hardhats and black jackboots play ball, slowly and rhythmically, before drawing Christ's body from a curtained backdrop with a surreal portrait of a pregnant Virgin Mary. The young men are ominous, faintly threatening, aggressive in their work and play. They are simultaneously workers, soldiers, doctors (at the moment of birth their tools suggest surgical instruments), and technocrats. The thwack of the ball in one player's glove alternates hypnotically with the softer sound of the hand-catch. The shrouded birth-bundle is unwrapped to reveal parts of a life-sized white figure which the workers assemble and nail to a giant metal cross which has been onstage from the beginning. The cross is then hoisted overhead and remains hanging above stage and audience for the duration of the play. Despite the obvious artificiality of the body, one flinches as the workers screw the hands and feet to the cross.[6] The young girl beside me in the theatre who had been giggling and talking throughout the first act gasped aloud as the giant cross was raised aloft, and remained rapt for the rest of the performance. The first act brilliantly demonstrates Herbiet's belief in theatrical forms other than the classical and the realistic.

The overhead cross is one of the dominating symbols of the play. Many of the scenes are actually anti-masses, parodies of the eucharistic act. The fourth one commemorates the Spaniards' slaughter of forty thousand persons in Mexico in the sixteenth century and their attempt to force the native emperor, by torture, to reveal the hiding place of the Aztec treasure. A flamboyant backdrop depicts the Emperor, strong, sexually potent, surrounded by sun. Above it rise four puppet profiles, in two groups, with fire between : a ruffled nobleman and priest on the left, and a torturer-cum-executioner with his victim on the right. One phrase is repeated hypnotically as the action of pushing the victim into the fire is repeated : question, silence, torture. Words, music and actions are dreamlike and hypnotic. Colours : red and black. After the surreal torture scene, two human actors enter and celebrate mass in the same place. When they leave, the eyes of the executioner glow. The juxtaposition of orthodox piety with violent cruelty makes words unnecessary. Conquest means "*My* will be done." Obey, or be destroyed.

The Jeanne d'Arc scene is particularly impressive. It follows, and contrasts with, the formal rhymed poetry, rich costumes, and mock-heroic posturings of the Crusades. Five men in red and white choir robes enter in a formal manner and unroll a life-size portrait of Joan : *nude*. An authoritative voice begins reading. "Joan" is posted on the backdrop. The men leave, only to return promptly with cut-out paper-doll clothing for Joan. While the solemn voice pontificates and wooden sticks are clicked (both voice and clicking accelerates), the portrait is robed and disrobed a half dozen times, leaving the audience helpless with laughter. After a final verdict, the portrait is laid on the floor and ritually whipped by the men in clerical robes. *Schismatic* ! (stroke) *Apostate* ! (stroke). The portrait's head is torn off and the portrait burned in a censer. The ecclesiastic judgment is then quickly reversed. Joan's rehabilitation takes the form of giant building blocks, put together to reveal a triumphal Joan on horseback. Never were irrational judgments, or vice masquerading as virtue, more effectively mocked.

The last scene is called Racisms or, in a literal translation of the more ironic French title, the Anatomy Lesson. As a background to the action, a voice reads from Hitler's finest rhetoric. The voice claims to have been chosen by providence to be one of the great liberators of humanity, one destined to free mankind from the restrictions of so-called conscience and to lead the German people towards their glorious destiny. Meanwhile, five men manipulate a 'body' in the form of a cloth picture on a stretcher. The body is dismembered, sawn into pieces, while the actors coil ropes like snakes and hiss steadily : *sale juif, sale nègre, maudit blanc, maudit jaunes*, and the multiple variations with which we are unfortunately familiar. The climatic lines of the hissed refrain are "Goddam you/Goddam me/Filthy humans/Filthy Jew". All hatred, as Herbiet dramatically illustrates, is ultimately self-hatred.

The dismembered portions of the corpse are held by the five men who kneel and reverently declaim "Lord, make me an instrument of thy peace" in English, Spanish, German, French and, finally, in the language of silence and gesture. The men put on the pieces of clothing which formed the corpse, while the silence is cut by a raucous folksong : "You never ask questions while God's on your side." And the great crucifix which has hung over the entire action swings down.

"The Christian Brothers" set also features a cross. Like the Canadian play, it shows not Christian but *human* actions, the acts of man *in need of* a sign of peace : a sign, as Herbiet puts it, of God's sufferance of our being.[7] Their ironic indirections speak louder than words.

REFERENCES

1. "Owning Things" is dated 4 April 1975 : "The Christian Brothers" is dated 10 April 1974, and was first performed at the Nimrod Street Theatre in Sydney, August 1975. *President Wilson in Paris* is Blair's only published play as of June 1976. "Flash Jim Vaux" was first performed at the Nimrod Street Theatre in Sydney on 28 August 1971; and "Kabul", by the University of New South Wales Drama Foundation and the Old Tote Theatre Company on 31 May 1973.

2. Ron Blair, *President Wilson in Paris*, Currency Methuen Play Series III, No. 3 (Sydney : Currency Methuen Drama, 1974), pp. 9-10.

3. "Entrevue avec Jean Herbiet", *Theatre Vivant*, No. 3 (June, 1967), p. 48. Herbiet says : "Je pense d'abord spectacle....Pour moi, l'ecriture theatrale est plus importante que l'ecriture romanesque ou poetique. Je suis surtout un dramaturge" (pp. 48-49).

4. "La Rose Rotie" (1972) was described as "not unlike a verbal cantata." See Zelda Heller, "A verbal cantata …,"*Montreal Star*, 17 April 1972.

5. See James Nelson, "In God's Name, Actors and puppets combine to break new theatrical ground," *The Ottawa Journal*, 22 November 1975, p. 39 : "He said in an interview that his reflections on man and Christianity were crystallised in re-reading the Book of Jacob after seeing the elaborate decoration of a seventeenth century baroque church, and thinking of the troubles Galileo faced with the Inquisition in his belief that the sun—and not the earth—is the centre of the universe. In short, Mr Herbiet said that man has frequently tried to mould the

world's concept of God to further man's ends, not God's. His conclusion is : 'If you want to have a relation with God, leave Him alone'...., But he said it is not his intention to preach, to be rude, or to offend people. The play is an attempt to prompt members of the audience to reflect on God and man."

6. This action is performed to the heavily ironic accompaniment of Bing Crosby's "I'm Dreaming of a White Christmas."

7. Letter from Jean Herbiet to the Rev. John F.H. Stewart, 11 December 1975.

24

Struggling with a Bugaboo :
The Priest-Character in
Achebe and Greene and Keneally

EDWARD P. VARGO, S.V.D.

"EVERY consciousness has its rainless lands and polar wastes, its undiscovered and unventured countries. And there are simply boring stretches, like the Western Plains or the dry mouth's taste. Certainly consciousness is capable of subtle, wonderful, and terrifying transformations. After all, it is the dream we live in, and like the dream, can harbour anything....It is our only evidence we live." Yet, as the philosopher-novelist William H. Gass continues to say in a critique of American popular culture written several years ago, most men fear and hold consciousness in contempt. They may sometimes find it useful, but most times it is embarrassing or even threatening and horrible. The generality of men prefer simple oblivion to consciousness. "Only an obstinate, foolish will to live, the simple insistence of the veins which leaves have, cowslips, oxen, ants have just as well, can account for most men's going on, since such a will moves blindly, in roots beneath the ground, in bottleflies and fish, and our feelings are the price we pay for being brained instead of finned. Perception, Plato said, is a form of pain."[1]

What Gass has written so lyrically about consciousness can serve as the starting point for an approach to the three apparently disparate novels which I have chosen to discuss—Chinua Achebe's *Arrow of God*, Graham Greene's *The Honorary Consul*, and Thomas Keneally's *Three Cheers for the Paraclete*. *Arrow of God*, Achebe's artistically most controlled and balanced work, deals with that period of African history when the foundations of British nineteenth century colonialism among the Igbo were already set, twenty years after the confrontation dramatised in *Things Fall Apart*. *Three Cheers for the Paraclete* provides a much more narrow setting, a House of Studies for priests of the Roman Catholic Church in Australia during the mid-1960's, when the first winds of change from the Second Vatican Council were only feebly blowing upon that continent.

The Honorary Consul, which Greene himself considers to be his best work, is placed in a seedy provincial town on the border between Argentina and Paraguay. This scene becomes the stage on which a hapless band of guerrillas act out their bit parts in the struggle for social justice currently racking South America. Three novels, three far-flung continents, three vastly different cultures.

Superficially, however, these novels invite comparison by the presence in each of a major priest-character. Ezeulu, the Chief Priest of Ulu, and Dr James Maitland, the young Church historian who has just returned from advanced studies in Europe to become a priest-teacher-of-priests in Australia, are the central characters in *Arrow of God* and *Three Cheers for the Paraclete.* While Father Leon Rivas, the ex-priest-turned-revolutionary, is not the key character in *The Honorary Consul,* his life and actions are intimately bound up with the fortunes of Charley Fortnum, the self-appointed honorary consul who is mistakenly kidnapped, and Doctor Eduardo Plarr, an old schooltime friend.

It is here that Gass's comments about consciousness have relevance. In every society where a priesthood has evolved, the priest has been set aside from that category called "most men." He has been perceived as somehow more in touch with transcendent realities than other men, as a spiritual leader, a divine spokesman, an intermediary beween men and the deity, and even the bearer of the people's spiritual burdens. He ministers at all stages of man's rites of passage, and his personality may at times be defined in terms of the attributes of the God whom he serves.[2] Even those who do not believe in his priestly power may insist that he cannot opt for simple oblivion in preference to consciousness as a way of life. He cannot live blindly by "the simple insistence of the veins" which all nature shares but should have the blood of God coursing through him. He is not excused from living a life of perception and feeling merely because it is a form of pain.

The novelist who chooses to depict the life of a priest in his daily communion with the world of men and the world beyond will have to keep these considerations in mind. Moreover, he will have to dramatise these realities in a convincing manner, especially as they impinge upon the consciousness of the priest himself. Lesser novelists than the three under discussion have failed miserably in the attempt, either through insensitivity to what is involved or through settling for didactic, sentimental, or peripheral themes. There is nothing less at stake than man's relationship with his God. To present this theme with artistic integrity to a secularised readership is no easy task.

With the completion of these remarks, it should now be possible to launch into a more specific examination of how these novelists actualise their priest-characters within the thematic structure of each novel. Baldly stated, *Arrow of God* pictures the clash of two cultures, both self-sustained systems of social and religious values, one represented by Captain Winterbottom and his district officers, the other represented by Ezeulu and the members of his tribe. But Achebe takes pains to demonstrate that the breakdown of Igbo society is possible only because of the inner conflicts which are already present—the rivalries between men, clans, villages, and even gods. For example, each of the six groups composing Umuafia is independent, each with its own gods. Is Ulu the leading god of the six villages or a god among gods ? Is Ezeulu, as the Chief Priest of Ulu, the leader of the six villages, or simply one among equals ? Both opinions have their adherents.

Caught between these polarities, Ezeulu does not always know how to react. It is, then, through the confrontations of Ezeulu with his enemies, his friends, and his god that Achebe dramatises his larger theme of man's relationship with his god. Being "the arrow in the bow of his god," half man, half spirit, in an entirely African-derived concept of priesthood, Ezeulu is conscious of himself as the carrier of the god's truth, as the one who must bear the heavy burden of decision, as a scapegoat to bear all the sins of the people, as one ready for the symbolic sacrifices regularly demanded by the deity. One of the most dramatic realisations of Ezeulu's central function as priest is achieved in the Festival of the First Pumpkin Leaves. Painted with white chalk, carrying in his right hand "Nne Ofo, the mother of all staffs of authority in Umuaro," Ezeulu is filled with a sense of his own divinity. After re-enacting the first coming of Ulu and the establishment of his power, Ezeulu breaks into the concluding ritual race to the safety of his shrine. The participating crowd understands that their Chief Priest is "triumphant over the sins of Umuaro which he was now burying deep into the earth with the six bunches of leaves."[3]

However, most of Ezeulu's actions are double-edged, producing both good and bad consequences for his society. When he testifies to Captain Winterbottom against his own village in the firm belief that Ulu does not fight a war of blame, he earns the animosity of the priest and followers of Idemili, the rival python god. Although he does not believe in Christianity, he plans a temporary alliance because he recognises its power. Consequently, he sends his son Oduche to join the white man's religion so that he may act as Ezeulu's "eyes and ears." He assumes that this action would assure his continuance in power as well as that of the religion, civilisation and tradition which he embodied. But in his zeal for the new religion, Oduche desecrates the sacred python and goes unpunished because of Ezeulu's fear of ridicule. When Captain Winterbottom, shrewd enough to know that Ezeulu is a man of honour, wishes to confer upon him the title of warrant chief, Ezeulu pridefully rejects the offer. Clapped into jail for his insult to the Empire, he is unable to eat the sacred yams which will mark the time for bringing in the harvest. Since he feels his people neglected him during his imprisonment, after his return he vindictively decides to punish them by still following the cycle of new moons in eating the yams, after having missed two. The harvest rots in the earth, and famine spreads over the land. In a final blow at the end of the novel, his favourite son Obika dies, and Ezeulu becomes totally disoriented :

> Why, he asked himself again and again, why had Ulu chosen to deal thus with him, to strike him down and cover him with mud ? What was his offence ? Had he not divined the god's will and obeyed it ? When was it ever heard that a child was scalded by the piece of yam its own mother put in its palm ? What man would send his son with a potsherd to bring fire from a neighbour's hut and then unleash rain on him ? Who ever sent his son up the palm to gather nuts and then took an axe and felled the tree ? But today such a thing had happened before the eyes of all. What could it point to but the collapse and ruin of all things ?[4]

While this process runs its course in society, Ezeulu tragically goes insane. At the deepest level, Ezeulu "suffers the agony of the priest who interprets his own vengeful will as that of his deity and is destroyed in the process."[5] Conscious of himself as a man apart, he is an intellectually aloof, proud and lonely man, by virtue of his character as much as by his priestly function. His great error is his assumption that he alone can provide solutions for society's dilemmas. Unbending as a man, he is also inadequate as a spirit.[6] Ulu himself chides Ezeulu for his audacity while he is contemplating the problem of the two wasted moons : " 'Who told you that this was your own fight ?...Go home and sleep and leave me to settle my quarrel with Idemili....' Who was Ezeulu to tell his deity how to fight the jealous cult of the sacred python ? It was a fight of the gods. He was no more than an arrow in the bow of his god."[7] The bow and the arrow are after all not to be totally identified.

As an artist, Achebe has not merely produced a faithful anthropological account. He has even more firmly grounded his tragic story in its culture by his remarkable ability to create an English style that clearly reflects his own Igbo idiom and rhythm and love for allusion, symbolism, colourful imagery, and proverbs. The citation from Ezeulu's thoughts at the novel's close should serve as a fine example. Although space does not allow a more thorough analysis, at least one technique can be singled out. Achebe commonly uses proverbs to sustain the themes which he is exploring and to dramatise significant aspects of the novel, as when Nwaka describes Ezeulu's predicament in this manner : " 'A man who brings ant-ridden faggots into his hut should expect the visit of lizards.' "[8]

While *Arrow of God* portrays the dangers of over-identification of the priest with his God in a context of two clashing cultures, *The Honorary Consul* dramatises the opposite—the alienation of a priest from his functions. In a country still suffering from its colonial past, the Church as an institution has nestled in the fist of a repressive government, whereas it should be serving, in the words of Father Rivas, "as Christ on earth." Ironically, churchmen serve to hide God from men, especially by the fact that they have settled for less than their calling demands. Father Rivas ascribes his departure from the priesthood to loneliness, but even more to anger with the Church that stands in God's name on earth. " 'I was a priest in the poor part of Asuncion near the river....''Sell all and give to the poor''—I had to read that out to them while the old Archbishop we had in those days was eating a fine fish from Iguazu and drinking a French wine with the General.' ''[9] Like Ezeulu, he is a thinking man who is more painfully aware of the evils in society than most men and, impatient of others, takes matters into his own hands. Unlike Ezeulu, he feels that he is a criminal, estranged from God. But he still feels himself as a bearer of the people's burdens and is still desperately struggling with the transcendent reality of God. How is he to reconcile the goodness of God with the evil which is so alive in the world of men ?

As Ezeulu suffers agony by confusing his own will with that of his deity, so Father Rivas agonisingly rationalises his own evil and that of the community of men into the essence of God himself. Using the manichean images of light and darkness, in a discussion with Doctor Plarr that comes perilously close to reading like a tract, Father Rivas verbalises a process theology in which God changes with the evolutions of man. " 'Every evil act of ours strengthens His night side, and every good one helps His day side. We belong to Him and He belongs to us. But now at least we can be sure where evolution will end one day—it will end in a goodness like Christ's. It is a terrible process all the same and the God I believe in suffers as we suffer while He struggles against Himself—against His evil side.' ''[10] Father Rivas admits he may be sick or mad, but this is the only way he can now believe in God.

Although the contradictions of love in a corrupt world are dramatised throughout this finely modulated novel, one scene can illustrate Greene's ironic and equivocal treatment. It is the episode where Father Rivas and Doctor Plarr are killed by the paratroopers who have come to rescue Charley Fortnum. Having recognised the genuine love that Fortnum has for his young wife Clara, Doctor Plarr experiences his first doubts about his cynical attitude toward all love and offers to negotiate with the police. When he is gunned down before he can speak, Father Rivas rushes out of the hut, as if he "had to come," as if Plarr 'might need" him. The last human acts of these two tormented men are unselfish acts of love. When Father Rivas is also shot, his last words approximate those of the whisky priest in Greene's earlier masterpiece, *The Power and the Glory* : " 'Father.... I am sorry....I beg pardon...' '' Are they spoken to Plarr or to God ? Attempting to joke, Plarr recites the words of absolution usually said by the priest over the person who is asking forgiveness of God in the rite of penance : " '*Ego te absolvo*,'... but he was too tired and the laugh shriveled in his throat."[11] Perhaps there is no more to it than that, but this scene still holds open the possibility that in the end these two men are seized out of the depths of their ridiculous misery and absurd shame by the mysterious love of God.

Arrow of God and *The Honorary Consul* both dramatise the interaction of good and evil in the world, though with vastly different results. The sense of tragedy and irreparable loss is not as great at the end of *The Honorary Consul* as in *Arrow of God*. Greene's novel suggests that imperfect and corruptible man is nevertheless redeemable. The human tragedy is paradoxically divine comedy. A Christian tragedy is impossible.

If *Arrow af God* and *The Honorary Consul* are dramatising man's relationship to God, it would be more accurate to say that *Three Cheers for the Paraclete* is dramatising man's relationship to Church. Ulu is almost as vividly drawn in *Arrow of God* as the characters themselves. God is hidden or obscured in *The Honorary Consul* by the corruptions of men and their institutions, but the presence of His loving action is still felt. In Keneally's novel God is an absence, a void in the heart, or at most, an ossified abstraction called Certitude.

Because Dr James Maitland has tasted some of the new freedom in priestly life and theology in Europe, he is suspect to the closed community of the Australian House of Studies, which is suffering from arteriosclerosis in its life style and theology. In a series of minor skirmishes, the battle lines between the opposing camps are made clear. At the outset, Dr Maitland offers an open-air Mass for a guild of graduates. He senses "that what he performed had an affinity to the earth and the elements and the blood" and, for the first time since his return, feels "at home". Stirred by his union with mystery, he spontaneously preaches an eloquent sermon that includes a dictum about "sapless priests": " 'Because they love no one, they imagine that they love God.' "[12]

Much of the novel is concerned with fleshing out this statement. In manifold ways, through dialogues and confrontations, it becomes apparent what the values of institutional authoritarianism are, as represented by Dr Costello or Monsignor Nolan. They are a demand for blind obedience which is often a cover for manipulative power-plays, an insensitive legalism in matters that concern the human person, a caution in preaching in order to safeguard the worldly status of the Church, an imprisonment of God in static formulas, an arrogant certitude that these conceptualisations are identical with the living Truth. For example, in the first glow of his election as bishop (an occasion which draws from Maitland the dry and ironic remark, "Three Cheers for the Paraclete"), Dr Costello triumphantly orates :

"The price we paid throughout centuries for this faith !... Our first priest a convict, political prisoner, shipped for months in a reeking hold, beaten in prison three hundred times with a wire cat. If we are not vigilant within our own ranks, within our own minds, we will find that a great part of that....will go for nothing...Will we be the so-called liberals, the so-called modernists, the so-called humanists, corrupted by expediencey, rotten with existentialism, at whose door will be laid the blame for the ruin of the Church as we know it ?"[13]

For people such as Costello or Nolan, the capital crime is being "out of tune," refusing to present a united front or join the masonry of clerical mateship. Dr Maitland is regularly reminded that he is disloyal, a proud and malicious trouble-maker, a man with no sense of belonging to the organisation.

Through most of the novel, the young priest seems to withstand these attacks. When Dr Costello is piously and smugly pressuring him to recant his secretly published book, Dr Maitland expresses his anger with a fine raciness : " 'The Church !... You think of the Church as Christ's young bride already come into the fullness of beauty. I think of her as a scruffy old eyesore with half her tats drawn who's whored around too much with politicians.' "[14]   He is as sensitive to the incongruities of a luxury-loving clergy as Father Rivas : "What was the sense in risking hell or its equivalent by becoming a priest if, like everyone else, you knew what was par on expensive golf courses and commended cynical waiters on the filet mignon?"[15]   He is as sensitive to the exploitation of the poor. But when he preaches against the deceptive advertising of Allied Projects and Investment General, he finds himself hedging : "one had to be careful with well-heeled congregations."

This last episode reveals the canker in the rose, for Dr Maitland suffers from an unresolved ambivalence. He consistently downgrades himself for a litany of tepidities ranging from glibness to lack of certitude. Hating himself even as he says it, he describes his attitude toward the other staff members in the following manner: ' "I judge *them* good because they're sure. I feel that being sure is a superior moral state, the sort of state a person should be relatively humble in front of.' "[16] How ironic that he cannot fully accept the open-ended uncertainty which he preaches and knows is necessary for the life of the spirit ! Unlike Ezeulu and Father Rivas, he seems incapable of any sustained effort, rather suffers from an inner paralysis that exhausts his spiritual resources. Perhaps he is floundering through an unrecognised dark night of the soul, but where is the spiritual master to aid him in its discernment ?

In the end, he begins to fit into the mould of the institution rather than face expulsion and the loneliness of freedom.[17]   Earlier, he had told a seminarian who was dismissed : " 'Some individuals—mystics, prophets, saints—outgrow institutions. But I never will,... I have to wait for the revelation within this framework.' "[18]   One can respect his choice but still have misgivings. His very passivity may stifle the winds of God. One fears that his vision and priesthood may be stillborn, that Dr Maitland may develop into still another organisation man. The breath of death hovers over the final sentences.

All three of these novels depict the failure of organised religion. While one system gives way to another in *Arrow of God*, strikingly similar abuses within the institutional church are presented in *The Honorary Consul* and *Three Cheers for the Paraclete* .   Reading these three novels together invites reflection on how the principle of entropy operates within religious institutions; conversion and renewal are certainly related to this phenomenon.   The three priest-characters who have been under discussion can be considered variants in the genre of the traditional intellectual hero.   Men of contemplation rather than action, they all share a heightened consciousness of themselves and of the world around and beyond them.   All three have some sense that they are intermediaries between God and men; the experience of God, however, is vastly different for each.   The great danger in their lives seems to be a kind of priestly arrogance, through which they appropriate to themselves the power of their God.

The chief paradox of the priesthood is that a finite, fallible and sinful man has to represent the infinite and holy God.   The priest is to reflect the restored and perfected image of his God, yet his pride, fear, fallibility and rebellion always distort that reflection.   Divine treasures are entrusted to earthen vessels.   Perhaps the inherent drama of that situation is one of the reasons why novelists have still found the priest an interesting challenge in a century when his role seems greatly diminished.   Whether one believes in his message or not, whether the priest himself fails or succeeds, he still points to man's search for a transcendent, a value or a person that will give his life experience an ultimate meaning.

Chinua Achebe and Graham Greene have given us two remarkable responses to the question of how to dramatise this relationship of man to God.   In the case of Thomas Keneally, his success rests rather in the fact that he has side-stepped this question and limited himself to dramatising Dr Maitland's relationship to the Church as an institution.   Dr Maitland has not yet grappled with the deeper issue — whether and how he believes in God.   *Three Cheers for the Paraclete* also walks a tight line between realism and propaganda.   I have known and lived with many clerical types like Costello and Nolan, but in their unguarded moments they have all shown some spark of divine fire or human warmth. The absence of such a spark is what makes Keneally's novel so devastatingly bleak.

In conclusion, I would like to comment on the problems of response to these three novels from literatures other than my own.   These difficulties are at once both linguistic and cultural.   Personally, I felt no great obstacles in the language of Greene and Keneally, aside from certain items of local vocabulary and phraseology, especially in *Three Cheers for the Paraclete*.   It is also not too difficult to experience the context of *Arrow of God* because of Achebe's skill in transferring Igbo idiom into English.   However, it would be next to impossible to savour the full sophistication of his linguistic achievement without the aid of studies by knowledgeable critics.

Understanding the cultural milieu of each novel is a greater problem.

Suppose one is reading his first novel from a country or culture of which he knows next to nothing. If there is anything of human value in the book, the reader will certainly be able to respond to it, but the chance of misreadings will be in direct proportion to the distance of that novel's background from the reader's own. What the alien reader obviously lacks is a frame of reference. Materials from other disciplines, literary criticism by indigenous scholars, a wide reading in the country's literature, can all help supply the lacunae. For example, after learning that the American culture hero Huck Finn's type of freedom, outside a community of some sort, is rare in Australian thought and literature, the American reader may considerably qualify his judgment of Dr Maitland's final decision.[19]

The need for a frame of reference applies to elements of a culture as much as to the entire milieu. Being a Catholic and a priest, I have a particular access to the theological underpinnings of *The Honorary Consul* or the subculture of Keneally's Australian clerics. This same personal history may work against my entering into the system of theology or belief underlying the rites of Ulu. It is all too easy for us to behave like Captain Winterbottom, presuming that any work of art, regardless of its place of origin, can be judged from the values and premises of one's own culture. What may be the most crucial qualities in our response to literatures other than our own are attitudes of the mind and heart. Such reading demands a greater effort of empathy, openness to new experiences, and suspension of judgment until we have assimilated as much as possible. Only then is the non-native critic ready to present insights which may have eluded the indigenous reader. Finally, if I have sometimes spoken like Captain Winterbottom and not the godlike critic sketchily outlined here, I beg your pardon.

REFERENCES

1. See Ray B. Browne et al., eds., *Frontiers of American Culture*, Purdue University Studies, 9, West Lafayette, Ind., Purdue Univ. Press, 1968, pp. 194-99.

2. For a brief discussion of the concept of priesthood in African societies, see Kofi Awoonor, *The Breast of the Earth : A Survey of the History, Culture, and Literature of Africa South of the Sahara*, Garden City, New York, Anchor Press, Doubleday, 1975, p. 273. For a more extended treatment of the African concept of priesthood, see John S. Mbiti, *Concept of God in Africa*, New York, Praeger, 1970. For an extensive investigation of the Catholic point of view, see Karl Rahner, S.J., ed., *The Identity of the Priest*, Concilium : Theology in an Age of Renewal, 43, New York, Paulist Press, 1969.

3. Chinua Achebe, *Arrow of God*, New York, John Day, 1967, pp. 85-90.

4. *ibid.*, p. 286.

5. Awoonor, p. 272.

6. See Achebe's own comments on Ezeulu in Bernth Lindfors et al., *Palaver : Interviews with Five African Writers in Texas*, Austin, African and Afro-American Research Institute, 1972, p. 9.

7. Achebe, pp. 240-41.

8. *ibid.*, p. 178.

9. Graham Greene, *The Honorary Consul*, New York, Simon and Schuster, 1973, p. 140.

10. *ibid.*, p. 270.

11. *ibid.*, p. 298.

12. Thomas Keneally, *Three Cheers for the Paraclete*, New York, Viking, 1969, pp. 1-3.

13. *ibid.*, pp. 148-49.

14. *ibid.*, p. 232.

15. *ibid.*, p. 110.

16. *ibid.*, p. 206.

17. See John R. Beston, "The Hero's 'Fear of Freedom' in Keneally," *Australian Literary Studies*, 5, 1972, 374-87.

18. Keneally, p. 205.

19. See Jerome H. Rosenberg, "Narrative Perspective and Cultural History in *Robbery Under Arms*," *Australian Literary Studies*, 6, 1973, 11-23.

25

George Lamming and Chinua Achebe :
Tradition and the Literary Chroniclers

CECIL A. ABRAHAMS

AT the end of Chinua Achebe's classic novel, *Things Fall Apart* (TFA), the obtuse colonial District Commissioner discusses the tragic hanging suicide of Okonkwo, the pulse of the Ibo tribe, as peculiar enough to warrant "a reasonable paragraph" in his book on *The Pacification of the Primitive Tribes of the Lower Niger*. For the District Commissioner, this momentous event in African history is dismissed as merely the act of a weird, uncivilised people with queer customs. Normally, to those elite black men and women in Africa and the Caribbean, agreement would be expressed with the clearly uninformed and colonialist position of the District Commissioner. One of Achebe's main tasks in writing his literary histories of Nigeria is to counteract the prejudiced view of the white officer and to inform the elite bourgeoisie of Africa and the Caribbean that Okonkwo's act was one of protest and courage rather than of "primitivism". Hence, he offers Okonkwo's great friend, Obierika, the opportunity to set matters straight. It is Obierika who says : "That man was one of the greatest men in Umuofia. You drove him to kill himself; and now he will be buried like a dog..." (TFA, p. 187). Achebe's aim is to redefine the African past and the present in the light of both the "official" history and the oral African tradition. For an Africa that had endured the evils of slavery compounded by wrong-headed Western forms of education and religion, Achebe must create again within the modern African a love for his past and dispel within him any belief that Africa's tribal tradition was evil and primitive.

George Lamming, who reacts to statements of the Caribbean such as "History is built around achievement and creation, and nothing was created in the West Indies,"[1] shares Achebe's concern for the need to instil a true sense of history into his fellow West Indian and to stir within the Caribbean soul a pride in the ancestral past from which it emerged. In this purpose, both Lamming and Achebe follow the great tradition of the tribal storyteller and as literary chroniclers they desire to reach the same glorious aims as their predecessors.

The ethos of traditional society was enshrined in an oral, religious, and literary tradition through which the community transmitted from generation to generation its customs, values, and norms. The poet and the storyteller stood at the centre of this tradition, as the community's chroniclers, entertainers, and collective conscience. Their contribution to society was considered of the greatest significance. The oral creative act was a communal act rather than the product of a particular genius. The story, often carried over from other generations but sometimes newly invented, was acted out in the marketplace or village square. It was a dramatic performance which not only attracted the entire village but demanded the participation of the villagers. Because of this instant feedback from the audience, the artists gave their best, and in return they had their repertoire of tales enriched both qualitatively and quantitatively.

The very nature of the artistic act ensured that the storyteller emphasised the communal value of art : that the story was intended to deal with the issues of life, death, and the many processes of living which circumscribed the existence of the villagers. The storyteller was always guided by a broad theme that centred around the need for an ordered society, a stable and harmonious community. For the artist in the traditional society there was not the luxury of being able to espouse a doctrine of "art for art's sake"; because art was not severed from the physical, social and religious needs of the community. Song, dance and music were an integral part of a community's grappling with its environment, part and parcel of the needs and aspirations of the ordinary man. Hence, even in their most disillusioned moments the traditional storytellers could not express themselves in the manner which James Joyce does in *A Portrait of the Artist as a Young Man* :

> I will tell you what I will do and what I will not do. I will not serve that in which I no longer believe, whether it call itself my home, my fatherland or my church; and I will try to express myself in some mode of life or art as freely as I can and as wholly as I can, using for my defence the only arms I allow myself to use— silence, exile and cunning.[2]

If, for example, one had to look at a Xhosa story such as "The Turban,"[3] one would be confronted by the seeming contradiction of the collective custom and the individual practice. In this story Nyengebule has two wives : one of them, the head wife, fulfils her function as wife, co-wife, and mother in proper traditional fashion, always adhering to custom, never stepping out of her role as the perfect wife. This, of course, is all that the traditional society demands of its married women. But the husband defies tradition by preferring the love of his second wife who does not satisfy the customary demands placed on a wife. The chorus, which in the traditional performance would be the moral which all the participants (i.e. the storyteller and the audience) will sing, summarises the paradox of the action :

> Nyengebule has killed his favourite wife,
> She discovered bees and gathered the honey,
> She ate and forgot to leave him a share;
> He buried her together with her festival dress,
> And saw not the turban dropping on the way.[4]

To add to her uncustomary behaviour of neglecting her husband, the junior wife is barren as well. Tradition demands, therefore, that Nyengebule take on another wife who can provide him with children. The storyteller has thus presented the dilemma to his community, and he is asking for the wisdom of the community to settle this question. This performance would normally occur on the village square. The heightening tension and the creative solution will mark the community's collective soul and wisdom.

The evidence that is presented to the community is that Nyengebule has acted contrary to custom in three important aspects : he loves his junior wife to the extent of ignoring the facts of her barrenness and her neglect of her husband; not only is his romantic love untraditional, but his killing of his wife through rage as a form of punishment is unwarranted and untraditional; and finally, his dishonesty and deception in an open society where all the problems of the community are laid bare, condemn him to the death which is meted out by the junior wife's relatives. Nyengebule's crime has been the disruption of the harmony on which the security of his society is based, and nature steps in in the form of the honeybird (and then its wing) to right the disrupted equilibrium. It is the honeybird that informs the relatives of the crime, and the in-laws do the rest. The collective will is supreme in the traditional society, and the chronicler is constrained to uphold this supremacy. Even Nature is subordinated to the collective will.

Nature brings harmony as well in another Xhosa story—"The Maidens of Bhakubha."[5] Here the crucial episode is the princess's wilful violation of her society's customs in two important respects : she goes counter to the custom of female purification rites by leaving her secluded place, and she further ignores custom by going to the forbidden pool to swim. In her arrogant reaction to the hallowed traditions of her people, she has become monstrous : poetically, she has become one with the monster. The beast retaliates by biting her so that she becomes as ugly as the monster itself; this is a metaphorical way of equating the girl's behaviour to the repulsiveness of the evil creature. Only when she and the other maidens of Bhakubha realise the enormity of their act is she cleansed, and this is symbolised in the milk-purification episode of the narrative.

Lamming, in *In The Castle of My Skin*, and Achebe, in *Things Fall Apart*, do not differ much in their conception of their traditional role as literary chroniclers. Their main concern is to redefine the past and the present of their people. Hence their themes evoke compassionate treatment of the family relationships, the economic welfare, the quarrels, the religion, the love and hatred which preoccupy man in his daily sojourn. For Lamming, the very act of writing a novel is "a way of investigating and projecting the inner experiences of the West Indian community."[6] It is the West Indian novelist, says Lamming, who "was the first to chart the West Indian memory as far back as he could go."[7] As a literary chronicler, the West Indian novelist has at his beck and call "the anthropologist and all other treatises" who wish to learn about West Indian history. And in recording his people's past, present and future, the West Indian peasant,

For the first time...became other than a cheap source of labour. He became, through the novelist's eye, a living existence, living in silence and joy and fear, involved in riot and carnival.[8]

In concentrating on the aspects that make and create life among his people, Lamming shares Achebe and the traditional chroniclers' belief that "Art for art's sake is just another piece of deodorised dog-shit."[9] For the traditional storyteller, no matter how despondent he may be, "art is, and was always, in the service of man."[10] Furthermore, says Achebe,

Our ancestors created their myths and legends and told their stories for a human purpose (including, no doubt, the excitation of wonder and pure delight); they made their sculptures in wood and terracotta, stone and bronze to serve the needs of their times. Their artists lived and moved and had their being in society, and created their works for the good of that society.[11]

For Achebe, as indeed it is for Lamming, the artist is a recorder of his people's history, and by doing so, he is able to cast light on his society's past and is able to assist his society to better understand their present and future. Achebe and Lamming wish to assert the strength of their people's past, and to demonstrate, most of all, that the people were not living in darkness and primitivism when the European invader arrived to put a knife in their society and split it apart. But the task of recording history and interpreting it for one's fellow participants is not an easy one. And hence both novels grow slowly and painstakingly as the artists grapple with the best technique to evoke creative responses from an audience whose passivity and obtuseness are unlike the traditional audience who anticipated and eagerly expanded the storyteller's tale.

Lamming and Achebe adhere further to the constraints of the story-teller by giving the distinct impression in their novels that the stories they are recording have been brought down to them by other storytellers of the collective soul of their people. In this regard, because both writers are quite young at the time of the telling of their tales, they humbly accept the awesome position which they hold. *In the Castle of My Skin* is a story of change which covers the ninth to eighteenth years of the life of the narrator. But the pulse and heart-beat of the history of the Barba-dian village is not the narrator, but the character called Pa, whose exis-tence precedes the community. But Pa is more than age (though age is a prerequisite for historical veracity in the traditional community), says Lamming :

> His age was not just years, but a whole way of being together with generations of children whom he had seen mature into fathers, or stumble, one way and another, into disgrace.[12]

Pa is the verbal historian to whom the young narrator goes for an understanding of the complexity of his growth and the change in his village.

Pa's knowledge of history goes beyond the years which he has eked out in Creighton village. Like Trumper, who has extended his horizon by spending time in the United States, Pa talks to the young boy of a harmonious, ancestral past where people were honest, hardworking, and trustworthy :

> ...time was I see by the sun how the season sail and the moon make warning what crops to expect. Leaf fall or blood stain by the edge of the sea was a way of leaving one thing for another. Wood work in the morning and the tale at night was the way we walk the world, and no one worry what wonders take place on the top of the sky. Star in the dark and stone in the shine of the sun sideways speak nothing but a world outside our world and the two was one. Fire heat in the daytime and the colour that come later to take light from the eye make small, small difference to my people. (CS, p. 232)

Pa remembers the time when the European invader arrived in Africa and bought Africa's best "produce" :

> A man walked out in the market square and one buyer watch his tooth and another his toe and the parts that was private for the coming of a creature in the intimate night. The silver sail from hand to hand and the purchase was shipped like a box of good fruit. (CS, p. 233)

As the custodian of the history of the community, Pa shows a perception which is deeper and has greater veracity than that which is held by the formally educated members of Creighton village. Pa is aware of his slave past and he is able to indicate the cause for this process. Pa is also not ashamed of his ancestral past as the schoolchildren who discuss slavery obviously are. The schoolchildren are, of course, products of a colonial education which desires to eradicate any blame the colonial power had in creating the cruel system of slavery. Furthermore, colonial education wishes to ensure an allegiance to the colonial power, and to do so, it must necessarily present the ancestral past of the children in a bad light. And to aid the colonial power, teachers are recruited from the indigenous population to provide authenticity. Lamming in *The Pleasures of Exile*, puts it as follows :

How in the name of Heavens could a colonial native taught by an English native within a strict curriculum diligently guarded by yet another English native who functioned as a reliable watch dog, the favourite clerk of a foreign administration : how could he ever get out from under this ancient mausoleum of historic achievement ?[13]

This is why there is a marked contrast in the historical perspective of Pa and the children who are taught history by colonised, elitist black men. The following passage from *In the Castle of My Skin* demonstrates this point :

He asked the teacher what was the meaning of slave, and the teacher explained. But it didn't make sense. He didn't understand how anyone could be bought by another. ... He told the teacher what the old woman had said. She was a slave. And the teacher said she was getting dotish. It was a long, long, long time ago. People talked of slaves a long time ago. It had nothing to do with the old lady. She wouldn't be old enough. And moreover it had nothing to do with people in Barbados. (p. 56)

For Lamming, the kind of education which is purveyed to the community is crucial. Lamming concentrates heavily in the discussion of slavery on showing his people that the devastating results that European colonialism has had (and continues to have) on the Caribbean people had in fact been engineered through the force of Christian education. Lamming shows that the success of the twin-evils of colonialism and capitalism could not have occurred without the assistance of Christianity and Christian-oriented education, whose duty it was (and is) to capture the soul and the mind as well. Thus, history and values are distorted and reversed, and social order, disrupted beyond recognition, is replaced by another that is both foreign and unjust. Colonial education produced subservience, self-hatred, and mutual suspicion. Furthermore, colonial education selected a few gifted people from the community and uprooted them from the mass of the people and even from their own friends, as the narrator, who receives a high school education, discovers when he is separated from his childhood friends, Bob, Trumper and Boy Blue. Not only does colonial education make these gifted people worship the achievements of the European but it sent them out as missionaries among their own people to instil the · achievements of Europe into their minds. The narrator at the end of the novel, having obtained the colonial stamp of approval, sets out for Trinidad to be a beacon of European light. And the black teachers who live in *In the Castle of My Skin* are more fastidious about celebrating Empire Day, singing "God Save the King", and fostering myths about Barbados' "Little England" status than were the zealous white missionaries before them.

Pa, as seen in an earlier passage from *In the Castle of My Skin*, is also the link with Africa, the original home from which the ancestors of the people in Creighton village emerged. But Pa's stories of slavery and "god worship" in Africa are not complete, and, consequently, he is unable to relate to the young narrator the glorious civilisation of the African past. It is to Achebe's *Things Fall Apart* that the West Indian and African must turn, because this book deals with the common cultural heritage of both peoples. *Things Fall Apart* is literary history at its best, and it serves as an excellent example of the writer's role as historian and teacher.

Achebe does not use the technique of an historian within a literary history as Lamming does with the use of Pa. But Achebe relies on the passed-on legends of the African people to fill in the past. Achebe recalls in *Morning Yet on Creation Day* the creative and fascinating environment of story-telling by relatives in which he was brought up. In particular, the stories always dealt with the glory and despair which embraced the tribal community. There is tremendous pride in the story-teller of *Things Fall Apart* when he reminds his audience of the legal machinery that the tribe employed when sitting in judgment. The marital dispute between Odukwe and Uzowulu is carried out in great pomp and ceremony and with due respect to the ancestral spirits of the tribe who provide the *egwugwu*, the disputants, and the audience with proper wisdom to settle the litigation. There is the dramatic opening greeting from the chief *egwugwu*, an indication of the communal atmosphere :

"Umuofia kwenu !" shouted the leading egwugwu, pushing the air with his raffia arms. The elders of the clan replied, "Yaa!"
"Umuofia kwenu !"
"Yaa!"
"Umuofia kwenu !"
"Yaa !"   (p. 81)

Because it is an occasion for justice to show its face, there is need to have the *egwugwu* dressed in appropriate clothes to show that this is a momentous and fearful happening :

> The egwugwu with the springy walk was one of the dead fathers of the clan.   He looked terrible with the smoked raffia body, a huge wooden face painted white except for the round hollow eyes and the charred teeth that were as big as a man's fingers.   On his head were two powerful horns.   (p. 82)

Like everything else in this closely related community, disputes are the property of the community, and, therefore, it is appropriate that the dispute be aired in the open and that the act of justice be a communal one.   As in the Xhosa story, "The Turban", disputes cause disharmony not only in the huts of the disputing parties, but in the huts of the entire community.   Therefore, the audience takes an active interest in the evidence presented by Odukwe and Uzowulu and is rightfully indignant when Odukwe accuses Mgbafo of the unutterable crime of having slept with "her lover" while she was pregnant :

> "Two years ago," continued Odukwe, "when she was pregnant, he beat her until she miscarried."
> "It is a lie.   She miscarried after she had gone to sleep with her lover."
> "Uzowulu's body, I salute you", said Evil Forest, silencing him.
> "What kind of lover sleeps with a pregnant woman?"   There was a loud murmur of approbation from the crowd.   (p. 83)

Later, the "crowd roars with laughter" when Odukwe threatens to "cut off" Uzowulu's "genitals" if "he ever beats" Mgbafo again (p. 84). After the *egwugwu* had retired to their underground home, which is symbolic of seeking the wisdom of the ancestral spirits, they reappear and appropriately pronounce a judgement of rehabilitation rather than punishment: "Our duty," says Evil Forest, "is not to blame this man or praise that, but to settle the dispute" (p. 84).   The judgement, therefore, contains both admonition for Ozowulu's behaviour and a renewed sign of friendship between the disputing parties as symbolised by the "pot of wine".   The judgement thus restores harmony to the disputants and to the community. Achebe is at pains to show his African audience that there is no costly prolonged and divisive litigation, and compared with the European model of justice, it is more equitable and regenerative.

Achebe parades before us a host of tribal customs, each one intending to show how these customs were functional, logical, and, above all, not "primitive".   The Mbaino incident seems to be a just way of settling a dispute between tribes (TFA, p. 11-14) : here the deliberate killing of Ogbuefi Udo's wife by the men of Mbaino can only be compensated by the demand for another wife for Udo and as punishment for the wilful act of the taking away of a young man such as Ikemefuna. For Achebe, who is fully aware that the tribes of Europe had gone to bloody war for similar or less cause (compare the Helen of Troy story), he wishes to demonstrate the "civilised" nature of the tribes of Africa. Furthermore, the traditional society does not differ from any other complex society in its belief in oracles (the *Agbala*), soothsayers (the priestess Chielo), and superstition (the *chi* and *iyi-uwo*).

The traditional storyteller sang truthfully of the hope and despair of the community. Achebe, in his role as storyteller and literary chronicler, records faithfully those customs which violated the value of life, with no doubt an eye towards teaching his countrymen not to descend into those vile practices again. Hence, he mentions the illogical killing of Obierika's wife's twin children, an occurrence which was regarded by the tribe as unnatural and therefore evil : "The Earth had decreed that they were an offence on the land and must be destroyed." (TFA, p. 114) Achebe singles out the practice of *ogbanje*, the belief that an *ogbanje* child was "one of those wicked children who, when they died, entered their mothers' wombs to be born again." (TFA, p. 70) Ekwefi, one of Okonkwo's wives, had suffered this fate no less than nine times. After this happened on the third occasion, Okonkwo summoned a famous medicine man named Okagbue Uyanwa. Uyanwa not only instructs Okonkwo to sleep with his wife in the future in his *obi* (hut) but he proceeds to mutilate the remains of the dead child Onwumbiko :

> The medicine-man then ordered that there should be no mourning for the dead child. He brought out a sharp razor from the goatskin bag slung from his left shoulder and began to mutilate the child. Then he took it away to bury in the Evil Forest, holding it by the ankle and dragging it on the ground behind him. After such treatment it would think twice before coming again, unless it was one of the stubborn ones who returned, carrying the stamp of their mutilation—a missing finger or perhaps a dark line where the medicine-man's razor had cut them. (TFA, p. 71)

Of course, Okagbue Uyanwa's solution does not work, because Ekwefi suffers the same fate six more times before Ezinma lives beyond age three.

But, most of all, Achebe revels in the glorious celebrations of the past : a time when the community is truly a unit, when they fully explore and enjoy the blessings of the Earth. Such for example was the "Feast of the New Yam", which was held before the harvest and the occasion for honouring Ani, the earth goddess and the source of all fertility, and the ancestral spirits of the clan. Huge quantities of yam foo-foo and vegetable soup were cooked and "no matter how heavily the family ate or how many friends and relations they invited from neighbouring villages, there was always a huge quantity of food left over at the end of the day." (TFA, p. 34) It was a time to invite relatives and neighbours from afar to share in the abundance of the Earth. It was also the time for the great wrestling matches when the strongest man in the village was determined. Again, as in the litigation scene, wrestling is as much a community affair as is a dispute or a marriage or a funeral. Before the wrestlers arrive on the village *ilo*, the drummers set the scene, a dramatic moment for the crowd that is gathered there and that is seated in an appropriately hierarchal manner :

> The wrestlers were not there yet and the drummers held the field. They too sat just in front of the huge circle of spectators, facing the elders. (TFA, p. 42)

Finally, the two teams of wrestlers dance into the circle while the crowd roars and the drums reach a level of frenzy. For the winner, in this case Okafo, there is song and praise and the promise of being promoted to a good position within the community. This is, of course, the way in which Okonkwo got promoted from the lowly son of Unoka to the most powerful man of Umuofia.

The Uri feast of Obierika's daughter gives Achebe an opportunity not only to discuss the feast of marriage but to demonstrate that marriage was treated with deep respect and joy by the community; that it was not a frivolous act, but one that has gone through the several stages of ritual and blessing of the community. Therefore, in such a community, divorce is often unheard of. As in all communal celebrations food is the major item, and song provides the closing when night falls :

> As night fell, burning torches were set on wooden tripods and the young men raised a song. The elders sat in a big circle and the singers went round singing each man's praise as they came before him. They had something to say for every man. Some were great farmers, some were orators who spoke for the clan; Okonkwo was the greatest wrestler and warrior alive. (TFA, p. 107).

The song reaffirms the unity of the community and the value of each member in the collectivity. Celebrations, therefore, are regenerative— they are meant to cement the unity of the tribe.

Achebe shows in painstaking manner that the Africa of the past was complex, hierarchal, proud, dignified and above all, not "primitive". Achebe writes sensitively about this period of African history and like the storyteller he is not afraid to sing of the Africa that was soon to be confronted by the Europeans with their arrogant belief in the superiority of their god, their educational, political and economic systems.

Both Lamming and Achebe regard Christianity as a disrupting force
in the lives of their people. Achebe shows the subtle, pervasive and devastating effects of Christianity in its mission to subjugate the African people.
The Christian missionaries, who had at first been welcomed as "crazy
men" and given an opportunity to build a church in the much-maligned
and feared Evil Forest, through building a school and a hospital and
demonstrating the essential superstition behind many of the tribal society's
fears, start to make converts among the tribe. Furthermore, through kind
though misguided men such as Reverend Brown, they begin to question
the basis of tribal society and insist that the gods that the tribesmen worship are "false gods, gods of wood and stone". (TFA, p.131) The Christian
teachings concentrate as well on the weaker and cruel aspects of the
society whereas the hierarchal structure of the tribe cannot accept the Osu
(the outcast) as part of the community, the missionaries preach that
"Before God there is no slave or free. We are all children of God and we
must receive these our brothers." (TFA, pp. 142-3) For a modern Africa
that has only lately come out of hundreds of years of enslavement from the
very people who preached this latter doctrine, the hollow ring of this pious
statement of brotherhood is devastating.

It is Christianity which proves more restrictive in the final analysis.
The Christian refuses to accept the essential truth of another's religion,
and hence, he begins to employ "the sword" of the colonial administration to bring the recalcitrant in line. European civilisation, then, which
had, from a naive liberal view, set out "to bring civilisation to a primitive
people", begins to show its greater primitiveness in administering its cruel
and hypocritical Christian justice. (TFA, p. 176) It is with the pernicious
help of Christianity that the soul of a once proud people is destroyed. And
this causes Okonkwo's revolt and his destruction at his own hands.

Even though Lamming treats the Christian influence in Creighton
village with some hilarity, he is no less cognizant of the powerful enslav-
ing effect which Christianity has had on the people of the Caribbean. One
of the aspects of traditional society which Christianity automatically reacts
to is that of polygamy. The Christian believes firmly in the practice of
one man one wife. The stories of Jon, Jen and Susie, and of Bambi,
Bambina and Bots treat this theme both comically and tragically. In the
case of Jon, Jen and Susie, Jon who has been living happily with Susie, is
suddenly converted to a religious sect led by Brother Bannister, who really
wants Jon for his daughter Jen. Jon makes Jen pregnant and his troubles
start with Brother Bannister threatening to shoot him if he does not marry
his daughter. Meanwhile, Susie swears to poison herself should Jon desert
her for Jen. To resolve the question, Jon promises to marry both Susie
and Jen, but at different churches on the same day and hour. He escapes
his dilemma on the wedding day by climbing up a tree in a graveyard halfway between the two churches where he "sit all the day before, turn' his
mind now this way, now that, like a fowl feather in the wind."(CS, p. 135).

In the case of Bambi, Bambina and Bots, Bambi has been living with the two women in the same house for years. The two women have children by him and 'Everybody sa ys there never know in all the village from top to bottom a set of people who live in love an' harmony like Bots, Bambina an' Bambi, with children..." (CS, p. 145) Then a German Christian woman comes to live in the village and persuades Bambi to "legally" marry one of the women. They each toss a coin, he marries Bots and they all continue living as before, but the strain of a legal contract brings a psychological change in Bambi, who starts beating the women indiscriminately. This results in a complete break-up of their lives.

It is passive Christianity which blinds the village people to the unequal situation which exists between Creighton and the villagers. Thus while they are being exploited they are led into Christian song by the evangelists who conduct services on the street at night. Belief in God and the resurrection of the poor in a prosperous after-life is also the chief reason why Ma cannot perceive as deeply as Pa. And it is only when this blind belief is removed that Creighton's dominance is rejected :

> They turn as dotish with all these nancy stories 'bout born again, an' we never ever give ourself a chance to get up an' get.Nothin' ain't goin' change here til we sort o' stop payin' notice to that sort o' joke 'bout a old man goin' born again. It ain't only stupid but it sound kind o' hasty, an' that's what Mr. Slime want to put an end to. He mention that said same thing last night in his speech. An' he call it tomfoolery. 'Tis what got us as we is, he say. (CS, p. 157)

But the change that comes transcends the perniciousness of Christianity as Pa reminds the narrator. Having seen man promise and having seen the failure of dreams so often before, it is Pa who resignedly says "The years had changed nothing." (CS, p. 231) For him, it is for the same price that Slime had preached against Christianity (as Christianity had earlier preached against the tribe), the "silver" that passed "from hand to hand" and caused the enslavement of his ancestors :

> If the islands be sick 'tis for no other reason than the ancient silver. Your motto now is price or power which mean the same same thing. Sinner and saint are alike in this matter. I see the purchase of tribes on the silver sailing vessels, some to Jamaica, Antigua, Grenada, some to Barbados and the island of oil and the mountain tops. (CS, p. 233)

The old man's vision is of the past and the effects on the present. Lamming, the literary chronicler of now and tomorrow, provides the reader with an enlarged view which counteracts the restrictive, hopeless vision of Pa. The narrator, informed by the wisdom of the old man's past, must now interpret and record his community's present and future.

To do so, he must become like Trumper and go into exile, but come back again to carry out his important task. "And this," says Lamming, "is [his] theme of [his] work for tomorrow."[14]

Achebe's task, throughout the writing of his Umuofia novels, that is, *Things Fall Apart*, *No Longer at Ease*, *The Arrow of God*, and *A Man of the People*, is to be the Bard of the Past, Present, and Future. Hence he does not suggest that the hanging suicide of Okonkwo is a hopeless defeat of the tribe. Neither does Achebe suggest that Okonkwo was too rigid to accept the "winds of change", as many critics of Achebe's work want us to believe. Okonkwo is not resistant to change at all—he is only against a change which is not operated by his soiety but one that has been cruelly imposed on them. His suicide, therefore, if it has any validity, and consequently underscores Obierika's observation, is a final monument to the tribe to take heed of their failure and to search for different approaches to overcome the colonial dominance. Okonkwo and Mr Slime mirror the tragedy of the oppressed, but in their actions the literary chroniclers affirm the essential power and aspirations of the oppressed.

REFERENCES

1. V.S. Naipaul, *The Middle Passage*, London, 1962.

2. James Joyce, *A Portrait of the Artist as a Young Man*, New York, 1953, pp. 246-247.

3. A.C. Jordan, *Tales from Southern Africa*, California, 1973, has a good selection of Xhosa folk legends.

4. *ibid.*, p. 25.

5. *ibid.*, p. 57.

6. George Lamming, *The Pleasures of Exile*, London, 1960, p. 37.

7. *ibid.*, p. 38.

8. *ibid.*, p. 39.

9. Chinua Achebe, *Morning Yet on Creation Day*, London, 1975, p. 19.

10. *ibid.*

11. *ibid.*

12. Lamming, *The Pleasures of Exile*, p. 227.

13. *ibid.*, p. 27.

14. *ibid.*, p. 229.

26

Colonialism as
Metaphor and Experience in
'The Grass is Singing' and 'Surfacing'

LOIS C. GOTTLIEB & WENDY KEITNER

THAT colonialism is a relationship of exploitation has been recognised for a considerable time. Recently, however, feminist criticism has extended the analysis of oppressive political relationships into the area of sexual relationships. Simone de Beauvoir, for example, argues that woman's conception of herself as inferior and dependent flows directly from her realisation that "the world is masuline on the whole; those who fashioned it, ruled it, and still dominate it today are men."[1] Thus woman is classified with "workers, black slaves [and] colonial natives [who] have also been called grown up children."[2] Similarly, but more forcefully, Sheila Rowbotham cites "economic dependence", "cultural takeover", and "the identification of dignity with resemblance to the oppressor" as some of the "similarities that exist between the colonisation of the underdeveloped country and female oppression..."[3] From both groups' lack of power— economic, political, and social—grows a host of corresponding psychological characteristics, the most noticeable of which is a conviction of the colonised that they are inferior to and dependent upon the colonisers.

This analogy between political and sexual colonialism opens a rich field of exploration for the literary critic. This paper is limited to an exploration of two fictional accounts of women's conflicts, set in the contexts of political colonialism in Rhodesia and in Canada and further complicated by the imbalance of power between the sexes. Although separated by a generation, Doris Lessing's *The Grass is Singing* (1950) and Margaret Atwood's *Surfacing* (1972) reinforce the thesis that women's lives constitute an experience of colonialism.

Lessing's novel begins shortly after the violent death of Mary Turner, a white Rhodesian farm woman, at the hands of her black houseboy, Moses, and then retrospectively seeks to understand the causes of such violence.

Lessing retraces the steps leading to the profoundly complicated, six-year relationship between white mistress and native servant, exploring both its extremes of racial domination—including Mary's physical brutalising and public humiliation of Moses—and the extreme of sexual domination— ending in the black man's vengeful stabbing of the white woman who was disloyal to him.   The colonial brutality has, rightly, received major atten- tion as the novel's most clearly articulated theme.   Nonetheless, the critic must also examine the premises by which the central woman's life is dis- torted by the power of political and sexual patriarchies.   This theme of sexual colonialism remains submerged throughout the novel, but its pre- sence explains the ambivalent role played by Mary, seemingly powerful but ultimately powerless, within the hierarchy of white rule.

What is common to the powerlessness of blacks and women is the dis- tortion of their human sexuality to fit the needs of the dominant group. For the civilised white man, the native man appears imbued with superior sexual powers, to be admired, envied, and feared. The primitive state of the native accounts, in the coloniser's mind, for both his greater sexual poten- cy and his incapacity to restrain his sexual appetite.   Thus the white man is forced to guard his white woman from the probability of sexual attack by the native, and he justifies many of the brutal aspects of his coloniser's code as a response to the "threat" of the native's sexuality.

Marston, the English outsider, draws explicit attention to the "sexual aspect of the colour bar, one of whose foundations is the jealousy of the white man for the superior sexual potency of the native."[4] Implicitly, from the first chapter of the novel, we are drawn to another "sexual aspect of the colour bar" and that is the objectification of white woman as the symbol of unattainable power, which is the exclusive property of the white man, and as a visible reminder of the native man's inferiority.   Further, by objectifying the white woman as a sexual symbol, the white man effec- tively denies the importance of her individual humanity.   This evidence of the colonised status of woman emerges most clearly from the treatment of the dead Mary by the official spokesmen for the white patriarchy of Rhodesia.

Mary's murder arouses fear and disgust in the white Rhodesians because of its suggestion of sexual intimacy between Mary and Moses. Thus, the whites reflexively deny that the murder contained anything more than the expected components : characteristic drunkenness on the part of the native and the expression of his natural proclivity to rob and rape. In this "conspiracy of ignorance", Marston recognises "white civilisation...fight- ing to defend itself" by refusing to admit "that a white person and most particularly a white woman, can have a human relationship whether for good or evil, with a black person." (p.12) But in their repulsion towards and execration of Mary, we recognise that the sexual mythology surrounding the white woman as white man's sexual property is central to maintaining the white structure. The fallen Mary, a defiled symbol of white superiority, must bedis missed as the "silly woman" who "got herself murdered" (p. 12) and whose body they leave to lie like a discarded rag.

An additional aspect of woman's powerlessness within the colonial and sexual patriarchies is her "natural" inability to wield effective power over black labour, thus demonstrating her unfitness to share power with white man. The Rhodesian farm women are indicted with humorous paternalism by their men for being notoriously "bad" managers of their houseboys. As Charlie Slatter, the area's most powerful man, spells it out : "Needs a man to deal with niggers...Niggers don't understand women giving them orders. They keep their own women in their right place" (p 27).

Mary's bad reputation with her houseboys becomes legendary in the course of the novel; but her obsession to gain control, to wield power over other humans, is compensation for her inability to wield power over her own destiny. During her husband's lengthy first malaria attack, Mary is forced to oversee the labourers in the field. Her time in power literally revitalises her from her former lethargic depression. As Lessing reports, "The sensation of being boss over perhaps eighty black workers gave [Mary] new confidence; it was a good feeling, keeping them under her will, making them do as she wanted" (p. 138). Mary displays the coloniser's brutal indifference to the humanity of her workers, refusing them rest periods, relaxation, or even the acknowledgement that they are more than animals. But Mary displays this brutal indifference in a hysterical style, so that the master/servant relationship, accepted as the inevitable domination of the powerful over the inferior, becomes exposed to a new point of view. When Mary slips the sambok over her wrist, as a sign of her authority, she is imitating Charlie Slatter whose harsh treatment of native workers sets the style for white rule; but Mary's horrible aping of Slatter's methods betrays another facet of her own colonised status. As Rowbotham notes, the colonised identifies "dignity" with "resemblance to the oppressor."[5]

The one black labourer against whom Mary applies the sambok in her fanatical display of power is Moses. Thus, ironically, through the wielding of colonial power, Mary initiates a chain of events that leads temporarily to the breakdown of the barrier between white woman and black man, mistress and servant, and ultimately to her own destruction.

Perhaps the most suggestive aspect of the theme of woman's colonised status is Lessing's portrayal of a social system which requires men to act out the role of the powerful adult or risk losing their identities as men (as does Mary's hapless husband, Dick) and which prescribes that women shape their lives along the dimensions of the dependent child. Mary is a child-woman in a society that glorifies the image of the immature and even physically underdeveloped woman. Mary models her dress and behaviour :"on the more childish-looking film stars" (p. 42), wears her hair in "little girl fashion" on her shoulder, and ties it with a girlish ribbon.

Dick's first image of Mary, the false image thrown up by the distorting lights in the movie house, causes him to dream about "the girl with the young, uptilted face and the wave of loose gleaming hair" (p. 55). Lessing exposes the grotesqueness of the entire concept of the child-woman when Mary, seeking to restore an "attractive" image of herself, instinctively returns to her little girl fashion even after years on the farm have rendered her desiccated, frowsy, and scrawny.

For the novel's purpose, the most significant aspect of Mary's child role is its asexual nature. This shields Mary from acknowledging her most feared and most desired sensation—her longing for and her revulsion from her father's sexuality. Moses specifically takes on fatherly qualities once Mary's open display of weakness puts their relationship on a new, human footing. He brings her food, urges her to eat, forces her to rest, and gradually confines her to a child-like and dependent role. Furthermore, father and lover are combined as Moses courts Mary with flowers, admiration, and a growing domination. In Mary's nightmares, a reflection of her madness, Moses and her father merge into one identity—the sexual identity of man. Thus, whatever beauty might have clung to the human relationship between Moses and Mary becomes distorted by the sexual battles. As Lessing notes, "they were like two antagonists, silently sparring. Only he was powerful and sure of himself, and she was undermined by fear, by her terrible dream-filled nights, her obsession" (p. 207).

Just as Mary is attracted and repulsed by the sexuality of Moses, the man, so she is attracted and repulsed by the humanity of Moses, the black. Madness sufficiently deranges Mary's senses so that she can ignore society's prohibitions against intimacy with blacks, and she can ignore her psychic rejection of intimacy with men. But she cannot overcome her compulsion to be punished for her transgressions. She has been disloyal to her race; she has been disloyal to her neurotic sexual ideals; and, furthermore, she has been disloyal to Moses in her dismissal of him, as both interpret this act. Thus both realise that Moses is the natural agent of her punishment, and Mary acts out woman's age-old role of sacrificial victim. Mary achieves an equilibrium with her environment only by presenting herself to her murderer and by permitting "the bush"—the Africa of the native people— to avenge itself on her.

In contrast to Lessing's novel where the power disparity between men and women is depicted principally in terms of physical violence, Atwood's *Surfacing* focuses more directly on the psychological dimensions and strategies of sexual politics. It traces the experiences of the unnamed central female character—including a devastating extramarital affair, abortion, and the death of her father—which lead to alienation and, ultimately, to her mad identification with the exploited Canadian wilderness. Fully expressing a post-sixties revulsion against international violence, American capitalist expansion, and pollution of environment,

Atwood implies a basic analogy between woman's personal victimisation by a male-dominated society and the ecological destruction of the land under American economic imperialism. While other critics have noted the importance of the nationalist theme, this paper redirects attention to an equally important aspect of the novel, the painful and erratic emergence of the narrator's feminist consciousness.

Growing up female in a father-dominated family within a priest-controlled rural Quebec community during the post-war years, the narrator has been subjected to a process of social conditioning. The main premise of this conditioning is that "men ought to be superior,"[6] and, by logical extension, that women, in their inferiority, ought to defer to the male's greater strength, wisdom, rationality, and his more direct links with divine authority. As a child, the narrator worships her father—a logical, scientific man—as a god; identifying with him, rather than with her faceless, invalid mother, she fantasises about becoming all-powerful herself by magical means. School, however, enforces the ideal of feminine passivity, and, as a young girl, the narrator learns not to question authority and to accept her dependent position. Thus she submits to the miniature chauvinists of the schoolyard who express the dictum of their society to be stronger than women, although they do not employ adult chivalric disguises : they torment, capture, and tie up the young narrator in her own skipping rope, silently underscoring how feminine playthings may themselves trap young girls into sexual stereotypes, thereby constraining their free development.

The models of older women in the community sanctify this forced submissiveness to masculine authority, even when the submission is to a definition of womanhood as corrupt or evil. For example, the narrator recalls that many of the local women, deferring to the old priest's ban on short skirts and bare arms, lived all their lives by the lake without ever learning to swim because they were too ashamed of their bodies to wear bathing suits. The distorted alternatives open to women within the spectrum of dependent and inferior beings are still more horrifically suggested by the narrator when she describes the effective reduction of woman's humanity in the accounts of women's lives in her youthful reading. Fairy-tale princesses, True Romance goddesses, and glossy magazine glamour queens inanely "holding up cans of cleanser, knitting, smiling, modelling toeless high heels" (p. 91) provide the range of women's lives from domestic drudge to sex symbol. And, according to photographs of her as a teenager, the narrator has conformed to her society's image of femininity, wearing "stiff dresses, crinolines and tulle, layered like store birthday cakes; I was civilised at last" (p. 108).

Forced in her adolescence to an awareness of international violence through her viewing of newsreels of Hitler and World War II, the narrator has had her political consciousness raised for many years. She is thus able to see immediately the destructive consequences inherent in American technological encroachment on Canadian natural resources; so she resists the national tendency to sell out by refusing to let go of her family's wilderness property. By contrast, however, she only gradually comes to the consciousness that she has given in to social pressures to exploit her own body, turning it into an artificial object, "the finished product' (p. 108), from which she feels estranged. And just as the narrator only gradually comes to judge her estrangement from her body, not as an individual sickness, but as a function of society's treatment of women, so she perceives only after a great deal of time that the disharmony characterising her relations with men has been a consequence of the imbalance of power between the sexes, an imbalance which gives men the right to dominate as colonisers of the social territory. Again, her enlightenment is not epiphanic, but gradual and piecemeal, forcing the reader to experience the narrator's visceral responses upon seeing disparate parts of the world through a new consciousness.

When the narrator is able to confront the realities of her recent and debilitating affair with a married, middle-aged man, her judgment is that he is "only a normal man...selfish and kind in the average proportion" (p. 189). Thus she understands the exploitative behaviour of her lover—who forced an unwanted pregnancy upon her — as normal in the context of sexual colonialism. Although she eventually has an abortion, during the short period of her pregnancy she feels that the foetus in her womb belongs not to her but to her husband, that "he imposed it on me, all the time it was growing in me I felt like an incubator...after it was born I was no more use" (p. 34). The inescapable conclusion which Atwood draws is that, like nature's resources exploited by the "fucking pig Americans" (p. 89), woman's body is exploited to supply men's needs, including their dynastic drive, their need for transcendence through children. Ultimately, even the uniquely female capacity to give birth seems to the narrator to be dominated by "their power, not yours'. (p. 80).

She gains further insight into her own and the female condition by observing the brutal tactics of her married friends, David and Anna. During their week-long wilderness quest together, the narrator relinquishes her youthful, romantic desire to believe that "what she called a good marriage had remained possible, for someone" (p. 99). Increasingly she becomes convinced that relations between the sexes, even between herself and the undemonstrative Joe, are like interactions between countries throughout the course of history : in essence, one long series of struggles for supremacy, "people taking and losing power over other people" (p. 97). That women as a sex have been the losers in this power struggle is luridly emphasised in David's disgusting corruption of the Canadian national song, "The Maple Beaver for Ever", which portrays Wolfe as a sexual as well as a military conqueror.

A fuller understanding of the sexual power struggle emerges as the narrator integrates what were formerly only flashes of consciousness of her colonised state; a series of bizarre and grotesque images succinctly sums up her situation. Estranged from her exploited body, she feels as theatrically victimised as a carnival woman, "Woman sawn apart in a wooden crate, wearing a bathing suit, smiling" (p. 108). "I was nothing but a head" (p. 108), she records, but then quickly corrects this image—with its overtones of reason, control, and importance--"or no, something minor like a severed thumb"(p. 108). As these images of dismemberment coalesce into a more unified consciousness, the narrator begins to react against her socially assigned inferior and powerless role. Significantly, she redirects the quest for her missing father to a quest for "the missing part of me" (p. 108). Contrary to her conditioning, she puts her own interests ahead of those of the male authority figure, her father, asserting : "It was no longer his death but my own that concerned me" (p. 107).

What the novel shows is that woman's increasingly independent role, her progress to sanity and wholeness, poses a threat to men. David caricatures "Women's Libbers" as preachers of random castration "roving the streets in savage bands armed with garden shears" (p. 111); even the feckless Joe appears to have "the defiant but insane look of a species once dominant, now threatened with extinction. That's how he thinks of himself too : deposed, unjustly" (p. 8). That a quiet sexual revolution is being waged by Margaret Atwood is suggested by the concluding portion of the novel; here the physical drowning of man finds an equal and opposite movement in the psychological surfacing of woman.

This revolution is not accomplished painlessly for the woman. The narrator has had to undergo an anguishing process of rebirth, which includes temporary madness, in order to reject the erroneous, repressive, but nonetheless comforting assumptions of man's superiority and of woman's child-like innocence. She can no longer play the feminine part of "eternal child."[7] She admits : "I have to recant, give up the old belief that I am powerless and because of it nothing I can do will ever hurt anyone. A lie which was always more disastrous than the truth would have been" (p. 191). Taking responsibility for her own actions, she achieves adult status, independence, and maturity.

Atwood's woman in the end is the antithesis of Lessing's. Thus, the two central female characters clearly express opposite possibilities for woman within the system of sexual colonialism. In Lessing's novel, Mary is imprisoned in her society's image of woman—dependent, inferior, helpless, requiring domination—and she acts out, to her own destruction, the role of sacrificial victim which has so often been thrust on women. In short, Lessing's woman epitomises the sickness of her society, and her death suggests the inevitable fatality of that social hierarchy. Lessing almost says as much in the second, anonymous epigram which stands as a foreword to the novel : "It is by the failures and misfits of a civilisation that one can best judge its weaknesses." In Atwood's novel, a generation

later, the woman's image, though in constant flux, distorted and fragmented, is, nevertheless, perceived by the heroine as flexible and capable of further change. The destructive image of the colonised woman, submissive and
inferior, is not fatal because the heroine's consciousness rises above that
of her society; she finally pierces through its stereotypes of women by
means of her new critical insight.   Atwood's woman, then, is infected
only partially by her society's sickness.   Once she recognises the value
and tactics of sexual colonialism, she refuses to be trapped by them and
so is psychically reborn. While the white Rhodesian woman perishes
childless at the hand of the black man, the Canadian woman surfaces
from her victim position, revitalised and pregnant with new life.   Thus,
The Grass is Singing and *Surfacing* reveal dissimilar prospects for the
assertion of autonomous female identity.

REFERENCES

1. Simone de Beauvoir, *The Second Sex*, trans. H.M. Parshley, 1949, rpt. London :
    Four Square Books, 1961, p. 298.

2. *ibid.*

3. Sheila Rowbotham, *Women, Resistance and Revolution*, London, Pelican Books,
    1974, p. 201.

4. Doris Lessing, *The Grass is Singing*, 1950, rpt. London, Heinemann Educational
    Books, Ltd., 1973, p. 230. All subsequent references to this edition will be found
    in the text.

5. Rowbotham, op. cit., p. 201.

6. Margaret Atwood, *Surfacing*, Toronto, Paper Jacks, 1973, p. 111. All subsequent
    references to this edition will be found in the text.

7. de Beauvoir, op. cit., p. 298.

27

African, Boer, and Indian Attitudes to an Imperialist War

ARTHUR RAVENSCROFT

I am uncertain whether this paper is mainly historical or literary in approach; if the former, it may not be altogether unfitting before this audience. Commonwealth literature may be said to consist of the best that has been experienced, thought, and expressed by acute and sensitive minds among the many peoples who once constituted that historical fact known as the British Empire. I intend to look at writings by three men who were personally much involved in a great Imperial crisis—the Boer War in South Africa, 1899-1902. In effect it means looking chiefly into three works written by non-Britishers : Mahadev Desai's translation from the Gujarati of M.K. Gandhi's *Autobiography or The Story of My Experiments with Truth*, Solomon T. Plaatje's *Boer War Diary : An African at Mafeking*, and Deneys Reitz's *Commando : A Boer Journal of the Boer War*.[1] I shall not be doing the justice to Gandhi's work that it deserves as a spiritual autobiography, because I shall be using it chiefly to ascertain Gandhi's attitudes to the Empire and the Boer War. Plaatje's *Diary* is hardly an example of the best that has been "experienced, thought, and expressed", but it is the earliest writing of the first Black South African novelist in English, and reveals the attitudes of a member of another of the subject peoples of the Empire. Reitz's book I believe to be one of the finest accounts of personal experience in war that has ever been written in English. I hope that in looking at these three figures, even as briefly as this occasion dictates, we shall adduce something about the relationship between history and literature, and that some understanding will emerge of how human minds are necessarily limited by the constrictions of the historical periods during which they exist. I fear that in the wisdom of hindsight both historians and literary critics often blame the writers of the past for not possessing omniscience. I begin with a quotation from Gandhi :

When the war was declared, my personal sympathies were all with the Boers, but I believed then that I had yet no right, in such cases, to enforce my individual convictions....Suffice it to say that my loyalty to the British rule drove me to participation with the British in that war. I felt that, if I demanded rights as a British citizen, it was also my duty, as such, to participate in the defence of the British Empire. I held then that India could achieve her complete emancipation only within and through the British Empire. So I collected together as many comrades as possible, and with very great difficulty got their services accepted as an ambulance corps.[2]

Writing in *Young India* on 17 November 1921, Gandhi quotes a letter from a correspondent who angrily takes him to task for having helped the British suppress the so-called Zulu Rebellion in South Africa in 1906 and for recruiting Indians for the Imperial forces in 1914. His correspondent asked bitterly : "Why then did you induce people to take part in a war the merits of which they knew not, and for the aggrandisement of a race so miserably wallowing in the mire of imperialism?"[3]

That Gandhi assisted the Imperial war effort against the Boers in 1899, against the Central powers in 1914, but especially against the Zulu uprising in 1906, is a fact still remembered in Southern Africa and even used in pseudo-part-justification for African attitudes to people of Indian origin in East Africa some seventy years later. His own participation, though sometimes under actual fire, was non-combatant, as a medical orderly. It is easy enough today to wonder whether the revered and wise Mahatma was perhaps playing a double political game or simply being unbelievably naive. To his correspondent's severe questioning in 1921, Gandhi made this reply :

I lost no occasion of serving the Government at all times. Two questions presented themselves to me during all these crises. What was my duty as a citizen of the empire as I then believed myself to be, and what was my duty as an out-and-out believer in the religion of *ahimsa* —non-violence ?

I know now that I was wrong in thinking that I was a citizen of the empire. But on those four occasions I did honestly believe that, in spite of the many disabilities that my country was labouring under, it was making its way towards freedom, and that on the whole the government from the popular standpoint was not wholly bad, and that the British administrators were honest though insular and dense. Holding that view, I set about doing what an ordinary Englishman would do in the circumstances....

The whole situation is now changed for me. My eyes, I fancy, are opened. Experience has made me wiser. I consider the existing system of government to be wholly bad and requiring special national effort to end or mend it. It does not possess within itself any capacity for self-improvement. That I still believe many English administrators to be honest does not assist me, because I consider them to be as blind and deluded as I was myself. Therefore I can take no pride in calling the empire mine or describing myself as a citizen. On the contrary, I fully realise that I am a *pariah* untouchable of the empire. I must, therefore, constantly pray for its radical reconstruction or total destruction, even as a Hindu *pariah* would be fully justified in so praying about Hinduism or Hindu society.[4]

To few political leaders is given the wisdom during their lifetimes to learn the obvious lessons of their own experience. To fewer still is given the honesty and humility that Gandhi showed in acknowledging past judgements to have been faulty, even if in good faith. Nevertheless, as Dr Raja Rao has reminded me, Gandhi never lost the vision of an international brotherhood of man leading to a World State, and continued to hope that the Empire (and later the Commonwealth) might still develop in that direction. Jawaharlal Nehru also consistently saw this ideal as a justification for India's continued membership of the Commonwealth.

Imperialism today takes much less obvious forms than it did in Gandhi's young manhood in the 1890s, of which he was to write : "I.... vied with Englishmen in loyalty to the throne. With careful perseverance I learnt the tune of the 'national anthem' and joined in the singing whenever it was sung."[5] Today the imperialism of uniform and gunboat is anathema to thinking people who have grown up at least since 1945, and some of us who cannot claim quite that degree of youth find it difficult to remember that we actually grew up in some corner or other of the British Empire and came under the influence of its sometimes persuasive ideas. After all, the worth of an idea does not necessarily depend on the motives that gave it birth, but rather on what men's minds make of it subsequently. This very gathering here in Delhi this week is one result (however much we may wince at the thought) of the historical fact of the British Empire. Allowing for the conference-monger in each of us, are our professed aims of mutual enlightenment and the "common pursuit of true judgement" thereby vitiated ?

Gandhi's autobiographical writings show conclusively that until 1919 he believed in the concept of imperial citizenship that transcended race and religion and national frontiers within the Empire, and carried with it the implications of common civic rights, privileges, and reponsibilities. It may have been a concept invented by the more idealistic among the British practitioners of imperialism, or it may have been no more than a chimera projected by the pragmatic agencies of imperial rule, but one can see now how it must have appealed to generous, large-hearted thinkers, like Gandhi, among the peoples who lived under the Empire. Beyond the immediate sordidness of the imperial fact, Gandhi certainly saw the vision of an international, imperial brotherhood of man.

Gandhi's adherence to Imperialism was certainly not singular in the 1890s among the many peoples subject to the Queen-Empress. During the Boer War, the Boers besieged Mafeking from October 1899 to May 1900. Among the besieged was a Black African member of the Cape Civil Service, a Morolong employed as an interpreter in the Mafeking Magistrate's Court and in the military Court of Summary Jurisdiction. He was Solomon Tshekisho Plaatje, later to become a distinguished journalist and linguist, the first General Corresponding Secretary of the South African Native National Congress (the predecessor of the African National Congress), and the first Black South African novelist. In the late 1960s, a South African anthropologist, John Comaroff, discovered the manuscript diary that Plaatje kept during the siege and his meticulous edition of it was published in 1973. Plaatje had no cause to rejoice in the Boer treatment of the Barolong people in the pre-war years, so he enthusiastically backed the British, and after the war continued to do so in the forlorn hope that British influence in South Africa would ease the lot of the Black South African people. Had he been with Gandhi in Natal (that colony of British settlers) as the Boer War began, he might have been disillusioned early, for Gandhi nearly was, as can be seen from these bitter comments that he made on the plight of the British Indian refugees from the Transvaal Republic who were being denied entry into the British colony of Natal :

> To find that British subjects cannot find shelter from danger on a British soil is truly heart-rending. The Natal Government would seem to have done their best, if they could, to shake the faith of the poor Indians in British justice, and in the enchanting power of the phrase "British subjects". Happily, they do not represent the whole of the British Empire. Strange as it may appear, a cablegram to-day announces that, in reply to repeated representations from Natal, the Imperial Government have ordered the despatch of 10,000 troops from India for the protection of Natal which refuses to give temporary shelter to the Indians from the Transvaal, to guard against which, the above troops are intended. Comment is superfluous.[6]

While the British in Natal were being hard pressed by the first spectacular successes of the Boer commandos, hundreds of miles to the west Mafeking was surrounded and Boer shells were exploding in the town. In fact, in true South African style, it was virtually two towns, for it consisted of the white settlement, and, physically separated from it, the Barolong capital Mafikeng (the Place of Rocks) founded in 1857, from which the white township took its name when *it* was set up in 1885. Like Gandhi, Plaatje was enchanted by the phrase "British subject", and throughout his political life laboured to turn its applicability to Black South Africans into hard reality. The British commander in Mafeking was, of course, Col. R.S.S. Baden-Powell, later to become the Great White Chief of the Boy Scouts Movement. During the siege, Barolong raids on the Boer herds of cattle contributed considerably to Baden-Powell's ability to hold out, though when rations had to be severely cut, the Barolong had their supplies reduced long before the same hardship affected the white inhabitants. Eventually Plaatje had to help organise the evacuation of hundreds of Barolong through the Boer lines under cover of night, in order to conserve food supplies. Nevertheless, thanks to traditional Barolong-Boer enmity, Plaatje identifies himself completely with the British in his *Diary*, and scathingly refers to the Boers as "Women Slayers" and "women murderers."[7] This entry, for 9 December 1899, shows the extent of that identification, despite the slightly sardonic edge to the comment :

> Too little, if anything, has been said in praise of the part played by that gallant Britisher—the Barolong herdboy. Cattle are now grazing on what may be termed "disputed" territory, just where the Dutch and English volleys cross each other; and it is touching to see how piccaninnies watch their flocks, and how in the bright sunshine along the wide plain south and west of the Stadt [i.e. Mafikeng]....the Dutch artillerist would turn his attention to them....They [herdboys] would quietly mind their stock or drive them home under a severe shell fire with the tenacity of the African in all matters where cattle are concerned.[8]

When news of the early British reverses in the war percolated into Mafeking in January 1900, Plaatje grew very despondent and wrote :

> I am inclined to believe that the Boers have fully justified their bragging, for we are citizens of a town of subjects of the richest and the strongest empire on earth and the Burghers of a small state have successfully besieged us for three months—and we are not even able to tell how far off our relief is. It is certain that this cannot be too near ...It is a shame on the part of the Imperial Government to "kgotla semane" [disturb a hornet's nest] before they have tested their abilities to face it. Now let us square the account while they lounge on couches in London City, reading their newspapers and smoking their half-crown cigars.[9]

Plaatje's *Diary* gives us the only authentic account there is of what the Black inhabitants suffered during the siege. Apart from those killed in action and as runners and cattle-raiders, many died of starvation. On 21 March 1900, Plaatje writes : "It is really pitiful to see one who was too unfortunate to hear soon enough that there was a Residency [with a soup kitchen] in Mafeking, and, being too weak to work, never had a chance to steal anything during the last 6 days, and so had nothing to eat.

Last month one died in the Civil Commissioner's yard. It was a miserable scene to be surrounded by about 50 hungry beings, agitating the engagement of your pity and to see one of them succumb to his agonies and fall backwards with a dead thud."[10]

I am sure that Comaroff is right in his view that Plaatje did not intend the diary to be published, that he kept it for his own personal satisfaction and perhaps in order to practise setting down his impressions and thoughts on paper, just as he used some of the entries to practise his newly acquired skill at shorthand. Most of it must have been written in the intervals in his activities as interpreter, as general liaison man between the Civil Commissioner and the Barolong, and as paid typist to various newspaper correspondents covering the siege. Here and there one finds him attempting an elegant turn of phrase, as on 13 November 1899, when he reports : "Only two shells came in from 'Sanna' [nickname of the Boer 94-pounder siege-gun] and Mausers not quite a thousand." Then, as an afterthought he adds in parenthesis : "(Shelling slow and Mausering mild.)"[11] On the other hand, the very first entry, for 29 October 1899, shows the embryonic stylist, who was to write the novel *Mhudi* some eighteen years later, attempting an experiment with imagery :

> To give a short account of what I found war to be, I can say : no music is as thrilling and as immensely captivating as to listen to the firing of the guns on your own side. It is like enjoying supernatural melodies in a paradise to hear one or two shots fired off the armoured train; but no words can suitably depict the fascination of the music produced by the action of a Maxim, which to Boer ears, I am sure, is an exasperation which not only disturbs the ear but also disorganises the free circulation of the listener's blood.[12]

This rather heavy-handed gunfire/music comparison continues for another half-page or so. On the whole, however, the diary is an unpolished, utilitarian document, and the impact that it makes depends almost entirely upon its eye-witness, on-the-spot, reportage quality.

In the years after the Boer War, Plaatje, like Gandhi, was to work with all his abilities for the freedom of his oppressed people. In India, Gandhi took on successfully the might of the Empire to whose service he had given himself in South Africa in 1899 and 1906, whereas by 1913 Plaatje found that, in his vain efforts to prevent the passing of the Natives' Land Act by the Parliament of the Union of South Africa, he was ironically not opposed obviously by the Imperial power, but by its successors in South Africa, the Boer generals, Botha and Smuts, whom the British had militarily defeated eleven years earlier. The Natives' Land Act fulfilled all Plaatje's fears, by becoming the foundation of subsequent South African apartheid legislation. As we all know, Plaatje's efforts for Black South Africans have proved as unavailing as Gandhi's years of South

African labour on behalf of the largest concentration of people of Indian origin who live beyond this subcontinent—the Indians of Natal.

As I remarked at the beginning, I have not attempted to do justice to Gandhi's *Autobiography*, but a glimpse of what I have ignored can be gathered from his description of how his thoughts were tending while he actively ministered to the Zulu wounded during the uprising of 1906, when he led the volunteer Indian Ambulance Corps : "Marching with or without the wounded, through these solemn solitudes, I often fell into deep thought. I pondered over *brahmacharya* and its implications, and my convictions took deep root...So thinking, I became somewhat impatient to take a final vow. The prospect of the vow brought a certain kind of exultation. Imagination also found free play and opened out limitless vistas of service."[13]

By contrast, it is doubtful whether "deep thought" ever enters into Deneys Reitz's *Commando*. The "limitless vistas" of its pages are almost wholly geographical, and yet at the heart of *Commando* is a thoroughly unselfish, vital commitment to service in a forlorn cause that Gandhi would have responded to immediately. It is a tale of extraordinary physical and moral endurance. Reitz's own account of how it was written in exile in Madagascar in 1902-1903 forms the last paragraph of a book about being at the receiving end of imperialist might, and I think that the tragedy of Afrikanerdom is that the Afrikaners were never able to understand that their Black and Brown fellow-South Africans were as much the victims of imperialism as they themselves. *Commando* ends like this : "At present we are eking out a living conveying goods by ox-transport between Mahatsara on the East Coast and Antananarive, hard work in dank, fever-stricken forests, and across mountains sodden with eternal rain; and in my spare time I have written this book."[14] That final, throwaway clause perhaps holds the secret of the enduring literary worth of *Commando*. The most remarkable feats of daring, endurance, and youthful zest, all of them factually true, most of them reading like the products of a skilful novelist's imagination, are retailed as if they were everyday occurrences that don't deserve wondering at.

Reitz's father, Francis William Reitz, was President of the Orange Free State Republic from 1889 to 1896. A year or two later, he moved to the Transvaal, where President Kruger appointed him Secretary of State (Foreign Minister). It was he who drafted the ultimatum to the Imperial Government that led to the outbreak of the Boer War in 1899. The father and three of his sons fought right through the war, refused to take the oath of allegiance to the British monarchy after the peace treaty in 1902, and went into voluntary exile as irreconcilables. Deneys Reitz was seventeen when the war began, and what particularly characterises *Commando* is his rare gift, in the use of the conqueror's language, for conveying the open-minded, ingenuous freshness of his seventeen-year-old perceptions when he wrote them down at the age of twenty-one or twenty-two. In a few words he captures the heady excitement produced by the outbreak of war :

> War was officially declared on October 11th. At dawn on the morning of the 12th, the assembled commandos moved off and we started on our first march.
>
> As far as the eye could see the plain was alive with horsemen, guns, and cattle, all steadily going forward to the frontier. The scene was a stirring one, and I shall never forget riding to war with the great host.[15]

And a little later, as they looked down upon Natal :

> With one accord the long files of horsemen reined in, and we gazed silently on the land of promise. General Maroola, with a quick eye to the occasion, faced round and made a speech telling us that Natal was a heritage filched from our forefathers, which must now be recovered from the usurper. Amid enthusiastic cries we began to ford the stream. It took nearly an hour for all to cross, and during this time the cheering and singing of the "Volkslied" were continuous, and we rode into the smiling land of Natal full of hope and courage.[16]

This boyish relishing of the glory of riding to war was soon to give way to Reitz's first experience of the grim reality, after the defeat of a detachment of British troops in which he took part : "Officers and men were dressed in drab khaki uniforms, instead of the scarlet I had seen in England, and this somewhat disappointed me as it seemed to detract from the glamour of war; but worse still was the sight of the dead soldiers. These were the first men I had seen killed in anger, and their ashen faces and staring eyeballs came as a great shock, for I had pictured the dignity of death in battle, but I now saw that it was horrible to look upon."[17]

The Boers routed the British in these first encounters in Natal, but lost the initiative when General Joubert, the aged and inept Commandant-General, failed to exploit his successes and quoted the old saying : "When God holds out a finger, don't take the whole hand."[18] Had Joubert pursued the retreating British while his army of 15,000 horsemen was still intact, it is very likely that the Boers would have occupied the whole of Natal and won the war. Instead they invested Ladysmith. In describing the fighting in these early days, Reitz mentions how with some of his fellows he had come upon "a party of Indian dhoolie bearers, who had brough down some wounded English soldiers."[19] They must have been member of the Indian Ambulance Corps that Gandhi had organised and was serving with on the Natal front.

Reitz took part in the Boer recapture of Spion Kop on the Tugela

River, which thwarted General Buller's second attempt to relieve Ladysmith. He tells of the carnage the Boers found on Spion Kop, after they had dislodged the troops who had held it for about twenty-four hours :

> In the shallow trenches where they had fought the soldiers lay dead in swathes, and in places they were piled three deep.

> The Boer guns in particular had wrought terrible havoc and some of the bodies were shockingly mutilated. There must have been six hundred dead men on this strip of earth, and there cannot have been many battlefields where there was such an accumulation of horrors within so small a compass.[20]

Once the British breached the Tugela line in Natal in February 1900, which coincided with the relief of Kimberley in the Cape Colony and the capture of General Cronje and 4,000 men at Paardeberg in the Orange Free State, large-scale battles were virtually at an end. The Boers, of course, had no professional army, no uniforms, no organised paraphernalia of war. Their forces consisted of ordinary citizens who supplied their own horses, rifles, ammunition, and such foodstuffs as they could cram into their saddle-bags, and they got no pay. For supplies in the field they relied on foraging, and, later in the war, on captured British supply wagons. Reitz himself was soon using a captured British Lee-Metford rifle, and once, when he and some companions had run out of ammunition, they simply followed in the wake of a British column and picked up unused cartridges dropped by British troops, until their bandoliers were full again. Then off they galloped to another skirmish with their suppliers. The Boer forces consisted of commandos of varying and constantly fluctuating size. Discipline was slack and men moved almost at will from one commando or makeshift unit to another.

In this way Reitz in the two-and-a-half years of the war covered a prodigious extent of the interior of South Africa. From the Natal defeat, he moved into the Transvaal and then down into the central Free State to join in the hopeless Boer rearguard actions against Lord Roberts's relentlessly advancing superior forces, which swept across the Free State plains, entered the Transvaal and occupied Johannesburg and Pretoria. In July 1900 began a similar Boer skirmishing withdrawal before the British drive east along the Johannesburg-Delagoa Bay railway line, and again Reitz was in the thick of it. When, after this drive, General Botha reorganised the scattered commandos and the conflict entered the bitter phase of guerrilla warfare that was to last for two years, Reitz again played an active part, narrowly escaping death and capture on innumerable occasions. Up into the Eastern Transvaal under Botha, then hundreds of miles across the country to the Western Transvaal under de la Rey, to within a day's ride of Mafeking, where the siege had been raised seven months before. Then

back again across the whole width of the Transvaal in response to a call
from Botha, hard-pressed by Kitchener's new tactics of great systematic
sweeps, with the British rounding up Boer women and children and sending them to concentration camps, while every Boer farm was burnt, crops
destroyed, livestock driven off or killed. Reitz's sparse, controlled style
conveys a dramatic sense of the resulting devastation—in the Free State,
for instance : "We passed the *dorp* of Bultfontein on our way and looked
in for what we could find, but the place was gutted. For the rest we rode
over interminable plains devoid of human beings. We did not see a single
homestead that was not in ruins, and at some places lay hundreds of sheep
clubbed to death or bayoneted by the English troops, in pursuance
of their scheme of denuding the country of live-stock to starve out the
Boers."[21]

During the last year of the war, Reitz was a member of General
Smuts's 300-strong commando that made an audacious raid into the Cape
Colony. This truly epic adventure occupies the second half of *Commando*,
and it is here that Reitz's vivid, racy narrative, unpretending, ingenuous,
and frank, becomes a compelling, epic-like account of what the human
body and spirit are capable of when tested to the uttermost limits. From
the Orange River, down into the plains and mountains of the Eastern
Cape, constantly harried by superior British forces that would otherwise
have been on the trail of the Boer units in the Transvaal, Smuts's
commando went moss-trooping, frequently evading capture by unbeliev-
able exploits on precipitous mountain-sides, through forests, in one of the
bitterest winters South Africa had ever known. For some time the only upper
garment Reitz had was a grain-bag with holes cut in it for neck and arms;
one bitterly cold night it froze solid on his body, "like a coat of mail."[22]
Twice they crossed the 5,000-foot Swartberg range in the South-Western
Cape, some 300 miles from Cape Town, and at one point were within sight
of Table Mountain, and, a little fancifully, contemplated a raid upon Cape
Town. Then back inland, across the semi-desert Great Karoo, until they
effectively controlled hundreds of square miles of the North-Western Cape
Colony, from the Orange River southwards to within some 200 miles of
Cape Town.

By simply recounting his personal experiences on horseback across the
vast distances of the South African landscape, Reitz's book generates a
design not unlike the related movements of a symphony. The physical
features of the landscape strip the human struggle being enacted upon it to
the most elemental levels of endurance and sheer survival, yet in the telling
the struggle is elevated to what I do not hesitate to call Homeric proportions. Of course, Reitz was by no means unacquainted with literature;
indeed he knew at least one work of what we now call Commonwealth
Literature, for on one occasion he writes of "a deep valley that reminded
me of Dreadful Hollow in *Robbery Under Arms*."[23]

In 1902 Smuts's commandos in the North-West Cape besieged the copper-mining town of O'Okiep, so that the British had to send a relief force by sea from Cape Town to Port Nolloth. At this point Smuts was summoned to the peace conference at Vereeniging in the Transvaal, and he took Reitz with him. It was the end for the exhausted and worn down Boer fighters, and the two republics became part of the British Empire.

Within two decades Smuts was a general in the British Army and a member of Lloyd George's Imperial War Cabinet. In 1940 he was made a British Field Marshal. Reitz, his companion in fighting and later in politics, underwent a similar metamorphosis. In 1918 he was a British colonel in command of the First Royal Scots Fusiliers in France, and recovered from severe wounds in time to lead his battalion into Germany. What turned the Boer general and the Boer irreconcilable of 1902 into fervent supporters of the Imperial concept only a few years before Gandhi abandoned that ideal, and started in earnest the long struggle for Swaraj in India ? It is a highly ironic reversal of roles, the irony doubled by the fact that Gandhi's major opponent in his efforts on behalf of the Natal Indians between 1910 and 1914 was no longer the Imperial Government, but Smuts, as a cabinet minister in the independent South African government. There is no doubt that Smuts, Botha, and Reitz regarded the granting of responsible government to the two conquered republics in 1907 as an imaginative act of British generosity. Perhaps, unconsciously, they also apprehended the truth that with the final departure of Imperial troops from South Africa in 1912, the coalition of Boers and settlers of British origin had become the inheritors of Imperial power in Southern Africa. It was possible because, as Plaatje reminds us in his quotation from a letter that Baden-Powell wrote to the investing Boer forces at Mafeking, and as Reitz openly reveals, there was a tacit understanding that the war between Britain and the Boers was a white men's war. Hence too, Gandhi's difficulty in getting even the non-combatant services of the Indian Ambulance Corps accepted by the military authorities. In violation of normal white South African political historiography, Botha, Smuts, and their supporters can therefore be regarded as Transitional Afrikaner Nationalists who made possible the reincarnation of both the old Boer policies and the old methods of empire, when Dr Malan's all-Afrikaner government came to power in 1948 as the ultimate upholders of the very imperialism they so bitterly execrated, and had so grievously suffered under.

I think the last words should be Gandhi's : "It has always been a mystery to me how men can feel themselves honoured by the humiliation of their fellow-beings."[24]

REFERENCES

1. M.K. Gandhi, *An Autobiography or The Story of My Experiments with Truth*, trans. Mahadev Desai, Ahmedabad, Navajivan Pblg. House, 1927; references 1959 edn., Solomon T. Plaatje, *The Boer War Diary of Sol T. Plaatje : An African at Mafeking*, ed. John L. Comaroff, London, Macmillan, 1973; references Sphere Books edn., 1976; Deneys Reitz, *Commando : A Boer Journal of the Boer War*, London, Faber & Faber, 1929; references 1935 edn.

2. Gandhi, op. cit., p. 156.

3. Gandhi, *Non-Violence in Peace and War*, Ahmedabad, Navajivan Pblg. House, 1942, 1948 edn., Vol. I, p. 21.

4. *ibid.*, pp. 22-23.

5. *Experiments with Truth*, p. 124.

6. *The Collected Works of Mahatma Gandhi*, Delhi, Publications Division, 1960, Vol. III, p. 112.

7. Plaatje, *Boer War Diary*, p. 134.

8. *ibid.*, p. 67.

9. *ibid.*, pp. 94-95.

10. *ibid.*, p. 144.

11. *ibid.*, p. 42.

12. *ibid.*, p. 34.

13. *Experiments with Truth*, p. 233.

14. Reitz, *Commando*, p. 325.

15. *ibid.*, p. 24.

16. *ibid.*, p. 26.

17. *ibid.*, pp. 30-31.

18. *ibid.*, p. 44.

19. *ibid.*, p. 41.

20. *ibid.*, pp. 79-80.

21. *ibid.*, p. 189.

22. *ibid.*, p. 223.

23. *ibid.*, p. 278.

24. *Experiments with Truth*, p. 112.

28

A Note from the Third World towards the Re-definition of Culture

LLOYD FERNANDO

I

THE recent discovery of the Tasaday tribe, in Southern Mindanao in the Philippines, is the latest and most striking instance of the impossibility of living apart from the entire community of man in the twentieth century.[1] To protect the Tasadays, the Philippine Government benevolently established a 46,000-acre forest reserve around their primitive valleys, but the anthropologists, journalists and television cameramen who have already passed through will no doubt be followed by countless others; and the Tasadays, just like the rest of us, are faced with the challenge of having to learn the difficult art of relating insistent, new complexities to old, stable ways. We should not commit the error of classing the outsiders as despoilers and the Tasadays as wholly innocent would-be victims. Already the Tasadays themselves are curious about the rest of the world, suggesting to a government official that "it might be good to have just a look outside the forest." How that look will modify their lives, what it will cost them, only time will tell. They do have a tribal saying which declared their kinship with us long before they knew us : "Let us call all men one man" —a reassurance that they do not need to be only learners in facing the twentieth century.

This example of the Tasadays illustrates one of the paramount problems of learning about culture in the modern era—that of understanding how individuals as much as whole societies cope with bicultural and multi-cultural contexts, that is, with situations in which differing cultural norms and ideals are found together. (For convenience I will use the word bicultural to cover multi-cultural contexts as well.) The proper

span for examining this topic is the last four hundred years, and if we do
our work well we should be able to discern the essentials of a humane
vision for the next four hundred. During the first three hundred and
fifty years of this period (beginning, say, with Magellan's and Drake's
voyages round the world in 1519 and 1577), bicultural contact was
enforced by curiosity, greed, missionising zeal, and military conquests on
the part of waves of European invaders beginning with the Spanish, going
on to the Portuguese, Dutch, British, French, and latterly, Americans.
The conquistadores, the military governors, the company agents, the Resi-
dents and their followers parcelled out the world between them. They
upheld a monocultural viewpoint. Their territories overseas were merely
extensions of their respective homelands, and the strange inhabitants over
whom they held sway people who would be assimilated to the "parent"
culture, or suffered to continue existence as secondary beings. In the
present century, the so-called Axis powers, Italy, Germany and Japan,
virtual newcomers in the techniques of territorial annexation, unwittingly
brought this phase of militarily enforced culture-contact to a ferocious
climax. By taking the principle of conquest and domination to its extreme
limits, they achieved a kind of *reductio ad absurdum* in which military
aggression against other cultures and exaggerated notions of cultural
purity were perceived to be anachronistic in the modern world.

But there has been no let-up. In the last fifty years the original
imperialistic impetus has been taken over by a technological one through
the proliferation and increasing sophistication of all forms of communication, whether through travel or the media. Very few nations or individuals can now remain in ignorance for long about details of the
dominant cultures of the world which, as it happens, are drawn from the
original colonial powers. In a slightly more enlightened age, and by a
kind of compensatory reverse logic which is worth examining in more
detail, the essential movement of peoples and cultures is now much more
a two-way process, with many Asians, Africans and others of the so-called
Third World moving to and settling down in the national territories of
former aggressors. The peaceful migration of other peoples as well in
different directions is one of the most interesting cultural phenomena of
post-World War II years. Poles, Yugoslavs, Indians, Chinese, Koreans,
Filipinos, Vietnamese and others have shifted to new homelands carrying
with them their cultural values including language, customs, food pre-
ferences and world views.

Nearly all of us, then, all over the world are united at least in facing
the problem presented by different cultural norms co-existing, easily or
uneasily, within the boundaries of our respective nations. We have to
re-order, accept, or discard elements from a diverse area of beliefs,
assumptions, modes of communication, customs and habits because,
despite significant variations, we have become aware of the new dimension
in the development of cultures : the last fifty years have confirmed us all

in a bicultural phase which had been building up for the previous three centuries. Cautiously, I advance this as a principle epitomising the underlying tension in everything we say and do nowadays. We search for unity, homogeneity, while being confronted by the reality of heterogeneity. The intermingling of races and cultures all over the world has compelled us to face the test of giving a valid meaning to the Tasadays' brilliantly pithy prescription from the Stone Age, "Let us call all men one man."

II

Joseph Conrad's *Heart of Darkness*, E.M. Forster's *A Passage to India*, William Faulkner's "A Rose for Emily", Raja Rao's *The Serpent and the Rope*, Wilson Harris's *Palace of the Peacock*, Shahnon Ahmad's *Ranjau Sepanjang Jalan*, Achdiat Mihardja's *Atheis*, Patrick White's *Voss*, and N.V.M. Gonzalez' *The Bamboo Dancers*, between them spanning the last seventy-five years, are examples of works which reveal the complexity of possible responses to the promise, or threat, of a bicultural universe.[2] Works of high literary merit such as these enlighten us directly or indirectly in this area of cultural relations, while lesser works and popular reading matter will do so unwittingly, if we know how to look. The entire spectrum of works from the serious to the popular deserves fresh scrutiny. While works of this century will attract prime attention, I have outlined historical reasons why one may go to works in previous centuries to increase one's understanding of the new ways of growth of cultures which are in enforced or involuntary contact.

There are enough hints in works of modern literature to suggest the classes of response (to this phenomenon) about which we need to know more. Firstly, there is the rejection of bicultural growth, and the resolution to go back to one's own heritage in the hope that homogeneity may be restored. The forms which this choice may take will be varied. The writer may be lyrical, dogmatic, idealistic, scholarly, despairing, or bitter. Few writers individually will exhaust the meanings and implications of such a decision; few also will be completely categorical in making this choice. To speak only of Asian writers in English, we see traces of this attitude in such writers as Manmohan Ghose (India), Lakdhas Wikkramasinha (Sri Lanka), and Mohammad Haji Salleh (Malaysia) who suddenly found a certain incongruity in writing in English, and either became completely silent or took to writing in their respective national languages.[3] All good writers seek to rediscover what the Tasadays call "the stump of our feelings", the native pith which could rearm them for the task of taking the jangling heterogeneity of the modern world in their stride. The discipline of seeking to be most oneself is the fundamental basis of cultural growth, and writers in post-colonial societies especially have realised that it is that basis which has become obscured, and in some cases even scotched, by centuries of foreign domination. The attempt to retrieve the essentials of a native past, far from being retrogressive, is vitally necessary, and the talented writer who sets out to rediscover the strength of his own linguistic heritage puts first things first, in wanting to know himself more truly to balance what he knows of others. In a very few instances a writer may believe he can help to restore a culture wholly to its original pristine identity by this or similar means. He finds that his culture has been too "open" to influences from everywhere and now wishes it wholly "closed". Given the complexities of the modern world, that is a near-impossibility.

There are questions of cultural and psychological ambivalence here which deserve exploring further. One has to look at the Malaysian novelist Shahnon Ahmad's *Ranjau Sepanjang Jalan* (1966) to see what the values and the hazards of a "closed" culture system might be. This superb novel, translated into English as *No Harvest but a Thorn* (1973), depicts a closed culture piercingly enough to celebrate it, but it also tacitly exposes its vulnerabilities. While it dramatises a bedrock of native vitality which vividly defines its characters, it equally highlights the physical and the moral toll of depending exclusively on traditional ways of living. The mention of the trader in the city to whom the Malay peasant hero's land is mortgaged, and of the tractor which alleviates the peasant family's misery temporarily, are striking reminders in the novel of the threat as well as the promise of heterogeneous growth in the offing, but somehow not faced. At the end of this novel, Lahuma the peasant has died, his body bloated through tetanus caught in the padi field, and Jeha his wife who has gone mad has to be put in a makeshift cage along with harvested rice. The symbolism of their fates, while obvious, is not the less powerful for that. William Faulkner's short story, "A Rose for Emily", similarly links compassionate concern for the Southern heritage to a clear-eyed recognition of the decay that has eaten into the heart of a culture which strove to be sufficient unto itself alone. This theme runs through Faulkner's major novels, too, such as *The Sound and the Fury* (1929) and *Light in August* (1932).

The second class of response is the opposite of the first. Here writers appear to face the challenge of bicultural development squarely, no matter which language they use. Raja Rao (India) and Achdiat Mihardja (Indonesia) are examples. The first is scholarly, the second coolly observant. The works of both writers are nevertheless suffused by a meditative melancholy which greatly increases the artistic impact of their creations. They show a rare ability to discriminate essentials from ephemera. They offer evidence of the immense intellectual and emotional energy needed to arbitrate between co-existing cultural norms. Mihardja's *Atheis* (1949) analyses both threat and promise in a homogeneous society similar to Shahnon's, but one which is open to the busy traffic of ideas and values in the world at large. The novel rests on a structure of unobtrusive symbols which hint at the submerged conflicts between old and new which the protagonist Hasan experiences. When Hasan involuntarily vomits on being told by his friends, Kartini and Rusli, that he has eaten pork at their table, his physical distress in unwittingly breaking a taboo of his faith signifies equally the repulsion he feels from the depths of his being for the Marxist ideas of his friends which he has just accepted with his mind but not with his innate spirit. The end of this novel is as stark as that in Shahnon's. Jakarta is blacked out in anticipation of a Japanese air raid. Searchlights scour the dark night-sky for the unseen enemy, while Hasan huddles in a makeshift shelter amidst strangers—symbolically as if, having been opened to the heterogeneity of the modern world, Hasan's society itself has had its vision obliterated and does not know which direction to take now. If reliance on "the stump of our feelings" has its hazards, so too does the unwary acceptance of heterogeneity.

These examples illustrate the point that biculturalism is a potent factor even in relatively homogeneous societies. Such societies cannot remain "closed" for long, for modernisation, or if they are not careful, Westernisation, or Americanisation—which are its adulterated forms—cannot be escaped. There must be numerous other similar works which throw additional light on this question, in apparently homogeneous contexts, which can enable us to learn more of the cultural problem bounded by these two works— Shahnon's depicting a "closed" culture, and Mihardja's an "open" one. Lesser writers in the same category reveal themselves to be whole-hearted followers of "influences" or currently dominant literary trends. These, by their readiness to be swamped by fads, cheapen literary controversies concerning the tension between what is foreign and what is native, but demonstrate thereby the hazards of "open" cultures—that is, cultures receptive to all influences without prejudice. Too many writers discover that simple, unbiassed openness is an impossibility. Dominant literary and artistic trends from the developed world overwhelm them too easily.

In the third category are those writers who deal with the contradictions, dilemmas, minor tragedies and minor successes of life in a confusing bicultural context where ultimate goals are undiscernible, and the meaning of the past is inexplicable. They document the detailed realities of private lives, their works represent the diverse partial visions of artists who may be talented enough but lack a driving thoroughness of perspective to raise their achievement to the first rank. Many writers in this category are possibly too enamoured of their "uniqueness" (which is the opposite concept to "national identity"). Blessed with a degree of talent, they are deceived into believing they have no responsibility to educate themselves outside their craft. As a result they know less than they should, missing the point that given equal literary skills, the writer who shows he knows more is the better. They do not seek wholeness of vision, which is only attainable by going outside oneself into the cultural and spiritual problems of the community in which one lives. In a bicultural world that community will not necessarily be confined to those within politically defined boundaries (which change, often anyway) although it must begin there.

The concept of a bicultural phase in human relations, then, is a fruitful point from which to learn from literature about the ways in which cultures grow in the modern world. Our original condition was a kind of homogeneity, real or illusory, currently possessed or long since lost, which creates a tension with everything which surrounds us today, and gives the writer his impetus for seeking a human continuity which could embrace us all. Most people believe the ideal of homogeneity realised in a place where the inhabitants are of the same ethnic stock, speak the same language, and have the same social, artistic and religious/spiritual systems. There are very few places in the world today where all these conditions are to be found. Writers who yearn for homogeneity nowadays are also more aware of the fascist implications of upholding cultural purity of such a concentrated kind. But even where some measure of homogeneity is to be found, the bicultural challenge cannot be avoided because modernisation and the spread of technology inevitably introduce fresh norms of conduct, value and belief which compete with existing cornerstones of the society, and open it to the interflow between cultures on a global scale. But whatever the additional variations which fresh examples may substantiate, they will be exceeded in complexity by the bicultural realities of plural societies.

III

In addition to the pressures of technological culture, linguistic, ethnic and ideological differences create a situation where different logics of conduct and value operate. The idea of multi-valued logics brought about by cultures which co-exist is one which has hardly been plumbed as yet. Among the few writers who have produced works which indicate the dimensions of the field are Joseph Conrad, James Joyce, E.M. Forster, William Faulkner, and Raja Rao. No one has exceeded Conrad in the power of his demonstration of the extremest challenge presented by differing cultural logics. His short novel, *Heart of Darkness* (1902), works to a terrifying revelation in which the essence of the conflict between alternative logics appears as the opposition between a practice which is at the heart of one culture, and the taboo of this very same practice at the heart of another. For the African tribe which eventually deifies Kurtz, ritual human sacrifice and ritual cannibalism constitute a key ceremony by means of which the chief of the tribe is rejuvenated to guarantee the continuation of good harvests and the maintenance of the general well-being of the tribe.[4] For people from Western countries and other parts of the world this idea is a taboo so ingrained as to evoke the deepest feelings of revulsion. Totally opposite logics upholding totally opposite ideas of right action are in conflict. The issue is so emotionally charged that Conrad approaches this revelation with artistic deliberateness. The density of his prose itself, and the circumspectness of his method suggest a formal and ceremonial approach to a deep mystery which remains hidden in primal mists. Kurtz who reaches the heart of all conflicts between cultures is brutally made aware of the supreme cost of seeking to supplant the logic of another culture with that of his own.

There is a morally disconcerting idea here that all cultural logics are of equal value. If we believe, out of a mistaken liberalism, that we really do subscribe to this view, we should ask ourselves where we stand regarding the cruel dilemma which confronted Kurtz. We may even conclude with Mrs Moore in E.M. Forster's *A Passage to India* (1924) that the opposite is true, that all logics are equally worthless: " 'Pathos, piety, courage—they exist, but are identical, and so is filth. Everything exists, nothing has value' " (Ch. 14). The dark caves at Marabar, the obscure forests in the heart of the Congo, are the ciphers of the respective writers for a terrain of extreme complexity which we must explore more thoroughly.

We will seek to distinguish between three principal kinds of reaction to co-existing cultural logics : that which insists on the primacy of one logic over the others (the colonial mentality); that which insists that logics of cultures are irreconcilable (the apartheid mentality); and that which explores the confusing ways in which cultures merge or interweave or seek to reconcile themselves to one another in the blind hope that we may, some day, be able to call all men one man. Even after a work is classed in any one of these categories, it is very likely that it will not illustrate any one of these reactions emphatically. In the nature of things the most we will be able to find is that a theme or a character tends in one of these ways. But by remaining aware of the three possibilities we have the essential topography of a highly problematic area which every work dealing with more than one culture will help illuminate, wittingly or unwittingly. It is very likely also that most works will fall into the third category, and we shall have to develop special skills to identify features which point to inner agitation colouring the moral impetus towards cultural adjustment. The agitation would be caused principally by the prospect of cultural loss as well as the prospect of adopting unknown new ways. A rather wobbly dream sequence in Lee Kok Liang's short story, "It's all in a dream" (in *Twenty-Two Malaysian Stories,* Heinemann, 1974), and the abstract, intellectual prose of Raja Rao's *The Serpent and the Rope* are revealing indicators by themselves of some of the kinds of responses which the thought of an ultimate confrontation of cultures can inspire.

IV

This brings us to the last of the major problem areas which I wish to touch upon here. It relates to the impact of bicultural realities on the individual psyche. I have dealt with this topic at some length in a long essay on Conrad's South-East Asian Fiction, and therefore I will not go into a detailed explication of it here.[5] Without a developed sensitivity to the nuances of cultural interaction we are likely to miss a large, key area of significance in many literary works, and be content instead with critical analyses of a conventional kind. In the explication of character, for example, Freudian notions are quite inadequate for analysing the psyche faced with confusing cultural norms; tenets of behavioural psychology are not a help, either. A character in a literary work of whatever quality, if we observe him with care, will reveal one of the three attitudes just outlined, to contexts in which cultures commingle. He will continue to assert and struggle to live exclusively by the norms of his own culture, like the British Resident in Borneo in Somerset Maugham's short story "The Outstation" who reads his six weeks' old copies of the London *Times* in sequence, one each morning at breakfast, unaware of either ridiculousness or futility.[6] By the end of that story, the Resident, Mr Warburton, has become psychotic in his efforts to ward off the threat to his deliberately insulated cultural identity. On the other hand the character may surrender his own norms in an effort to adjust to the norms of the dominant culture. This latter process is by no means simple, or brief, or painless, for it involves learning new habits, new customs, a new language, and much else for which no better phrase is available than Lionel Trilling's "culture's buzz and hum of implication"; additionally he will have to cope with the reluctance of some of the natives to accept him as one of them. At the same time he would be doing the reverse with his original culture. Probably no one completes this activity of simultaneous learning and unlearning, and literary criticism has hardly shown itself to be aware of the ways in which an author's interest in the process affects his art, and *vice versa*.

Thirdly, the character may seek out ways in which to adjust some at least of the values of his own culture to some of the values of the culture with which he is in unavoidable contact. Patrick White's *Voss* highlights the kind of faculty needed for intuiting the cultural reality of a "new" old country, Australia, in relation to diverse races, people and landscapes. Yet the sensitive German explorer of this novel dies without fully realising where even his understanding fell short. The aborigine whom Voss would naively befriend in the heart of the continent, as if by a simple offer of friendship he would solve all conflicts, responds to Voss's outstretched hand with instinctively devastating irony :"...[He] took the hand as if it had been some inanimate object of barter, and was turning it over, examining its grain, the pattern of veins, and, on its palm, the lines of fate. It was obvious he could not estimate its value" (Ch. 8). The Caribbean novelist, Wilson Harris, in *Palace of the Peacock* (the first volume of his *Guyana Quartet*), insists on a poetic vision of the unity of men which beautifully assuages the pain and bitterness of Guyana's culturally mixed history. All of James Joyce's works are gradually intensi- fying accounts of the author's efforts to reconcile his Irish heritage to the tradition of Western civilisation and the human race as a whole. *Finnegans Wake* is his final daunting effort in this direction.[7] The only Asian novel I know, where the author pursues the goal of satisfactory adjustment be- tween cultures with an intellectual energy comparable to Joyce's, is Raja Rao's *The Serpent and the Rope*. To discover compatibility with another tradition than one's own one must, in a sense, be a heretic. Rao's protagonist, Rama, finds his research into the Albigensian heresy leading suggestively to a confusing area of thought capable of accommodating simultaneously a version of Buddhism, another great historical heresy. In his intellectual disquisitions, Rama finds that these two major heresies of two of the world's great religious traditions, (Christianity and Hinduism), appear to share common ground, as if they had reached out towards each other. His discovery is ironically contrasted with the actual fate of his own marriage to a French woman, which ends in divorce—on the grounds of incompatibility. This theme deserves closer and more lengthy expli- cation than there is room for here; it is certainly added justification for the novel's deservedly wide popularity among scholars.

The intensive study of a variety of works from different countries against a backdrop of such abstruse possibilities should add significantly to our knowledge of the general processes by which different cultures and classes interweave or diverge. What we will get, if we are successful, will not necessarily be the true sociological picture, but an informed and artis- tic portrayal of how individual minds adapt to, or reject, or master, or are overpowered by conflicting norms within themselves, and in their respec- tive milieux.

But there is one final turn of the screw. A person's cultural substance being virtually second nature to him (it is, quite often, inseparable from his character), he will experience complex stresses and strains resulting from the fear of losing his identity on the one hand, and on the other the fear that he may not succeed in achieving the new identity which he seeks to assume. This condition for which I use the term "detribalisation anxiety" is exceeded in gravity by the ultimate threat, which Mrs Moore faced, and which many of Conrad's protagonists faced, of completely valueless or undifferentiated existence. A person becomes aware, at some point, that the effort of cultural growth and development and the dedica- tion to a widening sensibility have no foreseeable natural conclusion but are part of an unceasing process, capable of continuing as if in infinite series, with every stage of the series having no lasting validity. "One's own personality is only a ridiculous and aimless masquerade of something hopelessly unknown," Conrad wrote in one of his letters.[8] Since "we are 'ever becoming—never being,' " he concludes, in the same letter, that for sanity's sake he will adopt an arbitrary cultural stance—all cultural stances are in the last analysis arbitrary—and "shake my fist at the idiotic mystery of heaven." That is the position which Marlowe, Conrad's narrator, reaches at the end of *Heart of Darkness*, adopting a Buddhistic pose of non-attachment towards the dismaying truth which he has grasped. Heterogeneity in its ultimate forms threatens a kind of valuelessness which accompanies indiscriminate change, where homogeneity at the other end of the scale is a prison. With this realisation Marlowe is ready to reaffirm his native cultural origins with a new wisdom, albeit with a certain sadness as well. The furthermost reaches of cultural intermingling remain part of an original chaos which it is impossible to fathom.

I have sought to show that in seeking to understand the actions of characters in bicultural situations, conventional notions of character formation are undermined, and influential psychological theories are of very limited help. Few authors are concerned to penetrate this area; not many, apart from those whom I have mentioned, appear to be aware of it. But where the instincts and the artistry of other authors combine successfully, we should be able to contrast profitably what their themes and characters do demonstrate against this problematic reality.

V

To contemplate the problems outlined here is, for me, to realise the importance of comparative literary studies in a new way. To speak only of English literary studies, scholars have for too long tended to assume that a sufficient knowledge of the interaction between literature and society and culture may be had from the study of English literature alone or combined with some knowledge of the European tradition. In a bicultural age we need a knowledge of another literature from a quite different cultural area, preferably in the original, or at least in translation, so that we may prevent the study of literature itself from becoming more and more remote from present needs, or from becoming unnecessarily parochial. Western definitions of literary conventions—theatre conventions, for example—and of the image of man, the state and God are nowhere near self-sufficiency. In the field of cultures in contact, Asian literatures have as much to teach as literature elsewhere; the entire field offers a unique way of considering literature as a whole.

Besides being intercultural, our studies will be interdisciplinary as well, bringing in social and historical considerations of the kind mentioned here. The work of critics like T.S. Eliot, Lionel Trilling, L.C. Knights, Raymond Williams, and Northrop Frye and, latterly, George Steiner deserves to be extended beyond the frontiers of Western culture.[9] These have shown always the importance of remaining literary critics while benefiting from knowledge drawn from other disciplines : this seems to me to be crucial. Literary criticism as a form of discourse should always be hospitable to new ideas, but the challenge will be to learn how to use ideas to give the language of literary criticism greater fibre and not to fall between two stools nor embark on a phoney scientism. The hazard for the critic who would learn about culture through literature would be that he might put in jeopardy his primary responsibility to the author and his work through a false exercise in self-justification, and the easiest way to do that these days is to forsake his original premises and methods in favour of those of a more fashionably acceptable discipline.

But the critic will run a cultural gauntlet (besides a methodological one) very similar to that presented by the authors he studies. He will be intellectually aware of a matrix of ideas which the authors treat imaginatively. He too will wish for a simple order while being confronted by complexity. Like the Filipino critic, Rolando Tinio, he may yearn to grow "backwards", rejecting the confusion of the present.[10] On the other hand, he may tend to be too complacent and be content with proven methods applied to a comfortably defined, safe area of study. In between, as usual, will be the man who realises the possibility of new vistas if he is prepared to extend his range to include outstanding literary works from a quite different culture in, preferably, another language. In doing so he will embark upon a programme of redefining goals which might otherwise remain static. Good new work from another culture (or good old work encountered for the first time) is probably one of the best simple motivating forces to the reader to inquire into that culture, mainly because axioms of belief, norms which are held tightly, have a way of becoming unsettled by qualities in a work foreign to the reader. Needless to say, not every good foreign work will do this. Needless to say also, the instinct that the work is good or disconcerting (the words are not necessarily interchangeable) should offer the first impetus : nothing can replace that. Provided the adventurous reader begins there, he can be reasonably certain that he will be engaging in the kind of self-renewal we must all undertake from time to time. The major lesson he will learn is the inadequacy of the tenets of his chosen discipline when confronted by the stream of life whose humane values he wishes to safeguard. He will become freshly aware that the works he reads are compact constructions which alert him, wittingly or unwittingly, to complexities in the culture of the modern world. He may then ponder these complexities in their social, historical and psychological dimensions and bring his hypothesis back from these dimensions to a reinterpretation of the works which have moved him. The process is two-way, from the literature to the culture and back again. What we can reasonably expect from considering literature and culture together is more commerce between the two, and not the distortion of one for the purposes of the other.[11]

REFERENCES

1. See John Nance, *The Gentle Tasaday*, Harcourt Brace Jovanovich, 1975; reviewed in *Time*, June 1975.

2. Joseph Conrad, *Heart of Darkness* (1902); Dent Collected Edition 21 vols (1946-1955); E.M. Forster, *A Passage to India*, 1924, London, Everyman 1957; William Faulkner, "A Rose for Emily" in *The Collected Short Stories of William Faulkner*, 3 vols., London, 1958; Raja Rao, *The Serpent and the Rope*, London, John Murray 1960; Wilson Harris, *Palace of the Peacock*, 1960, London, Faber, 1968; Shahnon Ahmad's *Ranjau Sepanjang Jalan* (1966) translated as *No Harvest but a Thorn* by Adibah Amin, Kuala Lumpur, Oxford University Press, 1973; Achdiat Mihardja, *Atheis* (1949) translated under the same title by R.J. Maguire, St Lucia, Queensland University Press, 1972; Patrick White, *Voss*, London, Penguin, 1956, and N.V.M. Gonzalez, *The Bamboo Dancers*, Manila, Benipayo Press, 1959.

3. Manmohan Ghose is discussed in David McCutchion, *Indian Writing in English* : *Critical Essays*, Calcutta, Writers Workshop, 1964, pp 44-45; Lakdhas Wikkramasinha expresses his own decision forcefully in his Note to his volume of poems *Lustre*, Kandy, Ariya, 1965, p. 41; a selection of Mohammad Haji Salleh's poetry in English is included in *Seven Poets* ed. Edwin Thumboo, Singapore, University of Singapore Press, 1973, while his national award-winning volume of poetry in Malay, his native language, is *Sajak-sajak Pendatang*, Kuala Lumpur, Dewan Bahasa dan Pustaka, 1973.

4. See Stephen A. Reid, "The 'Unspeakable Rites' in *Heart of Darkness*," in *Conrad* : *A Collection of Critical Essays*, ed. Marvin Mudrick, New Jersey, Prentice-Hall, 1966.

5. See my essay, "Conrad's Eastern Expatriates : A New Version of his Outcasts", *PMLA*, 91, No 1 (January 1976), 78-90.

6. *The Collected Short Stories of Somerset Maugham*, London, Heinemann, 1951, vol 3.

7. I have given some grounds for this view in my article, "Language and Reality in *A Portrait of the Artist* : Joyce and Bishop Berkeley", *Ariel*, 2, No 1 (January 1971) 78-93.

8. *Letters from Joseph Conrad 1895-1924*, ed. Edward Garnett, 1928, New York, Charter Books, 1962, p 46.

9. See especially, T.S. Eliot, *Notes towards the Definition of Culture*, London, Faber, 1948; L.C. Knights, *Explorations*, London, Chatto, 1958; Raymond Williams, *The Long Revolution*, London, Chatto, 1960; Northrop Frye, "Literature and Myth" in *Relations of Literary Study*, ed. James Thrope, New York, Modern Language Association of America, 1961; and "The Critical Path : an Essay on the Social Context of Literary Criticism", *Daedalus*, 99, No 2 (1970). 268-342; and George Steiner, *In Bluebeard's Castle : Some Notes towards the Redefinition of Culture*, London, Faber, 1971.

10. Rolando Tinio, "Literature for National Unity", unpublished paper presented at the Afro-Asian Writers' Symposium in Manila, 31 January-3 February 1975, p. 5.

11. This essay was originally presented in a slightly different form at an international seminar on Literature and Culture at the East-West Center, 6-12 July 1975, and was first published in *Southern Review*, 10, No. 3 (November 1977).

29

The Expatriate Experience

EUNICE DE SOUZA

OUT of the many possibilities that a topic such as expatriate writers offers, I have chosen to discuss the work of four writers : Farrukh Dhondy will be compared with Dom Moraes, and Jean Rhys with Ruth Prawer Jhabvala. Each pair has something in common in terms of their situation, but they are different in terms of their attitudes and achievements. Through a comparison of these attitudes, I would like to point out what I consider to be the more worthwhile, the more relevant ways of writing about the Third World.

Reviewing V.S. Naipaul's *In a Free State* in 1971, Farrukh Dhondy made a point relevant to my purpose. (I don't intend to discuss Naipaul, nor do I regard Dhondy's statement on Naipaul as adequate, but the quotation contains some ideas I want to make use of.) Dhondy wrote, "We demand of an artist, especially a writer, that he have his finger on the pulse of the essential creation of his time, more today than ever before. The sustenance that Naipaul drew from the English literary tradition is now inadequate and starves his vision...Naipaul's characters are all emergents from a transient planetary age of mimic men. If we understand his characters better than he does, as I feel I understand Santosh and the other benighted of *An Area of Darkness*, it is because the world has caught up with the mimic men and is steadily decreasing their significance and the significance of looking at people through this assumption."[1]

To my mind, the mimic men are those who wish to be identified with the elite, and whose attitudes to their own people are in conformity with those of the empire builders and the Western elites, British and American. Dom Moraes whose prose works I am considering here belongs to this category. He is of course not the only one.

Dom Moraes, until very recently, made England his home, India an important source of income, and the English literary and social elite his society. The norms of this elite are his source of values, and the only norms he uses to evaluate other peoples. As Verrier Elwin observed to him in the remarks quoted in Mr Moraes' autobiography, *My Son's Father*, "You yourself are a very English person. Your reactions aren't Indian, are they ?...you seem quite naturally to live in a world of English poetry and English painting, and you are an English poet."[2] As if to prove this remark true, Mr Moraes has consistently adopted the Imperial English view of modern India. Standing at Kanheri, he feels, "a kind of vacancy, a hollowness waiting to be inhabited...in Europe I had positive emotions, in India I sank into the dream in which the whole country was sunk."[3]

Nevertheless, in the essay "Living in Delhi" in the collection *From East and West*, he talks of wanting to recapture his sense of identity with the country, despite the fact that he hasn't lived in the country for fifteen years. He attempts a rather romantic way of finding this identity. He tries to recognise the servant Mani as a person, he says, "and (to) be recognised, outside the relationship of employer and servant." "But I had failed," he writes, and then adds characteristically, "and I felt that it was some quality in Indian society that had caused my failure."[4] At no point does Mr Moraes see his attempts as superficial and romantic.

In *Gone Away*, Mr Moraes is content to sail past a few classrooms and observe that the students were noisy and the teachers were ineffectual. "The older and better colleges seemed to produce more disciplined but also more fatuous students. They ask questions but not very good ones."[5] Mr Moraes does not tell us whether he bothered to answer such questions or how. But a serious attempt at recapturing identity would have required him to probe why and how teachers become ineffectual, and students noisy and fatuous in this country. It is not possible to find an identity in a society which you don't make an effort to understand. Further, given Mr Moraes' own shyness as a young man which he talks about several times in his autobiography, one would have thought he would be more capable of understanding others who came from backgrounds much less sophisticated than his own and therefore were socially insecure.

The failure to achieve any sense of identity with the country or even to make any serious attempts in this direction have never, however, stopped Mr Moraes from writing a great deal about this country. He is the son of an illustrious father (this matters in India) and started with high level connections. His works include interviews with Nehru and Mrs Gandhi, the Chogyal of Sikkim whom he refers to by his first name, the Dalai Lama and so on. Unfortunately these connections have given him a fair amount of overconfidence verging on superciliousness, and over the years, a tone of increasingly lofty disdain and petulance. His access to high level contacts has further made him uncritical of himself so that he never stops to wonder whether he is at all adequate to deal with a subject.

A fellow spirit of Mr Moraes, Nirad Chaudhuri advises Mr Moraes to return to England. "If you stay here you will perish. They will not understand you here,"[6] he says. The other standby is of course that

Indians have no sense of humour and therefore cannot stand criticism.

I don't think it is very difficult to understand Mr Moraes or others of his ilk. They find favour in England and America because they do the white man's dirty work without running the risk of being called racial. They create a picture of a country peopled by grotesques and morons, totally incapable of doing anything about themselves or their situation. They do not bother to investigate what state the country was left in by the white men who took all they could from it, and continue to do so in more insiduous ways. Like many elitist liberals Mr Moraes is in fact entirely establishment-oriented. The point is not that there is nothing wrong with the country or that we reject criticism. The point is that Mr Moraes' facile, impressionistic style skims over scene after scene. Nowhere is there any analysis in depth, nowhere any attempt to understand the forces at work in the country he is writing about. There is no point telling us the obvious facts characterising a poor, underdeveloped country. Obvious facts do not turn into profundities because Mr Moraes has uttered them.

In contrast I would like to mention a writer relatively unknown, Farrukh Dhondy. He is Indian and lives in England. He has written poetry, some of which has been published in this country. Recently Macmillan in England published a book of short stories by him, *East End at Your Feet*. I would also like to mention that he has written on social and political subjects for various journals and that he has been for some years now a very successful teacher in a comprehensive school in London. I mention these facts because the experience they refer to are of a piece with the stories. The knowledge and understanding of, and the unbiased characterisation of the immigrant community in England would not be possible without the kind of educational and socio-political work that Farrukh Dhondy is doing in England. He makes no attempt to identify himself or even impress the London literary or social establishment, unlike educated Indians abroad who consider the 'other' immigrants an embarrassment.

It is necessary to mention here that *East End at Your Feet* was published in the Topliner Series for school leavers, and this is why all the stories concern themselves with the problems of adolescent immigrants. Nevertheless the stories have a wide appeal.

The stories concern the conflicts and dilemmas, sometimes poignant, sometimes humorous, that black or Asian immigrants face in England. The people, brown and white, are all recognisable human beings. The Asians are not the unthinking, submissive, static, helpless people that the India of Mr Moraes is peopled with. There is no rhetoric, no romantic glorification of the underprivileged (white or black), no facile denigration of the privileged white. I must mention too, because so many people assume that political and social concern is rarely accompanied by a sense of form, that there is a sure sense of form in the stories. This combination of understanding and a sense of form is a rare one in Indian writing in English, local or expatriate.

Only one story is overtly political, *KBW* (Keep Britain White). Soon after Taher and his family settle in a housing colony of white and Asian working-class families, there occurs a case of typhoid. Rumours in the colony and the papers blow this up as an epidemic, pointing to the immigrants as the source of infection. The white union leader who lives next door to Taher and who is not racial in his attitudes, is worried about the effects of the newspaper reports on the relationship between him and his neighbours. At cricket practice that day, Taher is bewildered to find that nobody will share his mug of cocoa with him. Later a white girl dies of typhoid. A white racist mob invades Taher's home. The white labour leader feels resentful about what the mob is doing to this innocent Asian neighbour but does not have the courage to encounter it. Both families, white and Asian, here were caught up in the pressures created by the racialist whites who want to *KBW* and the press which covertly feeds their frenzy. Each family suffers a humiliation, but in a contrasting way. Another story, *Pushy's Pimples*, deals in a humorous way with a painful situation for a young girl Pushpa from a conservative background, and her English school-friends who snigger at her as she doesn't know much about sex or that pimples are related to the lack of sexual experience. They suggest the way to get rid of them is to sleep with someone. A friend arranges a date, which tragi-comically does not work out.

Ruth Prawer Jhabvala's early novel, *The Householder* and some of her early stories such as *Like Birds, Like Fishes*, are uneven, but sensitive and perceptive in the way that Farrukh Dhondy's stories are. Unfortunately, these qualities have not lasted in her work, and over the years she has come to resemble Dom Moraes. In *An Experience of India*, a book of short stories published in 1966, Mrs Jhabvala says that there is a cycle that Europeans in India tend to pass through, "first stage tremendous enthusiasm—everything Indian is marvellous; second stage, everything Indian is not so marvellous; third stage, everything abominable." For some people, she says, "it ends there, for others it renews itself and goes on. I have been through it so many times that now I think of myself as strapped to a wheel that goes round and round, and sometimes I am up and sometimes I'm down."[7] Further on she says, "I must admit I am no longer interested in India. What I am interested in now is myself in India."[8]

There is a kind of honesty in this statement. But the mere knowledge that she is going through these stages does not produce creative work. As a writer, recognising what is happening to her, she should be careful to see that her writing is not unduly influenced by the phase she happens to be in—otherwise the writing will be unbalanced too—either uncritically enthusiastic or uncritically scathing. Her early and later works show such an imbalance.

After *Like Birds, Like Fishes*, Mrs Jhabvala's work displays too much self-indulgence. In *An Experience of India* she writes that the westernised strata is socially poised but empty. The rest of the people in India are people who "say yes and give in...and (are) meek and accepting and see God in a cow."[9] With attitudes like this, the characters in the books naturally become ethnic curiosities, like Moraes' morons. Formula characters recur throughout her later works, Indians who are grotesque or slothful or ill-mannered. In works in which she appears to like her characters, *The Nature of Passion*, for instance, her attitude is one of patronising affection, as if she were talking of overgrown babies.

In the books which contain characters that are not particularly sympathetic, it is difficult to say what these characters are representative of. What, for instance, does the slothful Gulab of *Esmond in India* represent ? In *Heat and Dust*, for which Mrs Jhabvala has received an award, she descends to third-rate adolescent fiction. The Nawab in this book is so virile that virtually no woman can resist him. He is also a dacoit in disguise.

As in Moraes, there is no attempt to analyse in depth what the characters signify in terms of the society they live in. It is not enough to observe that those of the upper Westernised strata are empty. The fact remains that this strata controls a great deal of power in society. As a result of this unanalytical approach, Mrs Jhabvala's insights are disastrously hackneyed, surfacial and repetitious. Her self-indulgence has destroyed her writing.

It is sometimes argued in defence of writers such as Jhabvala, and the Naipaul of *Area of Darkness*, that the writer's world is "within" and that he is entitled to it. The writer is certainly entitled to his world. But the critic is equally entitled to a value judgement of that world. David Craig puts the point well in his book *The Real Foundations* in a chapter in which he discusses T.S. Eliot. He writes, "Faced with this kind of argument that challenges the poet by relating him to the life he is imaging, the critics riposte subtly that it is naive to 'check' art against life...what matters is not the life we are being made to see anew but the artefact that results, which is sufficient unto itself and no longer relates significantly to what it was 'of' or 'about' in the first place. The one virtue of this view is that it warns us against referring back to life too quickly, before we have allowed the art to affect us fully in its own special way. But to speak as though referring back should never happen at all is wilfully to curtail our experience of art by denying its manifest rich relevance to our actual living..."[10]

In contrast to Jhabvala, it is worth looking at the work of Jean Rhys, a white woman of English descent who was born and grew up in the West Indies, and much later spent time in England and on the Continent. Though she wrote in the thirties, her work has come to be more widely known only in the last ten years or so.

In her stories *Tigers are Better Looking* and the recently published *Sleep It Off Lady*, and in her novels *Wide Sargasso Sea, Good Morning Midnight, Voyage in the Dark* she reveals a strong compassion for the down-and-out of society, the lonely and the vulnerable, the self-destructive personalities. Though English herself, she has not bent over backwards to find favour with the English establishment by caricaturing the 'natives'. Her books are in fact suffused with a deep nostalgia, though not an uncritical or sentimental one, for her West Indian childhood, and her heroines look longingly back from their freezing, bleak, cheap grey England lodgings. England is far from being paradise regained.   The privileged, particularly, are cold, hard, provincial, and seldom if ever manifest the cheerful tole- rance of eccentrics that we have been led to believe is such a character- istic of the British.

In the story *Let Them Call It Jazz*, the English neighbours take it for granted that the West Indian girl next door who likes loud music and dancing can only be a whore.   They persecute her till she retaliates, and then have her picked up by a police van for disorderly behaviour.   In the story *The Lotus*, Lotus is a fading middle-aged white woman who has taken to drink and goes mad from loneliness and runs naked in the street. Not one of the white tenants claims any knowledge of her when the police come to investigate.   The novel *Good Morning, Midnight* is, as Francis Wyndham who is quoted in a review of the book says, not only the story of a "lonely, ageing woman, who has been deserted by husbands and lovers and has taken to drink; it is the tragedy of a distinguished mind and a generous nature that have gone unappreciated in a conventional un- imaginative world."[11]

Though there is so much despair and disaster in the novels, there is a certain astringency of perception in the characters, a searching, unflinching honesty in their assessment of themselves and the society they inhabit, which helps the characters to hold their own, so that they are never merely pathetic or sentimental, and have a dignity denied to the cruel and unsee- ing.   They are the centres of our vision.   Characters—black, white or coloured—are recognisable human beings.   In addition, Jean Rhys has an unerring sense of form.

What we ask of the expatriate writer then is that he be both concerned and analytical as Farrukh Dhondy and Jean Rhys are and Dom Moraes and Jhabvala are not. If the expatriate writer leaves a developing country, for whatever reason, to live in a Western one, or leaves a European country and comes to live in an underdeveloped, neo-colonial country, he has a special responsibility.   His work is meaningful to the extent that he can interpret one group to the other, make these groups see how others see them.   The uncomprehending sneer of an 'outsider' is not merely the easy and irresponsible way out.   It is ultimately destructive, both of individuals and their writing.

REFERENCES

1. *Economic and Political Weekly*, Vol. VI, No. 52, Dec. 25, 1971.

2. *My Son's Father*, Vikas Publishing House, Delhi (date of pub. not mentioned), p. 164.

3. *ibid.*, p. 162.

4. *ibid.*, p. 123.

5. Heinemann, London, 1960, p. 36.

6. *ibid.*, p. 69.

7. John Murray, 1966, p. 7.

8. *ibid.*, p. 8.

9. *ibid.*, pp. 19-20.

10. Chatto & Windus, London, 1973, p. 204.

11. *London Magazine*, Nov. 1966, Vol. 6, No. 8, p. 101.

30

The Immigrant Indian Experience in Literature : Trinidad and Fiji

SATENDRA NANDAN

I

THE Immigrant Indian image in literature reflects essentially the Coolie predicament [which is a strand of the larger and more complex colonial experience. The sociology of slavery spawned the Indenture System— the official euphemistic term for the bondage under which the 'new slaves' were transported from India. The etiological exploration of slavery has, for a long time, dominated the educated consciousness. And rightly so. However, few readable accounts of the Indenture System have been written. The best to my knowledge is Hugh Tinker's *A New System of Slavery*[1]. It attempts a comprehensive and perceptive analysis of an aspect of the colonial reality.

The title of the book is taken from Lord Russell's announcement of 15th February, 1840, which forms its epigraph. Both the date and details are significant :

> I should be unwilling to adopt any measure to favour the transfer of labourers from British India to Guiana ...I am not prepared to encounter the responsibility of a measure which may lead to a dreadful loss of life on the one hand, or on the other, to a new system of slavery.[2]

The historical perspective of the whole adventure of uprooting and transplanting people, basically peasants most of whom hadn't travelled beyond their village, to alien lands across the black seas, is important to the understanding of the coolie predicament as portrayed in literary works. The Indian villagers—poor, oppressed, caste-ridden though most of them certainly were—possessed an extraordinary sense of continuity of tradition and community of life. This gave the vital spiritual resilience to the 'dumb millions' to survive under some of the most abject conditions of existence. With the advent of the coolie trade they had to confront a destiny in unknown lands amidst considerable human and natural hostility. Of course much before them, colonisers, colonists and slaves had made longer journeys but what gives a profound poignancy to the coolie is that, unlike most other migrants, he is often not given a sense of belongingness in countries which he helped create :

> They arrived as coolies, and in many people's eyes they are itinerant coolies still. For slavery is both a system and an attitude of mind. Both the system and the attitude are still with us.[3]

It is the recognition of this reality that has shaped the imagination of creative artists engaged in the exploration of this experience. I shall return to that shortly. For the moment back to the motes of history.

When slavery was abolished in 1833, at least on paper, the tropical planters began clamouring for cheap labour. India and China were the obvious sources : India more obvious because it was cheaper to transport labourers from here and it was a British colony. Thus shiploads of coolies were transported to many parts of the world and, 'the existence of these overseas Indians is the direct consequence of economic exploitation of the colonial power.' Significantly the end of the system was brought about by the outburst of public opinion in Gandhi's India, not, as in the case of slavery, in England. Ironically from most of the coolie countries the conquerors have vanished, their victims survive.

The coolies never really caught the imagination of writers, though they fitfully feature in the journalistic travelogues of some. Anthony Trollope, for instance, wrote in *The West Indies and the Spanish Main* (1859) :

> ...these men [coolies] could not be treated with more tenderness unless they were put separately each under his own glass case with a piece of velvet on which to lie. In England we know of no such treatment for field labourers.[4]

Naturally at a time when the measure for money was sterling and the measure for man was an Englishman, Trollope couldn't have seen things accurately or prophetically, especially as the passage smells of being written under the influence of Jamaican rum rather than any acquaintance with prevailing reality.

The literature of this historical experience has grown out of these wounds of history. The artist attempts to heal, but in the process a deeper vivisection is inevitable and often necessary. Here we are primarily concerned with writers in two contexts : the Caribbean and the South Pacific, more specifically Trinidad and Fiji. Several contemporary writers have attempted to create for us an imaginative understanding of this condition—V.S. Naipaul, Samuel Selvon, Wilson Harris, Shiva Naipaul from the Caribbean. In the South Pacific the first beginnings are being made by a host of writers.[5] For this paper V.S. Naipaul is the central figure in the literary landscape. With his novel, *A House for Mr Biswas*, as the focal point, we shall be exploring, in contrast, the emerging attitudes in the poetry of a couple of poets from the South Pacific. There is a creative nexus between Naipaul's works and these writers whose writings are set in a familiar context and arise out of a familiar pattern of experience.

II

The House that Biswas Built

No one
knows Tom now, no one cares.
Slave's days are past, forgotten. The faith, the dream denied,
the things he dared
not do, all lost, if un-
forgiven. This house is all
that's left of hopes, of hurt,
of history...

—Edward Brathwaite, *Rights of Passage*.

The Middle Passage, Naipaul's response to a journey into the Caribbean, has an epigraph from Thomas Mann's *The Tables of the Law* to reinforce the West Indian reality with an ancient myth :

Because several of their generations had lived in a transitional land, pitching their tents between the houses of their fathers and the real Egypt, they were now unanchored souls, wavering in spirit and without a secure doctrine. They had forgotten much; they had half assimilated some new thoughts; and because they lacked real orientation, they did not trust their own feelings. They did not trust even the bitterness that they felt towards their bondage ![6]

Virtually all of Naipaul's writings deal with the predicament of the 'unanchored souls'. In a dozen works, Naipaul's vision has never faltered; indeed it has widened, with a sense of urgency and immediacy, into a more universal fate, moving into other cultures, other lands, other peoples. However, the underlying, unifying reality is always the same. That he has made the Caribbean experience an integral strand in the pattern of human condition is his signal achievement.

A brief exposition of the historical milieu, which shapes Naipaul's vision and generates his writings, may give us a deeper insight into the writer's world. After Columbus' 'discovery' of the New World in the last decade of the fifteenth century, European settlers arrived and exterminated, with considerable efficiency and speed, the aboriginal Arawaks and decimated the gentle Caribs.[7] Thus the islands were deprived of any indigenous culture that is part of the inner landscape of a post-colonial African, Asian, or Pacific writer. The Caribbean writer therefore lacks a tradition of continuity and a sense of the wholeness of existence.

In the subsequent power struggles of Europe, the islands became vulnerable to pirates and buccaneers. As the potential for sugarcane was realised, slaves from Africa made the middle passage—millions of them. Unlike the situation in the slave states of America, the Caribbean plantocracy never looked at the West Indies as their home. Exploitation and brutality here meant gracious living in Europe. Inevitably, genocide was followed by servitude.

The great mass of the West Indian society is made up of the descendants of slaves; that inheritance has left deep psychic wounds' on the community. The uprooted, transplanted slave's new world was further fragmented as he was separated from his tribe lest he revolt with the others. He lost his landscape, his language and any other meaningful modes of being that he might have carried from his homeland. He was truly the damned of the earth, as Franz Fanon has cruelly but accurately defined him.

In 1833 when slavery was abolished the sugar barons had to look for 'new slaves' from elsewhere. Thus around 1850 the East Indians began to fill the Caribbean melting pot. Unlike the slaves, the East Indian was not totally deprived of his cultural modes and customs. His life was not so severely dislocated. But there was little doubt that he was the 'new slave'.

Naipaul writes primarily about the East Indian community in the Caribbean. Like its predecessors, this too is a destitute society. In *The Middle Passage* he writes about the Trinidad Indian Society as

A peasant-minded, money-minded community, spiritually cut off from its roots, its religion reduced to rites without philosophy set in a materialistic colonial society : a combination of historical accidents and national temperaments has turned the Trinidad Indian into a complete colonial, even more Philistine than the white. (p. 89)

It is this image—the essence of an historical experience—that Naipaul explores; it becomes a portrayal of failure, futility, isolation, dispossession, rootlessness moving inexorably towards a menacing void. The image has grown into a larger metaphor in his recent works, most notably in *In a Free State* and *Guerillas*; indeed it has become his way of seeing and apprehending the world.

In a chaotic, inorganic world, the problem of the talented individual without tradition is how to comprehend the core of this reality and give it significance beyond its locality. Naipaul consequently attempts to interpret and reconstruct a whole nations's unique history until it, like the legend of El Dorado which created that history, becomes 'the narrative within narrative, witness within witness, like finest fiction, indistinguishable from truth.'[8]

III

The post-colonial society—if ever it can become post-colonial—has produced at least three kinds of writers: those who search for roots in the lands of their ancestors; those who discover meaning and a sense of belonging in their own landscape; and those who reject their society and prefer the fate of the perennial exile. Naipaul belongs to the last category. For him such isolation has not meant 'withdrawal, but the detachment of the one from the many which is the necessary precondition of all original thought.'[9] It is his 'perpetual ostracism' that has led to the final triumph of an independent and ironic vision. Some hint of this is given in the characterisation of Anand, Mr Biswas' son :

Though no one recognised his strength, Anand was among the strong. His satirical sense kept him aloof. At first this was only a pose, an imitation of his father. But satire led to contempt and at Shorthills contempt, quick, deep, inclusive became part of his nature. It led to inadequacies, to self-awareness and a lasting loneliness. But made him unassailable.[10]

That Anand later grows into Naipaul is obvious to a reader who knows a little of the writer's background. It fact the fictive biography follows the factual one very closely indeed. As the work develops, it is the novelist's controlling imagination that gives power and depth to the novel, not the bare biographical details of the life of his father.

In his first three novels[11] it is this 'satirical sense' that is predominant. In *Miguel Street*, which epitomises the chain of islands, things are 'crazily mixed up'. The confusion of life, the chaos of values, the lack of norms in a community are reflected with a compassionate insight and the irony of acceptance. The street is the imprisoning world of its inhabitants. It is impotent and deprived : it lacks any meaningful features. The mongrel dog that roams the street is a revealing image.

His other two novels, *The Mystic Masseur* and *Suffrage of Elvira*, deal with religious frauds and political opportunists—clichés of an emerging colonial society. Race, religion and democracy made some colonial peoples fall apart and made them see possibilities which their colonial masters had probably never imagined ! Naipaul writes about a people 'unimportant except to themselves, and faced with all kinds of problems, exhausting their energies in petty power squabbles and maintaining the petty prejudices of petty societies.'[12]   The despair is enveloping and over-whelming. The satire reflects both the brutality and bastardy of the society.

Truth may be stranger than fiction but fiction in Trinidad seems truer. The three early works therefore deal essentially with a fossilised and static society.   The characters accept their condition : there is no character who struggles to assert his personality with an inner dignity and conviction; nor is there anyone whose quest involves going beyond the immediate environment, either morally or aesthetically.   For this personal odyssey we must turn to *A House for Mr Biswas*, Naipaul's next novel.

IV

Naipaul wrote this novel when he was 29. It is 'conceived and executed in the great tradition of the humanist novel, and is as subtle and comprehensive an analysis of the colonial experience as anything in imaginative literature.'[13]   We are given the first glimpse of the coolies :

> In the arcade of Hanuman House, grey and substantial in the dark, there was already the evening assembly of old men, squatting on sacks on the ground and on tables now empty of Tulsi store goods, pulling at clay cheelums that glowed red and smelled of ganja and burnt sacking. Though it wasn't cold, many had scarves over their heads and around their necks; this detail made them look foreign and, to Mr Biswas, romantic. It was the time of day for which they lived. They could not speak English and were not interested in the land where they lived; it was a place where they had come for a short time and stayed longer than they expected. They continually talked of going back to India, but when the opportunity came, many refused, afraid of the unknown, afraid to leave the familiar temporariness. And every evening they came to the arcade of the solid, friendly house, smoked, told stories, and continued to talk of India.[14]

However, the organising theme of the work is the idea of slavery—slavery as the essence of the historical experience. Naipaul explores the consciousness of those who have escaped historical slavery but "carry about them the mark, in their attitudes and sensibilities and convictions, of the slave, the unnecessary man."[15]   The theme is developed in a multitude of details, ideas, and images enacted in the organisation of the Tulsi family. It is a microcosm of a slave society. Hanuman House—the name is carefully chosen for its ironic and metaphorical purposes. It has a mythical dimension as well for Hanuman is the supreme servant of Rama in the *Ramayana*. Biswas' attempt to escape the confines of this stifling 'alien fortress' is the efforts of slaves and coolies to escape from their inhuman bondage, whether from the chains of slavery or caste.

At another level Hanuman House is more immediately symbolic of the

slave world. Mrs Tulsi needs workers to build her empire. She has grasped
the psychology of the slave system.   Like the Caribbean society, Tulsidom is constructed of a vast number of disparate families, gratuitously
brought together by the economic need of the high caste minority. To
accept Hanuman House is to acquiesce to slavery. Mrs Tulsi, the cunning
coloniser, justifies her exploitation with her foxy explanation that she is
really doing her subjects good. Seth in the baluchers is the slave master :
a brutal and brutalising symbol. Mr Biswas' rebellion against social and
personal slavery provides the motivating thrust of the book.

While slavery is the implicit force in the novel, it is the character
of Biswas and his Hindu world that give the work its other resonances.
Naipaul makes the struggle of Biswas so compelling and convincing
because he establishes the suffocating, Hindu world with vividness and
fidelity. Against the solidity of this world, Mr Biswas' efforts acquire
heroic dimensions. It is only when the claustrophobic world is coming
apart that Biswas feels some sense of freedom : his artistic gift—sign painting—leads him to his doom and later comes to his rescue. From disintegrating communalism the novel moves to displaced individualism. It is a
gradual growth for it encompasses a whole culture, a people's whole history.

The terrible inheritance of the past is not denied, but a few possibilities are also revealed through Mr Biswas' quest for a dignified existence.
Biswas' character shows enormous resilience, and a capacity for growth.
This springs from an inner faith in the value of human personality; after
all, 'Biswas' in Hindi means 'Faith'.

In Tulsidom he alone fights in his own ludicrous and brave way the
vulgar, emasculating Tulsi machinery. His struggles are heroic, in a world
where there are no heroes. So it becomes an ordinary, obscure man's
struggle against overwhelming odds. Because the battle involves the conflict between identity and nonentity, and because Biswas is embattled this
struggle with an inner belief, his simple acts are deeply moving.

His rebellion however, becomes positive in terms of human relationships, and his vision of a house of *his* own. His final relationship with
Shama, his wife, is a measure of his achievement. As he is dying in *his*
house :

It gave Mr Biswas some satisfaction that in the circumstances Shama
did not run straight off to her mother to beg for help. Ten years before that would have been her first thought. Now she tried to comfort
Mr Biswas and devised plans of her own.[16]

It is only when Biswas' rebellion is deepened by an awareness of his
human responsibilities and relationships that the house acquires a substantial force. Before this, his several efforts at building his house have resulted
in failure as reflected in his attempts to create a garden :

Untended, the rose trees grew straggly and hard. A blight made their stems white and gave them sickly, ill-formed leaves. The buds opened slowly to reveal blanched, tattered blooms covered with minute insects; other insects built bright brown domes on the stems. The lily-pond collapsed again and the lily-roots rose brown and shaggy out of the thick, muddy water, which was white with bubbles. The children's interest in the garden was spasmodic, and Shama, claiming that she had learned not to interfere with anything of Mr Biswas', planted some zinnias and marigolds of her own, the only things apart from an oleander tree and some cactus, that had flourished in the garden of Hanuman House.[17]

What gives significance to the quality of Biswas' experience is his persistent desire to understand life and to make sense of a chaotic world. This is an infinitely difficult task for a character who is historically displaced and lives in a destitute society in a derelict land. He is an orphan in more than one sense. Mr Biswas' appeal lies in the fact that he has remained himself and the author's achievement is that with creative wit and humour he enables the central character 'to balance his personal inadequacies against the contradictions of existence itself'[18] in a society that offers few possibilities.

Nevertheless, it is not the historicity of slavery, nor the personal history of Biswas that transform history and autobiography into art. The central, integrating and ever-expanding metaphor is the house. As Biswas moves from one strange house to another—be it his father's hut or the 'alien fortress' called Hanuman House—the metaphor gathers meanings and resonances that give a quality of mythical significance to an individual's experience. The final possession of the house, flawed though it must be, is truly a 'stupendous' achievement. Amidst the family, and amongst a lifetime's acquisitions, it stands out :

But bigger than them all was the house, his house.

How terrible it would have been at this time, to be without it : to have died among the Tulsis, amid the squalor of that large, disintegrating and indifferent family, to have left Shama and the children among them, in one room; worse, to have lived without even attempting to lay claim to one's portion of the earth, to have lived and died as one had been born, unnecessary and unaccommodated.[19]

Even for the children the house provides an ordered world, something missed in Mr Biswas' past.

Soon it seemed to the children that they had never lived anywhere but in the tall square house in Sikkim Street. From now on their lives will be ordered, their memories coherent. The mind, while it is sound, is merciful. And rapidly the memories of Hanuman House, the Chase, Green Vale, Shorthills, the Tulsi house in Port of Spain would become jumbled and blurred : events will be telescoped and forgotten.[20]

It is in this environment the children will discover themselves spiritually and aesthetically. It is at this human level the house becomes the central symbol of the novel with universal applicability. Of course it is open to other significances at historical, political, and even metaphysical levels, but because a whole historical experience is portrayed in human and individual terms that we realise, like Mr Biswas, we are all stiffening in rented mansions, though some of us like Mr Biswas, may be lucky enough to have our own laburnum tree. Naipaul's shaping imagination has through this metaphor seen beyond the particular and given it the dimension of a universal symbol. The vision of the house has sustained Mr Biswas through all his fears of a decadent void. The house becomes the creative and positive side of his rebellion. It acquires dimensions of his own identity. The final triumph of his own house is Mr Biswas' most meaningful though ambiguous achievement and in that metaphor lies the book's most enduring, human significance.

On revisiting the Caribbean, Naipaul wrote in *The Middle Passage* :

How can the history of this West Indian futility be written ?... The history of the islands can never be satisfactorily told. Brutality is not the only difficulty. History is built around achievement and creation— and nothing was created in the West Indies.[21]

A House for Mr Biswas repudiates that comment for it is a considerable artistic creation for the writer just as the house is a truly 'stupendous' achievement for Mr Biswas. (Possibly that is the vital difference between the historian and the artist—*The Middle Passage* is the observation of an historian's sensibility, *A House for Mr Biswas* is the vision of creative imagination.) The novel gives a deeper perspective to colonial experience and suggests wider affinities as Mr Biswas is an aspect of the world of Willy Loman and Stan Parker:[22] each attempts to find himself and give us a vision subtler than our own for they are fragments of a larger human quest. It is only when that experience is given the quality of myth that it becomes truly real. *A House for Mr Biswas* stands on that level of reality.

While Naipaul's artistic triumph is undoubtedly of the first order and universally acknowledged, his achievement at another level needs focussing. Until Naipaul wrote his novels, the indentured labourer was featureless. There had been some agitation against the coolie trade in India, but amidst the elemental political struggle for freedom, the coolie theme did not find adequate and sustained expression in the imagination of an enlightened public. Official documents, articles, and research papers on the subject lay gathering dust; a few Ph.D. theses have latterly resulted in books. But it is Naipaul's writings which have given these 'dregs of humanity' a place in the educated consciousness of the world community. For the first time the face of the coolie acquires distinctive features which have the power to disturb a conscience.

Of course the writer may not give a pleasant interpretation of this experience (that is his prerogative) but it is a profoundly compelling one, often poignantly moving. The detached commitment of the artist is not necessarily a negative vision; in fact, often it springs from the very centre of fierceness and concern within him.

That Naipaul has that quality of historical imagination which goes in the making of art is obvious to anyone who has read his formidable history : *The Loss of El Dorado*; that he should have used his powers to create the faceless men and women as images of reality of the colonial experience is his major and lasting contribution to our understanding of the condition of modern man : for Mr Biswas symbolises the irreducible individual's efforts to put 'up a structure in the face of shapelessness, building... a resistance to annihilation.'[23] This is the moving and central reality which confronts us, personally and universally, in literature, but more significantly in our daily lives.

In *The Middle Passage*, Naipaul wrote :

Living in a borrowed culture, the West Indian more than most, needs writers to tell him who he is and where he stands. Here the West Indian writers have failed.[24]

After *A House for Mr Biswas*, much of Naipaul's success in fiction could be interpreted as failure of a kind—of imagination, for it is no longer enough to tell the West Indian what he is but also to reveal in the inner landscape of his existence the possibilities of perpetual becoming. To create life out of life! An interesting contrast would be the works of Patrick White. At one time the Great Australian Emptiness stared him in the face but White with his gift has shown that the blowfly is indeed a variation of the rainbow. He enjoins one to accept and live out one's humanity, not to deny or reject it. Besides, as he said about *The Tree of Man* :

Because the void I had to fill was so immense, I wanted to try to suggest in this book every possible aspect of life, through the lives of an ordinary man and woman. But at the same time I wanted to discover the extraordinary behind the ordinary, the mystery and poetry which alone could make bearable the lives of such people...[25]

Even the poet who wrote *The Wasteland* and *The Hollow Men* could also produce *Four Quartets*. That quality of development doesn't seem to have taken place within Naipaul. He has certainly become a journalist of some genius, but his artistic growth appears to have been arrested and his recent works leave one with a feeling of unsubstantiality—a certain etiolated vision and desiccated spirit dominate. In *An Area of Darkness*, Naipaul took the Indian writers to task for ignoring the obvious. In his own writings he seems too obsessed by it. For too long he has stared at the void, now the void is staring back! Reviewing *In a Free State*, D.J. Enright commented :

> It might be feared that Naipaul is in the process of washing his hand of smelly humanity and therefore of the novel too. In the case of the man who wrote *A House for Mr Biswas* this would be a reason for distress.[26]

Exile, perhaps, always takes its toll—whether it is Rama's, or his children's, or the children of coolies.

V

Moving from Naipaul's world to the South Pacific is like changing to another smaller airline : some features are common, yet there are subtle and significant differences in one's experience of the flight. Historically Fiji is different from Trinidad. The tentacles of colonialism reached the South Pacific much later and by then a few enlightened people in power had realised its withering effects. In Fiji when Sir Arthur Gordon arrived as the Governor, he saw that the need for labour on the sugar plantations was breaking and fragmenting the Fijians' communal way of life. To preserve this and to make the recently ceded colony economically viable, Indian indentured labour was recruited. The coolies began arriving in 1879. Today their descendants outnumber the indigenous population. Thus you have a multicultural society with its tensions and possibilities. Life in Fiji has been looked at through racial and political glasses but rarely through poetic eyes. Of course the Fijians have a rich native oral tradition and the Indians a transplanted culture from India, or at least a semblance of it. But there is a whole unwritten world: to the Fiji Indian the Ganga is holy, seen only through Shiva's third eye, but not the Nandi, on whose banks he has built his home. The desire to nuzzle at the cultural teats of India has often stifled creative expression: cultural cringe is a complex not exclusive to our larger neighbour. That the Indian tradition can enrich and enhance local creativity is obvious but it cannot become a substitute for Fiji's own multicultural tradition, which alone will be the country's most enduring identity.

Consequently the tasks of the Fiji Indian writer are manifold : he has to create a sense of place, a sensitivity to other peoples, build cultural and emotional bridges, to humanise and mythologise the environment, to bring into imaginative existence the world around him, and, above all, to attempt to discover and reveal in art the images of reality in the multi-faceted society—in short, the creation and continuation of a whole local literary culture.

In Fiji Hindi there have been a few minor poets and short story writers. Most of the characters found in Naipaul's early works have become clichés in Fiji Hindi writing. However, there hasn't been a sub-stantial and sustained exploration of our society in images and metaphors that cultivate the imagination of a whole nation.

The first stirrings of self-expression in English by the locals began in the seventies. With the launching of *Mana*, the journal of the South Pacific Creative Arts Society, there was a prolific production of short stories and poems, many by the grandchildren of the coolies. Before these there was only one book in English with the theme of Cooliesm as its major preoccupation. It is a collection of reminiscences of a young Australian overseer in Fiji. It is a sharp and shrewd account of the system and the spirit which pervaded it—a series of pictures not unlike *Miguel Street*. But there is in *Turn Northeast at the Tombstone*[27] by Walter Gill, no pretensions to be artistic. It is not a novel, although it has within it most of the elements that go in the making of a novel.

Among the Fiji-Indian poets there are several and samples of their poetry are to be found in *Some Modern Poetry from Fiji*,[28] edited by Albert Wendt. The volume is slim but significant, not only because it is the first collection of poems by Fiji poets, but more importantly the poems reflect themes and preoccupations of a whole generation. Because the colonial experience is so deeply political in its orientation, as elsewhere in erstwhile countries so in Fiji, the political preoccupations dominate most writers' consciousness. This is a necessary and vital stage in Fiji's literary growth, besides, as Thomas Mann said, modern man's destiny *is* measured in political terms; one hopes that most of these writers will move beyond communal politics into larger concerns and look into the heart of the multicultural milieu, for at least in its writings, Fiji must be more than the sum of its racial parts. That is a major challenge confronting the Fiji writer.

In my volume of poems *Faces in a Village*[29] the concerns are slightly different. For a critical evaluation of the poems, perhaps, I should direct you to Mr Subramani's article.[30] My primary concern in these poems is to create an imaginative understanding of the indentured labourers and to make them part of the Fiji consciousness. Personally for me the dead or the dying old men and women embody the essence of a living reality. Although I write principally of old Indians, I hope that their existence in creative writing will bring to mind others : for old men and women die, always and everywhere, the same death. By exploring this aspect of the Indian experience, one attempts to give some idea of life. It will doubtless bring other realities to mind, but these spring ultimately from one's own.

The colonial educative process has often been the other way round : we memorised the daffodils but failed to notice the hibiscus in our own garden. Through writing one is endeavouring to make this connection; at least make others see the continuities. *Faces in a Village* takes the indentured labourer as the poetic image of the experience : it is rooted in the subterranean sorrows of a forgotten generation. The tensions between the sufferings of the past and the possibilities of the future are regenerative for on the debris life often flourishes with strange abundance.

In the Fiji context, therefore, creative writing in English is very much at an exploratory stage though there is a perceptible trend towards greater commitment both in terms of accepting one's history and living out one's humanity and in attempting to create the imaginative life of a multi-cultural nation, believing in Henry James' memorable phrase that "art makes life". Exile, whether Rama's or Naipaul's, is no answer to Mr Biswas' quest for life.

REFERENCES

1. London, OUP, 1974.

2. *A New System of Slavery*, p. v.

3. *ibid.*, p. 383.

4. *ibid.*, p. xvi.

5. See K. Arvidson's article in *The Mana Annual*—1973, South Pacific Creative Arts Society, Suva, Fiji.

6. *The Middle Passage*, Harmondsworth, Penguin, 1969, p. 42.

7. See Louis James' 'Introduction' in *The Islands in Between*, London, OUP, 1968.

8. Naipaul, *The Loss of El Dorado*, London, Andre Deutsch, 1969, p. 29.

9. Harry Levin, *Refractions*, New York, OUP, 1966, p. 81.

10. *A House for Mr Biswas*, Penguin, 1969, p. 413.

11. *The Mystic Masseur* (1957), *The Suffrage of Elvira* (1958), *Miguel Street* (1959, written first).

12. *The Middle Passage*, p. 253.

13. Francis Wyndham, *The Listener*, 7 October 1971, p. 1.

14. *A House for Mr Biswas*, p. 193.

15. William Walsh, *A Manifold Voice*, London, Chatto & Windus, 1970, p. 71.

16. *A House for Mr Biswas*, p. 7.

17. *ibid.*, p. 376.

18. Landeg White, *V.S. Naipaul : A Critical Introduction*, London, Macmillan, 1975, p. 92 (a valuable book to which I am indebted).

19. *A House for Mr Biswas*, pp. 13-14.

20. *ibid.*, p. 581.

21. *The Middle Passage*, p. 29.

22. See Arthur Miller's *Death of a Salesman* and Patrick White's *The Tree of Man*.

23. Patrick White, *The Living and the Dead*, London, Eyre & Spottiswoode, 1962, p. 20.

24. *The Middle Passage*, p. 73.

25. *Prodigal Son, Australian Letters*, 1, 3, 1958.

26. W. Walsh, *Readings in Commonwealth Literature*, London, OUP, 1973, p. 339.

27. Rigby, Adelaide, 1970.

28. South Pacific Creative Arts Society, Suva, Fiji, 1974.

29. New Delhi, Printsman, 1976.

30. *The Fiji Times*, November 6, 1976, pp. 12-13. See also *Mana Review*, Vol. I, No. II, pp. 72-74.

31

New Language, New World

W. H. NEW

IN 1947, the Canadian chemist Paul Hiebert published a mock literary biography called *Sarah Binks*. The "divine Sarah", as he called his creation—"the sweet songstress of Saskatchewan"—wrote the world's worst verse; the life he invented for her was also absurd; and as a result Hiebert's book is delightfully entertaining. It is also instructive. The satire draws attention to ways in which poets write badly and critics read badly, and implicitly calls for people to recognise how language in literature works. One of Sarah's most awful—and hence "best"—poems is called "Storm at Sea". Landlocked Sarah, Saskatchewan born and bred, had never been near the sea. She knew about prairie storms, railway cars, and woollen winter underwear more than about ships and oceans, so that when her marine knowledge failed her, she made substitutions, drawing on her prairie girl's vocabulary. The poem reads this way :

> A hail, for the sailor who puts to sea,
> When the wind is right, and the sky is free;
> But shed a tear for his sweetheart true,
> If he isn't home in a month or two—
> But shed more tears for the sailor lad,
> When the wind is east—and the weather's bad;
> > Then it's into your woolies
> > And heave, my bullies,
> > And wind up the sails,
> > And pull on the pullies,
> > And shout together, Ship Ahoy—
> > It's going to blow—and boy, oh boy !
> The storm clouds gather, the rigging hums,
> The captain shudders—and here she comes—
> Ripping the shingles from off the deck,
> The wind grows louder and louder, by Heck—
> Ah, many a vessel has been submersed,

> And gone to the bottom, caboose-end first—
>> So it's heave, my hearties,
>> And yell, my hearties,
>> And slug and batter the bell, my hearties,
>> And send out the S.O.L., my hearties,
>> The storm is at its worst.
>> Ah, many a sailor, when help is past,
> Has gone to the bottom, caboose-end last,
> And many a weeping sweetheart true,
> Has counted and waited a month or two,
> Has counted and waited a month at least,
> And written him off as predeceased—
>> So belay, my buddy,
>> And stay, my buddy,
>> And let them bloody-well weigh, my buddy,
>> And stay or stow away, my buddy,
>> When the wind is turning east.[1]

Our concern ought not to be to dwell on the clichéd rhymes, the jogtrot rhythms, the incongruities. *They* show Sarah's awfulness. Critically we should pay attention to *Hiebert's* skill. With a good ear and a sprightly sense of humour, he controls these technical devices, and the way he does so shows us how important a particular vocabulary is in conveying a writer's world.

As "biographer", tongue deeply in cheek, Hiebert declares that the poem shows Sarah being faithful "to the finest tradition of poetry in every age and clime." Of course it does nothing of the kind. More than that, it calls into question the very notion of universality upon which phrases like this one rest. Hiebert shows Sarah trying to write about something she doesn't understand and trying to adapt a vocabulary to fit a "foreign" situation. At the same time, her local vocabulary persistently shows her origins. Hiebert, for his comic purposes, keeps the "right" and the "wrong" vocabularies in balance, establishing his intentional incongruities. The point to understand, however, is the twin observation about language: a "wrong" vocabulary will create a distorted picture; a local vocabulary will reveal a world of its own.

In a general way, we have always known this. Young writers are advised often enough to "write about what they know". What I suggest, however, is that many Commonwealth writers have been the victims of having to use a language that wasn't really theirs, or victims of criticism which failed to appreciate the language they were using.

As an example of the first situation, I would cite John Kent, editor of *The Canadian Literary Magazine*, who in his first issue in 1833, declared in these words his intention to maintain high literary standards: "As far as lies in my power, I will tomahawk every ignorant and conceited

trespasser upon Parnassus, and hang up his scalp, as a trophy, in the
Temple of Apollo."[2]   The failure of idiom here is one caused by the
presence of a borrowed vocabulary. The incongruity is uncontrolled.
The other example I have to cite shows an even more familiar situation
that of the coloniser's attitude to anything colonial.   Here is Louisa Anne
Meredith, writing about Australian speech sound for the English readers
of her 1844 volume *Notes and Sketches of New South Wales* :

> The natives (not the aborigines, but the "currency", as they are termed,
> in distinction from the "sterling", or British-born residents) are often
> very good-looking when young; but precocity of growth and prema-
> ture decay are unfortunately characteristic of the greater portion. ...
> The boys grow up long, and often lanky, seldom showing the strong
> athletic build so common at home, or, if they do,it is spoiled by round
> shoulders and narrow chest, and what puzzles me exceedingly to
> account for, a very large proportion of both male and female natives
> *snuffle* dreadfully; just the same nasal twang as many Americans have.
> In some cases English parents have come out here with English-
> born children; these all speak clearly and well, and continue to do so
> whilst those born after the parents arrive in the colony have the
> detestable snuffle. This is an enigma which passes my sagacity to solve.[3]

Such explicit colonialism could be outgrown. But there is an implicit
kind which still operates if, as writers and critics, we mimic the words and
sounds and structures and values of writers in other cultures, or if we insist
upon interpreting the language of Commonwealth literatures either in the
European terms we have inherited by politics and education, or in the
American terms which the twentieth century has made visible to us.

In critical commentaries which have been published over the last few
decades, there has been some controversy about whether English is an
acceptable literary language in the Commonwealth. The arguments have
been variously literary and political. Some critics have rejected the English
language as a suitable vehicle for local expression, asserting the incompatibility of local thought and English words, English syntax, English style.
Others, adhering to the notion of a single English literary tradition, find England's literature to embody the excellences to which "peripheral" literatures
must aspire. Still other writers, spurning British literary models, accept American ones, and consequently run the risk of merely transferring their colonial allegiance; while those who totally reject America appear to ignore
how much their own cultures make use of the international technical language to which America has so largely contributed during the twentieth
century. Whether the impulse is to attach oneself to Great Traditions or to
sever oneself from them, there is general agreement in all these stances about
one thing: language affirms a set of social patterns and reflects a particular cultural taste.   Writers who imitate the language of another culture,

therefore, allow themselves to be defined by it. The best of the Commonwealth writers who do use English, however, have done more than just use the language; they have also modified it, in the process generating alternative literary possibilities.

They have not simply substituted one set of words for another. Sarah Binks' "Storm at Sea" showed the fallacies of such a mechanical procedure. The plain fact is that a new lexicon is not simple to use. English is an absorptive language and takes words like *Kookaburra* and *tomahawk* quite readily into its lexicon. But new words—invented, borrowed, or however devised in any given culture—have their own resonances, their own connotations. In use, they demand an appropriate formal context—sometimes even a new syntax—if they are to make sense.[4] Failing to control form would result in pastiche and be equally as barren as imitation. This problem is even more acute in the cases where a society has adapted old words to new situations. The Europeans who early arrived in Canada, for example, in effect rewrote the environment when they applied European terms to it. The largest tree that grows on Canada's Pacific Coast is called a "fir", but it isn't a fir tree, and the closest the *botanical* name gets to it is to call it a "false hemlock". Small wonder that Canadian writing [is so characteristically indirect; a political "riding" in Canada has nothing to do with Yorkshire's tripartite division and "Indians" have nothing to do with "India". Canadian writers use these words because they are their words. But a critic must be careful to distinguish not just between the European usage and the Canadian one, but also between the Canadian connotation (the image provoked by the term "Indian", for example) and an irrelevant one which American literature and American films have made familiar.

A further point about lexical variation derives from various Commonwealth writers' use (in English language works) of non-English words. Anthony Delius, writing in a *Times Literary Supplement* review of *A Dictionary of English Usage in Southern Africa*, observes :

> I very much doubt if such words as *knoppiesvelsiekte* (lumpy skin disease), *jeugweerbaarheid* (youth preparedness), *mapasjaan* (African word for tyre-sandal), or *aitsa* (Khoisan form of "Good God!") can really be put under the head of "English usage" in southern Africa. *Waterblommetjiebredie* (mutton stew made with water-flowers) can no more rightly be claimed for any form of English usage than *boeuf bourguignon* or *taramasalata* could be said to be Standard English even down Fulham Broadway.[5]

Neither are aboriginal songs in common Australian speech; nor is a word like *mashkinoje* widely known to Canadians. Yet Katharine Susannah Prichard's *Coonardoo* contains aboriginal songs and phrases, and Dave Godfrey's "The Hard-Headed Collector" uses *mashkinoje*. Plainly, writers

who are striving to evoke the voices of their society will make creative use
of the words in that society, whether or not they are all common parlance,
all from [the same rootstock, or all spoken by the same group. The
combination of words creates a formal context while it creates a literary
world. It establishes sound, structural order, and structural rhythm
both as inseparable extensions of a lexicon and as inherent contributors
to meaning.

Consider, for example, Richard Rive's "No Room at Solitaire". The
story opens conversationally, with a narrator setting the scene this way :

> Now Fanie van der Merwe had every right to be annoyed. Here he
> stood, owner of the only hotel in Solitaire, wiping glasses in an empty
> bar on Christmas Eve. The owner of the only canteen till Donkergat, and
> facing empty tables and chairs. Well, not quite empty, because old
> Dawie Volkwyn sat sullen and morose at the counter. But then Dawie
> Volkwyn always sat sullen and morose at the counter. Fanie couldn't
> remember when Dawie had not sat on the very same stool opposite the
> kitchen door. To have the only canteen for miles around empty on
> Christmas Eve.[6]

Later on, when a black man and his pregnant wife seek shelter, the innkee-
per turns them away, and we overhear his conversations with his servant,
with the man, and with Dawie Volkwyn — all of whom he despises, but in
different degrees, depending on their colour and station:

> In the doorway stood a bearded man of an indefinite age, holding a
> donkey by a loose rein. A black woman sat groaning on the stoep.
> "Ja?" said Fanie.
> "My wife, she is sick.."
> "So what is wrong?"
> "She is sick, baas."
> "But what is the matter?"
> "She is going to have a child."
> "I am not a verdomde midwife."
> "I look for a doctor, baas."
> "Yes?"
> "There is no one in the dorp."
> "So what can I do?"
> "They all at Bo-Plaas, baas."
> "So?"
> "I need help, baas, my wife is sick."
> "Go to Bo-Plaas."
> "She is sick, baas."
> "Come on, get away."
> "Please, baas."
> "Voetsak!" Fanie turned on his heels, followed by Dawie. They settled

down to their disturbed drink.
"As if I'm a verdomde midwife."
"Kaffirs are getting more cheeky."
"They come to me of all people."
"Wragtig."[7]

The Afrikaans words evoke not just a place, but also a cultural attitude. A
word like *voetsak* is carefully placed, so that we recognise its meaning—from
context it means "Get out ! Go !—and at the same time, from its abrupt
sound and its position in sequence with oaths like *verdomde* and *wragtig*,
deduce the quality of the insult it conveys. To know that it is a term used
with animals—the term used to send a dog running—is to realise in full
the insult being aimed at the black man, an insult neither as powerful nor
as culturally descriptive had it been rendered in the lame English equivalent, "Leave, you dog!", which is merely the stock phrase of melodramatic romance.

A strong political consciousness lies behind this story and gives it much
of its moral force. Yet its aesthetic quality comes not from the fact of
its political message but from the writer's control over the language he is
using to communicate it. The actual lexicon is part of this control. It
will be clear from what I have been saying, however, that a lexicon by itself is an abstract notion. Put into use, words have sound and structure
and grammatical relationships as well. If we return then to the opening
paragraph of "No Room at Solitaire" and listen to its pattern, we will
hear how Rive uses the conversational tone, right from the opening "now",
to set up the idiom that follows, and orders the statements so that we
sense the structures and contradictions of the society that is his subject.
Let me read it again :

Now Fanie van der Merwe had every right to be annoyed. Here he
stood, owner of the only hotel in Solitaire, wiping glasses in an empty
bar on Christmas Eve. The owner of the only canteen till Donkergat,
and facing empty tables and chairs. Well, not quite empty, because
old Dawie Volkwyn sat sullen and morose at the counter. But then
Dawie Volkwyn always sat sullen and morose at the counter. Fanie
couldn't remember when Dawie had not sat on the very same stool
opposite the kitchen door. To have the only canteen for miles around
empty on Christmas Eve.[8]

This is a world in which absolute judgments are made. The most repeated
word in the paragraph is "only"; followed by "always" and "empty", it
tells us in unmistakable terms of an absolute truth—except that it also tells
us that this is a "truth" which isn't true. The canteen is "not quite
empty"—but then in Fanie's mind Dawie doesn't count, and the black men
count even less, so the canteen is empty after all and the "truth" is preser-

ved. Through his technique, Rive dismisses such illogicality; but rather than argue his case directly—as though he considered the subject past debate—he lets his world and the characters in it quietly suffer their slow illumination.

When we read Allen Curnow's 1941 poem "House and Land", we are conscious of a related literary device. Once more there are hints of the English language being used outside the English cultural ambience and once more it is not the lexicon alone which is creating the difference. Here, however, we are aware not so much of a combination between a non-English vocabulary with English principles of structure as of a marriage between the poem's structural organisation and its dependence on idiom and accent. It is a poem to be heard, a poem that depends on the nuances of the spoken word, and it appears straightforward only if as critical listeners we fail to perceive its four separate voices. Three of its personae are clearly specified : old Miss Wilson, remnant of a transplanted English family, with English attitudes to language and landscape; the cowman, phlegmatic and idiomatic; and the historian, educated out of the broadest of local accents and intellectualising about the identity of this locale. Responding to all three and providing a context for them is the fourth voice, the ironic one of the narrator. The resulting poem is a play of separate monologues, which sounds something like this (I have distorted Curnow's stanzaic pattern to separate the four voices) :

Wasn't this the site, asked the historian, of the original homestead?

> Couldn't tell you, said the cowman;
> I just live here, he said,
> Working for old Miss Wilson
> Since the old man's been dead.

> Moping under the bluegums
> The dog trailed his chain
> From the privy as far as the fowlhouse
> And back to the privy again,
> Feeling the stagnant afternoon
> Quicken with the smell of rain.

> There sat old Miss Wilson.
> With her pictures on the wall,
> The baronet uncle, mother's side,
> And one she called
> Taking tea from a silver pot
> For fear the house might fall.

> People in the *colonies*, she said,
> Can't quite understand...
> Why, from Waiau to the mountains
> It was all father's land.

> She's all of eighty said the cowman,
> Down at the milking-shed.
> I'm leaving here next winter.
> Too bloody quiet, he said.

The spirit of exile, wrote the historian,
Is strong in the people still.

> He reminds me rather, said Miss Wilson,
> Of Harriet's youngest, Will.

> The cowman, home from the shed, went drinking
> With the rabbiter home from the hill.
> The sensitive nor'west afternoon
> Collapsed, and the rain came;
> The dog crept into his barrel
> Looking lost and lame.

> But you can't attribute to either
> Awareness of what great gloom
> Stands in a land of settlers
> With never a soul at home.[9]

Quite clearly this poem has Curnow's own stamp on it. But if it is obviously not written by countrymen like William Pember Reeves or Kendrick Smithyman, it still reveals overtones which outsiders to New Zealand could not manage. The language has contrived to convey a recognisable cultural sensibility, not just an individual one. Part of this sensibility derives from Curnow's use of the single word "home", which carries characteristically ambivalent New Zealand reverberations, from the nineteenth century, through Mansfield and Mulgan, down to Curnow's world. "Home" is both *here* and *abroad—overseas*—and so in neither place, satisfactorily, by itself. Curnow's narrator, moreover, by closing his observations with this word, leaves the ambivalence hanging in the air. His irony reflects his recognition of his own inability to identify with any one of the three characters he observes—or perhaps it is fairer to say that he recognises all three of these identities as contemporaneous components in his own portrait of a land and its house. The trouble is, to outsiders they appear disparate, not coherent, and if insiders reject this view it is still hard for them to articulate their vantage point. Hence the poem. But if this is so, the poem *is flitse attempting an articulation*, and these voices are less separate monologues than at first seemed. They sound, rather, a kind of counterpoint, in which even the cowman's world is permeated by its British origins (one hears in it echoes of Stevenson's "Home is the sailor, home from the sea,/And the hunter home from the hill"), but which expresses—to quote from another Curnow poem, "The Unhistoric Story"—"something different, something/Nobody counted on."[10]

This situation is not unrelated to the point which John Figueroa makes about Creole syntax and dialect in Derek Walcott's "Tales of the Islands, Chap. VI." Showing how Walcott holds standard and non-standard lexical and grammatical items in a tightly controlled relationship, Figueroa writes that Walcott is

> an innovator. He is not only reproducing "the dialect" as the "true" speech of a certain person; he is also embodying and expressing through the very heterogeneity of our language situation a certain basic relationship (in the West Indies) between "fete" and *angst*; between "Oxbridge guys" and "native art"; between two kinds of celebration. And he does this partly by his masterly use of the Creole base which breaks through all the Oxbridge and the existentialist "philosophy" in the shape of "we has none".
>
> In the space of one sonnet he significantly uses the variety of speech and language which exists in the Creole situation—he uses this variety to do what could not be done in an homogeneous speech community. In other words he turns a situation often considered to be confusing and somehow "backward" entirely to his, and our, advantage.[11]

Literature which uses the actual language—the sounds and syntax—of the people becomes, then, an arena in which the people's political and psychological tensions can find expression. The linguistic contrarieties that are part of such "actual language" both derive from and convey the tensions in the society. And the literary form that can sustain the verbal tensions becomes a means of celebrating, or exposing, or at least recognising and communicating particular social realities. The realities existed before the form was devised; the language also existed before the form was found that could accommodate it. The problem of writing, which authors faced and resolved, turns at this point into a problem of reading, for critics to appreciate and unravel.

Turning to Edward Brathwaite's trilogy *The Arrivants*, we are made aware of yet another extension of literary uses of language. A work like Curnow's makes us conscious of the relationship between lexicon and phonology, conscious of the simple fact that we must hear the sounds of the words we read. A work like Brathwaite's focuses our attention on sound itself, on ways in which sound—by both rhythm and syllable—communicates meaning. That Brathwaite makes deliberate use of a number of different rhythms in his poem is obvious even at first listening. Calypso, limbo, blues, reggae, speech rhythms, drum rhythms, syllables that mimic crow noises and syllables that emulate rain: all these are sounded. They provide some of the clearest examples of poetic lines being crafted with movement in mind as well as literal meaning. Part of the "Calypso" section, for example, reads as follows :

Steel drum steel drum
hit the hot calypso dancing
hot rum hot rum

who goin' stop this bacchanalling?

For we glancé the banjo
dance the limbo
grow our crops by maljo

have loose morals
gather corals
father our neighbour's quarrels

perhaps when they come
with their cameras and straw
hats : sacred pink tourists from the frozen Nawth

we should get down to those
white beaches
where if we don't wear breeches

it becomes an island dance
Some people doin' well
while others are catchin' hell

o the boss gave our Johnny the sack
though we beg him please
please to tak 'im back

so the boy now nigratin' overseas...[12]

A section from "Caliban" sounds the limbo rhythms :

And limbo stick is the silence in front of me

limbo
limbo
limbo like me
limbo
limbo like me
long dark night is the silence in front of me
limbo
limbo like me
stick hit sound
and the ship like it ready
stick hit sound
and the dark still steady

limbo

limbo like me

long dark deck and the water surrounding me
long dark deck and the silence is over me

limbo
limbo like me

stick is the whip
and the dark deck is slavery

stick is the whip
and the dark deck is slavery

limbo
limbo like me.[13]

Another powerful section from early in "Masks" renders the voices—the naming—of the drums that the narrator goes back to Africa to hear:

THE GONG-GONG

God is dumb
until the drum
speaks.

The drum
is dumb
until the gong-gong leads

it. Man made,
the gong-gong's
iron eyes

of music
walk us through the humble
dead to meet

the dumb
blind drum
where Odomankoma speaks :

ATUMPAN

Kon kon kon kon
Kun kun kun kun
Funtumi Akore
Tweneboa Akore
Tweneboa Kodia

that he has come from sleep
that he has come from sleep
and is arising
and is arising

Kodia Tweneduru

like *akoko* the cock
like *akoko* the cock who clucks

Odomankoma 'Kyerema se
Odomankoma 'Kyerema se

who crows in the morning
who crows in the morning

oko babi a
oko babi a
wa ma ne-ho mene so oo
wa ma ne-ho mena so oo

we are addressing you
ye re kyere wo

akoko bon anopa
akoko tua bon
nhima hima hima
nhima hima hima...

we are addressing you
ye re kyere wo

listen
let us succeed

Funtumi Akore
Tweneboa Akore
Spirit of the Cedar
Spirit of the Cedar Tree
Tweneboa Kodia

listen
may we succeed...[14]

Odomankoma 'Kyerema says
Odomankoma 'Kyerema says
The Great Drummer of Odomankoma says
The Great Drummer of Odomankoma says

Some of the effect in all this is that of simple onomatopoeia. And the fact that there is a definite relation between sound and sense fends off any possible charge that emotionalism has been substituted for ideas. But to make these observations is still not to have got to the significance of the rhythmic variations, nor to have appreciated the intellectual force that the oral voice possesses, both in traditional Africa and to the Caribbean historian trying to locate his African roots.

The uprooting and transplanting of African culture that took place when Africans were taken to the Caribbean led inevitably to variations on the parent pattern. The development of European languages as native tongues was one of them. As Brathwaite's poem emphasises, the people of the West Indies are no longer wholly "African", whatever their ancestral origins, no more than Curnow's New Zealanders are wholly English. Part of Brathwaite's intent is to make this point, and having made it, to return his questing narrator to the islands in order to find his future. All this is bound with a search for godhead and an exploration of what is meant by *possession* : *possessing* and *being possessed*. The themes of godhead and possession coalesce in the *vodun* motifs that run through the poem, and my point is that the *vodun* references are not casual allusions nor exotic adorn-ments but an integral element in the poem's structure and meaning. One must appreciate that this religion was one of the features of African culture which survived the Atlantic crossing in a changed form. The Caribbean rituals (the *Petro* rites) differ in various respects, therefore, from the Dahomeyan *Rada* rites, not the least observable in the drumming. Maya Deren writes :

> ...the conditions of the new world were not those of Dahomey. The stability, the integration, the traditional, established patterns were disrupted, diffused, broken and violated, often brutally. The traditional defensive, protective attitude could not suffice where there was no longer anything organised or solid to defend. It was a moment of specific and urgent need : the need for action. In the new world there arose a new nation of loa, the loa of the Caribbean : the Petro nation. The difference between Rada and Petro is not to be understood on a moral plane, as an opposition between good and evil, although its violence and its closeness to magic has given Petro a reputation for malevolence... If the Rada loa represent the protective, guardian powers, the Petro loa are the patrons of aggressive action.

> This is apparent in the nervous tension that is the emotional "colour" of the Petro rites. Whereas most of the Rada drumming and dancing is on the beat, the Petro drumming and dancing is off-beat.[15]

When we turn back to Brathwaite's poem, then, it is to hear it in a new way. The on-beat speech rhythms of the central African section, "Masks", are clear. Surrounding them are the two Caribbean sections, which provide the poem with its cultural perspective. "Rights of Passage" emphasises its consciousness of deracination and various kinds of dislocation by the way it characteristically uses the rhythmic movement of the poetic line. In this section from "New World A-Comin", for example, the actual print rendering of the lines points to the breaks in the stress pattern :

> How long have we
> travelled down
> valleys down
> slopes, silica
> glinted, stones
> dry as water,
> to this flash
> of flame in the forest.
> O who now will help
> us, help-
> less, horse-
> less, leader-
> less, no
> hope, no

> Hawkins, no
>
> Cortez to come.
> Prempeh imprisoned,
>
> Tawiah dead,
> Asantewa bridled
>
> and hung.
> O who now can help
>
> us :   Geronimo, Tackie,
> Montezuma to come.[16]

The African section does not resolve these rhythmic tensions, and "Islands" returns to them. But there is by now some acceptance where there was once only disruption, and when the poem closes, in "Jou'vert", it refers to the future hopefully :

> flowers bloom
> their tom tom sun
>
> heads raising
> little steel pan
>
> petals to the music's
> doom
>
> as the ping pong
> dawn comes
>
> riding
> over shattered homes
>
> and furrows
> over fields
>
> and musty ghettos
> over men now
>
> hearing
> waiting
> watching
> in the Lent-
>
> en morning
> hurts for-
>
> gotten, hearts
> no longer bound
>
> to black and bitter
> ashes in the ground
>
> now waking
> making

> making
> with their
> rhythms some-
> thing torn
> and new[17]

The terms in which it does so involve drumming (but steel drums, not African ones), and rhythm (still "broken", but accepted now as part of the new culture and not rejected because it lacks the characteristics by which the old culture defined order).

Writers themselves have been among the clearest observers of their own linguistic environments, and among the clearest commentators on the relation they find between the language they live with, the culture they live in, and the world they create. In a laconic interview with Graeme Gibson, for example, Dave Godfrey enunciates his sense of a particular literary challenge he faces as a Canadian writer : "Well", he said,

> one of the problems is that I work a lot backwards from language, you know; that is, just almost visually I work with words, and musical-ly I work with words... I start with the words, put the words together and the content of the people grows out of the words...in a sense you're trying to say things in a different way. You're really trying to open up the language and then you move back to the form part of it. Now in Africa that was very easy to do. I mean you have different dialects, different] languages, you have strange kinds of English, you have a lot of new writers writing in different ways. You have a real richness in the people's vocabulary, in the conflicting vocabularies of a different culture and whatnot. Once you start writing about Canada you get into the problem which I ran into in DEATH GOES BETTER WITH COCA COLA, and that is, reticence is the natural form, you know, and you write these kind of tight-lipped stories.[18]

His book of integrated short stories, *Death Goes Better with Coca Cola*— the title a mordant, culturally activist allusion to an American advertising commercial—is one of his attempts to meet the challenge. Like Dennis Lee and Margaret Laurence, he has attempted to render Canadian caden-ces. Like his adopted compatriot Malcolm Lowry, who observed some years before the publication of *Hear Us O Lord From Heaven Thy Dwell-ing Place* that

> it is possible to compose a satisfactory work of art by the simple process of writing a series of good short stories, complete in them-selves,... full of effects and dissonances that are impossible in a short story, but nevertheless having its purity of form,[19]

he has relied upon the multiple perspectives of the short story sequence for reflections on society which the traditional novel form did not seem to provide. He has contrived a world in which form itself is meaning, a meaning which involves a sense of his own society's structure, cultural values, and social dilemmas. In India, in 1937, Raja Rao observed in his foreword to *Kanthapura* that

> the telling has not been easy. One has to convey in a language that is not one's own the spirit that is one's own... We cannot write like the English. We should not... Our method of expression therefore has to be a dialect which will some day prove to be as distinctive and colourful as the Irish or the American. Time alone will justify it.[20]

And when Chinua Achebe, in the series of essays collected in *Morning Yet on Creation Day*, calls openly and directly for an end to "colonialist criticism",[21] and for asserting the link between language and truth,[22] and for respecting the language which writers actually use,[23] he, too, calls attention to the relation between the writer's medium and the writer's world. He reiterated the Commonwealth literary challenge in 1964 when he enunciated clearly his feeling that "the English language will be able to carry the weight of [his] African experience. But it will have to be a new English, still in full communion with its ancestral home but altered to suit its new African surroundings".[24] What the anonymous Canadian writer in the *Dominion Annual Register* wrote in 1881—that a new literature "may borrow the literary forms of the authorcraft of the Old World, but its themes must be those of the New"[25]—only went halfway. There are a good many abstract themes one would expect to find straddling international borders, but colonial form will always stand in the way of what, from our various Commonwealth vantage points, we consider creative expression.

In exploring form, the writers I have quoted have done more than simply declare their artistic independence. They have all underscored the fact that Commonwealth societies are rich in speech *sounds*—in the cadences and intonations that constitute Commonwealth voices. The inference to draw is that, even when written, literature in the Commonwealth is an oral art. To comprehend it, we must *hear* how it works. What we require, therefore, is a greater sensitivity to English in the process of being born. We need the ability to distinguish between writers who explore the suppleness of their own idiom and writers who substitute a safe vocabulary for the words which their own tongue would utter. We need an increased appreciation of the tempos and cadences of Commonwealth language, a greater exchange of recordings and tapes, improved access to *voice*, so that we can more clearly understand the aural aesthetic upon which Commonwealth literatures rely. If we exercise such critical skill, we may find new force in "regional" writings; we may look for the coherent reasons behind contemporary writers' adaptations of fabular form; we may explore the links between documentary purpose and lyric and narrative method; we may examine how a culture and a cultural rhetoric combine. But if, instead, we insist on reading Commonwealth words with "foreign" English sounds in our ears, we perpetuate the myth of "universal" critical standards, we remain lodged in the land of themes, and we take language away from our writers at the very time they have made their language into a world of their own.

REFERENCES

1. Paul Hiebert, *Sarah Binks*, 1947, rpt; Toronto McClelland & Stewart, 1964, pp. 137-38.

2. I, no. 1 (April 1833), p. 2.

3. Mrs Charles Meredith, *Notes and Sketches of New South Wales During a Residence in That Colony from 1839 to 1844*, London, John Murray, 1844, 50. The volume is dedicated "To those dear English friends for whose amusement, and at whose request, the following pages have been written...."

4. There have been several dictionaries and guidebooks to local English published, including *A Concise Dictionary of Canadianisms*, Toronto, Gage, 1973; K.A. Sey's *Ghanaian English*, London, Macmillan, 1973; D.R. Beeton & H.H.T. Dorner's *A Dictionary of English Usage in Southern Africa*, London, Oxford, 1976; F.G. Cassidy and R.B. LePage's *Dictionary of Jamaican English*, Cambridge, University Press, 1967; Sidney J. Baker's *The Australian Language*, Sydney, Currawong, 2nd ed., 1966; and G.W. Turner's *The English Language in Australia and New Zealand*, London, Longman's, 1966.

    Black Aesthetics, ed. Andrew Gurr and Pio Zirimu, Nairobi, East African Literature Bureau, 1973, collects a number of colloquium papers on the connections between African writing and African perspectives. *Language and Learning*, ed. Janet Emig et al., New York, Harcourt, Brace & World, 1966, contains a series of essays (by Ezekiel Niphahlele, Arthur Delbridge, J. L. Dillard, and P. Lal) on the use of English in the Commonwealth. Other useful recent commentaries include those by Andre P. Brink, "English and The Afrikaans Writer", *English in Africa*, 3, no. 1 (March 1976), 35-46; John Spencer, ed., *The English Language in West Africa*, London, Longman, 1971; R.B. LePage, *The National Language Question : Linguistic Problems of Newly Independent States*, London, Oxford University Press, 1964; and Douglas Killam, "Notes on Adaptations and Variations in the Use of English in Writing by Haliburton, Furphy, Achebe, Narayan and Naipaul", in Alistair Niven, ed., *The Commonwealth Writer Overseas*, Brussels, Librairie Marcel Didier, 1976, 121-35.

5. "Aardvark to Zulu", *Times Literary Supplement*, 21 May 1976, p. 617.

6. In Richard Rive, ed., *Quartet*, 1963, rpt; London, Heinemann Educational, 1965 p. 82.

7. *ibid.*, pp. 87-88.

8. *ibid.*, p. 82.

9. *A Small Room With Large Windows*, London, Oxford University Press, 1962, pp. 5-6.

10. *ibid.*, p. 7.

11. "Our Complex Language Situation" in his *Caribbean Voices*, Vol. 2 : *The Blue Horizons*, London, Evans, 1970, pp. 227-28. The poem, anthologised here on p. 208, reads as follows :

> Poopa, da' was a fete ! I mean it had
> Free rum free whisky and some fellars beating
> Pan from one of them band in Trinidad
> And everywhere you turn was people eating
> And drinking and don't name me but I think
> They catch his wife with two tests up the beach
> While he drunk quoting Shelley with 'Each
> Generation has its *angst*, but we has none'
> And wouldn't let a comma in edgewise.
> (Black writer chap, one of them Oxbridge guys.)
> And it was round this part once that the heart
> Of a young child was torn from it alive
> By two practitioners of native art,
> But that was long before this jump and jive.

12. *The Arrivants*, London, Oxford University Press, 1973, pp. 49-50.

13. *ibid.*, p. 194.

14. *ibid.*, pp.97-9.

15. Maya Deren, *Divine Horsemen : Voodoo Gods of Haiti*, 1953, rpt; London, Thames and Hudson, 1970, p. 61.

16. *The Arrivants*, p. 10,

17. *ibid.*, pp. 269-70.

18. Interviewed by Graeme Gibson, *Eleven Canadian Novelists*, Toronto, Anansi, 1972, pp. 163-64.

19. *Selected Letters of Malcolm Lowry*, ed. by Harvey Breit and Margerie Bonner Lowry, Philadelphia and New York, Lippincott, 1965, p. 28.

20. "Author's Foreword", to *Kanthapura*, 1938, rpt; New York, New Directions, 1963, p. vii.

21. "Colonialist Criticism", *Morning Yet on Creation Day*, London, Heinemann Educational, 1975, pp. 3-18.

22. "Language and the Destiny of Man", *ibid.*, p. 37.

23. "Thoughts on the African Novel", *ibid.*, p, 50.

24. "The African Writer and the English Language", *ibid.*, p. 62.

25. *The Dominion Annual Register and Review*, ed. Henry J. Morgan, Montreal, John Lovell, 1882, p. 282.

32

The Creation of National Images in Indian and Pakistani Speeches to the United States Congress

ALAN L. McLEOD

OF all the literary genres, the speech has been most intimately associated with politics. Stories such as James Joyce's "Ivy Day in the Committee Room" and novels like Wole Soyinka's *Kongi's Harvest* have political themes and subjects. but they are about politics rather than of it; they explore political situations rather than influence them; that is, they are non-rhetorical. But the best speeches of the major politicians and statesmen—Pericles and Demosthenes, Cicero and Churchill, Danton and Lenin, Tilak and Gokhale—have had considerable effect on the course of history.

It is for this reason, surely, that Aristotle in the *Rhetoric* says that of the three branches of rhetoric (deliberative, forensic, and epideictic) he prefers "the deliberative branch, that of the statesman, which is nobler, since it deals with communal interests, and affords less room for... biasing the audience by playing on their emotions."[1] One of the principal communal interests of any nation is the creation of a favourable image in other countries, especially in those of wealth, power, and prestige, such as the United States today. Accordingly, it is instructive to consider the speeches delivered in America by representatives of ¦India and Pakistan soon after Partition to discover the national image that they projected.

In the United States great attention has always been given to public address; speeches from pulpits, platforms, courtrooms, and legislatures have been enshrined in the national literary heritage. But the attention of readers and critics seems to focus particularly on political speeches— the deliberative orations of which Aristotle spoke. The great speeches of Lincoln, Webster, and Roosevelt are familiar to most Americans and well known to many. In fact, it might fairly be claimed that nowhere outside Asia has the successful political speech been more highly valued since eighteenth-century England than in the United States today.

A tradition of the United States Congress (one that has recently been adopted by other national legislatures), is to extend to visiting foreign statesmen and dignitaries an invitation to deliver an address to the House of Representatives, the Senate, or the Congress assembled in joint session for that purpose.[2]

The format for such speeches was established when Charles Stewart Parnell, the celebrated Irish member of the House of Commons, visited the United States in 1880. On that occasion Congress met in joint evening session, not to honour Parnell with an address (as it had General Lafayette, Louis Kossuth, and Toku Iwakura beforehand), but "to hear an address on Irish affairs, and because of the great interest which the United States take in the condition of Ireland."[3] Quite predictably, Parnell censured the British government for its failure to remedy recurrent famines, and criticised the archaic land-tenure laws. The immediate effect of his speech was a Congressional allocation of $300,000 for relief of the Irish famine, and provision of free passage of donated commodities. Successive speakers have likewise emphasised the bonds that tie their country to the United States, have directly or indirectly invited the sharing of the national bounty, and expressed the desire to perpetuate peace and friendship.

In all, there have now been 113 addresses to Congress by the representatives of 54 countries. Most have addressed both houses of Congress separately, though since 1958 joint sessions have been convened wherever feasible. Some 47 speakers have addressed joint sessions, which were discontinued after Parnell's speech, but reintroduced in 1941 on the occasion of Winston Churchill's visit.

The invitation to address Congress is formally extended by the Speaker of the House of Representatives and the President of the Senate after consultation with the majority and minority leaders of the two chambers. It is assuredly not an automatic honour, for numerous are the prime ministers and presidents who visit Washington while Congress is in session but are not extended an invitation. It is virtually impossible to learn what criteria are employed in the selection, the subject being obfuscated with protocol more appropriate to Medieval courtship or Renaissance diplomacy.

The address to Congress offers an exceptional means of becoming known to the leaders of American politics, provides the speaker with "high-profile exposure", guarantees widespread reporting of the message, and permits direct access to those legislators who possess the power to implement programmes of assistance, development, or defence. Furthermore, because the speech is published in full in the *Congressional Record*, is usually broadcast and televised, is printed in full, precis or paraphrase in newspapers, and is commented on or alluded to in editorial commentary, it has a vast and singular propaganda potential for the creation and dissemination of a national image in the Unites States. And since the Congressional audience at the higher levels of power is reasonably stable, there are no unusual rhetorical problems of audience adaptation.

In 1942 President Roosevelt invited Jawaharlal Nehru to visit the United States, but he was unable to accept, because, as he later explained, the situation in India was too difficult for him to leave.[4] When President Truman repeated the invitation, it was accepted, and Nehru arrived on 11 October 1949 for a three-week visit. Two days later, he delivered his first speech, planned as "the only major address of his stay,"[5] first to the Senate, and then to the House.

The speakers who had over the years preceded Nehru had been introduced in brief, bland, and formal fashion, so that they found it necessary to establish their ethical proof themselves. Prime Minister Clement Attlee, for instance, devoted over a third of his speech to the task of establishing personal proof and rapport with his audience before proceeding to the discussion of his theme. But for Nehru the President of the Senate drew the picture of a man of intelligence and experience, of high character, and of goodwill; that is, of impeccable personal, or ethical proof. He described Nehru as

A distinguished statesman, lawyer, and scholar of India. We have been familiar with his life, his career, and his services in behalf of his people for many years. He early became a follower of the immortal Gandhi. He has suffered the hardships of imprisonment which so often accompany the life of men who have devoted themselves to liberty, freedom, and the welfare of their people. He is now prime minister of India, a position which he has reached through merit, service, and distinction in many fields. We are honoured by his presence, and are happy to honour him in return.

After the formalities in the Introduction to his address, Nehru states the purpose of his visit and speech as "To create a greater understanding between our respective peoples, and...those strong and sometimes invisible links that bind countries together." Thereupon, he proceeds to disabuse the skeptical or cynical; he is not a mendicant, a sycophant, or an apologist, but an equal: "I have come here, therefore, on a voyage of discovery of the mind and heart of America, and to place before you our own mind and heart." It was not inadvertence, surely, that determined the order of "mind and heart", for the substance of the speech explores ideas and follows unassailable logic; there is little recourse to the heart, to the emotions. In treating of communal interests dispassionately, therefore, Nehru is following the Aristotelian dictates implicitly.

He does make allusions that carry emotional connotations: for example, to the American Founding Fathers; but it is balanced by allusion to India's Father of the Nation, Gandhi, the better to demonstrate the common moral foundation of the two nations and the better to create an acceptable image. Furthermore, there are passages of deeply poetic quality, as when he alludes to Washington, Jefferson, and Lincoln and says that all of us "must catch something of the fire that burned in the hearts of these who were the torchbearers of freedom, not only for this country, but for the world."

And in this passage, as elsewhere, we witness Nehru's characteristic and inimitable alchemy whereby he transforms a particular achievement into a universal benison, endowing the individual with a vaster merit. In a speaker of less adequate ethical proof this would sound hollow, would smack of insincerity; from Nehru it is a deeply felt acknowledgment of worth.

He follows this tribute with a reference in quasi-Biblical language to Gandhi : "In India there came a man in our own generation who inspired us to great endeavour, ever reminding us that thought and action should never be divorced from moral principle, that the true path of man is truth and peace. We called him reverently and affectionately the Father of our Nation." As a result, he further stresses the essential equality of the two nations.

In like manner he develops other parallelisms : (1) the United States and Indian Constitutions guarantee the same basic personal freedoms—often in identical language; (2) the United States is in the old European tradition, but India is in the older Asian tradition; (3) the United States won its independence militarily; India won its independence peaceably. From these points there is an inescapable conclusion: that India, "though new to world politics...is old in thought and experience, and has travelled through trackless centuries in the adventure of life," yet is devoted to the fulfilment of the legitimate aspirations of modern man.

The communal interest that Aristotle stresses is further developed by Nehru when he realistically identifies Indian problems and achievements, wisely stressing the amelioration: the anachronistic land-tenure system is being replaced as quickly as feasible ; living standards are being raised, and the goal is "To remove this poverty by greater production, more equitable distribution, better education, and better health." Here the important element is the comparative: greater, more, and better; these things are all being done, and they are being improved.

Positive audience response is induced by a variety of linguistic means. By indicating that the Indian Constitution is modelled on the American, Nehru is acknowledging emulation, which Aristotle described as "a good emotion, and characteristic of good men."[6] When he voices the aphorism, "Self-help is the first condition of success for a nation no less than for an individual," he is paraphrasing the American folk-hero, Benjamin Franklin, and repeats what appears to be a tenet of popular wisdom. In *The Discovery of India* Nehru wrote, "It is difficult to capture the meaning, much less the spirit, of an old word or phrase,"[7] but he manages to do so, and with consummate skill.

The maxim is one of the tropes that characterise Nehru's style, and in his speech to Congress he includes several : "Out of understanding grows fruitful cooperation"; "Victory without the will to peace achieves no lasting result"; Where freedom is menaced, or justice threatened, we shall not be neutral"; The force employed must be adequate to the purpose." Of the maxim Aristotle said:

> People like to hear stated in general terms what they already believe in some particular connection. Another advantage, and a greater, is that it invests a speech with moral character. This quality is present in every speech that clearly evinces a moral purpose. Now, maxims always produce the moral effect, because the speaker, in uttering them, makes a general declaration of ethical principles, so that, if the maxims are sound, they give us the impression of a sound moral character in him who speaks.[8]

By extension, this impression of sound moral character is transferred to the nation or cause represented by the speaker.

In *Independence and After* Nehru had written, "...foreign policy is the outcome of economic policy, and until India has properly evolved her economic policy, her foreign policy will be rather vague, rather inchoate, and will be groping."[9] It is not surprising, then, that his treatment of foreign affairs is couched in vague, though not ambiguous or ambivalent terms. India's objectives, he says simply, "are the preservation of world peace and the enlargement of human freedom," and in support of his assertion, he adds:

> Throughout her long history she has stood for peace, and every prayer that an Indian prays ends with an invocation to peace. It was out of this ancient yet young India that Mahatma Gandhi arose and taught us a technique of action that was peaceful, and yet it was effective and yielded results that led us not only to freedom, but to friendship with those with whom we were, till yesterday, in conflict.

Nehru's speech, then, portrays India as ancient yet young; poor but improving; bothered by major problems, though tackling them resolutely; committed to peace, yet resolved to resist aggression. In other words, it presents an image of a country of noble heritage and laudable goals, or moral principles and sound judgments, of intelligent policies and stalwart resolution.

Prime Minister Liaquat Ali Khan of Pakistan bore a political relationship to Nehru rather like that of Jinnah to Gandhi, Attlee to Churchill, Evatt to Menzies, Bustamante to Manley, or Jagan to Burnham. Somehow he seemed dour, uninspired and uninspiring, deficient in the culture, the dignity, the presence, the style, the charismatic qualities that set one apart as a leader, and proceed, apparently, from superior intellect, patriarchal tradition, and literary accomplishment.

After Partition, Liaquat Ali became increasingly critical of British policy in Asia. At first he intimated, then stated openly with increased petulance and undisguised opportunism, that Pakistan would remain in the Commonwealth only so long as it proved beneficial to it. The higher good—the furtherance of peace and prosperity through cooperation and mutual assistance that Nehru frequently alluded to—seems not to have weighed significantly in his thinking.

Immediately prior to Liaquat Ali's arrival in the United States, Arthur Symonds' *The Making of Pakistan*, "that had the blessing of the Pakistan government,"[10] was published. In it the author wrote, "Alienation from Britain has to some extent inclined Pakistan to America for friendship and assistance."[11] In this context, Liaquat Ali's visit to America can be seen as an integral part of Pakistan's diplomacy, of which the speech to Congress would be a major component; accordingly, it would be appropriate to think of its preparation as a matter of moment, since it could create a sufficiently attractive image of Pakistan to influence legislative and public opinion in its favour, *vis a vis* India. Apparently this was the intention, for in the preface to *Pakistan: The Heart of Asia*, the Prime Minister said that, in the almost forty speeches that he delivered on his visit, he "reiterated with monotonous regularity" the content of his speech to Congress.

Unfortunately, the introductory remarks by the President of the Senate did not provide for Liaquat Ali anything comparable to the ethical proof that had been provided for Nehru. In part this is explicable : Nehru's voluminous publications, widely publicised incarcerations, and contretemps with the British government, together with his close identification with the Mahatma, had already made him a world figure; by contrast, Liaquat Ali was virtually unknown in the councils of the West. But the deficiency was hardly compensated for by these words :

> The whole world knows the process by which in recent years India and Pakistan, which were originally united as India, have acquired their independence.

> We are glad to welcome the prime minister of Pakistan, which originally was part of India, and which, through negotiation and friendly cooperation, has become a free and independent nation—as free and independent as India itself is at this time.

By inadvertence or design, Liaquat Ali's accomplishments were unmentioned, his merits unstated, and his role in the administration of his country undiscovered. Nehru had been introduced as "a follower of the immortal Gandhi," who had suffered imprisonment in his pursuit of liberty, freedom, and national welfare and had become prime minister "through merit, service, and distinction in many fields." The effect of so remarkable a disparity can be imagined : the speaker arose, in effect, as an anonymous parvenu, and under this circumstance could hardly be expected to create in his audience an appropriate personal or national image.

Furthermore, Pakistan was presented in a relationship inferior to India. "The whole world," we are told, "knows the process by which India and Pakistan, which were originally united as India, have acquired their independence." To any audience mindful of recent sad events, the oblique reference to Partition would not be ineffective; but to a Congressional audience familiar with the American Civil War, fought over an attempted secession, the allusion would be salutary. In addition, the order of national names is significant: *India* precedes *Pakistan* and it is repeated in association with *united*. In the second paragraph, *India* is mentioned twice, while *Pakistan* is mentioned just once, and on that occasion as the inferior component in a comparison : "as free as India itself."

For a nation attempting to enhance its national image, it is a burden to be referred to only in terms of another nation from which it is attempting to be differentiated.

Conforming to tradition, Liaquat Ali acknowledges the privilege of being invited to address Congress, recounts his visit to the national shrines, and in contrast to Nehru's recital of India's antiquity, sagacity, and pacificism, advises that "Pakistan's name is not yet three years old...it is a new state on the map of Asia." Then follows a substantial development that creates a not entirely favourable impression.

The major point is that Pakistan was founded "by the indomitable will of a hundred million Muslims who felt that they were a nation too numerous and too distinct to be relegated forever to the unalterable position of a political minority." The point is not that the Muslims sought religious freedom, but that they wanted political autonomy, and the emphasis provided through repetition in the speech suggests not deprivation, but disaffection, as the motivation; it is therefore counterproductive. An attempt to present Pakistanis as analogous to America's pilgrims is ineffectual, and when the speaker admits that Partition did not eliminate or efface minorities, one wonders whether he recognised the inexorable logic that these groups should likewise seek independent nationhood.

In all this, Liaquat Ali does not offer example or illustration in support of his contention that religious freedom was impossible in a united India. He explains that the proposed Pakistani constitution will guarantee religious freedom to minorities; but Nehru had quoted the already enacted Indian Constitution which has identical provisions. In view of the minuscule number of American Muslims, and of the general lack of appreciation for Islam in the United States, it must be considered disadvantageous for Liaquat Ali to have stressed Muslim political concerns rather than generalising the problem as one of the fundamental human right to religious freedom.

He incorporates no maxims, though he occasionally uses the longer, and hence less impressive, enthymeme. It would appear, furthermore, that a better case could have been made for Pakistan than Liaquat Ali's.

While it is no disservice to speak of "youthful countries liks ours" and to allude to "our short life as a free nation," it would seem prejudicial to the development of an enhanced image to refer to "our immature years," to the nation as "under a number of handicaps, both natural and man-made," to the task ahead as being "truly immense," and to admit that "recent centuries of progress and advancement in the world have bypassed us, leaving our resources untapped, our capacities unused, and our genius inactive." There is a distinction between candour and deprecation, but it is not always recognised.

In sum, Liaquat Ali's speech presents Pakistan in a very unenviable light, and the responsibility for its perilous condition, by not being assigned, must be borne by the speaker and his own people.

Five years after Nehru's address to Congress, Dr Sarvepalli Radhakrishnan, President of India's Rajya Sabha, delivered an address to the United States Senate on the occasion of the presentation of an ivory gavel to replace the one that had been used since 1789.[12] The visitor was introduced simply by name and title, and the epithet, "one of the world's great scholars," and delivered a brief speech appropriate for a nonpolitical national representative.

In language remarkable for its aphoristic quality, for beauty of cadence and balance of statement, he transforms political platitudes into philosophical concepts, and readily displays the same moral concerns as Nehru : "We realise that political freedom is not an end in itself; it is a means to social equality and economic justice"; "We are interested not only in our objectives, but in our methods"; "We must not cut the knots with the sword, but we must have the patience to untie them." He says,

> Even if we meet defeat in our attempt to replace force by persuasion, the politics of power by the politics of brotherhood, we are convinced that the defeat will be only temporary, for goodness is rooted in the nature of things; kindness and love are as contagious as unkindness and hate.

As with Nehru, the speaker expresses his concern with the fundamental philosophical issues rather than with sectional, sectarian, or secular ones.

On 11 July 1957 Prime Minister Husseyn Shaheed Suhrawardy of Pakistan spoke to the two houses of Congress; though the language of his speeches is varied slightly, the substance is identical. His three points are that the United States has "reconstructed and put on their feet" many countries, which is praiseworthy; it has refrained from using atomic weapons, which is commendable; and that affairs in Hungary are a warning of the consequences if nations "should become victims of what is called a socialist regime."

While an expression of gratitude for American foreign assistance is assuredly not misplaced, it is rather fatuous to suggest that failure to use atomic weapons is simply an instance of gentlemanly restraint. And to so imply the consequences of socialist government must have struck the speaker as ill-conceived, for he immediately qualified his statement by adding, "if one considers socialism in its best aspect, all of us desire and all of us believe in social equality."

Suhrawardy observed before the Senate that "What has taken place in Hungary can never be forgotten by this generation, nor even by succeeding generations."[13] This itself suggests that he was unable to differentiate between a minor episode and a major event, but this rather jejune judgment is not the least of his deficiencies. Periphrastically, he casts animadversions on India by reminding the House that "In Southeast Asia, as we all know, there are possibilities of trouble... about 1200 to 1500 miles of foreign territory separate our two wings"; but he then loses the presumed advantage when he continues, "I am determined that there will be a general election, and a fair and free election." The audience's presumption is that fair and free elections in Pakistan are not normal.

Suhrawardy's speeches have minimal literary merit: they are marred by the commonplaces of argument, by trite expressions such as "a satisfying picture" and "the road to imperialism," by puerilities such as "naughty countries," and the unfortunate figure, "give power to the elbow of the United Nations." In sum, the content is pusillanimous and the form is pedestrian, so that they add no stature to the speaker or Pakistan, and denigrate rather than enhance its image.

Of the several speeches under consideration, indubitably the least helpful in creating a positive national image is that of Mohammad Ayub Khan, President of Pakistan, delivered before a joint session of Congress on 12 July 1961. It is the longest of the five, and one of the longest of the addresses to Congress.

The speaker opens with that universal plaint, "I am told my time is short," and thereupon promises "to go over the ground rapidly." This ground he explains as "the problems that we in Pakistan face, what sort of mistakes we have made, and what sort of remedies we are trying to evolve." There follows an analysis and enumeration of such extent, and in such a manner, that an audience would not be excited to sympathy and understanding, but instead depressed to the point of despair.

Initially, General Ayub recapitulates the circumstances of his country's birth, though less eloquently than Liaquat Ali, and regrettably notes that the Muslims "made a *demand* that they should have a separate homeland." So forceful a term does not comport with the subsequent assertion that this was "not based on bigotry or intolerance," and almost implies the contrary. He proceeds with a catalogue of Pakistan's problems : "Our society, apart from being feudal, is very tribal, with a tribal consciousness; politically, we have not gone very far"; "We had a succession of bad leadership" (implying that Liaquat Ali and Suhrawardy were bad leaders); "In the economic field we were badly off. The problem of our balance of payments was going wrong. Our agricultural production was not in a healthy state. From being a surplus food producing area, we became a deficit area." There is no corresponding list of remedies being applied or considered except this : "Today we want you to assist us to develop. We need foreign capital. We need machines. We need this and we need that ...You had better not get tired of this story...You have to give it to us."

But this is not the worst of it. In mentioning Mohammad Jinnah as the father of his country, Ayub adds, "of whom you might have heard," which casts Jinnah into the role of some minor and inconsequential politician. Likewise, in alluding to Liaquat Ali, he reminds his audience that "he was assassinated some years ago." Finally, he reminds his listeners that "There was a revolution in our country. I was the head of the revolution." Though Generals Lafayette and Washington are held in esteem in the United States, their role was in effecting independence from a distant colonial power; there is little probability that Ayub would have been seen as belonging to their tradition. Rather, he must appear in the tradition of African and South American colonels who have led anti-democratic *coups d' etat*. And to add that "In Muslim society there is no such thing as colour prejudice or race prejudice," is (for his American audience) unnecessarily gauche.

Ayub's picture of Pakistan is an unfortunate one, and does more to provide a negative national image than a positive one. If he had given a shorter speech, it might have been better; and we can surmise the audience reaction when he concluded with a self-evaluation : "I have a lot of other things here, but I do not think I will waste your time."

From the foregoing, it is clear that the national image created by the Indian speeches to the United States Congress is positive : it is of age, experience, and wisdom, of work and progress in a democratic and pacifist republic. In contradistinction, the Pakistani speeches produce a negative image, one that results from repeated allusions to secession, Muslim discontent, war, political incompetence, revolution, assassination, and insuperable economic problems.

REFERENCES

1. Aristotle, *Rhetoric*, trans. Lane Cooper, New York, Appleton-Century, 1932, p. 4.

2. Provided for by Rule XXXIV of the House of Representatives, which grants admission to the floor of the House to "representatives of foreign governments which are duly accredited to this government," and by Rule XXXIII of the Senate, which extends the privilege to "members of national legislatures of foreign countries." General Lafayette was invited in 1824 to receive an address by the Speaker

of the House, the distinguished orator, Henry Clay. Louis Kossuth, the leader of the movement for Hungarian independence, sought United States intervention in 1852; he was honoured by being invited to hear an address delivered by the then Speaker, and responded in a brief, unrecorded speech. A Japanese mission to negotiate a trade treaty in 1872 was accorded the same honour; on this occasion the leader, Toku Iwakura, responded with a speech that praised the United States and pledged lasting friendship.

3.   *Congressional Record*, vol. 10, Pt. 1, p. 664.

4.   Jawaharlal Nehru, *Visit to America*, New York, John Day, 1950, p. 173.

5.   *The New York Times*, 14 October 1949, p. 1.

6.   Aristotle, op. cit., p. 129.

7.   Jawaharlal Nehru, *Discovery of India*, London, Meridian, 1946, p. 155.

8.   Aristotle, op. cit., p. 151.

9.   Jawaharlal Nehru, *Independence and After*, New York, John Day, 1950, p. 201.

10.   W. Norman Brown, *The United States and India, Pakistan, Bangladesh*, Cambridge, Mass., Harvard University Press, 1972, p. 347.

11.   Arthur Symonds, *The Making of Pakistan*, London, Faber, 1950, p. 173.

12.   The President of the Senate, *pro-tem.*, advised the audience immediately after the speech that "The Sergeant at Arms of the Senate set about to find a piece of ivory large enough from which to carve a gavel similar to the one which the Senate had traditionally used. He was unable to find the proper sized piece through the usual commercial sources, and consequently contacted the commercial attache of the Embassy of the Government of India."

13.   It is of interest to note that President Ford, during the 1976 presidential election campaign debates with Governor Carter, expressed the view that eastern European countries were no longer under Soviet domination. This suggests that the Hungarian episode, in fact, had been forgotten well within the present generation of which Suhrawardy spoke.

33

Audience and Argument in the Speeches of R.G. Menzies and Krishna Menon on the Suez Canal Crisis in 1956

MARIAN B. McLEOD

THE circumstances and events of the Suez Canal crisis in 1956 provided a significant rhetorical opportunity for spokesmen of the Commonwealth--one that brought forth two main themes, enunciated most clearly by Robert Menzies and Krishna Menon, whose speeches at the London Conference I shall examine to reveal their distinctive integrative rhetorical features, as well as to evaluate their merit as oratorical literature.

President Nasser's sudden and apparently unforeseen nationalisation of the Suez Company, on 26 July 1956, abruptly burst the calm complacency of those returning home from the Commonwealth Prime Ministers' Conference in London at which, according to Prime Minister Sidney Holland of New Zealand, "there was no thought of this crisis developing."[1] The shock of Suez drew an angry denunciation from Anthony Eden, who viewed the matter as "a seizure of Western property," and declared that "a man with Colonel Nasser's record" could not be allowed "to press his thumb on our windpipe," since the canal was "an international asset," and Britain's "essential interest must be safeguarded, if necessary, by military action...Even if Her Majesty's Government had to act alone they could not stop short of using force to protect their position"; he rejected referral of the problem to the United Nations Security Council, for the "precedents were discouraging."[2]

Among the Commonwealth countries, Eden's view of the Suez crisis seemed at the outset not to provoke serious disagreements. As the crisis developed, however, it was clear that there was no single unified Commonwealth point of view; different official government views are discernible in the speeches of Menzies and Menon. Their divergent views seem both rooted in and expressive of differing views of the Commonwealth itself.

The Australian reaction, led by Prime Minister Menzies, gave unequivocal, whole-hearted support to the initial and subsequent British behaviour;

support of British militancy made sense to Australians, who were accustomed to think of the Suez Canal as vital to their economic well-being. The Indian position, as enunciated by her principal spokesman, Krishna Menon, then Minister Without Portfolio, was as supportive of President Nasser as the Australian position was denunciatory. India was a canal user; thus, Menon's stance was to express concern equally for both sides in the dispute and to stress the role of Third World nations in securing a rational, pragmatic settlement.

One of the early opportunities for expression of differing Commonwealth views was provided by the First London Conference, convened on 16 August, and to which were invited the twenty-four principal canal users. Canada and South Africa alone of the eight Commonwealth nations did not attend, since they did not qualify as users. By the time the conference opened, all the nations invited were in attendance except Greece and Egypt—the latter declined on the ground that no outside body had a right to discuss what she regarded as her internal concern, but she offered to convene a users' conference to guarantee free passage through the canal.[3]

When the London Conference closed a week later, two plans had been produced for internationalising the canal : (1) the American plan, supported by Menzies, which recognised Egypt's right to nationalise the canal, created an international managerial body, and gave it "effective sanctions"; (2) the Indian plan, promulgated by Menon, which permitted the international body to function only in a consultative way with the controlling Egyptian authority.[4] The American proposals were eventually approved by a majority of eighteen nations, which ultimately appointed a committee of five under the chairmanship of Menzies to present their plan to Nasser.

An examination of the conference speeches of both Menzies and Menon reveals their underlying assumptions, as well as their choice of speech materials designed to harmonise audience differences and secure acceptance of their proposals. The audience of nations gathered for the conference, while united in seeking continued free passage through the Suez Canal, were far from agreeing on any plan for this accomplishment; moreover, they did not all subscribe to Britain's view that Nasser's move was illegal and that the decisions of the conference should be imposed on him. Menzies, who was Eden's principal supporter at the conference, shared these views and agreed to the twin objectives of Anglo-French policy: international control of the canal and its enforcement by the withholding of transit dues from Egypt should she refuse to agree to such a plan.[5]

It was Eden's opinion that Anglo-French policies would receive the support of the Afro-Asian nations, whom he described as "alarmed that Nasser might be allowed to get away with his pillage."[6] In fact, most of those nations fully supported Nasser's right to nationalise the canal and were apprehensive because they were convinced that the military preparations of Britain and France meant that they really intended a settlement by

force rather than by negotiation.   Prime Minister Jawaharlal Nehru spoke
for these countries when he said: "In Asia as a whole, with its colonial
memories, great resentment has been aroused.   Threats to settle this
dispute or enforce their views in this matter by the display or use of force
are the wrong way.   It does not belong to this age and it is not dictated
by reason."[7]

India's position was extremely important, for she was not only a member of the Commonwealth, but was friendly to Egypt and had been in
close consultation with her prior to the London Conference. It was India's
position, a conviction which she shared with Russia, that the conference
could reach no final decision, since that required Egypt's agreement; like
Russia, she felt that international control was unnecessary and that primary reliance should be placed on promises of fair behaviour by Egypt
as a sovereign country.[8]

Thus, before the conference convened, basic differences were obvious
between Britain and France on the one hand, and the majority of participants (including India and Russia) on the other.   The United States
occupied a position somewhat between the Anglo-French view that the
crisis was mainly political and that a settlement by force should not be
ruled out, and the Asian-Russian view that the crisis was chiefly
economic and Egyptian sovereignty must be respected. Dulles was fully
aware of these differences, but felt that the conference could at least be a
means of gaining time for diplomacy, moderation, and reason.[9]

One of the principal addresses, because representative of the majority
position, was Menzies' speech to the London Conference on 18 August 1956.
As a delegate to the London Conference, Menzies had an opportunity not
only to bridge the gap between the United States and Britain, but also to seek
to harmonise the aims of Asian nations with the views of the three powers.
Since Commonwealth membership was shared by countries on both sides
of the argument over legality and internationalisation, it presumably could
have served as the ground for establishing agreement between them. There
was also the possibility that Menzies could have chosen to speak indepen-
dently... to hear both sides and form a disinterested opinion. On this occasion, however, while Menzies does attempt to speak to both sides, he seems
to combine the roles of advocate and arbiter, for he urges the adoption
of the American proposals as the means of solving common problems.

Menzies' rhetorical task, then, included the necessity to restore unity
between the United States and Britain as a step toward the fulfilment of
his larger purpose of mobilising conference support for international control of the canal.   In the process he made some accommodation to Asian
views to the extent that he waived questions of the legality of Nasser's
action; however, Menzies would not relinquish tripartite insistence on the
establishment of an international regime for canal management.   His
course was dictated as much by logic as by emotion, since a disagreement
between Britain and the United States would obviously lessen the chances

for success of their objectives. His decision was also influenced by the fact that both countries were indispensable to the conduct of Australian foreign policy.

Menzies would have found little difficulty in speaking for the American plan, for there were many points of similarity between American and Australian views. Both countries shared the primary, tangible concern for efficient operation of the canal. In the matter of the use of force, the American view was that force should not be used unless every possible alternative had been attempted. This was in keeping with Menzies' view that force, although a very real aspect of diplomacy, should nonetheless be a veiled threat, to be invoked when all other attempts at settlement had failed.[10] America's colonialist reservations appear not to have been important to him. Eden had been susceptible to American pressure from the outset of the crisis; his wavering approach to the Suez problem no doubt made it easy for Menzies to support the specific proposals of Dulles, whom he described as "*the* man of the Conference, clear, eloquent, moderate but grave."[11]

Menzies' support for Anglo-American views did not mean that India, Pakistan, and Ceylon were unimportant to him, for maintenance of friendly relations with those countries and other Asian nations was the third element in Australia's triangular foreign policy; however, the Commonwealth connection, which Menzies had on numerous instances cited as an important "third force" in the world, and which he asserted "must remain our first preoccupation," was apparently consigned on this occasion to a secondary position.[12] In overlooking Australia's Commonwealth associations in Asia at the time of the Suez crisis, Menzies gave the impression that the British aspects of the Commonwealth were more significant to him than its Asian elements.

No doubt Menzies' choice in this case was influenced to some extent by his view that the Commonwealth had been changed, not wholly for the better, by the admission of India as a republic in 1948: "In one stroke, the common allegiance to the Crown ceased to be the bond of union, and the 'British Commonwealth' became the 'Commonwealth.'"[18] In Menzies' view, such changes inevitably made it more difficult for Commonwealth prime ministers to arrive at any common view of events unless the Commonwealth countries could present "constructive views to the world as representing a group of nations," their effectiveness as a "third force in the world" would be severely impaired.[14]

In addition to Menzies' regret over the passing of the old Commonwealth ties, his feelings toward India were further affected by his apparent personal dislike of Krishna Menon, the Indian representative to the conference, and to a degree by a distaste for Prime Minister Jawaharlal Nehru himself.[15] When Menzies learned that Krishna Menon would substitute for Nehru at the Commonwealth Prime Ministers' Conference in London in 1956, he expressed his regret that "that dreadful man...Menon is going to be there"; his feelings towards Nehru were reported to be little better, having been derived from the unfavourable reactions that his former professor and mentor, Sir Owen Dixon, had to Nehru when Sir Owen served as United Nations mediator in the Kashmir dispute between India and Pakistan in 1950.[16] Such items may be discounted as trivial, but they should be viewed in the light of Menzies' reservations, expressed at the time of India's independence, concerning the capacity of the new Indian state for self-government:

I have grave fears about the fate of the institution of self-government in a country which, quite obviously, has not reached the stage at which the majority of its people are by education, outlook and training fit for self-government...The action...may precipitate very great civil disorder in India.[17]

Nor would Menzies have felt sympathetic to Indian attempts during the 1950's to assert the role of the Third World: the neutralism of the uncommitted countries must have been anathema to his legal proclivities for disjunction. One must conclude that psychological, emotional, and logical factors impelled Menzies to support Anglo-American rather than Asian views at the conference, although he went at least part of the way to meet them. In Menzies' view, harmony was essential among Australian, American, and British views; this was the critical core of Australian foreign policy, and other considerations, including the Commonwealth and Australia's Asian policies, took second place.

Within the limitations of Menzies' identification as a spokesman for the western powers and an advocate of the internationality of the canal, he sought strategies that would conciliate his audience and enable him to win their approval. He attempted to establish a relationship with his audience-that revealed him as their colleague, trusted adviser, and fellow canal-user rather than as a legal expert or an avowedly nationalist spokesman, in which roles he had characteristically been seen. He attempted to show himself as a preserver of common economic interests rather than of national interests. Had he been too authoritarian he might have destroyed communication, for there were some who did not concede his authority.

Nevertheless, Menzies' speech is marked by individuality. For example, while he agreed with the general opinion of the conference in accepting the nationalisation of the Suez Canal Company, he made no concurrent affirmation of Nasser's legal right to take such action. In fact, in a brief paralipsis Menzies reserves his private opinion that nationalisation was illegal:

For myself, I believe that the long-standing contract with the company, and its intimate association with the 1888 Convention, possessed an international quality which excluded it from nationalisation. But that does not matter for purposes of the present debate. The deed has been done...[18]

Thus, while Menzies professes to waive the issue of legality, he manages to insert material which not only implies his unfavourable estimation of Nasser's, but also enhances his own, ethos by suggesting that his disposition is to compromise rather than squabble over legal details.

Menzies does not neglect to employ emotional proof, although his use of it in the body of his speech is sparing. In the following passage, illustrative of his customary method in this speech of combining emotional appeals with a plea for reason, he appeals to his audience's fears of the threat to their economic stability should the conference not solve the problem of the canal: "If the Conference fails,/then/ quite plainly the harmony of the world will be left in jeopardy; and if the Conference succeeds then, as I hope to show in a few minutes, every nation in the world, including Egypt, will secure peaceful advantages."

The advantages that Menzies sets out in the body of the speech, when examined in the framework of the whole speech, are an essential part of the argumentative, enthymematic structure of the speech, for they connect the conclusion—that international controls (Dulles' plan) must be adopted—to the stated needs of freedom of passage and respect for "Egypt's legitimate territorial rights." Menzies encountered difficulty, however, in gaining Asian and Soviet support for the Dulles plan since it mandated the establishment of on international board of control. The Russian and Indian delegates envisioned a board which would have only advisory function; therefore, since they did not agree with Menzies' definition of an international presence, they could not really accept his proposals. Menzies' statements about the board are brief and general: control, he says, "ought to be in one set of hands...the fingers of which represent a variety of nations with no dominant interest in the possession of any one nation." Perhaps with such generalities he hoped to gain wider support, but the creation of such a board, with its designated function of control, was the very thing which was the sticking point in the proposals. In the minds of some of Menzies' audience, colonialist exploitation was synonymous with such a controlling presence; Shepilov subsequently called Menzies' speech "an expression of colonialism in a somewhat modernised form."[19]

The speech also shows that Menzies uses elements of style so as to elicit the responses that will help him accomplish his purpose. One of the chief characteristics of his style in this speech is its conversational quality, which provides an impression of self-confidence, sincerity, and easy association with equals that could be helpful in countering any audience feeling that he intended to force through action at their expense. The absence of legal terms and obscure expressions contributes to the simplicity of his style, as does his occasional use of such expressions as, "In our own homely phrase, they amount to pushing something down Egypt's throat." His choice of language provided admirable clarification of his points, as in the following illustration:

I myself am rather attracted by the idea that the right method in terms of form would be for Egypt as the owner, as the landlord, to grant to the new authority a perpetual lease under which it would pay a rental adjusted from time to time as the business of the Canal grows....Egypt would secure from this property a substantial, steady, and assured return.

Menzies frequently inserts important qualifying and modifying elements into his sentences so as to enhance the clarity of his speech; they are not confusing circumlocutions. His proclivity for qualification is a marked characteristic which no doubt derives from his legal training and seems designed to suggest his concern for accuracy and to attempt to counteract any impression that he is doctrinaire in his approach to the problem.

Examples of parallelism, an attribute which conduces to the impressiveness of the speech, are so numerous that only a few need be quoted: "Nations east of Suez and nations west of Suez"; "the advantages of an open canal or the disadvantages of an uncertain one." Another element of impressiveness, which is characteristic of both legal and eighteenth-century literary style, is the triadic expression of ideas, as in the following excerpt: "canal work, canal maintenance, and canal development."

On the whole, Menzies' speech is well conceived and exhibits many compositional excellences. The exigencies of the situation surrounding his speech on that occasion, however, made it nearly impossible for him to succeed; his failure to persuade the Asian and Soviet delegates should be attributed not to any weakness in form or manner, but to the impossibility of discovering any means of harmonising the mutually exclusive aims of the two audiences.

The impelling need to find suitable ground for agreement led Krishna Menon to produce an alternative line of argument, including a plan which was compatible with Egyptian sovereignty and that he insisted had the virtue of being acceptable to Nasser, in contrast to the Dulles plan, which he correctly assessed as anathema to that country.[20]

In brief, Menon's plan, which gained the support of Indonesia, Ceylon, and the Soviet Union, was designed to safeguard the interests of users by mandating compensation, providing for canal maintenance, guaranteeing non-discriminatory access, and providing for United Nations action should Egypt violate users' rights. Egypt's sovereignty would be guaranteed; she and her people would work the canal.

Analysing the reasons for the failure of the Indian plan, Hugh Thomas, in his book, *Suez*, theorises that Menon's authorship was the source of discord : "India who could have exercised an influence for compromise was unfortunately represented by Menon, who always maddened British Conservative politicians and who acted as Egypt's advocate."[21]

Menon himself felt that Dulles' double-dealing and temporising was largely responsible for the failure of the conference to reach consensus:

> It all turned on 1888: I think Dulles played a double game here; probably he talked about it one way to us and to the British differently. He was the person who actually killed the London Conference. We could have got an agreement in London if the United States played the role that she had to and did play afterwards, at the United Nations.[22]

Apparently the crucial factor was Menon's *ethos*; there is some basis to assume that if someone other than Menon had presented his proposals, there would have been a greater chance of their success. Menon, like Menzies, had to remove or minimise unfavourable impressions of himself held by some of his audience. In Menon's case those perceptions arose partly from his frequent, intensely emotional condemnations of United States' economic penetration as neo-colonialism,[23] and partly from the fact that he was seen as a spokesman for Egypt, for he had remained in constant touch with Ali Sabry, Nasser's "observer" who was in London during the conference.

Menon sought to counter those impressions as inimical to the success of his proposals by identifying himself as sharing his audience's need for the economic security that an open canal would provide, and by assuming the role of mediator and colleague. Stressing the urgency of the situation, he reveals his good will to his audience when he pledges that his only concern is "to assist if we can in opening the way for a peaceful settlement... Whatever contribution my Delegation makes in this matter is directed to that end."[24]

Furthermore, Menon takes the role of conciliator when he declares that he has no wish to place blame : "So far as my delegation is concerned it is not our business at the present stage to enter into discussions of... rightness or wrongness... We have to take... their leaders as they are." Such statements tend to create the impression that Menon is completely sincere in his efforts, thereby enlarging his capabilities as an arbitrator. The impression that he seeks conciliation not confrontation is reiterated throughout the speech and is effectively combined with his final moving appeal to his audience to act

> not as parochial citizens of one country, or as parochial people in one part of the world, but with the full responsibility and realisation of our obligations to the international community and our appreciation of the ways in which settlement can be reached. I plead with you to adopt the part of conciliation and not the part of dictation.

To offset any unfavourable impression that he is a special pleader for Nasser, Menon articulates a distinct Indian view. While he says that

Egypt was within her rights in nationalising the canal company, he points out :

> My Government would like it to be stated that there are, in the manner in which the nationalisation was carried out, features which have led to the present aggravated situation. We would like to have seen that nationalisation carried out in the normal way of international expropriation, where there is adequate notice, and the way of taking over is less dramatic and does not lead to these consequences.

And later in the speech he reinforces the point in a more succinct way when he says, "We cannot speak for the Egyptian Government—we can only convey to this conference what is our understanding."

The sense of Menon's candour and individualism would also be promoted by the clear, straightforward way he states his basic assumptions to his audience. He says : "No final solutions...are possible without the participation of the country most concerned." These sentiments are repeated in various paraphrases throughout the speech and give thematic unity to his message.

Menon eschews the use of narrow legalistic grounds of settlement and asserts instead the need for practical common sense, thus seeming to underscore the impression of his own good sense, as in the following passage :

> So we will not approach this problem from an academic or legalistic sense but with a full sense of the reality of its impact upon countries all over the world, particularly the countries of Asia, and so far as we are concerned, with understandable self-interest, our own.

On the whole, Menon's strategies in the use of *ethos* seem well designed to foster trust in him, thus facilitating communication. His efforts to establish the impression of his probity, sagacity, and good will are linked with appeals to the audience's desire for security and their fears of the economic ruin that would attend any interference with trade through the canal. When he presents India as a user nation who has the same concerns as other participants in the conference, he builds a strong emotional identification with his audience. Their fears are legitimate, he says, given the "context of tension and suspicion and fear... alarm that is felt in the minds of people about the grim prospect if failure of our efforts should eventuate."

But an important part of Menon's strategy of playing upon the audience's fear is to focus that fear not on Nasser, as untrustworthy, but to translate it into a fear of failure of the conference. Nasser, Menon says, must be taken at his word. Menon insists that Egypt would carry out her promises to honour user interests; however, he offers in support only

Nasser's own assurances—evidence that would hardly be very effective with listeners who agreed with Britain that Nasser had wronged them and must be punished. Menon might have enhanced his persuasion had he been able to establish Nasser's probity and thus mitigate audience fears. Menon' appeals to economic security and common interests would have been extremely salient to all of his audience, but the forcefulness of those appeals was impaired when he claimed that Egypt must be given primary responsibility for safeguarding that security.

In developing rational strategies in his speech, Menon bases his arguments on the assumption that Egyptian sovereignty must be respected because, as he says, "the rulers of Egypt are really the only people who can guarantee freedom of navigation." Throughout the speech Menon reiterates the warning that Egypt would never accept any derogation of her authority : "responsible public officials of Egypt will not be favourable and will not take kindly to the imposition of a regime that is not their own." Since Menon's assumptions were not shared by all of his audience, the strength of his arguments would thus be diminished. A more serious weakness, however, is that he does not successfully overcome his listeners' mistrust of Nasser. In this regard, his flat assertions of Egypt's reliability are insufficient. Since he eschews the role of apologist for Nasser, he might have employed more strategies of adjustment to audience concerns.

A feature of the argumentative strategies in Menon's speech is his use of refutation, which he combines with organisational techniques of elimination of residues. He demonstrates the impracticality and undesirability of Dulles' plan, arguing at length that India's proposals are feasible and ought to be acceptable since they are built on the common ground of mutual usership.

Menon's use of language shows both clarity and appropriateness. His style is not marked by any striking figures; however, his orderly presentation of points is noteworthy on account of his skilful use of rhetorical question and answer and authoritative transitions such as "thus" and "therefore," which impart a sense of command and direct address to his speech.

Menon employs numerous refutational strategies, but they are not couched in the language of acid invective and disdain so common in many of his speeches. There is deliberate restraint in his speech on this occasion, as when he remarks almost euphemistically on "precautionary military movements of a character which has created alarming reactions." And, at the end of the speech he makes a very understated reference to the adverse effect that the imposition of international control would have on Asian and African countries when he says :

But we are even more concerned, if I may say so, at the dreadful consequences which would in effect reverse the currents that have been set in motion in regard to the relations between the Western countries and peoples, including the peoples of Asia and Africa, during the last thirty or forty years.

In sum, Menon shows considerable ability to use speech materials that seem designed to enhance his personal credibility in the role of mediator. With the exception of his neglect to discover a means to overcome unfavourable audience reaction to Nasser, his methods seem well-chosen for his purpose, despite the fact that he was not successful in persuading his listeners to accept his proposals.

The presence of both Menzies and Menon on a common stage affords an opportunity for comparison. There are some observable similarities between the two speakers in their use of argument and adaptation to the audience. Both men represented the views of powerful and important segments of the audience; each was labelled a spokesman for another party. Hence, to a considerable extent each attempted to modify prevailing impressions of his *ethos* and to portray himself as a conciliator. While neither speaker used his customary methods of invective or biting sarcasm, Menon appears more controlled and restrained than Menzies, whose frequent forthright digressions in the form of paralipsis reveal a tinge of animosity that seems to belie his moderate stance. At the same time, Menzies' style is more interesting on account of his conversational tone and homely figures.

Both speakers present their proposals in general terms, but with clear articulation of basis assumptions and well-defined appeal to practicality and common sense that does not rest on argument from legal authority. It is in the matter of basic principles that the two speakers are most far apart; furthermore, neither is diligent in seeking strategies of common middle ground, although each cites the necessity for accommodation and consensus.

Having examined the speeches of two equally capable men who represented different sides of the argument, it seems apt to conclude that there is a distinct set of rhetorical commonplaces available to the diplomatic speaker, and that these are derived primarily from the constraints and restraints of the speaking situation itself and necessity for the speaker to discover means of communicating effectively with the audience in that situation.

REFERENCES

1. Quoted in James Eayrs, *The Commonwealth and Suez : A Documentary Survey*, New York, Oxford University Press, 1964, p. 6.

2. Anthony Eden, *The Suez Crisis of 1956*, Boston, Beacon Press, 1968, pp. 51, 53-54 respectively.

3. Egyptian statement on the Anglo-French-United States statement of 2 August and the invitation to the London Conference, 12 August 1956, cited in Royal Institute of International Affairs, *Documents on International Affairs* 1956, New York, Oxford University Press for the Royal Institute of International Affairs, 1959, pp. 168-173. Hereinafter cited as *RIIA Documents*.

4. Full texts of both proposals in *The Suez Canal Conference (Selected Documents) : London, August 2-24, 1956*, London, Her Majesty's Stationery Office, 1956, pp. 5-7.

5. Eden, pp. 86-87.

6. *ibid.*, p. 73.

7. Text of speech by Nehru; in *Manchester Guardian*, 9 August 1956, p. 1.

8. *Manchester Guardian*, 15 August 1956, p. 5.

9. *ibid.*

10. Robert Gordon Menzies, *Afternoon Light : Some Memories of Men and Events*, London, Cassell, 1960, pp. 165-66.

11. *ibid.*, p. 153.

12. Press conference in Ottawa, reported in *Manchester Guardian*, 27 July 1956; also Menzies, "The British Commonwealth of Nations in International Affairs", in *Speech is of Time ; Selected Speeches and Writings*, London, Cassell, 1958, p. 8.

13. Menzies, *Afternoon Light*, p. 188.

14. Press conference, cited in *Manchester Guardian*, 27 July 1956, p. 7.

15. Kevin Perkins, *Menzies : Last of the Queen's Men*, San Francisco, Tri-Ocean Press, 1968, p. 250.

16. *ibid.*

17. Commonwealth of Australia, *Parliamentary Debates*, 18th Parliament, 1st Session, 190 (19 March 1947), 855.

18. Menzies, "Speech of 18 August 1956, to the London Conference" (London : Australian News and Information Bureau, 1956). Subsequent quotations from the speech are from this text.

19. Text of speech on 21 August 1956, in *RIIA Documents*, pp. 177-86.

20. Michael Brecher, *India and World Politics : Krishna Menon's View of the World*, New York, Praeger, 1968, p. 64.

21. Hugh Thomas, *Suez*, New York, Harper, 1966, p. 65.

22. Brecher, p. 64.

23. *ibid.*, p. 311.

24. Krishna Menon, "Statement and Proposal at the 22-Power London Conference, 20 August 1956." Text in United States Department of State, *The Suez Canal Problem*, Documentary Publication 6392, Washington, D.C. : Government Printing Office, 1956, pp. 159-178. Subsequent quotations from the speech are from this text.

34

Difficulties of Communicating an Oriental to a Western Audience

G.V. DESANI

AT Bombay airport, on my way to New Delhi to meet you, I had a bag full of books, manuscripts, and things, stolen. I have strained my memory and expect somehow to put this paper together.

My lost paper was entitled *Certain Difficulties in Communicating an Oriental to a Western Audience.* I imagine the western audience to be an average audience to whom the book page of a Sunday newspaper is addressed. It is difficult to define an oriental. I am concerned with the Indian oriental. One cannot treat the Hindus and the Muslims of India as a group and label them oriental. These two communities are distinguished by their traditional attitudes towards beef and pork, for instance.

A Hindu reader was enchanted by a European novel till he chanced upon the page which described the heroine having breakfast in bed. She was relishing a boiled egg and that fact, to this reader, an oriental Brahmin vegetarian from South India, was too disgusting for words, and she was breakfasting without having brushed her teeth. An Indian doctor told me recently that an English colleague of his in a Madras hospital had said to him that but for being dirty, there wasn't much difference between his Indian and English patients. The Indian was dirty.

Kalidas's Shakuntala made such an impression in the west, it is worth recalling, and the oriental cinema-going audiences have adopted western actors and actresses as idealised human beings. Shakuntala and the actors might have certain admired qualities. They certainly dispense feelings. In spite of our individual differences, we are related to all creatures who have feelings. There is of course the creative process at work in the presentation of Shakuntala and the characters impersonated by actors.

I do not feel disposed to explain the creative process. One recognises it. It is, as often, unrecognised. Entirely workable techniques exist today to convert a taped conversation into a short story or a chapter of a novel. A work of literary art, however—as a result of the creative process—has something additional and undefined. It has something to do with its creator. It is his or her uniqueness that is the factor.

Writers have written for purely professional reasons, which is to say, to entertain and to claim rewards as entertainers. One is grateful to story-tellers too. Now, John Milton, in a letter, replying to an inquiry about what he was thinking of, wrote to his correspondent that he was thinking of immortality. Obviously, a man like that was not writing as a professional. A man like that, in his own estimation, feels responsible to generations. Some men have felt themselves to be "the custodians of the uncreated unconscious of mankind." A man needs to cultivate himself, and to make himself exceptional, so as to make something that the generations to come might witness as exceptional. A great work of art, quite obviously, is an effect of a great personality, by whatever standard you may have it, the eastern or the western.

To believe in art as a purpose has been a western tradition. It has been an eastern tradition, too, I dare say, but we have little biographical data of oriental artists and writers. To experiment with life, and to feel truly, and objectively, and to master the technique, and to excel in the craft, is pursuit of perfection. And poetry is the right medium to aim at beauty. All kind of writing that deals with life—additionally—is an inquiry into the truth. Literary criticism, in the last analysis, is criticism of life. Edgar Allan Poe's vision of a kingdom under the sea, howsoever strange, borrows its imagery from life. That being so, I cannot see how a so and so aspiring assistant professor or a pushing Ph.D. candidate or a budding critic—without having had a violent personal encounter with life—can possibly understand Othello's love, as revealed in his last speech, which Matthew Arnold might have found poignant and T.S. Eliot somewhat wanting, by virtue of his own (Eliot's) experiment with love. A character of mine heard the ghost of her lover cry out to God for comfort. It was years after that I knew that the poor woman might feel an additional pang of regret that her lover did not cry out for her.

I happen to know that anybody recommending the credo of artists—as a pursuit of perfection and beauty and the truth—is likely to be considered irrelevant. One expects this sort of response from immature individuals, people who believe in short cuts, instant success, and in collecting recipes, rather than dedicating a lifetime to cultivating a personal aesthetic taste which any great cook needs to cultivate to be a great cook. The professionals who teach the craft of writing—following the questionable theory that anything at all can be taught—themselves have not dared to compete with Milton or Shakespeare or Tolstoy.

I need now to share a few confidences with you, if I may, about my own difficulties and their resolution in communicating strange yet distinctively oriental characters to western audiences. I am presuming, not from vanity but of necessity, that some of you might be acquainted with my *All About H. Hatterr* and *Hali*. The first book has intrigued several translators. But the difficulties of style, and the personal syntax—rather than my man H. Hatterr as a personality—have made them give up. A highly spoken of Italian translator, not knowing its significance, let stand untranslated my *"Hail Kerlumby!"*—New York campus slang for *"Hail Columbia!"*—and, unable to identify Shakespeare's diction, or, possibly, treating it as one more occasion for playing the clown, dared to translate Shakespeare (*Henry the VIII*) and my blended Shakespeare—not mock-Shakespeare, but Shakespeare added to Shakespeare—in modern Italian of the *mezzo-signori*. Everybody wants to be a clown. It is pathetic. I cannot see my book in any language other than the English language. The entirely wasteful Indian debate—for my specific intention—whether one should write in English or Punjabi or Hindi or Urdu or whatever, is altogether irrelevant. It is the demands of the craft that matter.

My man H. Hatterr, moreover, hasn't much to do with the problems of an Anglo-Indian individual, if any such problems exist, or with the alleged problems of an Indian in search for a theory or a way or a philosophy of life. Parrots imitate and what passes for an alleged sickness among some Anglo-Indians or Indians as a struggle to choose a way of life, the British way, or the Indian, is no sickness. This kind of searching is no conflict in the soul of the victim, but a desire to imitate, to be led, and so strive for status. Whether one would imitate the once successful British thoughtlessly, or the not so successful Indians, equally thoughtlessly, might be appearing to some as a sickness or spiritual struggle or search.

Now this fellow, H. Hatterr, in spite of his innocence, can and does distinguish between "a mix up" involving "mysticism and brain failure." As far back as in 1951, if this is of any *possible* interest to anybody—it ought to be—I said H. Hatterr was a portrait of man, the common vulgar species, found everywhere, both in the east and the west. His fears, desires, appetites, aspirations—not his experiences—are the same as those of any man, east, west, north, or south. At the end of the book, he gives us the list of his feelings, the feelings he had lived through, and his list does conform to Carl Jung's list of human emotions. He did include in his feelings, the attraction for the Unknown, the Mysterious, and the desire to submit to the authority of an Overlord. This sort of thing in our make-up, and the resulting behaviour, is often mistaken for a spiritual struggle which—oriental and occidental symbols vary—is, if anything, a struggle between material and the spirit, between God and Mammon, between self-love or the love of God. Anyway, my man does not, thoughtlessly, imitatively, deny God or infer God or presume himself to be God from somebody else's formula. He has a direct realisation of God. He has a religious experience by the Ganges, in spite of what he himself says about it. It is sacred. If a professional book reviewer or an aspiring critic cannot see this, he or she is deficient, as far as I am concerned, 'and he or she is not making a statement about H. Hatterr but about himself or herself.

So absorbed was George Orwell with the problems of the underprivileged that he wrote a letter of protest to me that I occupied myself with
H. Hatterr at all.   That was a wrong thing to do, he thought, when a war
was on.   Edmund Blunden, on the other hand, rejoiced that I occupied
myself with H. Hatterr.   That I did so when a war was going on, he
thought, was a measure of my courage.   T.S. Eliot was mostly concerned
with literary virtue—with the management of images and words—and his
response to *H. Hatterr* and indeed *Hali*—he considered its imagery "often
terrifyingly effective"—was approval.   I want to draw a conclusion.   It is
that one hast o bring with oneself to an author a certain skill, or talent,
to get on terms with one's author.   There are some unfortunate people
who have failed to be touched by beauty.   Some human beings, and children, and saints, and indeed all genuine acts of love, of compassion, are
capable of blessing us with beauty-experience, if one is conscious enough
of beauty.   An impassioned speech by Romeo makes a certain kind of
insensitive lout giggle.   It is all unreal to some men and women.   These
people's notion of realism in literary art is an image of a woman of flesh
and blood and sweat and feminine odours.   If these specifics are missing,
she is not a real woman.   The divinity of Beethoven, the music-maker, is
as *real* as the flesh and blood Beethoven.

Ask me, why should one write about H. Hatterr ?   Because, as man,
he is a legitimate topic in literature and his singularity is justification
enough for his appearance.   I happen also not to be an admirer of H.
Hatterr although I am sympathetic to H. Hatterr.   He is to me a comic
character, and my treatment of him is bound to be satirical.   I have tried,
you see, *per pro* H. Hatterr, to minimise man somewhat.   And the very
personal language he uses, and other characters do, has nothing to do
with the species of English called *babu*.   Actually, *babu* is spoken by
incompetent people and—apart from now and then amusing better
speakers of English—it has little virtue as a means of expression.   An
equally ignorant form of Hindi is being used in India today by highly
paid foreign advertisement copywriters.   I have picked up two examples
at random.   First, a washing powder is described in these terms :   *"haee
power"* (Lever Bros. merchandise)   *"me jyada alishan safed dhulai ki
shakti hai."*   *"Haee power"* is the genuine bastard fathered by the English
"high powered," and *"alishan"* is Urdu (whose parents are Persian and
Arabic), and *"shakti"* is Sanskrit for power.   Next, *"is-a pain-a..."* —for the
English "this pen," *"...ki gold-plated-a"*—for the English "gold-plated"—
tip'd-a —for "tipped" —*"nib-a"*—for "nib" ... (I am not striving for
effect but these Hindi words carry the terminal vowel, hence "pen-*a*"
and "nib-*a*").   Anyway, after describing their fountain pen in these
self-righteous and self-indulgent terms, they add, "...*achhe parinama ke
liye*"—"for good results" "...*hamari*"—our—"...*sihai*" —ink—"...*istemal
kijiye*" (put into use, yourselves).   The Urdu *"istemal"* with the Sanskrit
"parinama" is much too offensive and I will not comment. These examples

show the depraved *babu* Hindi being written in India today.

Language, as employed in literary composition, is a manifestation of feeling too. This statement is an over-simplification. Anyway, a successful communication of feeling must produce in the reader a response. The reader must have access to the language and, above all, he and she must have a certain equipment—I have earlier used the words skill and talent—so as to respond to the words, words which evoke in the reader the writer's feeling or tension.

An aspiring Indian writer has shown me a short story in which a young Indian woman is described as travelling by train. She is reported as grievously afraid because her male companion, in the men's compartment, does not show up at the next stop, to reassure her, that is. The author of the story, a young woman herself, had felt the girl's predicament, I dare say, and she had described it faithfully and at length. But the English magazine editor wasn't moved by it. He thought the girl was stupid. He actually called her a dam' fool. She might have got out of the women's compartment and looked into the men's compartment for her young man. Yet, the situation was real enough and the girl's response, helplessness and fear, genuine. For her, to expose herself to strange men, would be unthinkable. Now, an Indian father of sixty, with tears streaming from his eyes, reviews his predicament. His daughters have grown up, have become *sayani*—know what is what—and he has failed to find suitable matches and the dowries for them. This situation, if ably played on the stage, or the screen, is perfectly intelligible to an Indian audience. This is a genuine predicament. A western audience might dismiss the tragic figure of the father as unreal. His tears might merit a laugh. Both these people, the frightened girl in the train and the defeated father of the worldly-wise girls—always allowing for talent, the magic of a gifted writer—do not have a universal appeal. Their appeal might be local. There are people in certain parts of the world today, I imagine, who are worried to death and cannot decide as a matter of national or tribal policy, whether to file or not to file their teeth. Their ancestors had always filed their teeth and achieved masculine beauty. This is a genuine predicament. Elsewhere, in certain islands of the Pacific, I assume, currently, the issue to resolve is whether or not you should be acknowledged a man, if you hunted down and consumed at least two of your fellow men. The reformers among them, I suspect, say, to vanquish one man might do. It is a local problem. Yet, Cervantes' man, who fights the windmills—and most of us are conditioned not to drift into war against windmills—is emotionally acceptable, and so is Alice in *Alice in Wonderland*, intelligible and acceptable. An analytical approach—social, linguistic, sociological, psychological, anthropological—cannot account for the mystery of art and for the makers of art. If T. S. Eliot feels awe in the presence of Dante's power to realise the inapprehensible in visual images, that would seem to me appropriate enough a response. The lesser folk, in the arm chairs, judge and analyse anybody at all, and instead of explaining anybody at all, end up by exposing themselves.

So much for my preoccupation with the common man. Now, Hali is my image of the excellent man. He is, in every particular, the opposite of H. Hatterr. He is sinless. I do not find any ethical or moral lapses in him. Faced with sorrow and defeat, his search is after peace. Most men and women, after they have done with pursuit of money, progeny, status and the rest, seek peace. His tormentor, a voice within himself, promises him freedom. And Hali, at the conclusion of the work, addresses him as "forebearing friend", and says to him, "I seek no love of the living, and I seek no commerce with the dead, but I wish to be nigh, I wish to be nigh, as air, as air bearing love." There is, it might be obvious, no basis for conflict in such an attitude, and he does attain peace. I had been satisfied with Hali's "I do not long to die, for death might not be fulfilment," and, years after, changed the phrase to, "I do not long to die, for death might deny me peace." I have no formula to explain the reason for the change except that the whole of a personality might be involved in making such a choice. I need readers with *soul*, and very special sensibility, to understand *Hali* and its very special idiom. Its fewer than six thousand words, published in 1950, have occupied me for years. I last revised the work in 1964.

Your committee has generously permitted the speakers to unburden themselves to the extent of four thousand words each. I do not think either of us, yourselves or myself, would benefit from this concession. I am convinced that the genuine approach to my deliberately contrasted two characters, or profiles of man, the common and the excellent—I am still on H. Hatterr and Hali—is to recognise them as contradictions in my own personality during the years I was occupied with them. In order to communicate these, impersonally, I needed a craft, and I have chosen the craft of writing. And my entire linguistic creed—an Indian Professor of English has, recently, asked me a question about this in a letter—is simply to find a suitable medium. I find the English language is that kind of a medium. It needs to be modified to serve my purpose. Mrs Sita Rambeli, a character in *All About H. Hatterr*, writing to the publishers, signs herself, "Yours happy, Sita (Mrs Rambeli)." That phrase might be a device to make her tangible to a western audience, as indeed H. Hatterr being the son of a European, or his owning a dog, might be a device to make him tangible. I would rather not have "Yours happily, Sita (Mrs Rambeli)," because my modified form, in my view, is better. In my judgment, it is characteristic of her. A personal sensibility is decisive. It is this factor that makes the language of *Hali* as strange and personal and deliberate as H. Hatterr's.

"Man is born to make," Hilaire Belloc has writen. "That human art in which it is most difficult to achieve this end is the art of writing..." "Yet," he continues, "this much is certain, that unconstructed writing is at once worthless and ephemeral and nearly the whole of our modern English writing is unconstructed. The great majority of men do not attempt it—you can discover in their slip-shod pages nothing of a seal or a stamp... The thing is extremely rare." This is as true today as it was in his day. Something might be done about this.

REFERENCES

George Orwell, letter dated December 17, 1944. "...I have read this Ms. (*All About H. Hatterr*) with a great deal of astonishment, even bewilderment...I don't think this is the time for literary high jinks...in the sense that all sensitive people are much too aware of the outside world and its menaces to be able to play the fool single-mindedly."

Edmund Blunden, letter addressed to the High Commissioner for India, London, February 1952. "...I am sorry we are to lose Mr Desani and wish him ..at least some leisure—which even the most imaginative minds must have. He has lived in this country in times full of anxiety and trial but his personal courage has been reflected in his literary enterprise : and that Tristram Shandy character he invented will stay in our memory—Mr H. Hatterr. I am proud of having been one of the earliest readers who made the acquaintance of that "poor gentleman" ...but better critics have recognised the originality of that character, and I only have to add that I admired not only the finished study but the untiring labours of the artist (which I happen to know of) as he strove for the best effect,"

E.M. Forster, letter dated December 9, 1947. "...*Hali* does seem to me genuine and personal. I get a view through it though I should be hard put to it to describe what I see. The moral I find on page 20, 'I do not long to die, for death might not be fulfilment.' Treating life as if it is what death might be—that seems to be the method in its wild pilgrimage...Private mythologies are dangerous devices. You have succeeded wonderfully with yours. The emotion is direct. I was constantly moved and hearing overtones."

E.M. Forster, letter dated April 19, 1948. "...I have read *All About H. Hatterr*, again... as I read in it, bewilderedly entertained and wondering how it keeps up the pace. The pace, wherever I opened it, seems the same...I shall go through the whole of it again...on a long journey."

35

Method or Madness : How May We Expect Commonwealth Studies to Affect the Teaching of English ?

JOSEPH JONES

FROM an Indian platform I hope I may be privileged to speak in large terms, transcending the *karma* of our day-to-day routine and our mundane short views of human endeavour. At least that is what, briefly, I intend trying to do. There are, as I see the situation, several important questions to be asked : (1) How does the profession now look to those who, after long careers inside it, have been privileged to step outside ? (2) How does the profession look to the overwhelming majority who have never been inside it ? (3) How do these points of view relate to one another ? —i.e., how should the profession be commencing to look, to those still closely occupied with its details ? If they begin to take Commonwealth studies—language and literature—seriously, what can that do to help them discover some truths about themselves as teachers and scholars; about what their profession should mean to the entire field of education, both national and international, in today's world ?

Let me preface my remarks by quoting from two books which appeared in London during 1976. The first is a work of reference, *Contemporary Novelists* (St. James Press, 1976), a comprehensive dictionary of over 1600 pages listing and briefly analysing the fiction of about 600 current novelists writing in English. In the preface to this most useful compilation the British novelist Walter Allen cites "the sudden and unexpected appearance of the novel written within the past three decades or so in the new countries where English is spoken." Continuing :

For a congenital reader and student of the novel it has been a moving experience to watch these new literatures come into existence during one's reading lifetime, for they are surely signs of life, not of death. The task of these men and women making these new literatures is, no doubt, different from that of contemporary English and American white novelists, for it is to forge, in Joyce's words, the uncreated conscience of their race. But their novels testify to the variety and diversity of human experience and to the human need to set it down and rejoice in it. (p.xii)

The second excerpt is from a novel entitled *The Glass Zoo* (Hodder & Stoughton, 1976), by James McNeish of New Zealand. A teacher in one of London's more difficult comprehensive schools is reflecting on current educational problems :

The trouble with schools is that they're artificial. With prisons and ships, they're the most artificial communities on earth. It is the demands they make. If the demands weren't unnatural, they wouldn't have to rest on a system of reward and punishment as a substitute for a natural rhythm of things. The system is so clean it organises instinct out of it. No love, no hate, no fear, no lust, all wrong. When the hormones play, the system can't take it. It turns and bites. (p. 159)

I hope I can make clear, in the remainder of this discourse, a firm connection between these two quotations.

Commonwealth language and literature study demonstrates, conclusively, the impossibility of perpetuating a closed system of instruction, restricted to a predetermined sequence of English "masterpieces" arbitrarily so defined. This proposition carries wide-sweeping implications for linguistic instruction as well as literary, if any such distinction is in fact a proper one to make. Unless I read the signs altogether wrongly, we shall be called upon, very soon and very imperatively, to examine the structure of our English curriculum along with the methods through which we present it. When that time—already overdue—is full upon us we should not spare ourselves; not try to inflate the *status quo* or invent alibis for not doing better. Well, then, what is there still remaining to be discovered by the majority of English teachers everywhere ? In another connection I have given a good bit more space to what I think must be done if English is to fulfil its destiny. Here I can attempt only to review the main heads.

First of all, let us emphasise the necessity of seeing Commonwealth literature as a part of world literature in English. It is certainly not the whole show, and I should hope nobody here supposes it is, or ever will be. Nor is English as viewed by most teachers and professors of English the whole show, either : world literature in English is far too vast a subject to "cover" by courses and lectures, and we should be looking for some other way to approach it. What direction will our search most profitably take ? We have too much to be taught to too many by too few : how can we ever escape such a dilemma as that ? Not by compounding the errors already too plainly apparent. "Business as usual", but in greater volume, most emphatically is *not* going to work. Forget that delusion !

If language and literature is to serve the individual as the groundwork of his life we must begin early to persuade him this is true—or, as I would prefer to think of it, we must be sure to ratify and keep alive and open for him the natural interest, the miraculous degree of easy motivation that we observe in very young children. We must do everything possible to help each person help himself, not merely baptize him, anoint him with formalised, ritualistic procedures, and exhort him to do right. To force the individual into the English classroom is to fragment and mutilate the most precious endowment, gift, treasure—call it what you will—that he brings with him when he starts to school.

Very well, you may ask, if this is so good why haven't we been doing it all along ? One compelling reason, no longer really a serious problem, has been lack of equipment. Another reason, not so easily disposed of, is the lack of a full-bodied conception, by English teachers themselves, of how large the subject is and of what it means in broad terms. Suppose we say this still is a serious problem but not insurmountable. Finally, there is a widespread lack of understanding, both inside and outside the school system, of the nature and importance of language study, by which I mean both reading and expression. This is a very serious difficulty, surmountable only after long, hard effort. But let us at least explore, or set out to explore, the alternative.

Instruction in English, all too commonly, is built upon a foundation of monumental passivity. That is why, in large part, it accomplishes so little; why "standards" so-called are falling and will continue to fall, and why teaching is coming under peremptory challenge from all sorts of groups, including—ominously enough—politicians. Passivity, tractability, shallow-rooted skill at short-term memorisation, aptitude for push-pull ingestion and regurgitation of masses of facts—are these the values which democratic education really cherishes ? I hope not, but they are what I see when I look at the system I have lived with for my past forty years as teacher and for an earlier twenty as student.

Would we not do far better, I wonder, to take the individual out of such a stultifying context, setting to work to persuade him, from the very earliest beginnings of his schooling, that he is the one forever responsible—the only one who really *can* be responsible—for improving his knowledge of language and literature, though not without constructive assistance and continuing challenge from a well-trained staff of English teachers? Are we capable of nothing more imaginative, more productive, than the dreary routine of classroom lecturing inherited from the medieval pulpit and the pre-Gutenberg university system? How seriously do we take our jobs? How much of our pay-check do we well and truly earn? Perhaps these are rude questions to be asking, but if we are unwilling to ask them of ourselves and try to answer them, let us not become too righteously indignant when others begin to fish about for their own answers.

I can see Commonwealth studies, therefore, as one of the most important links in a chain of events which have already brought us to what I should call a constructive crisis.   Until recently we were well content, too many of us, to busy ourselves with whatever specialities seemed naturally attractive or professionally promising, while we gave our students and the larger aspects of our study only as much time and attention as was thought decently necessary.   This attitude was approved and encouraged by the structure of rewards and penalties within which we worked, a structure for which we were only in part responsible, perhaps, but to which we quite willingly conformed.   But we were in fact narrowing and impoverishing our subject by the behaviour that supposedly was enriching it.   Worst of all, we were gradually but quite certainly losing the interest of our students, processing them through short-term, low-yield courses in which their role was chiefly that of the passive receptor.   In the face of all that, how did they respond?   Naturally enough : instead of seeing English as a creative, expanding discipline they came to see it as an imposed requirement which once satisfied, was for the most part mercifully self-destructing : they were happy to forget it. How else do we explain a steadily deteriorating level of performance, a a precipitate exodus from English classrooms, a general malaise among both teachers and taught?

But how, you may say, can I view this dismal assessment (if true) as in any way "constructive"? First, because we are clearly under pressure to act, to temporise and compromise no further. The watchword is no longer "publish or perish" for the individual but "reform yourselves or perish" for the whole profession. Once we see that this is our true condition, the way is open for at least some very frank discussion of basic problems and possibilities. It is in this context of searching for a workable alternative to fragmentation and impersonality that I call for an approach which assumes the individual student as the natural centre of attention.   This would make it possible to use, in the most flexible way possible, the personal resources of a broadly educated English staff.   Moreover, through the ever-improving techniques already available to consultative individual instruction at all stages, there could be intelligent development of the ongoing experience of language and literature, the continuum each of us lives in. Any rational approach to English in today's world, and tomorrow's as well I make bold to believe, needs to erase in so far as possible the dividing lines between school years and the increasingly long life-span that succeeds them. Clearly this is still an artificial separation which too often splits the individual himself.   In the effort to minimise it, English teaching rightly conceived would play a central role, one that would not be tied inexorably to a job-market or even to length of attendance at school. By contrast, the present conditions under which it is doomed to operate can only serve to reinforce the division, insuring that intellectual paralysis will become the norm for most of the population pushed through the assembly-line and rubber-stamped EDUCATED.

I conclude, then, that we need very much to rethink our position. We can do far better than we are doing now, and it is high time for us to try. Commonwealth studies can serve us as a useful and needful means of helping to keep the doors open.

36

The Probles of Teaching
Indian Fiction in Commonwealth Countries

SAROS COWASJEE

MINE is a paper about the classroom—a classroom in which the instructor knows the aesthetic limitations of his subject but dares not stress them if he wishes to teach the subject; and the students—if the facts were acknowledged—couldn't care less whether Indian fiction is good literature or not. The majority of foreign students study Indian fiction not because it is good literature but because it is Indian. They are not looking for literary merits, but are asking themselves questions such as "What does this novel tell us about India? In what ways is this novel Indian?" As David McCutchion says in *Indian Writing in English*, it is not scornful to face this fact.

It is not scornful for two reasons. First, those who contend that literature must reflect life have been so vocal in our own time that even the word "documentary" has lost much of its stigma, and "the ivory tower" has become a lonely place. For the majority of readers everywhere, what the writer has to say is more important than how he says it. This is not a healthy trend, but it is there. At the Sorbonne I found that students preferred Mulk Raj Anand's *Coolie* to R.K. Narayan's *The Guide*. The latter is a more sophisticated work, but then *Coolie* is a commentary on India in the way *The Guide* is not. It should not be our purpose to belittle the documentary approach (much of Indian fiction is sociologically and historically oriented), but rather to show how the documentary itself, with skill, can become a work of art. Anand's *Private Life of an Indian Prince* is a fine example in which history and literature have been fused into a work of art. However, this novel raises another problem to which I shall turn later.

The second reason why we need not be scornful of Indian fiction is that it can hold its own in relation to fiction from other Commonwealth countries : notably Canada and New Zealand. The writers from these countries have an advantage over their Indian counterparts, for they are writing in a language that is their own. The advantage that the Indian writer has is that India has generated more interest than English-speaking

Commonwealth countries because of the impact of Indian thought on writers like Shelley, Wordsworth, Tennyson, D.H. Lawrence, T.S. Eliot, W.B. Yeats, Emerson, Thoreau and Walt Whitman. The mystery, the "unknown quality about India"—whether it be fact or fiction—has also gone to kindle interest in India, and it is not surprising that readers should turn to Indian fiction for information for which they should perhaps look to non-fiction.

C.D. Narasimhaiah, speaking of the neglect American literature suffered until recently, says that this neglect "is one of the worst things that can befall a country that has emerged from colonial status." If this is true for the United States, which has been an independent nation for two hundred years, what must we say for India which got its independence barely thirty years ago ? Furthermore, as Narasimhaiah points out, everything written in English has "to be routed through England" if it is to win even partial approval by the English-speaking world. Except for the works of R.K. Narayan, who has shown concern for nothing else but his art, and G.V. Desani, who wrote a highly original book, most Indian novels channelled through Britain have had strong social content. Novels were promoted in England for the light they threw on India rather than their literary excellence. Bhabani Bhattacharya's *So Many Hungers* (dealing with the Bengal famine of 1942) was applauded by *The Times Literary Supplement* as being "a factual and vivid account of one of the most shocking disasters in history." Anand's *Untouchable*, which figures repeatedly in courses in Indian fiction around the world, was recommended by Bonamy Dobrée to the publisher Rupert Hart-Davies of Jonathan Cape as being "an extremely interesting book...about things we don't know anything about, written by someone who obviously does."

The danger in an approach like that of Dobrée is that we are urged to read a novel for what it tells us about India, with no inducement to evaluate it as literature. The gentle and balanced writing in *Untouchable*, the measured regularity with which Anand alternates episodes, some happy and some unhappy, are ignored in the presence of the social issues—the most significant being that a large segment of mankind is ostracised for being unclean, and condemned to misery. It is, of course, easier to underline the social significance of a book than draw attention to its technical excellence, and this is what happens with much of Indian fiction. While teaching *Untouchable* to a none-too-bright class, I said : "There are sixty million untouchables in India ! Do you know what that means ? It means that three times the total population of Canada is subjected to the fate of Bakha [the hero of *Untouchable*]." It worked. At the end of the hour I took a vote and found that students preferred *Untouchable* to Mark Twain's *Huckleberry Finn*. Arthur Koestler says in *The Lotus and the Robot* that "statistics neither bleed nor smell." But they do. Why else should Manohar Malgonkar in his prefatory note to *A Bend in the Ganges* (a novel about Indian independence and its bloody aftermath) announce that "freedom brought on a kind of havoc rarely seen in war; twelve million people were rendered homeless, three 'hundred thousand were slaughtered, more than a hundred thousand women were abducted, raped, mutilated" ?

Though the Western reader is often guilty of taking a purely documentary approach to Indian fiction, Indian writers such as Anand, Bhabani Bhattacharya and Manohar Malgonkar have encouraged this approach by writing socially competent novels. Of the major Indian novelists, only Narayan seems to steer clear of the larger social and political issues, maintaining "that historical forces need not have anything to do with the production of great art."   His work relies on the interaction of character and situation, and in portraying life he transcends what is local and national in order to reveal those human traits which are a common denominator to all mankind. Alone among Indian writers, he makes no conscious attempt to use Indian-English, Indian myths, or the theme of East-West encounter which bulks so large in Indian fiction. Narayan's novels pose no serious problems to the discerning reader, and if his name does not recur in this paper it should be taken as a tribute to him. But let his achievements not disparage the works of those Indian writers who are striving to make the documentary artistic—which is a mark of much great literature.

If one were required to sum up in a phrase what constitutes the basic problem in teaching Indian fiction to Commonwealth students, the answer would be : the students' lack of familiarity with India. And in a country as large and as complex as India, there is no easy road round the problem. This lack of familiarity can have two effects on a work of fiction : it could lead to misinterpretation, which in turn could affect its proper evaluation. Second, it could prevent the reader from seeing the subtleties, the fine distinctions, the slight gradations which contribute so much to our enjoyment to literature. Let me illustrate what I have just said with two political novels : Anand's *Private Life of an Indian Prince* and Khushwant Singh's *Train to Pakistan.*

Private Life of an Indian Prince is the case-history of Maharaja Ashok Kumar (better known as Vicky), as recorded by the Maharaja's personal physician for the benefit of Dr Bhagwat—the superintendent of a mental asylum to which the Prince is finally admitted. The story offers no opportunity to the narrator to explain the political background of the princes, for Dr Bhagwat presumably knows as much about it as the narrator. The result is that the reader is left uninformed. The political background, however, is vital to the understanding of Vicky's character. To those unfamiliar with the history of the princes and what the British Government had led them to believe for a century, Vicky's bid for independence might seem the act of a lunatic. But to look on the Prince as a lunatic is to misconstrue the novelist's purpose; it is to make meaningless the Prince's confrontation with his people and the new Government of India. Vicky's actions are as much a result of the shameless schooling he has received in his father's harem as it is of his faith (one shared by Maharaja Hiroji in Manohar Malgonkar's *The Princes*) that his dynasty will endure. The faith owed itself largely to the promises given by the British Government to the princes. Her Majesty Queen Victoria, in 1858, gave her celebrated pledge to "respect the rights, dignity and honour of the native princes as our own." Representatives of the Crown in successive years repeated the promises, but when Independence came to India and Pakistan, all that the princes received from the British was advice and admonitions. The novel centres on the betrayal of trust : the trust between the princes and the British Government, the trust between Vicky and his mistress Ganga Dasi, and the trust between Vicky and the Indian States Department. The clue to the understanding of Vicky's character is not supplied by Anand, and we have to turn to sources outside the novel for it.

Khushwant Singh's *Train to Pakistan* also deals with the fateful year 1947. In unimpassioned prose, and with biting economy of words, he tells how communal frenzy engulfs the remote village of Mano Majra where Hindus and Muslims have lived in peace. But before the last train-load of Muslims crosses the border into Pakistan, Khushwant Singh abandons the detached stance of the narrator (which, by now, has served its purpose), and through the magistrate Hukum Chand gives expression to his own bitter disillusionment :

Where was the power ? What were the people in Delhi doing ? Making fine speeches in the assembly ! Loudspeakers magnifying their egos; lovely-looking foreign women in the visitors' galleries in breathless admiration. "He is a great man, this Mr. Nehru of yours. I do think he is the greatest man in the world today. And how handsome ! Wasn't that a wonderful thing to say ? 'Long ago we made a tryst with destiny and now the time comes when we shall redeem our pledge, not wholly or in full measure but very substantially.' " Yes, Mr. Prime Minister, you made your tryst. So did many others—on the 15th August, Independence Day.

The full effect of the above passage, with all its vibrations and implications, can only be felt by those who are well conversant with Nehru's personality and his speech to the Constituent Assembly on the night of August 14, 1947. Nehru made his tryst with destiny and became India's first Prime Minister. But what of the others ? What about the man whose penis was cut off and presented to his newly-wed wife ? Just one of a thousand horrors ! In Nehru's speeches there is a sentence (not quoted in the novel) which reads : "A moment comes, which comes, but rarely in history,...when the soul of a nation, long suppressed, finds utterance." The soul of India, professedly wedded to non-violence, found utterance in atrocities of which there are few parallels in human history. But Khushwant Singh is not attacking Nehru, as critics have asserted; he is contrasting

Nehru's idealism with the painful grossness of life.   To see this one needs to know more about Nehru than the novel itself offers.

The indiscriminate use of Indian-English, a conscious infusion of myths into novels, and the lack of objective critical studies frustrate the foreign reader.   Indian-English is a legitimate means of giving an Indian flavour to writing, and it is achieved primarily by literal translations of Indian idioms and proverbs into English.   Idioms such as "Is this any talk" by Anand, "...gone to eat the Indian air" by Khushwant Singh, or a proverb such as "When an ant grows wings and starts flying in the air, it is not far from its doom" by Bhabani Bhattacharya have a charm of their own. But writers in their zeal to be distinctive have translated idioms that have lost their uniqueness in translation and have become purposeless verbiage in English.

Among the devices to create a new mode of expression are the changing of the spellings of English words to conform to Indian pronunciations, and interpolating Indian with English words in speech.   The first has comic possibilities : "Yus" for yes, "Gut noon" for Good afternoon, create no special problems for the reader.   The second device occasionally does. Here are two quotations from Anand.   The first is from *The Road*, where a character cries out : "Maro salè ko kill him."   The second is from *The Sword and the Sickle* and reads, " 'Chup salè !' shouted Ram Din, striking Gupta a 'thappar' on the head."   The first quotation, despite the three Hindi words in it, does not create difficulties [re-read it]. A reader who is unconversant with Hindi can still get the meaning from the context, and from the key words—"kill him."   The question here is not that of obscurity, but straightforwardly one of authenticity.   No Indian in his speech is likely to juxtapose Hindi and English words in the order in which they appear in Anand.   But this is something we cannot expect a foreigner to know. In the second quotation, the word "thappar" will intrigue a foreign reader.   When, by the aid of a dictionary or by some other means he finds out that "thappar" simply means a slap, he is sure to ask what is achieved by inserting this particular Hindi word in an English sentence.   Certainly nothing Indian has been created !

Raja Rao in the "Author's Foreword" to *Kanthapura* pleaded for "a dialect which will some day prove to be as distinctive and colourful as the Irish or the American."   This has not come into being, and is now unlikely to develop. Indian-English has added quaintness and a certain charm to Indian fiction, but it has also led to obscurity, pretentiousness and unreality. Furthermore, Indian-English is seldom suitable for moments of heightened drama, and even those writers who have been its strongest advocates have turned to standard English when dealing with elemental passions and the most crucial events in the lives of their characters.

Of the Indian novelists read in Commonwealth countries, Raja Rao and Mulk Raj Anand have made conscious use of myth in their works, but for diametrically opposed purposes. For Raja Rao, who is steeped in religion and philosophy, the myths offer sustenance by taking him back to India's oldest rituals, beliefs and values. In *The Serpent and the Rope* he deals with the quest of the individual to work out his own salvation. There are allusions to Rama's self-imposed exile and the Radha-Krishna legend. But more alien to the foreign reader would be the Advaita (Non-dualistic) Vedanta of Sankara in which the hero finds comfort. No less intriguing will be the narrative technique of Raja Rao, which he models on the *Puranas* with their interminable weaving of history, literature, philosophy and religion.

If Raja Rao uses myth to broaden our understanding and to show how human impulses go back to man's primal state, Anand uses myth to show its limitations and its irrelevance to our times. Gauri in *The Old Woman and the Cow* is likened to Sita in her predicament. Like Sita she has to leave home, and her stay with the banker in Hoshiarpur parallels Ravana's abduction of Sita and her forced exile in Lanka. Just as Sita is returned to her husband, so is Gauri to her husband, Panchi. However, in the *Ramayana* the earth swallowed Sita to save her from further humiliation. But the earth is not going to open up for Gauri. For her the only solution lies in freeing herself from the fetters of her village and "taking the road to the town." Anand's technique is to follow the mythical parallel to a point and then break away, thereby indicating that the old myths have no answer to man's present-day problems.

Successful as Anand's technique is, *The Old Woman and the Cow* is marred by serious flaws and it is to *Kanthapura* and *The Serpent and the Rope* we must turn to enhance our understanding of the Indian spiritual and philosophic temperament. In novels dealing with myths, the key to success lies in sharing a common mythology between narrator and the reader. The Western reader often knows little about Indian myths. Raja Rao creates additional problems by referring to local myths.

Modern Indian fiction in English dates from the mid-thirties, and only since the early sixties has it been included in university curriculums. And that, too, in a small way. It is, therefore, understandable that there is a dearth of first-rate criticism. Serious criticism of Indian fiction began with K.R. Srinivasa Iyengar's *Indian Writing in English* in 1962. Despite its shortcomings, this book is widely consulted by foreign students. Iyengar's study paved the way for nearly a dozen surveys, most of them mediocre. But there are a couple of good ones too, notably Meenakshi Mukherjee's *The Twice Born Fiction*. In addition to surveys, there have been a few essays and studies on individual novels and novelists. Among those who have added to our appreciation of Indian fiction I should like to mention C.D. Narasimhaiah, V.V. Kantak, William Walsh, Paul Verghese and Haydn Moore Williams.

The bane of much Indian criticism is that it is subjective, the critics substituting emotion for judgement and using the novels to substantiate their own pet opinions. No critical tradition has so far emerged; there are no standards to go by. The Western reader is left at a loss. National pride, and a passionate desire to promote a national product, have led the critics to make fantastic claims for the Indian novel. In this they are occasionally aided by the novelists themselves, who answer their queries, supply them with favourable reviews to quote from, and furnish additional information such as the number of languages into which their works have been translated. Perhaps their work is better in translation, for very recently the poet Dom Moraes wickedly remarked that most of them cannot write English !

I have touched on some of the problems of teaching Indian fiction to Commonwealth students. I am glad I don't have to offer a solution. We have to work with existing material. We can no more ask the critics to give us sound criticism than we can ask the novelists to give us good novels. We take what we get. This reminds me of a letter I got from a lecturer in Bhubaneswar telling me that she found my novel *Goodbye to Elsa* "nauseating." But she did not think I was devoid of talent, and she concluded her epistle with this modest request : "One thing—may I request you to write something like Emily Bronte's *Wuthering Heights* ? Please. I love the book."

I replied by return post that I shall certainly do so. But don't expect all writers and critics to be that obliging !

37

The Caste of English

RAJA RAO

THE East India Company, that honourable company of astute traders, discovered that there were many Portuguese and Indian children that needed schooling,—children of the servants of the Company. So in the year 1677, it engaged a young Englishman called Ralphe Orde, on the magnificent salary of £50 a year, in order to establish "a convenient school for the teaching of the 'gentes' and native children to speak and read and write the English language and to understand arithmetic and merchants' accounts." We have for each caste and subcaste in India, the founder—the genealogical originator—of the sect or subcaste, and we name him in our prayers. And if ever we should name an originator, a founder for the English language in India, we should all have to take the name of Ralphe Orde, that humble English school-teacher who started so meritorious a task in my country. Since Ralphe Orde and the East India Company, Macaulay wrote his famous Minute on Indian Education, wanting to make of us Englishmen in custom, morality and intellect—all in fact, except in colour etc. etc.—and thus unintentionally created the new India. It can be said, and without fear of contradiction, without the English language there would never have been the India of Gandhi and Pandit Nehru. If a monument has to be set up for the contribution of British Rule to India, it cannot be for the building of our railway system or for the growth of our industries, it will not even be for the great administrative system that the British built up and beqeathed to us. It will have to be for Ralphe Orde and for the many illustrious and humble men (and may be sometimes even women,) who taught the English language in our universities—Grierson, Wordsworth, Elton, Bain, Miller, Dickinson—and gave us a *new sensibility*, to feel with and to know with. The French language is more akin to our own, and might have made us very Gaulois, the Germans might have given us the apotheosis of compound words and of high confusion, but the English language brought us Shakespeare. If any one is so honoured, almost a saint in a country of saints, it is William Shakespeare. And that this great English poet should be happy amongst us is not because he finds us so drunk with his metrics or his sense of the tragic, but the perception he has of values. It is ultimately the spiritual tradition of India that has incorporated the English language to itself. (One must remember Raja Rammohun Roy's first desire was to reach the spiritual tradition of English—and so he learnt English.)

Truth, said a great Indian sage, is not the monopoly of the Sanskrit language. Truth can use any language, and the more universal, the better it is. If metaphysics is India's primary contribution to world civilization, as we believe it is, then must she use the most universal language for her to be universal. Once again the Indian sage said, what is universal is always Indian. And as long as the English language is universal, it will always remain Indian. And the most remarkable books published in the English language in India, in the last hundred and fifty years and the most original are the works, not of poets and novelists, but of philosophers and sages—Raja Rammohun Roy, Keshub Chandra Sen, Vivekananda, Sri Aurobindo, J. Krishna Murti, and Sri Krishna Menon (Sri Atmanda Guru of Travancore).

It would then be correct to say as long as we are Indian—that is, not nationalists, but truly Indians of the Indian psyche—we shall have the English language with us and amongst us, and not as guest or friend, but as one of our own, of our caste, our creed, our sect and of our tradition.

What caste will English have then ? Like that pioneer Raja Rammohun Roy, we too may make singular changes in English syntax, make its grammar suit our philosophical predilections; we may make use of long Indian words from Sanskrit or Malayalam (say like 'brahmacharya' or 'harikathakalakshepam',); we may offend the ears of the good Englishman by our inability to use the letter V. and W. as though they came from the same posture of tongue and labial disposition; we may still think Charles Dickens the greatest writer of fiction, and wonder that no Englishman quotes Tennyson any more; we may know by heart and recite like Sanskrit verse, with rhythm, hand-clap and foot-beat, passages from John Stuart Mill with the firm conviction that never was philosophy more at home with us than with this great Englishman on our tongues; we may even now read Marie Corelli and regard her outlook on love as the very English of English, and the most eternal of eternal; we may hear Mr Stephen Spender recite his melodramatic poetry, and say to each other, "And, Kitta, but that is not as good as Coventry Patmore;" we may write editorials in our papers reminding ourselves that C.P. Scott wrote such and such an editorial during the Boer War that made Queen Victoria ask Disraeli, who it was that dare write such impertinences about the realm (our English History may be wrong, but we are earnest); and our young men may still know little of T.S. Eliot or Dylan Thomas nor understand what the Logical Positivists in England have discovered, but we shall continue to read and speak English. It has settled in India, and I repeat, we will not let her go.

Hindi is our national language. It is spoken and understood by nearly three hundred and fifty million out of the six hundred million people of India. But then one could say and rightly : look at the Brahmins, they were not even proportionately as numerous as those who speak English and yet they were so powerful. Though this statement is strictly correct, you should not, in all frankness use it, for India today is a secular state, and there is neither Brahmin nor non-Brahmin, Hindu or Muslim. We all are Sri. There is neither Pandit nor Maulana, nor that extraordinary combination of symbols represented by M.R. Ry (which meant Maharaja Raja Sri, a south Indian honorific). Pandit Nehru is Sri Nehru. Maulana Azad is Sri Azad. Thus Mr Frank Anthony, the Anglo-Indian leader, is Sri Anthony. Likewise, since India is secular, the English language too loses its superior caste, and becomes the language of India.

38

Toward a View of
Commonwealth Poetic Tradition

SYED AMANUDDIN

CRITICAL evaluation of Commonwealth poetry in terms of its tradition implies a comparative approach to the various regional or national
literatures. Isolation of each national literature for analysis, specialised
study, and assessment by only those who are formally initiated into its tradition, is a disservice to both the cause of literary scholarship and specific
literatures and writers. It is now time for aggressive scholarship in Commonwealth studies, and we need more and more comparatists who would
use their background and training in developing the vocabulary and structure of criticism and critical approaches bearing in mind the peculiar
characteristics of this still new branch of world literature which cannot be
approached successfully with the traditional European canons of literary
criticism. In my essay "World Writing in English and English Studies",
I wrote: "In recent years several new literary centres have emerged, and
looking at the quality of writing being produced at these centres one
would say that many important writers of the later part of the twentieth
century are going to be from these centres. It is time that the comparatists
and other specialists including modernists started exploring this poorly
charted area and developed critical approaches for its study, analysis and
evaluation...a writer writing in English is also contributing to English-
language literature, and therefore he must be able to stand comparison
with at least his contemporaries writing in English both in his own region
and in other parts of the world."[1] Our task as comparative critics is simplified to some extent by the fact that we would be confining our discussion to only English-language writers. These writers, however, come from
diverse cultures and even literary traditions far older than those of England.
Language too has its regional variations. There are also certain common
features among these writers. They try to assume one or more of the
following voices in their poetry : individual voice, national voice, and
cosmopolitan voice. They write about their personal and private experience or about the landscape of their region, social issues and national

concerns, or treat the themes of general human interest or universal concern. While there are several elements common to all national literatures, there are also elements which are unique to individual literatures. The purpose of this paper is to trace some of these common and uncommon elements shaping the tradition of Commonwealth poetry and deduce from them certain bases for Commonwealth criticism. This paper is intended to be only a brief introduction to the subject which I hope to develop later into a book-length study. The terms "national literature", "regional literature", and "individual literature", will be used as synonyms in this study. "English-language literature" will be used to mean the entire body of world literature in English including British and American.

The term "tradition" as a frame of reference in our discussion of Commonwealth poetry needs some clarification. The Canadian writer Miriam Waddington sees it as "agglomeration of artistic and literary principles based on a continuous usage," extending a writer's life-range backward into the collective past and forward into collective future.[2] It is sometimes seen as a series of revolts of generation against generation, age against age.[3] A critic of African literature thinks that it is a cultural and linguistic experience shared by readers and writers.[4] For T.S. Eliot, tradition involves a historical sense with a perception not only of the pastness of the past, but also of its presence. "No poet, no artist of any art, has his complete meaning alone...,You cannot value him alone; you must set him for contrast and comparison, among the dead...what happens when a new work of art is created is something that happens simultaneously to all the works of art that preceded it."[5] Eliot suggests the condition of poetry as a living whole of all the poetry that has ever been written.[6] Obviously we cannot expect a Commonwealth poet to create his works in a vacuum and his works cannot be evaluated in total isolation from the works of other writers. Who, then, are the "dead" writers he should be compared with ? If the condition of poetry is accepted to be a living whole of all the poetry that has ever been written, shouldn't we place the writer among the writers of the same language no matter what region the poet comes from ? Also, comparison with the living writers of the same language is as important as comparison with dead writers. Eliot finds "an unconscious community" between the true artists of any time.[7] Being the users of the same language and sharing many common problems of the shrunken world, one may say the Commonwealth poets function as a single community at least unconsciously, thus creating a peculiar living tradition of their own. But what should be their relation to the writers of the past ? Where do we place them for the purpose of comparison ? Certainly not with Homer, Sophocles or Sappho although comparison with any significant writers would have its own value. More meaningful comparison would be to place them in the tradition of English-language literature which is more than a thousand years old.

It is interesting to see how the Commonwealth poets themselves

look at this problem of tradition and their relationship to it. One early
New Zealand poet wrote in his "Song of Allegiance":

> Shakespeare Milton Keats are dead
> Donne lies in a lowly bed
>
> ...   .
>
> They are gone and I am here
> stoutly bringing up the rear
> Where they went with limber ease
> toil I on bloody knees
> Though my voice is cracked and harsh
> stoutly in the rear I march
> Though my song have none to hear
> boldly bring up I the rear.[8]

Commonwealth poetry began thus, emulating the British masters, toiling
on bloody knees, and often content with "stoutly bringing up the rear."
The poets considered themselves a part of the British tradition and did
not think that they were capable of creating a regional tradition of their
own or creating poetry of merit that would rank them with the British
masters. A critic of Indian poetry writes : "Hero-worshipping the British
poets, and piously imitating their form and metre, even at times their
themes and moods, the Indo-Anglian poets of the nineteenth century
recollected their emotions almost in futility."[9] Early Commonwealth poets
did not feel that they could reshape the British tradition itself by their own
creative genius. Fortunately this is no longer the attitude of Commonwealth poets. They do not refuse to admit the genius of the former users
of the English language who forged a poetic tradition, but they do not
consider themselves merely as "bringing up the rear." The tradition of
the English-language poetry is there to be used and reshaped if necessary.
Addressing the major romantics, a contemporary poet from India
writes :

> i am my brothers part of the stream
> flowing downhill from you
>
> shakespeare used this language
> blake yeats n hopkins too
> ae hart crane thomas n ginsberg
> we are dreamers n visionaries
> our consciousness milk of paradise[10]

It is this consciousness—the milk of paradise—that the users of the same
language for creative expression have access to. A contemporary Commonwealth poet (or English-language poet) writes with definite loyalties to
his region or race, to the poets of the English language, and to the speakers

(or users) of the English language who are primarily his audience. An Australian poet, for example, writes for an Australian audience with an awareness of Australian poetic tradition, and at the same time he is conscious that he is using a medium that is used in several other regions of the world for creative expression. He also knows that it was the language of Shakespeare, Wordsworth and Keats. This is true of poets of Canada, Ceylon (Sri Lanka), India, Nigeria, and New Zealand.

A Commonwealth poet thus is a poet of his region, a Commonwealth poet, and a world poet writing in English. This does not mean, however, that he lacks national or ethnic identity although his very medium forces him to get out of the insularity that regional, national, or ethnic pressures may impose on him. At the same time, his aspirations, values and perceptions are influenced by his immediate environment. Ultimately, however, all traditions are forged, sustained, and reshaped by poets who are distinctive voices in each national tradition. It is these significant poets who really matter in the discussion of both common and uncommon elements that form Commonwealth poetic tradition. A major Commonwealth poet is one who is a distinctive voice in his region and stands comparison with distinctive voices in other regions, and thus contributes to both national poetic tradition and Commonwealth poetic tradition. One may even say he belongs to the tradition of English-language literature.

As every writer must begin somewhere, possibly in his own regional tradition, before he is able to give it a new direction and also have his impact on Commonwealth tradition, national traditions within the broad Commonwealth tradition cannot be ignored in any discussion of Commonwealth tradition. But writers do not seem to agree on what constitutes national or regional tradition. Some writers believe in the individual or national voice and some in the cosmopolitan voice. Some assert the nativeness of their writing and some aim at the more general and universal concerns. New Zealand poets such as R.A.K. Mason and Allen Curnow seek themes in the "peculiar character of the country, the individuality of New Zealandness", while later poets such as James K. Baxter and Louis Johnson care for a private reality, "an individual truth".[11] A critic may see in these later poets a "growth towards maturity and freedom from the preoccupations of time and place evident in these older poets."[12] Canadian poet and critic A.J.M. Smith finds both nativeness and cosmopolitanism in Canadian poetry. He emphasises what he calls "eclectic detachment" in Canadian poetry—the capacity of Canadian poets to draw freely on diverse cultures and traditions.[13] It should be pointed, however, that eclectic detachment is not peculiar to Canadian poets—this may be regarded as a characteristic of Commonwealth poetry. While working within their distinctive regional traditions, the Commonwealth poets draw freely from diverse cultures and traditions.

Is there any link between the socio-political nationality and literary nationality ? How far should we emphasise the passport of a writer in our critical evaluation of his work ? Poetry is not a guidebook for a tourist or a "sociological survey bundled up in verse."[14] An Indian writer, B. Rajan, writes : "To create an identity is part of the essential business of the artist; to arrive at, or even to contribute towards a declaration of literary nationality, is not necessarily relevant to his concern and may even infringe on the honesty of those concerns."[15] Miriam Waddington emphasises the human element in Canadian poetry rather than the peculiarly Canadian element : "The truth is that the Canadian writer is neither abroad nor in the backwoods. He is, as A.M. Klein understood twenty years ago, in the world with other men, other writers."[16] An Australian critic declares the same way : "Our best poetry is written by poets who know they are human beings by necessity and Australians by accident."[17] A.M. Klein's comment on the local colour in Canadian poetry underscores the above views : "The writer who is more concerned with his writing and not with his passport, neither stresses nor ignores that background."[18] Most Commonwealth poets and critics seem to agree that while a writer may develop national identity, it is not his passport that makes him a good writer. His primary commitment is not so much to his region, race, or sex, as to his writing. While working within the limitations of time and space, he attempts to transcend them in his mature writing. Ethos of the writer's community or region may influence his writing as also the landscape of his environment. But ethos and landscape are mere themes as are love, death, seasons, and the poet must move from personal, private and local experience to general and universal if he is aiming at reaching a larger audience whose interest in his poetry is not merely that of a tourist or sociologist. Perhaps, it is possible to seek the essentially human experience even while dealing with the local and the immediate. Every topical experience has the implications of a universal experience in it for those who seek it and poets ought to be such seekers by both necessity and choice. An Indian writer writes in a letter to a reader : "My national heritage ? I recognise only human heritage. I was born in India but now I am fast progressing towards the citizenship of the universe. Would you like to join me? You don't need a passport, only an attitude."[19]

Whether a writer's thematic base is geographical or social landscape of his region or his own personal vision and individual experience, his significance is not because of his region, race, or his themes, but because he is a creative writer. He is a manipulator of words, an experimenter with technique and modes. For the purpose of evaluating him, we need a set of standards which are not necessarily national standards. The pitfalls of national standards are obvious. "Cultural nationalists can be simplistic and levelling in their tastes. Local colour, dialects, and facile optimism are sometimes preferred to the serious and profound."[20] Literary historians and national historians in collaboration with national critics may look for extra-literary aspects that make writers significant nationalists even when the works of these writers may be far inferior to the works of writers whose preoccupations may not be with the myth of nationalism. Australian poet Bernard O'Dowd by espousing the national cause "attained a far greater reputation in history"[21] than his contemporary Christopher Brennan who was a better poet than O'Dowd. Sometimes national temper may influence the judgement of critics such as the Indian interest in religious philosophy which often prompts critics in India to overrate the poetry of Sri Aurobindo who is certainly a better yogi and religious philosopher than a poet. It was Sarojini Naidu's involvement in politics which probably brought her the title "The Nightingale of India" from her admirers, but her title often misleads readers in India to imagine that she is a major poet. Political honours and titles such as Poet Laureate are bestowed on poets often for wrong reasons. National pride and national aspirations often create hurdles in a detached appraisal of regional literature using the national standards. And this is especially true when the same medium is used for creative expression in other countries. We need a set of valid standards in order to study, analyse, compare, and evaluate Commonwealth poets, and these standards should help up in placing them both in their own regional tradition and Commonwealth tradition. Norman Jeffares rightly demands cosmopolitan standards : "True, one reads them (Commonwealth writers) because they tell us about the way their countries are evolving; true, one reads them because they enrich our pleasure in the English language, but in the cold light of judgement one reads them for their supranational qualities in their work. One reads them because they bring new ideas, new interpretations of life for us. One reads them, in short, because they are good writers. The standards of judgement are not national standards. Standards of the critic must be cosmopolitan; only the best must be praised."[22]

While recognising the need for objective standards so that only the best could be praised, we should remember that we cannot impose these standards from outside. We must develop these standards only in relation to the existing elements of Commonwealth literature. The chief common element in Commonwealth poetic tradition is obviously language. In the words of William Walsh, "Language, then, is the substance of literature and its modification is the spring of literary development."[23] This close link between language and literature cannot be ignored in any literary evaluation. Literature primarily is a verbal art. While literature has its birth in language, it is literature that develops, vitalises, and sustains language. The most remarkable thing that has happened to the English language recently is that it is being used as the language of creative expression in many parts of the world. Modern age and the English language arrived hand-in-hand in many parts of Asia and Africa. As one writer puts it : "The twentieth century is known to have arrived in India and the language of its arrival is probably English."[24] In the multi-lingual societies of Asia and Africa, using English for creative expression is as natural as breathing which persons growing up in a mono-lingual situation can hardly understand. West African poets and Indo-Anglian poets have one thing in common—they use English as a matter of choice for creative expression instead of choosing one of the languages of their regions. While the Indian writer has a tradition of written literature which is at least three thousand years old, the African writer has an oral tradition which may be equally old, and naturally "the communal creative genius"[25] dominates African poetry much more than any other. There is also clash of indigenous and imported cultures in these poets as symbolised by the drum and the piano in Gabriel Okara's poem "Piano and Drum". Indian poets such as Dom Moraes and A.K. Ramanujan also have this clash of cultures as their theme. But poems such as "Speech in the Desert" by Moraes, "Self-Portrait" by Ramanujan, and "The Stars Have Departed" by the African poet Christopher Okigo are examples of poetry in which we find an indivisible bond between the poetic experience and its expression. After all, all poetry is a translation of what the poet experienced into words—but these poets are not translating their expression from one language to another. They are creative users of English.

Poets of Australia, New Zealand, Canada, white poets of Rhodesia and South Africa, being transplanted Europeans, use English as the medium of expression naturally, as it is not a matter of choice for them. Writers of these regions have been making conscious attempts to eliminate the colonial spirit and the mood of exile from their poetry. It is interesting to see how an Australian critic Alec King quarrels even with the label "Australian poetry". He declares : "...our language is English and our poetry is essentially English poetry."[26] However, these writers gradually seem to be losing the feeling that they are transplanted Europeans in an alien landscape. This is particularly true of writers in Australia, Canada, and New Zealand. Judith Wright's words apply not only to Australian writing, but Canadian and New Zealand writing as well : "We are beginning to write, no longer as transplanted writers, nor as rootless men who reject the past and put their hopes only in the future, but as men with a present to be lived and a past to nourish us."[27]

Obviously Judith Wright is not endorsing conscious attempts to express Australianism in poetry. It is interesting to see how a mature poet like A.D. Hope deals with the problem of Australianism in his poem, "Australia" :

> They call her a young country, but they lie.
> She is the last of lands, the emptiest,
> A woman beyond her change of life, a breast
> Still tender but within the womb is dry.
>
> ....
>
> Yet there are some like me turn gladly home
> From the lush jungle of modern thought to find
> The Arabian desert of the human mind,

Hoping, if still from the deserts the prophets come.[28]

Australian poets have contributed significantly to Commonwealth poetic tradition not so much as landscape poets of Australia, but as the explorers of the landscape of the human mind, personal experience or general human experience. Some of the best poems of Robert FitzGerald and Judith Wright have nothing peculiarly Australian about them. Yet they are major Australian and Commonwealth poets at the same time. Accident of birth or residence makes them Australian poets. Use of the English language makes them Commonwealth poets. But their chief importance is because of their own individual creative genius which makes them handle the medium, technique, and theme creatively.

Medium, technique, and theme are the three important elements we should consider in our discussion of Commonwealth poetry. We have discussed the use of English for creative purpose by the Commonwealth poets : (1) the poets use the same language with some regional variations; (2) there is a poetic tradition at least a thousand years old in the English language; (3) poets know their fellow poets are writing in the same language in various parts of the world and they realise that they must make a conscious attempt to write poetry of quality for a cosmopolitan audience if they want to reach distant readers; (4) the medium compels them by its very nature to write both for a regional audience and a world audience. To be understood and appreciated by readers in various parts of the world, a Commonwealth poet along with his peculiarly personal and national themes, must also choose cosmopolitan and universal themes of general human interest and concern and his ultimate contribution should be not only to his regional or national culture, but to human culture. The writer's primary concern being writing itself, he should pay particular attention to tone control, imagery, mode, and form, without which poetry would be bad prose. Technique and medium are interlinked because without conscious control of words, there cannot be control of tone and mode. Similarly, medium and themes are also related and without the expression, experience by itself has no meaning in poetry. These are the elements common to all Commonwealth poetry. We should also try to understand and appreciate elements unique to each regional literature for a deeper understanding of the Commonwealth poetic tradition. They are chiefly three : (1) regional peculiarities of the language; (2) regional culture and social environment; and (3) regional landscape and geography.

An analysis of the various common and uncommon elements in the works of Commonwealth poets should help us in comparing them with one another and in evaluating their collective as well as individual achievement, and in placing them in the tradition of Commonwealth poetry. The following questions directly related to the elements discussed above should be helpful in the evaluation of Commonwealth poets :

(1) Are they imitators who think that great writers are others, especially those of the past or of regions such as England and America, and the only way to become good poets is by imitating such poets ?

(2) Are they peculiarly regional poets exploring their regional culture, local idiom, and landscape at both descriptive and interpretive levels ?

(3) Are they movement writers, who instead of being individual voices, belong to an "ism", a movement, or a group with common interests and loyalties ?

(4) Are they distinctive individual voices using their regional and general human experience as a thematic base in their poetry ?

(5) Are they interested in the exploration of their own states of mind in an idiom peculiarly their own yet intelligible to others ?

(6) Do these writers care for the technique, tone and rhythm control, dramatisation of experience (as opposed to mere statement of it or description of it), word choice and effective imagery ?

The imitators can be easily dismissed as minor writers. But poets who meet other standards need careful assessment. Voguishness would destroy movement or group poets. Singers of landscape and local issues have naturally a limiting vision of life if they don't write about other themes. It is poets who can dive deep into themselves and those who can respond to both their immediate environment and to general human experience, and those who can, using these experiences, create poetry of distinctive quality in style and technique and in the creative use of language, who are the masters of Commonwealth poetic tradition. They are also the major voices of their regions and significant writers of world literature.

REFERENCES

1. Syed Amanuddin, "World Writing in English and English Studies", *Creative Moment*, III, 2 (1974), pp. 25-26.

2. Miriam Waddington, "Canadian Tradition and Canadian Literature", *The Journal of Commonwealth Literature*, 8 (December, 1969), pp. 125-126.

3. Irving Howe quoted in Waddington's article, p. 125.

4. Peter Young, "Tradition, Language and the Reintegration of Identity in West African Literature in English", *The Critical Evaluation of African Literature*, ed. Edgar Wright, London, Heinemann, 1973, p. 24.

5. T.S. Eliot, "Tradition and the Individual Talent", *Selected Essays*, New York, Harcourt, Brace and Co., 1950, pp. 4-5.

6. *ibid.*, p. 7.

7. T.S. Eliot, "Function of Criticism", *Selected Essays*, p. 13.

8. Quoted in W.H. Pearson, "The Recognition of Reality", *Commonwealth Literature: Unity and Diversity in a Common Culture*, ed., John Press, London, Heinemann, 1965, p. 38.

9. John B. Alphonso-Karkala, *Indo-English Literature in the Nineteenth Century*, Mysore, The Literary Half Yearly, University of Mysore, 1970, p. 34.

10. Syed Amanuddin, "British Museum : Manuscripts", *The Age of Female Eunuchs*, Sumter, South Carolina, Poetry Eastwest, 1974, p. 64.

11. A.J. Gurr, "The Two Realities of New Zealand Poetry", *The Journal of Commonwealth Literature*, 1 (September, 1965), p. 122.

12. W.H. Pearson, p. 39.

13. A.J.M. Smith, *Towards a View of Canadian Letters—Selected Essays* 1928-1971, Vancouver, The University of British Columbia, 1973, p. 23.

14. Alec King, "Contemporary Australian Poetry", *The Writer in Australia*, (ed.) John Barnes, New York, Oxford University Press, 1969, p. 324.

15. Balachandra Rajan, "Identity and Nationality," *Commonwealth Literature*, ed. John Press, p. 106.

16. Miriam Waddington, p. 128.

17. Alec King, p. 330.

18. Quoted in Waddington, p. 128.

19. Syed Amanuddin, "Letters to a Reader", *The Age of Female Eunuchs*, p. 10.

20. Bruce King, "Introduction", *Literatures of the World in English*, London, Routledge and Kegan Paul, 1974, p. 21.

21. Judith Wright, "Introduction", *A Book of Australian Verse*, New York, Oxford University Press, 1968, p. 6.

22. A. Norman Jeffares, "Introduction", *Commonwealth Literature*, ed. John Press, p. xiv.

23. William Walsh, "England", *Literatures of the World in English*, ed. Bruce King, p. 63.

24. B. Rajan, "India", *Literatures of the World in English*, p. 80.

25. K.E. Senanu, "The Literature of West Africa," *The Commonwealth Pen*, (ed.) A.L. McLeod, Ithaca, N.Y., Cornell University Press, 1961, p. 168.

26. Alec King, p. 323.

27. Judith Wright, "Australia's Double Aspect", *An Introduction to Australian Literature*, ed. C.D. Narasimhaiah, Ja Brisbane, Q, Jacaranda Press, 1965, p. 11.

28. A. D. Hope, "Australia", *A Book of Australian Verse*, ed. Judith Wright, p. 123.

39

Literature as Culture

GUY AMIRTHANAYAGAM

THERE are many ways of studying a culture different from one's own. Perhaps the best, most complete, and comprehensive is to take the step, sometimes irretraceable, of living in another culture and learning in a direct way the language or languages of the people, becoming familiar consciously and subconsciously with the customs, social habits, mores, thoughts, religions, literature and art, popular culture and other aspects of the culture's way of life. But for most of us, indeed for all of us, this way of learning cultures is not practicable. To begin with, it is not at all clear that one has learned another culture merely because one has lived several years in it. Apart from degrees of percipience and discernment which vary among individuals, a problem arises when one has identified oneself so closely with the culture one studies that one loses the objectivity which is essential for any kind of balanced study. Again, there is such an overwhelming number and variety of cultures in the world that one has to consider economies not only of time and money and place, but also of spirit. Thus, the student of culture has to limit his area, choose his focus, and do what is possible, given the inevitable brevity of the time he has at his disposal. There are the separate ways of the anthropologist, the sociologist, the philosopher, the historian, the litterateur or merely that of the intelligent and curious traveller.

However, it has been said that study of the literature is a unique and perhaps one of the best ways of apprehending a culture in its complex particularities, its nuances and its own characteristic tone. It has been emphasised that literature is a most valuable cultural expression because it springs from its cultural nexus with an immediacy, a freshness, a concreteness, an authenticity and a power of meaning which are not easily found in other emanations or through other channels. If, for example, you read of the tea ceremony in Japan as presented by Kawabata, you proceed from the intricacies of the ceremony to the complexities of

Japanese social life; if you read R.K. Narayan's *The Financial Expert* you are plunged into the actualities of a small town in southern India and immersed in the vivid realities of a small town's business life. Let me now take some familiar American examples as illustrations. Whether for me as an outsider or for Americans themselves, the examples cited, while universal in some senses, are also national, regional, particular and time-bound. I am thinking of Mark Twain's *Adventures of Huckleberry Finn*, Henry James' *The American* or *Portrait of a Lady* and F. Scott Fitzgerald's *The Great Gatsby*. *Huckleberry Finn*, besides being a novel of universal appeal, is also a book set in a specific context—post-Civil War America. It opposes nature and the machine, the pre-industrial and the industrial way of life. While its morality is not a simple repetition of ethical principles found in codes of conduct, it does associate ther iver, for example, with moral meanings and a moral aura. Huck's morality is based on nature of which the river is a powerful symbol, and while it is different from the conventional Christian morality of the day, it is an example of a complex, evolving moral imagination and sensibility. The current worship of the machine, of money, of what Ruskin called "the Goddess of getting on" is what Mark Twain inveighs against. He describes the offensive credo elsewhere as follows : "Get money. Get it quickly. Get it in abundance. Get it in prodigious abundance. Get it dishonestly if you can, honestly if you must". Against this he places the old America, simpler, with its own mix of good and evil but somehow to be preferred. The concrete setting of the story in a particular time and place is the source of its value as cultural knowledge and also the source of its artistic excellence.

Henry James' *The American* also belongs to a specific time and place, while being concerned with the international theme, with America's relationship to its past, and to the old Europe. The protagonist Christopher Newman embodies a particular aspect of the American dream of that time. As he tells his expatriate friend Tristram :

"I want the biggest kind of entertainment a man can get. People, places, art, nature, everything ! I want to see the tallest mountains, and the bluest lakes, and the finest pictures and the handsomest churches, and the most celebrated men, and the most beautiful women".

He uses a metaphor from his business past when he says that he wants a woman who would be the "best article in the market". Even his business mentality is idealised as having "undefined and mysterious boundaries, which invite the imagination to bestir itself on his behalf."

Even though he is crude compared to the Europeans—he has often admired the copy more than the original—he has such a strong streak of decency that he refuses to exploit his knowledge of the skeleton in their cupboard in order to get even with his European associates. The novel is too simplified, as it opposes not American innocence to European sophistication but American nobility of mind to European villainy. But it looks forward to the later novels where James was to treat the "international" theme with greater psychological depth and maturity, where the American-European exchange was more subtle and more of a two-way business, where James' main preoccupation was the theme of freedom and the circumstances in which freedom had to operate, where James was able to project his opposition between American and European cultures in terms of an ideal civilization which though nowhere to be found could nevertheless be posited as a humanly satisfying scale of reference. It looks forward to *The Portrait of a Lady* which examines more seriously the possibilities of freedom in the real world of circumstances, and uncovers a tragic reality which endures.

F. Scott Fitzgerald's *The Great Gatsby* is a later variant of the American dream and reflects a changed society. I do not want to dwell on the complex cultural meaning of this novel, but I would like to draw attention to the quality of Gatsby's corrupt greatness which can still cling to an incorruptible dream. The earlier widespread respect for "getting rich quickism" has already turned somewhat sour in American culture though his love for Daisy redeems to some extent his unscrupulously acquired wealth and other faults of character. The description of Gatsby at the graveside as the 'poor son of a bitch' is derogatory as well as pathetic. Gatsby differs from the typical American self-made man by his greater imaginative desire for self-renewal, for wanting to be reborn, to spring from his own Platonic conception of himself. This feeling though somewhat individualised in Gatsby has its links with the original American desire to begin all over again in a new country with ever expanding frontiers. I have no space to chart the further disintegration of the American dream in later times, as for example in Arthur Miller's *Death of a Salesman*, where the pressures exercised by the still sufficiently pervasive belief that only "making it" matters can but lead to tragic collapse.

The use of literature for culture learning is one of the important new directions taken by literary studies in recent times. Though it has been known for a long time that one of the ways in which culture reveals itself most fully is in the thinking that guides it, shapes its values and gives rise to its various creative expressions, and that the literary or artistic achievements of a culture are among its deepest and most authentic manifestations, there have been in the past relatively few systematic or sustained attempts to study cultures in this way, to 'possess' them intellectually as it were and to relate the humanistic achievements to the 'totality' or 'wholeness' of cultures. Traditionally, the teaching of literature has been concerned with the literary text as being worthy of study because of its artistic merit or moral value. The most common way in which the literary text has been extended has been in the direction of relating it to, and seeing it as a part of the history of literary tradition in a particular language. While the major literary works of past historical periods have been regularly used as source material for the study of the social life of the period in question, little contemporary work has been examined in this way. In recent years, though, considerable momentum has developed toward regarding the social context of literature as essential to its understanding.

Though the literary critic in particular has resisted any attempt to "sociologise" the work of art, he is now willing to approach it through concepts of medium, channel, genre or ambience. The conviction has gained ground that the study of society is a necessary dimension of the study of literature itself, that the sensitive literary critic or the sensitive social scientist will not do any disservice either to literary or to social studies. In fact without sensitiveness, moral sensitivity and imagination, neither the literary critic nor the social scientist is likely to be a good practitioner of his own chosen speciality.

The sociological implications of such phenomena as alienation, the loss of identity in mass society, the changing ecological scene and the bureaucratisation of modern life are reflected in fiction, poetry and drama, and the sociological studies of these matters provide useful background for literary study. On the other hand, the literature is itself important documentation for social studies and the scientist cannot ignore it. Particularly since the nineteen-fifties there has been a renaissance in the area of the relations of literature and society, the position of the writer in society, and in social problems as material for the creative artist.

However, it must be emphasised that even though literature introduces the reader to the culture with an immediacy and a concreteness which cannot otherwise be duplicated, there are several pitfalls which have to be borne in mind. Most critics and lovers of literature claim that literature is its own end and justification, that one must first learn to read and appreciate literature before moving from it to cultural studies of any kind. In fact they would reverse the process and say that one must study the culture in order to appreciate the literature and not vice versa, because literature represents the greater value, and should therefore be the prime concern. More people are interested in Homer than in the specifics of Homeric times.

The work of literature is surrounded by many concentric circles. There is the author's character, his life story, his health or illness, his place within his family and immediate social circumstances; his receptivity to the ideas and ideologies current in his time, and, remembering T.S. Eliot's remark that a major Western poet should write with a sense of the tradition from Homer onwards in his bones, his place in the literary tradition which may extend backward for thousands of years. There is also, and importantly, the writer's relation to his own times. In addition to all these there is the quirk of his own creativity, that special gift which is unique to him and which interacts with all the other factors, somewhat in the nature of a catalytic agent, to produce the special and irreplaceable work of art. To be able to read literature well one must be perceptive and sensitive to all these factors: to read it perfectly would therefore be nearly impossible.

It may be that a culture is more accurately studied in some respects by reading its newspapers than its works of serious art. It may also be true that best sellers are more representative of some aspects of the time than its works of major literature. It is undeniable that popular books like *Uncle Tom's Cabin* or even *Gone With The Wind* which have defensible claims to authenticity are better source material for the study of the age than the more recondite masterpieces. In our own time soap operas on television may tell us more about what that indefinable character known as the common man really feels and thinks. The point, however, is that literature is the fruit of the most creative and often the most interesting minds in a society. And therefore, what is found therein is significant in a different way and at a different level. Great literature may capture what is happening in the depths of the individual and social mind; it may engage the deeper preoccupations which in further times may surface and become prominent so that students of later periods are ready to identify these interests as the most important realities of the times in question. But one has to have the required critical sense to recognise that some works may be merely idealistically nostalgic or even utopian or future-oriented. The novel may deal with the emergent aspects of the future as for example George Orwell's *1984*. The "feel" of reality may be deceptive: if you read Tolstoy's short story *Master and Man*, you cannot conclude that the aristocrat who gave his life to prevent his servant from dying of cold is in any way typical of relations between master and man in 19th century Russia. Tolstoy is more concerned with communicating a human sympathy which transcends time and place. It is in this sense that one has to reckon with literature's engagement in the universal arena of experience. The writer's enduring value may subsist in what he gives to his time and not so much in what he derives from it. One has therefore to take into account in an interrelated way all these possible facets of a work of art before determining their relevance for cultural knowledge.

Great literature is concerned with truth while soap operas may merely reflect the fantasies, dreams and pathologies of the producer and the audience. In so far as man is a social animal, even the most private experiences treated in literature have a social context and therefore they help to determine and complete our knowledge of the human and cultural condition. The Chinese poet's attitude to nature and the passage of time, and Wordsworth's sense of the non-human tell us not only of the individual sensibilities of the poets concerned but also of their respective societies and the different periods in which they wrote. As even the most intimate experiences of, say, love, nature or death have a social context, their recreation by artists has profound social meanings. There is therefore no substitute for the cognitive value of great literature: it is an

invaluable source of the ongoing movements of communion between individuals and cultures.

There are other tendencies, not yet dominant but becoming more and
more vocal in our culture, which have given the study of literature
additional new dimensions. Literature has acquired a special value in the
so-called age of science to the extent to which purely scientific education
has been seen to be incomplete. Science, of course, is not expected to
yield values or guide conduct, but the scientific approach seen as a total
attitude is now largely discredited, if not finally laid to rest. Every partial
approach such as the scientific, however ethically or morally neutral, tends
to create its own mythologies and the gray mythologies of science have
proved themselves life-defeating.

The social sciences enjoyed till recently a period of fitful bloom but
they too seem to have lost their confidence. More and more people are
turning to the humanities to seek the values whose life-support was once
provided by religion and philosophy. Critics and scholars nowadays increasingly tend to busy themselves with the cultural situation in which
literature finds itself and with the insistent demands being made upon
literature to provide an education in moral sensibility and critical intelligence. They tend to approach literature with the expectation that the
principle which should direct and inform educational effort is to be found
primarily in literary study. Since literature expresses the lived actualities
of the time, it is seen as an authentic source not only of the realities of
society as experienced by its most intelligent and sensitive members but
of life-giving values and value-judgments. Literary study is seen to lead
not only to enlargement or refinement of sensibility but to training in
discrimination, aesthetic and moral; the moral judgment is not separate
from the aesthetic in the sense that it is subsequently super-imposed on it;
they are composite, and form a unity.

Unlike in the past where the experience of literature was sought to
clarify and extend moral insights, as for example of one's reading of Blake
would modify one's traditional interpretations of Christian world-views,
today one goes to literature for the very creation of values. Literature
no longer offers the mere alteration of, or escape from, traditional belief
systems; it is called upon to provide substitutes for what is no longer believed in.

It is in this context that extreme and exaggerated demands are made
from poetry and nearly impossible claims made on its behalf. For a poet
like Wallace Stevens, poetry belongs to the highest rung in the caste-
system of human knowledge. He says in one of his essays, "After one
has abandoned the belief in God, poetry is that essence which takes its
place as life's redemption." This is indeed the supreme claim; it goes far
beyond even the Shelleyan position for the poet as the unacknowledged
legislator. Stevens may not be representative. There are other views,
notably that of T.S. Eliot, a poet equally dedicated to his calling but for

whom the poetic discipline was not self-sufficient and needed completion by a moral or even theological discipline. But Eliot's view is even less accepted today. For Stevens' poetry makes life "complete in itself"; that his assertion is not as fantastic as it appears is seen in his long poem *Notes Toward a Supreme Fiction*. The subject is the relation between Imagination and Reality; the imagination which is the golden solvent brings the vivid transparence which in turn renovates experience. Reality is not realism, which is a corruption; it is the "ultimate value," the spirit's "true centre." Imagination, "man's power over nature," confronts reality in all its fullness: what ensues is a fruitful interchange, a supreme fiction, a poetry which is life's sustaining ailment:

> Is it he or is it I that experience this ?
> Is it I then that keep saying there is an hour
> Filled with inexpressible bliss, in which I have
>
> No need, am happy, forget need's golden hand
> Am satisfied without solacing majesty,
> And if there is an hour there is a day,
>
> There is a month, a year, there is a time
> In which majesty is a mirror of the self:
> I have not but I am and as I am, I am

That, in a secular age, a poet should fabricate an experience which may be described as a 'pagan' equivalent of the beatific vision is in itself an achievement: that he should make it appear so nearly credible is a poetic triumph. In another poem, *The World as Meditation*, Stevens expressed the sense in which, even though there is no longer any fury in transcendent forms, his actual candle blazes with artifice. Though God is dead, the imagination takes his place as the mirror and the lamp, the source and giver of life:

> We say God and the imagination are one
> How high that highest candle lights the dark
>
> Out of this same light, out of the central mind
> We make a dwelling in the evening air
> In which being there together is enough

Despite the fact that high claims are made for literature and that it has been pressed into service for a variety of scholastic purposes, the most notable of which is its use for cultural studies, I would like to conclude by stressing that there is no substitute for the close, unremitting, disinterested reading of the literary text with a view to extracting the total

meaning. There is no surrogate for literary analysis and comparison.
All cultural study of literature must begin from there, before proceeding
to aesthetic, moral or cultural extensions and judgments. This is not to
minimise the information and the knowledge that is afforded by the study
of history, sociology and other relevant disciplines, but merely to stress
that the reality of the creative personality must spill over into the history
of the mythology of the human imagination. To understand the individual creative personality, one must read the text as carefully as possible.
It is only then that one can demonstrate how effective or ineffective it is.
Only after fully saturating oneself in the work, penetrating and evaluating
its significance can one move into cultural studies. The movement into
cultural studies as well must be informed by the same intense, humane
concern for the dynamics of civilization, which in itself has close relationships to the original creative pressure.

40

Variety of Ways :
Is There a Shared Tradition in
Commonwealth Literature?

MULK RAJ ANAND

IF autobiographical reminiscence be forgiven, may I tell you of the small beginnings from which this big conference has grown?

Already in the twenties some of the British intellectuals and creative men and women had accepted the young hopefuls among the writers from the colonies as equals without patronage.

Apart from the respect paid to the doyen Tagore, the Bloomsbury group, specially Leonard Woolf, Laurence Binyon, E.M. Forster, T. S. Eliot, Arthur Waley (and his wife Beryl de Zoete) and the Stracheys sponsored young authors from India, Ceylon, Africa and the Carribean. In Soho, Nancy Cunard sang the praises of the American Negro poets. And soon Paul Robeson was to be the rage of London, when Maurice Browne presented him in the role of *Othello.*

In the thirties Bonamy Dobrée became Professor of English literature at Leeds University. And, by sheer coincidence some Indian, Australian and African students began to hear his lectures and a few researched under him. Not only was he a teacher with a style, but he was casual, un-buttoned and hospitable, in the manner of the Egyptians with whom he had spent long winters in Cairo and Alexandria.

It was not strange, therefore, that, later, Professor Norman Jeffares should have taken the initiative to urge the formation of the Common-wealth Association of Writers. The minds and hearts opened by Bonamy Dobrèe were to accept the once suppressed voices, of even those who had launched out on unknown seas.

Luckily, F.R. Leavis had been offering friendship to students from the colonies in Cambridge. As he had championed the cause of 'bottom dogs' like D.H. Lawrence, so he took up the fight on behalf of the 'un-touchables' of the Empire. (I shall never forget the way he boosted my own low morale after several rejections of my first novel, by saying:

'Anand, you wait—truth will win through ! I have written to Edgell Rickward to welcome a new rebel !'

And the coincidence of the world-wide thirties movement, sponsored by the liberals, radicals and communists, against Fascism, brought pioneers like Gorky, Gide, Malraux, John Strachey, C. Day Lewis, Stephen Spender, Ernest Toller, Hemmingway, Dos Passos and many other western intellectuals on the same platform of life against death, as Paul Robeson, Mulk Raj Anand, Peter Ahrahms, Langston Hughes, Pablo Neruda and Shelley Wang.

The defence of the Spanish Republic against the dictators rallied the advance guard intelligentsia of the whole world.

And the gruelling years of the second world war united, under the leadership of George Orwell, in the *Voice* magazine of BBC men and women of letters like E.M. Forster, T.S. Eliot, Herbert Read, Storm Jameson, Naomi Mitchison, Mulk Raj Anand, Stephen Spender, Dylan Thomas, Narayana Menon, Louis MacNiece, Arthur Koestler, J.B.S. Haldane, Balraj Sahni and Zulfikar Bukhari.

I have referred to the friendship, in spite of the differences of opinion, of the various pre-war writers, as I wished to emphasise the fact that the western intelligentsia had accepted the concept of a variety of ways of life and expression, in the spirit of the 'Atlantic Charter', in spite of the snobs. The stresses of the common struggle for decencies against world reaction, through the prolonged seven-year bloodbath, brought even the most whimsical individualists together.

And, with the coming of political freedom for almost all the colonies of the various empires (the chain effect having been started by Gandhian India), the acceptance of a more congenial, egalitarian and mutually helpful attitude for pooling the resources of the Commonwealth, had become a happy augury for the future growth of solidarities. The openmindedness of the sponsors of the Commonwealth Association has prospered through the emergence of new, fresh and ardent young talents from all parts of the world.

The thing which unites us is the English language, which will come to be recognised as the one positive residuum of the erstwhile British Empire, as a link language among vast peoples.

Curiously, however, the English language which we Indians inherited from the British-Indian universities, has changed in the hands of our creative writers and become Indian-English.

Only a very few of the new generation of writers use what is called the 'Queen's English', whatever that may mean in the polyglot that is current in the United Kingdom. Like the Irish, the Scotch, the Welsh. the Americans, the Australians, the Newzealanders, the West Indians, the Nigerians, the Kenyans, the Ugandans, the new young of India often seem to echo either the intonation, or the rhythm, or the atmosphere of the mother-tongue. Specially is this so in the writing of fiction, where dialogue

is involved.   Almost all Indian writers in English have given up the 'thee'
and 'thou' used as a convention by the British writers about India.

And it is no longer possible for even the most blatant denigrators of
Indian-English writing, to dub the style as 'Babu English'. The truth is that
most Indian writers in English have a fair command of English grammar
and know what is cliche and what is clap-trap in the English language, as
it is being written in various countries, where English is the mother-tongue.

Consciously or unconsciously, they have also seized on the fact that the
19th and early 20th century narrative prose of English and American
literatures, has changed from the twelve- to seventeen-word sentence to a
seven- to eleven-word sentence.   And many new words from all parts of
the world have entered the 'Queen's English'.

The Indian-English writers (and this may be true of most of the Commonwealth writers), have thus found themselves giving up the old closed
literary language of the coteries of London and New York.   They have,
sometimes deliberately, and often from the need to reproduce local characters, introduced vibrations, sounds and words from their mother-tongues, as
also sometimes coined synthetic words to introduce new metaphors and
imagery into the Commonwealth literature.

This phenomena has sometimes disturbed the literati of the cosmopolises.
Also, the 'little critics', in the pockets of reaction within the ex-colonies
(now free countries), have been throwing jibes at the various new expressions of our talents for seeking to express themselves in free, expressio-
nist, vital words, even if they should seem odd to the ears of the remaining
'Brown Sahibs.'

The fact that the African, Australian and Caribbean writers in English
have also been writing in a spontaneously mixed speech, or in the
peculiarly expressive English dialect of their own peoples, in their novels
and short stories, adds force to my argument that 'Pigeon-Indian' (by which
I mean the Indian-English which coos messages of love) is the right name
to use for the new Indian-English rather than 'Pidgin-English'.

All the emergent styles of the different Commonwealth countries
reinforce Professor Dobrée's hunch that there are a 'variety of ways' in life
as in literature.

I suggest that we make 'variety of ways' a motto of our conference.

It is too early to say, at this juncture, which writers, of what country,
will succeed in creating more authentic expressions of the genius of their
people, of their joys and pains, and of their imperceptible feelings.

Some of us feel that it is necessary to keep an open mind and allow the
flood of creative expression to fertilise the consciousness of these vast
peoples, who could not enter literature during the prolonged era of one-
man rule.   Criticism can, at best, only interpret an emergent style : it
should not be used to inhibit innovation, experiment and genuine
utterance.

I would like to recall here the way in which Irish-English came into being under the patronage of W.B. Yeats, A.E. (George Russell) and Lady Gregory, through the recognition of the brave initiatives of the pioneer Irish writers like William Allingham, Samuel Ferguson, Maria Edgeworth, Charles Lever, Standish O'Grady, Douglas Hyde, John Millington Synge, Sean O'Casey, Frank O'Connor, Paeder O'Denniel, Elizabeth Bowen, Francis Stuart and others.

At the end of the 19th century Yeats and his colleagues realised that, before them, Irish writers had not dared to bring in their native genius, as well as their inheritance of old Gaelic myths, but had approximated to the English heroic ideals, influenced by the Graeco-Roman tradition.

This had made their verse into 'literary poetry' and their prose into the prolonged cadences of Richardson and Smollet and the archetectonics of Thomas Hardy. The Irish exuberance, which was to come into the new novels and stories from the love of the folk, and Ireland itself, arose from the deliberate introduction of the folk dialectic particularly by Synge, Lady Gregory and Sean O'Casey.

This style of Irish-English, which Lady Gregory humorously called 'Kiltartan' (as I call Indian-English 'Pigeon-Indian'), was defined by Yeats in the following words :

"The Anglo-Irish idiom is a form of English, modified by Gaelic habits of thought, speech, imagery and syntax: the words and meanings are English, but the word order corresponds to the word order of Gaelic". [*Synge and the Irish Drama*, page 38]

Later on he insisted :

"The English idiom of the Irish speaking people of the west, is the only good English, spoken by any large numbered Irish people today And we must, found good literature on a living speech . ' [*Plays and Controversies*, page 28].

The admiration which Yeats had for Synge, particularly, was for his renunciation of literariness of its 'hollow images' and for treating of characters, like the fisherfolk of the west coast, in all their heroism against the sea, face to face with poverty, their sense of humour, their passion for life, against all the odds.

In fact the naked truth came into Irish-English writing. All the embroidery and decorativeness was discarded. The later writers even dissolved the 'Celtic Twilight', taking from it only the emotions, moods and physical realities of Irish legends into their humanist framework, uplifted their works into the world of imagination. In turning to life, away from sentimental sadness of 'the country of shadows', and upturning the earth of fresh fields, they gathered harvests in every season.

All the writers of the Comonwealth countries, I feel, will find themselves in similar situations.

They are bound to recreate the authentic lilts of their peoples. They will find themselves confronting the realities of the fundamental situations of their own landscapes. They will realise that no language is inherently more poetical than another. And they will realise that if they resort more to the rhythms of their own ballads, they will be far more allied to the consciousnesses of their own people. The distinctive idiom of their characters, when transcreated into English, will bring new metaphors and imagery into their writings.

And it is these fresh flavours exuding the expression of the new hearts, the new minds and the different imaginations, which the world is looking for, beyond the classics, in the changing situations of the contemporary world. This does not mean that we have to accept from the late Henry Ford the dictum that 'History is bunk !' No. We will still read Palgrave's *Golden Treasury*. The students will open the old books in the libraries. But we may want to adventure out on our different quests, in our journeys to the interior as well as the open spaces of our lands, with light hearts and as little luggage as possible.

We have to go and meet millions of those peoples in our countries, who have come newly from one-man rule into the pool of the world democracy. We have to recognise the human dignity of each of these individuals. We have to concern ourselves with the well-being of each one of them. And we have to help bring them into the first and last freedoms.

Thus we have to worship the new consciousnesses of our people as part of love of man himself—urged by the exigencies of a tragic age, where we all stand on crossroads of possible death through the enormous armaments piled up and of abounding life in co-existence. Our beloved friend, leader and guide, Jawaharlal Nehru, often reminded us that it is co-existence or co-death.

May I add to this magic word co-existence—co-discovery.

This will involve exchange, and mutual aid as well as solidarity or friendship.

I consider literature as a means of communication, which connects, and this connection is the extension of love. Because it is not possible anymore to be an island, on one's own, in this world.

Paradoxically, the same forces which divide the world today through rigid frontiers, have united the world, even against their will, by faster means of communication.

And we are already ushered, on several planes, into a one world culture. This means that we are likely to meet each other, to visit different countries frequently. And we will have to find out the inner patterns of the lives of our brethren, to appreciate the variety of ways of life, and to taste different cultures. Indeed, we have to pursue co-discovery.

I suggest that the English language which connects us has already become one of the most important mediums of co-existence and co-discovery. Our books are in the libraries of different universities of the world.

And, currently, we are unconsciously in the process of 'connect'.

I think writing arises from the deepest urges for communication.   And communication ends our loneliness and fosters friendships, intimacy, and brings love.

If someone asks me why I have written so many books, I find myself answering : I love.

Notes on Contributors

J.J. HEALY : Professor of English at the University of Carleton, Canada, was Secretary of ACLALS, and in that capacity organised the Second Triennial conference of ACLALS at Kingston, Jamaica.

DANIEL MASSA : Teaches at the Royal University of Malta, organised a conference of Commonwealth Literature in March 1978 at Malta under the auspices of the European branch of ACLALS. Has attended previous Conferences of ACLALS.

ALASTAIR NIVEN : Holds a Ph.D. from Leeds. Teaches at the University of Stirling. Member of ACLALS Executive and Commonwealth Library Holdings Committee ; organised a regional conference of ACLALS at Stirling in 1974.

BERNTH LINDFORS : Professor, Department of English, University of Texas at Austin, specialist in African Literature. Editor of *Researches in African Literature*.

ROBERT M. WREN : Teaches English in the University of Houston, Houston, Texas, USA.

WILLIAM WALSH : Professor of Commonwealth Literature at the University of Leeds. Formerly Dean of the Faculty of Education and Pro-Vice-Chancellor, University of Leeds. Author of *The Human Idiom*, *A Manifold Voice*, *Commonwealth Literature* and books on Coleridge and D.J. Enright.

SYD HARREX : Lecturer in the Department of English, University of Flinders, South-Australia and Director of the recently founded Centre for New Literatures in English in the same University. He obtained his Ph.D. from the University of Tasmania for his dissertation on Indian Writing in English.

MEENAKSHI MUKHERJEE : Teaches at Lady Shri Ram College, New Delhi. Has published a book of criticism on Indian fiction *Twice Born Fiction*. Editor, *Vagartha* a quarterly journal of Indian Literature and *Essays in Indian Literature*.

PETER ALCOCK : Teaches at Massey University ; contributed a bibliography of Newzealand Literature to *Commonwealth Literature* : *A Handbook*. He has been offering courses in Commonwealth Literature and has published many articles on Newzealand Literature. Has attended ACLALS conference previously.

G.S. AMUR : Professor and Head of the Department of English at Marathwada University, Aurangabad. Author of *A Concept of Comedy* and a book on Manohar Malgonkar in the series, *Indian Writers in English* (Arnold-Heinemann).

CLARKE BLAISE : Teaches at Concordia University. His stories have appeared in Canadian and American Journals. Author of *A North American Education*, a novel. Currently working on a novel *Lunar Attractions*.

CHRIS TIFFIN : Teaches at the University of Queensland. Secretary of SPACLALS, currently Asst. Chairman, ACLALS.

HELEN TIFFIN : Teaches at the University of Queensland. Secretary of SPACLALS and ACLALS.

LEE BRISCOE THOMPSON : Teaches at the University of Vermont, Burlington, Vermont, USA.

NICK WILKINSON : Teaches at the University of Nigeria : author of a book on African Literature.

PETER NAZARETH : is in the International Writing programme at the University of Iowa. Poet, Novelist, Playwright and Critic. Recent publication : *An African View of Literature*.

A. J. GUNAWARDANA : Teaches at the Vidyawardhaka University, Sri Lanka, held a Senior Fellowship for 1976-77 at Culture Learning Institute, East-West Center, Hawaii.

D.V.K RAGHAVACHARYULU : Professor and Head of the Department of English at Nagarjuna University, Guntur, Andhra Pradesh. Obtained Ph.D. at the Universities of Andhra Pradesh and Pennsylvania. Author of a book on *Eugene O'Neill*, edited *Essays in Indian Writing in English* and contributed several essays on American Literature and Indian Writing in English.

EDWARD BAUGH : Teaches at the University of West-Indies; is Chairman of the West-Indian branch of ACLALS.

K. AYYAPPA PANIKER : Reader in English, Kerala University; obtained a Ph.D. from Indiana University, writes poetry, drama and criticism in Malayalam, a South Indian language.

K.L. GOODWIN : Professor of English at the University of Queensland, Australia. Currently Chairman of ACLALS; has published a book on Ezra Pound and edited *National Identity* containing select papers read at ACLALS Conferences held in Australia, 1968.

VICTOR J. RAMRAJ : Teaches at the University of Calgary, Alberta, Canada. Edited a recent number of the Carribean number of *Ariel*.

PATRICIA MORLEY : Professor of English at the University of Concordia, Sir George Williams Campus, Canada; teaches Canadian Literature. Important publications : *The Mystery of Unity*; *Theme and Technique in the Novels of Patrick White*; *The Immoral Moralists; Robertson Davies* and a score of articles on Canadian Literature.

EDWARD P. VARGO : Teaches at the Fu Jen University, Taipei, Taiwan.

CECIL A. ABRAHAMS : Teaches at Bishop's University, Lennoxville, Quebec, Canada; Chairman, Canadian branch of ACLALS.

WENDY KEITNER : Teaches at the University of Guelph, Canada; Co-editor with R.T. Robertson of a bibliography of Canadian Literature.

LOIS C. GOTTLIEB : Teaches in the University of Guelph, Canada.

ARTHUR RAVENSCROFT : Teaches at the University of Leeds, Editor of *Journal of Commonwealth Literature;* Specialisation: African Literature on which he has contributed many scholarly papers; author of a monograph on Chinua Achebe.

LLOYD FERNANDO : Professor of English at the University of Malaysia, Kuala Lumpur; has organised the Malaysian branch of ACLALS; author of a novel *Scorpion Orchid* ; edits *Tenngara*, a journal of Malaysian Literature.

EUNICE DE SOUZA : Lecturer in English at St. Xavier's College, Bombay. Her poems have been published in several journals; reviews books for Bombay papers.

SATENDRA NANDAN : Graduate of the Universities of Delhi and Leeds. Teaches at the University of South Pacific. Presently working on Patric White for his Ph.D. at the National University, Canberra.

W.H. NEW : Teaches at the University of British Columbia, Vancouver; has compiled a comprehensive bibliography of Commonwealth Literature; currently editor of *Canadian Literature*.

ALAN L. McLEOD: Teaches at Trenton State College, Trenton, N.J. Edited with introduction a book on Whitman by Field Marshall Smuts.

MARIAN B. McLEOD : Teaches at Trenton State College, Trenton, N.J.

G.V. DESANI : Professor of Philosophy at the University of Texas, Austin. Author of a novel *All About H Hatterr* and *Hali*, a poetic play.

JOSEPH JONES : Professor Emeritus, Department of English, University of Texas. General Editor of books on Commonwealth Literature in Twaine series.

SAROS COWASJEE : Professor of English at the University of Saskatchewan at Regina. Author of a novel *Goodbye to Elsa; Letters of Anand*.

RAJA RAO : is a Professor of Buddhist Philosophy in the University of Texas, Austin, USA and author of *Kanthapura, The Serpent and the Rope, The Cat and Shakespeare;* the recipient of Padma Bhushan and National Literary Akademi Award for his *The Serpent and the Rope*.

SYED AMANUDDIN : A University lecturer. Edits a journal *Poetry East-West*.

GUY AMIRTHANAYAGAM : Research Associate at the Culture Learning Institute, East-West Center, Hawaii. Formerly a senior member of the Diplomatic Service, Sri Lanka.

MULK RAJ ANAND : Indian Novelist. Prolific Writer. Editor of *Marg,* an Art Magazine, Author of books on Indian Art, Humanist who considers Humanism the only 'ism' possible. Recent publication : *Confessions of a Lover* the third in the series of autobiographical novels, *The Seven Ages of Man*.